Human-Centered Approaches in Industry 5.0:

Human-Machine Interaction, Virtual Reality Training, and Customer Sentiment Analysis

Ahdi Hassan
Global Institute for Research Education and Scholarship, Amsterdam, The Netherlands

Pushan Kumar Dutta
Amity University Kolkata, India

Subir Gupta
Swami Vivekanand University, India

Ebrahim Mattar
College of Engineering, University of Bahrain, Bahrain

Satya Singh
Sharda University, Uzbekistan

IGI Global
PUBLISHER of TIMELY KNOWLEDGE

A volume in the Advances in Business Information Systems and Analytics (ABISA) Book Series

Published in the United States of America by
IGI Global
Business Science Reference (an imprint of IGI Global)
701 E. Chocolate Avenue
Hershey PA, USA 17033
Tel: 717-533-8845
Fax: 717-533-8661
E-mail: cust@igi-global.com
Web site: http://www.igi-global.com

Library of Congress Cataloging-in-Publication Data

CIP PENDING

TITLE: Human-Centered Approaches in Industry 5.0: Human-Machine Interaction, Virtual Reality Training, and Customer Sentiment Analysis
ISBN: 9798369326473
eISBN: 9798369326480

This book is published in the IGI Global book series Advances in Business Information Systems and Analytics (ABISA) (ISSN: 2327-3275; eISSN: 2327-3283)

British Cataloguing in Publication Data
A Cataloguing in Publication record for this book is available from the British Library.

All work contributed to this book is new, previously-unpublished material. The views expressed in this book are those of the authors, but not necessarily of the publisher.

For electronic access to this publication, please contact: eresources@igi-global.com.

Advances in Business Information Systems and Analytics (ABISA) Book Series

Madjid Tavana
La Salle University, USA

ISSN:2327-3275
EISSN:2327-3283

Mission

The successful development and management of information systems and business analytics is crucial to the success of an organization. New technological developments and methods for data analysis have allowed organizations to not only improve their processes and allow for greater productivity, but have also provided businesses with a venue through which to cut costs, plan for the future, and maintain competitive advantage in the information age.

The **Advances in Business Information Systems and Analytics (ABISA) Book Series** aims to present diverse and timely research in the development, deployment, and management of business information systems and business analytics for continued organizational development and improved business value.

Coverage

- Forecasting
- Strategic Information Systems
- Data Governance
- Business Systems Engineering
- Performance Metrics
- Data Analytics
- Data Strategy
- Business Intelligence
- Legal information systems
- Statistics

IGI Global is currently accepting manuscripts for publication within this series. To submit a proposal for a volume in this series, please contact our Acquisition Editors at Acquisitions@igi-global.com or visit: http://www.igi-global.com/publish/.

The Advances in Business Information Systems and Analytics (ABISA) Book Series (ISSN 2327-3275) is published by IGI Global, 701 E. Chocolate Avenue, Hershey, PA 17033-1240, USA, www.igi-global.com. This series is composed of titles available for purchase individually; each title is edited to be contextually exclusive from any other title within the series. For pricing and ordering information please visit http://www.igi-global.com/book-series/advances-business-information-systems-analytics/37155. Postmaster: Send all address changes to above address.

Titles in this Series

For a list of additional titles in this series, please visit: http://www.igi-global.com/book-series/advances-business-information-systems-analytics/37155

Leveraging ChatGPT and Artificial Intelligence for Effective Customer Engagement
Rohit Bansal (Department of Management Studies, Vaish College of Engineering, Rohtak, India) Abdul Hafaz Ngah (Faculty of Business Economics and Social Development Universiti Malaysia Terenganu, Malaysia) Aziza Chakir (FSJES AC, Hassan II University, Casablanca, Morocco) and Nishita Pruthi (Maharshi Dayanand Universit, India)
Business Science Reference • © 2024 • 320pp • H/C (ISBN: 9798369308158) • US $265.00

Intersecting Environmental Social Governance and AI for Business Sustainability
Cristina Raluca Gh. Popescu (University of Bucharest, Romania & The Bucharest University of Economic Studies, Romania & The National Institute for Research and Development in Environmental Protection, Romania & INCDPM, Bucharest, Romania & National Research and Development Institute for Gas Turbines (COMOTI), Bucharest, Romania) and Poshan Yu (Soochow University, China & Australian Studies Centre, Shanghai University, China)
Business Science Reference • © 2024 • 310pp • H/C (ISBN: 9798369311516) • US $275.00

Leveraging AI and Emotional Intelligence in Contemporary Business Organizations
Dipanker Sharma (Central University of Himachal Pradesh, India) Bhawana Bhardwaj (Central University of Himachal Pradesh, India) and Mohinder Chand Dhiman (Central University of Himachal Pradesh, India)
Business Science Reference • © 2024 • 300pp • H/C (ISBN: 9798369319024) • US $270.00

Data-Driven Intelligent Business Sustainability
Sonia Singh (Toss Global Management, UAE) S. Suman Rajest (Dhaanish Ahmed College of Engineering, India) Slim Hadoussa (Brest Business School, France) Ahmed J. Obaid (University of Kufa, Iraq) and R. Regin (SRM Institute of Science and Technology, India)
Business Science Reference • © 2024 • 320pp • H/C (ISBN: 9798369300497) • US $265.00

Advancement in Business Analytics Tools for Higher Financial Performance
Reza Gharoie Ahangar (Lewis University, USA) and Mark Napier (Lewis University, USA)
Business Science Reference • © 2023 • 321pp • H/C (ISBN: 9781668483862) • US $250.00

Cases on Enhancing Business Sustainability Through Knowledge Management Systems
Meir Russ (University of Wisconsin-Green Bay, USA & Stellenbosch University, South Africa)
Business Science Reference • © 2023 • 366pp • H/C (ISBN: 9781668458594) • US $240.00

IGI Global
PUBLISHER of TIMELY KNOWLEDGE

701 East Chocolate Avenue, Hershey, PA 17033, USA
Tel: 717-533-8845 x100 • Fax: 717-533-8661
E-Mail: cust@igi-global.com • www.igi-global.com

Table of Contents

Detailed Table of Contents

solutions. It concludes by looking ahead, outlining promising areas for future research at the intersection of BDA and AI to foster well-informed decision-making in Industry 5.0.

Recent advancements in physiological monitoring tech have eased the adoption of a human-centric strategy in factories, despite challenging working conditions that typically impede research on operator user experience (UX). These innovations offer various methods to assess overall UX, including aspects like mental workload, stress, and ergonomics. The current training efforts aim to create a comprehensive UX index for early identification of user discomfort root causes and system design improvements. Virtualizing and simulating production processes yield cost and time savings, while enabling research on human-machine interaction and assembly line design enhancements. Moreover, this research introduces a novel method for ergonomic analysis of automobile assembly line workplaces in a virtual setting. This preventive ergonomic approach holds the potential to revolutionize human-centered workplace design, leading to cost savings and improved job quality.

This chapter examines an innovative strategy for attaining environmental sustainability in manufacturing, particularly emphasizing the idea of a "green factory" and its component "green unit processes." Innovative approaches to industrial production are essential when environmental degradation and resource depletion are causing growing worry. This chapter explores a cooperative process that brings together a range of stakeholders in pursuing sustainable manufacturing practices, including manufacturers, academics, policymakers, and local communities.

3D printing (3DP), also known as additive manufacturing (AM), is a popular method used in Industry 4.0 that involves using machines and pens to create customized and complex 3D objects from a digital file by layering materials. This technology is widely used in industries such as aerospace, automotive, healthcare, and consumer goods for prototyping, rapid tooling, and production of end-use parts. 3DP offers companies a low-risk, low-cost, and fast way to produce prototypes, allowing them to test new products and speed up development without expensive models or specialized tools. Machines are more

of emerging trends and challenges. It serves as a persuasive call to prioritize IoT device protection to preserve user privacy and interconnected system integrity.

Kriti Saroha, Centre for Development of Advanced Computing, Noida, India
Vishal Jain, Sharda University, India

This chapter explores the ethical considerations that arise at the intersection of artificial intelligence (AI) and virtual reality (VR). It examines the multifaceted ethical challenges posed by the integration of AI and VR technologies, focusing on issues such as privacy, bias, autonomy, social impact, and regulatory frameworks. By analyzing existing literature and real-world cases, this chapter seeks to provide a comprehensive understanding of the ethical dimensions of AI-driven virtual reality experiences.

Sourav Madhur Dey, University of Burdwan, India
Pushan Dutta, Amity University, India

Artificial intelligence (AI) has become a transformative force in the healthcare industry, offering unprecedented opportunities for improved diagnostics, patient treatment, and outcomes. However, its integration into healthcare systems has also brought to light a host of ethical concerns that require careful scrutiny. This chapter delves into the intricate nexus of ethics and AI in healthcare, shedding light on the multifaceted implications and challenges that arise. AI technologies such as machine learning (ML) and data analytics (DS) have immense potential to revolutionize healthcare. They can enhance diagnostic accuracy, enable the treatment of a larger number of patients, and improve patient outcomes. However, their implementation is not without ethical quandaries. These primarily revolve around data privacy, bias mitigation, transparency, responsibility, and patient independence. Transparency and interpretability are other essential aspects of the ethical discourse surrounding AI in healthcare.

Namita Sharma, Sharda University, India
Vishal Jain, Sharda University, India

In today's digitally interconnected world, customer feedback has become a goldmine of valuable information for businesses seeking to improve their products, services, and overall customer experience. Analysing this data is instrumental in boosting business. Machine learning and sentiment analysis have emerged as powerful tools in processing and extracting valuable insights from customer feedback. MonkeyLearn, Lexalytics are some of the sentiment analysis tools which are well suited for processing customer feedback. Sentiment analysis powered by machine learning algorithms automates the process of extracting insights from unstructured textual data. This chapter will explore the underlying principles of machine learning algorithms and their roles in automating sentiment analysis from diverse sources such as online reviews, social media, surveys, and customer support interactions. Through real-world case studies and practical examples, readers will discover how to harness the power of sentiment analysis to gain actionable insights and effectively measure customer satisfaction.

A significant amount of user-generated material, notably in the form of customer evaluations, has been produced in recent years as a result of the exponential rise of digital platforms. Utilizing this vast amount of data through cutting-edge methods like machine learning and sentiment analysis has become essential for organizations looking to learn insightful things about their customers' attitudes. This chapter explores how machine learning and sentiment analysis dynamically intersect when used to analyze customer evaluations. The chapter analyses how machine learning algorithms can be efficiently used to uncover complex patterns and feelings hidden in various consumer feedback through a thorough study. By using cutting-edge methodology, it reveals the intrinsic polarity and emotional undertones of these evaluations, offering insightful information about how customers feel. The chapter further illustrates how machine learning-driven sentiment analysis is used in practice across a variety of industries, shedding light on how it influences strategic business choices.

This chapter explores the integration of machine learning with customer sentiment analysis to unveil insights from customer feedback. It emphasizes the importance of understanding customer sentiment for enhancing satisfaction and making informed decisions. The chapter covers various machine learning approaches including supervised and unsupervised learning, as well as deep learning models. Preprocessing techniques and feature engineering methods for textual data are discussed. The challenges of sentiment analysis, such as sarcasm and context, are addressed, along with practical applications in product development, brand management, and personalized marketing. Ethical considerations are highlighted. Overall, this chapter provides valuable insights on leveraging machine learning for customer sentiment analysis.

The Metaverse is a network of 3D virtual worlds that combines real-world and virtual experiences and offers ways for multimodal communication and experiences in a range of settings. The third wave of the World Wide Web revolution, known as the metaverse, is based on cutting-edge technologies like

Preface

As editors of this comprehensive reference book, we are delighted to present *Human-Centered Approaches in Industry 5.0: Human-Machine Interaction, Virtual Reality Training, and Customer Sentiment Analysis*. This book is the culmination of extensive research and collaboration among experts in the fields of digital manufacturing and smart factories. It offers a deep exploration of the latest developments and emerging trends that are shaping the future of manufacturing, with a specific focus on human-centered approaches.

In a world rapidly transforming through digitalization, manufacturing industries find themselves at the forefront of change. The advent of Digital Manufacturing and Smart Factories has the potential to revolutionize the way we produce goods. The integration of advanced technologies such as Artificial Intelligence, Robotics, Internet of Things (IoT), Augmented Reality (AR), Virtual Reality (VR), Big Data Analytics, Cloud Computing, and Additive Manufacturing presents new possibilities and challenges in the manufacturing landscape.

This book is a response to the ever-increasing need for a comprehensive guide that not only explores these technologies but also highlights their impact on human-machine interaction, virtual reality training, and customer sentiment analysis. We believe that a human-centered approach is essential in harnessing the full potential of Industry 5.0. This approach emphasizes the importance of optimizing user experiences, enhancing ergonomics, and ensuring responsible development in the age of emerging technologies.

We invite a diverse audience to explore the content of this book. Researchers and academics will find cutting-edge research on emerging trends, providing insights into the future of manufacturing. Practitioners and professionals seeking to implement new strategies by leveraging technological innovations will discover valuable guidance. Policymakers and government officials interested in staying up-to-date with global developments in digital manufacturing will find a wealth of information. Entrepreneurs and innovators exploring opportunities through disruptive technology innovations will uncover essential insights for their ventures.

This book aims to accomplish several objectives. Firstly, it provides readers with an in-depth understanding of the latest technologies driving digital manufacturing and smart factories globally. Secondly, it explores how these technologies can be leveraged to enhance efficiency, productivity, and sustainability across different stages of the manufacturing process. Thirdly, the book highlights standalone innovations in fields that have successfully implemented emerging technologies in manufacturing, demonstrating practical applications in real-world contexts. Most importantly, we hope this book will foster innovation by providing insights into how new ideas can be developed by leveraging cutting-edge technology trends while addressing the increasing demands for quality products at lower costs through efficient production methods.

By bringing together contributions from leading experts across related fields, this book also aims to foster collaboration between researchers working on similar topics. It advances current research further by identifying gaps in existing knowledge and proposing solutions based on interdisciplinary approaches.

In summary, this book serves as a comprehensive guide for individuals interested in exploring the possibilities offered by emerging technologies, such as AI, ML, IoT, AR, VR, BDA, Cloud Computing, and Additive Manufacturing, and their potential impact on Digital Manufacturing and Smart Factories. We believe that our publication holds significant potential not only for academic purposes but also for commercial use cases, making it highly relevant both domestically and internationally.

We envision that this book will be particularly useful to researchers, academics, practitioners, students, policymakers, entrepreneurs, and innovators working across different disciplines, such as mechanical and electrical engineering, computer science, and industrial economics. It provides a comprehensive overview of emerging technologies with potential applications to enhance efficiency, productivity, and sustainability across various stages of the manufacturing process.

Furthermore, this book includes case studies from diverse industries such as automotive, aerospace, pharmaceuticals, demonstrating successful implementations within real-world contexts. These case studies make it highly relevant for professionals seeking practical insights into how these emerging technologies can be leveraged to achieve better results.

Lastly, students pursuing degrees related to mechanical, electrical, or computer science will significantly benefit from gaining knowledge of future-proofing skills required in today's job market.

In summary, our audience includes a wide spectrum of individuals, including but not limited to researchers, academics, practitioners, professionals, policymakers, government officials, entrepreneurs, and innovators. We are confident that the knowledge presented in this book will empower and inspire our readers to explore and embrace the incredible potential of emerging technologies in the context of digital manufacturing and smart factories.

We, the editors, express our heartfelt gratitude to all the contributors who have dedicated their time and expertise to make this book a reality. We believe that this publication will not only inform but also inspire, fostering collaboration and innovation in the ever-evolving landscape of digital manufacturing and smart factories. Thank you for joining us on this journey, and we encourage you to explore the chapters within this book to discover the boundless potential of these emerging technologies.

CHAPTER OVERVIEW

As editors of this edited reference book, we are pleased to present an overview of the chapters included in *Human-Centered Approaches in Industry 5.0: Human-Machine Interaction, Virtual Reality Training, and Customer Sentiment Analysis*. This book provides a comprehensive exploration of emerging technologies in the context of Industry 5.0, focusing on their impact on human-machine interaction, virtual reality training, and customer sentiment analysis.

Chapter 1: Emerging Technologies to Enhance Human-Machine Interaction and to Facilitate Industrial Paradigm Shift to Industry 5.0 – A Comprehensive Review

This chapter offers a comprehensive review of emerging technologies that enhance human-machine interaction and drive the paradigm shift to Industry 5.0. It emphasizes the integration and advancement of digital technologies in manufacturing and their transformative potential, highlighting the challenges and opportunities.

Chapter 2: A Review of Big Data Analytics and Artificial Intelligence in Industry 5.0 for Smart Decision-Making

This chapter delves into the profound impact of Big Data Analytics and Artificial Intelligence on smart decision-making in Industry 5.0. It showcases how these technologies play a pivotal role in data acquisition, storage, processing, and improved decision-making across various industrial sectors, with real-world case studies.

Chapter 3: Ergonomic Prevention Method Based on the UX Index to Assess Industrialized Tasks From a Human-Centered Standpoint

This chapter focuses on ergonomic prevention methods, based on the User Experience (UX) index, for assessing industrialized tasks from a human-centered perspective. It explores recent advancements in physiological monitoring technology and its application in improving user experiences in factories.

Chapter 4: A Collaborative Model for Green Factory Through Green Unit Processes

This chapter discusses innovative strategies for achieving environmental sustainability in manufacturing, with a focus on the concept of a "Green Factory" and its component "Green Unit Processes." It emphasizes the importance of collaboration among stakeholders in pursuing sustainable manufacturing practices.

Chapter 5: A Study of Additive Manufacturing Using 3D Printing Machines and Pens – A Review

This chapter explores the applications of additive manufacturing (3D printing) using machines and pens in various industries. It delves into the advantages, limitations, and potential uses of 3D printing technology, shedding light on its role in prototyping, tooling, and production of end-use parts.

Chapter 6: Unleashing the Future Potential of 4D Printing – Exploring Applications in Wearable Technology, Robotics, Energy, Transportation, and Fashion

This chapter explores the emerging field of 4D printing, which combines additive manufacturing with materials capable of self-assembly and shape transformation. It investigates the potential applications of 4D printing in wearable technology, robotics, energy systems, transportation, and the fashion industry.

Chapter 7: Security Incidents and Security Requirements in Internet of Things (IoT) Devices

This chapter delves into the security incidents and requirements associated with Internet of Things (IoT) devices. It highlights the importance of safeguarding IoT devices and their data, discussing historical security incidents and practical measures to enhance IoT security.

Chapter 8: Ethics in AI and Virtual Reality – Ensuring Responsible Development

This chapter explores the ethical considerations at the intersection of artificial intelligence (AI) and virtual reality (VR). It analyzes ethical challenges related to privacy, bias, autonomy, social impact, and regulatory frameworks, providing a comprehensive understanding of the ethical dimensions of AI-driven VR experiences.

Chapter 9: From Code to Care and Navigating Ethical Challenges in AI Healthcare

This chapter examines the ethical challenges that arise with the integration of artificial intelligence (AI) in healthcare. It focuses on topics such as data privacy, bias mitigation, transparency, responsibility, and patient independence in AI-driven healthcare, emphasizing the importance of ethical considerations.

Chapter 10: Machine Learning and Sentiment Analysis – Analyzing Customer Feedback

This chapter explores the applications of machine learning and sentiment analysis in analyzing customer feedback. It delves into the principles of machine learning algorithms and their role in automating sentiment analysis, showcasing practical examples and real-world case studies.

Chapter 11: Machine Learning and Sentiments Analysis Analyzing Customer Reviews

This chapter further investigates the intersection of machine learning and sentiment analysis, specifically focusing on the analysis of customer reviews. It explores how machine learning algorithms can be effectively used to uncover patterns and emotions hidden in customer feedback, providing insights on their intrinsic polarity and emotional undertones.

Chapter 12: Unleashing Customer Insights – Harnessing Machine Learning Approaches for Sentiment Analyzing and Leveraging Customer Feedback

This chapter emphasizes the integration of machine learning with customer sentiment analysis to unveil insights from customer feedback. It discusses various machine learning approaches, preprocessing techniques, and feature engineering for textual data, with a focus on their practical applications in product development, brand management, and personalized marketing.

Chapter 13: Safety for Digital Immersive Environments and Social Economic Dynamics Based on Designing the Metaverse

This chapter explores the safety considerations for digital immersive environments and the social economic dynamics related to designing the metaverse. It discusses the potential of the metaverse, its role in creating virtual worlds, and how it can be leveraged for scientific empirical research in economics.

Chapter 14: Critical Success Factors (CSFs) of Industry Centre of Excellence (ICoE) Performance at Majlis Amanah Rakyat (MARA) Technical and Vocational Education

This chapter addresses the challenges and critical success factors (CSFs) related to Industry Centre of Excellence (ICoE) performance at Majlis Amanah Rakyat (MARA) Technical and Vocational Education institutions. It emphasizes the importance of industry collaboration and discusses how to overcome organizational obstacles for successful ICoE performance.

We believe that the collective insights from these chapters provide a comprehensive understanding of the latest developments and emerging trends in the digital manufacturing landscape, with a particular focus on human-centered approaches and their impact on the Industry 5.0 paradigm shift. We invite readers to explore the individual chapters to gain in-depth knowledge on these topics and their practical applications in various industries.

IN SUMMARY

As editors of this comprehensive reference book, *Human-Centered Approaches in Industry 5.0: Human-Machine Interaction, Virtual Reality Training, and Customer Sentiment Analysis*, we have had the privilege of compiling an insightful collection of chapters that delve into the cutting-edge technologies shaping the future of digital manufacturing.

The industrial landscape is undergoing a profound transformation with the advent of Industry 5.0, a paradigm shift that emphasizes human-technology collaboration. This book has explored the integration and advancement of digital technologies, particularly in the context of manufacturing, and has highlighted the significant role they play in redefining how we approach production, interaction, and data analysis.

Throughout the chapters, you have been exposed to a diverse array of topics, ranging from enhancing human-machine interaction, leveraging virtual reality for training, and harnessing the power of customer sentiment analysis to drive business decisions. We've delved into the ethical considerations that arise in the intersection of AI and virtual reality and have examined the potential applications of 4D printing in various industries.

The critical insights offered by each chapter contribute to our understanding of the profound impact of these emerging technologies. From enhancing ergonomics in industrialized tasks to addressing security incidents in IoT devices, and from analyzing customer feedback using machine learning to exploring the possibilities of the metaverse, the topics covered reflect the multidisciplinary nature of the digital manufacturing landscape.

We believe that this book provides valuable resources for researchers, academics, practitioners, policymakers, students, and innovators who seek to navigate the complex terrain of Industry 5.0. The contributions of the authors, who are experts in their respective fields, offer practical insights and critical knowledge that will undoubtedly inspire further exploration and innovation.

In conclusion, we hope that this book serves as a catalyst for new research, innovation, and transformative practices within the realm of digital manufacturing and Industry 5.0. The collaboration of experts from around the world has created a resource that holds significant potential for both academic and practical use cases, making it highly relevant in the domestic and international arenas.

We extend our heartfelt gratitude to the contributors who have shared their expertise and insights, as well as to the readers for embarking on this journey of exploration with us. As we move forward into this exciting era of digital manufacturing, may the knowledge and ideas within these pages continue to shape the landscape of Industry 5.0, fostering innovation, improving human experiences, and driving sustainable progress in manufacturing and beyond.

Thank you for joining us on this intellectual adventure.

Sincerely,

Ahdi Hassan
Global Institute for Research Education and Scholarship, Amsterdam, The Netherlands

Pushan Kumar Dutta
Amity University, India

Subir Gupta
Swami Vivekanand University, India

Ebrahim Mattar
College of Engineering, University of Bahrain, Bahrain

Satya Singh
Sharda University, Uzbekistan

Chapter 1
Emerging Technologies to Enhance Human-Machine Interaction and to Facilitate Industrial Paradigm Shift to Industry 5.0: A Comprehensive Review

R. Raffik
https://orcid.org/0000-0001-8806-193X
Kumaraguru College of Technology, India

K. B. Sanjeev
https://orcid.org/0009-0000-3919-0313
Kumaraguru College of Technology, India

R. P. Roshan
https://orcid.org/0009-0006-6096-7530
Kumaraguru College of Technology, India

C. Subash
Kumaraguru College of Technology, India

ABSTRACT

Industry 4.0 connects machines and systems, merging the physical and digital worlds using IoT (internet of things), robotics, AI (artificial intelligence), and more. Industry 5.0 integrates humans with advanced tech like quantum computing, digital twins, and cobots for collaborative and efficient production. Digital manufacturing's CAGR (compound annual growth rate) is predicted to rise, reaching $450 billion by 2027. Challenges include human-robot communication. VR plays a significant role in marketing and product promotion. Additive manufacturing reduces waste and is expected to grow to $150 billion. Industry 4.0 and 5.0 roadmap future industrial progress, with Industry 5.0 emphasizing human-robot collaboration. This chapter encourages further exploration of these transformative technologies.

DOI: 10.4018/979-8-3693-2647-3.ch001

INTRODUCTION

Industry 4.0 connects machines and systems in the factory. It is easy to access the equipment via mobile applications, remote sensing, and drones; briefly, it connects the physical world with the digital world. (EHDR da Silva et al.,2019) The key technologies of Industry 4.0 are IoT, robotics, artificial intelligence, computing, additive manufacturing, cyber-physical systems (CPS), AR (Augmented Reality), and VR (Virtual Reality). However, manufacturers are increasing their expenditures on IoT, machine learning, and automation. For the next 5–10 years, the compound annual growth rate (CAGR) of digital manufacturing will rise. Industry 5.0 is like the fourth industrial revolution with some changes; Industry 5.0 is an integration of machines and humans, which is an automatically operated system. With technologies like quantum computing and cyber-physical systems such as digital twins, blockchain, and cobots, digital manufacturing represents the fifth phase, or Industry 5.0. Work is done collaboratively and using robots makes difficult activities done by humans easier and increases mass production compared to manually operated systems. In 2027, the global market for digital manufacturing will be valued more 450 billion United States dollars and raise at a CAGR of 12.9%. The vast amount of data that these linked items produce serves as the 21st century's raw material (Yuval Cohen et al.,2019). Furthermore, as manufacturers increase the level of automation made feasible with Al, which is machine vision, real-time information analytics, and Edge Computing, which is discrete production is predicted to expand quickly.

The main challenge of Industry 5.0 is that workers cannot collaborate with robots because the robots cannot understand the workers' communication and cannot understand what they are saying. Industry 5.0 is the result of the convergence of advanced technology and design that is oriented towards people. Together, machines and human beings generate products in a symbiotic way, with each bringing a separate set of strengths to the process. Cobots (collaborative robots) are key components of Industry 5.0, as they can be easily and quickly programmed to adapt to changing production demands, boosting industrial flexibility (Sahan A. M. et al., 2023). Industry 5.0 influenced industries other than manufacturing, such as healthcare, education, and coordination, which embraced similar concepts of human-machine collaboration. Manufacturing has improved greatly because of the quick transition from industrial 4.0 to 5.0.

The fifth generation of industry efforts to overcome the issues highlighted by Industry 4.0 while developing a more productive, customised, and ecological manufacturing method by focusing on the merging of physical, digital, and biological systems. This transition will be facilitated by the deployment of modern innovations such as artificial intelligence and the IoT, which can enhance productivity, consumer health and happiness (Abilesh, K. S. et al., 2023). One of the major technologies in Industry 4.0 was Virtual reality (VR) is a significant advancement in the merging of software and hardware technologies. A human can interact with a three-dimensional virtual environment in virtual reality by using interactive gear, such as goggles, headsets, gloves, or body suits, that transmit signals and information (Raffik R. et al., 2023). Internet and various digital communication channels are utilized to interact with potential customers for their brand promotions in digital online marketing. Digital marketing also includes marketing channels, text messaging, multimedia marketing, all social networking platforms, emails, and web-based solutions for product advertisements.

Virtual reality might develop into a more potent and useful tool in the future. Hospitals, schools, the automobile industry, marketing, tourism, engineering, gaming, and entertainment are just a few of the industries that benefit from it. Businesses in the quick-paced digital world are always looking for fresh ways to connect with customers and set themselves apart from the competition. The benefits of employing virtual reality in digital manufacturing go beyond the enhancement of individual process efficiency and competence. VR has the potential to be a fantastic tool for product promotion on a digital marketing platform. The digital marketing platform may approach or offer its products in a three-dimensional simulation using VR-integrated devices. The customer might thus enjoy the gratification of reviewing a new product without visiting a store.

Virtual reality in digital marketing is primarily used to increase customer interaction by enabling customers to research new products from the comfort of their homes. In a congested digital world, virtual reality is a great tool for grasping and retaining customers' attention. Through appealing three-dimensional simulations, virtual reality enables companies to engage emotionally with their customers. As a result, the consumer becomes pickier and more discerning. Virtual reality may effectively link a product or brand to the consumer emotionally. Virtual reality helps the brand attract customers by elevating their experience. Brands and companies can create a Virtual showroom for their products where customers can purchase and evaluate the products, allowing them to experience unpredictable reality while still being in their comfort zone. Through virtual reality, customers can experience personalization and privacy throughout their purchases, which may help gather information on the customer's tailoring and optimising of their search for products, which will be beneficial to the customer in purchasing a product that will truly satisfy them (Raffik R. et al., 2023).

The most powerful and significant digital marketing tactic is brand storytelling, which uses narrative to explain and transmit the historical core, values, and personality of a brand to its target market. Innovative technology businesses from all sectors will continue to use virtual reality as the most important and practical approach to using this game-changing technology to forge remarkable relationships with their consumers. The future of digital marketing is driven by virtual reality. For a prolonged period, companies produced products using the subtractive manufacturing approach, in which a certain shape of the material is taken and processed with operations such as cutting and moulding to create the desired output. The huge disadvantage of this technology is the waste of raw materials. However, Additive manufacturing has emerged as a new industrial revolution in recent years. Predictive manufacturing process trends that are connected to the growth of novel innovations might vary by region (Bojana Nikolic et al.,2017).

Additive Manufacturing has the advantage of reducing material waste by creating items using 3D CAD modelling software. Additive Manufacturing creates products with more complexity while still maintaining dimensional accuracy, precision, tolerances, and required material properties. It also reduces prototype time and cost. Many consider additive manufacturing to be a disruptive innovation for society since it allows customers to produce their items. In this decade, the Additive manufacturing industry is expected to grow from $12 billion to about $150 billion as it shifts from prototype to mass production. Integration of smart technologies and production systems, such as additive manufacturing, promotes Industry 4.0 and plays a vital role in solving some of the essential requirements of the 4th Industrial Revolution. Additive manufacturing will be the next paradigm for futuristic production, and as the technology for additive manufacturing advances, more innovative technologies will be created. In addition, despite the reality that Industry 4.0 is still in its initial stages of development and the major breakthroughs cannot be anticipated till the period between 2020 and 2025 (Skobelev P. O. & Borovik S. Yu,2017).

This article briefly discusses the industrial applications, difficulties, and opportunities of additive manufacturing technology. It will also concentrate on presenting difficulties, advances, and future trends for the research community and integrate techniques in Additive manufacturing-related domains to assist in future research. Industry 4.0 started to emerge to manage industrial problems. The main objective of Industry 4.0 is integrating machines, humans, IoT, cloud computing to achieve maximum performance. Industry 5.0 increases the industry's efficiency and productivity by combining the human creative ability with precision and accuracy of robotic systems to create unique solutions for industrial demands. It considers the potential advancements and futuristic predictions based on collaboration with robots and humans. Industry 5.0 is the new industrial paradigm that frequently results in efficient and effective solutions. Industry 4.0 and 5.0 have developed a roadmap for organisations to follow to thrive. The co-habitation between the two Manufacturing Revolution generates necessitate discussions and justifications (Xun Xu et al.,2021). There is more discussion on the practical uses and innovations made possible by Industry 5.0, such as production growth, high profit, supply chain, and more. Further understanding of this technology, this research also takes notes on the suggestions and difficulties presented by Industry 5.0. This article intends to discuss these technologies and encourage more insights into these domains.

INDUSTRIAL REVOLUTION'S HISTORY

The primary industrial revolution became a turning point in the development of industrialization in the late 18th century when products were created using processes created and approved for machine production. This revolution had an impact on industries by moving the economy from handicrafts to machines. Industry 2.0, the following industrial revolution, occurred between 1871 and 1914, allowing for a speedier spread of breakthrough ideas. Modern technologies like big data, artificial intelligence, digital twins, and future-oriented wireless networks are going to have a considerable influence on Industries 5.0 and Society 5.0 (Sihan Huang et al.,2022). This revolution fosters innovation and considerable progress in Industry 1.0, and this period is characterized by economy growth and increased company productivity.

The Digital Revolution, also known as Industry 3.0, occurred in the second half of the 20th century, and was characterized by the incorporation of computers and digital technology into several sectors. Today's industrial revolution, known as Industry 4.0, integrates physical assets with innovative technology like the Internet of Things (IoT), the cloud, robotics, 3D printers, machine learning, and more. The structure is being strengthened by emphasizing "smart operators" as tools for human-centricity (Mariia Golovianko et al.,2020). The forthcoming industrial revolution, called Industry 5.0, was about robots helping people perform faster and better tasks by leveraging modern technology such as IOT and data analytics. It humanizes the industry 4.0 pillars of automation and efficiency. Several enabling technological trends, such as Digital Twin, Artificial Intelligence, Mixed Reality, Additive Manufacturing, 5G and beyond, Cobots, Blockchain, and IoE are shown in Figure 1. Those will make Industry 5.0 an advanced production model with a focus on human-machine interactions. It humanizes the industry 4.0 pillars of automation and efficiency.

Figure 1. Enabling Technologies in Industry 5.0

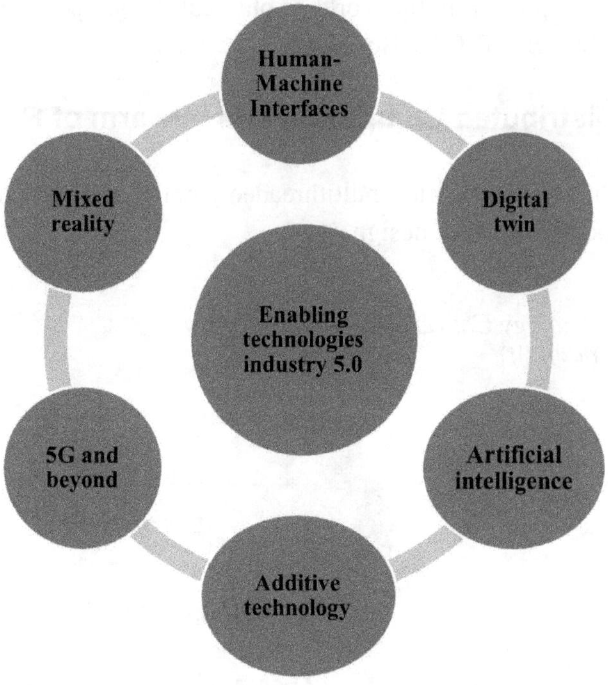

INDUSTRY 4.0 TO 5.0 EVOLUTION IN DIGITAL MANUFACTURING

The expression "Industry 4.0" refers to new technological developments in manufacturing that enable personalised manufacturing and rely on digital and virtual technology. (Jon Kepa Gerrikagoitia et al.,2019) These advancements are meant to help the industry respond to some major global concerns. According to Hartmann et al, who include Digital Manufacturing underneath the aegis of industry 4.0 technologies, business executives concur that technologies of digital manufacturing will alter facets of value chains' production processes. Computer Integrated Manufacturing (CIM), and Cyber-Physical Systems (CPS) (Thomas Kurfess et al.,2020) which was created in the early 1980s, early on in CPS's development (Anbesh Jamwal et al.,2021). Then the computer was being used significantly for machines and automated control, and planning transformed into Digital Manufacturing technologies. It may have been unavoidable for manufacturing to become more interdisciplinary. The notion of industry 5.0 in digital manufacturing - which underlined the more cooperative design of products and procedures is required from the fusion of organisational sciences such as Lean Manufacturing, also known as the concept of TQM- total quality management, and concurrently integrating with the engineering sciences of the CIM. shows the typical "pyramid of sciences and technologies," whose confluence, in our view, can lead to the transformation to Societies 5.0. In a method of abstractions from the environment of actual objects (with certain elements of AI), the layers of the pyramid are distributed from the bottom to the top of it leading to principles of society 5.0, addressed how 4.0 industry practises and ethical manufacturing may increase resource efficiency, reduce waste, and boost the use of energy (Farhan Aslam et al.,2020). It might involve emergent intelligence (AI), an innovative theory of intersubjective management processes in daily life. Figure 2 shows the typical "pyramid of sciences and technologies" whose convergence can help with the transition to Society 5.0. The distribution of layers in a pyramid to its top begins from the bottom in a process of abstraction from the world of physical things (perhaps with some AI items) to concepts of Society 5.0 (Skobelev P. O. & Borovik S. Yu,2017).

Fresh Varieties of Distributed Computing and "Swarm of Robots"

Decentralised networks of computers offer multithreaded parallel and asynchronous computation and feature a complicated topology network design.

Figure 2. Science and Technology Convergence in Society 5.0
[(Skobelev P. O. & Borovik S. Yu,2017)]

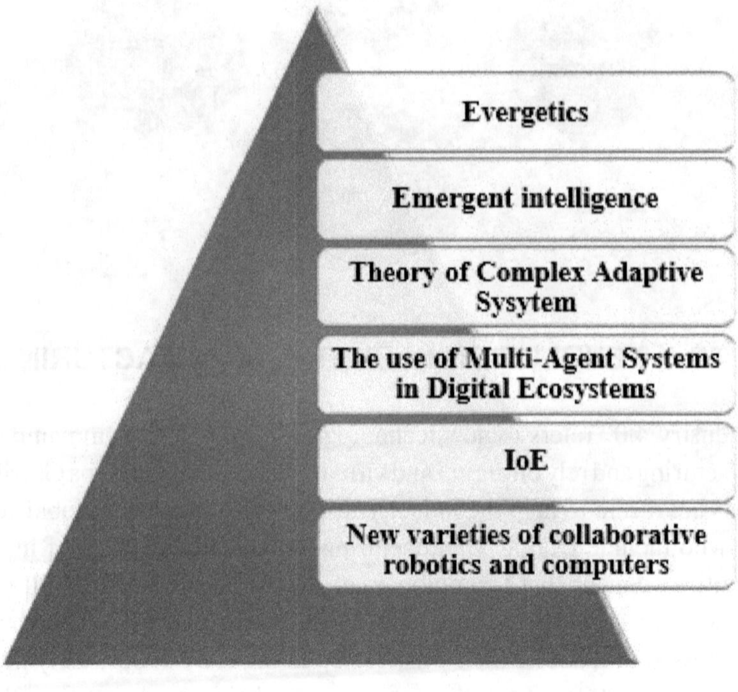

Self-contained robot groupings are referred to as "swarms of robots". And in this case, we are not only talking about anthropomorphic robots; we are also talking about distributed smart technological systems. This concept may be shown via intelligent gas turbines with intelligent blades. Every single blade of these engines "agrees with neighbours" regarding where it should be in the air-gas channel (how it should be spun) to create the best circumstances for the operating medium's (gas) flowing and avoid the generator reaching a state of emergency status (Elias Ribeiro da Silva et al.,2020). These innovations additionally involve independent collection of tiny spacecrafts (nano- and piko- satellites), that like a hive of bees, can be multifaceted and adaptably setup to solve a specific issue while remaining stable and reliable in the most diverse circumstances during Earth observations, object study in wide-open space, communications troubleshooting, and other various tasks. Another instance is a "swarm" of pilotless trucks and other agricultural machinery that are communicating with every other and is in continuous interaction amongst oneself, cooperating with one another.

People and the Internet of Things

The Internet of Things (IoT) is a rapidly evolving technology field that complements regular internet usage for humans. It includes the Industrial Internet of Things (IIoT) and serves as a foundation of society, playing a crucial role in the fourth industrial revolution, known as Manufacturing 5.0. According to the ITU-Y.2060 recommendation, the World Wide Web of Things is an international infrastructure that advances services through the information age. It establishes connections between both real and virtual objects by utilizing adaptable and accessible information and modern methods of communication. In broader terms, a "thing" refers to any object in the physical or virtual world that is recognizable and can be integrated into communication networks. In 2013, Cisco introduced the term "Internet of Everything" (IoE), which is a broader concept than IoT. According to Cisco, IoE encompasses the networked connectivity of people, data, processes, and objects. While IoT is a part of the technologies that make up IoE, it is not limited to Industry 4.0. The deployment of IoT (including IIoT and IoE) requires the development of various technologies such as telecommunications, intelligent sensors, smart dust, Wi-Fi, 6LoWPAN, RFID (Radio Frequency Identification), NFC, and others. These technologies enable "things" to incorporate "intelligence" at various stages of development and production. In our society, focused on Manufacturing 5.0, IoT and IoE should not be viewed solely as innovations benefiting Industry 4.0 technologies.

Multi-Agent Systems and Technologies

The Internet of Things (IoT) technology has expanded into the virtual realm, commonly known as the "cloud." In this digital environment, physical objects are represented by corresponding "virtual twins" that follow specific algorithms and rules. Intelligent agents play a crucial role in enabling communication, collecting information from the physical world, making decisions, and collaborating with other objects or individuals in real time, both in real-life and online settings. These physical objects can operate autonomously or as part of complex systems, including household appliances, manufacturing lines, or fleets of aerial vehicles. To manage this diversity, a multi-agent structure is employed to create a network of interconnected private agents. These agents exist within a broader context and collaborate for various purposes to achieve system objectives. These agents can interact directly through message exchange or indirectly by modifying their immediate environment. Multi-agent systems and technologies are crucial in building digital environments where services can collaborate and compete effectively. They are highly effective in addressing complex issues, such as resource optimization, planning, and information extraction from extensive datasets, both large and small (Raffik R. et al., 2023). In summary, IoT technology has gone beyond simple device connectivity to become a sophisticated Internet of entities and objects, known as the "internet of agents."

Scientific and Technical Backlogs: Eligibility and Development

Researchers and IT developers are focusing on, and will continue to focus on, the essential fields of science and technology that enable the transition to a society of 5.0. These fields were briefly mentioned in section 2. Author-represented organisations are not a unique case. Since we were early adopters in many of the directions, we possess the essential knowledge and background in the construction of comparable systems (Dilberoglu U. M. et al., 2017). The creation of systems with several agents, ontology analysis of data, and energetics are our primary areas of interest and accomplishment in the relevant context. Samara has been developing multi-agent systems and techniques for almost 25 years (since 1990). Initially, there was a focus on creating novel approaches and tools to address difficult issues related to the concept of organizing themselves and development ("emerging intelligence"). In specific instances of multi-agent evolution that have been effective, devices were coupled with simulations of needs networks and chances (NO-networks) and the conjugate technique of real-time communication for resource management (Qiu X et al.,2023). This strategy was created in the efforts of P. Skobelev and V. Vittikh and led to the formation of NO-networks. The roles of wants and opportunities both carry an understanding of the "past" or "in the future" inside themselves. With such a strategy, it is possible to see the many procedures for resolving complicated multicriteria management of resource tasks of any sort (static or mobile, split up, reusable, etc.) from a completely new angle.

Many Industries 4.0 technologies are not fully implemented yet, especially in SMEs or across entire value chains (Alejandro Germán Frank et al., 2019). In this instance, they are viewed as an organized process that includes recognizing conflicts and settlement among agents through discussions with concessions to obtain their permission (consensus). As previously mentioned, the organization of knowledge bases about detail domains and methods of information deployment in systems with several agents is done on the foundation of ontologies, which allow for the description of the diverse, multicopying, and unfinished knowledge that might include false knowledge and can be linked not only hierarchically but additionally by structures of networks, etc. S. Smirnov created groundbreaking achievements in ontological data analysis (Yasmin A et al., 2015). He contributed an important solution to some of the serious issues in this field: the automated process of the creation of ontology for data fields based on observations, which is founded on the examination of fundamental notions. The common object-and-features data arrangement was expanded upon, and multiple-valued vectorial logic was employed to analyses the data (Leng J et al., 2021).

Furthermore, it is essential to note that formalized ontology can serve as a scientific and methodological framework for the application of the foundational ideas of the developed framework for intersubjective management processes and energetics. It is feasible to utilize an approach of ontology data analysis, especially to identify the emotions of a problem scenario for the actor. The theoretically sound and logical examination of the formal notions serves as the method's foundation.

DIGITAL MANUFACTURING

Digital technologies are becoming increasingly essential across various industries, revolutionizing manufacturing in what is known as Industry 4.0. This digital transformation empowers businesses to enhance their production processes and compete globally. In the earlier industrial phases (1.0 and 2.0), information was primarily conveyed through physical prototypes and drawings during research and development. Physical prototypes were a necessity to validate the alignment of virtual models with the actual product's structure, ergonomics, and performance. Industry 3.0 introduced concepts like virtual prototypes and digital prototypes, replacing the need for physical ones. Information models took precedence over physical representations, including PTC, Siemens, ANSYS, and Dassault. In a sense, physics is replaced in a digital prototype by the information model (Fast-Berglund Å et al.,2018). Industry 4.0, or smart manufacturing, presents a global perspective on the fourth industrial revolution. It emphasizes integrating information and communication technologies (ICT) into manufacturing to create intelligent factories with fully integrated production processes. This marks a new era in industrial technology, focusing on maximizing productivity and efficiency while minimizing resource consumption. Industry 4.0 has transformed every aspect of manufacturing, from product design to production, resource management, and customer satisfaction. Digital manufacturing streamlines processes and its importance were represented in below Table.1., fosters innovation, improves customer interactions, and enhances cost efficiency. It leverages computerized technology, artificial intelligence, and machine learning to optimize manufacturing processes and introduces digital tools and automation to improve industrial output and development.

Table. 1. Digital Manufacturing Process

S. No.	Digital Manufacturing Process	Process Enablers and its Importance
1	Collaborative Design	VR enables the entire design team to collaborate within virtual environments, enhancing visual representation and facilitating interaction with product models (Pérez, L et al.,2020).
2	Design Evaluation	The capability of three-dimensional (3D) visualization ensures that professionals can utilize it as a shared place to create and share design entities. This platform gives authorized users in different geographical areas access to the company's product data, such as product drawing files kept on designated servers, and allows them to collaborate on product design work simultaneously and cooperatively on any operating system (Pappas, M. et al.,2006).
3	Production Planning	The combination of these two technologies, assembly simulation and virtual reality, enables the construction of fully interactive and immersive 3D visualisations of assembly lines and factories. Users can experience their simulation model, travel through their virtual factories, visually check the different stations, interactively assess bottlenecks, and so on in these virtual interactive settings.
4	Training	VR is an effective tool for assembly Training. It provides a risk-free digital environment with superior input and output devices that allow the user to interact with the digital components intuitively. It helps to bridge the actual and digital worlds. This reduces risk and workers can safely practice both new and existing tasks
5	Quality Appraisal	VR is employed to evaluate part designs, machinery selections, and factors impacting quality, machining duration, and expenses through modelling and simulation (Pérez, L et al.,2020).
6	Rapid Prototyping	The Virtual Prototyping system improves the collaboration and communication of a product development design team. It provides simulation approaches for analysing and improving a product's design and manufacture processes. The assessment and adjustment of a product design can be iterated using simulations without having to worry about the production and material expenses of prototypes (Choi, S. H., & Cheung, H. H. ,2008).
7	Inspection	Customers can inspect a design and adjust using VR technology during the early stages of the product development process. By creating virtual environments that accurately simulate real-world inspection scenarios, researchers can analyse and improve various aspects of the inspection process. This includes studying the effectiveness of different inspection techniques, identifying potential collision risks, and fine-tuning the precision of the overall process.

VIRTUAL REALITY

The foundation of the digital realm hinges on swift connectivity and rapid processing, alongside the evolution of augmented reality (AR) and virtual reality (VR) as emerging display platforms for more immersive interactions between humans and computers. Virtual reality is a technology that immerses the user in a computer-generated, three-dimensional environment that is simulated, and it is a platform that is comprised of specialized hardware and software. This makes the attraction more dynamic and realistic for people than standard projectors or displays. VR has emerged as one of the most intriguing and disruptive technical breakthroughs of our time, with the capacity to transport users to a digital environment (Wohlgenannt, I et al.,2020). During the 1960s and 1970s, visionaries like Ivan Sutherland established the groundwork for VR through their basic head-mounted displays, which served as the precursor for the advancement of virtual reality (VR), augmented reality (AR), and mixed reality (MR) (Mujber, T. S et al.,2004). Although virtual reality did not emerge until the 2010s, it swiftly became mainstream. Virtual reality cemented its position in 2014 with the company's Oculus VR headsets.

The primary objective of virtual reality is to allow people to interact with their surroundings as if they were in the real world. Virtual reality strives to convey a sense of presence and the environment even when it is not present. It was made feasible through the integration of software and hardware. Spatial audio enhances the experience by immersing users in a soundscape that adjusts to their movements. Depending on the VR system and software, users can interact with the digital environment via motion controllers, their own motions, or vocal commands. Unlocking the Future of Manufacturing: Embracing Virtual Reality in Industry 4.0 for Enhanced Efficiency, Training, and Innovation is shown in Figure 3. The technology development of virtual reality has diverse applications in many disciplines, such as training and simulation, enhanced learning, architectural and design visualization, healthcare and therapy, remote collaboration, gaming and entertainment, art and creative expression, tourism and travel, data visualization, reduced risk and cost accessibility, marketing and branding, innovative storytelling, environmental and social impact, and product design and prototyping.

Figure 3. Benefits of Virtual Reality in Digital Manufacturing Industry 4.0

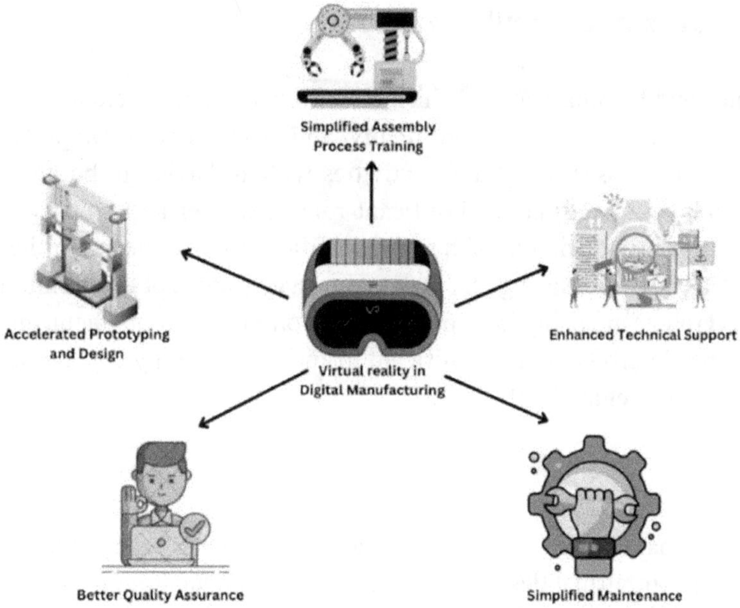

Fundamentals of Virtual Reality in Digital Manufacturing

The modern digital world relies on automated and computerized manufacturing units to produce commodities that fulfil the expectations of customers in terms of use, functionality, and quality. "Lean automation" refers to the combination of automation technology and lean production. These Cyber-Physical Production Systems (CPPS) monitor real operations, reach independent judgments, and immediately initiate responses (Abishek, B. A. et al., 2023). They engage in communication and collaboration with both each other and individuals. Networked machines perform better in terms of efficiency, collaboration, and resilience (Raffik R. et al., 2023).

The precise and enhanced production of final products is now accomplished through the utilization of contemporary CPPSs and unsupervised robots or machinery, which constitutes a pivotal element of Industry 4.0. The use of unsupervised robots or machinery that are supervised by CPPS and human operators is necessary for intelligent automation. Robots are used in agricultural sectors and landmining processes (Zhe An et al., 2022). Enhancing worker safety and efficiency, previously limited by labor-intensive processes, are the main objectives (Raffik R. et al., 2023). Safety issues have limited the employment of robots in industrial settings; they are frequently kept far from people, and some jobs are thought to be too expensive (Zhang, L et al.,2019). Wireless autonomous systems with sensor fusion techniques are deployed for effective industry performance (Vanteru, M. K. et al., 2022). The versatility and scalability of VR also enables the accurate simulation of complicated and dynamic trends. VR's capacity to portray a model as realistically as possible, along with a user-friendly interface, may simplify and hasten a work. VR can help with more than one element of production, including factory layout planning, product design, maintenance, CNC machining, robotics, and assembly design.

Virtual Factory Tours and Familiarization

Virtual Factory Tours and Familiarization, which give workers an intellectual and engaging experience as well as hands-on experience using virtual reality, allows workers to comprehend, investigate, and become acquainted with industries and their activities without having to be physically there. Virtual factory tours and familiarization play a significant role in worker and employer safety by allowing workers to learn about safety standards and hazard identification in a safe, controlled environment. This improves worker efficiency by ensuring that personal mistakes are kept to a minimum. Automation and smart interconnected robots are being incorporated into commercial manufacturing processes, which is resulting in a sharp rise in productivity, significant material and energy cost reductions, and improved workplace safety (Zhang, L et al.,2019).

Design

Industry 4.0 creates a dynamic environment for designers, engineers, and manufacturers to generate and assess 3D models, perform virtual design reviews, and plan production processes with unprecedented efficiency and precision. The virtual reality platform provides a personalized platform for a large industrial team to review the 3D CAD model design and check for mistakes. This element reduces mistakes in design creation, evaluation, and manufacturing. This enables employees and designers to create a product model through creative thinking and invention, resulting in more efficient and visually beautiful goods. Furthermore, VR enables the quick production and assessment of prototypes, minimizing the time and expenses associated with traditional physical prototyping. The design of complicated items frequently includes several skills and domains. Different domains are included in the design of distinct items. Statics, dynamics, kinematics, fluid mechanics, and thermodynamic simulation are all included in structural simulation, which frequently combines with the finite element analysis methodology. These are structural analyses conducted over 3D CAD designs. The real operation of electronic circuits is reproduced in electronic circuit simulation using the defined model. Physical circuit design is expensive, especially for sophisticated integrated circuits (Yasmin, A et al.,2015).

Production

A critical and difficult phase of the product life cycle that directly affects the outcome as well as the effectiveness of the finished product is the manufacturing execution process. The result is the most vital component of the process and improves industrial output by providing immersive simulations and training environments that increase design, assembly, quality control, maintenance, and cooperation. It lowers costs, decreases mistakes, improves processes, and raises product quality. VR also allows for remote help, predictive maintenance, and tailored training, all of which contribute to greater production efficiency and competitiveness (Yasmin, A et al.,2015). By providing creative ways to track, arrange, and optimize inventory, virtual reality (VR) is positioned to transform inventory management. Managers may tour virtual places to evaluate inventory levels, organization, and layout by using VR to turn warehouses and inventory storage systems into immersive 3D settings. Additionally, VR-based training programs may effectively onboard inexperienced staff by enabling them to master inventory management operations in a virtual warehouse environment, lowering the learning curve and improving accuracy. By giving employees visual overlays and instructions, speeding the process, and reducing mistakes, VR also helps with order picking and fulfilment. VR technology may also be quite helpful for stocktaking and audits by offering an interactive and effective way to confirm inventory correctness. The use of VR in inventory management often promises increased effectiveness, fewer mistakes, and increased production in the warehouse. Furthermore, it might completely alter how companies track and manage their inventory. Workers can readily access real-time data and information on inventory levels thanks to VR technology, making it simpler to track and manage stock. Along with saving time, this lowers the potential for human mistakes during manual inventory checks. Additionally, VR can provide remote inventory management, which enables companies to keep an eye on and manage their stock from anywhere in the globe, further boosting productivity and efficiency. The potential influence of VR on inventory management is genuinely revolutionary as it develops and becomes more widely available.

Testing

In general, the use of virtual reality for training is not a novel notion. Virtual reality is also used to monitor and compare the actual performance of a design or manufacturing process (Peng Q,2007, pp.1-2). Virtual model's functionalities can be increased by leveraging their scalability and adaptability to serve as a training ground for operators without incurring major additional costs. Virtual reality allows for the monitoring and scheduling of all manufacturing processes, including assembly line production, packing, stocking, and scheduling. This improves productivity and optimization, decreases movement and transportation, and opens the door to potential future additions (Yasmin A et al.,2015).

VR allows users to experience difficult-to-access scenarios, providing immersive experiences that closely resemble reality. It accelerates comprehension and reduces uncertainty. Moreover, VR enables users to view hidden objects not visible in traditional 3D models. Beyond these advantages, VR can significantly cut product lead times and costs, enhance product quality and reliability, and seamlessly integrate the entire product design and manufacturing processes into a virtual environment, revolutionizing the way industries approach design, testing, and production (Veleva, S. S & Tsvetanova, A. I., 2020). By delivering realistic and engaging learning experiences, virtual reality (VR) is changing maintenance and assembly training. Staff and workers can practice difficult activities in a secure virtual setting where they can engage with lifelike models of tools and machinery. This hands-on method minimizes mistakes, increases learner confidence, and hastens the development of skills.

In addition, VR provides remote training, allowing instructors to mentor and evaluate students from a distance, promoting effective knowledge transfer and raising worker proficiency in assembly and maintenance jobs. Additionally, virtual reality (VR) gives businesses a practical way to deliver training programs without having to buy expensive tools or technology. This lowers the likelihood of mishaps during actual hands-on training while also saving money on procurement and maintenance expenditures. VR is redefining product testing by providing a diverse platform for analyzing and enhancing items across sectors. VR allows designers and engineers to construct virtual prototypes, simulate product behavior realistically, and immerse testers in virtual worlds for user experience and safety evaluations. It shortens the feedback loop, lowers the cost of physical prototypes, and improves testing accessibility by permitting remote cooperation. VR also allows for more efficient and informed decision-making through training and personalized test situations. As VR technology advances, its application in product testing can streamline product development processes and increase product quality.

Sales and Digital Marketing

The digital world has had a major influence on the globe's marketing platform, forcing businesses to adopt and accept innovative technology for marketing strategies. Digital marketing using virtual reality is the use of modern technology to promote or denigrate a product, service, or brand directly to targeted consumers via online platforms. The progression of VR technology has opened doors for the emergence of digital marketing platforms, including online advertising, email marketing, social media marketing, text messaging, affiliate marketing, search engine optimization, and more. Digital marketing through virtual reality encompasses a wide range of promotional tactics that leverage digital technology to engage and attract clients. This disruptive technological wave has completely transformed how businesses engage with their existing and prospective customers. Recent studies show that over 75% of consumers now devote a massive portion of their daily lives to digital environments, making it an integral and genuine companion when making choices about companies, products, and services (Peng, Q ,2007, pp.1-2).

Traditional marketing relies heavily on offline mediums such as magazines, newspapers, billboards, resulting in less contact with customers and a lack of faith in the marketing of the product. Traditional marketing focuses on a specific target, whereas traditional product marketing is mostly determined by geographical location. As a result, the product has less influence on customers. Traditional marketing lacks real-time engagement and communication between companies or brands and their customers. This may diminish customer loyalty to specific products, companies, or brands. Open marketing has a lower influence on consumer personalization. This minimizes personalization to safeguard the clients' selection of brands and desired items (Bala M & Verma D,2018). The shortcomings of traditional marketing are addressed by digital marketing, which employs innovative technologies. Digital marketing using virtual reality is mostly based on Internet marketing and the social media market.

Digital marketing using virtual reality has an impact on a worldwide audience that is not restricted by location. It offers real-time analytics and monitoring capabilities, allowing organizations to assess campaign effectiveness, click-through rates, conversion rates, and other crucial indicators. Leveraging virtual reality in digital marketing fosters a tailored setting for customers to acquire products. The rising trend of personalized marketing, which entails offering product recommendations based on user behaviors and preferences, is gaining momentum. This approach enhances the user experience and has the potential to boost conversion rates. Through digital marketing technology, customers gain the advantage of accessing corporate updates and information about products or services at their convenience, irrespective of location and time. It empowers customers to interact with businesses by exploring websites, making online transactions, and leaving feedback.

Digital marketing ensures customers have access to comprehensive product details, minimizing the risk of misunderstandings compared to face-to-face interactions. One of the significant benefits for consumers lies in their ability to efficiently compare products and services from various suppliers, a particularly valuable feature as more businesses shift to online marketing. Online purchasing is accessible 24/7, offering flexibility to buyers. Furthermore, digital marketing simplifies the process of sharing product or service content, allowing viewers to discuss features with others. Pricing is transparent, and companies can adjust rates or provide discounts as needed. Offering complicated prices is challenging in traditional marketing; however, information in digital marketing could explain all the pricing options that potential customers would find appealing (Todor R.D., 2016). The transformative power of Virtual Reality in Digital Manufacturing in Industry 4.0 is represented as a flow graph in Fig.4.

Figure 4. Impact of Virtual Reality in Industry 4.0

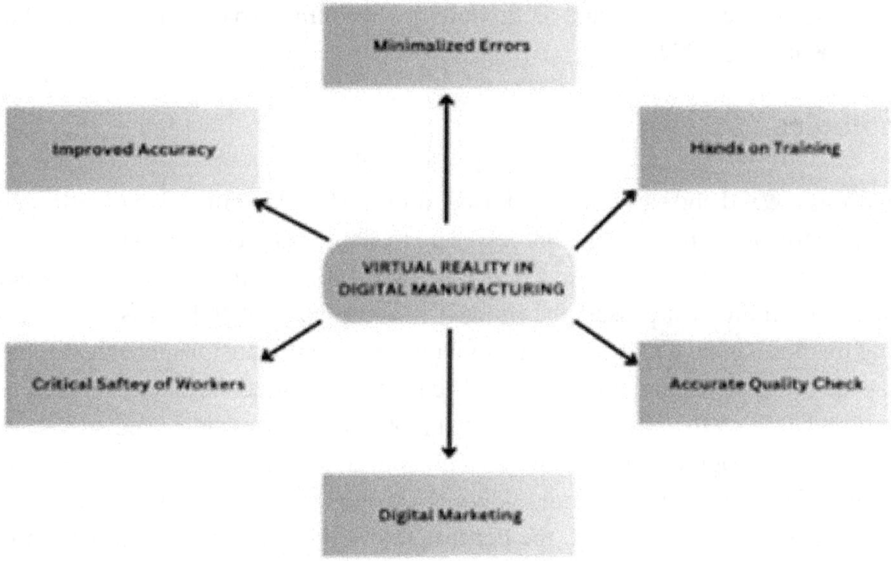

ADDITIVE MANUFACTURING

For a long time, industries used a traditional manufacturing process known as subtractive manufacturing. It is a type of procedure that involves processes such as grinding, cutting, drilling, cutting, and boring to make the product by eliminating the material. Unlike traditional subtractive processes, which create a product from a big piece of material by machining it, additive manufacturing develops a final product by adding layers on top of each layer (Di Nardo, M & Yu, H., 2021). CNC machining and CAD software have typically been used in this process. The greatest disadvantage was the high percentage of raw material wastage (Abdulhameed, O et al.,2019). However, our technologies are continually improving, and additive manufacturing has emerged as a new industrial revolution in recent years. It is defined as a process of producing items via layer-by-layer deposition of material utilizing 3D CAD modelling software. To create products, additive manufacturing melts, fuses, or cures liquid polymer material. It builds products layer by layer using 3D CAD drawings.

Current terminologies for additive manufacturing methods include 3D printing, rapid manufacturing, direct digital manufacturing, rapid prototyping, and solid freeform fabrication. Using 3D computer data or Standard Tessellations Language (STL) files that include geometric data about an item, additive manufacturing builds components (Raffik R. et al., 2023). When high design complexity and low production volume are required, additive manufacturing is quite useful. Additive manufacturing can be done by processes such as SLA, SLS, FDM (Fused Deposition Modelling), SLM, DMLS, EBM, material jetting, and binder jetting, with each process differing depending on the material used. Even though additive manufacturing has many benefits, its applications remain limited as it is less accurate and takes longer to create products than CNC machines (Bikas, H et al.,2016).

The additive manufacturing process is composed of three phases: design, processing, and testing. Recent advancements in industrial applications of metal-based additive manufacturing have made it possible to manufacture products like car engines, power tools, manufacturing equipment, and others. Many industry sectors, including the automotive, medical, and aerospace industries, are quickly adopting additive manufacturing technologies and methodologies, and this expansion is expected to continue in upcoming years (Kumar, S., 2020).

AM Technologies

A CAD design was created and saved in STL format for transfer to the machine (post-processing) in the first phase of the additive manufacturing process. The machine was set up, and the product was created and removed in the next phase (Abdulhameed, O et al.,2019). In the third phase, the product is inspected against the specified limit; if it passes, the product is accepted; if it fails, it is rejected. The additive manufacturing method can be classified depending on machine dimensions, nozzle dimensions, nozzle speed, workspace dimensions, and other factors. Figure 5 shows that additive manufacturing technologies are classified based on the type of raw material (solid, liquid, powder) used.

SLA: SLA (Stereolithography Apparatus) is a process of making use of a laser to solidify tiny layers of ultraviolet (UV) light-sensitive liquid polymer (Wohlers, T et al.,2016), for manufacturing final products. After each new layer is cured, the construction platform slides down the item as layers are produced. These layers are continually cured or hardened using ultraviolet light, which creates a pattern on the liquid resin's surface. Supporting structures are required for SLA to connect the component to the construction platform and to hold the product while it floats in liquid resin. In 1987, 3D Systems' stereolithography (SL), a process that employs the ultraviolet laser (UV) to solidify the layers of liquid polymer, was the first commercial use of AM (Wong, K. V. & Hernandez A., 2012).

Figure 5. Additive Manufacturing technologies
[Abdulhameed, O et al.,2019]

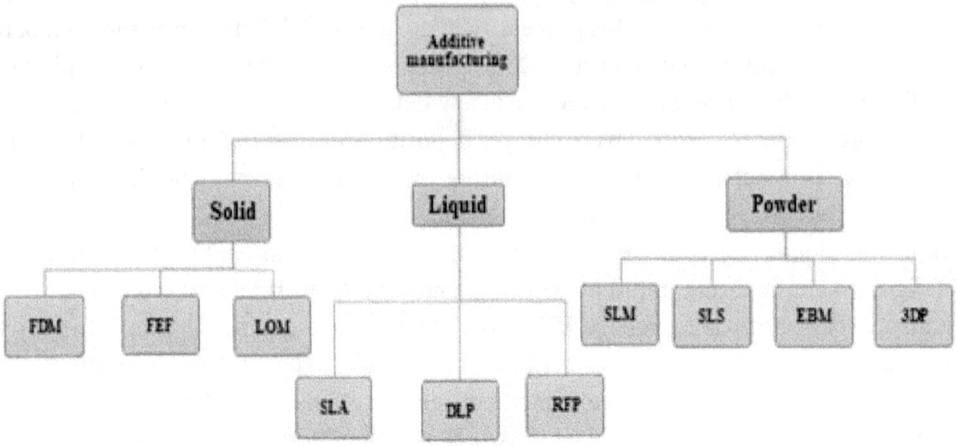

SLS: SLS (Selective Laser Sintering) is a method of sintering or melting spread layer powder particles that use high-intensity CO2 layers. The bed is slowly lowered with each successive layer scan, and a new powder layer is put on top; the same process is repeated. The fundamental advantage of SLS is that it is a self-supporting additive manufacturing process because the object is placed in a bed of powder as it builds, and no further supports are required. It utilises production-grade nylon materials, resulting in flexibility, toughness, heat resistance, and flame retardancy.

FDM: FDM (Fused deposition modelling), is based on the layer-by-layer deposition of raw material along a specified path. FDM uses thermoplastic polymers as raw materials, which are melted and extruded through the nozzle. The nozzle head moves in a predetermined path to generate layers and create the product. ABS, PLA (POLYLACTIC ACID), PET, and PETG are some of the materials used in FDM (Rasheed R. et al., 2023). The main advantages of this method are less expensive, no chemical post-processing is required, there are no resins to cure, and the equipment and materials are less expensive, resulting in a more cost-effective procedure (Sun, C et al.,2021).

SLM: SLM (Selective Laser Melting), is a method of fabricating a part layer by layer by selectively melting the powder with a laser. It can be used to make complicated components that would be impossible to make using any other manufacturing method.

EBM: EBM (Electron beam melting) is a new additive manufacturing process that has found widespread use in the medical and aerospace industries. It is a process in which powdered metal is melted using a high-energy electron beam. This beam generates a stream of electrons that follow a magnetic field, melting powdered metal layer by layer to build a product that meets the specifications given in a CAD model (Guo, N & Leu, M. C, 2013). Impurities are eliminated and high strength is produced since the entire process is carried out in a vacuum. Arcam, in Sweden invented and marketed the EBM process (Vafadar, A et al.,2021).

Real World Applications

Automotive: One of the market leaders for additive manufacturing is the automobile sector, the advancements in metal additive manufacturing have opened possibilities for more flexible, optimized, and durable designs of automobile parts. BMW, a German vehicle manufacturer, claims that it had additive manufacturing technology 28 years ago. Every year, almost 100,000 precision components are made at the automaker's additive manufacturing centre in Munich. Similarly, in 2018, Volkswagen opened an additive manufacturing centre that uses binder jetting 3D printing for prototype and tool production. Honda Motor Company, a Japanese automaker, is also using additive manufacturing technology to create body cell parts for electric vehicles. Audi, a German automaker, has collaborated with SLM solution groups to produce customised product spare parts (R. Leal et al.,2017). Stamped parts used in the car industry include chassis components such as the A-pillar, B-pillar, bumper, roof rail, rocker rail, and tunnel (Blakey-Milner B et al.,2021). For example, an additively made water adaptor for the Audi w12 engine. Automakers and tier manufacturers can successfully produce new components with complicated designs and structures using additive manufacturing, resulting in weight reduction and greater efficiency of working components.

Aerospace: The aircraft sector was one of the first to use additive manufacturing technology. Additive manufacturing technologies are being used in all fields of aerospace, including military applications, missile systems, and commercial aircraft. Because of the excessive cost of fuel, the best option to reduce fuel consumption is to build lighter-weight parts, which can be accomplished by additive manufacturing. Mass reduction strategies are one of the most effective ways to improve aircraft energy efficiency. The technology of additive manufacturing can reduce frame weight by 25% while boosting structural integrity. For example, lowering the bulk of a Boeing 787 by 20% increases fuel economy by 10% to 12% while enhancing acceleration and other performance characteristics (Javaid, M et al.,2021). Airbus manufactures metal brackets and bleed pipes for their aircraft using EOS and concept laser equipment. In partnership with Acronis, this company is also creating large-scale airframe components using additive manufacturing technology. General Electric (GE) Aviation manufactures fuel nozzles for its new LEAP engines with Concept lasers and Arca metal printers. Compared to the previous nozzle, the LEAP nozzle is 25% lighter and stronger. This element improves the engine's energy efficiency over the previous model by up to 15%. It is clearly seen that the aerospace industry is receiving benefits from additive manufacturing technologies.

Medical: The rapidly evolving medical industry is utilising additive manufacturing solutions to provide advances to specialists, patients, and research centres. Customised prosthetics can be created using additive manufacturing. For example, a 3D-printed prosthetic hand can be customised to match the patient's remaining hand. Additive manufacturing allows for bone and joint repair, such as hip replacements, jaw reconstructions, and knee replacements. A few companies that have produced medical devices using additive manufacturing technology include OMX Solution, Johnson & Johnson Medical Devices, Egan Dental Laboratory, and Endocon GmbH.

Construction: Creating an architectural model can be a challenging task for architects. Architects typically make their models by hand; however, creating complicated-shaped models is a challenging task. Models are essential for architects to examine the model's functionality and convey the design plan to their clients. Even if the design is complex, additive manufacturing technologies provide a significant benefit in terms of constructing a physical model faster. SLA is a very suitable process for architects to build their models because of the material used and printing resolution.

CHALLENGES AND FUTURISTIC SCOPE OF ADDITIVE MANUFACTURING

Additive manufacturing has several advantages, including design flexibility, the ability to print complex structures, and simplicity of use. Addictive manufacturing technology, on the other hand, has yet to advance to the point where it can be applied in real-world applications. The obstacles that require additional advancement and study are path size limitations, excessive costs, limited manufacturing efficiency, low accuracy, layer misalignment, and slow production speeds. Despite these challenges, additive manufacturing outperforms traditional manufacturing processes in object construction. Furthermore, hybrid manufacturing reduces some disadvantages, such as product surface quality and the ability to repair or reconfigure existing pieces.

A hybrid manufacturing process is a mix of additive and subtractive manufacturing methods that are used sequentially or in conjunction to produce a product, including proper fixing and orientation control. This procedure is used to improve dimensional accuracy while also speeding up the whole production process. Equipment makers recognise the problems and are working hard to increase production speed. For example, SLS printers have two print heads to sinter powder faster. Most additive manufacturing parts necessitate post-processing, which requires additional effort and expense. Some additive manufacturing processes require support removal, cleaning, sanding, curing, and so on. Manufacturers are attempting to reduce these difficulties by automating the entire process with robotics and automated material handling systems. In 2017, the aerostructure providers Premium AeroTEC and Daimler joined up with EOS, a technology supplier for industrial 3D printing. As part of the "NextGen AM" project, these three entities plan to advance current additive manufacturing technology to next level (Schleifenbaum, J. H. et al.,2020). The objective of this project is to create a completely automated and integrated production unit that eliminates the need for manual intervention.

This method offers unmatched design freedom and complexity since different materials—such as polymers, metals, and ceramics—are deposited precisely and under control. The technique of additive manufacturing is finding uses in the automotive, aerospace, and healthcare industries, among others, by facilitating personalised production, fast prototyping, and decreased waste. To maximise the manufacturing process and drive innovation and breakthroughs in production technology, science requires a grasp of material qualities, thermo-dynamics, and computer algorithms.

ADVANCEMENTS AND INNOVATION IN ENABLING TECHNOLOGIES

Digital Twin: A "digital twin" is a working replica of a physical asset or system that continually adjusts to operational changes based on data and information acquired online and may even predict the future of its real counterpart. Digital Twin can provide real-time input on machine performance as well as feedback from the manufacturing line. It enables the maker to predict problems earlier. A virtual depiction of the complete supply chain is created in Industry 5.0 using digital twins. Consequently, inventory control, demand forecasting, and organization are improved (Raffik R. et al., 2023).

5G and Beyond: Because it offers the connection, speed, and reliability required to support advanced industrial applications and transformations, 5G technology is crucial to Industry 5.0. By offering high-speed and low-latency communication networks that provide real-time data transfer and analysis, 5G technology can support Industry 5.0. The effectiveness, precision, and adaptability of industrial processes and supply chains may be enhanced as a result.

Human-Machine Interfaces: By combining the creativity, problem-solving abilities, and emotional intelligence of human workers with the accuracy and efficiency of robots, Industry 5.0 strives to create a more human-centred and sustainable production process. This effort concentrates on the human component of technology by aiming to use and expand the present technical advancements to build an extremely intelligent and smart society. As a result, it would be wise to say that the three terms (i) human-centric, (ii) sustainable, and (iii) resilient best describe Society 5.0 (Müller, J. 2020, pp.9). Recent Technologies used in Human-Machine Interaction are represented in Table 2.

Artificial Intelligence: In Industry 5.0, AI enables robots to collaborate with people, supporting them in making complicated decisions, solving problems, and boosting productivity. To create a connected and intelligent production environment, IoT devices are essential. They enable real-time monitoring of machines, predictive maintenance, and data-driven decision-making. IoT data may be utilized to enhance quality assurance, decrease downtime, and optimize manufacturing operations.

Table. 2. Technologies in Human-machine interaction

TECHNOLOGY	DEFINITION	ADVANTAGES	DISADVANTAGES
Natural Language Processing (NLP)	Natural Language Processing is an artificial intelligence area that focuses on enabling computers to understand, interpret, and synthesize human language for a variety of applications.	Improved Human-Computer Interaction Time Efficiency Data Generation and New content creation Advances in Artificial Intelligence	Limited understanding of context and meanings Biased results for Biased training data Struggles with rare or out-of-vocabulary words.
Voice User Interface (VUI)	A Voice User Interface (VUI) is a technology that allows users to interact with devices or software by speaking to them, making communication more intuitive and hands-free.	Multi-Tasking Accessibility-interaction through voices Efficiency- Faster than typing	Not suitable for all user tasks Voice clashes Limited languages and dialects
Brain Computer Interface (BCI)	Brain-computer interfaces (BCIs) allow direct brain-to-external device contact. They provide assistive technology, control, and communication for people with impairments, as well as prospective uses in human-machine interaction and healthcare.	Assistive Technology- allows paralysed people to control prosthetic limbs. Used for Neurofeedback and Neurorehabilitation Enhanced data processing	Invasive procedure- risks at surgical implantation of electrodes Expensive Limited speed and precision
Gesture Based Interaction	Gesture-based interaction provides intuitive, touchless, and immersive user experiences by using hand or body movements to operate software and devices.	No physical contact is required. Spatial control Hands-free operation	Environmental challenges – poor lighting Limited feedback Inaccuracy

CONCLUSION

The digital world uses high-speed connectivity, processing, augmented reality (AR), and virtual reality (VR) for in-depth human-computer interactions. VR has applications in various disciplines, including training, simulation, healthcare, and remote collaboration. Industry 4.0 incorporates ICT into manufacturing to achieve maximum efficiency and minimal resource use. Virtual reality simplifies projects, improves worker efficiency, and introduces automation and collaborative robots. Industry 4.0 creates a dynamic environment for designers, engineers, and manufacturers to generate and assess 3D models, plan production processes, and perform virtual design reviews. Virtual reality (VR) is revolutionizing the manufacturing execution process by providing immersive simulations and training environments that enhance design, assembly, quality control, maintenance, and cooperation. It can lower costs, reduce mistakes, improve processes, and raise product quality. VR also transforms inventory management by allowing remote help, predictive maintenance, and tailored training. It also enhances testing by allowing designers and engineers to construct virtual prototypes, simulate product behaviour, and immerse testers in virtual worlds. In sales and digital marketing, VR is a key tool for attracting clients and offering real-time analytics, impacting a global audience.

REFERENCES

Abdulhameed, O., Al-Ahmari, A., Ameen, W., & Mian, S. H. (2019). Additive manufacturing: Challenges, trends, and applications. *Advances in Mechanical Engineering*, *11*(2), 1687814018822880. doi:10.1177/1687814018822880

Alqoud, A., Schaefer, D., & Milisavljevic-Syed, J. (2022). Industry 4.0: A systematic review of legacy manufacturing system digital retrofitting. *Manufacturing Review*, *9*, 32. doi:10.1051/mfreview/2022031

Aslam, F., Aimin, W., Li, M., & Ur Rehman, K. (2020). Innovation in the era of IoT and industry 5.0: Absolute innovation management (AIM) framework. *Information (Basel)*, *11*(2), 124. doi:10.3390/info11020124

Bala, M., & Verma, D. (2018). A critical review of digital marketing. M. Bala, D. Verma (2018). A Critical Review of Digital Marketing. International Journal of Management. *IT & Engineering*, *8*(10), 321–339.

Bikas, H., Stavropoulos, P., & Chryssolouris, G. (2016). Additive manufacturing methods and modelling approaches: A critical review. *International Journal of Advanced Manufacturing Technology*, *83*(1-4), 389–405. doi:10.100700170-015-7576-2

Blakey-Milner, B., Gradl, P., Snedden, G., Brooks, M., Pitot, J., Lopez, E., Leary, M., Berto, F., & Du Plessis, A. (2021). Metal additive manufacturing in aerospace: A review. *Materials & Design*, *209*, 110008. doi:10.1016/j.matdes.2021.110008

Cohen, Y., Faccio, M., Pilati, F., & Yao, X. (2019). Design and management of digital manufacturing and assembly systems in the Industry 4.0 era. *International Journal of Advanced Manufacturing Technology*, *105*(9), 3565–3577. doi:10.100700170-019-04595-0

da Silva, E. H. D. R., Shinohara, A. C., de Lima, E. P., Angelis, J., & Machado, C. G. (2019). Reviewing Digital Manufacturing concept in the Industry 4.0 paradigm. *Procedia CIRP*, *81*, 240–245. doi:10.1016/j.procir.2019.03.042

Da Silva, E. R., Shinohara, A. C., Nielsen, C. P., de Lima, E. P., & Angelis, J. (2020). Operating Digital Manufacturing in Industry 4.0: The role of advanced manufacturing technologies. *Procedia CIRP*, *93*, 174–179. doi:10.1016/j.procir.2020.04.063

Di Nardo, M., & Yu, H. (2021). Special issue "Industry 5.0: The prelude to the sixth industrial revolution". *Applied System Innovation*, *4*(3), 45. doi:10.3390/asi4030045

Dilberoglu, U. M., Gharehpapagh, B., Yaman, U., & Dolen, M. (2017). The role of additive manufacturing in the era of industry 4.0. *Procedia Manufacturing*, *11*, 545–554. doi:10.1016/j.promfg.2017.07.148

Fast-Berglund, Å., Gong, L., & Li, D. (2018). Testing and validating Extended Reality (xR) technologies in manufacturing. *Procedia Manufacturing*, *25*, 31–38. doi:10.1016/j.promfg.2018.06.054

Frank, A. G., Dalenogare, L. S., & Ayala, N. F. (2019). Industry 4.0 technologies: Implementation patterns in manufacturing companies. *International Journal of Production Economics*, *210*, 15–26. doi:10.1016/j.ijpe.2019.01.004

Gerrikagoitia, J. K., Unamuno, G., Urkia, E., & Serna, A. (2019). Digital manufacturing platforms in the industry 4.0 from private and public perspectives. *Applied Sciences (Basel, Switzerland), 9*(14), 2934. doi:10.3390/app9142934

Ghobakhloo, M., & Iranmanesh, M. (2021). Digital transformation success under Industry 4.0: A strategic guideline for manufacturing SMEs. *Journal of Manufacturing Technology Management, 32*(8), 1533–1556. doi:10.1108/JMTM-11-2020-0455

Golovianko, M., Terziyan, V., Branytskyi, V., & Malyk, D. (2023). Industry 4.0 vs. Industry 5.0: Co-existence, Transition, or a Hybrid. *Procedia Computer Science, 217*, 102-113.

Guo, N., & Leu, M. C. (2013). Additive manufacturing: Technology, applications, and research needs. *Frontiers of Mechanical Engineering, 8*(3), 215–243. doi:10.100711465-013-0248-8

Gupta, N., Weber, C., & Newsome, S. (2012). *Additive manufacturing: status and opportunities*. Science and Technology Policy Institute.

Huang, S., Wang, B., Li, X., Zheng, P., Mourtzis, D., & Wang, L. (2022). Industry 5.0 and Society 5.0—Comparison, complementation, and co-evolution. *Journal of Manufacturing Systems, 64*, 424–428. doi:10.1016/j.jmsy.2022.07.010

Jamwal, A., Agrawal, R., Sharma, M., & Giallanza, A. (2021). Industry 4.0 technologies for manufacturing sustainability: A systematic review and future research directions. *Applied Sciences (Basel, Switzerland), 11*(12), 5725. doi:10.3390/app11125725

Javaid, M., Haleem, A., Singh, R. P., Suman, R., & Gonzalez, E. S. (2022). Understanding the adoption of Industry 4.0 technologies in improving environmental sustainability. *Sustainable Operations and Computers, 3*, 203–217. doi:10.1016/j.susoc.2022.01.008

Javaid, M., Haleem, A., Singh, R. P., Suman, R., & Rab, S. (2021). Role of additive manufacturing applications towards environmental sustainability. *Advanced Industrial and Engineering Polymer Research, 4*(4), 312–322. doi:10.1016/j.aiepr.2021.07.005

Kumar, S. (2020). Additive manufacturing processes. Springer.

Kurfess, T. R., Saldana, C., Saleeby, K., & Dezfouli, M. P. (2020). A review of modern communication technologies for digital manufacturing processes in industry 4.0. *Journal of Manufacturing Science and Engineering, 142*(11), 110815. doi:10.1115/1.4048206

Leal, R., Barreiros, F. M., Alves, L., Romeiro, F., Vasco, J. C., Santos, M., & Marto, C. (2017). Additive manufacturing tooling for the automotive industry. *International Journal of Advanced Manufacturing Technology, 92*(5-8), 1671–1676. doi:10.100700170-017-0239-8

Leng, J., Wang, D., Shen, W., Li, X., Liu, Q., & Chen, X. (2021). Digital twins-based smart manufacturing system design in Industry 4.0: A review. *Journal of Manufacturing Systems, 60*, 119–137. doi:10.1016/j.jmsy.2021.05.011

Mujber, T. S., Szecsi, T., & Hashmi, M. S. (2004). Virtual reality applications in manufacturing process simulation. *Journal of Materials Processing Technology, 155*, 1834–1838. doi:10.1016/j.jmatprotec.2004.04.401

Müller, J. (2020). Enabling technologies for Industry 5.0. European Commission.

Nikolic, B., Ignjatic, J., Suzic, N., Stevanov, B., & Rikalovic, A. (2017). Predictive manufacturing systems in industry 4.0: Trends, benefits and challenges. *Annals of DAAAM & Proceedings, 28.*

Peng, Q. (2007). Virtual reality technology in product design and manufacturing. *Proceedings of the Canadian Engineering Education Association (CEEA).*

Pérez, L., Rodríguez-Jiménez, S., Rodríguez, N., Usamentiaga, R., & García, D. F. (2020). Digital twin and virtual reality-based methodology for multi-robot manufacturing cell commissioning. *Applied Sciences (Basel, Switzerland), 10*(10), 3633. doi:10.3390/app10103633

Qiu, X., Cai, Z., & Peng, H. (2023). Predefined Time Consensus Control of Nonlinear Multi-agent Systems for Industry 5.0. *IEEE Transactions on Consumer Electronics*, 1. doi:10.1109/TCE.2023.3319477

Skobelev, P. O., & Borovik, S. Y. (2017). On the way from Industry 4.0 to Industry 5.0: From digital manufacturing to digital society. *Industry 4.0, 2*(6), 307-311.

Sun, C., Wang, Y., McMurtrey, M. D., Jerred, N. D., Liou, F., & Li, J. (2021). Additive manufacturing for energy: A review. *Applied Energy*, *282*, 116041. doi:10.1016/j.apenergy.2020.116041

Vafadar, A., Guzzomi, F., Rassau, A., & Hayward, K. (2021). Advances in metal additive manufacturing: A review of common processes, industrial applications, and current challenges. *Applied Sciences (Basel, Switzerland), 11*(3), 1213. doi:10.3390/app11031213

Vafadar, A., Guzzomi, F., Rassau, A., & Hayward, K. (2021). Advances in metal additive manufacturing: A review of common processes, industrial applications, and current challenges. *Applied Sciences (Basel, Switzerland), 11*(3), 1213. doi:10.3390/app11031213

Veleva, S. S., & Tsvetanova, A. I. (2020, September). Characteristics of the digital marketing advantages and disadvantages. *IOP Conference Series. Materials Science and Engineering*, *940*(1), 012065. doi:10.1088/1757-899X/940/1/012065

Wohlers, T., Gornet, T., Mostow, N., Campbell, I., Diegel, O., Kowen, J., ... Peels, J. (2016). *History of additive manufacturing*. Academic Press.

Wohlgenannt, I., Simons, A., & Stieglitz, S. (2020). Virtual Realist. *Business & Information Systems Engineering*, *62*(5), 455–461. doi:10.100712599-020-00658-9

Wong, K. V., & Hernandez, A. (2012). A review of additive manufacturing. *International Scholarly Research Notices*.

Xu, X., Lu, Y., Vogel-Heuser, B., & Wang, L. (2021). Industry 4.0 and Industry 5.0—Inception, conception, and perception. *Journal of Manufacturing Systems*, *61*, 530–535. doi:10.1016/j.jmsy.2021.10.006

Yasmin, A., Tasneem, S., & Fatema, K. (2015). Effectiveness of digital marketing in the challenging age: An empirical study. *International Journal of Management Science and Business Administration, 1*(5), 69-80.

Zhang, L., Zhou, L., Ren, L., & Laili, Y. (2019). Modeling and simulation in intelligent manufacturing. *Computers in Industry*, *112*, 103123. doi:10.1016/j.compind.2019.08.004

Chapter 2
A Review of Big Data Analytics and Artificial Intelligence in Industry 5.0 for Smart Decision-Making

Kassim Kalinaki
https://orcid.org/0000-0001-8630-9110
Islamic University in Uganda, Uganda

Umar Yahya
https://orcid.org/0000-0002-4255-0364
Islamic University in Uganda, Uganda

Owais Ahmed Malik
Universiti Brunei Darussalam, Brunei

Daphne Teck Ching Lai
https://orcid.org/0000-0001-8290-8941
Universiti Brunei Darussalam, Brunei

ABSTRACT

Globally, the industrial landscape is witnessing a significant transformation with the emergence of Industry 5.0, marking a new era characterized by seamless convergence of digital technologies, physical systems, and human expertise. This shift hinges on the dynamic interplay between big data analytics (BDA) and artificial intelligence (AI), becoming the cornerstone of intelligent decision-making in Industry 5.0. Accordingly, this study explores the profound impact of integrating BDA and AI in Industry 5.0, emphasizing the pivotal roles of data acquisition, storage, and processing. Additionally, it examines how AI improves human decision-making across various industrial sectors like manufacturing, retail, automotive, energy grid management, and healthcare, showcasing real-world case studies. Moreover, the chapter addresses the challenges associated with managing large-scale data and offers innovative solutions. It concludes by looking ahead, outlining promising areas for future research at the intersection of BDA and AI to foster well-informed decision-making in Industry 5.0.

DOI: 10.4018/979-8-3693-2647-3.ch002

INTRODUCTION

The world continues to experience a transformative shift in the way industries operate, with the emergence of Industry 5.0. The seamless integration of digital technologies, physical systems, and human expertise characterizes this new industrial era. At the center of this evolution lies an evolving synergy between BDA and AI, which is rapidly becoming the cornerstone of intelligent decision-making in Industry 5.0 (Leng et al., 2022). Consequently, it is important to understand the profound implications of this integration and its immense potential for transforming the future of industries across the globe. To comprehend the significance of BDA and AI in Industry 5.0, a reflection upon the journey that has led us here must first be highlighted. The previous industrial revolutions have laid the groundwork for this current transformation. Industry 1.0 brought mechanization, while Industry 2.0 introduced mass production through electrification. Industry 3.0 ushered in the era of automation, characterized by the use of computers and electronics. Subsequently, Industry 4.0 marked the advent of the Internet of Things (IoT) and the digitalization of industrial processes. Industry 4.0 witnessed the emergence of smart factories and interconnected systems, setting the stage for Industry 5.0 (Yin et al., 2017).

Marked by the fusion of the physical and digital realms in a way that transcends mere automation and autonomation, Industry 5.0 represents a significant leap forward. In this era, machines and systems work harmoniously with humans, coexisting to leverage their strengths. Human-machine collaboration is not just an option; it is the essence of Industry 5.0 (Leng et al., 2022; Xu et al., 2021). What distinguishes Industry 5.0 from its predecessors is the seamless convergence and flow of information between these elements of a heterogenous ecosystem. Data, continuously generated by sensors, machines, and humans, and constantly analyzed for insights, essentially becomes the lifeblood of this new industrial ecosystem. Moreover, it is this data that makes smart decision-making possible and allows industries to operate with unprecedented efficiency and precision (Fazal et al., 2022). Central to this paradigm shift is the concept of Big Data. With the proliferation of sensors and interconnected devices, industries are now generating vast volumes of data at an unprecedented rate. This data, often characterized by its volume, velocity, variety, and veracity, has become a potent resource (Xian et al., 2023). In Industry 5.0, data is not merely a byproduct but a strategic asset, serving as the foundation upon which intelligent decisions are built. From real-time monitoring of machinery to predictive maintenance schedules, supply chain optimization to personalized customer experiences, Big Data forms the backbone of these transformative processes (Leng et al., 2022). However, the true value of Big Data lies not in its quantity but in the insights it can yield. This is where BDA comes into play.

Defined as the process of examining large and complex datasets to uncover hidden patterns, correlations, and trends, BDA enables organizations to derive actionable insights from the deluge of data they generate (Belhadi et al., 2019). In the context of Industry 5.0, BDA plays a pivotal role in translating data into intelligence. The capabilities of BDA are manifold. For instance, in the case of machinery for manufacturing, studies have shown that it can aid in predicting equipment failures before they happen, thus preventing costly downtime (Dai et al., 2019). It optimizes supply chains, ensuring that products are manufactured and delivered with maximum efficiency (Lee & Mangalaraj, 2022). Furthermore, it enhances product development by analyzing customer feedback and market trends (Awan et al., 2022). In short, BDA empowers industries to make informed effective decisions, optimize processes, and create value like never before. While BDA provides the means to process and derive insights from data, it is AI that infuses intelligence into these insights. AI, particularly machine learning (ML) and deep learning (DL) algorithms can learn from data, recognize patterns, and make predictions or decisions autonomously.

In Industry 5.0, AI augments human capabilities, making them more efficient and effective. Moreover, it analyzes data at speeds and scales that are beyond human capacity and can sift through vast datasets to identify anomalies or opportunities (Rožanec et al., 2023). Additionally, it provides real-time recommendations and predictions, allowing for agile decision-making (Zhang et al., 2023). As a result, AI becomes the cognitive engine that powers Industry 5.0. The true transformative potential of Industry 5.0 emerges at the convergence of BDA and AI. These two technologies are not isolated but complementary, working in tandem to empower smart decision-making. BDA provides the raw material (data) and processes it to yield insights. AI, on the other hand, takes these insights to the next level. It continuously learns from the data, adapts to changing conditions, and refines its decision-making processes. This synergy between BDA and AI is what yields the fascinating seemingly magical possibilities and opportunities of Industry 5.0. Together, they enable industries to achieve levels of automation, optimization, and decision-making precision that were previously quite unimaginable. Processes become not just automated but intelligent, adapting in real-time to changing circumstances. Decisions are data-driven and predictive, leading to enhanced productivity, reduced costs, and improved customer experiences (Rožanec et al., 2023).

While the integration of BDA and AI holds immense promise, it is not without its challenges. The volume of data generated requires robust data management and storage solutions. Privacy and security concerns loom large, necessitating stringent cybersecurity measures (Alli et al., 2021; Kalinaki, Thilakarathne, et al., 2023). It is important to address ethical considerations when implementing AI in decision-making processes. Yet, the challenges posed by this technology are offset by the opportunities it provides. Industry 5.0 has the potential to generate new industries and job opportunities, fueling economic growth, among several other socio-economic transformations. With data-driven resource management, sustainable practices can be achieved. Additionally, AI can provide individuals and organizations with unprecedented seamless access to information and insights, empowering them in ways previously unimaginable (Adel, 2022). Overall, the integration of BDA and AI in Industry 5.0 heralds a new era of hybridized intelligent decision-making. From the genesis of Industry 5.0 to the challenges and opportunities that lie ahead, this chapter provides a comprehensive exploration of the transformative potential of these technologies within the industrial landscape. Furthermore, it delves deeper into how BDA and AI are reshaping industries, offering insights into both opportunities and challenges, and propelling them into a future characterized by enhanced productivity, efficiency, and innovation.

Chapter Contributions

The following are the main contributions of this chapter:

1. We provide a clear and concise overview of Industry 5.0, emphasizing the convergence of physical and digital systems and the pivotal role of data and AI in this transformative era.
2. We highlight how data generation, acquisition, storage, and management are foundational to the entire evolution of the industrial ecosystem, making it clear that data is not just a byproduct but a critical resource.
3. We elucidate the significance of AI, particularly machine learning and deep learning algorithms, in augmenting human decision-making in Industry 5.0.
4. We highlight the different BDA and AI-powered tools for smart decision-making in Industry 5.0.

5. Through examples and real-world case studies, the chapter illustrates how the integration of BDA and AI is applied across industries such as manufacturing, retail, automotive, energy grid management, and healthcare.
6. We provide valuable insights into the formidable challenges posed by the management of large-scale data and present innovative solutions to surmount these obstacles.
7. We highlight the future prospects of BDA and AI in Industry 5.0 for informed decision-making.

Chapter Organization

After the introduction in section 1, the remainder of this chapter is organized as follows; Section 2 details the data acquisition, storage, and processing of big data in Industry 5.0. section 3 delves into the AI's role in enhancing human decision-making in industry 5.0. Section 4 details the different AI and BDA tools for smart decision-making in Industry 5.0. Section 5 explores the real-world case studies of Big Data and AI in Industry 5.0. Section 6 details the Challenges of Big data and AI in Industry 5.0 along with proposed solutions. The future directions are depicted in section 7 and the conclusion is shown in section 8.

BIG DATA ACQUISITION, STORAGE, AND PROCESSING IN INDUSTRY 5.0 FOR SMART DECISION-MAKING

Industry 5.0 signifies a monumental leap in the evolution of industries, where automation and technology converge to birth intelligent, interconnected systems. At its core, this transformation hinges upon the seamless integration of Big Data and Artificial Intelligence (AI). These potent technologies empower industries to collect, store, and process vast and diverse data streams from myriad sources, heralding an era of intelligent decision-making. Accordingly, this section explores the critical facets of big data acquisition, storage, and processing in the context of Industry 5.0, highlighting their profound influence on intelligent decision-making.

Data Acquisition

Data acquisition is the bedrock upon which Industry 5.0 builds its capacity for smart decision-making. It entails the systematic collection of data from a plethora of sources, encompassing sensors, machines, devices, and even human interactions. In Industry 5.0, data acquisition has reached unprecedented levels of sophistication, driven by the proliferation of IoT devices, smart sensors, and cutting-edge analytics. For instance, at the forefront of data acquisition in Industry 5.0 lies the ecosystem of IoT, an intricate network of interconnected devices and sensors, extending into industrial machinery, infrastructure, and even wearable gadgets, generating a ceaseless torrent of data (Alojaiman, 2023). These sensors are adept at capturing real-time data on variables such as temperature, pressure, humidity, speed, and other pivotal parameters, thus offering a holistic perspective of industrial operations (Chander et al., 2022). The data sourced from IoT devices plays a pivotal role in predictive maintenance, ensuring that machines are preemptively serviced or repaired to circumvent breakdowns, thereby curtailing downtime and financial losses (van Oudenhoven et al., 2022). Moreover, Industry 5.0 also underscores the significance of human-machine interaction in the realm of data acquisition (Xian et al., 2023). Equipped with augmented reality (AR) tools and wearable technologies, human workers contribute valuable input and feedback. This human-generated data introduces a qualitative dimension to the quantitative data amassed from sensors, endowing us with a more comprehensive understanding of industrial processes.

Furthermore, data acquisition in Industry 5.0 surpasses the realm of individual data sources. It entails the integration of data from various systems and platforms, creating a unified data ecosystem comprised of heterogeneous data sources. Integration ensures that data is not segregated in isolated silos, enabling cross-functional insights and fostering intelligent decision-making throughout the organization (Ivanov, 2023).

Data Storage

With the influx of data in Industry 5.0, effective data storage solutions are paramount. Traditional databases and storage methods are often insufficient for handling the sheer volume, variety, and velocity of data generated (Xian et al., 2023). Besides, with data sources being heterogeneous, storage mechanisms are increasingly expected to accommodate multiple data formats, moreover in a dynamic manner. Consequently, new storage approaches have emerged to address these challenges. For instance, Big Data storage technologies such as Hadoop and Spark are foundational cloud-based computing systems in Industry 5.0 for storing and processing large datasets efficiently (Paschek et al., 2022). These distributed storage systems enable organizations to scale their data storage infrastructure dynamically, ensuring that they can accommodate growing data volumes. Additionally, Cloud computing platforms including Amazon Web Services (AWS), Google Cloud, and Microsoft's Azure offer scalable cloud-based storage solutions that can be tailored to the specific needs of each organization. The cloud also provides flexibility and accessibility, allowing users to access data from anywhere, which is crucial in a world where remote work and collaboration are increasingly prevalent (Adel, 2022). Moreover, data lakes and data warehouses are becoming essential components of data storage in Industry 5.0. due to their ability to store raw, unstructured data as well as organize and structure data for easy analysis (Nambiar & Mundra, 2022). These repositories empower organizations to store vast amounts of data while maintaining data integrity and ensuring that data is readily available for analysis.

Data Processing and Visualization

Data acquisition and storage are only a part of the data management equation as required in Industry 5.0. To harness the true potential of data, organizations must invest in advanced data processing and visualization techniques powered by AI, particularly machine learning and deep learning. For instance, Industry 5.0 demands real-time data processing capabilities to make instantaneous decisions. In this case, AI algorithms are now capable of analyzing incoming data streams in real time, identifying patterns and anomalies. This real-time processing is invaluable for applications like quality control, and process optimization, where defects and flaws can be detected and addressed accordingly as soon as they occur (Nguyen et al., 2023). Additionally, AI-driven predictive analytics is a game-changer in Industry 5.0 whereby ML models can predict equipment failures, demand fluctuations, and market trends with high accuracy (Leng et al., 2023; van Oudenhoven et al., 2022). These predictive capabilities enable proactive decision-making, allowing organizations to optimize production, reduce costs, and seize new opportunities. Moreover, cognitive computing, which includes technologies like natural language processing (NLP) and computer vision, is being deployed in Industry 5.0 due to its ability to empower machines to understand and interpret human-generated data (Panagou et al., 2023). This capability is particularly useful in industries where textual or visual data is abundant, such as healthcare, where AI can assist in diagnosing medical conditions based on patient records and medical imaging (Fahim et al., 2023; Kalinaki, Fahadi, et al., 2023).

In a nutshell, big data acquisition, storage, and processing are at the core of smart decision-making in Industry 5.0. The integration of Big Data and AI technologies enables organizations to harness the power of data to improve efficiency, reduce costs, drive innovation, and gain a competitive edge. As industries continue to evolve, those who prioritize data-driven strategies will be best equipped to not only thrive but also survive obsolesce in this new era of smart manufacturing and decision-making.

AI'S ROLE IN ENHANCING HUMAN DECISION-MAKING IN INDUSTRY 5.0

Unlike the earlier industrial revolutions that primarily focused on automation and autonomation, Industry 5.0 emphasizes the synergy between human expertise and technological capabilities as illustrated in Figure 1.

Figure 1. Industry 5.0 as an intersection of automation, autonomation, and human intelligence

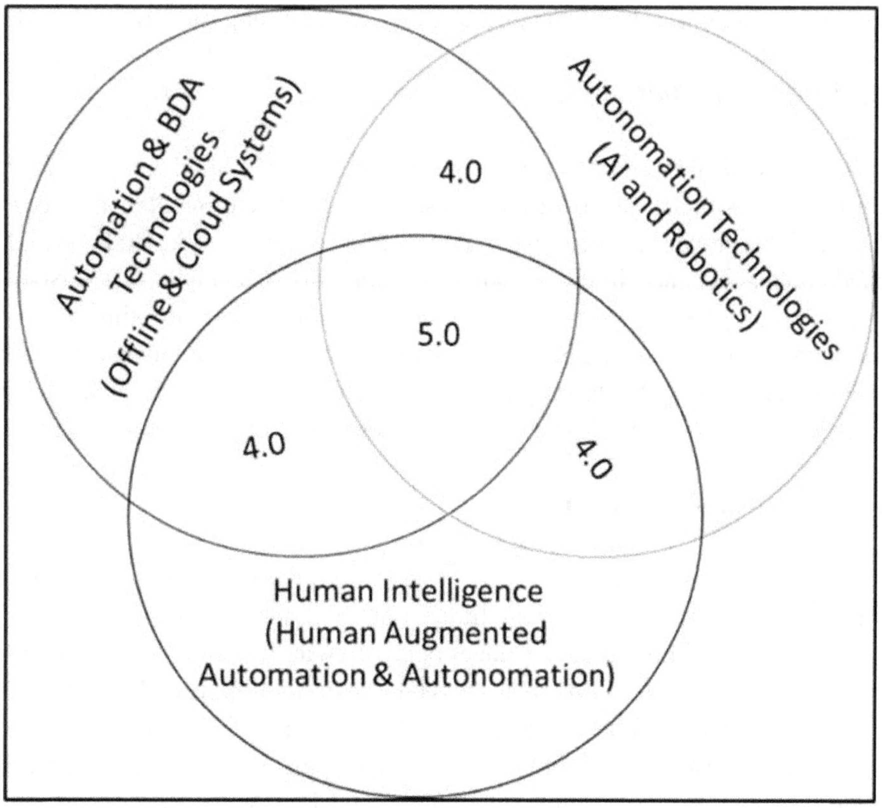

This synergy is facilitated by AI, which plays a pivotal role in enabling robots and machines to analyze data, learn from it, and make intelligent decisions. Accordingly, this section delves into AI's role in Industry 5.0, exploring its applications and the profound impact it has on enhancing human decision-making. More specifically, we emphasize the role of intelligent automation, a subset of AI that combines ML, robotic process automation (RPA), and NLP to perform tasks that traditionally require human intelligence.

Streamlining Processes and Operations

AI-driven intelligent automation plays a pivotal role in simplifying intricate operational processes. For instance, in agriculture, autonomous drones equipped with AI-driven cameras are used for precision agriculture (Kalinaki, Shafik, et al., 2023). These drones can monitor crop health by analyzing images of fields and detecting pests, diseases, and nutrient deficiencies. This allows farmers to apply treatments precisely where needed, optimizing crop yields and minimizing the use of pesticides and fertilizers, which is both cost-effective and environmentally friendly. Moreover, in the healthcare industry, AI-driven intelligent automation can significantly streamline the processing of insurance claims, a complex and time-consuming task due to the sheer volume of claims. Here, Optical Character Recognition (OCR) technology combined with NLP can extract relevant information from both digital and paper claims. Well-trained AI algorithms can identify patient details, diagnosis codes, treatment procedures, and provider information with high accuracy (Amponsah et al., 2022; Davenport & Kalakota, 2019).

Enhancing Predictive Maintenance

In the aviation industry, airlines are increasingly relying on AI for predictive maintenance of their aircraft. AI algorithms analyze data from various sensors and historical maintenance records to predict component failures. This proactive approach not only minimizes the risk of in-flight breakdowns but also reduces unscheduled maintenance, improving aircraft availability (Çinar et al., 2020; Soori et al., 2023).

Moreover, in the energy sector, power plants and utility companies are adopting AI-driven predictive maintenance (Alvarez Quiñones et al., 2023; Franki et al., 2023). By continuously monitoring equipment such as turbines and generators, AI algorithms can anticipate issues like wear and tear, enabling timely maintenance scheduling to avoid costly unplanned shutdowns and ensuring a reliable energy supply.

Optimizing Resource Allocation

In urban planning, AI is being employed to optimize resource allocation in transportation systems. ML algorithms analyze traffic patterns, public transportation usage, and real-time data to dynamically adjust traffic signal timings. This not only reduces congestion and commute times but also lowers fuel consumption and emissions, contributing to sustainable urban development (Bharadiya, 2023).

Furthermore, in the context of renewable energy, AI plays a crucial role in optimizing the allocation of renewable resources like solar and wind power. AI algorithms predict weather patterns and energy demand, allowing power grids to efficiently distribute electricity from renewable sources. This ensures reliable and sustainable energy generation while reducing reliance on fossil fuels (Khan et al., 2023; Mhlanga, 2023).

Improving Supply Chain Management

In the fashion industry, AI-driven supply chain management is revolutionizing inventory control. AI algorithms analyze fashion trends, customer preferences, and sales data to predict which clothing items will be in high demand (Mohiuddin Babu et al., 2022). Retailers can adjust production and inventory accordingly, reducing overstock and the need for clearance sales. Additionally, in the healthcare sector, AI enhances supply chain logistics for pharmaceuticals and medical equipment. AI-powered systems monitor inventory levels of critical medical supplies in hospitals and clinics in real time (Bag et al., 2023; Vora et al., 2023). When supplies are running low, automated orders are placed, ensuring the availability of essential items and preventing stockouts during emergencies.

Personalizing Customer Experiences

Recommendation algorithms analyze viewing history and user preferences to suggest personalized content. This not only keeps users engaged but also helps platforms like Netflix and Spotify retain subscribers (Starke & Lee, 2022; Velankar & Kulkarni, 2023). Moreover, in the financial sector, AI-driven chatbots and virtual assistants provide personalized customer support (Kalinaki, Namuwaya, et al., 2023). These AI systems can understand customer queries, analyze transaction history, and provide tailored financial advice. This not only improves customer satisfaction but also streamlines customer service operations for banks and financial institutions.

Data-Driven Decision-Making

In the field of climate science, AI is used to analyze vast datasets of temperature, atmospheric, and oceanic data. ML models can identify climate trends, predict extreme weather events, and assist in climate modeling (Jain et al., 2023; Karanth et al., 2023). These insights inform policymakers and aid in the development of climate change mitigation strategies. Furthermore, in the legal profession, AI-powered tools are used for legal research and analysis. NLP algorithms can review and categorize legal documents, extract relevant case law, and provide recommendations for legal strategies (Baser & Saini, 2023; Bhatt et al., 2022; Silva et al., 2022). This not only saves time for legal professionals but also improves the accuracy of legal research and decision-making.

AI AND BDA TOOLS FOR SMART DECISION-MAKING

AI and BDA tools are essential for smart decision-making in Industry 5.0. These tools enable organizations to extract valuable insights from large datasets, automate decision processes, and optimize operations. Accordingly, this section details some of the AI and BDA tools for smart decision-making in Industry 5.0.

ML Platforms

ML platforms, such as TensorFlow and PyTorch (Abadi et al., 2016; Imambi et al., 2021), represent versatile toolkits for creating, training, and deploying ML/DL models. These platforms offer a rich assortment of pre-built algorithms and libraries, facilitating applications like predictive maintenance in

Industry 5.0. For instance, a steel plant used TensorFlow to develop predictive maintenance models that monitor equipment failures using sensor data to anticipate maintenance needs, thereby preventing costly breakdowns (Choi et al., 2023).

Business Intelligence (BI) and Data Visualization tools

BI tools, exemplified by QlikView and Tableau (Beard & Aghassibakes, 2021; Shukla & Dhir, 2016), offer interactive dashboards and reports that empower data-driven decision-making. QlikView can compile sales and inventory data from various locations, enabling retail managers to make real-time decisions on inventory restocking and allocation (Baruti, 2023). Also, data visualization tools, like Tableau and Matplotlib, are indispensable for transforming complex data into comprehensible graphical representations. These tools are of paramount importance for Industry 5.0, enabling decision-makers to gain insights from vast datasets. For example, in the aircraft assembly field, Tableau is used to create interactive real-time monitoring and information traceability, allowing manufacturing supervisors to identify trends and optimize processes swiftly (Li et al., 2023).

NLP Libraries and AI-Powered Chatbots

NLP libraries such as spaCy have a pivotal role in analyzing and extracting insights from unstructured text data (Fantechi et al., 2021). These tools are highly relevant for sentiment analysis in Industry 5.0. In the context of customer feedback analysis particularly in the tourism industry, spaCy can be utilized to process and categorize customer reviews, extracting sentiment scores that inform product improvements and marketing strategies (Puh & Bagić Babac, 2023). Moreover, AI-driven chatbots, based on platforms like Dialogflow and Microsoft Bot Framework, enhance customer service and automate routine tasks in various industries. For instance, in healthcare, Dialogflow can be integrated into a patient support system, providing quick responses to common medical queries and guiding patients to appropriate resources (Fenza et al., 2023).

Predictive Analytics Software

Predictive analytics software, such as SAS, is vital for forecasting future trends and outcomes. In Industry 5.0, this software can be applied for predictive maintenance, where algorithms in SAS are harnessed to anticipate equipment failures and optimize maintenance schedules, resulting in reduced downtime and enhanced operational efficiency (Daoudi et al., 2023).

Big Data Processing Frameworks

Big Data processing frameworks like Hadoop and Spark are the bedrock of large-scale data analysis in Industry 5.0. These frameworks facilitate distributed data processing and are invaluable for handling the vast data streams characteristic of this industrial paradigm. For example, Spark can process real-time sensor data from a smart factory, enabling timely decision-making on production adjustments (Putrama & Martinek, 2023).

Cloud-Based AI Services

Cloud providers, such as AWS, Azure, and Google Cloud, offer a suite of AI and Big Data services. These services, for instance, AWS SageMaker, provide a platform for developing, training and deploying ML models. Organizations can leverage scalable computing resources for AI-driven insights without heavy upfront infrastructure investments (Nigenda et al., 2022).

REAL-WORLD CASE STUDIES OF BDA AND AI IN INDUSTRY 5.0 FOR SMART DECISION-MAKING

This section discusses five case studies describing real-world applications of big data and AI in Industry 5.0 for smart decision-making:

Predictive Maintenance in Manufacturing (General Electric - GE)

GE, a pioneer in predictive maintenance, equips its jet engines with an array of sensors that continuously monitor various parameters like temperature, pressure, and vibration. These sensors generate massive amounts of real-time data. AI algorithms process this data, looking for patterns and anomalies (GE Research, 2023). The AI system can predict when a particular engine component is likely to fail, analyze historical data to fine-tune predictions, and suggest maintenance actions, when necessary, well in advance of a potential issue. Deploying this technique led to reduced downtime in which airlines can plan maintenance during scheduled stops, minimizing disruptions. Moreover, GE saves millions by avoiding unscheduled maintenance and optimizing parts inventory. Furthermore, the early detection of impending issues serves as a crucial safety net, averting catastrophic engine failures, and ultimately elevating safety standards across the aviation industry. In summary, General Electric's innovative approach to predictive maintenance exemplifies the quintessence of smart decision-making in Industry 5.0. Through the strategic integration of big data and AI, GE not only predicts issues but harnesses historical data to refine those predictions, leading to reduced downtime, significant cost savings, and heightened safety standards.

Supply Chain Optimization in Retail (Amazon)

Amazon's supply chain optimization relies on a complex network of data sources, including historical sales data, real-time inventory levels, weather forecasts, and transportation data. AI algorithms analyze this data to make real-time decisions (Sherrod, 2023). The AI system can adjust inventory levels at fulfillment centers based on demand forecasts, optimize shipping routes and modes based on real-time traffic and weather conditions as well as predict potential supply chain disruptions and proactively address them. The outcomes of this seamless integration of data and AI-driven smart decisions are unequivocally significant. Customers experience swifter delivery times, as products are strategically placed for quick access. Simultaneously, the system effectively minimizes storage costs and optimizes transportation routes, exemplifying the harmonious marriage of economic and ecological considerations. Ultimately, this smart decision-making approach not only fuels Amazon's operational excellence but also enhances the customer experience by ensuring products are available precisely when and where customers require them.

Quality Control in Automotive Manufacturing (BMW)

BMW employs computer vision and ML algorithms in its paint quality control process. High-resolution cameras capture images of car bodies from multiple angles, while machine learning algorithms inspect the images for defects, such as paint inconsistencies or scratches (Hemmerle, 2020). The AI system detects minor defects that may not be visible to the human eye, ensures consistent quality across all vehicles, and reduces the need for manual inspection and rework. Through its deployment, many benefits have been realized such as improved product quality where fewer defects reach the market, enhancing brand reputation. In essence, BMW's innovative employment of AI and ML for quality control epitomizes the essence of smart decision-making within Industry 5.0. It leads to swift and accurate quality control, resulting in heightened operational efficiency. This paradigm shift in quality control is a testament to the transformational potential of AI and ML, as it empowers BMW to set new standards in the automotive manufacturing industry, ensuring the delivery of top-tier products while simultaneously optimizing their manufacturing processes.

Energy Grid Optimization (Enel)

Enel uses big data and AI to manage its energy grid efficiently. They collect data from various sources, including sensors on power lines, LiDAR point clouds, satellites, weather forecasts, and renewable energy production (Namtao et al., 2023). Their AI-powered system can predict and prevent grid failures by identifying potential issues in advance, optimizes the distribution of electricity based on real-time demand and supply and maximizes the use of renewable energy sources when conditions are favorable. This leads to enhanced reliability by having fewer power outages and improved grid stability. Moreover, there's reduced waste in energy distribution leading to energy efficiency. Finally, there's greater utilization of renewable energy sources, reducing environmental impact. In summation, the Enel case study vividly exemplifies how the amalgamation of big data and AI, can metamorphose the energy grid landscape within Industry 5.0. The underpinning theme is smart decision-making, whereby Enel leverages a wealth of data to avert grid mishaps, optimize energy distribution, heighten reliability, elevate energy efficiency, and reduce environmental repercussions. This paradigmatic shift encapsulates the essence of Industry 5.0, where the synthesis of data and AI augments the intellect of decision-makers, fostering a more sustainable and efficient future.

Healthcare Diagnostics and Treatment (PathAI and Harvard's Beth Israel Deaconess Medical Center)

PathAI is a healthcare AI company that specializes in pathology and diagnostic solutions. They collaborated with Harvard's Beth Israel Deaconess Medical Center (BIDMC) to harness the power of AI and big data in improving the accuracy and efficiency of diagnosing diseases through pathology. PathAI's AI algorithms are trained on a massive dataset of medical images, including pathology slides, radiology images, and patient records (Prescott, 2016; Santosh & Gaur, 2021). These algorithms can analyze images with incredible precision and speed. In radiology, for example, AI algorithms can assist radiologists in identifying and classifying anomalies in X-rays, CT scans, and MRI images. This can be particularly helpful in early detection of diseases like cancer. The system integrates data from various sources, including patient histories, genetic information, and medical literature, to provide a comprehensive view of a patient's condition and risk factors. What makes this initiative particularly remarkable is its integration of data from a myriad of sources. These encompass patient medical histories, genetic information, and insights from the wealth of medical literature. Through this comprehensive data integration, a holistic view of a patient's condition and the associated risk factors is offered. This approach significantly enhances the smart decision-making process in healthcare diagnostics and treatment, representing a beacon of hope for more precise and timely healthcare interventions.

In summary, these case studies illustrate how big data and AI technologies are applied in Industry 5.0 to optimize decision-making processes, resulting in significant benefits such as cost savings, increased efficiency, and improved product quality. These advancements play a crucial role in shaping the future of various industries.

CHALLENGES OF BIG DATA AND AI IN INDUSTRY 5.0 ALONG WITH PROPOSED SOLUTIONS

In this section, we explore the different challenges of BDA and AI along with proposed solutions to mitigate them.

Data Volume and Variety

The advent of Industry 5.0 has ushered in an influx of data from diverse sources, encompassing IoT devices, sensors, and intricate production processes. This inundation of data, characterized by its multifarious formats and structures, constitutes a formidable challenge (Alabdulatif et al., 2023; Arshad et al., 2023; B. Singh & Verma, 2021). Solutions to this conundrum involve the judicious application of data preprocessing techniques, including data filtering, aggregation, and compression. These methods serve to distill the essential components of data while rendering it more manageable. Concomitantly, the implementation of robust data management systems emerges as a requisite strategy, facilitating the efficient handling of disparate data formats and structures (Nguyen et al., 2023).

Data Security and Privacy

The heightened utilization of data in Industry 5.0 underscores the pivotal importance of data security and privacy. Safeguarding sensitive information from the omnipresent specter of cyber threats and concomitantly adhering to data protection regulations, notably the General Data Protection Regulation (GDPR), becomes an exigent imperative (Alli et al., 2021). The ramifications of a data breach reverberate throughout an organization, tarnishing its reputation and imperiling its decision-making acumen. Strategies addressing this issue encompass investments in state-of-the-art cybersecurity measures, inclusive of encryption and multi-factor authentication. Moreover, the regular conduct of security audits stands as a cornerstone for ensuring the sanctity of data. Concurrently, the imposition of stringent data access controls and compliance protocols crystallizes a commitment to the secure handling of sensitive data in alignment with pertinent regulatory mandates (Kalinaki, Thilakarathne, et al., 2023).

Lack of Data Standards

Industry 5.0 is characterized by data emanating from diverse sources and systems that often eschew standardized conventions. This dearth of data standardization engenders complexities in data aggregation and analysis, thereby engendering incongruities in the decision-making processes (Espinoza et al., 2021). The remedy to this quandary resides in the advocacy for the universal adoption of data standards within the industry's purview. Such advocacy extends to suppliers and partners, who are encouraged to assimilate these standardized paradigms into their data generation and transmission practices (Agrawal & Madaan, 2023). Concurrently, the deployment of data integration platforms, characterized by their capacity to translate and harmonize data originating from heterogeneous sources, emerges as an indispensable solution to bridge the chasm of standardization heterogeneity.

Data Access and Ownership

The issue of data ownership and access allocation, compounded by the participation of myriad stakeholders, bespeaks a complexity that necessitates elucidation (Wang & Yin, 2023). Resolving this conundrum mandates the meticulous delineation of data ownership prerogatives and access privileges through the prism of collaboration agreements and contractual instruments. Augmenting this endeavor, the integration of blockchain or distributed ledger technology serves as a potent means to establish a transparent and immutable ledger of data ownership and access history, thus redressing this intricate matter (Das et al., 2023; Di Francesco et al., 2023).

Complexity of AI Models

The utilization of highly intricate AI models as decision-making tools in Industry 5.0 poses a formidable challenge of interpretability. The elucidation of the inner workings of these models, an attribute essential for engendering trust and informed decision-making, embodies an ongoing challenge (Afzal et al., 2023; Lu et al., 2022). Addressing this conundrum necessitates an investment in research endeavors about Explainable AI (XAI). The development of AI models that offer explicable rationales for their decisions stands as a pivotal goal within this context. Concurrently, periodic auditing and validation of AI models become imperative to ensure conformity to established norms and the eradication of latent biases (Königstorfer & Thalmann, 2022; Koshiyama et al., 2022; Munechika et al., 2022).

Scalability

As the industrial landscape embraces the pervasive integration of BDA and AI, challenges of infrastructure and computational resources loom large. The fundamental imperative is to ensure that systems remain amenable to scale, accommodating the burgeoning volumes of data and increasing complexities intrinsic to Industry 5.0. To achieve this, organizations are well-advised to harness the capabilities afforded by cloud computing services (Adel, 2022). These services facilitate the provisioning of scalable infrastructure on-demand, enabling the orchestration of resources in consonance with the evolving needs of the enterprise. Furthermore, the implementation of load balancing and auto-scaling mechanisms stands as a prudent strategy, ensuring the resilience of systems in the face of heightened workloads during peak operational periods (Yao et al., 2022).

Talent Shortage

The endemic shortage of proficient professionals adept in the domains of BDA and AI engenders substantial impediments within the era of Industry 5.0. The demand for data scientists, machine learning engineers, and AI specialists perennially outpaces the supply, creating a palpable deficit that encumbers the capacity of organizations to cultivate and sustain a proficient workforce (Johnson et al., 2021). Remedying this scarcity necessitates a multi-pronged approach. To redress the talent shortfall, organizations must commit to substantial investments in employee training and development programs. These initiatives serve to upskill extant personnel in the intricate arts of data science and AI. Furthermore, the cultivation of strategic alliances with academic institutions and research establishments is paramount. Such partnerships not only facilitate the identification and nurturing of prospective talents but also invigorate the establishment of talent pipelines. In instances where immediate expertise is imperative, organizations may strategically engage external experts, thereby circumventing immediate talent shortages and ensuring the seamless progression of Industry 5.0 initiatives.

Change Management

The integration of Industry 5.0 technologies into traditional manufacturing paradigms engenders a requisite cultural metamorphosis within organizations. The profound exigencies of change management, characterized by resistance to transformative shifts and the imperative of comprehensive training and education, assume a paramount role in navigating this transition (Meinert et al., 2022; Nti et al., 2022). Organizations are encouraged to methodically engineer change management strategies that pivot upon the pillars of clear communication, comprehensive training regimens, and robust support mechanisms. This holistic approach, resonating with the stakeholders involved, facilitates the seamless assimilation of Industry 5.0 technologies. Additionally, the active involvement of employees in the decision-making process serves to impart a sense of agency and ownership, thus ameliorating apprehensions concerning technology-induced obsolescence. Organizations must underscore the value of AI in enhancing the roles of employees, reframing AI not as a replacement but rather as an augmentation of human capabilities.

Costs and ROI

The implementation and sustenance of BDA and AI systems are often characterized by substantial financial outlays. Measuring the return on investment (ROI) vis-à-vis these expenditures presents a notable challenge, particularly for entities of limited financial bandwidth (Kejriwal, 2023). A judicious approach involves the solicitation of expert counsel, who undertakes thorough cost-benefit analyses, ensuring the alignment of technological investments with overarching strategic objectives. Post-implementation, the diligent monitoring and measurement of the impact of these technologies on key performance indicators (KPIs) emerges as a sine qua non for the precise and judicious quantification of ROI. Such rigorous analysis serves as a lodestar for future financial decisions within the framework of Industry 5.0.

Ethical Considerations

The ascendancy of AI within the realm of decision-making begets a veritable Pandora's box of ethical considerations. Chief among these are concerns encompassing algorithmic bias and the potential for the displacement of human labor by automation. The resolution of these ethical quandaries and the steadfast enshrinement of principles of fairness and accountability within AI-driven decision-making processes represent an intricate endeavor. Enterprises are encouraged to embark upon the establishment of ethical guidelines and governance frameworks, which underscore the ethical dimensions of AI development and utilization within their organizational domains. Furthermore, the application of bias detection and mitigation techniques in AI algorithms attests to a commitment to ethical propriety. The cultivation of a continuous dialogue with stakeholders, characterized by transparency and a willingness to address concerns, crystallizes a proactive approach to upholding ethical integrity within the context of Industry 5.0 (Koshiyama et al., 2022; Munechika et al., 2022). In conclusion, the advent of Industry 5.0 has ushered in a transformative era characterized by unprecedented challenges and opportunities in the realms of Big Data and Artificial Intelligence. While the journey has been arduous, the solutions forged to address these challenges reflect a dynamic synthesis of innovation, strategy, and ethical responsibility.

Insufficient Regulatory Frameworks

The similitude of the risks and the immense potential and opportunities that lie within the Industry 5.0 revolution, is that of a double-edged sword. As organizations at both private and state levels scramble to adopt and adapt these emerging technologies, an underlying inherent concern is the legal and regulatory frameworks within which technologies should operate. On this aspect, a critical challenge is the inadequacy of the existing regulatory frameworks that are largely inflexible and static, especially within the developing world. It is therefore paramount for all societies to develop and streamline strong and dynamic legal and regulatory regimes, as a prerequisite to transitioning to Industry 5.0 technological ecosystem.

FUTURE DIRECTIONS OF BDA AND AI IN INDUSTRY 5.0 FOR SMART DECISION-MAKING

The future of BDA and AI in Industry 5.0 promises to be transformative, ushering in new directions that will further enhance decision-making, efficiency, and innovation. Here are some key future directions for these technologies: -

Explainable AI (XAI)

As AI systems are increasingly integrated into critical decision-making processes in Industry 5.0, the need for transparency and interpretability becomes paramount. XAI techniques aim to make AI models more understandable and interpretable by humans. This ensures that decisions made by AI systems can be explained and justified, enhancing trust and accountability (Rožanec et al., 2023).

AI-Driven Sustainability

Industry 5.0 will witness a growing emphasis on sustainability. AI will be used to optimize resource allocation, reduce energy consumption, and minimize waste. AI-powered simulations and analytics will help industries achieve environmental goals, making operations more sustainable and eco-friendlier (Ghobakhloo et al., 2022).

Ubiquitous Computing, Edge AI, and IoT Integration

Edge computing, coupled with AI, will become more prevalent. AI algorithms will be deployed directly on edge devices, such as sensors and cameras, enabling real-time data processing and decision-making at the source. This reduces latency and enhances responsiveness in Industry 5.0 applications (Xian et al., 2023).

Federated Learning and Privacy-Preserving AI

Privacy concerns will drive the development of federated learning and privacy-preserving AI techniques. These methods enable AI models to be trained on decentralized data sources while preserving data privacy. Industries can collaborate and share insights without compromising sensitive data (Chi & Radwan, 2023; S. K. Singh et al., 2023).

Quantum Computing and AI

As quantum computing matures, it will have a profound impact on BDA and AI. Quantum computers promise to solve complex optimization and machine learning problems at speeds unattainable by classical computers, unlocking new frontiers in AI applications (Nguyen & Tran, 2023).

AI-Driven Cybersecurity

In an era of increased digitalization, AI will be central to cybersecurity efforts. AI-driven threat detection and response systems will continuously adapt to evolving cyber threats, enhancing the security of Industry 5.0 systems.

These future directions underscore the continued evolution and integration of BDA and AI into Industry 5.0. They reflect the growing importance of responsible and ethical AI, the need for seamless human-AI collaboration, and the potential for these technologies to drive sustainability and innovation across industries. As Industry 5.0 unfolds, organizations that embrace these directions will be better equipped to navigate the evolving landscape and harness the full potential of AI and BDA.

CONCLUSION

In conclusion, this chapter offers a comprehensive examination of the intricate relationship between BDA and AI within the context of Industry 5.0, highlighting their pivotal roles in shaping informed decision-making processes. We commenced with a meticulous exposition, presenting an exhaustive panorama of the evolving landscape, affirming the indispensable status of these technologies within the industrial sphere. Subsequently, we embarked on a methodical exploration of the multifaceted dimensions of Big Data acquisition, storage, and processing in the specialized context of Industry 5.0, elucidating their integral contributions to the facilitation of informed decision-making. Furthermore, we illuminate the transformative potential of AI in elevating human decision-making capabilities within the realm of Industry 5.0. We furnish compelling evidence of its prowess in orchestrating operational refinement, enhancing predictive maintenance protocols, optimizing resource allocation strategies, enhancing supply chain management practices, personalizing customer experiences, and instilling a culture of data-driven decision-making. Our discourse is enriched by a compendium of real-world case studies culled from esteemed organizations, affording tangible insights into the pragmatic applications and advantages stemming from the convergence of BDA and AI. These cases span several industries, including manufacturing, retail, automotive, energy grid management, and healthcare. Yet, our narrative transcends mere accolades, engaging earnestly with the multifarious challenges confronting organizations as they endeavor to integrate BDA and AI. Our discerning analysis encompasses a spectrum of obstacles, ranging from grappling with issues on data volume, diversity, and security, data standards, accessibility, and ownership, AI model complexity, scalability hurdles, talent scarcity, change management, cost considerations, and the intricate ethical dimensions that accompany this paradigm shift to offering nuanced resolutions for the mentioned challenges. In anticipation of the future, we catch a glimpse of the promising horizons that beckon BDA and AI within the framework of Industry 5.0. Emerging trends, including XAI, AI-driven sustainability, the seamless integration of Edge AI and IoT, the advent of Federated Learning and Privacy-Preserving AI, the convergence with Quantum Computing, and the pivotal role of AI in fortifying cybersecurity, collectively point to an era of innovation. These transformative trajectories herald not only heightened operational efficiency and economic viability but also a path forward characterized by responsible and fortified practices. In summary, the convergence of BDA and AI within the ambit of Industry 5.0 epitomizes a seismic shift in the operational ethos of enterprises and their decision-making paradigms. This chapter serves as a meticulous roadmap, deftly navigating the contemporary landscape, adroitly addressing formidable challenges, and charting an expansive course toward the horizon, where data-driven intelligence reigns supreme, and industry metamorphosis finds its zenith.

REFERENCES

AbadiM.AgarwalA.BarhamP.BrevdoE.ChenZ.CitroC.CorradoG. S.DavisA.DeanJ.DevinM.GhemawatS. GoodfellowI.HarpA.IrvingG.IsardM.JiaY.JozefowiczR.KaiserL.KudlurM.ResearchG. (2016). *TensorFlow: Large-Scale Machine Learning on Heterogeneous Distributed Systems*. https://arxiv.org/abs/1603.04467v2

Adel, A. (2022). Future of industry 5.0 in society: human-centric solutions, challenges and prospective research areas. *Journal of Cloud Computing, 11*(1), 1–15. doi:10.1186/s13677-022-00314-5

Afzal, M. A., Gu, Z., Afzal, B., & Bukhari, S. U. (2023). Cognitive Workload Classification in Industry 5.0 Applications: Electroencephalography-Based Bi-Directional Gated Network Approach. *Electronics, 12*(19), 4008. doi:10.3390/electronics12194008

Agrawal, D., & Madaan, J. (2023). A structural equation model for big data adoption in the healthcare supply chain. *International Journal of Productivity and Performance Management, 72*(4), 917–942. doi:10.1108/IJPPM-12-2020-0667

Alabdulatif, A., Thilakarathne, N. N., & Kalinaki, K. (2023). A Novel Cloud Enabled Access Control Model for Preserving the Security and Privacy of Medical Big Data. *Electronics (Basel), 12*(12), 2646. doi:10.3390/electronics12122646

Alli, A. A., Kassim, K., Mutwalibi, N., Hamid, H., & Ibrahim, L. (2021). Secure Fog-Cloud of Things: Architectures, Opportunities and Challenges. In M. Ahmed & P. Haskell-Dowland (Eds.), *Secure Edge Computing* (1st ed., pp. 3–20). CRC Press. doi:10.1201/9781003028635-2

Alojaiman, B. (2023). Technological Modernizations in the Industry 5.0 Era: A Descriptive Analysis and Future Research Directions. *Processes, 11*(5), 1318. doi:10.3390/pr11051318

Alvarez Quiñones, L. I., Lozano-Moncada, C. A., & Bravo Montenegro, D. A. (2023). Machine learning for predictive maintenance scheduling of distribution transformers. *Journal of Quality in Maintenance Engineering, 29*(1), 188–202. doi:10.1108/JQME-06-2021-0052

Amponsah, A. A., Adekoya, A. F., & Weyori, B. A. (2022). A novel fraud detection and prevention method for healthcare claim processing using machine learning and blockchain technology. *Decision Analytics Journal, 4*, 100122. doi:10.1016/j.dajour.2022.100122

Arshad, M., Brohi, M. N., Soomro, T. R., Ghazal, T. M., Alzoubi, H. M., & Alshurideh, M. (2023). NoSQL: Future of BigData Analytics Characteristics and Comparison with RDBMS. *Studies in Computational Intelligence, 1056*, 1927–1951. doi:10.1007/978-3-031-12382-5_106

Awan, U., Bhatti, S. H., Shamim, S., Khan, Z., Akhtar, P., & Balta, M. E. (2022). The Role of Big Data Analytics in Manufacturing Agility and Performance: Moderation–Mediation Analysis of Organizational Creativity and of the Involvement of Customers as Data Analysts. *British Journal of Management, 33*(3), 1200–1220. doi:10.1111/1467-8551.12549

Bag, S., Dhamija, P., Singh, R. K., Rahman, M. S., & Sreedharan, V. R. (2023). Big data analytics and artificial intelligence technologies based collaborative platform empowering absorptive capacity in health care supply chain: An empirical study. *Journal of Business Research, 154*, 113315. doi:10.1016/j.jbusres.2022.113315

Baruti, R. (2023). *Analysis and Implementation of a Business Intelligence QlikView application for logistic and procurement management. Sews Cabind case for the shortage problem.* Academic Press.

Baser, P., & Saini, J. R. (2023). AI-Based Intelligent Solution in Legal Profession. *Lecture Notes in Networks and Systems, 516*, 75–84. doi:10.1007/978-981-19-5221-0_8

Beard, L., & Aghassibakes, N. (2021). Tableau (version 2020.3). *Journal of the Medical Library Association: JMLA, 109*(1), 159. doi:10.5195/jmla.2021.1135

Belhadi, A., Zkik, K., Cherrafi, A., Yusof, S. M., & El fezazi, S. (2019). Understanding Big Data Analytics for Manufacturing Processes: Insights from Literature Review and Multiple Case Studies. *Computers & Industrial Engineering, 137*, 106099. doi:10.1016/j.cie.2019.106099

Bharadiya, J. P. (2023). Artificial Intelligence in Transportation Systems A Critical Review. *American Journal of Computing and Engineering, 6*(1), 34–45. doi:10.47672/ajce.1487

Bhatt, H., Bahuguna, R., Singh, R., Gehlot, A., Akram, S. V., Priyadarshi, N., & Twala, B. (2022). Artificial Intelligence and Robotics Led Technological Tremors: A Seismic Shift towards Digitizing the Legal Ecosystem. *Applied Sciences, 12*(22), 11687. doi:10.3390/app122211687

Chander, B., Pal, S., De, D., & Buyya, R. (2022). Artificial Intelligence-based Internet of Things for Industry 5.0. *Internet of Things : Engineering Cyber Physical Human Systems*, 3–45. doi:10.1007/978-3-030-87059-1_1

Chi, H. R., & Radwan, A. (2023). Full-Decentralized Federated Learning-Based Edge Computing Peer Offloading Towards Industry 5.0. *IEEE International Conference on Industrial Informatics (INDIN)*. 10.1109/INDIN51400.2023.10218137

Choi, J.-S., Choi, S.-W., & Lee, E.-B. (2023). Modeling of Predictive Maintenance Systems for Laser-Welders in Continuous Galvanizing Lines Based on Machine Learning with Welder Control Data. *Sustainability (Basel)*, *15*(9), 7676. doi:10.3390u15097676

Çinar, Z. M., Nuhu, A. A., Zeeshan, Q., Korhan, O., Asmael, M., & Safaei, B. (2020). Machine Learning in Predictive Maintenance towards Sustainable Smart Manufacturing in Industry 4.0. *Sustainability, 12*(19), 8211. doi:10.3390/su12198211

Dai, H. N., Wang, H., Xu, G., Wan, J., & Imran, M. (2019). Big data analytics for manufacturing internet of things: Opportunities, challenges and enabling technologies. *Enterprise Information Systems, 14*(9–10), 1279–1303. doi:10.1080/17517575.2019.1633689

Daoudi, N., Smail, Z., & Aboussaleh, M. (2023). *Machine Learning Based Predictive Maintenance: Review, Challenges and Workflow*. doi:10.1007/978-3-031-43524-9_6

Das, L., Bibhu, V., Logeswaran, R., Dadhich, K., & Sharma, B. (2023). *AI Model for Blockchain Based Industrial IoT and Big Data*. doi:10.1007/978-3-031-31952-5_3

Davenport, T., & Kalakota, R. (2019). The potential for artificial intelligence in healthcare. *Future Healthcare Journal, 6*(2), 94–98. doi:10.7861/futurehosp.6-2-94 PMID:31363513

Di Francesco, M., Marchesi, L., & Porcu, R. (2023). Kryptosafe: managing and trading data sets using blockchain and IPFS. *Proceedings - 2023 IEEE/ACM 6th International Workshop on Emerging Trends in Software Engineering for Blockchain, WETSEB 2023*, 5–8. 10.1109/WETSEB59161.2023.00006

Du Nguyen, H., & Tran, K. P. (2023). Artificial Intelligence for Smart Manufacturing in Industry 5.0: Methods, Applications, and Challenges. *Springer Series in Reliability Engineering*, (Part F4), 5–33. doi:10.1007/978-3-031-30510-8_2

Du Nguyen, H., Tran, P. H., Do, T. H., & Tran, K. P. (2023). Quality Control for Smart Manufacturing in Industry 5.0. *Springer Series in Reliability Engineering*, (Part F4), 35–64. doi:10.1007/978-3-031-30510-8_3

Espinoza, J., Xu, N. Y., Nguyen, K. T., & Klonoff, D. C. (2021). The Need for Data Standards and Implementation Policies to Integrate CGM Data into the Electronic Health Record. *Journal of Diabetes Science and Technology, 17*(2), 495–502. doi:10.1177/19322968211058148 PMID:34802286

Fahim, K. E., Kalinaki, K., & Shafik, W. (2023). Electronic Devices in the Artificial Intelligence of the Internet of Medical Things (AIoMT). In Handbook of Security and Privacy of AI-Enabled Healthcare Systems and Internet of Medical Things (pp. 41–62). CRC Press. https://doi.org/ doi:10.1201/9781003370321-3

Fantechi, A., Gnesi, S., Livi, S., & Semini, L. (2021). A spaCy-based tool for extracting variability from NL requirements. *ACM International Conference Proceeding Series, Part F171625-B*, 32–35. 10.1145/3461002.3473074

Fazal, N., Haleem, A., Bahl, S., Javaid, M., & Nandan, D. (2022). Digital Management Systems in Manufacturing Using Industry 5.0 Technologies. *Lecture Notes in Mechanical Engineering*, 221–234. doi:10.1007/978-981-16-8341-1_18

Fenza, G., Orciuoli, F., Peduto, A., & Postiglione, A. (2023). Healthcare Conversational Agents: Chatbot for Improving Patient-Reported Outcomes. *Lecture Notes in Networks and Systems, 661*, 137–148. https://doi.org/ doi:10.1007/978-3-031-29056-5_14/COVER

Franki, V., Majnarić, D., & Višković, A. (2023). A Comprehensive Review of Artificial Intelligence (AI) Companies in the Power Sector. *Energies, 16*(3), 1077. doi:10.3390/en16031077

Ghobakhloo, M., Iranmanesh, M., Mubarak, M. F., Mubarik, M., Rejeb, A., & Nilashi, M. (2022). Identifying industry 5.0 contributions to sustainable development: A strategy roadmap for delivering sustainability values. *Sustainable Production and Consumption, 33*, 716–737. doi:10.1016/j.spc.2022.08.003

Hemmerle, A. (2020). *BMW Group applies AI solutions to increase paint shop quality*. BMW. https://www.press.bmwgroup.com/global/article/detail/T0307724EN/bmw-group-applies-ai-solutions-to-increase-paint-shop-quality?language=en

Imambi, S., Prakash, K. B., & Kanagachidambaresan, G. R. (2021). PyTorch. *EAI/Springer Innovations in Communication and Computing*, 87–104. https://doi.org/ doi:10.1007/978-3-030-57077-4_10/COVER

Ivanov, D. (2023). The Industry 5.0 framework: Viability-based integration of the resilience, sustainability, and human-centricity perspectives. *International Journal of Production Research, 61*(5), 1683–1695. doi:10.1080/00207543.2022.2118892

Jain, H., Dhupper, R., Shrivastava, A., Kumar, D., & Kumari, M. (2023). AI-enabled strategies for climate change adaptation: Protecting communities, infrastructure, and businesses from the impacts of climate change. *Computational Urban Science, 3*(1), 1–17. doi:10.100743762-023-00100-2 PMID:36685089

Johnson, M., Jain, R., Brennan-Tonetta, P., Swartz, E., Silver, D., Paolini, J., Mamonov, S., & Hill, C. (2021). Impact of Big Data and Artificial Intelligence on Industry: Developing a Workforce Roadmap for a Data Driven Economy. *Global Journal of Flexible Systems Managment, 22*(3), 197–217. doi:10.100740171-021-00272-y

Kalinaki, K., Fahadi, M., Alli, A. A., Shafik, W., Yasin, M., & Mutwalibi, N. (2023). Artificial Intelligence of Internet of Medical Things (AIoMT) in Smart Cities: A Review of Cybersecurity for Smart Healthcare. In Handbook of Security and Privacy of AI-Enabled Healthcare Systems and Internet of Medical Things (pp. 271–292). CRC Press. https://doi.org/ doi:10.1201/9781003370321-11

Kalinaki, K., Namuwaya, S., Mwamini, A., & Namuwaya, S. (2023). Scaling Up Customer Support Using Artificial Intelligence and Machine Learning Techniques. In *Contemporary Approaches of Digital Marketing and the Role of Machine Intelligence* (pp. 23–45). IGI Global. doi:10.4018/978-1-6684-7735-9.ch002

Kalinaki, K., Shafik, W., Gutu, T. J. L., & Malik, O. A. (2023). Computer Vision and Machine Learning for Smart Farming and Agriculture Practices. In *Artificial Intelligence Tools and Technologies for Smart Farming and Agriculture Practices* (pp. 79–100). IGI Global. doi:10.4018/978-1-6684-8516-3.ch005

Kalinaki, K., Thilakarathne, N. N., Mubarak, H. R., Malik, O. A., & Abdullatif, M. (2023). Cybersafe Capabilities and Utilities for Smart Cities. In *Cybersecurity for Smart Cities* (pp. 71–86). Springer. doi:10.1007/978-3-031-24946-4_6

Karanth, S., Benefo, E. O., Patra, D., & Pradhan, A. K. (2023). Importance of artificial intelligence in evaluating climate change and food safety risk. *Journal of Agriculture and Food Research, 11*, 100485. doi:10.1016/j.jafr.2022.100485

Kejriwal, M. (2023). *AI in Practice and Implementation: Issues and Costs.* doi:10.1007/978-3-031-19039-1_2

Khan, S. U., Khan, N., Ullah, F. U. M., Kim, M. J., Lee, M. Y., & Baik, S. W. (2023). Towards intelligent building energy management: AI-based framework for power consumption and generation forecasting. *Energy and Building, 279*, 112705. doi:10.1016/j.enbuild.2022.112705

Königstorfer, F., & Thalmann, S. (2022). AI Documentation: A path to accountability. *Journal of Responsible Technology, 11*, 100043. doi:10.1016/j.jrt.2022.100043

Koshiyama, A., Kazim, E., & Treleaven, P. (2022). Algorithm Auditing: Managing the Legal, Ethical, and Technological Risks of Artificial Intelligence, Machine Learning, and Associated Algorithms. *Computer, 55*(4), 40–50. doi:10.1109/MC.2021.3067225

Lee, I., & Mangalaraj, G. (2022). Big Data Analytics in Supply Chain Management: A Systematic Literature Review and Research Directions. *Big Data and Cognitive Computing, 6*(1), 17. doi:10.3390/bdcc6010017

Leng, J., Sha, W., Wang, B., Zheng, P., Zhuang, C., Liu, Q., Wuest, T., Mourtzis, D., & Wang, L. (2022). Industry 5.0: Prospect and retrospect. *Journal of Manufacturing Systems, 65*, 279–295. doi:10.1016/j.jmsy.2022.09.017

Leng, J., Zhong, Y., Lin, Z., Xu, K., Mourtzis, D., Zhou, X., Zheng, P., Liu, Q., Zhao, J. L., & Shen, W. (2023). Towards resilience in Industry 5.0: A decentralized autonomous manufacturing paradigm. *Journal of Manufacturing Systems, 71*, 95–114. doi:10.1016/j.jmsy.2023.08.023

Li, Y., Liu, W., Zhang, Y., Zhang, W., Gao, C., Chen, Q., & Ji, Y. (2023). Interactive Real-Time Monitoring and Information Traceability for Complex Aircraft Assembly Field Based on Digital Twin. *IEEE Transactions on Industrial Informatics, 19*(9), 9745–9756. doi:10.1109/TII.2023.3234618

Lu, Y., Zheng, H., Chand, S., Xia, W., Liu, Z., Xu, X., Wang, L., Qin, Z., & Bao, J. (2022). Outlook on human-centric manufacturing towards Industry 5.0. *Journal of Manufacturing Systems, 62*, 612–627. doi:10.1016/j.jmsy.2022.02.001

Meinert, E., Khan, A., Iyawa, G., & Vărzaru, A. A. (2022). Assessing Artificial Intelligence Technology Acceptance in Managerial Accounting. *Electronics, 11*(14), 2256. doi:10.3390/electronics11142256

Mhlanga, D. (2023). Artificial Intelligence and Machine Learning for Energy Consumption and Production in Emerging Markets: A Review. *Energies, 16*(2), 745. doi:10.3390/en16020745

Mohiuddin Babu, M., Akter, S., Rahman, M., Billah, M. M., & Hack-Polay, D. (2022). The role of artificial intelligence in shaping the future of Agile fashion industry. *Production Planning and Control*, 1–15. Advance online publication. doi:10.1080/09537287.2022.2060858

Munechika, D., Wang, Z. J., Reidy, J., Rubin, J., Gade, K., Kenthapadi, K., & Chau, D. H. (2022). Visual Auditor: Interactive Visualization for Detection and Summarization of Model Biases. *Proceedings - 2022 IEEE Visualization Conference - Short Papers, VIS 2022*, 45–49. 10.1109/VIS54862.2022.00018

Nambiar, A., & Mundra, D. (2022). An Overview of Data Warehouse and Data Lake in Modern Enterprise Data Management. *Big Data and Cognitive Computing, 6*(4), 132. doi:10.3390/bdcc6040132

Namtao, M., Larcher, S., Gavazzeni, C., & Angelo Porcelli, G. (2023). *Enel automates large-scale power grid asset management and anomaly detection using Amazon SageMaker | AWS Machine Learning Blog*. Amazon. https://aws.amazon.com/blogs/machine-learning/enel-automates-large-scale-power-grid-asset-management-and-anomaly-detection-using-amazon-sagemaker/

Nigenda, D., Karnin, Z., Zafar, M. B., Ramesha, R., Tan, A., Donini, M., & Kenthapadi, K. (2022). Amazon SageMaker Model Monitor: A System for Real-Time Insights into Deployed Machine Learning Models. *Proceedings of the ACM SIGKDD International Conference on Knowledge Discovery and Data Mining*, 3671–3681. 10.1145/3534678.3539145

Nti, I. K., Quarcoo, J. A., Aning, J., & Fosu, G. K. (2022). A mini-review of machine learning in big data analytics: Applications, challenges, and prospects. *Big Data Mining and Analytics*, *5*(2), 81–97. doi:10.26599/BDMA.2021.9020028

Panagou, S., Neumann, W. P., & Fruggiero, F. (2023). A scoping review of human robot interaction research towards Industry 5.0 human-centric workplaces. *International Journal of Production Research*, 1–17. Advance online publication. doi:10.1080/00207543.2023.2172473

Paschek, D., Luminosu, C.-T., & Ocakci, E. (2022). *Industry 5.0 Challenges and Perspectives for Manufacturing Systems in the Society 5.0*. doi:10.1007/978-981-16-7365-8_2

Prescott, B. (2016). *Artificial intelligence approach improves accuracy in breast cancer diagnosis*. Harvard Medical School. https://hms.harvard.edu/news/better-together

Puh, K., & Bagić Babac, M. (2023). Predicting sentiment and rating of tourist reviews using machine learning. *Journal of Hospitality and Tourism Insights*, *6*(3), 1188–1204. doi:10.1108/JHTI-02-2022-0078

Putrama, I. M., & Martinek, P. (2023). A hybrid architecture for secure Big-Data integration and sharing in Smart Manufacturing. *Proceedings of the International Spring Seminar on Electronics Technology*. 10.1109/ISSE57496.2023.10168508

Research, G. E. (2023). *Predictive Maintenance*. General Electric. https://www.ge.com/research/project/predictive-maintenance

Rožanec, J. M., Novalija, I., Zajec, P., Kenda, K., Tavakoli Ghinani, H., Suh, S., Veliou, E., Papamartzivanos, D., Giannetsos, T., Menesidou, S. A., Alonso, R., Cauli, N., Meloni, A., Recupero, D. R., Kyriazis, D., Sofianidis, G., Theodoropoulos, S., Fortuna, B., Mladenić, D., & Soldatos, J. (2023). Human-centric artificial intelligence architecture for industry 5.0 applications. *International Journal of Production Research, 2023*(20), 6847–6872. doi:10.1080/00207543.2022.2138611

Santosh, K., & Gaur, L. (2021). *Artificial Intelligence and Machine Learning in Public Healthcare.* Springer Singapore. doi:10.1007/978-981-16-6768-8

Sherrod, L. (2023). *Supply Chain Optimization: How AI is Improving Efficiency and Reducing Costs.* LinkedIn. https://www.linkedin.com/pulse/supply-chain-optimization-how-ai-improving-efficiency-larry-sherrod

Shukla, A., & Dhir, S. (2016). Tools for data visualization in business intelligence: Case study using the tool Qlikview. *Advances in Intelligent Systems and Computing*, *434*, 319–326. doi:10.1007/978-81-322-2752-6_31

Silva, H., António, N., & Bacao, F. (2022). A Rapid Semi-automated Literature Review on Legal Precedents Retrieval. Lecture Notes in Computer Science (Including Subseries Lecture Notes in Artificial Intelligence and Lecture Notes in Bioinformatics), 13566, 53–65. doi:10.1007/978-3-031-16474-3_5

Singh, B., & Verma, H. K. (2021). Dawn of Big Data with Hadoop and Machine Learning. *Machine Learning and Data Science: Fundamentals and Applications*, 47–65. doi:10.1002/9781119776499.ch3

Singh, S. K., Yang, L. T., & Park, J. H. (2023). FusionFedBlock: Fusion of blockchain and federated learning to preserve privacy in industry 5.0. *Information Fusion*, *90*, 233–240. doi:10.1016/j.inffus.2022.09.027

Soori, M., Arezoo, B., & Dastres, R. (2023). Artificial intelligence, machine learning and deep learning in advanced robotics, a review. *Cognitive Robotics*, *3*, 54–70. doi:10.1016/j.cogr.2023.04.001

Starke, A. D., & Lee, M. (2022). Unifying Recommender Systems and Conversational User Interfaces. *ACM International Conference Proceeding Series*. 10.1145/3543829.3544524

van Oudenhoven, B., Van de Calseyde, P., Basten, R., & Demerouti, E. (2022). Predictive maintenance for industry 5.0: Behavioural inquiries from a work system perspective. *International Journal of Production Research*. Advance online publication. doi:10.1080/00207543.2022.2154403

Velankar, M., & Kulkarni, P. (2023). Music Recommendation Systems: Overview and Challenges. *Signals and Communication Technology*, 51–69. doi:10.1007/978-3-031-18444-4_3

Vora, L. K., Gholap, A. D., Jetha, K., Thakur, R. R. S., Solanki, H. K., & Chavda, V. P. (2023). Artificial Intelligence in Pharmaceutical Technology and Drug Delivery Design. *Pharmaceutics, 15*(7), 1916. doi:10.3390/pharmaceutics15071916

Wang, C., & Yin, L. (2023). Defining Urban Big Data in Urban Planning: Literature Review. *Journal of Urban Planning and Development*, *149*(1), 04022044. doi:10.1061/(ASCE)UP.1943-5444.0000896

Xian, W., Yu, K., Han, F., Fang, L., He, D., & Han, Q. L. (2023). Advanced Manufacturing in Industry 5.0: A Survey of Key Enabling Technologies and Future Trends. *IEEE Transactions on Industrial Informatics*, 1–15. Advance online publication. doi:10.1109/TII.2023.3274224

Xu, X., Lu, Y., Vogel-Heuser, B., & Wang, L. (2021). Industry 4.0 and Industry 5.0—Inception, conception and perception. *Journal of Manufacturing Systems*, *61*, 530–535. doi:10.1016/j.jmsy.2021.10.006

Yao, Z., Desmouceaux, Y., Cordero-Fuertes, J. A., Townsley, M., & Clausen, T. (2022). Aquarius - Enable Fast, Scalable, Data-Driven Service Management in the Cloud. *IEEE Transactions on Network and Service Management*, *19*(4), 4028–4044. doi:10.1109/TNSM.2022.3197130

Yin, Y., Stecke, K. E., & Li, D. (2017). The evolution of production systems from Industry 2.0 through Industry 4.0. *International Journal of Production Research*, *56*(1–2), 848–861. doi:10.1080/00207543.2017.1403664

Zhang, C., Wang, Z., Zhou, G., Chang, F., Ma, D., Jing, Y., Cheng, W., Ding, K., & Zhao, D. (2023). Towards new-generation human-centric smart manufacturing in Industry 5.0: A systematic review. *Advanced Engineering Informatics*, *57*, 102121. doi:10.1016/j.aei.2023.102121

Chapter 3

Ergonomic Prevention Method Based on the UX Index to Assess Industrialized Tasks From a Human-Centered Standpoint

M. S. Hemawathi
The Kavery Engineering College, India

R. Sivaramakrishnan
KPR Institute of Engineering and Technology, India

P. Dhanasekaran
The Kavery Engineering College, India

R. Pavithra
Dr. N.G.P. Institute of Technology, India

S. Illavarasi
Sengunthar Engineering College, India

ABSTRACT

Recent advancements in physiological monitoring tech have eased the adoption of a human-centric strategy in factories, despite challenging working conditions that typically impede research on operator user experience (UX). These innovations offer various methods to assess overall UX, including aspects like mental workload, stress, and ergonomics. The current training efforts aim to create a comprehensive UX index for early identification of user discomfort root causes and system design improvements. Virtualizing and simulating production processes yield cost and time savings, while enabling research on human-machine interaction and assembly line design enhancements. Moreover, this research introduces a novel method for ergonomic analysis of automobile assembly line workplaces in a virtual setting. This preventive ergonomic approach holds the potential to revolutionize human-centered workplace design, leading to cost savings and improved job quality.

DOI: 10.4018/979-8-3693-2647-3.ch003

1. INTRODUCTION

One of the most important control points in the industry focuses on the specifications in particular fields. Since these factors help to provide a safe and healthy working environment, ergonomic criteria and safety standards are related. While safety requirements focus on identifying and reducing risks that could result in mishaps, illnesses, or harm, ergonomic requirements involve creating work environments, tools, and technology to lessen the physical strain on employees and support their well-being. Taking into account ergonomic elements including body placement, equipment design, and improved job organization can lower the incidence of musculoskeletal illnesses and prevent ergonomic hazards (Arciniega-Rocha et al., 2023). By incorporating ergonomic principles into safety procedures, workers are given the knowledge and tools to identify and mitigate ergonomic risks. This leads to a thorough method of managing occupational health and security that raises worker happiness, security, and output.

The procedures utilized for tool selection are one of the main concerns for ergonomic management. To lessen the likelihood that a worker will develop an illness in the future, it is vital to analyze how repetitive and physically demanding the work is before implementing the workstation and after using a systematic tool selection.

Figure 1. User-centered design methodology for commercial settings

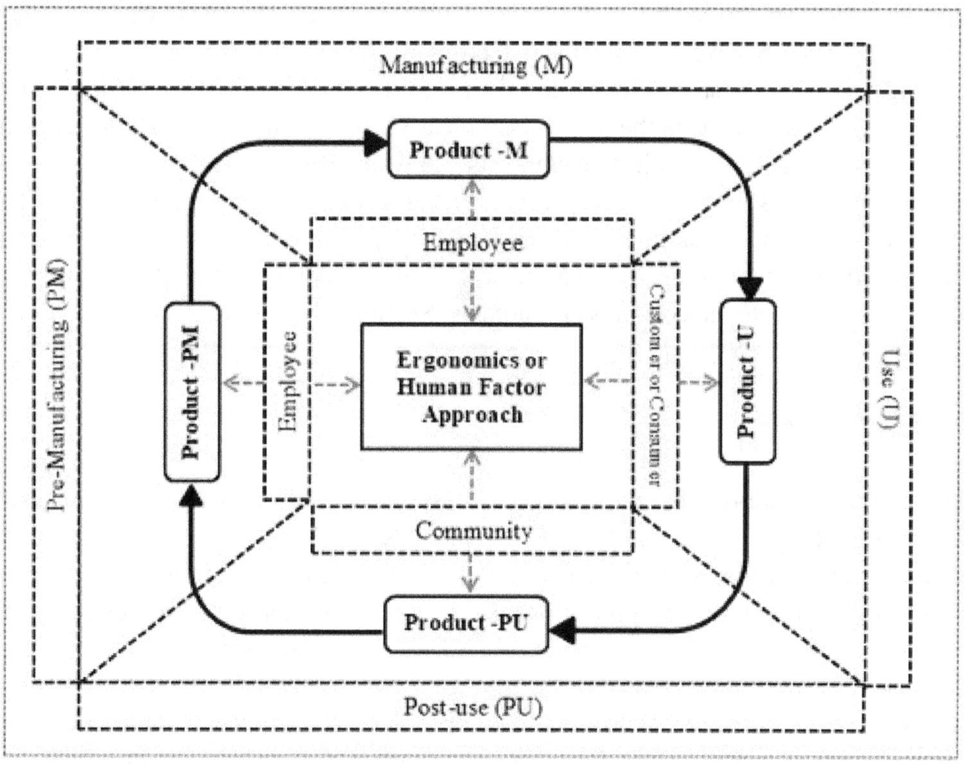

This method enables the design of human-inspired workspaces that maximize ergonomics while upholding production norms in Figure 1 (i.e., task completion times) (Panariello et al., 2021). To achieve this, the design of human-oriented workspaces will consider both objective measurements derived from biosignals on humans and subjective measurements taken from the employees. From the perspective of objective measurements, biomechanics, and motion analysis are utilized to comprehend the physiological behavior of people while they are carrying out industrial work. Ad-hoc surveys are developed from the standpoint of subjective analysis to assess the opinions of the workers and thereafter take into account their sentiments while doing a task in various configurations.

Ergonomic workplace designs: The ergonomic parameters achieved in the preceding step are translated into engineering solutions during the workplace design stage. In particular, the objective is to design a workstation that minimizes workers' workloads and weariness while simultaneously maximizing production and winning over the worker.

Validation in a true industrial environment: Wearable sensors (such as inertial sensors, wearable force meters, and surface electromyography) that record the worker's actions, burdens, and attempts can be used to validate the methodology in actual industrial situations.

As a result, the designers must work extensively on ergonomics from all perspectives, and the ergonomic component might be challenging. It is never easy for the decision-makers to compare several plans to determine which one is better during the development process since there are too many things to take into account. Many businesses and institutes, like Motion Evaluation, Tekscan, and Advanced Science Laboratories, have been building gear and software to imitate real-world usage scenarios and gather data. When used, this apparatus provides a wealth of information about the human body and may, in certain cases, reflect ergonomic effectiveness (Arkouli et al., 2022). On the other hand, architects and decision-makers frequently have a strong understanding of the product's ergonomic performance, and they consistently evaluate the suggestions using their experiences. The data from a single piece of gear can only reflect a few parameters in the first ergonomic assessment solution, while the latter ergonomic evaluation solution incorporates subjective elements and is insufficiently accurate.

The rest of this essay is structured as follows. The related efforts on ergonomic evaluation are discussed in Section 2. In Section 3, we outline our procedure for ergonomic evaluation and decision-making. To start, we construct an ergonomic evaluation tree. Section 4 details the method's use and provides examples of how to evaluate the cockpit's ergonomics. Section 5 concludes.

2. RELATED WORKS

Many scholars and programmers have been engaged in system creation and administration in ubiquitous computing environments during the last few years (Jeong & Yi, 2014). A service is an online application procedure that may be used remotely. The creation and development of user-centric services and a computing environment focused on applications is the key component of ubiquitous computing. Since space within the environment supports the interactive sharing of data between learners and is coupled to the service applications, these settings differ from the current computing models in that respect.

The deployment of a PFL and SSM collaboration mode calls for the evaluation of human-robot contacts in particular (Gualtieri, 2021). Even if there are acceptable approximations, modeling a touch between a human body part and the robot systems is often difficult. The contact is typically thought to be a somewhat inelastic impact. The dynamic consists of a first swift section where two moving objects clash more or less intensely, followed by a brief and slight physical separation. Following that, the two objects can either continue moving in the same direction together or be distinct based on the contact conditions.

The twentieth-century World Wars served as the primary impetus for the shift from the trial-and-error methodology to the organized methodology of human factors and ergonomics, or HFE (Kilkki, 2011). Although the theory and science of HFE were eventually modified to fit other uses as well, labor productivity was the focus of the first published and extensively used practical approaches to HFE. Although the ergonomic approach has its roots in creating effective working practices and workforce training, the idea has shown to be quite helpful in the fields of contemporary technology and product creation.

Preventive occupational safety and health, balancing work and life, worker engagement, and human-centered design of work are some of the primary issues that social innovation must deal with (Papetti et al., 2020). To address current ergonomics-related issues and improve the wellbeing of the managers, human-focused best practices are required to be defined and put into practice. Reducing physical work-related diseases and mental stress can be achieved by monitoring important factors and subsequently modifying jobs, workplaces, instruments, and gear to match the worker. Social innovation is greatly facilitated by IoT and data.

The physical demands of manual materials handling jobs could be reduced with the use of effective ergonomic evaluation methods (such as checklists) (Dündar, 2018). Injury to the musculoskeletal system may decline. Hence, ergonomic Assessments are practical strategies for enhancing a business's Productivity, Good Products, and Business Overall competition as a result of cutting expenses associated with injuries to identify and avoid patterns with prevalent causes of risks in workplaces, effective workplace analysis should include injury and illness trends across time, based to the Elements of an Effective Safety and Health Programmer (Occupational Safety and Health Management).

The idea of process sustainability, one of the forces behind the fourth industrial revolution, is multifaceted and encompasses social, environmental, and economic considerations (Gualtieri et al., 2020). Occupational health and safety (OH), as well as the happiness and contentment of operators, are essential components of social sustainability in business. By enhancing working conditions and creating production methods that are centered on people, manufacturing organizations should see the human aspect as their core and an important component. Workplace ergonomics play a big part in this situation.

Deep learning techniques for assessing human posture in 2D have advanced dramatically in recent years (Paudel et al., 2022). When estimating human stance, there are primarily two methods. The first is a bottom-up strategy that locates all human bodily key points in an image before grouping those using clustering techniques. A second is a top-down approach that forms bounding boxes to first detect humans. These techniques make use of improvements in human recognition technology and extra person limit identifying data. Satisfactory performance is required under the top-down paradigm but at extra cost for personal box identification.

Ergonomics investigates how the working environment is changed to accommodate the talents of the individual employee (Anshasi et al, 2022). By tailoring the task to the worker rather than the other way around, it is possible to work smarter rather than harder. Ergo-dentistry, often known as dental ergonomics, focuses on creating dental tools and techniques that provide the healthiest possible working conditions for dental staff members. It prioritizes dental professionals, ensuring that they are compatible with their environment. Dental organizations, universities, medical centers, and other healthcare facilities must adopt an "ergonomics mindset" and participate actively in this program. In dentistry colleges, fundamental ergonomics instruction is rarely embraced. It would be preferable for future dental graduates, though, if dental ergonomics were taught in schools.

Think of ergonomics as the study of individuals in their work surroundings, with an emphasis on office desk layout, temporal and environmental assessments, as well as the mental and physical tasks of the worker (Hoyos-Ruiz et al., 2017). Currently, there is an area of ergonomics specifically intended for health care related to the prevention of occupational and psychosocial risks, safety hazards, and management of prevention, entailing elements taken from judiciary ergonomics by analyzing work, and the standards of impairment, unintentional event reconstruction, and professional maladies originated from ergonomic hazards and injury generates.

3. METHODS AND MATERIALS

In order to incorporate ergonomics into manufacturing, it is necessary to record how operators carry out and feel about their work. There are numerous techniques for gathering data, some of which solely include specialists (such as observers) while others also include the actual operators (such as self-evaluations). The sections that follow give an overview of these techniques organised according to physical and cognitive ergonomics as well as information on their effectiveness and drawbacks.

Figure 2. Design of ergonomic workplace

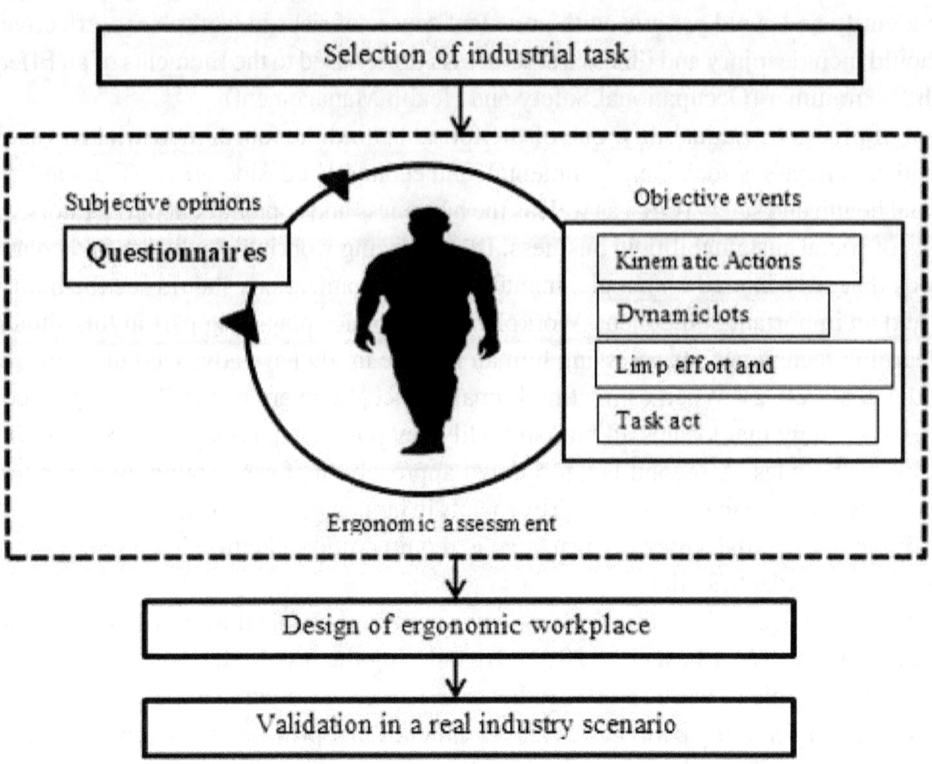

Strategies for Evaluating Ergonomics

When trying to implement ergonomics into production, it needs to be done to keep track of how employees conduct and perceive their work a variety of multiple information gathering strategies using Experts. The actual operators (e.g., observations) may also be used as an alternative. The portions that proceed offer a synopsis of these strategies arranged by physical and cognitive ergonomics along with details regarding the benefits and disadvantages in Figure 2.

Figure 3. Process of extended human-centered design

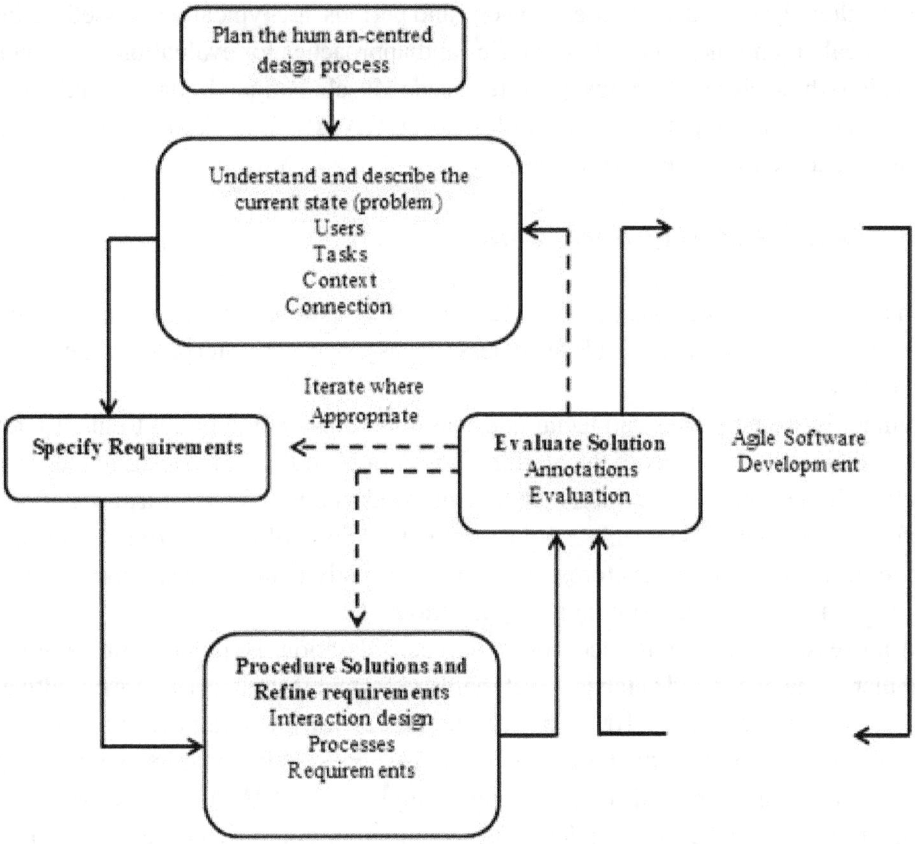

We use the HCD process (as an example method) to support each phase with specific modules to give a structured and consistent method for software development (see Figure 3). All of the process's outcomes may be applied to the implementation procedure to profit from it (Paul et al., 2014). For this task, the requirements are very well suited.

A user interface design method is supported by a User module in some ways. Information collected in one module may be connected to data collected in other modules. These references make it easier to comprehend development choices made during evaluation, architecture, or assessment since they can be traced back to the relevant requirements.

Fitness Ergonomics

The study of physical ergonomics focuses on issues like part handling, workspace health and security, and working postures. Physical ergonomics have been examined often during manufacturing because these are significant factors for system layout and adherence to current regulations. Such research is usually carried out when the goods and procedure designs have grown and matured and usually depends on the knowledge and hypotheses of mechanical design engineering professionals. The methodologies applied are aimed at helping engineers in structuring their evaluations, prioritizing concerns by determining those that might pose the greatest likelihood of damage, ranking by seriousness, and discovering the vulnerable body parts.

Physical loading factors, such as poses, powers, and periods, are typically assessed during the examination of physical ergonomics. Indicative metrics and approaches for evaluation are shown, which has been divided into three different groups: posture based (Muscle Fatigue Equations, NIOSH, etc.) which integrates biomechanical computations and multi-aspects (EWAS, RAMP, etc.) examines biomechanics-based methods that are usually experimental.

Limitations and Method Performance

- When an actual prototype has been established, investigations can be made easily, inexpensively, and with beneficial outcomes. Nevertheless, an assessor can interpret the person's experience inaccurately.
- Instrument-based addresses and techniques based on observation ought to incorporate an assortment of sufficient size to record the working population's traits such as population density, anthropometry, biomechanics, etc. which may be employed as obstacles for purposes of design, such as the laboring population's mean height governing the sizing of the shelving systems.
- Despite instrument-based structures are a bit more costly than observations, they can be utilized for both manufacturing and simulation applications.
- DHM possesses the ability to incorporate into consideration the demographics of the population being that of the integrated databases, yet there are certain techniques where cognitive ergonomics has been incorporated into DHM. The lengthy process of modeling every process, nevertheless, restricts the total length of the tasks' chain that is suggested for such investigations due to DHM demands an extended period for preparing a single step. DHM is an appropriate fit for initial computational design because it allows the consumption of numerous human examples or a wide range of anthropometric traits, but it is expensive and typically concentrates on short-duration jobs because of the time needed for development.
- Before the real-world layout of the workstation is finalized, virtual reality may enable genuine employees to successfully carry out their job duties digitally, enabling spectators and detectors to keep track of the staff members. But VR expertise is essential.
- Given that heuristic strategies demand a solid basis in theory, a professional's engagement is required to allow one to recognize the assessment as accurate.
- Because bodily responses to mental stress are incredibly scenario-dependent, various solutions have different impacts on conditions that are not identical. More importantly, there are currently no measurements that are applicable worldwide.

- Discussions and unannounced remarks from employees can help reveal task ergonomics limitations (physical and mental stress) as well as avoid erroneous interpretations of the operators' actions.
- Surveys and interviews commonly provide an aggregated evaluation of all steps taken throughout a task. They are consequently appropriate for a quick succession of procedures.
- MWL is capable of being estimated through self-reporting, physiological, and performance-associated parameters, but professionals believe that none of these precautions is a trustworthy independent MWL indicator.

Human-Centered Design's Implications

Numerous healthcare providers worldwide demand confirmation that additional advantages for low-resource demographics will ultimately result from using human-centered design methods. In their investigation, the author analyzed 21 publications from thoroughly reviewed and gray research sources that had been selected due to their ability to describe how various characteristics of HCD impact the health consequences. One of their discoveries was that the association between HCD and health consequences has not yet been extensively investigated in the scientific literature. Several weaknesses in the literature were additionally noted by this famous professor, particularly a shortage of articles that outline the entire project cycle, the thin description of the HCD tackles employed, and the unavailability of in-context feedback from stakeholders acquiring. None of the 21 publications that were picked responded to medical devices or diagnostics; alternatively, they primarily focused on software apps, clinical choice aids, and webpages that influence global health.

Even though we do not offer any measurable information to connect the use of HCD to adverse health outcomes in this article, we supply resources to demonstrate how HCD has an effect in other domains. User experience design and human factors engineering have been shown that they will have an effect on a good's capacity to earn money, in accordance with assessments. The primary argument is that minimal time and economic investment in early adoption of HCD will produce immense savings in costs afterward during the manufacturing procedure. For example, a famous professor cites an examination of a software program in which $20,700 dedicated to accessibility modifications generated a $47,700 return on investment on the very initial day they were put into action, while $68,000 invested in enhancing usability generated a $6,800,000 payback in the initial year of use for a different platform. Furthermore, after investigating the implications of human factors engineering on healthcare device architecture, the US FDA medical gadget oversight agency published the following conclusion:

Figure 4. Index for a new ergonomic triad model for sustainable working

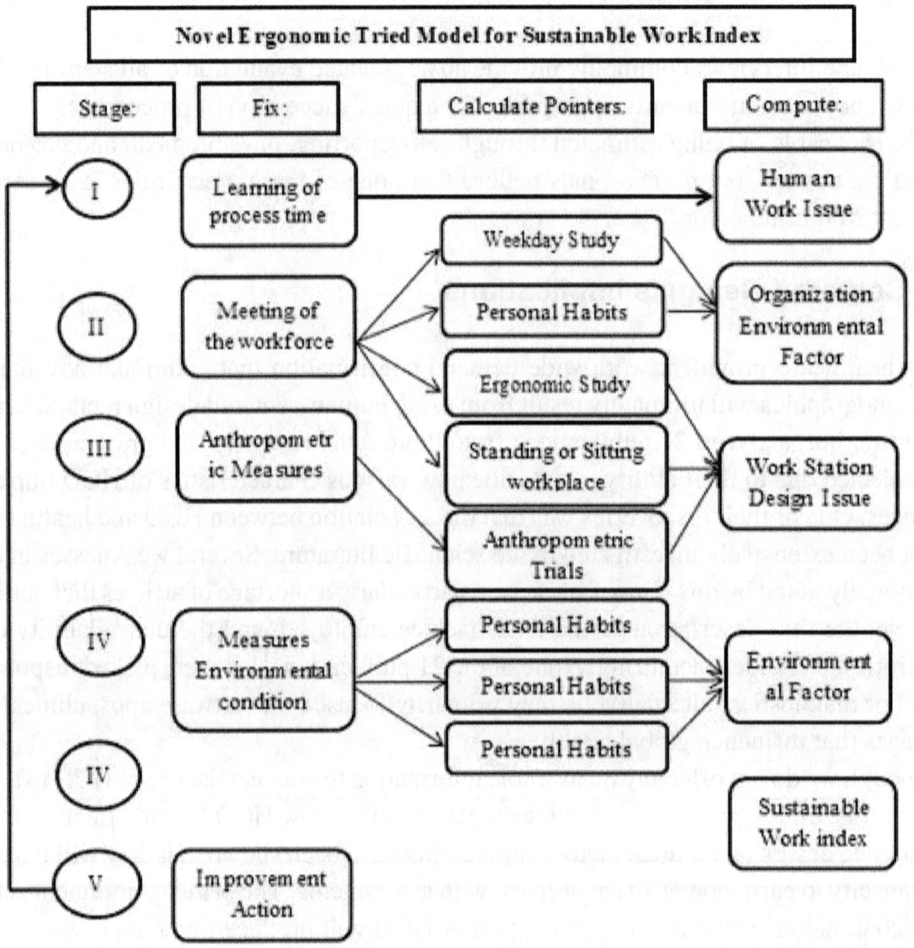

The new ergonomic triad approach to sustainable employment (see Figure 4) is made up of six phases in which process time analysis (Montoya-Reyes et al., 2020). It is remarkable that these kinds of evaluations concentrate on product economic achievement as opposed to positive neighborhood effects. In the opinion of experienced professor, the commercial achievement of a product is not undoubtedly closely associated with its benefiting impact on humanity. However, in our observations, designing products in partnership with groups enables impoverished global health projects to avoid pricey remakes which frequently fail to pay off in an end product. HCD can be applied to quickly create an assortment of healthcare equipment and diagnostic ideas for concepts that are compelling to stakeholders. Secure and reliable medical equipment needs both adequate usage and positive business perception. We believe that through better honing the architectural thoughts to fulfill the demands of stakeholders at the beginning of the design stage of HCD expands opportunities for positive impact.

The Procedure of Human-Centered Design

When executed correctly, HCD comprises an extensive spectrum of abilities and governs every aspect of the manufacturing process, from selecting the best team to delivering the final product. We believe that the use of HCD boosts the potential for successful product acquisition in the medical field. Figure 5 explains how human-centered planning originates by taking stakeholders' demands into consideration. The crew then has to search for opportunities where productive companies and viable solutions overlap. While financial viability and technical sustainability are not addressed in greater length in this paper, engineers and scientists typically have the skills to cope with the former issue but not the latter. Engineers and scientists who found organizations should early on encompass entrepreneurs to serve as instructors or colleagues. The establishment of an appealing, workable, and feasible approach is fundamental to the marketing or healthcare profitability of any good.

Figure 5. Procedure for integration of human-centered design process with the product development

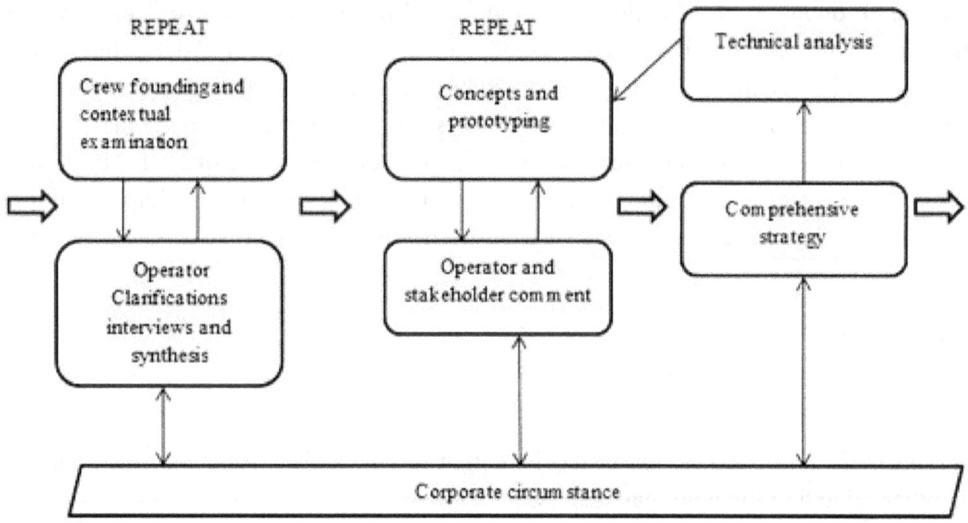

We provide sporadic proof of the intrinsic worth of human-centered designs as professionals with involvement in deploying HCD in more than twenty international medical technology campaigns focused on low-resource communities. We offer a real-life study of Planning That Matters' Firefly phototherapy for treating neonatal jaundice alongside brief instances from various other initiatives that demonstrate the procedures and positive aspects of HCD. HCD can be employed to produce investigations along with healthcare equipment and also to develop intellectual advancements that comprise global health systems, services, and regulations. The methodologies we supply during this project are aimed primarily at an increased risk of diagnostic procedures and healthcare devices for worldwide wellness.

Methodology for Human Reliability Evaluation of Management Interfaces

According to the complexity of human behavior and actions, both objective and subjective components need to be completely considered consideration when measuring personal trustworthiness. The strengthened AHP algorithm is employed for computing the subjective weights of indicators alongside the decision matrix based on fuzzy mathematics, whereas the stochastic weight take-on is utilized to figure out the quantitative weights of warning signs in conjunction with the TOPSIS-based judgment matrix. The objectives, as well as subjective evaluations of human reliability, are made using the preceding methodologies, accordingly. In order to validate the worth and efficiency of the human reliability assessment method, eye-tracking trials are employed.

Picked Evaluation Indexes to Design an Ergonomic Interface

A simulated attempt focusing on a complicated interface layout (the CNC machine tool operating system) has been performed. These factors were merged with the physical features with complicated interface architecture and ergonomics specifications for the design. Meanwhile, CREAM primarily concentrates on cognitive error algorithms and structures, and the factor "Adequacy of MMI (Man-Machine Interface) and operational assistance" has merely one requirement of CPCs, making it less than ideal for the comprehensive and exhaustive assessment of targeted ergonomic interface design. On the basis of CPCs, the human reliability evaluation index technique has been altered to be adequate for both the objective and subjective wide-ranging technique. Entropy, additionally referred to as anticipated information is the outcome of every connected with every single bit of information:

$$F(V)=\sum_{j=1}^{m}V_j i(V_j)=\sum_{j=1}^{m}V_j log\left(\frac{1}{V_j}\right) \tag{1}$$

Theil's entropy is employed to figure out the extent to which data collected from one category as well as the other related to the aggregate gap:

$$U=\log m-F(V) \tag{2}$$

Since $\sum_{j=1}^{m}V_j=1$,

$$\log m=\sum_{j=1}^{m}V_j\log m \tag{3}$$

Formula (2) needs to be substituted with equations (3) and (1) then;

$$U = \log m - F(V) = \sum_{j=1}^{m} V_j \log m - \sum_{j=1}^{m} V_j \log\left(\frac{1}{V_j}\right) = \sum_{j=1}^{m} V_j \left[\log m - \log\left(\frac{1}{V_j}\right)\right] = \sum_{j=1}^{m} V_j \left(\log m V_j\right) \tag{4}$$

The formula (4) may also be expressed in the following form: b_j is the total number of errors a specialist commits while utilizing the user interface corresponding to the j-th measure, and V_j is the proportion of the incorrect number relying on the j-th index in addition to the total amount of errors $V_j = b_j / \sum_{j=1}^{m} b_j$ and average value $\bar{b} = \sum_{j=1}^{m} b_j / m$

$$U = \sum_{j=1}^{m} \frac{b_j}{\sum_{j=1}^{m} b_j} \left(\log m \frac{b_j}{\sum_{j=1}^{m} b_j}\right) = \frac{1}{m} \sum_{j=1}^{m} \frac{b_j}{\sum_{j=1}^{m} b_j / m} \left(\log \frac{b_j}{\sum_{j=1}^{m} b_j / m}\right) = \frac{1}{m} \sum_{j=1}^{m} \frac{b_j}{\bar{b}} \log \frac{b_j}{\bar{b}} \tag{5}$$

Under the j-th participant, the characteristic weight of i-th index has been provided by

$$Q_{jk} = \frac{b_{jk}}{\sum_{j=1}^{m} b_{jk}}, j=1,2,\ldots,m \tag{6}$$

Following Theil's entropy, i-th index seems to appear as

$$f_j = \frac{1}{m} \sum_{j=1}^{m} \frac{b_{jk}}{Q_{jk}} \log\left(\frac{b_{jk}}{Q_{jk}}\right) \tag{7}$$

The explanatory value of the statistics in the various grouping and identical set might be improved evident on a general level through the utilization of this particular kind of expanded entropy. Theil's entropy defines the amount of weight for every index in the following manner:

$$x_j^2 = \frac{1 - f_j / \sum_{j=1}^{m} f_j}{\sum_{j=1}^{m} \left(1 - f_j / \sum_{j=1}^{m} f_j\right)} \tag{8}$$

where n represents the index number and m represents the participant number. The index value's less amount of variation degree demonstrates that consumers are more likely to engage in the identical mistakes as they navigate the interface, and one specific index's weight calculated using Theil's entropy is stronger.

The hierarchy of faults has been generated by implementing this human trustworthiness assessment index system, and TOPSIS was implemented for calculating it. The assessment decision matrix was constructed using the extremely vital degree.

The probability importance of key occurrences $U_g(j)$ needs to be projected for the purpose to evaluate how modifications in the likelihood of happening for necessary circumstances will impact the possibility of the existence of the highest circumstances. A multiple linear function describes the possibility parameter g of the chance that the top occasion is going to happen. The probability relevance coefficient of the primary incident can be referred to below by picking a partial derivative of the independent variable Q_j.

$$U_g = \frac{\gamma g}{\gamma Q_j} \tag{9}$$

The variance between the proportional rate of shift concerning the chance of the fundamental occurrence happening and that about the likelihood of the top occasion arising demonstrates the significance level of the straightforward event, which means that the possibility and vulnerability of the events happening with reference to itself constitute the foundation of the significant guidelines for each basic incident. In turn, the crucial importance is expressed as

$$U_G(j) = \frac{\gamma lng}{\gamma lnQ_i} = \frac{\gamma g / g}{\gamma Q_j / Q_j} \tag{10}$$

The following graph depicts the correlation between statistical information's important degree and critical magnitude.

$$U_G(j) = \frac{Q_j}{g} U_g(j) \tag{11}$$

where $U_G(j)$ is the probability of an extremely important degree, Q_j is the possibility that a situation is going to happen, and g is the chance that things will occur even overall. A non-normalized independent full evaluation is shown in the following format:

$$e_{lj} = 1 - \frac{U_G(j)}{\sum_{j=1}^{m} U_G(j)} \tag{12}$$

where M is the defect tree's entire amount of evidence for the starting point event.

The standardized matrix of m indicators for assessment for every subsequent occurrence of the fault hierarchy is as listed below: There are l interfaces to be inspected.

$$E = \begin{bmatrix} e_{11} & e_{12} & \cdots & e_{1m} \\ e_{21} & e_{22} & \cdots & e_{2m} \\ \vdots & \vdots & \ddots & \vdots \\ e_{l1} & e_{l2} & \cdots & e_{lm} \end{bmatrix} \tag{13}$$

Following is an examination by TOPSIS of the human reliability evaluation judgment matrix developed for the essential degree. This is how the upper limit score is established:

$$E^{+} = \left(E_1^{+}, E_2^{+}, \ldots, E_j^{+}\right) = \left(max\left\{e_{11}, e_{21}, \ldots, e_{l1}\right\}, max\left\{e_{12}, e_{22}, \ldots, e_{l2}\right\}, \ldots, max\left\{e_{1m}, e_{2m}, \ldots, e_{lm}\right\}\right) \tag{14}$$

The minimum value is defined as follows

$$E^{-} = \left(E_1^{-}, E_2^{-}, \ldots, E_j^{-}\right) = \left(min\left\{e_{11}, e_{21}, \ldots, e_{l1}\right\}, min\left\{e_{12}, e_{22}, \ldots, e_{l2}\right\}, \ldots, min\left\{e_{1m}, e_{2m}, \ldots, e_{lm}\right\}\right) \tag{15}$$

The below equation describes the distance between the l-th assessment indicator value and the maximum value where (l=1,2,…,o)

$$O_l^{+} = \sqrt{\sum_{j=1}^{m} x_{jk} \left(E_j^{+} - e_{lj}\right)^2} \tag{16}$$

The below equation describes the distance between l-th assessment indicator value and the minimum value where (l=1,2,…,o)

$$O_l^{-} = \sqrt{\sum_{j=1}^{m} x_{jk} \left(E_j^{-} - e_{lj}\right)^2} \tag{17}$$

The optimal solution's proximity to the k-th (k=1,2,…,l) assessment indicator is then evaluated.

$$T_l = \frac{x_j O_l^{-}}{x_j O_l^{+} + x_j O_l^{-}} \tag{18}$$

One can figure out the goal of the human reliability assessment vector as follows:

$$G_l = \frac{\left(1 - U_{gl}\right) \times T_l}{\sum_l^0 \left(1 - U_{gl}\right) \times T_l} \tag{19}$$

$I_0{:}q$ indicates the unrelated or random n group assessment whereas $I_1{:}q$ indicates positively correlated and more or less consistent.

Kendall coefficient of concordance:

$$X = \frac{12T}{n^2\left(m^2 - m\right)} \tag{20}$$

$$T = \sum_{j=1}^{m}\left(S_j - \frac{n(m+1)}{2}\right)^2 \tag{21}$$

In the above equation S_j is the sum of ranks in the i-th object, n indicates the judge number and m represents the object number. When f is comparable information is present, the tailored empirical X_d will be shown as follows:

$$X_d = \frac{12\sum_{j=1}^{m} S_j^2 - 3n^2 m\left(m+1\right)^2}{n^2\left(m^3 - m\right) - m\sum_{l=1}^{f}\left(u_l^3 - u_l\right)} \tag{22}$$

where u_l is the aggregate amount of knots within each f set of knots for rank l. It is advisable to make use of the vital parameters table for X if $m \leq 7$ and $n \leq 20$. The massive batch guess tactics are applied to derive the chi-square variables if the m and n parameters are bigger than the values shown in the Kendall coordination coefficient X value table:

$$Y^2 = n(m-1)X \tag{23}$$

Verify the chi-square threshold list shortly after determining the coefficient of chi-square for the freedom degree δ=m–1, to discover if the positions of n professionals are accurate. The I*0* hypothesis is refused and I*1* is approved whenever the critical value is $Y^2_{0.05,m-1} < Y^2$, then $q<0.05$, respectively. This implies that the scoring of each index in the m criterion layers by the n participants is consistent.

The assessment matrix is produced depending on the AHP's basic principles, and the shortest judgment matrix for each of the indexes in the identical system is produced as afterwards.

$$C_l^{(i)} = \frac{\sum_{j=1}^{n} m_j}{n} \tag{24}$$

$$C^{(l)} = \begin{bmatrix} 1 & \frac{C_2^{(i)}}{C_1^{(i)}} & \cdots \frac{C_l^{(i)}}{C_1^{(i)}} \\ \frac{C_1^{(i)}}{C_2^{(i)}} & 1 & \cdots \frac{C_l^{(i)}}{C_2^{(i)}} \\ \frac{C_1^{(i)}}{C_l^{(i)}} & \frac{C_2^{(i)}}{C_l^{(i)}} & \ldots 1 \end{bmatrix} = \left(\frac{C_m^{(i)}}{C_n^{(i)}} \right)_{l \times l} \tag{25}$$

$$\left(n, m = 1, 2, \ldots, l; C_l^{(i)} = 1, 2, \ldots, l\right)$$

$C_l^{(i)}$ in the earlier formula represents the overall grade of the participate ranking. The subsequent characteristics apply to the essential judgment matrix (25).

$$\left(C_m^{(i)} / C_m^{(i)}\right) = 1, \left(C^{(i)} / C_n^{(i)}\right) = 1 / \left(C_n^{(i)} / C_m^{(i)}\right) > 0.$$

Since $C_m^{(i)} / C_l^{(i)} \times C_l^{(i)} / C_n^{(i)} = 1 / \left(C_m^{(i)} / C_n^{(i)}\right)$, there is not anymore a requirement for verification of the uniformity of the matrix due to the fact it corresponds with its threshold.

Having a consistency matrix, $C^{(i)}$ has a rank of 1, a single nonzero eigenvalue of l, each column vector of $C^{(i)}$ is the eigenvector associated with k (Sgarbossa et al., 2020; Liu et al., 2021), and the normalized eigenvector of $C^{(i)}$ can be employed as the weight vector of $C^{(i)}$; in simple terms, $C^{(i)}$ has a weight vector.

$$C^{(i)} x = lx, x = \left(x_1, x_2, \ldots . x_l\right) \tag{26}$$

The derived vector $x^{(i)}$ post x normalization displays the corresponding weights of every element in the threshold layer of the lowest stage.

$$X_k^{(i)} = \begin{cases} \dfrac{1 - x_k}{\sum_{k=1}^{l} \left(1 - x_k\right)} x_k \geq 0, \\ \dfrac{1 + x_k}{\sum_{k=1}^{l} \left(1 + x_k\right)} x_k < 0 \end{cases} \tag{27}$$

The complete significance of every component at each of the layers can be assessed from the top to the bottom shortly after computing the corresponding relevance of the substances at each stage. Considering that we are right now in the i layer, a subsystem is composed of l elements, $C_1^{(i)}$ through $C_l^{(i)}$, each featuring a weight coefficient of $x_1^{(i)}$ through $x_l^{(i)}$, and in the layer below it, $C_k^{(i+1)}$, corresponding to $x_k^{(i)}$, $C_{k1}^{(i+1)}, C_{k2}^{(i+1)}, \ldots, C_{km}^{(i+1)}$, with $x_{k1}^{(i+1)} + x_{k1}^{(i+1)} + \ldots + x_{km}^{(i+1)}$, correspondingly. If $C_k^{(i+1)}$ and $C_l^{(i)}$ are separate from one another, then $x_k^{(i+1)} = 0$, and $x_k^{(i)} = \sum_{j=1}^{m} X_{kj}^{(i+1)}$ (k=1,2,…,l) are true, respectively.

Hence $X_{kj}^{(i+1)}$ which is the weight coefficient of factor $C_{kj}^{(i+1)}$ is indicated as

$$X_{kj}^{(i+1)} = x_{kj}^{(i+1)} x_k^{(i)} \tag{28}$$

The consistency index of hierarchical overall standing similarly needs to be 0, in compliance with the AHP principle. This avoids the requirement for stability inspection and modification and eliminates computer calculation. While analyzing information obtained by an improved AHP, a complicated mathematics principle is applied to highlight the degree of ambiguity of people's emotional sensations such as

$$A = X_k D = \left(x_1, \ldots, x_k\right) \begin{bmatrix} d_{11} & d_{12} & \cdots & d_{1w} \\ d_{21} & d_{22} & \cdots & d_{2w} \\ \vdots & \vdots & \ddots & \vdots \\ d_{k1} & d_{k2} & \cdots & d_{kw} \end{bmatrix} \tag{29}$$

$$d_{kw} = \frac{h_{kw}}{r} \tag{30}$$

A_i(h=1,2,…,o) projects the location of the i-th conclusion among the chain of selections; D is a vague analysis matrix $A=(A_1,A_2,\ldots,A_o)$ indicates a fuzzy assessment outcome; h_{kw} is the aggregate amount of contributions associated with the w-th degree of the k-th element concerning the interface portion of the function assessment and r is the number of participants enrolled in voting.

Every combined factor is having the result which is indicated as

$$G_a = AW^U \tag{31}$$

In the above equation, W is represented as the evaluation grade level vector while A is shown as the qualitative evaluation matrix.

Personalized Solutions Applying Human-Centered Workplace Design Techniques

According to the author in the opening, there is an immediate need for a generation of particular, personalized approaches to control the growing diversity of employees that involves a wide range of perceptual and mental abilities as well as physical talents and needs. Particularly when we take into account the so-called "aging-challenge" of the industrial job market, these become far more crucial. By proactively implementing their professional knowledge and exceptional abilities without stressing employees, all of these tools have the ability to preserve the productivity, quality, and assistance of older employees.

Implementing smart, age-friendly organizations that work together with human employees and expand their capabilities, instead of substituting them should be the objective. A famous author has created a prototype of a future assisting desk for elder workers that will enable individuals to manufacture bespoke items close to the consumer.

Surely this technique is equally suitable for the generation of tailored remedies for different consumers, encompassing newcomers and professionals, young and old, and individuals with and without physical challenges. Expanding companies to include disabled people who are normally prohibited from labor is an opportunity throughout these tactics to additionally promote the bigger community goals of career openness. Multidisciplinary studies covering the disciplines of manufacturing engineering, operations research, social science, ergonomics, management science, digital technologies, and data science can be employed to do this.

As a consequence, an entirely novel transdisciplinary attitude has to be fostered that encourages the creation and deployment of technology and multiculturalism in the labor force, effectively assisting business goals.

Using Assistive and Collaborative Technologies for Human-Centered Workplace Design

A widely recognized scholar described Operator 4.0 as the "operator of the future," a smart and talented employee who accomplishes projects "aided" by modern technology as required. Scalable production and distribution systems that merge workers and technologies via human cyber-physical systems, such as virtual twins, are recommended. Furthermore, it requires incorporating a comprehensive tracking system where data concerning the system's performance, from humans as well as machines, is compiled and evaluated in real-time through proficient predictive analytics algorithms.

Augmented truth and video recording infrastructure, two innovative methods that enable the creation of virtual copies of human-centered workplaces are extremely beneficial for refining and assessing working environments with a particular emphasis on customer demands along with the way they correspond to system efficiency.

But the implementation of collaborative and assistive technology through production and logistical systems is still unpredictable. The invention of highly accurate and extensive systems for decision assistance is essential for examining the situations under which the use of interconnected and assistive gadgets is financially cost-effective.

Difficulties in Human-Centered Working Space Design

Additional data about the links between community needs and system functionality has been officially offered by researchers. A heavy reliance on observation might end up in mistakes errors, and low-quality results. Excessive cognitive requirements could end up resulting in high stress, mistakes, poor health, and inferior quality as a result. High physical demands directly affect quality by causing fatigue and injury. To professionally incorporate these variables in their conceptual work, engineering teams need to have an in-depth comprehension of architectural level understanding as well as techniques.

In addition, professionals should have to concentrate on the high side effects of robotic and harmonious and assistive methodology. It's important to comprehend the ideal ratio between automating manual operations and those that should still be performed by humans. The likelihood of overwhelming the staff member with tedious duties that harm his or her health and accordingly, the viability of the framework, exists. Engineers additionally require to take into account the demands of other clients, such as the administration and deployment of staff members as technology systems grow increasingly tricky. If HF is not enough for these commitments, errors and outages will rise, system long-term expenses will rise dramatically, and the expense of investing in cutting-edge technology will be threatened.

The aesthetic and physical taxation of cutting-edge technology on labor are further important considerations. Plenty of questions maintain unnoticed in this situation, that include: "What is the outcome of font size and reflections using machines for technological worker guidance (e.g., laptops, virtual reality, and laser therapy and light support tools)?"; "What are the requirements of putting on a smart glass gadget of 1 kg for 8 hours?"; and "Are robotic bodies beneficial for the employees or do their bodies just modify the work to other areas of the physique, generally lesser parts?" Hence, while developing innovative work environments, it is vital to have instruments and processes that can guide engineering professionals in evaluating those requirements. Lacking methods and understanding, manufacturers might accidentally generate fresh issues for staff members while they strive to fix older ones.

Simulation for Production and Logistics Systems That Is Age-Friendly

Regardless of its strategic reliability, a significant number of study outcomes evaluated below have skipped over the age group of the labor force. With the goal to strengthen the assignment of duties in production and distribution systems, which might involve sorting of jobs in hand-held manufacturing/alignment workstations or workload controlling in manual processing mechanisms, new mathematical frameworks ought to be taken into account both intellectual and physical load obstacles for mellowing workers.

The successful implementation of imaginative, age-oriented techniques for governing the production and transportation networks would be corroborated by such frameworks. The hurdle for chief executives in the aforementioned scenario is to fully take advantage of their understanding along with the expertise of older staff members while obeying the steady decrease of professional opportunities that all individuals undergo as they age. Some instances of fresh methodologies that are necessary to accommodate retirement include learning curve calculation, rest-allowance testing, or in the context of learning of newcomers, job extension and improvement, or "age-oriented" shift work.

Production and Delivery System Simulation in the Context of Cooperative Technologies

It is critical to construct new operational planning techniques during collaborative human-robotic production as well as for intelligent and electronic workspaces. It might be highly important in this scenario to consider account and forecast the human implications of employing an unfamiliar device or gadget, as well as the impact of HF on system functionality in contrast to just the expense of investment. This highlights the problem of what new technology' supporting expenses are regarding the system's lifecycle. As an example, damage, turnover of employees, fatigue-related inaccuracies, and absences from work, there certainly will be a requirement for fresh approaches for measuring these secondary expenditures that also factor into consideration how well-liked these devices are within the workforce.

Constraints in Human-Centered Modeling in Production as Well as Distribution Systems

Upcoming simulation initiatives must consider this whenever making choices about scheme complexity and spatial resolution. When investigating emotional dizziness and excessive stress as an outcome of overwork, its effects on humans might require months compared to milliseconds, for instance, while researching electrophysiological tiredness conclusions in muscular contraction patterns.

Equal challenges emerge while selecting the vital refinement threshold for human modeling. "Make sure whether we should simulate pressures at every single human joint, for each muscle, or for every motor unit?" What exactly are the adverse effects of burnout on the same physical architecture? What is the only thing that is wrong with the requirements imposed on subjective and frightened operations? How can these be adequately accounted for in an individual model?

We believe that choosing which HF features ought to be incorporated and which ought to be excluded from an individual simulation attempt will involve an analysis technique. To support them in choosing an option for these challenges, trained professional designers will require appropriate devices and methods.

Effective Management Techniques for Manufacturing and Supply Chain Systems in Perspective of the Community's Elderly Workforce

The previously discussed shifts in population indicate that unique scrutiny should be considered to the developing capacities, physical endurance, and cognitive skills of the staff over the age of 55, especially when they are working in manufacturing and supply chain systems that encompass a lot of resource handling.

Starting from the viewpoint of management, it is going to become fundamentally crucial in this scenario to estimate the expense of implementing assistive technologies (in addition to coordinating learning efforts) alongside the ability to successfully engage the labor force and win their sustained approval. Economic forecasting techniques will excessively exaggerate the positive effects of applying the latest technology, contributing to what has been nicknamed "phantom profits," lacking simulations that can project supplementary, notably negative, human adverse effects of the system's architecture.

Future Production and Logistics Systems Will Implement Strategies for Management Utilizing HF Principles

Both ecological sustainability and the efficient functioning of the manufacturing and transportation networks are influenced by HF. Yet, in real life, the research streams and their implications for HF and organizational management have remained frequently separated. Indeed, it is established that supervisory inquiry and decision-making will be cut off from aesthetics if they are merely viewed from a social and ethical standpoint without dealing with financial and economic considerations. These novel procedures require promoting envisioning brand-new workplaces for engaging skillful persons. The acceptance of novel approaches to leadership that are more decentralized, self-sufficient, and clever and depend on techniques from data science, which include sophisticated predictive analytics, experiment, and predictive optimization, can be altered by the introduction of the most recent technologies.

To foster the enforceable utilization and application of these innovations by staff Members methods for knowledge management must also serve as tweaked and adjusted effectively. Ultimately, an organizational planner must consider and take responsibility for every factor that could potentially have an influence on staff productivity, from advancement in their careers to well-being and health. Depending on this vantage point, the success rate of the companies' efforts will be significantly impacted as well by the condition of their work atmosphere. As a result, it will be vital to create a new set of indicators or indices for measuring the various human-centered procedures and approaches that these businesses are implementing.

Managerial and Intellectual Abilities

On top of that, it persists be unusual to find projects that take seriously multiple objectives and emphasize the necessity of governing both operational efficiency and staff happiness at the same period. Investigators in this field of study must continuously pay attention to indications of human overall health, such as exhaustion, workload, annoyance, and risk of accident, as well as human performance. For more susceptible team members and throughout a long period, this is particularly significant. Another benefit is that a few articles validated the outcomes of their algorithms with actual information or real-life examples.

If trustworthy forecasting algorithms need to be developed, additional evidence-based study is required. In manufacturing and transportation systems, for illustration, there is an urgent demand for sophisticated analytical frameworks, numerical methods, and simulation-based research, however, there is also an appetite for qualitative strategies and empirical research that provide a deeper understanding of psychological problems and the connections between human beings and emerging tools.

The investigation needs to take into consideration of concerns about quality, including human errors and needs to focus on the tangible, intellectual and psychological human aspects in production and practical operations. There is an obvious demand for study on the acceptance of technology, trustworthiness, and sustainability in these structures, all of which come with an impact on HF, in conjunction with the possibilities and barriers of incorporating supportive and joint technology in human industrial duties.

Designers and managers should consider human factors (HF) when designing or redesigning traditional labor activities in order to keep enhancing the efficiency and effectiveness of production and logistics infrastructures in light of advancements in demographics. HF, in particular, the distinct requirements and skills of laborers, deserve to be taken into consideration.

4. IMPLEMENTATION AND EXPERIMENTAL PARTS

The execution of the architecture encompassed a broad range of subject matter, encompassing a clarification of the system's technical requirements, limitations on how computer programs could potentially be carried out, the execution of techniques, and the utilization of graphical interfaces. MoFi is carried out by making use of the user-centered design methodology. The first handheld device, which is the tiniest and is 4 inches, is closely followed by the second, which is 5.3 inches in size, and the final one, which is 7 inches in size; all of them are outfitted with the MOFI-controlled system. The gadget's touchscreen is lightly touched by the consumer's fingertips on a wide range of icon panel sizes. The audio response that grows will be outdated if the user depends on a finger tap with a stretched touch duration. The operating system will fail to respond to the sound of the user's double-finger taps with a long touch time or more than thrice. With an extensive range of menu screen dimensions, the fingers of the user effortlessly slide to the right and left on the screen of the gadget by adjusting it once.

Table 1. Census of participants

Participants = 11	
Age	>41*th*=11 and <41*th*=0
Sexual category	Female = 5 and Male = 6
Effort	Farmer = 5 Entrepreneur = 2 Employee = 2 Housewife = 2
Long manifestation of thump	> 1year = 7, <1year = 4
Concentration of portable device use	Often (≥1*x*/*day*)=9 Rarely (≤1*x*/3-7 *day*)=2

The functional necessities formerly listed in Table 1 constitute the foundation for the system specification to be implemented in the present test. The pragmatic screening methodology uses a "black box," and test models are implemented to verify the functional criteria.

User Center Design (UCD) Method of Launch

Depending on ISO 13407:1999, there are currently four phases to User Center Design (UCD):

1. **Identify and indicate the user circumstance**: MOFI was developed in order to help consumers whom, as an outcome of cerebral infarction, are unable to speak (aphasia) with the people around them. Activity Daily Living (ADL) will be commonly utilized throughout this program. There is a choice on the menu in the current application for conveying the user's emotions, such as discomfort, vomiting, heat, dizziness, fear, and so on.
2. **Figure out what the users' and corporate requirements are**: Reviewing the operational as well as content necessities listed in Table 2 will help clarify the needs and wants of MOFI users.
3. **The conclusive design response:** The user experience design methodology (UX), encompassing architecture tactics, domain layout, architecture design, which is skeleton construction, and surface design, is the starting point for the MOFI application's layout. Each design's consequences are highlighted in a sectional graph.
4. **Validation of consumer needs in architecture**: Whenever the app is presented to the client for testing and evaluation, its architecture is evaluated. Ten users (stroke survivors as well as healthy individuals) engaged in a trial implementation of this investigation, after which questionnaires were utilized to record user responses and analyze them.

Evaluation

Both operational and inactive testing will be featured in the assessment discussion. A functional examination is a trial done to assess if the technological infrastructure has been successfully constructed according to the operational demands that were originally mentioned. Any individual's entry point to the computer system can potentially be mimicked using an appropriate test case. The experiments generated observations demonstrating the reliability of the functional examination as an entire system. It suggests that the equipment was able to adjust positions, manipulate noises, exhibit photos, and show text.

Non-functional inspection is a test performed to appraise the technology that was successfully established and its reliability (Priana et al., 2018). The gadget's control circumstances and attractiveness indicators are to be employed in this non-functional evaluation strategy. MoFi's program menu choice methodology requires using your fingertips. Depending on the final results of each device's management tests, an equipment control examination was then generated, and it came out at 75% for the product control score 1, which has been classified as a fulfilment group. On equipment 3, a baseline score of 82% was achieved, sorting the category as extremely satisfactory, whereas device 2 acquired a supervision rating of 76%, classifying it as a satisfaction category.

Usefulness is the following non-functional evaluation trait, and it can be utilized to figure out the extent to which users are satisfied with the usefulness of the designed system. This test is carried out by giving the system that was designed for an assortment of volunteers. A questionnaire with certain comments on the system's simplicity and effectiveness will be given to the respondents.

The queries that will be included in this research questionnaire have been adapted from a previous investigation titled "Toward Standard Reliability Questionnaires for Handheld Augmented Reality," which contains the usability testing of handheld technology on Android phones. Very satisfaction (0-19%), not satisfaction (20-39%), neutral (40-59%), satisfaction (60-79%), and very satisfaction (80-100%) are the five categories employed for categorizing the outcomes of the survey.

Figure 6. Usability experiment results

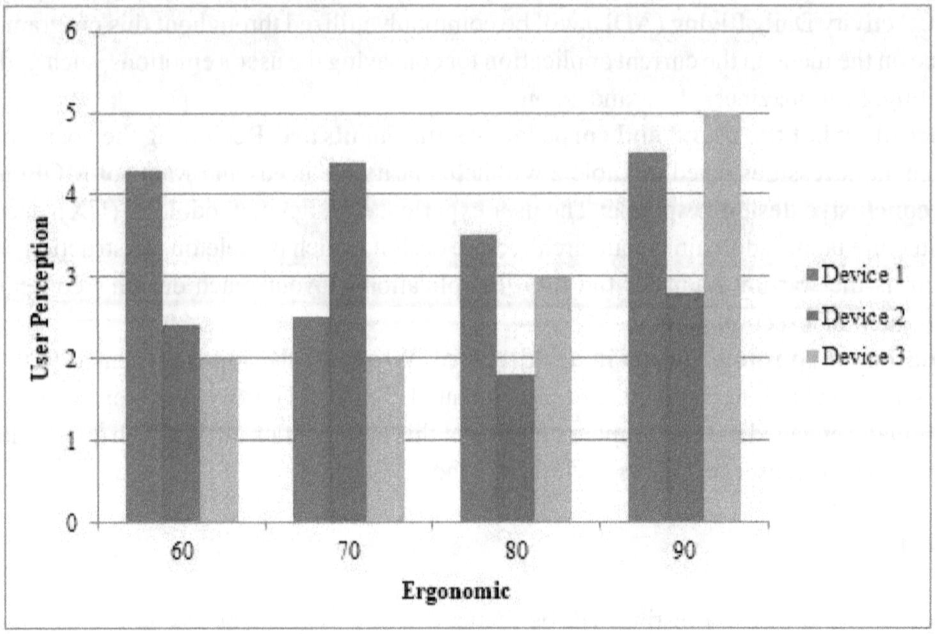

In accordance with the results of each gadget's functionality parameter examination in Figure 6, the average practicality of the first smartphone is 74.6% (satisfaction category), the mean convenience of the second gadget is 76%, and the normal suitability of the third phone is 82.4% (very satisfaction category). The primary claims that "the quantity of information exhibited on the smartphone's screen is adequate"

achieves the highest possible rating out of the three gadgets' contentment indices for customer opinion. The eighth affirmation, "Interaction with the program does not require much muscular effort," obtains the highest rating on the level of satisfaction index for the ergonomics of employing the application. The entire set of test results indicates that the system that was constructed offers users fulfilment.

Table 2. Outcomes of Gadgets 1, 2, and 3 through the experiments

Sl. No.	Usability	Gadget 1	Gadget 2	Gadget 3
1	View of user	74.2%	77%	81.8%
2	Comfort	75%	75%	82%
Aggregate		74.6%	76%	82.4%
Level of Usability		Satisfaction	Satisfaction	Very satisfaction

In line with an examination of such results, higher consumers of apps are at comfort in integrating an additional device, a tablet-smartphone having a bigger screen size (7.5 inches), in comparison to the first and second devices' (6 inches and 6.3 inches, correspondingly). The research results suggest that the recursive nature will be more pleased with the bigger device. However, when considered in terms of everyday use, the massive device should render it more challenging and heavier for an individual to carry around. It may be asserted that the utilization of apps on cell phones can be tailored to the circumstances, demands, and convenience of the customer, notably for the sick. Mobile gadgets shouldn't stress patients or jeopardize their sense of well-being.

5. CONCLUSION

Many problems relating to health, safety, comfort, and efficiency can be resolved with the help of ergonomics considerations. It might be a very promising topic on a societal, economic, and human level if goods are built with ergonomic requirements in mind within a certain setting, enhancing user experience as well as performance and adaptability for target users.

The development of goods can be done using a wide range of processes, tools, and design techniques. Some of them include a verification of ergonomics criteria throughout the user analysis phases, although this verification only involves qualitative user analysis and literature research. Because designers frequently have different mental models than users, they rarely consider the human model of activities (the product operability) while creating designs, which reduces task quality and satisfaction. A method or explicit tool was then established inside systemic design processes in order to incorporate functional concerns as well as biomechanical, anthropometric, and cognitive variables, among other.

According to the implementation and testing results, the application accessibility levels in the three devices are satisfactory (devices 1 and 2) and extremely satisfactory (device 3), respectively, when viewed from the perspectives of perception and ergonomics. Therefore, it can be said that the system developed provides satisfactory results to consumers. For additional study, this application will be given more developed characteristics, evaluated once more utilizing some metrics for user satisfaction with more respondents, and used with a wider range of gadget sizes for more effective outcomes.

REFERENCES

Anshasi, R. J., Alsyouf, A., Alhazmi, F. N., & AbuZaitoun, A. T. (2022). A Change Management Approach to Promoting and Endorsing Ergonomics within a Dental Setting. *International Journal of Environmental Research and Public Health, 19*(20), 13193. doi:10.3390/ijerph192013193 PMID:36293773

Arciniega-Rocha, R. P., Erazo-Chamorro, V. C., & Szabo, G. (2023). The prevention of industrial manual tool accidents considering occupational health and safety. *Safety (Basel, Switzerland), 9*(3), 51. doi:10.3390afety9030051

Arkouli, Z., Michalos, G., & Makris, S. (2022). On the selection of ergonomics evaluation methods for human centric manufacturing tasks. *Procedia CIRP, 107*, 89–94. doi:10.1016/j.procir.2022.04.015

Dündar, C. (2018, September). A Human-Centered Approach to Hazard Evaluation Checklists for the Risk of Back Pain in Manual Handling Tasks. *Proceedings of the Human Factors and Ergonomics Society Annual Meeting, 62*(1), 870–874. doi:10.1177/1541931218621198

Gualtieri, L. (2021). *Methodologies and guidelines for the design of safe and ergonomic collaborative robotic assembly systems in industrial settings* [Doctoral dissertation]. Free University of Bozen-Bolzano.

Gualtieri, L., Palomba, I., Merati, F. A., Rauch, E., & Vidoni, R. (2020). Design of human-centered collaborative assembly workstations for the improvement of operators' physical ergonomics and production efficiency: A case study. *Sustainability (Basel), 12*(9), 3606. doi:10.3390u12093606

Hoyos-Ruiz, J., Martínez-Cadavid, J. F., Osorio-Gómez, G., & Mejía-Gutiérrez, R. (2017). Implementation of ergonomic aspects throughout the engineering design process: Human-Artefact-Context analysis. *International Journal on Interactive Design and Manufacturing, 11*(2), 263–277. doi:10.100712008-015-0282-3

Jeong, H. Y., & Yi, G. (2014). A service based adaptive u-learning system using UX. *TheScientificWorldJournal, 2014*, 2014. doi:10.1155/2014/109435 PMID:25147832

Kilkki, D. S. K. (2011). *User-centered design of an instruction manual for a research vehicle*. Academic Press.

Liu, X., Liu, Z., Chen, P. Q., Xie, Z. Y., Lai, B. J., Zhan, B., & Lao, J. R. (2021). Human reliability evaluation based on objective and subjective comprehensive method used for ergonomic interface design. *Mathematical Problems in Engineering, 2021*, 1–16. doi:10.1155/2021/5560519

Montoya-Reyes, M., Gil-Samaniego-Ramos, M., González-Angeles, A., Mendoza-Muñoz, I., & Navarro-González, C. R. (2020). Novel ergonomic triad model to calculate a sustainable work index for the manufacturing industry. *Sustainability (Basel), 12*(20), 8316. doi:10.3390u12208316

Panariello, D., Grazioso, S., Caporaso, T., Di Gironimo, G., & Lanzotti, A. (2021). User-centered approach for design and development of industrial workplace. *International Journal on Interactive Design and Manufacturing, 15*(1), 121–123. doi:10.100712008-020-00737-x

Papetti, A., Gregori, F., Pandolfi, M., Peruzzini, M., & Germani, M. (2020). A method to improve workers' well-being toward human-centered connected factories. *Journal of Computational Design and Engineering*, *7*(5), 630–643. doi:10.1093/jcde/qwaa047

Paudel, P., Kwon, Y. J., Kim, D. H., & Choi, K. H. (2022). Industrial Ergonomics Risk Analysis Based on 3D-Human Pose Estimation. *Electronics (Basel)*, *11*(20), 3403. doi:10.3390/electronics11203403

Paul, M., Roenspieß, A., Mentler, T., & Herczeg, M. (2014). The usability engineering repository (UsER). *Software Engineering*.

Priana, A. J., Tolle, H., Aknuranda, I., & Arisetijono, E. (2018). User Experience Design of Stroke Patient Communications Using Mobile Finger (MOFI) Communication Board With User Center Design Approach. *International Journal of Interactive Mobile Technologies*, *12*(2), 162. doi:10.3991/ijim.v12i2.7937

Sgarbossa, F., Grosse, E. H., Neumann, W. P., Battini, D., & Glock, C. H. (2020). Human factors in production and logistics systems of the future. *Annual Reviews in Control*, *49*, 295–305. doi:10.1016/j.arcontrol.2020.04.007

Chapter 4
A Collaborative Model for Green Factory Through Green Unit Processes

Amber Batwara
https://orcid.org/0000-0003-4666-426X
LNM Institute of Information Technology, India

Vikarm Sharma
LNM Institute of Information Technology, India

Mohit Makkar
LNM Institute of Information Technology, India

ABSTRACT

This chapter examines an innovative strategy for attaining environmental sustainability in manufacturing, particularly emphasizing the idea of a "green factory" and its component "green unit processes." Innovative approaches to industrial production are essential when environmental degradation and resource depletion are causing growing worry. This chapter explores a cooperative process that brings together a range of stakeholders in pursuing sustainable manufacturing practices, including manufacturers, academics, policymakers, and local communities.

1. INTRODUCTION

Green factories are crucial for the future because they uphold sustainability, environmental stewardship, and responsible resource management. They contribute to environmental protection and economic growth, improved brand recognition, and a more sustainable and resilient future for businesses and society throughout the globe. Processes for creating green units are essential to the creation of a green factory (Dong et al., 2018). They make it possible for industries to lessen their adverse effects on the environment, increase resource efficiency, adhere to regulations, boost competitiveness, and help create a more sustainable future. Adopting these procedures is not only environmentally responsible but also crucial

DOI: 10.4018/979-8-3693-2647-3.ch004

for long-term economic success in a world increasingly emphasizing sustainability(Kumar et al., 2020) (Batwara et al., 2022). The manufacturing industry may shift towards sustainability and environmental responsibility using the roadmap provided by this collaborative concept. We may start along a road that reduces ecological impact, boosts competitiveness, propels economic development, and promotes a better and more sustainable future for future generations by adopting Green Unit Processes within the framework of a Green Factory.

Sustainable development is a trendy topic worldwide in the twenty-first century. Sustainable development is a development that meets current demands without affecting generations to come the ability to satisfy their requirements." SM (Sustainable Manufacturing) can be applied to various domains, including stakeholders, technology, services, and the supply chain. In addition, there are contradictions in using the life cycle view, temporal perspective, and integrating viewpoint (Moldavska & Welo, 2017). The idea of sustainable development should be adapted to protect the environment, linking with a selection of materials, design, and production to waste management; the fundamental objective of this "green" innovation in the value chain of trade production in the industry from a strategic level(Liu & Ling, 2020). To achieve long-term sustainable development, a factory must balance environmental, economic, and social sustainability considerations. Applications of green manufacturing have a considerable favorable outcome on ecological and performance in social situations. (Sezen & Çankaya, 2013).

The green factory model aimed to identify green process parameter settings for the unit manufacturing process. Improving energy and resource efficiency is a top priority for manufacturers. Adapting some energy-efficient technologies gives wrong estimates and might affect output (Thiede et al., 2013). While considering efficiency-improving technology, the industry is concerned about certain constraints (Ghadimi et al., 2014). A green factory has two main constraints: resource consumption and work environment. Figure. 1 shows various green controls throughout the unit manufacturing process, from its initial stages to the concluding steps, essential for minimizing environmental impacts and promoting sustainability. Here are some important green measures that can be integrated at various phases of the manufacturing process: Eco-friendly Materials, Design for Sustainability, Implementing design principles that prioritize energy efficiency, reduced waste and recyclability, and Life Cycle assessment. By incorporating these green controls at various phases of the unit manufacturing process, businesses can reduce their environmental impact, save costs, enhance their reputation, and contribute to a more sustainable future. Some green processes used in conventional machining for better machinability and sustainability include cryogenic cooling, dry cutting, MQL, using green and solid lubricants, treating, coating, and texturing tools (Gupta, 2020).

Globalization of manufacturing, sustainable supply chains, and digitizing payment systems are all current trends. The need for novel optimization techniques is at an all-time high due to rising competition among diverse organizations. For long-term stability, both manufacturing processes and businesses must be continuously improved. Numerous supply chain bottlenecks have been resolved due to IT integration (Yousefnezhad et al., 2020)(Batwara et al., 2023). The fourth industrial revolution is also influencing drone applications in the manufacturing industry. Applications that enable manufacturers to "see" (visual inspection, monitoring) and "sense" (heat inspection, hazard detection, inventory management) data in their plants are emerging and cost-effective. (Maghazei & Netland, 2020). Inventory management, item intralogistics, and inspection and surveillance are warehouses' three most potential indoor drone use cases (Wawrla et al., 2019). Smart, sustainable systems are becoming more innovative, adaptive, and collaborative due to the introduction of technologies like IoT, virtualization, and control outsourcing. However, there are now significant security issues. Manufacturing cybersecurity had substantial gaps before introducing modern production systems powered by evolving technological equipment (Ervural & Ervural, 2018).

Figure 1. Green factory constraints

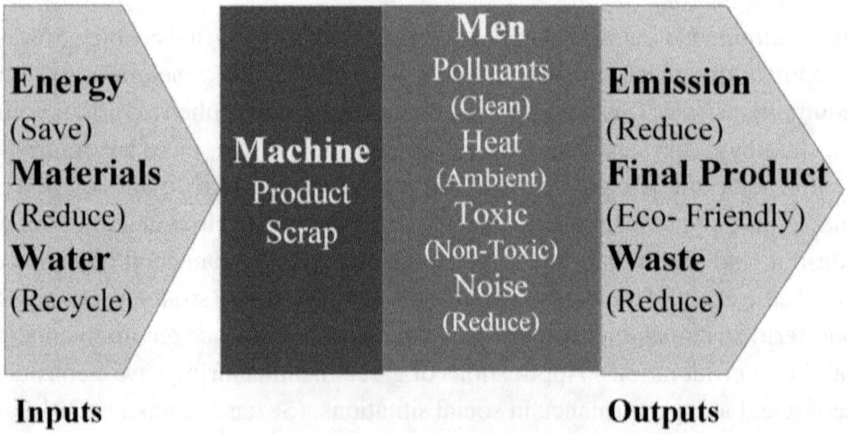

This chapter explores a cooperative process that brings together a range of stakeholders in pursuing sustainable manufacturing practices, including manufacturers, academics, policymakers, and local communities. We look at the guiding principles of Green Unit Processes and how to incorporate them into a comprehensive Green Factory architecture. We demonstrate the revolutionary potential of this collaborative concept through actual case studies and practical examples. A manual for utilizing vegetable oil and the Minimum Quantity Lubrication (MQL) approach to convert a unit production measure to be more environmentally friendly must be created as part of this endeavor. A case study for a circumstance focus comprises minimizing waste streams produced by cutting fluids and adverse effects on the operator and the environment. The impact of drilling process parameters on surface roughness responses was examined using an "analysis of variance" (ANOVA), and Monte Carlo simulation was employed for the probabilistic uncertainty analysis. Case studies show that sunflower oil did not perform as well while drilling E350 HT Steel because of the different lengths of the carbon chains. This demonstrated that speed and cutting medium have the greatest influence on surface roughness. Three cutting methods have produced model equations. However, when error analysis is done, they have a solid association with forecasting the same components. A FICEP DB 363 CNC drilling device from KEC in Jaipur was used for all experiments. The experiment used the Minimum Quantity Lubrication (MQL) approach in a dry and vegetable oil-cutting fluid (canola and sunflower).

This chapter further emphasizes how vital open innovation and information sharing are to building a solid ecosystem for green factories. We emphasize Life Cycle Analysis, Cutting Fluids, Waste Stream MQL, Waste Streams in Machining, and Global Networks in spreading best practices, encouraging innovation, and tackling common concerns.

2. LITERATURE REVIEW

Green manufacturing development depends on regular research and development (Garetti & Taisch, 2012). The European Commission's IMS2020: Supporting Global Research for IMS2020 Vision initiative highlighted the significant evidence on research difficulties envisaged for sustainable development manufacturing in a roadmap for future (2020) manufacturing research. The role of government (Mathiyazhagan et al., 2019) and stakeholder expectations (Silva et al., 2019) in removing the vast majority of issues have been emphasized mainly by most researchers.

A holistic view of the entire supply chain, including manufacturing systems, processes, and various product life cycles, is required to achieve overall sustainability(Batwara et al., 2022). It necessitates improved product performance models, predictive process models, and individual manufacturing optimization. A green factory must integrate the different steps of the 6R approach of the product's whole life cycle across the entire supply chain(Jayal et al., 2010). According to (Ahmad et al., 2018), two areas of sustainability were 12classed as partial sustainable product design (P-SPD) tools, while those that covered three aspects were classed as sustainable product design (SPD) tools. It will help lessen their doubt and increase their trust in using the tools for green factory development. CSM (competitive, sustainable manufacturing) is the primary facilitator of SD since it generates money, supports jobs (directly and indirectly), and oversees people and physical resources, from materials to energy. (Jovane et al., 2008)

Unit manufacturing is an individual device or machine tool that performs a unit process like drilling, milling, turning, etc.(Duflou et al., 2012). Improvements considerably aid green factories in the unit production process's green index. (Singh et al., 2016a). Cutting Force, Cutting Time, Torque, and process efficiency dominate energy consumption at the most basic level in industrial operations. (Borgia et al., 2014) The study focused on a module manufacturing process to measure and characterize the first parts of a comprehensive model required to represent a green factory. In our case study, sizeable green production in drilling unit processes is needed. Table 1 shows a different green unit manufacturing process application to improve green factories.

Table 1. Application of unit manufacturing process in green factory

Unit Manufacturing Process	Sustainability Performance Indicator	Source
Milling Process	Reduce energy consumption	(Borgia et al., 2014)
Grinding Process	Noise intensity, Aerosol concentration, Minimum Quantity Lubrication	(Singh et al., 2015)
Drilling Process	Noise intensity, Aerosol concentration, Minimum Quantity Lubrication	(Singh et al., 2016b)
Gear Machining	Minimum quantity lubrication, environmentally friendly machining	(Gupta et al., 2016)
Gear Hobbing	Minimal quantity lubrication	(Zhang & Wei, n.d.) (Matsuoka et al., 2013)
Abrasive Processes	energy-efficiency	(Aurich et al., 2013)
Gear Milling	Near-dry machining Minimal quantity lubrication	(Fratila, 2009)(Fratila & Radu, 2010)
Metal Cutting	Minimal quantity lubrication	(Taylor et al., 2007)

Solid lubricant-based machining has received a lot of interest recently due to its improved machinability and sustainability. These solid lubricants have outstanding lubricity and are biodegradable, sustainable, and recyclable. A unique setup or a high-pressure MQL(minimum quantity lubrication) system is used to secure their supply. MQL is a technology that uses a compressed air jet to spray tiny oil droplets. The lubricant is spread right into the cutting area as a substitute for the massive amounts of typical flood coolant. Because the oil droplets are transported instantly into the cutting region by the air jet, efficient lubrication is ensured (Burton et al., 2014) (Obikawa et al., 2006). As a result, vegetable oil reduces MQL cutting temperatures by around 5%–12% compared to dry machining at average cutting temperatures. A minimum amount of lubrication is employed in various manufacturing processes, including drilling, milling, and turning. The efficiency of MQL in grinding processes was investigated by (Rabiei et al., 2015). (Heisel & Schaal, 2009) examined how MQL in up-, down-, and face-milling affected burr development. Similar milling operations were carried out to demonstrate technical advancements and the use of MQL at the Ford Motor Company (Furness et al., 2006). The major conclusions reveal that introducing MQL resulted in a 15% operational cost decrease over a ten-year flood cooling comparison for each unit. MQL have various application in drilling(Singh et al., 2016b) (Singh et al., 2015) and turning operation(Mishra et al., 2020) as well. Improvement of turning process performance by efficient hybrid nanofluid and MQL application(Junankar et al., 2020).

According to (Kunle & Corresponding, 2013), cutting force was assessed using various vegetable cutting fluids like groundnut oil, coconut oil, palm kernel oil, and shea butter oil during the turning operation. Although the effects of cutting fluids made by vegetables were shown to be material-dependent, groundnut oil outperformed the other three vegetable-based cutting fluids tested. In another study, coconut oil topped the other two cutting fluids (soluble oil and straight cutting oil) to reduce the cutting force and temperature. MQL fluid application method (for mineral and canola oil) is compared with other methods(Singh et al., 2016b) (Singh et al., 2015). MQL can effectively lubricate the cutting process with minimal oil, enabling higher cutting speeds and longer tool life without needing to condition or dispose of cooling lubricants, resulting in increased productivity and environmental friendliness(Gupta et al., 2016). (Tai et al., 2014) says cooling and chip-evacuation ability have challenges during MQL machining.

3. METHODOLOGY

Various methodology is suggested below to reduce waste in adapting the green unit machining process.

3.1 Waste Streams in Machining

The wastage produced by machining is a significant environmental concern for society. The waste streams created and their transportation varies depending on the process and even within the process. In addition, each sort of waste has a particular environmental impact, including solid, liquid, gaseous, and thermal waste.

3.2 Life Cycle Analysis of Manufacturing Waste

Material, energy, cutting fluid, and tooling are examples of waste from manufacturing in the life cycle; the mass balance of the material entering the machining operation must account for the materials lost in an LCA (Life Cycle Analysis). Due to the depletion of material and energy consumed during extraction and processing, material waste has significant environmental repercussions during manufacturing. CO2 emissions occur during the processing procedure, which should be acknowledged. In addition, manufacturing operations necessitate energy, and the ecological consequences of toxic and hazardous gases must be studied. It should be emphasized that a manufacturing activity cannot avoid producing waste material throughout the machining process. However, recycling a portion of the material, waste cutting fluid, and worn-out equipment will lessen the waste stream's environmental impact. The shape and size of the chips created during the metal-removal process are influenced by the physical qualities of the work material and the machining conditions. Therefore, recycling large quantities of chips rather than tiny amounts is more cost-effective. Contamination of the recycling stream due to different materials is another limitation.

The sustainable life-cycle is achieved by planning each step precisely, and product development is a critical component in controlling environmental impacts and determining process efficiency(Vila et al., 2015). (Gbededo et al., 2018) addressed various methods to sustainable manufacturing, the trend toward a holistic LCSA, and the significance of a comprehensive analysis of the three sustainability criteria.

3.3 Cutting Fluid Heat Transfer

The heat transfer between the fluid and the workpiece is a significant energy consideration. The amount of heat transfer, or heat transfer rate, is a clear indicator of the cutting fluid's performance. The cutting fluid composition and the fluid application strategy affect cutting fluid heat transfer in machining operations. The heat transfer between the liquid and the workpiece is assumed to be primarily due to convection.

3.4 Cutting Fluids Waste Stream.

The adverse effects on the environment, health, and safety outweigh the benefits of employing cutting fluids. Manufacturers provide a safe and healthful working environment by considering worker safety, lighting, and noise, for example, hypertension(Chang et al., 2012) and noise-induced cardiovascular consequences on employees (Teodorico et al., 2014). The waste streams generated by cutting fluids impact both the environment and the operator. Dermal and eye irritation are caused by the fluid's fumes, odor, and smoke. Some waste streams are also carcinogenic and poisonous.

Cutting fluids produces mist, which is one of the waste streams. The heat generated during the machining process causes cutting fluids to evaporate. After that, the vapors condense as mist droplets. The cutting fluid's non-aqueous components, such as biocides, become a fine aerosol (Atmadi et al., 2001). Atomization techniques can also produce cutting fluid mists. When a cutting fluid stream comes into contact with a stationary surface, it may splash and generate a mist) (Taylor et al., n.d.) . The buoyancy, aerodynamic drag, and gravity forces affect the drops created by vaporization, condensation, or atomization. If the mist is not collected, it remains in the air and eventually settles on a vast work surface. (Djebara et al., 2013). According to "Occupational Safety and Health Administration requirements (OSHA)," most companies use managing systems to ensure that their personnel are exposed to as little fluid mist as possible.

3.5 Minimum Quantity Lubrication

A crucial technology in the context of environmentally friendly companies and sustainable production is minimum quantity lubrication (MQL). Green factories seek to minimize their adverse environmental effects while preserving their effectiveness and production. For several reasons, MQL is crucial in attaining these objectives. In order to solve the difficulties of environmental intrusiveness and occupational danger connected with airborne cutting fluid particles, the idea of MQL was first put out ten years ago. By lowering lubricant expenses, reducing fluid minimization has a positive economic impact. Time spent cleaning tools, machines, and workpieces is decreased. The MQL method involves misting or atomizing a tiny amount of lubricant in an air flow aimed at the cutting zone, generally at a flow rate of 50 to 500 ml/h(Gupta et al., 2016). An external delivery system of one or more nozzles sprays the lubricant. Compared to the quantity typically utilized under flood-cooling conditions, the amount of coolant used in MQL is less than 3–4 orders of magnitude (Boubekri et al., 2010).

MQL delivery methods may be divided into external spray and internal mixing. The coolant tank, reservoir, and tubes with one or more nozzle-equipped nozzles make up the exterior spray system. The system features separate adjustable air and coolant flow for balancing the coolant supply, and it may be built close to or on the machine. It is suitable for practically all machining processes, affordable, and portable. The internal mixing or two-channel systems represent the second arrangement. In a two-channel system, oil and air are often brought to an external mixing unit next to the tool holder, where the mist is produced using two parallel tubes routed through the spindle. This method necessitates the use of a unique spindle. These systems may produce mist with bigger droplet sizes than external mixing devices since they have less dispersion and dropouts. Additionally, they change tools between cuts and dispense oil more quickly when cutting. Critical components are housed within the spindle, making maintenance of the systems more challenging (Boubekri et al., 2010).

Despite the emissions caused by the usage of MQL, this lubricating method has no pollution effects, even though MQL is an environmentally friendly procedure. By incorporating MQL (Fratila, 2009) and modeling of stationary thermal state (Fratila & Radu, 2010) into the gear wheel milling process, it can be concluded that it is more significant and cost-saving. MQL also uses hole drilling to provide tool life comparable to gun drills, allowing for better penetration rates (Tai et al., 2014). When utilizing various cutting tools, hobbing with dry cutting in flank wear, crater wear, and completed surface roughness. (Zhang & Wei, n.d.)(Matsuoka et al., 2013)

MQL can effectively lubricate the cutting process with minimal oil, enabling higher cutting speeds and longer tool life without needing to condition or dispose of cooling lubricants, resulting in increased productivity and environmental friendliness (Gupta et al., 2016).

4. MODEL

The green factory concept seeks to meet the increasing need for industrial processes to be more sustainable. While significant progress has been achieved in energy conservation, workplace enhancement, and product ecological design, it is accepted that the present status of individual green processes is inadequate to assure long-term sustainable growth. The model acknowledges the urgency of environmental degradation and the necessity for high-performance buildings to maintain long-term ecological sustainability. Foreign academics have undertaken a related study on the integrated implementation of lean-green manufacturing; for example, (Zhu et al., 2022) developed a collaborative model for the performance of a Lean-Green Manufacturing System. The green manufacturing concept is founded on the creation of system models. Systems models are high-level frameworks that aid in understanding numerous criteria, sub-criteria, and linkages in the context of green manufacturing. These models give a formal means to analyze a manufacturing system's current green status, which is critical for identifying improvement areas. A green transformation strategy is included in the green manufacturing model. This plan details the ideas and activities required to convert a manufacturing plant into a more sustainable and environmentally friendly business. It acts as a road plan for meeting environmental objectives while preserving or boosting production. The model includes a variety of control measures and tools to aid in the transition. These are used to track and evaluate the advancement of green efforts inside the production system. Control measures help in measuring environmental performance, while tools aid in implementing adjustments and improvements. The system model architecture for creating and managing green unit manufacturing systems is shown in Figure 2. This architecture is a graphic depiction of the structure and components of three modules. 6R principles emphasise the necessity of reducing, reusing, and recycling, as well as resource recovery, reconsidering our consumption patterns, and avoiding unsustainable goods and practises. Individuals and organisations may contribute to a more sustainable and ecologically responsible future by adopting these concepts into their everyday lives and business operations.

Energy-saving procedures: The architecture's initial module is devoted to energy-saving procedures. This module will most likely concentrate on technology and practices that minimize energy usage in the industrial plant. This might include lighting upgrades, equipment efficiency, and renewable energy sources.

Product Ecology: The second module focuses on product ecology, which entails developing goods and processes that reduce resource use and waste creation. This might include efforts for sustainable material procurement, recycling, and waste reduction.

Work Environment: The third module is on the workplace. It emphasizes the need for a healthy and safe working environment for workers. This includes appropriate ventilation, ergonomic design, and safety standards to help reduce workplace accidents and health concerns.

This green manufacturing model aims to combine and optimize three major aspects: energy efficiency, environmental responsibility, and a safe and healthy work environment. By doing so, the manufacturing system will not only be able to satisfy its present production demands. Still, it will also be able to contribute to a more sustainable and ecologically responsible future. The model directs the development of procedures and practices that adhere to green manufacturing principles, eventually boosting eco-efficient systems and limiting the negative implications of environmental deterioration.

Figure 2. Model for green factory through unit manufacturing process

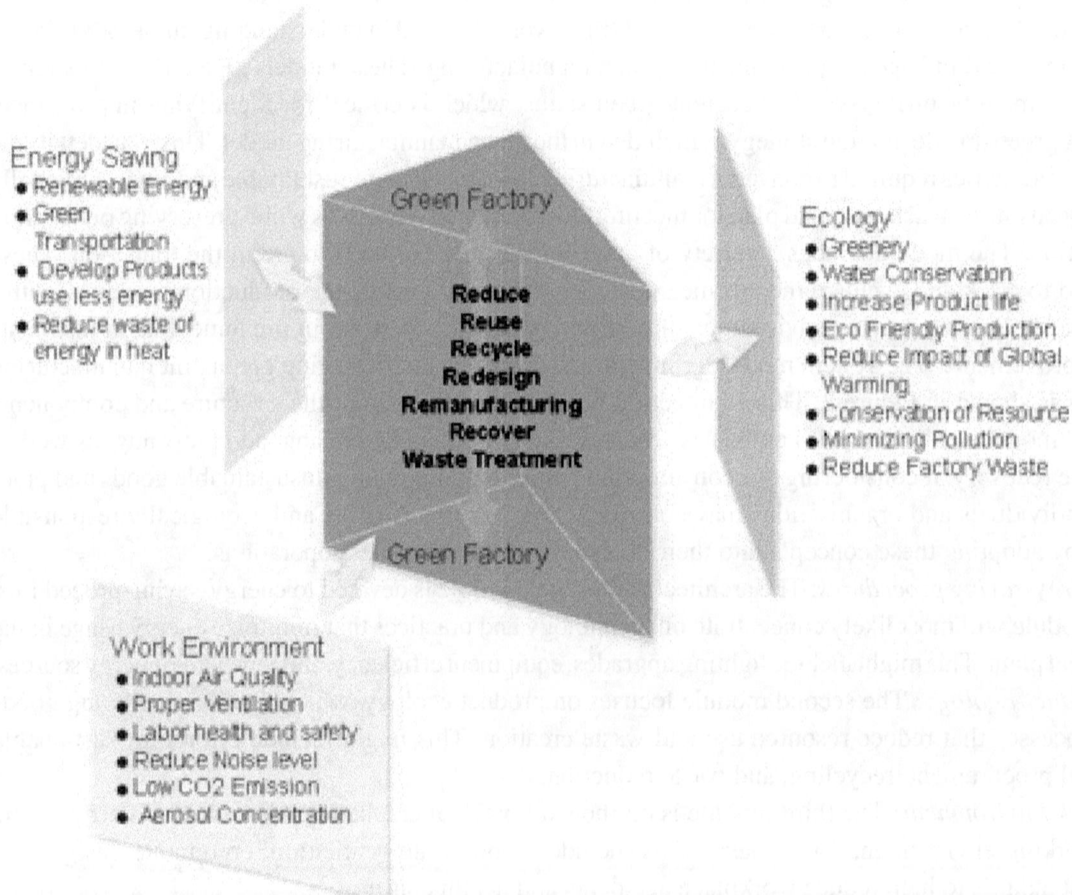

5. CASE STUDY

Cutting fluid supply and cleaning consume a significant amount of energy in production. It has been estimated that cutting fluids accounts for up to 32% of a manufacturing plant's overall energy consumption in some cases. So nowadays, researchers have targeted environmentally friendly cutting fluids, such as canola and sunflower vegetable oil, for a healthy working environment.

This case study focuses on optimizing the drilling process for E350 HT Steel using a sustainable approach. The process parameters for drilling were experimentally investigated, and the Plackett-Burman Design was employed to create 12 runs with three factors and one replicate each. The experiments were conducted on a FICEP DB 363 CNC drilling machine, and two cutting fluids, namely canola and sunflower oil, were utilized under the Minimum Quantity Lubrication (MQL) technique. The main objective of this study is to optimize the drilling process for E350 HT Steel in terms of greenness by reducing energy consumption and waste generation while maintaining or improving machining performance. This research contributes valuable insights into eco-friendly manufacturing practices, offering potential solutions for sustainable drilling processes in the metalworking industry.

5.1 Objective of Case Study

The objectives of the study include:

- To compare the effect of process parameters on surface roughness while drilling on a CNC machine utilizing the MQL technique under various cutting circumstances, such as canola and sunflower vegetable oils, to the dry state.
- The DOE model (Plackett-Burman) is designed to identify the best value for various parameters that determine the response of specific experiments.
- Using multiple regression modeling, create the regression model equations.
- Monte Carlo simulation and sensitivity analysis are used to predict and analyze results.

5.2 Methodology

In the present study, drilling is designed as a "unit manufacturing process," data on the characteristics above of greenness was collected using this unit process. The design of the experimental approach used and the process parameters for drilling E350 HT Steel test pieces are experimentally investigated. Plackett- Burman Design creates 12 runs for three factors and one replicate. All investigations used a FICEP DB 363 CNC drilling machine from KEC in Jaipur.

Drilling Machine: FICEP DB 363 CNC drilling machine from KEC in Jaipur.

Cutting Fluids: Canola oil and sunflower oil.

Lubrication Technique: Minimum Quantity Lubrication (MQL), MQL flow rate (ml/hr): 20

Factors: Spindle Speed: Two levels (Low and High) (rpm-217, 310).

Feed Rate: Two levels (Low and High) (mm/min-50, 100)

Hole diameter (mm) (18.5, 26.5).

Cutting depth (mm): 16

Cutting Fluid Type: Two levels (Canola oil and Sunflower oil).

Coolant flow rate (liter/minute):4.5

Density of Workpiece (gm/mm3): 0.0078

The experiment was conducted in a dry and vegetable oil cutting fluid (canola and sunflower), using the Minimum Quantity Lubrication (MQL) technique. The data will be analyzed to pinpoint the key determinants of the drilling process's greenness features. This study will assist in identifying the best cutting speed, feed rate, and cutting fluid type to reduce waste production and energy consumption while preserving or enhancing machining performance.

Figure 3. FICEP DB – 363 CNC machine

Figure 4. HT 200 x 200 x 16 angle workpiece

The MITUTOYO 178 portable surface roughness tester, available at KEC in Jaipur, was used to measure the surface roughness in all 36 cases. Even though surface roughness is good in all circumstances due to CNC machine standard accuracy, Different cooling mediums, such as dry, (MQL)c, and (MQL) v ('Canola' and sunflower vegetable oil), cause various variances. Therefore, this instrument has a high accuracy level and an accuracy error equal to 3. Table 2 shows the Surface Roughness Measurements for all experimental runs under three conditions.

Table 2. Surface roughness for all experiments

	Process Parameter			Surface Roughness		
No. of Runs	Spindle Speed	Feed Rate	Hole dia.	Dry	(MQL)s	(MQL)c
1	310	50	26.5	1.57	0.85	0.82
2	310	100	26.5	1.11	0.82	0.83
3	217	50	26.5	1.75	0.95	0.89
4	217	100	26.5	1.68	0.92	0.84
5	217	100	18.5	1.55	0.98	0.90
6	217	50	18.5	1.77	0.95	0.91
7	217	100	26.5	1.52	0.98	0.61
8	310	50	18.5	1.07	0.75	0.74
9	310	50	26.5	1.15	0.87	0.88
10	310	100	18.5	1.05	0.86	0.79
11	310	100	18.5	1.05	0.86	0.79
12	217	50	18.5	1.36	0.98	0.83

Figure 5. Time series graph for surface roughness

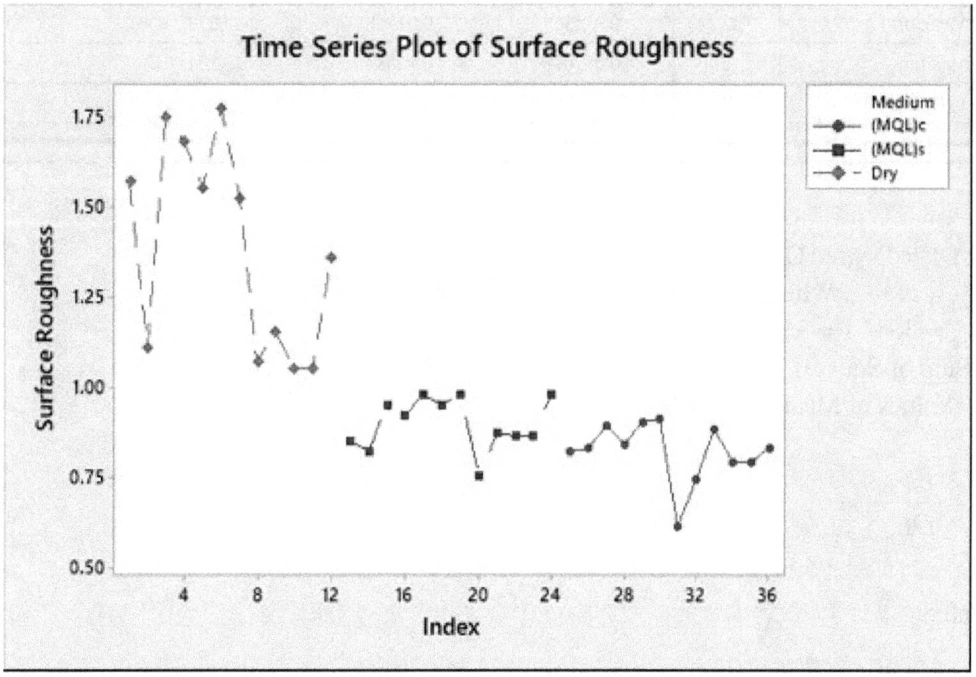

Figure 5 shows a graph based on time series on various groups. Time series analysis aims to detect patterns in data and utilize them to make predictions for every unique combination of cutting medium (Dry, $(MQL)_C$, and $(MQV)_S$, Minitab generates a graph. These data graph patterns show that Canola vegetable oil has a superior surface to other mediums.

5.4 ANOVA Analysis for Surface Roughness

An ANOVA analysis can determine the significance of input parameters on response. Table 3 shows the related ANOVA multiple regressions for Surface Roughness.

Table 3. Analysis of variance for surface roughness

Source	DF	Adj SS	Adj MS	F-Value	P-Value
Model	14	3.06249	0.2187	19.17	0.000
Linear	15	2.67170	0.5343	46.84	0.000
Spindle speed (1)	1	0.37700	0.3770	33.04	0.000
Feed rate (2)	1	0.01150	0.01150	1.01	0.327
Hole dia. (3)	1	0.02033	0.02033	1.78	0.196
Medium (4)	2	2.26287	1.1314	99.17	0.000
2-Way Interaction	9	0.41226	0.04581	4.02	0.004
Spindle speed*Feed rate	1	0.00073	0.00073	0.06	0.802
Spindle speed*Hole dia.	1	0.01590	0.01590	1.39	0.251
Spindle speed*Medium	2	0.28247	0.14123	12.38	0.000
Feed rate*Hole dia.	1	0.03511	0.03511	3.08	0.094
Feed rate*Medium	2	0.02536	0.01268	1.11	0.348
Hole dia.*Medium	2	0.05269	0.02634	2.31	0.124
Error	21	0.23958	0.01141		
Total	35	3.30207			

Here, DF = Degree Of Freedom

$DF_{Total} = N - 1$, Where N = Total no. of Runs = 36

$DF_{Total} = 36 - 1 = 35$

SS= Sum of Squares

MS = Values of Mean of Square.

$$MS_{value} = \frac{SS_{Factor}}{DF_{Factor}}$$

F - Value

$$F_{value} = \frac{MS_{Factor}}{MS_{Error}}$$

The P-value is used to reject the null hypothesis in a hypothesis test. The available P-value range is 0 to 1. This study's 95% CI (Confidence interval) is compared as an alpha value, with 0.05 being the value for alpha. The factor is significant if the p-value is less than 0.05

ANOVA analysis reveals that the medium components' spindle speed has a low p-value (0.000) and an acceptable p-value. As a result, speed and cutting medium have the most significant impact on surface roughness. Three cutting mediums have model equations created; however, they show a good relationship with predicting the same components when error analysis is performed. Minitab software calculates variance analysis for a 95 percent confidence interval (CI) for controller design. Table 4 shows the Surface roughness model equations. The squared multiple correlation coefficient is defined as $SS_R/SS_T = R^2$. This R2 value represents the proportion of variation in the response variable. The square root of R^2 is called the multiple correlation coefficient, the correlation between the observations. $R^2 = SS_R/ SS_T = 3.06249/ 3.30207= 0.92744$, suggesting that the squared multiple correlation explains 92.74 percent of the variability. The model equation for all three conditions is represented in Table 4.

Table 4. Regression equation for surface roughness

Medium	Regression Equation
(MQL)c	Surface Roughness = 1.265 - 0.00348 Spindle speed + 0.00563 Feed rate- 0.0082 Hole dia.+ 0.000004 Spindle speed*Feed rate+ 0.000120 Spindle speed*Hole dia - 0.000331 Feed rate*Hole dia.
(MQL)s	Surface Roughness = 1.494 - 0.00459 Spindle speed + 0.00690 Feed rate -0.0061 Hole dia. + 0.000004 Spindle speed*Feed rate+ 0.000120 Spindle speed*Hole dia - 0.000331 Feed rate*Hole dia.
Dry	2.634 - 0.00796 Spindle speed + 0.00430 Feed rate + 0.0130 Hole dia + 0.000004 Spindle speed*Feed rate + 0.000120 Spindle speed*Hole dia - 0.000331 Feed rate*Hole dia.

The regression models' relevance should be checked to ensure they have extracted all relevant data from experimental situations. The distribution of residues should be expected if the regression equations' results are appropriate. Figure 6 illustrates the normal probability of surface roughness. A linear red line with small residual values represents all experimental data points. The discrepancy between the observed and corresponding corrected values is known as residuals. The residual value in regression and ANOVA is helpful because it reveals how well a model accommodates variation in observed data. It provides strong proof for the accuracy of future applications(Batwara & Verma, 2016).

Figure 6. Normal probability for surface roughness

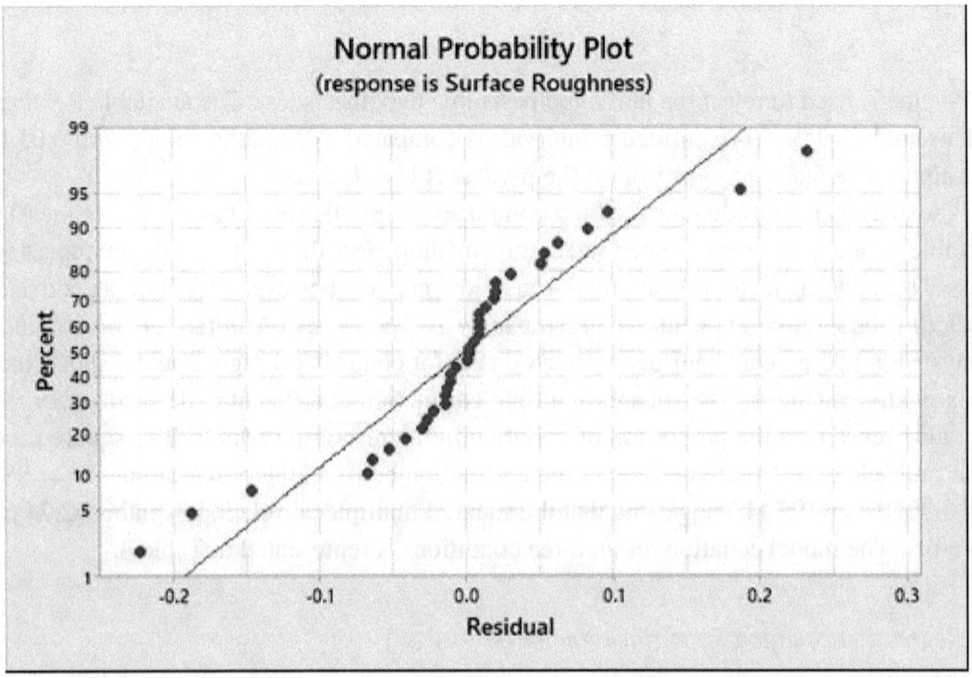

5.5 Monte Carlo Simulation

Physicists S. Ulam, E. Fermi, J. von Neumann, and N. Metropolis invented the Monte Carlo (MC technique) in the 1940s under "statistical sampling." This method has been used in practically every field of study since the pioneering research in the 1940s and 1950s. (Yang, X. S., 2010). It's a versatile simulation tool that can handle many realistic scenarios. (Marseguerra & Zio, 2000). (Fatih & Öztürk, 2019) (Öztürk & Fatih, 2019) identifying surface roughness uncertainty that deterministic methods could not capture.

Monte Carlo simulation techniques exploit stochastic uncertainty in predictions that deterministic approaches could not capture. The generated model equation has been made more realistic using Monte Carlo uncertainty analysis, allowing it to estimate surface roughness more precisely and boost the process's sustainability. This simulation applies to all three model equations which ANOVA generates. Simulation done by Minitab Workspace, total 50,000 runs considered. As per the suggestion operator of KEC, Jaipur select upper and lower specification limits roughness is 1.2 and 0 .75. Parameter setting for model assumptions spindle speed (263.5, 46.54), Feed rate (75, 25.2), and hole diameter (25.4, 4).

Figure 7. Monte Carlo simulation results

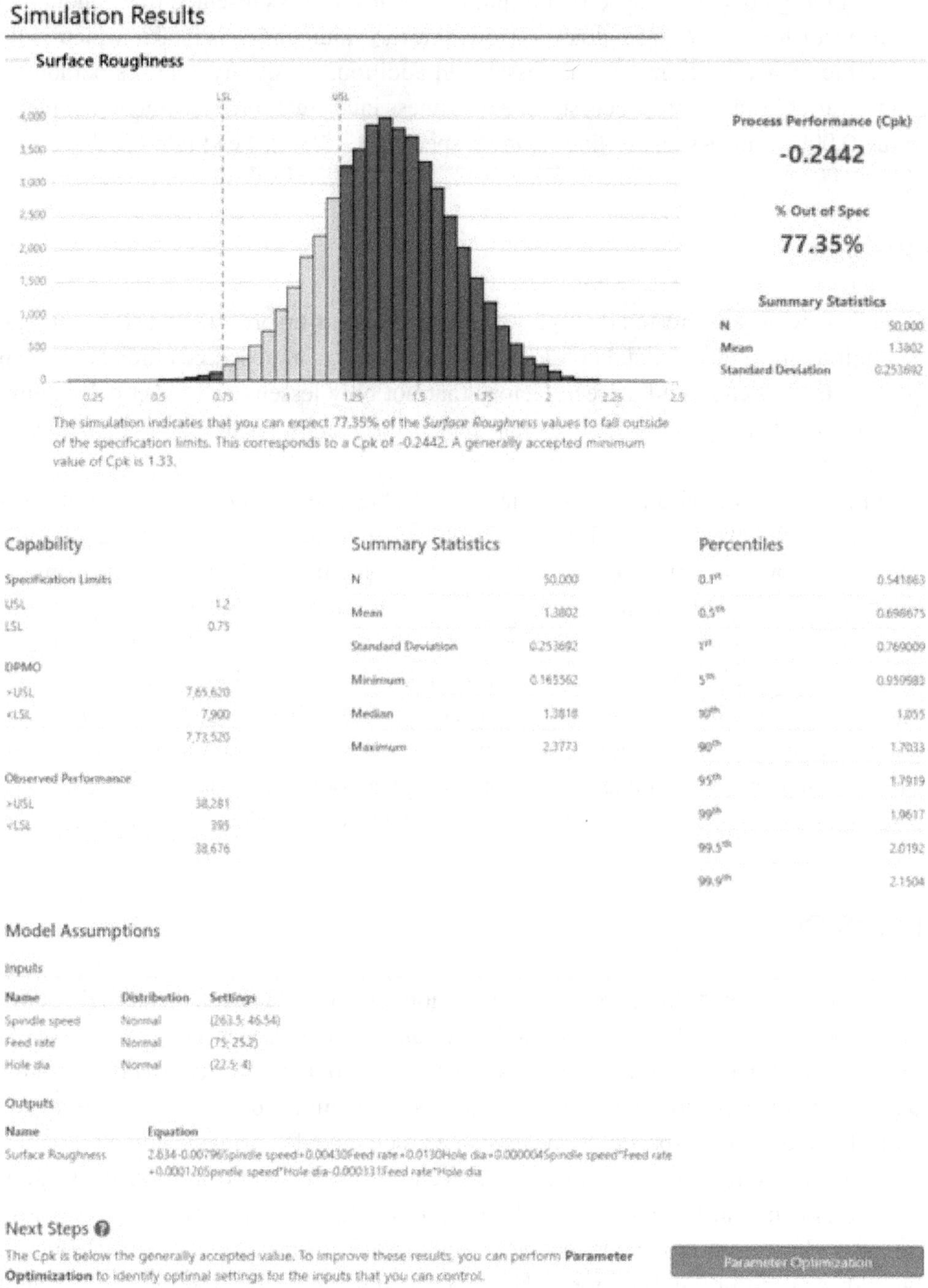

For the dry condition Figure. (a), the simulation results indicate that 77.35% of the surface roughness value falls outside the specific limits, and the value of C_{Pk} is -0.2442. Generally, the minimum value of C_{Pk} accepted is 1.33. The C_{Pk} below the accepted value can then perform parameter optimization to identify optimal input settings that we can control.

Simulation results for sunflower and canola oil are shown in Figures (b) and (c), with just 4.56% and 2.04% of cases falling outside the specified limitations. Thus, it is represented that canola oil achieves a better surface finish with 97.96 accuracies. However, the value of C_{Pk} is 0.532, which is lower than the allowed value; hence performing is necessary. In addition, sensitivity analysis demonstrates how changing input variable variation affects surface roughness interpretation. New input parameter settings to achieve the 0.00% Out-of-specific limit spindle speed (217, 23.2), Feed rate (50.3, 12.6), and hole diameter (25.4, 4).

5.6 Discussion

- A green factory may be created through the unit manufacturing process by using sustainable practices, minimizing environmental consequences, and improving resource efficiency. Adopting this suggested strategy can build a green factory that not only lessens its impact on the environment but also gains advantages like cost savings, enhanced brand recognition, and a competitive edge in the market.
- Minimum Quantity Lubrication is essential in green factories because it aligns with sustainability principles, energy efficiency, and environmental responsibility. It helps reduce waste, improve worker safety, lower operating costs, and promote a healthier work environment while contributing to the overall goal of minimizing the environmental impact of manufacturing processes.
- As a consequence of the case study, speed, and cutting medium has the most significant influence on surface roughness. Three cutting mediums have generated model equations, yet they are strongly associated with forecasting the same components when conducting error analysis.
- Vegetable oil has shown superior performance as a sustainable substitute for mineral oil, with no negative consequences on human health or ecological systems. (Wickramasinghe et al., 2020). According to case study results, Canola vegetable oil has a superior surface to other mediums.

6. CONCLUSION

This case study looks at the drilling process optimization for E350 HT Steel, emphasizing environmentally friendly production. The Plackett-Burman Design and MQL approach and vegetable oils as cutting fluids are used to minimize the drilling process's negative environmental effects while guaranteeing that performance goals are satisfied. The study's findings and recommendations may be utilized to direct future sustainable machining procedures and advance green manufacturing techniques.

The case studies of sunflower and canola oil-based cutting fluids show canola oil gives a good surface finish—compression of sunflower oil in a drilling operation. Dry cutting conditions were also used in the experiments, which resulted in rapid tool wear and fracture. Because of the various lengths of carbon chains, canola-based cutting fluids performed better than sunflower-based cutting fluids. Canola oil has three additional carbons in its formulas and a longer carbon chain that excels at high cutting temperatures, enhancing surface protection.

Furthermore, the high viscosity of canola oil tended to resist flow. This high viscosity lubricates the tool-chip interface more effectively, minimizing friction between the tool and the workpiece and swiftly eliminating heat generated at the contact. Surface roughness ratings in vegetable-based cutting fluids with a high percentage of extreme pressure additives were higher. According to the findings,

8% of revolutionary pressure additives, such as canola oil cutting fluid, performed better than the rest. Vegetable-based cutting fluids have been proposed to replace mineral and semi-synthetic cutting fluids in drilling operations. Cutting forces were also reduced when MQL was replaced with vegetable oil, and the fatty acid content of vegetable-based cutting fluids resulted in longer tool life.

Regressions using multiple variables apply to surface roughness, showing Spindle speed and cutting medium are the most significant factors, and model equations are generated for three cutting mediums. Even though, when performing error analysis on model equations, these equations show an excellent relation with predicting the same factors. It implies that a greater focus on numerical modeling and experimental design is required for future reference. The Monte Carlo approach revealed that future tests should be designed to reduce uncertainty. This technique predicts the surface roughness measurement uncertainty of the drilling operation under different cutting mediums, which is quite beneficial in a new precision process assigning high accuracy.

Other Green Parameters can consider a future case study representing a green factory model through unit manufacturing; Vibrations generated during machining might cause product deformation. So, in a prospective study, vibrations are considered for production quality.

REFERENCES

Ahmad, S., Yew, K., Lang, M., & Peng, W. (2018). Resources, Conservation & Recycling Sustainable product design and development : A review of tools, applications and research prospects. *Resources, Conservation and Recycling*, *132*(January), 49–61. doi:10.1016/j.resconrec.2018.01.020

Atmadi, A., Stephenson, D. A., & Liang, S. Y. (2001). *Cutting Fluid Aerosol from Splash in Turning: Analysis for Environmentally Conscious Machining*. Academic Press.

Aurich, J. C., Linke, B., Hauschild, M., Carrella, M., & Kirsch, B. (2013). CIRP Annals - Manufacturing Technology Sustainability of abrasive processes. *CIRP Annals - Manufacturing Technology, 62*(2), 653–672. doi:10.1016/j.cirp.2013.05.010

Batwara, A., Sharma, V., Makkar, M., & Giallanza, A. (2022). An Empirical Investigation of Green Product Design and Development Strategies for Eco Industries Using Kano Model and Fuzzy AHP. *Sustainability (Basel)*, *14*(14), 8735. Advance online publication. doi:10.3390u14148735

Batwara, A., Sharma, V., Makkar, M., & Giallanza, A. (2023). Towards smart sustainable development through value stream mapping – a systematic literature review. *Heliyon*, *9*(5), e15852. doi:10.1016/j.heliyon.2023.e15852 PMID:37215771

Batwara, A., & Verma, P. (2016). *Influence of process parameters on surface roughness and material removal rate during turning in cnc lathe – an artificial neural network and surface*. Academic Press.

Borgia, S., Pellegrinelli, S., Bianchi, G., & Leonesio, M. (2014). A reduced model for energy consumption analysis in milling. *Procedia CIRP*, *17*, 529–534. doi:10.1016/j.procir.2014.01.105

Boubekri, N., Shaikh, V., & Foster, P. R. (2010). A technology enabler for green machining: Minimum quantity lubrication (MQL). *Journal of Manufacturing Technology Management*, *21*(5), 556–566. doi:10.1108/17410381011046968

Burton, G., Goo, C., Zhang, Y., & Jun, M. B. G. (2014). Use of vegetable oil in water emulsion achieved through ultrasonic atomization as cutting fluids in micro-milling. *Journal of Manufacturing Processes, 16*(3), 405–413. Advance online publication. doi:10.1016/j.jmapro.2014.04.005

Chang, T., Liu, C., Young, L., Wang, V., Jian, S., & Bao, B. (2012). Science of the Total Environment. *The Science of the Total Environment, 416*, 89–96. doi:10.1016/j.scitotenv.2011.11.071 PMID:22221876

Djebara, A., Songmene, V., & Bahloul, A. (2013). *Effects of machining conditions on specific surface of PM 2 . 5 emitted during metal cutting*. Academic Press.

Dong, F., Hua, Y., & Yu, B. (2018). Peak carbon emissions in China: Status, key factors and countermeasures-A literature review. *Sustainability (Basel), 10*(8), 2895. Advance online publication. doi:10.3390u10082895

Duflou, J. R., Sutherland, J. W., Dornfeld, D., Herrmann, C., Jeswiet, J., Kara, S., Hauschild, M., & Kellens, K. (2012). CIRP Annals - Manufacturing Technology Towards energy and resource efficient manufacturing : A processes and systems approach. *CIRP Annals - Manufacturing Technology, 61*(2), 587–609. doi:10.1016/j.cirp.2012.05.002

Ervural, B. C., & Ervural, B. (2018). *Overview of Cyber Security in the Industry 4.0 Era*. doi:10.1007/978-3-319-57870-5_16

Fatih, M., & Öztürk, S. (2019). Experimental study of newly structural design grinding wheel considering response surface optimization and Monte Carlo simulation. *Measurement, 147*, 106825. doi:10.1016/j.measurement.2019.07.053

Fratila, D. (2009). Evaluation of near-dry machining effects on gear milling process efficiency. *Journal of Cleaner Production, 17*(9), 839–845. doi:10.1016/j.jclepro.2008.12.010

Fratila, D., & Radu, A. (2010). *Modeling and comparing of steady thermal state at gear milling by conventional and environment-friendly cooling method.* doi:10.1007/s00170-009-2238-x

Furness, R., Stoll, A., Nordstrom, G., Martini, G., Johnson, J., Loch, T., & Klosinski, R. (2006). Minimum Quantity Lubrication (MQL) machining for complex powertrain components. *Proceedings of the International Conference on Manufacturing Science and Engineering,* 1–9. 10.1115/MSEC2006-21112

Garetti, M., & Taisch, M. (2012). Production Planning & Control : The Management of Operations Sustainable manufacturing : trends and research challenges. Taylor & Francis.

Gbededo, M. A., Liyanage, K., & Garza-Reyes, J. A. (2018). Towards a Life Cycle Sustainability Analysis: A systematic review of approaches to sustainable manufacturing. *Journal of Cleaner Production, 184*, 1002–1015. doi:10.1016/j.jclepro.2018.02.310

Ghadimi, P., Li, W., Kara, S., & Herrmann, C. (2014). Integrated Material and Energy Flow Analysis towards Energy Efficient Manufacturing. *Procedia CIRP, 15*, 117–122. doi:10.1016/j.procir.2014.06.010

Gupta, K. (2020). A review on green machining techniques. *Procedia Manufacturing, 51*(2019), 1730–1736. doi:10.1016/j.promfg.2020.10.241

Gupta, K., Laubscher, R. F., Davim, J. P., & Jain, N. K. (2016). Recent developments in sustainable manufacturing of gears: A review. *Journal of Cleaner Production*, *112*, 3320–3330. doi:10.1016/j.jclepro.2015.09.133

Heisel, U., & Schaal, M. (2009). Burr formation in short hole drilling with minimum quantity lubrication. *Production Engineering*, *3*(2), 157–163. doi:10.100711740-009-0153-5

Jayal, A. D., Badurdeen, F., Dillon, O. W. Jr, & Jawahir, I. S. (2010). Sustainable manufacturing: Modeling and optimization challenges at the product, process and system levels. *CIRP Journal of Manufacturing Science and Technology*, *2*(3), 144–152. doi:10.1016/j.cirpj.2010.03.006

Jovane, F., Yoshikawa, H., Alting, L., Boër, C. R., Westkamper, E., Williams, D., Tseng, M., Seliger, G., & Paci, A. M. (2008). The incoming global technological and industrial revolution towards competitive sustainable manufacturing. *CIRP Annals - Manufacturing Technology, 57*(2), 641–659. doi:10.1016/j.cirp.2008.09.010

Junankar, A. A., Parate, S. R., Dethe, P. K., Dhote, N. R., Gadkar, D. G., Gadkar, D. D., & Gajbhiye, S. A. (2020). A review: Enhancement of turning process performance by effective utilization of hybrid nanofluid and MQL. *Materials Today: Proceedings, 38*, 44–47. doi:10.1016/j.matpr.2020.05.603

Kunle, S., & Corresponding, K. (2013). *Performance Evaluation of Vegetable Oil-Based Cutting Fluids in Mild Steel Machining*. Academic Press.

Liu, H., & Ling, D. (2020). Sustainable Computing : Informatics and Systems Value chain reconstruction and sustainable development of green manufacturing industry. *Sustainable Computing : Informatics and Systems*, *28*, 100418. doi:10.1016/j.suscom.2020.100418

Maghazei, O., & Netland, T. (2020). Drones in manufacturing: Exploring opportunities for research and practice. *Journal of Manufacturing Technology Management*, *31*(6), 1237–1259. doi:10.1108/JMTM-03-2019-0099

Marseguerra, M., & Zio, E. (2000). Optimizing maintenance and repair policies via a combination of genetic algorithms and Monte Carlo simulation. *Reliability Engineering & System Safety*, *68*(1), 69–83. doi:10.1016/S0951-8320(00)00007-7

Mathiyazhagan, K., Sengupta, S., & Mathivathanan, D. (2019). Challenges for implementing green concept in sustainable manufacturing: a systematic review. In Opsearch (Vol. 56, Issue 1). Springer India. doi:10.100712597-019-00359-2

Matsuoka, H., Ryu, T., Nakae, T., Shutou, S., & Kodera, T. (2013). *Fundamental Research on Hobbing with Minimal Quantity Lubrication of Cutting Oil*. Academic Press.

Mishra, R. R., Sahoo, A. K., Panda, A., Kumar, R., Das, D., & Routara, B. C. (2020). MQL machining of high strength steel: A case study on surface quality characteristic. *Materials Today: Proceedings, 26*, 2616–2618. doi:10.1016/j.matpr.2020.02.552

Moldavska, A., & Welo, T. (2017). The concept of sustainable manufacturing and its definitions: A content-analysis based literature review. *Journal of Cleaner Production*, *166*, 744–755. doi:10.1016/j.jclepro.2017.08.006

Obikawa, T., Kamata, Y., & Shinozuka, J. (2006). *High-speed grooving with applying MQL*. doi:10.1016/j.ijmachtools.2005.11.007

Öztürk, S., & Fatih, M. (2019). *Modeling and optimization of machining parameters during grinding of flat glass using response surface methodology and probabilistic uncertainty analysis based on Monte Carlo simulation*. doi:10.1016/j.measurement.2019.05.098

Rabiei, F., Rahimi, A. R., Hadad, M. J., & Ashrafijou, M. (2015). Performance improvement of minimum quantity lubrication (MQL) technique in surface grinding by modeling and optimization. *Journal of Cleaner Production*, *86*, 447–460. doi:10.1016/j.jclepro.2014.08.045

Sezen, B., & Çankaya, S. Y. (2013). Effects of green manufacturing and eco-innovation on sustainability performance. *Procedia: Social and Behavioral Sciences*, *99*, 154–163. doi:10.1016/j.sbspro.2013.10.481

Silva, S., Nuzum, A. K., & Schaltegger, S. (2019). Stakeholder expectations on sustainability performance measurement and assessment. A systematic literature review. *Journal of Cleaner Production*, *217*, 204–215. doi:10.1016/j.jclepro.2019.01.203

Singh, A., Philip, D., & Ramkumar, J. (2015). Quantifying green manufacturability of a unit production process using simulation. *Procedia CIRP*, *29*, 257–262. doi:10.1016/j.procir.2015.01.034

Singh, A., Philip, D., & Ramkumar, J. (2016a). Green Index quantification of a unit manufacturing process through simulation experiments. *Procedia CIRP*, *41*, 1131–1136. doi:10.1016/j.procir.2016.05.073

Singh, A., Philip, D., & Ramkumar, J. (2016b). Green Index Quantification of a Unit Manufacturing Process through Simulation Experiments. *Procedia CIRP*, *41*, 1131–1136. doi:10.1016/j.procir.2016.05.073

Tai, B. L., Stephenson, D. A., Furness, R. J., & Shih, A. J. (2014). Minimum Quantity Lubrication (MQL) in Automotive Powertrain Machining. *Procedia CIRP*, *14*, 523–528. doi:10.1016/j.procir.2014.03.044

Taylor, P., Dasch, J., Arcy, J. D., Gundrum, A., Sutherland, J., Johnson, J., Dasch, J., Arcy, J. D., Gundrum, A., Sutherland, J., Johnson, J., & Carlson, D. (n.d.). *in Automotive Plants. December 2014*, 37–41. doi:10.1080/15459620500377659

Taylor, P., Filipovic, A., & Stephenson, D. A. (2007). *Machining Science and Technology : A Minimum Quantity Lubrication (MQL) Applications in Automotive Power-Train Machining*. doi:10.1080/10910340500534258

Teodorico, C., Carmina, S., Anastasia, S., Roberto, G., Francesco, T., & Maria, R. (2014). Noise and cardiovascular effects in workers of the sanitary fixtures industry. *International Journal of Hygiene and Environmental Health*. Advance online publication. doi:10.1016/j.ijheh.2014.09.007 PMID:25455423

Thiede, S., Posselt, G., & Herrmann, C. (2013). CIRP Journal of Manufacturing Science and Technology SME appropriate concept for continuously improving the energy and resource efficiency in manufacturing companies. *CIRP Journal of Manufacturing Science and Technology*, *6*(3), 204–211. doi:10.1016/j.cirpj.2013.02.006

Vila, C., Abellán-nebot, J. V., Albiñana, J. C., & Hernández, G. (2015). An approach to Sustainable Product Lifecycle Management (Green PLM). *Procedia Engineering*, *132*, 585–592. doi:10.1016/j.proeng.2015.12.608

Wawrla, L., Maghazei, O., & Netland, P. D. T. (2019). Applications of drones in warehouse operations. *ETH Zurich*, (August), 13.

Wickramasinghe, K. C., Sasahara, H., Rahim, E. A., & Perera, G. I. P. (2020). Green Metalworking Fluids for sustainable machining applications: A review. *Journal of Cleaner Production*, *257*, 120552. Advance online publication. doi:10.1016/j.jclepro.2020.120552

Yousefnezhad, N., Malhi, A., & Främling, K. (2020). Security in product lifecycle of IoT devices: A survey. *Journal of Network and Computer Applications*, *171*(June), 102779. doi:10.1016/j.jnca.2020.102779

Zhang, G., & Wei, H. (n.d.). *Selection of optimal process parameters for gear hobbing under cold air minimum quantity lubrication cutting environment*. Academic Press.

Zhu, X., Xiao, Y., Xiao, G., & Deng, X. (2022). Research on Driving Factors of Collaborative Integration Implementation of Lean-Green Manufacturing System with Industry 4.0 Based on Fuzzy AHP-DEMATEL-ISM: From the Perspective of Enterprise Stakeholders. *Processes (Basel, Switzerland)*, *10*(12), 1–24. doi:10.3390/pr10122714

Chapter 5
A Study of Additive Manufacturing Using 3D Printing Machines and Pens:
A Review

Archisman Dasgupta
https://orcid.org/0000-0003-4292-2831
National Institute of Technology, Agartala, India

Prasenjit Dutta
National Institute of Technology, Agartala, India

ABSTRACT

3D printing (3DP), also known as additive manufacturing (AM), is a popular method used in Industry 4.0 that involves using machines and pens to create customized and complex 3D objects from a digital file by layering materials. This technology is widely used in industries such as aerospace, automotive, healthcare, and consumer goods for prototyping, rapid tooling, and production of end-use parts. 3DP offers companies a low-risk, low-cost, and fast way to produce prototypes, allowing them to test new products and speed up development without expensive models or specialized tools. Machines are more suitable for creating larger and more complex objects with high accuracy, while pens are better for smaller and simpler designs. Machines can be expensive and require training, while pens are more affordable and easy to use. Overall, AM with 3DP has provided new possibilities for designers and manufacturers. This chapter will further explore different printing methods, materials, advantages, limitations, software applications, potential uses, and future prospects of this technology.

DOI: 10.4018/979-8-3693-2647-3.ch005

1. INTRODUCTION

The advantages of AM are numerous. It makes possible to create complex and intricate designs that are previously impossible to produce by traditional manufacturing methods. AM is also providing more flexibility and customization options, allowing designers to create one-of-a-kind products for specific needs. Medicine, engineering, and education have all benefited from this AM technology. Besides this, AM is more environmentally friendly method of manufacturing because it can reduces waste materials and uses fewer materials (Bogue, 2013; Gogoi & Jeyapoovan, 2016; Shahrubudin et al., 2019; Takahashi & Kim, 2019; Yang, 2022; Zolotareva et al., 2021).

Filament and resin-based 3D printers are the two most common methods of printing 3D parts that are relevant for 3DP machines (Gokhare et al., 2017; Ngo et al., 2018). The machine starts with plastic filament as a raw material and then melts it down to give the required dimension to the material that has been programmed to get the final layer. Throughout the printing process, the printer only considered parts of a mono and 2D layer at a time. A 3D printer that uses filament obtains all of the pathways along which it intends to lay down material in each layer, then moves up a little and begins working on a new set of movements. In this manner, a new layer will be printed on top of each previous layer.

A transparent resin material melts together and resembles an injection-molded plastic part rather than a 3D printed part in resin-based 3D printers, usually stereolithography (SLA). This liquid resin is an adhesive and non-sticky film that is poured into a vat with a transparent bottom and is used to cover a liquid crystal display (LCD) screen. Instead of a monitor's actinic rays, it incorporates a powerful actinic radiation LED that shines. Most vats can have this film replaced. The UV semiconductor diode and the LCD masking screen, on the other hand, have a limited life span. The entire layer is exposed and cured at the same time on an LCD or, more commonly, a Masked Stereolithography Apparatus (MSLA) printer. As a result, regardless of the size of the part being printed, it will always take the same amount of time per layer. It will always build the print up at a similar speed vertically, and as a result, these machines will always produce the same product faster than filament printers. There are resins that are "water washable," which means they can be easily rinsed with regular water. Resin-based 3D printers are capable of producing highly intricate resin products with ultra-fine layers (Guerra et al., 2019; Hmeidat et al., 2018; Lopatina & Filippova, 2020; Tosto et al., 2020).

Peter Dilworth, Maxwell Bogue, and Daniel Cowen of Wobble Works, Inc. (formerly Wobble Works LLC) created the epitome of 3Doodler, which could be a 3D pen, in 2012 (Gogoi & Jeyapoovan, 2016; Takahashi & Kim, 2019). The fact that it conjures up power and aids in the development of skills in sketching with 3D pens, which is a recent trend on the planet. However, hand-drawn drawings do not appear to be as accurate and precise as machine-drawn drawings. However, the 3D pen may be a promising tool for encouraging inventive imagination. The difference between traditional ink-based pens and 3D printing pens is that the extruder tip of a 3D printing pen produces liquid plastic filament. To begin writing, a plastic filament that can be heated to the desired temperature is required, and this liquid plastic is used to design the desired look. The 3D pen attracts and deposits plastic filament material through the nozzle and the speed is controlled by a motor (Gogoi & Jeyapoovan, 2016).

2. PRINTING METHODS

For various applications, various methods of 3DP have been developed. Solidification of photo-curing materials, deposition of melted plastic materials, printing radiopaque ink on paper-based phantoms, melting or binding plastic powder, and bio-printing are some of the most commonly used methods (Murkute et al., 2022; Okkalidis, 2022). The method chosen is determined by the properties and needs of the printable material or composite, as well as the end-use application. Electro spinning and casting, for example, are two methods used to prepare aripiprazole and polyvinyl alcohol odispersible films (ODFs) (Łyszczarz et al., 2021). Fly ash-based fiber-reinforced geopolymer composites can be made in civil engineering applications using casted or injected samples, which simulate the 3DP process (Korniejenko et al., 2020). 3DP is a novel approach to producing 3D pharmaceuticals from digital designs in a layer-by-layer fashion in pharmaceutical manufacturing (Warsi et al., 2018). Traditional manufacturing processes, on the other hand, continue to be carried out using well-established manufacturing processes and regulatory guidelines (Warsi et al., 2018). The development of appropriate printing materials is also critical, as these materials should ideally be able to emulate the entire range of soft and bone tissues while still matching human anatomy (Okkalidis, 2022). Here are the 3DP methods explained below:

2.1 Fused Deposition Modeling (FDM)

This is a popular 3DP method that creates 3D objects layer by layer using a thermoplastic material. This method involves melting the thermoplastic material and then extruding it in a specific pattern onto the build platform via a nozzle. The extruded material fuses with the previously deposited layers to form a solid 3D object as it cools and solidifies. This method is used in the majority of 3D printers and pens. The machine's extruder is moved back and forth, layer by layer, until the object is complete. Direct material extrusion encourages the doodling method, which involves using a 3D printing pen to create free-form designs and shapes. As the material cools and hardens, the pen is used to draw directly onto the surface, creating a three-dimensional object. A stencil or template, on the other hand, is used to guide the 3D printing pen as it moves along the stencil to create a specific design and shape. While FDM has many advantages, it also has some disadvantages. The finished product may lack the detail and accuracy of other 3DP processes, such as SLA or SLS. Furthermore, the layer-by-layer assembly method can result in visible seams or lines in the final product. Because of these constraints, FDM is better suited to creating functional objects rather than aesthetic ones. Overall, FDM is a powerful and user-friendly 3DP technology that has enabled a diverse range of creations and innovations (Msallem et al., 2020).

2.2 Stereolithography (SLA)

To create solid objects, this 3DP technology employs a laser to cure photopolymer resin layer by layer. Charles Hull invented it in the 1980s and it was the first 3DP technology to be developed. SLA has grown in popularity as a rapid prototyping method, particularly in industries such as aerospace, automotive, and consumer goods. SLA's ability to produce highly accurate and detailed models with smooth surfaces is one of its primary advantages. SLA resin is cured by a laser that moves across the surface of the resin. This enables the creation of intricate shapes and fine details that would be impossible to achieve using traditional manufacturing methods. Because of its ability to print precise geometries, SLA has become a popular choice for applications such as dental implants, jewellery, and architectural models. Another advantage of SLA is its quick turnaround time. SLA machines can produce parts in hours, making it a quick and efficient method for rapid prototyping. Furthermore, the cost of SLA equipment has decreased over time, making it more accessible to small businesses and hobbyists. Overall, SLA has transformed the manufacturing process, enabling faster prototyping and product development at a lower cost (Abdella et al., 2021; Msallem et al., 2020; Suta et al., 2022).

2.3 Selective Laser Sintering (SLS)

It is an AM technique that fuses small particles of powdered material together to form a solid object using a high-powered laser beam. The procedure begins with a CAD file of the object that is then sliced into thin layers. A layer of powdered material is then spread over a build platform, and the laser selectively fuses the particles in the first layer's pattern before lowering the build platform and repeating the process until the object is complete. SLS has a number of significant advantages over other 3DP techniques. SLS has the advantage of being able to use a wide range of materials, including plastics, metals, and ceramics. Engineers and designers can use this flexibility to create parts that are perfectly suited to their application, with the right combination of strength, durability, and other properties. Furthermore, SLS is capable of producing complex geometries that would be difficult or impossible to achieve using other techniques such as injection moulding or CNC machining. Despite its advantages, SLS has some drawbacks. One disadvantage is that the surface finish of SLS parts is rougher than that of other techniques. Furthermore, the process can generate a significant amount of waste, which must be properly disposed of. Nonetheless, SLS is a valuable tool for a wide range of manufacturing applications, particularly those requiring complex geometries or specific material properties. As technology advances, it is likely to become even more widely used (Msallem et al., 2020; Yuri et al., 2022).

2.4 Digital Light Processing (DLP)

Digital Light Processing (DLP) is an advanced technology that allows for precise and fast printing in AM. DLP technology employs a digital light projection system to produce a series of high-resolution images. The images are projected onto a vat of liquid photopolymer, and the resin is cured layer by layer through light exposure. The end result is a solid object that accurately and precisely replicates the digital model. The use of DLP in AM provides numerous advantages to the manufacturing process. The technology allows for the production of complex geometries with high precision, detail, and consistency. DLP can create parts with features as small as 10 microns (0.01 mm), which other technologies cannot. Furthermore, DLP is a fast process, capable of printing up to four inches (10 cm) per hour. As a result, DLP provides a viable solution to the growing demand for personalised and on-demand manufacturing. While DLP has several advantages in AM, the technology is still in its infancy. DLP printers are still relatively expensive when compared to other technologies such as FDM and SLA. Furthermore, to achieve optimal results, DLP requires additional post-processing of the printed parts, such as cleaning and curing. Nonetheless, DLP's potential in AM is clear, and as the technology advances, it is likely to become more accessible, affordable, and operationally efficient, allowing more businesses and industries to reap its benefits (Abdella et al., 2021; Yuri et al., 2022).

2.5 Binder Jetting

Binder jetting is an AM process that uses two materials: a powder-based material and a binder. The binder acts as an adhesive between powder layers, and it is usually in liquid form, while the build material is in powder form. The two-material approach allows for a large number of different binder-powder combinations and various mechanical properties of the final model to be achieved by changing the ratio and individual properties of the two materials. This is one of the most popular AM methods for producing complex 3D printed parts. A print head moves horizontally along the x and y axes of the machine and deposits alternating layers of the build material and the binding material. After each layer, the object being printed is lowered on its build platform. This technology creates an object by dispensing a liquid binder on a thin layer of powder. Binder jetting necessitates the use of a CAD model to generate a digital file that controls the path of the printer's nozzle. Layer by layer, the binder is dispensed onto the powder in a precise pattern until the object is complete. The binder jetting process allows for colour printing and uses metal, polymers, and ceramic materials. The process is generally faster than others and can be further quickened by increasing the number of print head holes that deposit material. When compared to other 3DP methods, one of the significant advantages of binder jetting printers is their ability to produce high-quality parts at a faster rate. These printers can print on a wide range of materials, including sand, ceramics, and metals. Furthermore, because the unused powder around the object acts as a support structure, binder jetting does not require the use of support structures. This eliminates the need for post-processing of parts, lowering the cost of producing 3D printed parts significantly. Binder jetting printers, on the other hand, have some limitations. For one thing, the final product's quality is determined by the quality of the powder used. This means that the overall quality of the part will be determined by the particle size, shape, and composition of the powder used. Furthermore, the technology is still in its early stages, and improvements are needed to enable the printing of larger parts. However, the benefits of binder jetting printers make them an appealing option for businesses looking to reduce the cost and time associated with 3DP (Msallem et al., 2020; Shakor et al., 2019; Yuri et al., 2022).

2.6 Material Jetting

Material jetting is a popular AM technique. Layers of material are deposited onto a substrate using inkjet technology, creating 3D objects layer by layer. The technology is divided into two categories: drop on demand (DOD) and continuous inkjet (CIJ). DOD works by ejecting droplets of material through a nozzle, whereas CIJ sprays a thin stream of material continuously. Ceramics, metals, plastics, and composite mixtures are among the materials used in material jetting. One advantage of this technique is its ability to produce highly complex objects with great detail and accuracy, making it ideal for prototyping and small batches of customised products. Despite this advantage, material jetting has drawbacks such as high production costs and limited capacity. However, its precision engineering potential is significant if properly implemented in conjunction with other available experimentation instruments (Elkaseer et al., 2022; Suta et al., 2022).

2.7 Direct Energy Deposition (DED)

DED is a type of AM process that involves melting and fusing metal powders or wire using a focused energy source such as a laser or electron beam. Because it allows for precise control over material deposition and melting, this technique is ideal for creating complex geometries and repairing damaged parts. DED is used in a variety of industries, including aerospace, automotive, and biomedical engineering. Despite some limitations, such as high equipment costs and material selection limitations, this method has produced functional prototypes and end-use parts with excellent mechanical properties. Because of its versatility and potential, it is an exciting area of research in the ever-expanding field of AM (Elkaseer et al., 2022; Shakor et al., 2019; Yuri et al., 2022).

2.8 Cool Ink 3D Pens

To create the object, these pens use a special ink that hardens when it comes into contact with air. Because of its precise heating technology and smooth ink flow, this innovative device easily creates intricate designs and structures. With a wide range of coloured inks available, it will be possible to add depth and dimension to all printing projects (Jaksic, 2015).

2.9 Laser 3D Pens

A laser is used in these pens to fuse powdered material into a solid object layer by layer. Laser 3D pens are an innovative tool that enables users to create 3D drawings or objects by curing a special resin with a laser. These pens are ideal for artists, designers, and architects because they provide a new way to realise their visions. The process of creating with a pen is extremely simple. Unlike other 3DP tools, these pens provide greater versatility and flexibility because they can create freehand designs with no software constraints. Furthermore, there is no need to worry about wire connections or computers because the pen is portable and easy to use anywhere. Overall, laser 3D pens are a great addition for anyone who enjoys making physical objects and learning about new technologies in art and design (Asicioglu et al., 2022).

3. PRINTING MATERIALS

Materials for 3DP are constantly evolving and expanding. Here are some of the materials that are used in the AM process, which allows the creation of 3D solid parts from a digital file (Srinivasan et al., 2021).

3.1 Thermoplastics

Thermoplastics are plastic polymers with low melting points that will melt when heated, solidify when cooled, and can be re-melted after curing without damaging the physical integrity of the material. They are strong yet flexible, shrink-resistant and shock-absorbent, and easy to use since no post-processing is required. Common applications include prototyping and a wide range of consumer products, such as trash bags, cookware, children's toys, and even automotive parts. Engineers can add fillers and additives to thermoplastics to enhance their properties, such as greater strength or biocompatibility. 3DP technologies such as SLS and FDM can use thermoplastics to fabricate production components or prototypes. The properties used to determine the performance of thermoplastic materials are mainly mechanical and thermal. Standard thermoplastics, also known as commodity plastics, are the most widespread and, by far, the most produced. The followings are the most common materials used in 3DP. Thermoplastics are simple to use, inexpensive, and can be used to make a wide variety of objects (Nofar et al., 2022).

Because of their ability to be melted and reshaped multiple times, it is widely used in 3DP. The various types of thermoplastics used in 3DP are,

- *Polystyrene:* This is a lightweight, rigid plastic commonly used in 3DP. It is simple to print and inexpensive (Self et al., 2022). Polystyrene is a popular material in AM due to its low cost, ease of processing, and dimensional stability. It is a synthetic polymer derived from the aromatic hydrocarbon styrene monomers. Polystyrene is used in a variety of forms, including foam, film, and rigid plastic, for applications ranging from food packaging to electronics protection. Polystyrene is an addition polymer formed by the polymerization (interconnection) of styrene monomers (Sieradzka et al., 2021).
- *Polyethylene terephthalate-glycol (PETG):* This is a tough and flexible plastic that is commonly used in 3DP. It is moisture and chemical resistant, with a high impact resistance (Furka et al., 2021). PETG can be produced through recycling processes from either products made with PETG or virgin PET produced by adding glycol. PETG is widely used in the field of AM, but little is known about its instantaneous mechanical properties. PETG is one of the most widely used FDM filaments. PETG parts with and without short fibre reinforcement were tested and compared (Ferreira et al., 2019; Romeijn et al., 2022).
- *Polylactic acid (PLA):* This biodegradable plastic is commonly used in 3DP. It is derived from renewable, organic sources such as corn starch or sugar cane. It's simple to print and has a low melting point, so it's ideal for use with low-cost 3D printers (Furka et al., 2021). PLA is a flexible polymer that can be used to create a wide range of parts, packaging, and prototypes for various industries, including medical, food, cosmetics, and textile
- *Cyclic olefin copolymer (COC):* COCs are created by chain copolymerizing cyclic monomers with ethene, such as norbornene or tetracyclododecene. COCs have gained popularity in AM as a material for 3DP in recent years. COR, for Cyclic Olefin Resin, is a family of additive materials developed by polySpectra, with its first material, COR Alpha, demonstrating an unrivalled combination of properties. COCs have also found application in microfluidics and microdevices. This is a clear plastic with high heat resistance and excellent chemical resistance. It is widely used in medical and optical applications (Self et al., 2022). COCs were characterised for insulin reservoirs in an artificial pancreas in a recent study, demonstrating their potential in medical applications (Agha et al., 2022; Mallegni et al., 2023).
- *Trimethylene carbonate:* This is a biodegradable plastic with excellent mechanical properties that is widely used in medical applications (Self et al., 2022). The polymer poly(trimethylene carbonate) (PTMC) has been used in AM to create micro-porous vascular structures. PTMC has also been used to create 3D-printed scaffolds for tissue engineering applications, frequently in conjunction with other materials such as poly(-caprolactone) and tricalcium phosphate. Various techniques, such as stereolithography and two-photon polymerization, have been used to demonstrate PTMC's suitability for AM. Because of its biodegradability and biocompatibility, the use of PTMC in AM is promising for biomedical applications (Guo et al., 2020; Weisgrab et al., 2020; Zheng et al., 2023).
- *Acrylonitrile butadiene styrene (ABS):* ABS (acrylonitrile butadiene styrene) is a thermoplastic polymer that is commonly used in AM. ABS is made from a polymer blend of acrylonitrile, butadiene, and styrene. ABS is a terpolymer formed by polymerizing styrene and acrylonitrile in the presence of polybutadiene, with acrylonitrile proportions ranging from 15% to 35%, butadiene

proportions ranging from 5% to 30%, and styrene proportions ranging from 40% to 60%. ABS is used in 3DP as a long filament wound around a spool in FDM. ABS is well-known for its chemical and fatigue resistance, as well as its hardness, rigidity, and toughness. ABS can be manufactured using a combination of material extrusion AM and injection moulding, according to a recent study (Faidallah et al., 2021; Gong et al., 2022).

- *Nylon:* Nylon, also known as Polyamide (PA), is a tough and flexible plastic widely used in 3DP. It is available in powder or filament form for SLS, Multi Jet Fusion, and FDM technologies. Because of its flexibility, strength, and durability, nylon is a very useful and versatile material. It is used in the production of machine parts, brushes, fishing lines, and even food packaging films that require an oxygen barrier. When it comes to 3DP, nylon powder can be reused for multiple prints, and it has a higher refresh rate than SLS technology. However, nylon has been the subject of debate regarding its sustainability, and its environmental impact is dependent on the type of polyamide, its origin, and composition. Despite this, the AM industry is progressing towards more sustainable solutions for nylon and other materials (Faidallah et al., 2021; Farina et al., 2019).
- *Polypropylene:* Polypropylene (PP) is a widely used plastic that is now being used in AM. PP is well-known for its chemical resistance, low density, and mechanical properties. However, due to its high shrinkage and warpage, 3DP PP has proven difficult. Braskem has recently developed a portfolio of PP products that address the issue of excessive warpage in 3DP applications (Additive Manufacturing, n.d.). PP feedstock material has been optimised for extrusion-based AM by researchers (Jin et al., 2020). The mechanical properties of PP processed using Multi Jet Fusion technology were investigated, and it was discovered that PP has excellent mechanical properties. The average mechanical properties of a design of experiment on commercial PP powder using laser-based powder bed fusion were 19.9 MPa for ultimate tensile strength, 2.9% for elongation at break, and 9.21% for porosity. PP is used less frequently in AM than it is in the plastic injection industry (Faidallah et al., 2021; Flores Ituarte et al., 2018; Šafka et al., 2021).

In addition to these thermoplastics, efforts are being made to develop new 3DP materials, such as bio-derived terpene camphene, which can be used as a solvent and porogen for the freezecasting of thermoplastic parts under mild conditions (Self et al., 2022). Moreover, foam 3DP of thermoplastics has been proposed as an alternative to foam injection moulding, which involves the combination of foaming and printing technology to produce foamed printed structures (Nofar et al., 2022).

3.2 Cementitious Materials

In the construction industry, these materials are used to print cementitious structures. They are combined with water and other ingredients to form a printable mixture (Shakor et al., 2019). Cementitious materials, particularly in the construction industry, are becoming increasingly important in AM. Finding the right mix design that balances the need for high plastic yield stress to retain the shape of printed layers with the ease of pumping the cementitious system is the challenge. A vibration-based active rheology-controlled system that temporarily reduces plastic yield stress during pumping is one solution (Peerzada et al., 2022). Various prototyping technologies for printing cementitious materials have been reviewed, and benchmark examples for comparing different printing techniques have been provided (Shakor et al., 2019). The use of graphene oxide as a nano reinforcement material has shown promise in improving the printing feasibility and quality of 3D printed cementitious matrices, with viscosity modifying agents used to achieve the required consistency and flow (Mohammed & Al-Saadi, 2020). The effect of different process parameters on part quality has been investigated, and an alternative process-control strategy for controlling the width of the extruded path has been proposed (Foteinopoulos et al., 2020). Overall, there is a growing demand for higher productivity and part quality in cement-based AM, and research is ongoing to find new mix designs and optimise the printing process (Liu, Nguyen-Van, Panda et al, 2022).

3.3 Foam

In 3DP, foam materials can be used to create lightweight structures. A combined foaming and printing technology can provide an excellent alternative to currently used foam manufacturing technologies such as foam injection moulding (Nofar et al., 2022). Because of their lightweight and low cost, foam materials are becoming increasingly important in AM (Nofar et al., 2022). Here are some examples of foam material research in AM:

- *Thermoplastic foam 3DP:* This is a novel technology that combines foaming and printing technology to create foam structures. Attempts to create foamed printed structures are divided into four categories: architected porous structures, syntactic foaming, post-foaming of printed parts, and printing of saturated blowing agents filaments (Nofar et al., 2022).
- *In situ foam 3DP of microcellular structures:* This method allows for thermoplastic in situ foam 3DP. Thermally expandable microspheres (TEMs) are incorporated into the filament during the extrusion process to create an expandable feedstock filament. The material formulation and extrusion process are both designed to prevent TEM expansion during filament fabrication. Expandable filaments are then fed into a material extrusion AM process, which allows for the in situ foaming of microcellular structures during layer deposition (Kalia et al., 2022).
- *Core-shell material extrusion AM of carbon fibre and syntactic foam hybrid materials:* This method 3D prints core-shell architectures composed of a syntactic epoxy foam core surrounded by a stiff carbon fiber-reinforced epoxy composite shell using a core-shell print head capable of printing highly loaded fiber-filled inks and a new low-density syntactic foam ink. It has been demonstrated that test specimens and structures with controlled geometry, composition, and architecture can be printed effectively (Pack et al., 2020).
- *Tunable large-scale compressive strain sensor made by AM from carbon nanotube/polydimethylsiloxane foam composites:* Using material extrusion 3DP, a carbon nanotube/polydimethylsiloxane compressive strain sensor is created. The foam microstructure formed by removing sodium chloride exhibits at least 50% compressive strain and excellent elasticity on a large scale. The strain sensor has a gauge factor of 17.4 (Liu, Le, Zhang et al, 2022) and can withstand 10,000 cycles.
- *Pressure drops measured during water flow into porous materials created using AM:* The goal of this research is to create open-cell foams using AM, test them, and then generate a simulation model based on the real geometries to numerically optimise each parameter. The current manuscript describes the 3DP construction of open-foam and experimental pressure drop measurements when water flows through the foam (Righetti et al., 2021).

These studies show that foam materials have the potential to be used in AM for a variety of applications such as sensors, hybrid materials, and porous structures.

3.4 Metals

Metal is one of the most common materials used in the AM process, as it is great for designing and creating industrial-grade parts that are durable enough to handle. The process is additive in nature, with layers being successively added to build a part, as opposed to subtractive technologies, where material is removed or shaped by machining, milling, or forming. Metal AM offers the possibility to produce complex parts without the design constraints of traditional manufacturing routes. The process offers unsurpassed design freedom and the ability to manufacture parts from a variety of metal-based materials. Metal AM is an important part of manufacturing industry growth, as it helps manufacturers improve efficiencies, reduce waste, lower emissions, and increase the speed to market of stronger and lighter parts. The number of industries and individuals using metal additive technologies today represents a growing trend, including artists, designers, jewellers, and manufacturers of medical and engineering goods. Renishaw's metal powder bed fusion is an advanced AM process that builds complex metal parts directly from 3D CAD data in a variety of metals. Metal powders can be used to create metal parts in 3DP. This method is referred to as metal AM or metal 3DP (Srinivasan et al., 2021). Metal AM technologies have nearly unlimited potential in recent years, and the range of applications has expanded (Vafadar et al., 2021). The following metals are used in AM:

- *Titanium:* Because of their unique properties and potential applications, titanium-based alloys are increasingly being used in AM. To better understand the mechanical behaviour of additively manufactured titanium alloys, various types of mechanical testing have been performed. Because of its excellent biocompatibility and ability to promote bone growth and regeneration in its interior, titanium 3DP has distinct advantages in the medical industry. Titanium is a popular metal in AM due to its high strength-to-weight ratio, corrosion resistance, and biocompatibility. It finds widespread application in aerospace, medical implants, and automobiles (Revilla-León et al., 2020). The microstructure and mechanical properties of a titanium-molybdenum alloy created using the laser AM technique have been thoroughly investigated. The development of materials and methods for AM of titanium-based alloys, including their properties, challenges, and prospects, has been reviewed (Tshephe et al., 2022).
- *Stainless Steel:* Because of its excellent mechanical properties, corrosion resistance, and weldability, stainless steel is a popular material in AM (Wagner et al., 2022). Austenitic 316L stainless steel has excellent mechanical properties and is widely used in AM (Bedmar et al., 2021; Han et al., 2023). 316L VPro, 254, Super Duplex, 17-4PH, PH1 (15-5), and CX alloys are some other stainless steel powders used in AM. The austenitic stainless steel EOS Stainless Steel 254 has excellent corrosion resistance, making it ideal for demanding conditions and difficult environments such as chlorinated seawater handling equipment, pulp and paper manufacturing devices, and chemical handling equipment. Current research in steel AM has resulted in superior properties that cannot be achieved using traditional manufacturing methods (Haghdadi et al., 2021). Selective laser melting is an efficient method of producing steel metal parts (Gatões et al., 2022). It is commonly used in aerospace, automotive, and medical applications (Andreacola et al., 2021).
- *Cobalt-Chromium (CoCr):* CoCr is a metal superalloy that is widely used in AM, particularly in direct metal laser sintering 3DP processes. Because of its excellent mechanical properties, corrosion resistance, and biocompatibility, CoCr is ideal for use in biomedical and high-temperature engineering applications, as well as aerospace and dental applications (Konieczny et al., 2020;

Revilla-León et al., 2020). EOS, a leading manufacturer of industrial 3DP systems, provides a selection of CoCr powders, such as MP1, SP2, and RPD, which are specifically designed and tested for use in their metal systems (Eos, n.d.). The CoCr powders are shipped with an inspection certificate demonstrating the results of extensive quality assurance testing, and EOS provides a variety of validated processes to ensure that the properties of 3D printed parts are consistently achieved. Recent studies have focused on advancing the laser AM of CoCr alloys, with researchers developing analytical models for the laser powder bed fusion process and investigating the mechanical properties of 3D printed CoCr parts (Barazanchi et al., 2020; Mahmood et al., 2022; Wanniarachchi et al., 2022).

- *Aluminum:* Aluminium AM has grown in popularity in recent years, particularly in the aerospace and automotive industries, due to its high strength-to-weight ratio, recyclability, and chemical resistance (Zadpoor, 2018). Many specialised aluminium alloys for 3DP are available, with silicone for flowability and magnesium for strength. Because of their excellent strength-to-weight ratio, high-strength aluminium alloys are widely used in the aerospace industry for structural component manufacturing. Metal AM-fabricated high-strength aluminium alloys, on the other hand, tend to produce fatal metallurgical defects, which are a challenge that must be addressed (Altıparmak et al., 2021; Dixit & Liu, 2022). Despite these obstacles, AM with aluminium have a lot of potential for use in a variety of industries, as long as these technical and industrial issues are solved.
- *Nickel-Based Alloys:* Because of their excellent high-temperature strength, corrosion resistance, and ability to withstand extreme environments, nickel-based alloys are a popular material used in AM. Nickel superalloys are made up of a nickel alloy matrix to which a series of elements are added to improve their mechanical properties (Vafadar et al., 2021). To process nickel-based superalloys, AM methods have been developed, and the influence of process parameters on the microstructure and mechanical properties of the final product has been studied (Graybill et al., 2018). Nickel-based superalloys are commonly found in jet turbines, gas turbines, oil and gas, pressure vessels, and chemical processing components. The use of nickel-based superalloys in AM presents both opportunities for innovation and qualification challenges (Babu et al., 2018). The current state of materials development of nickel-base superalloys for AM processes and the associated challenges are discussed in detail in a recent article (Graybill et al., 2018).
- *Copper:* Copper is a material that is gaining popularity in AM. AM techniques such as selective laser melting, selective electron beam melting, and binder jetting have been used by researchers to fabricate parts with pure copper (Jiang et al., 2021; Sakib-Uz-Zaman & Khondoker, 2023; Vafadar et al., 2021). Until recently, printing three-dimensional objects with copper was difficult due to the metal's reflectivity and high thermal conductivity, making it difficult to use conventional 3D printers. Copper's material properties make it ideal for any application requiring good thermal and electronic conductivity. Copper 3DP now allows for the creation of much more complex geometries, which improves the efficiency of electric motors and enables new types of heat sinks in power electronics.

Each metal has distinct properties that make it suitable for a variety of applications. The metal used is determined by the application's specific requirements.

3.5 Ceramics

Ceramic powders can be used to make ceramic parts in 3DP. This method is referred to as ceramic AM or ceramic 3DP (Srinivasan et al., 2021). In AM, ceramic powders are increasingly being used to create complex geometries and customised parts. However, even after sintering, the low density of the fabricated parts has been a limitation. In order to address this, researchers investigated the effects of mixing powders with varying particle sizes on powder bed packing density and sintered density (Du et al., 2018). A linear packing model was used to guide the selection of particle sizes and fractions of constituent powders, and a selection process was built to achieve the highest mixed packing density. Binary and ternary mixtures have higher powder bed packing densities and sintered densities than their constituent powders, according to the results. Another study proposed a novel selective powder deposition process for producing glass-ceramic parts from recycled glass powders (Vasconcelos et al., 2022). The produced specimens had significant geometrical deviations, which could be related to some of the tested parameters. With proper control of the powder's coalescence, distortions could be mitigated by adding sand to the tested specimens. Material preparation techniques (powder granulation, mixing powders of different sizes, using slurry feedstock, and mixing different materials) and post processing techniques (sintering, chemical reaction, infiltration, and isostatic pressing) are also used to increase part density (Du et al., 2020). Lithography-based ceramic manufacturing, in which a light source with a specific wavelength is used to cure and structure ceramic-filled photosensitive resins, has been chosen as an optimal manufacturing process (Schönherr et al., 2020). Finally, bioactive glass-ceramic scaffolds have been successfully manufactured using two different AM techniques: powder-based 3DP and DLP, in combination with the sinter-crystallization of glass powders of two different compositions (Elsayed et al., 2018). Despite differences in manufacturing technology and crystallisation, all samples had very high strength-to-density ratios, making them suitable for bone tissue engineering applications.

3.6 Living Cells

In 3DP, living cells can be used to create biological structures such as tissues and organs. This is referred to as bio-printing (Srinivasan et al., 2021). Living cells and tissues have been subjected to AM for a variety of applications in tissue engineering and regenerative medicine. Using ring-shaped building units, researchers developed methods for automated AM of living bio-tubes (Manning et al., 2020). Living materials, which are composites of living cells in a polymeric matrix, have been designed to take advantage of the innate functionalities of the cells in a variety of applications such as fermentation and bio-sensing (Saha et al., 2018). For the production of a peptide, a yeast-laden hydrogel ink was developed and printed using a direct-write 3D printer (Johnston et al., 2019). Hard tissue replacements, such as implants made of Ti64 ELI titanium alloy, polyetheretherketone (PEEK), bio-ceramic, and magnesium alloys, have also been produced using AM (Hudak et al., 2021). Some of the complexities involved in 3D bio-printing are the selection of materials, cell types, growth and differentiation factors, and technical challenges related to the sensitivities of living cells and the construction of tissues (Hudak et al., 2021). The development of living materials for AM is still ongoing, and it is driving new frontiers in AM, such as multi-material 3DP, artificial intelligence for material design, and 4D printing with smart materials (Chua & Sing, 2022).

3.7 Photopolymers

Photopolymers are liquid resins that harden when they come into contact with light. They are commonly used in 3DP technologies such as SLA and DLP (Elbardisy et al., 2020). Photopolymers are AM materials that can be rapidly polymerized using light. They are used in the manufacture of medical devices, renewable materials, and other items. However, due to a lack of information on the biological risks of these materials, biocompatibility is a concern. The zebra fish embryo model has been used for toxicological testing (Alifui-Segbaya, 2018). Lignin-containing photopolymers have also been studied for their potential use in AM, with excellent print quality and increased ductility in cured parts (Sutton, 2019). For large-format AM, photoinitiator selection and concentration in photopolymer formulations have been studied, with bis(2,4,6-trimethylbenzoyl)-phenylphosphine oxide being a useful photoinitiator system for thick-section cure applications (Stiles et al., 2022). The behaviour of rubber-like photopolymers in AM processes has also been described using hyperelastic modelling (Hoque et al., 2011). Overall, photopolymers are a promising material for AM, but more research is needed to ensure biocompatibility and optimise their properties for different applications.

3.8 Blowing Agents

To create printed foam structures, blowing agents can be added to filaments (Nofar et al., 2022). To create foam structures with varying densities and hardnesses, blowing agents are added to polyurethane polymers (Rad, 2008). Carbon to carbon and hydrogenated fluoro hydrogenated chlorofluorocarbons, as well as perfluoroalkyl ethers, can be used as blowing agents in AM (Willson et al., 1998). A blowing agent is introduced into molten aromatic vinyl polymer to produce pellets of expandable vinyl aromatic polymers in the manufacturing process of expandable vinyl aromatic polymers (カサルト et al., 2011). Catalysts, surfactants, cross linkers, flame retardants, light stabilisers, and fillers are also used to control and modify the polymer's reaction process and performance characteristics (Rad, 2008). Non-toxic and inexpensive vitamins were used as active agents in one study to improve the photophysical properties and stability of perovskite nanocrystals via post-synthetic ligand surface passivation. The combination of vitamins and perovskite nanocrystals aided in the chemical formulation of composites that could be processed using AM (Recalde et al., 2023). To improve osseointegration, AM technology such as laser powder bed fusion can be used to create alloys with intricate shapes. Texturing the surfaces of these samples at the nanoscale, on the other hand, has proven difficult (Dzogbewu & du Preez, 2021). Another study immersed test specimens made of two different elastomeric filaments commonly used in 3DP in an abrasive fluid (commercial automotive petrol) to investigate their physical and mechanical properties.The effect of volume filling on mechanical properties as well as the petrol effect was investigated (Paz et al., 2021).

3.9 Architected Porous Structures

These structures are made by designing a lattice structure and printing it with a thermoplastic material (Nofar et al., 2022). In AM, architected porous structures refer to the use of 3DP technology to create complex, lattice-like structures with high porosity and specific mechanical properties. Thermal management, energy storage, and filtration are just a few of the applications for these structures. One study (Dominguez & Gonzalez, 2022), for example, presented a novel application of micro architected lattice structure to construct fibre filtering meshes attached to drainage channels, all in a "Integrated Mould." The methodology presented in this study defines a new approach for MFM design that offers a wider range of porosity and improves water drainage capabilities without compromising structural performance. Another study (Nofar et al., 2022) proposed a merged foaming and printing technology as a viable replacement for currently used foam manufacturing technologies such as foam injection moulding. This perspective review article focuses on the efforts made to launch this novel technology for simultaneously foaming and printing thermoplastics. Architected porous structures, syntactic foaming, postfoaming of printed parts, and eventually printing of blowing agent saturated filaments are among the attempts. Among these, the most recent approach is the most practical, though it has not yet been thoroughly studied.

3.10 Syntactic Foaming

To create a foamed structure, hollow microspheres are mixed with a thermoplastic material. Syntactic foaming is a novel technology that combines AM and foaming technology to create lightweight, low-cost cellular thermoplastic foams (Nofar et al., 2022). This technology has the potential to provide an excellent alternative to current foam manufacturing technologies such as foam injection moulding. Architected porous structures, syntactic foaming, post-foaming of printed parts, and printing of blowing agent saturated filaments are some of the attempts made towards generating foamed printed structures while highlighting their challenges (Nofar et al., 2022). Among these, the most recent approach is the most practical, though it has not yet been thoroughly studied. Syntactic foams are lightweight composites made of hollow particles reinforced in a polymer matrix, such as Glass Micro Balloons (GMBs) or cenospheres (Tewani et al., 2022). The GMB size controls the interior micro scale architecture of syntactic foams, with matrix segregation achieved via the SLS - AM process (Tewani et al., 2022). This manifests as paradoxical mechanical responses at the macro scale. GMBs with a diameter greater than the gaps between the segregated matrix's cell walls become lodged between and inside the cell walls, whereas those with a diameter less than the gaps become lodged inside the cell walls. As a result, larger particles significantly contribute to the stiffness of syntactic foams, while smaller particles have a negligible effect (Tewani et al., 2022). Combining reinforcement and print parameters allows for the design and fabrication of hierarchical customised structures and functional features in 3D printed syntactic foams (Tewani et al., 2022).

3.11 Binder Jetting

Binder jetting is unique among AM technologies because it does not employ heat during the process like others to fuse the material. Binder jetting is a 3DP process that involves depositing a liquid binder onto a powder bed to create a solid object. Here are some key points:

- Binder jetting is a flexible method for producing articles made of various materials, including magnesium oxychloride cement-based materials, stainless steel, and porcelain (Lecis et al., 2021; Pires et al., 2023; Salari et al., 2022).
- The mechanical properties of 3D-printed objects produced by binder jetting can be influenced by various factors, including particle size, the amount of binder, layer thickness, and binder liquid composition (Kreft et al., 2022; Salari et al., 2022).

- Binder jetting can be used to produce pharmaceutical solid products for oral drug delivery. The technology allows for flexible modifications on microstructure, material composition, and dose in the printed pharmaceutical products (Wang et al., 2022).
- Manufacturing time per part depends heavily on the geometry, orientation, printing process, and amount of parts manufactured in a single build. Manufacturing time per part varies substantially between different 3DP technologies. Powder bed fusion and binder jetting are optimal processes in regards to production speed (Salmi et al., 2016).

Overall, binder jetting is a promising 3DP technology that can be used to create objects of various materials with flexible microstructure and material composition modifications. Binder jetting 3D-printed objects' mechanical properties can be influenced by a variety of factors, and the technology has potential applications in pharmaceutical solid products for oral drug delivery.

4. PRINTING PARAMETERS

The printing parameters of AM are important factors that affect the quality and properties of the final product. These parameters include manufacturing speed, material flow, infill density, pattern orientation, printing layer height, number of shells, and infilling type. The influence of these parameters on the width of printed rods for a copper ink was analyzed in a study using a Design of Experiments. Another study investigated the effects of print parameters on the mechanical properties of additively manufactured metallic parts using a tensile test. The two significant print parameters emphasized in this study were infill density and pattern orientation. A meta-analysis study focused on layer thickness and sample orientation and showed that optimizing the printing parameters using an approved mathematical model enhanced the strength of a printed sample (Bonada et al., 2019; Farashi & Vafaee, 2022; Fongsamootr et al., 2022; Ingrassia et al., 2017; Khalid & Peng, 2021). The printing parameters for 3DP can differ depending on the application and type of printer used. Some of the printing parameters that can be changed are as follows:

4.1 Infill Raster Density (ID)

The density of the internal structure of the printed object is determined by this parameter. A higher infill density produces a stronger object but requires more material and time to print (Vidakis et al., 2023). ID is one of the FFF/FDM 3DP control parameters that affects the energy consumption and mechanical properties of the printed parts. The ID of a 3D printed object refers to the density of the internal structure, which can be adjusted by changing the spacing between the infill lines. Here are some important points to remember about ID in 3DP:

- ID affects the energy consumption of 3DP. In a study investigating the impact of six printing parameters on energy metrics, including energy printing consumption, specific printing energy, and specific printing power, ID was found to be one of the parameters that significantly affect energy consumption.

- ID affects the mechanical properties of 3D printed parts. In several studies investigating the mechanical response of 3D printed parts made from different materials, including PLA and polycarbonate, ID was found to be one of the most influential control parameters on mechanical strength.
- ID can be adjusted to optimize energy consumption and mechanical properties. By varying ID along with other control parameters, such as nozzle temperature, printing speed, and layer thickness, it is possible to find an optimal combination that balances energy efficiency and mechanical strength.
- ID is not the only control parameter that affects energy consumption and mechanical properties. Other parameters, such as raster deposition angle, nozzle temperature, printing speed, layer thickness, and bed temperature, also play a significant role.

In summary, ID is a critical control parameter in FFF/FDM 3DP, influencing both energy consumption and mechanical properties. It is possible to optimise both energy efficiency and mechanical strength by adjusting ID in conjunction with other control parameters.

4.2 Raster Deposition Angle (RDA)

The angle at which each layer of the object is printed is determined by this parameter. The angle can have an effect on the object's strength and surface finish (Vidakis et al., 2023). RDA is an FFF/FDM 3DP control parameter that influences the mechanical response and energy consumption of printed parts. The angle at which the printer head lays down each layer of material is referred to as RDA. Here are a few key RDA findings:

- RDA significantly impacts the mechanical response of 3D printed PLA parts.
- RDA is one of six printing parameters that affect energy consumption in 3DP, along with ID, nozzle temperature, printing speed, layer thickness, and bed temperature.
- RDA is one of six generic and device-independent control parameters that impact material deployment, flexural response, and energy consumption in MEX AM with PLA.
- The effect of RDA on actuating performance was investigated in a study on reversible thermo-responsive composites using PLA/paper bi-layer. Horizontal-type TRCs exhibited a greater range of average actuating performance compared with vertical-type TRCs.
- RDA is one of two printing parameters (along with infill density) that were optimized to improve the mechanical properties and electrical conductivity of 3D printed PLA composites reinforced with zinc oxide.

In general, RDA is an important parameter to consider when optimizing the mechanical response, energy consumption, and other properties of 3D printed parts.

4.3 Nozzle Temperature (NT)

The temperature at which the printer's extruder melts the filament is determined by this parameter. Temperature can have an impact on the quality and strength of a printed object (Vidakis et al., 2023). Here are a few key points to consider:

- NT affects the bending strength of 3D printed objects made of ABS material. In a study, it was found that the combination of nozzle temperature and layer height affected the flexural strength of the printed objects (Ilham et al., 2022).
- For printing with PEEK, a high-temperature material, a 3DP setup equipped with thermally stabilized modules of the printing nozzle and building chamber was developed to ensure successful manufacturing. Under optimized printing conditions, the maximal mechanical strength of the 3D printed sample attained over 80% of the original bulk property of PEEK (Jung et al., 2019).
- The emission rate of ultrafine particles during 3DP increases as nozzle temperature increases. To reduce particle emissions from 3DP, it is recommended to print at the lowest temperature possible or use low-emission materials (Jeon et al., 2020).
- NT affects the accuracy of 3DP PETG filament. In a study, it was found that layer height had the most dominant influence on accuracy, followed by nozzle temperature and printing speed (Muhammad et al., 2022).
- Jammed micro gel-based inks containing precursors of stimuli-responsive hydrogels for extrusion-based 3DP were developed. The inks exhibited shear-thinning and self healing properties that allowed extrusion through a nozzle and rapid stabilization after printing. Stimuli-mediated volume changes were observed for the extruded structures when they were post-cross linked by ultraviolet light to form interpenetrating networks of PAAm micro gels and stimuli-responsive hydrogels (Moon et al., 2022).

In review, nozzle temperature is an important parameter in 3DP that affects various aspects of the printing process and properties of the printed object. It is important to optimize nozzle temperature for specific materials and applications to achieve desired results.

4.4 Printing Speed (PS)

This setting controls how fast the printer's extruder moves across each layer of the object. A faster print speed can save time, but it can also result in lower quality or weaker objects (Vidakis et al., 2023). Printing speed is an important factor in 3DP because it influences the quality and efficiency of the process. Here are some important facts about printing speed:

- The printing speed is one of the process parameters that affect the accuracy of 3DP. The effect of changing the printing speed on the printing accuracy has been studied in experiments. The results show that the higher printing speed can lead to the defects like incomplete fill up of material in the printed parts.
- 3DP technologies manufacture objects layer by layer where each layer is composed of one or more closed 2D polygons (named as slices). As a result, the number of slices will directly affect the printing time. In addition, most 3DP technologies need extra supporting structures to support overhang regions during printing, which will largely increase manufacturing time. Therefore, optimizing the printing direction and minimizing the amount of supporting structures can reduce the number of slices and overhang areas, and thus reduce the printing time (Wang et al., 2020).
- The total cost of production must include the cost of labor, the process, and the manufacture of a product which is of utmost importance. The importance of 3DP lies in its ability to render a customized product at high speeds and with high precision (Wani & Abdullah, 2020).

- The aim of a study was to establish optimal 3DP parameters (printing direction, layer height, and percent of infill) that will allow printed gears to replace failed steel gears for at least some time, enough for spare steel gears to be produced and delivered on site. The study found that all characteristics of the manufactured parts depend on these parameters, including the percentage of infill, number of shells (outline/perimeter shells), layer height, extruder temperature, and printing speed (Mitrovic et al., 2018).

In summary, printing speed is an important parameter in 3DP that affects accuracy, efficiency, and cost. Optimizing this parameter along with other process parameters can improve the quality and efficiency of 3DP.

4.5 Layer Deposition Thickness (LT)

This parameter specifies the thickness of each layer of the object. A thicker layer can reduce print time, but it can also lead to lower quality or weaker objects (Vidakis et al., 2023). In 3DP, this parameter can also affect the quality and properties of the printed object. The following findings can be identified as important for this parameter:

- The thickness of the deposited layer determines the dimensional accuracy of products and the thickness of the deposited layer (Abramushkina et al., 2021).
- The thickness of the 3D printed tin sulfide (SnS) thin film was optimized by additive layer deposition using liquid deposition modeling (LDM) (Daniel et al., 2022).
- The residual stresses are reduced and improved mechanical properties can be achieved by increasing the value of layer thickness (Patel et al., 2022).
- The quality of parts produced by FDM process mainly depends on the selection of process parameters such as layer thickness, infill density, and speed of deposition (Sumalatha et al., 2021).
- The impact of 3DP parameters such as temperature, print speed, and layer height on mechanical parameters (strength, elasticity module), as well as on the accuracy of printing and roughness of the surface of a specimen based on thermoplastic (PLA plastic) was studied. Regression analysis was carried out to establish functional dependences of strength, elasticity module, printing precision, roughness of a surface on 3DP parameters (temperature, speed, thickness of the layer) (Vambol et al., 2021).
- A technique to improve print accuracy for layered manufacturing by filament deposition is to perform a local anti-aliasing, working at a sub-layer accuracy to produce slightly curved deposition paths and reduce approximation errors (Song et al., 2017).

In short, layer deposition thickness affects various aspects of 3DP such as dimensional accuracy, mechanical properties, and surface roughness. It is important to optimize this parameter based on the specific material and application to achieve desired results.

4.6 Bed Temperature (BT)

The temperature of the printer's build platform is determined by this parameter. The temperature of the object can affect how well it adheres to the platform during printing (Vidakis et al., 2023). The temperature of the bed is an important factor in 3DP because it affects the quality and mechanical properties of the printed parts. Several studies have been conducted to investigate the effect of bed temperature on the 3DP process. One study (Tichý et al., 2021) presented a mathematical model that describes the temperature distribution in various parts of a 3D printer that is based on AM and uses filament extrusion during operation. The model can estimate otherwise immeasurable properties such as the internal temperature of the filament during printing by calculating temperature changes in the filament (and the resulting print) during an FFF (fused filament fabrication) process.

Another study (Kechagias et al., 2022) looked at the effect of six control parameters, including bed temperature, on the mechanical properties of 3D printed PLA parts at the same time. The findings revealed that bed temperature has a significant impact on the mechanical response of 3D printed PLA parts. Furthermore, a study (Barbosa et al., 2021) assessed the effectiveness of a proposed housing for reducing the influence of printing bed temperature on electret microphone response, which is widely used as a low-cost and precise measuring device for 3DP process monitoring. The microphone housing was 3D-printed with ABS filament to separate the sensor from the heated bed and create an acoustic shell. The results showed that when operating at room temperature, the housing has a positive impact on the microphone's response. Overall, controlling the temperature of the bed is critical for producing high-quality 3D printed parts with the desired mechanical properties. Other factors that can influence 3DP include the material used, the object's design, and post-processing treatments such as annealing or polishing (Stefano et al., 2022). It is critical to optimise these parameters in order to achieve high-quality prints with few defects (Ferretti et al., 2021; Jiang et al., 2022; Kristiawan et al., 2021; Tay et al., 2022).

5. MAINTENANCE AND TROUBLESHOOTING

The importance of maintenance and troubleshooting (Bell, 2014) in 3DP cannot be overstated. Regular maintenance and proper troubleshooting techniques can assist in ensuring that the 3D printer runs smoothly and produces high-quality prints. The following are some guidelines for keeping the 3DP machine in good working order.

- Regular cleaning of the printer can prevent dust and debris from accumulating on the components and also, store the printer at a dry and cool place to prevent from moisture. A soft cloth or brush can be used to clean the exterior and compressed air canister to clean the interior.
- Apply lubricant to moving parts such as the rods and bearings to prevent friction and wear. Inspect the printer regularly for any signs of wear and tear, such as loose belts or damaged wires. Replace any worn-out parts immediately.
- Before attempting any fixes, identify the problem by observing the printer's behaviour and checking for error messages on the display or software. Make sure all cables and connections are secured and properly plugged in. Adjusting settings such as temperature, speed, and layer height can sometimes solve printing issues.
- A clogged nozzle can cause printing issues. Clean it using a nozzle cleaning kit or by heating it up and manually removing any debris.
- Updating the printer's firmware can sometimes fix bugs or issues with the software.

6. APPLICATIONS

AM has numerous applications in fields such as medicine, aerospace, automobiles, construction, the food industry, electronics, and many others. It enables the creation of personalised dosage forms and customised objects with complex geometries and integrated functional designs that would be difficult or impossible to produce using traditional manufacturing processes. Here are some examples of AM applications (Dodziuk, 2016; Muhindo et al., 2023; Parupelli & Desai, 2019; Straub, 2015; Ventola, 2014; Zhang et al., 2019):

- *Drug delivery:* 3DP has been investigated for biomedical and pharmaceutical applications and drug delivery in particular. The unique opportunity for the fabrication of personalized dosage forms is an important aspect in addressing diverse patient medical needs.
- *Customized objects:* Customized 3D objects with complex geometries and integrated functional designs can be created using 3DP. This makes it possible to create objects that would be difficult or impossible to produce using traditional manufacturing processes.
- *Electronics:* Electronic components such as sensors, antennas, and batteries have been created using 3DP. Conductive 3DP enables the development of conductive electronic devices such as LED lights and touch sensors. This technology can be especially beneficial in the development of IoT projects. 3DP enables the fabrication of low-cost sensors with unique shapes and sizes based on resistive and capacitive technologies. By enabling faster prototyping, customization, and the creation of complex components, 3DP technology is transforming the electronics industry. It also makes electronic devices more affordable and accessible to broader consumers.
- *Medical industry:* Prosthetics, implants, and surgical tools have all been created using 3DP. It's also been used to make organ models for surgical planning and training. One of the most promising medical applications of 3DP is bio-printing tissues and organoids. Using 3DP, this technique creates living tissues and organoids that can be used for drug testing, disease modelling, and even transplantation. 3DP can also be used to create patient-specific organ replicas for surgeons to practise on prior to performing complex operations. This technique has been shown to expedite procedures while minimising patient trauma.
- *Aerospace:* 3DP has been used to make lightweight aircraft and spacecraft parts. This reduces weight while improving fuel efficiency. By producing fully-functional parts, 3DP technologies enable aerospace companies to produce and evaluate multiple design variations. The engineers can put the parts through functional and durability tests. 3DP technology is used by aerospace manufacturers to design, build, and maintain both commercial and military aircraft. Some manufacturers use 3DP technologies to design and evaluate complex aircraft parts, while others 3D-print replacement parts.
- *Automobile:* 3DP has been used to make car parts such as engine components and body panels. Automotive designers can use 3DP to quickly create a prototype of a physical part or assembly, ranging from a simple interior element to a complex engine component. With manufacturing aids such as custom jigs and fixtures, 3DP can be used to reduce overhead and increase efficiency. The drive for continuous improvement in vehicle performance frequently necessitates the creation of custom tooling. Custom tooling for manufacturing processes can be created using 3DP.
- *Construction:* Building components such as walls, floors, and roofs have been created using 3DP. This method of producing construction elements or entire buildings by printing concrete, polymer,

metal, or other materials layer by layer on a 3D printer. This 3DP can save money by printing the exact measurements needed for materials, which is both cost-effective and environmentally friendly because this process produces less waste. It enhances project planning by allowing the creation of 3D construction models based on building CAD plans. This can assist in meeting clients' expectations and displaying the best design solutions. It can also produce precise and accurate sustainable construction projects with low environmental impact.

- *Food industry:* Customised food products such as chocolates, candies, and cakes have been created using 3DP. 3D printed food can give us the control we need to put a specific amount of protein, sugar, vitamins, and minerals into the foods we eat. This is especially beneficial for elderly nutrition. By allowing for precise portion control and the ability to print only what is required, this technology can help reduce food waste.
- *Defect detection:* AM can be used for defect detection in bespoke industrial manufacturing, which may be safety-critical and reduce or eliminate the need for testing of printed objects. In consumer and prototype printing, early defect detection may facilitate the printer taking corrective measures (or pausing printing and alerting a user); preventing the need to re-print objects after the compounding of a small error occurs.
- *High-performance liquid chromatography-amperometric analysis:* AM has been used to create a versatile wall-jet flow cell for high-performance liquid chromatography-amperometric analysis.

7. ADVANTAGES AND DISADVANTAGES

7.1 Advantages of AM (Carausu, n.d.; Wu et al., 2022; Zhu et al., 2021):

- Complex geometries can be produced with ease. AM allows for customization of products, as each object can be designed and printed to meet specific needs and requirements.
- Reduced waste and material usage compared to traditional manufacturing methods. AM can be more accurate than traditional processes, as it doesn't require human intervention, leaving less room for error. AM generates little waste, creating products by adding layers of material as needed. Any excess filament or powder used to create the product can also be recycled.
- Faster production times and reduced lead times. AM can produce prototypes quickly, which can be beneficial for rapid prototyping and iteration of parts and assemblies. AM can be used to produce products on demand, as needed. This means that manufacturers can make only the products that they need when they need them and don't have to worry about keeping excess inventory on hand.
- AM machines are smaller, use less energy, and don't need secondary tools, such as cooling systems. The energy savings can be significant enough to offset the cost of purchasing equipment in just a few years.

7.2 Disadvantages of AM (Carausu, n.d.; Kozak et al., 2021; Tang et al., 2021; Wu et al., 2022; Zhu et al., 2021):

- Limited material selection compared to traditional manufacturing methods. AM can be limited by the materials that are available for printing, as not all materials are suitable for the process.
- Surface finish and dimensional accuracy may not be as good as traditional manufacturing methods. AM requires strict quality control to ensure that the printed object meets the desired specifications, which can be challenging. Quality control can be challenging due to the layer-by-layer nature of the process.
- High initial investment cost for equipment and materials. AM can be more expensive than traditional manufacturing methods, as the equipment and materials required can be costly.
- Post-processing may be required to achieve desired surface finish or mechanical properties.
- Limited production volume compared to traditional manufacturing methods. AM is limited by the size of the printer, which can be a disadvantage for larger products.

8. CHALLENGES

There are currently a number of technological challenges. The high cost of AM equipment and materials, which require trained personnel to operate, is one of the most significant challenges. Furthermore, AM can have lower accuracy and repeatability than traditional methods, and there may be issues with the surface finish of 3D printed objects. Slow production speeds, materials development, and inconsistencies in material properties, manual post-processing, size limitations, and the inability to produce parts in multiple materials are among the other challenges. The adoption of globally recognised standards in a variety of industries will also aid AM in gaining a stronger foothold in the manufacturing landscape. To overcome these obstacles, it is critical to collaborate with an experienced AM partner who understands the entire workflow, including pre- and post-processing.

9. FUTURE SCOPE

Since its inception in the 1980s, AM has come a long way and has quickly taken over the manufacturing industry. The future scope of AM is vast and has the potential to revolutionise a variety of industries; it appears limitless and is expected to have a significant impact on a variety of sectors, including medicine, aerospace, and automotive, to name a few. Here are a few examples of how AM is expected to shape the future (Gao et al., 2015; Parupelli & Desai, 2019; Uriondo et al., 2015; Yang, 2022):

9.1 Mass Customization

AM enables the mass production of customised products. This technology is expected to be used in the future to create personalised products for individuals, such as custom-fit shoes or prosthetics. The aerospace and automotive industries will benefit greatly from AM as well. 3DP, with its ability to create complex structures and geometries that traditional manufacturing processes cannot, can help reduce the weight of parts and increase the efficiency of engines and other systems.

9.2 Sustainable Manufacturing

Because it produces less waste and uses fewer materials, AM is a more environmentally friendly option. This technology is expected to be used in the future to create more sustainable products, lowering the manufacturing industry's carbon footprint. Furthermore, the use of 3DP in these industries could result in shorter design-to-production cycles, lowering costs and increasing market speed.

9.3 Medical Advancements

The potential for AM to revolutionise healthcare is one of the most exciting prospects. In the medical industry, AM is already being used to create custom implants and prosthetics. 3DP has the potential to change the face of medicine, from customised prosthetics to personalised implants. The ability to print human organs from a patient's own cells has the potential to transform transplant surgeries. This technology is expected to be used to create organs and tissues for transplantation in the future, revolutionising the medical field. Furthermore, 3DP has the potential to accelerate the development and testing of new medicines, making it an indispensable tool for pharmaceutical companies.

9.4 Space Exploration

Parts for space missions have already been created using AM. This technology is expected to be used in the future to build structures and habitats in space, allowing for long-term space exploration missions.

9.5 Smart Manufacturing

AM is a critical component of Industry 4.0, which entails the integration of cutting-edge technologies such as the Internet of Things (IoT) and artificial intelligence (AI). In the future, AM is expected to play a significant role in the smart manufacturing revolution, allowing factories to operate more efficiently and effectively.

In general, the future of AM is bright, and the technology's potential applications are numerous. Technology is expected to transform various industries and lead to new innovations as it continues to evolve.

CONCLUSION

To summarise, the research on AM using 3DP machines and 3DP pens has shown great promise in terms of revolutionising the manufacturing industry. This technology has made it possible to create complex and intricate designs that were previously impossible to create using traditional manufacturing methods. 3D printers and pens also provide greater flexibility and customization options, allowing designers to create one-of-a-kind products for specific needs. Furthermore, because it reduces waste and uses fewer materials, the technology is more environmentally friendly. The various 3DP methods and machine and pen types available on the market provide a diverse range of AM applications. The future scope of

AM is vast, ranging from creating customised products to revolutionising the medical field and even space exploration. However, there are still limitations and challenges to overcome, such as the high cost of materials and machines, a lack of standardisation, and the need for more research and development. These obstacles can be overcome as technology evolves and becomes more accessible. Overall, 3DP technology has enormous potential in AM, and it has already made significant contributions to a variety of industries. This research provided an overview of the current state of technology, as well as its potential applications and limitations. Further research and development in this field will almost certainly result in new innovations and advancements, making AM an even more important part of the manufacturing industry in the future.

REFERENCES

Abdella, S., Youssef, S. H., Afinjuomo, F., Song, Y., Fouladian, P., Upton, R., & Garg, S. (2021). 3D Printing of thermo-sensitive drugs. *Pharmaceutics*, *13*(9), 1524. doi:10.3390/pharmaceutics13091524 PMID:34575600

Abramushkina, O.I., Uzorina, M.I., Surikov, P.V., & Ushakova, O.B. (2021). Investigation of the rheological behavior of ABS plastic grades for the production of filaments for 3D printing by layer-by-layer deposition. *Plasticheskie Massy*.

Additive Manufacturing. (n.d.). https://www.additivemanufacturing.media/articles/finally-a-polypropylene-you-can-3d-print

Agha, A., Waheed, W., Alamoodi, N., Mathew, B., Alnaimat, F., Abu-Nada, E., & Alazzam, A. (2022). A review of cyclic olefin copolymer applications in microfluidics and microdevices. *Macromolecular Materials and Engineering*, *307*(8), 2200053. doi:10.1002/mame.202200053

Alifui-Segbaya, F. (2018). Toxicological assessment of photopolymers in additive manufacturing using the innovative zebrafish embryo model. School of Dentistry and Oral Health, Griffith Health, Griffith University.

Altıparmak, S. C., Yardley, V. A., Shi, Z., & Lin, J. (2021). Challenges in additive manufacturing of high-strength aluminium alloys and current developments in hybrid additive manufacturing. *International Journal of Lightweight Materials and Manufacture*, *4*(2), 246–261. doi:10.1016/j.ijlmm.2020.12.004

Andreacola, F. R., Capasso, I., Pilotti, L., & Brando, G. (2021). Influence of 3d-printing parameters on the mechanical properties of 17-4PH stainless steel produced through Selective Laser Melting. *Frattura ed Integrità Strutturale, 15*(58), 282-295.

Asicioglu, F., Yilmaz, A. S., de Kinder, J., Pekacar, I., & Gelir, A. (2022). A novel 3D scan-based optical method for analyzing lines drawn at different pen pressure. *Forensic Science International*, *338*, 111388. doi:10.1016/j.forsciint.2022.111388 PMID:35907278

Babu, S. S., Raghavan, N., Raplee, J., Foster, S. J., Frederick, C., Haines, M., & Dehoff, R. R. (2018). Additive manufacturing of nickel superalloys: Opportunities for innovation and challenges related to qualification. *Metallurgical and Materials Transactions. A, Physical Metallurgy and Materials Science*, *49*(9), 3764–3780. doi:10.100711661-018-4702-4

Barazanchi, A., Li, K. C., Al-Amleh, B., Lyons, K., & Waddell, J. N. (2020). Mechanical properties of laser-sintered 3D-printed cobalt chromium and soft-milled cobalt chromium. *Prosthesis*, *2*(4), 28. doi:10.3390/prosthesis2040028

Barbosa, L., Lopes, T. G., Aguiar, P. R., de Oliveira, R. G. Junior, & França, T. V. (2021). Evaluating Temperature Influence on Low-Cost Microphone Response for 3D Printing Process Monitoring. *Engineering Proceedings*, *10*(1), 67.

Bedmar, J., Riquelme, A., Rodrigo, P., Torres, B., & Rams, J. (2021). Comparison of different additive manufacturing methods for 316l stainless steel. *Materials (Basel)*, *14*(21), 6504. doi:10.3390/ma14216504 PMID:34772039

Bell, C. (2014). *Maintaining and troubleshooting your 3D printer*. Apress. doi:10.1007/978-1-4302-6808-6

Berselli, G., Vertechy, R., Pellicciari, M., & Vassura, G. (2011). Hyperelastic modeling of rubber-like photopolymers for additive manufacturing processes. In M. Hoque (Ed.), *Rapid Prototyping Technology-Principles and Functional Requirements* (pp. 135–152). IntechOpen Ltd. doi:10.5772/20174

Bogue, R. (2013). 3D printing: The dawn of a new era in manufacturing? *Assembly Automation*, *33*(4), 307–311. doi:10.1108/AA-06-2013-055

Bonada, J., Xuriguera, E., Calvo, L., Poudelet, L., Cardona, R., Padilla, J. A., Niubó, M., & Fenollosa, F. (2019). Analysis of printing parameters for metal additive manufactured parts through Direct Ink Writing process. *Procedia Manufacturing*, *41*, 666–673. doi:10.1016/j.promfg.2019.09.056

Carausu, C. (n.d.). *Selection of Subtractive Manufacturing Technology Versus Additive Manufacturing Technology for Rapid Prototyping of a Polymeric Product*. Academic Press.

Chua, C. K., & Sing, S. L. (2022). Editors' foreword to the inaugural issue of Materials Science in Additive Manufacturing. *Materials Science in Additive Manufacturing*, *1*(1), 2. doi:10.18063/msam.v1i1.2

Daniel, T. O., Nmadu, D., Ali, S. O., Amadi, S. O., & Onuegbu, S. C. (2022). Liquid deposition modelling 3D printing of semiconductor tin sulphide (SnS) thin film for application in optoelectronic and electronic devices. *Revista Mexicana de Física*, *68*(5). Advance online publication. doi:10.31349/RevMexFis.68.051001

Dixit, S., & Liu, S. (2022). Laser Additive Manufacturing of High-Strength Aluminum Alloys: Challenges and Strategies. *Journal of Manufacturing and Materials Processing*, *6*(6), 156. doi:10.3390/jmmp6060156

Dodziuk, H. (2016). Applications of 3D printing in healthcare. *Kardiochirurgia i Torakochirurgia Polska/ Polish. The Journal of Thoracic and Cardiovascular Surgery*, *13*(3), 283–293.

Dominguez, J., & Gonzalez, P. (2022, June). Micro-Architected Lattice-Based Mesh for Fiber Filters: A Novel Additive Manufacturing Architecture for Molded Fiber Tooling. In *International Manufacturing Science and Engineering Conference* (*Vol. 85802*, p. V001T04A002). American Society of Mechanical Engineers. 10.1115/MSEC2022-85305

Du, W., Ren, X., Chen, Y., Ma, C., Radovic, M., & Pei, Z. (2018, June). Model guided mixing of ceramic powders with graded particle sizes in binder jetting additive manufacturing. In *International Manufacturing Science and Engineering Conference* (*Vol. 51357*, p. V001T01A014). American Society of Mechanical Engineers. 10.1115/MSEC2018-6651

Du, W., Ren, X., Pei, Z., & Ma, C. (2020). Ceramic binder jetting additive manufacturing: A literature review on density. *Journal of Manufacturing Science and Engineering*, *142*(4), 040801. doi:10.1115/1.4046248

Dzogbewu, T. C., & du Preez, W. B. (2021). Additive manufacturing of titanium-based implants with metal-based antimicrobial agents. *Metals*, *11*(3), 453. doi:10.3390/met11030453

Elbardisy, H. M., Richter, E. M., Crapnell, R. D., Down, M. P., Gough, P. G., Belal, T. S., & Banks, C. E. (2020). Versatile additively manufactured (3D printed) wall-jet flow cell for high performance liquid chromatography-amperometric analysis: Application to the detection and quantification of new psychoactive substances (NBOMes). *Analytical Methods*, *12*(16), 2152–2165. doi:10.1039/D0AY00500B

Elkaseer, A., Chen, K. J., Janhsen, J. C., Refle, O., Hagenmeyer, V., & Scholz, S. G. (2022). Material jetting for advanced applications: A state-of-the-art review, gaps and future directions. *Additive Manufacturing*, *60*, 103270. doi:10.1016/j.addma.2022.103270

Elsayed, H., Zocca, A., Schmidt, J., Günster, J., Colombo, P., & Bernardo, E. (2018). Bioactive glass-ceramic scaffolds by additive manufacturing and sinter-crystallization of fine glass powders. *Journal of Materials Research*, *33*(14), 1960–1971. doi:10.1557/jmr.2018.120

Eos. (n.d.). https://www.eos.info/en/3d-printing-materials/metals/cobalt-chrome

Faidallah, R. F., Szakál, Z., & Oldal, I. (2021). Introduction to 3d printing: Techniques, materials and agricultural applications. *Hungarian Agricultural Engineering*, (40), 47–58. doi:10.17676/HAE.2021.40.47

Farashi, S., & Vafaee, F. (2022). Effect of printing parameters on the tensile strength of FDM 3D samples: a meta-analysis focusing on layer thickness and sample orientation. *Progress in Additive Manufacturing*, 1-18.

Farina, I., Singh, N., Colangelo, F., Luciano, R., Bonazzi, G., & Fraternali, F. (2019). High-performance nylon-6 sustainable filaments for additive manufacturing. *Materials (Basel)*, *12*(23), 3955. doi:10.3390/ma12233955 PMID:31795290

Ferreira, I., Vale, D., Machado, M., & Lino, J. (2019). Additive manufacturing of polyethylene terephthalate glycol/carbon fiber composites: An experimental study from filament to printed parts. *Proceedings of the Institution of Mechanical Engineers, Part L: Journal of Materials: Design and Applications*, *233*(9), 1866-1878.

Ferretti, P., Leon-Cardenas, C., Santi, G. M., Sali, M., Ciotti, E., Frizziero, L., & Liverani, A. (2021). Relationship between FDM 3D printing parameters study: Parameter optimization for lower defects. *Polymers*, *13*(13), 2190. doi:10.3390/polym13132190 PMID:34209372

Flores Ituarte, I., Wiikinkoski, O., & Jansson, A. (2018). Additive manufacturing of polypropylene: A screening design of experiment using laser-based powder bed fusion. *Polymers*, *10*(12), 1293. doi:10.3390/polym10121293 PMID:30961218

Fongsamootr, T., Thawon, I., Tippayawong, N., Tippayawong, K. Y., & Suttakul, P. (2022). Effect of print parameters on additive manufacturing of metallic parts: Performance and sustainability aspects. *Scientific Reports*, *12*(1), 19292. doi:10.103841598-022-22613-2 PMID:36369254

Foteinopoulos, P., Esnault, V., Komineas, G., Papacharalampopoulos, A., & Stavropoulos, P. (2020). Cement-based additive manufacturing: Experimental investigation of process quality. *International Journal of Advanced Manufacturing Technology*, *106*(11-12), 4815–4826. doi:10.100700170-020-04978-8

Furka, S., Furka, D., Dadi, N. C. T. C. T., Palacka, P., Hromníková, D., Santana, J. A. D., & Bujdak, J. (2021). Novel antimicrobial materials designed for the 3D printing of medical devices used during the COVID-19 crisis. *Rapid Prototyping Journal*, *27*(5), 890–904. doi:10.1108/RPJ-09-2020-0219

Gao, W., Zhang, Y., Ramanujan, D., Ramani, K., Chen, Y., Williams, C. B., Wang, C. C. L., Shin, Y. C., Zhang, S., & Zavattieri, P. D. (2015). The status, challenges, and future of additive manufacturing in engineering. *Computer Aided Design*, *69*, 65–89. doi:10.1016/j.cad.2015.04.001

Gatões, D., Alves, R., Alves, B., & Vieira, M. T. (2022). Selective Laser Melting and Mechanical Properties of Stainless Steels. *Materials (Basel)*, *15*(21), 7575. doi:10.3390/ma15217575 PMID:36363178

Gogoi & Jeyapoovan. (2016). Design and analysis of 3d printing pen. *International Journal of Engineering Sciences & Research Technology*.

Gokhare, V. G., Raut, D. N., & Shinde, D. K. (2017). A review paper on 3D-printing aspects and various processes used in the 3D-printing. *International Journal of Engineering Research & Technology (Ahmedabad)*, *6*(06), 953–958.

Gong, K., Liu, H., Huang, C., Cao, Z., Fuenmayor, E., & Major, I. (2022). Hybrid Manufacturing of Acrylonitrile Butadiene Styrene (ABS) via the Combination of Material Extrusion Additive Manufacturing and Injection Molding. *Polymers*, *14*(23), 5093. doi:10.3390/polym14235093 PMID:36501488

Graybill, B., Li, M., Malawey, D., Ma, C., Alvarado-Orozco, J. M., & Martinez-Franco, E. (2018, June). Additive manufacturing of nickel-based superalloys. In *International Manufacturing Science and Engineering Conference* (*Vol. 51357*, p. V001T01A015). American Society of Mechanical Engineers.

Guerra, A. J., Lammel-Lindemann, J., Katko, A., Kleinfehn, A., Rodriguez, C. A., Catalani, L. H., & Dean, D. (2019). Optimization of photocrosslinkable resin components and 3D printing process parameters. *Acta Biomaterialia*, *97*, 154–161. doi:10.1016/j.actbio.2019.07.045 PMID:31352105

Guo, Z., Grijpma, D., & Poot, A. (2020). Leachable poly (trimethylene carbonate)/CaCO3 composites for additive manufacturing of microporous vascular structures. *Materials (Basel)*, *13*(15), 3435. doi:10.3390/ma13153435 PMID:32759759

Haghdadi, N., Laleh, M., Moyle, M., & Primig, S. (2021). Additive manufacturing of steels: A review of achievements and challenges. *Journal of Materials Science*, *56*(1), 64–107. doi:10.100710853-020-05109-0

Han, S. B., Lee, Y. S., Park, S. H., & Song, H. (2023). Ti-containing 316L stainless steels with excellent tensile properties fabricated by directed energy deposition additive manufacturing. *Materials Science and Engineering A*, *862*, 144414. doi:10.1016/j.msea.2022.144414

Hmeidat, N. S., Kemp, J. W., & Compton, B. G. (2018, March). High-strength epoxy nanocomposites for 3D printing. *Composites Science and Technology*, *160*, 9–20. Advance online publication. doi:10.1016/j.compscitech.2018.03.008

Hudak, R., Schnitzer, M., & Zivcak, J. (2021, January). Additive Manufacturing in Medicine and Tissue Engineering: Plenary Talk. In *2021 IEEE 19th World Symposium on Applied Machine Intelligence and Informatics (SAMI)* (pp. 11-12). IEEE.

Ilham, A., Arafat, A., Rifelino, R., & Nurdin, H. (2022). Pengaruh nozzle temperature dan layer height hasil 3d printing terhadap uji bending materiai abs. *Jurnal Vokasi Mekanika*, *4*(1), 144–150. doi:10.24036/vomek.v4i1.332

Ingrassia, T., Nigrelli, V., Ricotta, V., & Tartamella, C. (2017). Process parameters influence in additive manufacturing. In *Advances on Mechanics, Design Engineering and Manufacturing: Proceedings of the International Joint Conference on Mechanics, Design Engineering & Advanced Manufacturing (JCM 2016), 14-16 September, 2016, Catania, Italy* (pp. 261-270). Springer International Publishing. 10.1007/978-3-319-45781-9_27

Jaksic, N. I. (2015, June). BYOE: Using 3D Pens for Enhancement and Rework of 3D-Printed Parts. In *2015 ASEE Annual Conference & Exposition* (pp. 26-317). 10.18260/p.23656

Jeon, H., Park, J., Kim, S., Park, K., & Yoon, C. (2020). Effect of nozzle temperature on the emission rate of ultrafine particles during 3D printing. *Indoor Air*, *30*(2), 306–314. doi:10.1111/ina.12624 PMID:31743481

Jiang, C. P., Cheng, Y. C., Lin, H. W., Chang, Y. L., Pasang, T., & Lee, S. Y. (2022). Optimization of FDM 3D printing parameters for high strength PEEK using the Taguchi method and experimental validation. *Rapid Prototyping Journal*, *28*(7), 1260–1271. doi:10.1108/RPJ-07-2021-0166

Jiang, Q., Zhang, P., Yu, Z., Shi, H., Wu, D., Yan, H., & Tian, Y. (2021). A review on additive manufacturing of pure copper. *Coatings*, *11*(6), 740. doi:10.3390/coatings11060740

Jin, M., Neuber, C., & Schmidt, H. W. (2020). Tailoring polypropylene for extrusion-based additive manufacturing. *Additive Manufacturing*, *33*, 101101. doi:10.1016/j.addma.2020.101101

Johnston, T. G., Fellin, C. R., Carignano, A., & Nelson, A. (2019, May). Additive manufacturing of catalytically active living material hydrogels. In *Micro-and Nanotechnology Sensors, Systems, and Applications XI* (Vol. 10982, pp. 19–26). SPIE. doi:10.1117/12.2518653

Jung, H. D., Jang, T. S., Lee, J. E., Park, S. J., Son, Y., & Park, S. H. (2019). Enhanced bioactivity of titanium-coated polyetheretherketone implants created by a high-temperature 3D printing process. *Biofabrication*, *11*(4), 045014. doi:10.1088/1758-5090/ab376b PMID:31365916

Kalia, K., Francoeur, B., Amirkhizi, A., & Ameli, A. (2022). In situ foam 3D printing of microcellular structures using material extrusion additive manufacturing. *ACS Applied Materials & Interfaces*, *14*(19), 22454–22465. doi:10.1021/acsami.2c03014 PMID:35522894

Kechagias, J. D., Vidakis, N., Petousis, M., & Mountakis, N. (2022). A multi-parametric process evaluation of the mechanical response of PLA in FFF 3D printing. *Materials and Manufacturing Processes*, *38*(8), 941–953. doi:10.1080/10426914.2022.2089895

Khalid, M., & Peng, Q. (2021). Investigation of printing parameters of additive manufacturing process for sustainability using design of experiments. *Journal of Mechanical Design*, *143*(3), 032001. doi:10.1115/1.4049521

Konieczny, B., Szczesio-Wlodarczyk, A., Sokolowski, J., & Bociong, K. (2020). Challenges of Co–Cr alloy additive manufacturing methods in dentistry—The current state of knowledge (systematic review). *Materials (Basel)*, *13*(16), 3524. doi:10.3390/ma13163524 PMID:32785055

Korniejenko, K., Łach, M., Chou, S. Y., Lin, W. T., Cheng, A., Hebdowska-Krupa, M., & Mikuła, J. (2020). Mechanical properties of short fiber-reinforced geopolymers made by casted and 3D printing methods: A comparative study. *Materials (Basel)*, *13*(3), 579. doi:10.3390/ma13030579 PMID:31991886

Kozak, J., Zakrzewski, T., Witt, M., & Dębowska-Wąsak, M. (2021). Selected problems of additive manufacturing using SLS/SLM processes. *Transactions on Aerospace Research*, *2021*(1), 24–44. doi:10.2478/tar-2021-0003

Kreft, K., Lavrič, Z., Stanić, T., Perhavec, P., & Dreu, R. (2022). Influence of the Binder Jetting Process Parameters and Binder Liquid Composition on the Relevant Attributes of 3D-Printed Tablets. *Pharmaceutics*, *14*(8), 1568. doi:10.3390/pharmaceutics14081568 PMID:36015194

Kristiawan, R. B., Imaduddin, F., Ariawan, D., & Arifin, Z. (2021). A review on the fused deposition modeling (FDM) 3D printing: Filament processing, materials, and printing parameters. *Open Engineering*, *11*(1), 639–649. doi:10.1515/eng-2021-0063

Lecis, N., Beltrami, R., & Mariani, M. (2021). Binder jetting 3D printing of 316 stainless steel: Influence of process parameters on microstructural and mechanical properties. *La Metallurgia Italiana*, *113*, 31–41.

Liu, C., Le, L., Zhang, M., & Ding, J. (2022). Tunable Large-Scale Compressive Strain Sensor Based on Carbon Nanotube/Polydimethylsiloxane Foam Composites by Additive Manufacturing. *Advanced Engineering Materials*, *24*(6), 2101337. doi:10.1002/adem.202101337

Liu, J., Nguyen-Van, V., Panda, B., Fox, K., du Plessis, A., & Tran, P. (2022). Additive manufacturing of sustainable construction materials and form-finding structures: a review on recent progresses. *3D Printing and Additive Manufacturing*, *9*(1), 12-34.

Lopatina, Y., & Filippova, A. (2020). Research of composition porosity based on 3d-printed frames and impregnated with epoxy resin. *Modern Power Engineering (MPMB 2020) IOP Conf. Series: Materials Science and Engineering*, *963*.10.1088/1757-899X/963/1/012031

Łyszczarz, E., Brniak, W., Szafraniec-Szczęsny, J., Majka, T. M., Majda, D., Zych, M., & Jachowicz, R. (2021). The impact of the preparation method on the properties of orodispersible films with aripiprazole: Electrospinning vs. casting and 3D printing methods. *Pharmaceutics*, *13*(8), 1122. doi:10.3390/pharmaceutics13081122 PMID:34452083

Mahmood, M. A., Ur Rehman, A., Ristoscu, C., Demir, M., Popescu-Pelin, G., Pitir, F., & Mihailescu, I. N. (2022). Advances in Laser Additive Manufacturing of Cobalt–Chromium Alloy Multi-Layer Mesoscopic Analytical Modelling with Experimental Correlations: From Micro-Dendrite Grains to Bulk Objects. *Nanomaterials (Basel, Switzerland), 12*(5), 802. doi:10.3390/nano12050802 PMID:35269291

Mallegni, N., Milazzo, M., Cristallini, C., Barbani, N., Fredi, G., Dorigato, A., & Danti, S. (2023). Characterization of Cyclic Olefin Copolymers for Insulin Reservoir in an Artificial Pancreas. *Journal of Functional Biomaterials*, *14*(3), 145. doi:10.3390/jfb14030145 PMID:36976069

Manning, K. L., Feder, J., Kanellias, M., Murphy, J. III, & Morgan, J. R. (2020). Toward automated additive manufacturing of living bio-tubes using ring-shaped building units. *SLAS Technology*, *25*(6), 608–620. doi:10.1177/2472630320920896 PMID:32452278

Mitrovic, R., Miskovic, Z., Ristivojevic, M., Dimic, A., Danko, J., Bucha, J., & Rackov, M. (2018, July). Determination of optimal parameters for rapid prototyping of the involute gears. *IOP Conference Series. Materials Science and Engineering*, *393*(1), 012105. doi:10.1088/1757-899X/393/1/012105

Mohammed, A., & Al-Saadi, N. T. K. (2020). Ultra-high early strength cementitious grout suitable for additive manufacturing applications fabricated by using graphene oxide and viscosity modifying agents. *Polymers*, *12*(12), 2900. doi:10.3390/polym12122900 PMID:33287399

Moon, D., Lee, M. G., Sun, J. Y., Song, K. H., & Doh, J. (2022). Jammed Microgel-Based Inks for 3D Printing of Complex Structures Transformable via pH/Temperature Variations. *Macromolecular Rapid Communications*, *43*(19), 2200271. doi:10.1002/marc.202200271 PMID:35686322

Msallem, B., Sharma, N., Cao, S., Halbeisen, F. S., Zeilhofer, H. F., & Thieringer, F. M. (2020). Evaluation of the dimensional accuracy of 3D-printed anatomical mandibular models using FFF, SLA, SLS, MJ, and BJ printing technology. *Journal of Clinical Medicine*, *9*(3), 817. doi:10.3390/jcm9030817 PMID:32192099

Muhammad, A. R., Sakura, R. R., Dwilaksana, D., & Trifiananto, M. (2022). Layer Height, Temperature Nozzle, Infill Geometry and Printing Speed Effect on Accuracy 3D Printing PETG. *REM (Rekayasa Energi Manufaktur) Jurnal*, *7*(2), 81–88.

Muhindo, D., Elkanayati, R., Srinivasan, P., Repka, M. A., & Ashour, E. A. (2023). Recent advances in the applications of additive manufacturing (3D printing) in drug delivery: A comprehensive review. *AAPS PharmSciTech*, *24*(2), 57. doi:10.120812249-023-02524-9 PMID:36759435

Murkute, Gaikwad, Kathar, Sanap, & Raut. (2022). 3D printing technology and short introduction in 3D bio-printed matrices for in vitro tumor model. *International Journal of Science & Engineering Development Research, 7*(2), 217 – 228.

Ngo, T. D., Kashani, A., Imbalzano, G., Nguyen, K. T., & Hui, D. (2018). Additive manufacturing (3D printing): A review of materials, methods, applications and challenges. *Composites. Part B, Engineering*, *143*, 172–196. doi:10.1016/j.compositesb.2018.02.012

Nofar, M., Utz, J., Geis, N., Altstädt, V., & Ruckdäschel, H. (2022). Foam 3D printing of thermoplastics: A symbiosis of additive manufacturing and foaming technology. *Advancement of Science*, *9*(11), 2105701. doi:10.1002/advs.202105701 PMID:35187843

Okkalidis, N. (2022). 3D printing methods for radiological anthropomorphic phantoms. *Physics in Medicine and Biology*, *67*(15), 15TR04. doi:10.1088/1361-6560/ac80e7 PMID:35830787

Pack, R. C., Romberg, S. K., Badran, A. A., Hmeidat, N. S., Yount, T., & Compton, B. G. (2020). Carbon fiber and syntactic foam hybrid materials via core–shell material extrusion additive manufacturing. *Advanced Materials Technologies*, *5*(12), 2000731. doi:10.1002/admt.202000731

Parupelli, S., & Desai, S. (2019). A comprehensive review of additive manufacturing (3d printing): Processes, applications and future potential. *American Journal of Applied Sciences*, *16*(8), 244–272. doi:10.3844/ajassp.2019.244.272

Patel, R., Dhimmar, V., Kagzi, S., & Patel, M. (2022). Investigation of Fused Deposition Modelling Process Parameters in 3D Printing for Composite Material (Poly Lactic Acid and Banana Fibre). *International Journal of Automotive and Mechanical Engineering*, *19*(3), 10028–10038. doi:10.15282/ijame.19.3.2022.14.0774

Paz, E., Jiménez, M., Romero, L., Espinosa, M. D. M., & Domínguez, M. (2021). Characterization of the resistance to abrasive chemical agents of test specimens of thermoplastic elastomeric polyurethane composite materials produced by additive manufacturing. *Journal of Applied Polymer Science*, *138*(32), 50791. doi:10.1002/app.50791

Peerzada, A. B., Rangaraju, P., Roberts, J., & Biehl, A. (2022). Influence of External Vibration on the Gravitational Flow Characteristics of Cementitious Materials: A Perspective from Application in Additive Manufacturing. *Transportation Research Record: Journal of the Transportation Research Board*, *2676*(7), 379–394. doi:10.1177/03611981221078572

Pires, L. S. O., Afonso, D. G., Fernandes, M. H. F. V., & de Oliveira, J. M. M. (2023). Improvement of processability characteristics of porcelain-based formulations toward the utilization of 3D printing technology. *3D Printing and Additive Manufacturing, 10*(2), 298-309.

Rad, A. S. (2008). *Persual on synthesis, pattern and applications of polyurethane as functional macromolecule*. Academic Press.

Recalde, I., Gualdrón-Reyes, A. F., Echeverría-Arrondo, C., Villanueva-Antolí, A., Simancas, J., Rodriguez-Pereira, J., & Sans, V. (2023). Vitamins as Active Agents for Highly Emissive and Stable Nanostructured Halide Perovskite Inks and 3D Composites Fabricated by Additive Manufacturing. *Advanced Functional Materials*, *33*(8), 2210802. doi:10.1002/adfm.202210802

Revilla-León, M., Sadeghpour, M., & Özcan, M. (2020). A review of the applications of additive manufacturing technologies used to fabricate metals in implant dentistry. *Journal of Prosthodontics*, *29*(7), 579–593. doi:10.1111/jopr.13212 PMID:32548890

Righetti, G., Zilio, C., Savio, G., Meneghello, R., Calati, M., & Mancin, S. (2021, November). Experimental pressure drops during the water flow into porous materials realized via additive manufacturing. *Journal of Physics: Conference Series*, *2116*(1), 012059. doi:10.1088/1742-6596/2116/1/012059

Romeijn, T., Behrens, M., Paul, G., & Wei, D. (2022). Instantaneous and long-term mechanical properties of Polyethylene Terephthalate Glycol (PETG) additively manufactured by pellet-based material extrusion. *Additive Manufacturing*, *59*, 103145. doi:10.1016/j.addma.2022.103145

Šafka, J., Ackermann, M., Véle, F., Macháček, J., & Henyš, P. (2021). Mechanical properties of polypropylene: Additive manufacturing by multi jet fusion technology. *Materials (Basel), 14*(9), 2165. doi:10.3390/ma14092165 PMID:33922827

Saha, A., Johnston, T. G., Shafranek, R. T., Goodman, C. J., Zalatan, J. G., Storti, D. W., & Nelson, A. (2018). Additive manufacturing of catalytically active living materials. *ACS Applied Materials & Interfaces, 10*(16), 13373–13380. doi:10.1021/acsami.8b02719 PMID:29608267

Sakib-Uz-Zaman, C., & Khondoker, M. A. H. (2023). A Review on Extrusion Additive Manufacturing of Pure Copper. *Metals, 13*(5), 859. doi:10.3390/met13050859

Salari, F., Bosetti, P., & Sglavo, V. M. (2022). Binder Jetting 3D Printing of Magnesium Oxychloride Cement-Based Materials: Parametric Analysis of Manufacturing Factors. *Journal of Manufacturing and Materials Processing, 6*(4), 86. doi:10.3390/jmmp6040086

Salmi, M., Ituarte, I. F., Chekurov, S., & Huotilainen, E. (2016). Effect of build orientation in 3D printing production for material extrusion, material jetting, binder jetting, sheet object lamination, vat photopolymerisation, and powder bed fusion. *International Journal of Collaborative Enterprise, 5*(3-4), 218–231. doi:10.1504/IJCENT.2016.082334

Schönherr, J. A., Baumgartner, S., Hartmann, M., & Stampfl, J. (2020). Stereolithographic additive manufacturing of high precision glass ceramic parts. *Materials (Basel), 13*(7), 1492. doi:10.3390/ma13071492 PMID:32218270

Self, J. L., Xiao, H., Hausladen, M. M., Bramanto, R. A., Usgaonkar, S. S., & Ellison, C. J. (2022). Camphene as a Mild, Bio-Derived Porogen for Near-Ambient Processing and 3D Printing of Porous Thermoplastics. *ACS Applied Materials & Interfaces, 14*(43), 49244–49253. doi:10.1021/acsami.2c16192 PMID:36279408

Shahrubudin, N., Lee, T. C., & Ramlan, R. (2019). An Overview on 3D Printing Technology: Technological, Materials, and Applications. *2nd International Conference on Sustainable Materials Processing and Manufacturing (SMPM 2019).*

Shakor, P., Nejadi, S., Paul, G., & Malek, S. (2019). Review of emerging additive manufacturing technologies in 3D printing of cementitious materials in the construction industry. *Frontiers in Built Environment, 4*, 85. doi:10.3389/fbuil.2018.00085

Sieradzka, M., Fabia, J., Biniaś, D., Graczyk, T., & Fryczkowski, R. (2021). High-impact polystyrene reinforced with reduced graphene oxide as a filament for fused filament fabrication 3D printing. *Materials (Basel), 14*(22), 7008. doi:10.3390/ma14227008 PMID:34832407

Song, H. C., Ray, N., Sokolov, D., & Lefebvre, S. (2017). Anti-aliasing for fused filament deposition. *Computer Aided Design, 89*, 25–34. doi:10.1016/j.cad.2017.04.001

Srinivasan, D., Meignanamoorthy, M., Ravichandran, M., Mohanavel, V., Alagarsamy, S. V., Chanakyan, C., Sakthivelu, S., Karthick, A., Prabhu, T. R., & Rajkumar, S. (2021). 3D printing manufacturing techniques, materials, and applications: An overview. *Advances in Materials Science and Engineering, 2021*, 1–10. doi:10.1155/2021/5756563

Stefano, J. S., Kalinke, C., da Rocha, R. G., Rocha, D. P., da Silva, V. A. O. P., Bonacin, J. A., & Muñoz, R. A. A. (2022). *Electrochemical (bio) sensors enabled by fused deposition modeling-based 3D printing: A guide to selecting designs, printing parameters, and post-treatment protocols*. Academic Press.

Stiles, A., Tison, T. A., Pruitt, L., & Vaidya, U. (2022). Photoinitiator selection and concentration in photopolymer formulations towards large-format additive manufacturing. *Polymers*, *14*(13), 2708. doi:10.3390/polym14132708 PMID:35808752

Straub, J. (2015). Initial work on the characterization of additive manufacturing (3D printing) using software image analysis. *Machines*, *3*(2), 55–71. doi:10.3390/machines3020055

Sumalatha, M., Malleswara Rao, J. N., & Supraja Reddy, B. (2021). Optimization Of Process Parameters In 3d Printing-Fused Deposition Modeling Using Taguchi Method. *IOP Conference Series. Materials Science and Engineering*, *1112*(1), 1112. doi:10.1088/1757-899X/1112/1/012009

Suta, M. J., Béresová, M., Csámer, L., Csík, A., & Hegedűs, C. (2022). Evaluation of Polyjet and SLA 3D printers. *Fogorvosi Szemle, 115*(2), 64-68.

Sutton, J. (2019). *Evaluation of Lignin-containing Photopolymers for use in Additive Manufacturing*. Academic Press.

Takahashi & Kim. (2019). 3D Pen + 3D Printer: Exploring the Role of Humans and Fabrication Machines in Creative Making. *Conference: the 2019 CHI Conference*.10.1145/3290605.3300525

Tang, S., Ummethala, R., Suryanarayana, C., Eckert, J., Prashanth, K. G., & Wang, Z. (2021). Additive Manufacturing of Aluminum-Based Metal Matrix Composites—A Review. *Advanced Engineering Materials*, *23*(7), 2100053. doi:10.1002/adem.202100053

Tay, Y. W. D., Lim, J. H., Li, M., & Tan, M. J. (2022). Creating functionally graded concrete materials with varying 3D printing parameters. *Virtual and Physical Prototyping*, *17*(3), 662–681. doi:10.1080/17452759.2022.2048521

Tewani, H., Hinaus, M., Talukdar, M., Sone, H., & Prabhakar, P. (2022). *Architected syntactic foams: a tale of additive manufacturing and reinforcement parameters*. arXiv preprint arXiv:2211.00955.

Tichý, T., Šefl, O., Veselý, P., Dušek, K., & Bušek, D. (2021). Mathematical Modelling of Temperature Distribution in Selected Parts of FFF Printer during 3D Printing Process. *Polymers*, *13*(23), 4213. doi:10.3390/polym13234213 PMID:34883715

Tosto, C., Pergolizzi, E., Blanco, I., Patti, A., Holt, P., Karmel, S., & Cicala, G. (2020). 18 July 2020, Epoxy Based Blends for Additive Manufacturing by Liquid Crystal Display (LCD) Printing: The Effect of Blending and Dual Curing on Daylight Curable Resins. *Polymers*, *12*(7), 1594. doi:10.3390/polym12071594 PMID:32708360

Tshephe, T. S., Akinwamide, S. O., Olevsky, E., & Olubambi, P. A. (2022). Additive manufacturing of titanium-based alloys-A review of methods, properties, challenges, and prospects. *Heliyon*, *8*(3), e09041. doi:10.1016/j.heliyon.2022.e09041 PMID:35299605

Uriondo, A., Esperon-Miguez, M., & Perinpanayagam, S. (2015). The present and future of additive manufacturing in the aerospace sector: A review of important aspects. *Proceedings of the Institution of Mechanical Engineers. Part G, Journal of Aerospace Engineering*, *229*(11), 2132–2147. doi:10.1177/0954410014568797

Vafadar, A., Guzzomi, F., Rassau, A., & Hayward, K. (2021). Advances in metal additive manufacturing: A review of common processes, industrial applications, and current challenges. *Applied Sciences (Basel, Switzerland)*, *11*(3), 1213. doi:10.3390/app11031213

Vambol, O., Kondratiev, A., Purhina, S., & Shevtsova, M. (2021). Determining the parameters for a 3D-printing process using the fused deposition modeling in order to manufacture an article with the required structural parameters. *Eastern-European Journal of Enterprise Technologies*, *2*(1 (110)), 70–80. doi:10.15587/1729-4061.2021.227075

Vasconcelos, J., Sardinha, M., Vicente, C., & Reis, L. (2022). Additive Manufacturing of Glass-Ceramic Parts from Recycled Glass Using a Novel Selective Powder Deposition Process. *Applied Sciences (Basel, Switzerland)*, *12*(24), 13022. doi:10.3390/app122413022

Ventola, C. L. (2014). Medical applications for 3D printing: Current and projected uses. *P&T*, *39*(10), 704. PMID:25336867

Vidakis, N., Kechagias, J. D., Petousis, M., Vakouftsi, F., & Mountakis, N. (2023). The effects of FFF 3D printing parameters on energy consumption. *Materials and Manufacturing Processes*, *38*(8), 915–932. doi:10.1080/10426914.2022.2105882

Wagner, M. A., Engel, J., Hadian, A., Clemens, F., Rodriguez-Arbaizar, M., Carreño-Morelli, E., & Spolenak, R. (2022). Filament extrusion-based additive manufacturing of 316L stainless steel: Effects of sintering conditions on the microstructure and mechanical properties. *Additive Manufacturing*, *59*, 103147. doi:10.1016/j.addma.2022.103147

Wang, W., Shao, H., Liu, X., & Yin, B. (2020). Printing direction optimization through slice number and support minimization. *IEEE Access : Practical Innovations, Open Solutions*, *8*, 75646–75655. doi:10.1109/ACCESS.2020.2980282

Wang, Y., Müllertz, A., & Rantanen, J. (2022). Additive manufacturing of solid products for oral drug delivery using binder jetting three-dimensional printing. *AAPS PharmSciTech*, *23*(6), 196. doi:10.120812249-022-02321-w PMID:35835970

Wani, Z. K., & Abdullah, A. B. (2020, September). A Review on metal 3D printing; 3D welding. *IOP Conference Series. Materials Science and Engineering*, *920*(1), 012015. doi:10.1088/1757-899X/920/1/012015

Wanniarachchi, C. T., Arjunan, A., Baroutaji, A., & Singh, M. (2022). Mechanical performance of additively manufactured cobalt-chromium-molybdenum auxetic meta-biomaterial bone scaffolds. *Journal of the Mechanical Behavior of Biomedical Materials, 134*, 105409.

Warsi, M. H., Yusuf, M., Al Robaian, M., Khan, M., Muheem, A., & Khan, S. (2018). 3D printing methods for pharmaceutical manufacturing: Opportunity and challenges. *Current Pharmaceutical Design*, *24*(42), 4949–4956. doi:10.2174/1381612825666181206121701 PMID:30520367

Weisgrab, G., Guillaume, O., Guo, Z., Heimel, P., Slezak, P., Poot, A., Grijpma, D., & Ovsianikov, A. (2020). 3D Printing of large-scale and highly porous biodegradable tissue engineering scaffolds from poly (trimethylene-carbonate) using two-photon-polymerization. *Biofabrication*, *12*(4), 045036. doi:10.1088/1758-5090/abb539 PMID:33000766

Willson, J. M., Grinshpun, V. S., & Santos, R. (1998). *U.S. Patent No. 5,789,456*. Washington, DC: U.S. Patent and Trademark Office.

Wu, Y., Lu, Y., Zhao, M., Bosiakov, S., & Li, L. (2022). A Critical Review of Additive Manufacturing Techniques and Associated Biomaterials Used in Bone Tissue Engineering. *Polymers*, *14*(10), 2117. doi:10.3390/polym14102117 PMID:35631999

Yang, S. (2022, September). Introduction and future outlook of the 3D printing technology. In *International Conference on Mechanical Design and Simulation (MDS 2022)* (Vol. 12261, pp. 240-246). SPIE. 10.1117/12.2639668

Yuri, K., Hyun-Jung, Y., Bum-Keun, K., & Hee-Don, C. (2022). Choi Yun-Sang, 3D Printing Technology: Food Tech Analysis. *Resour Sci Res*, *4*(1), 1–11. doi:10.52346/rsr.2022.4.1.1

Zadpoor, A. A. (2018). Frontiers of additively manufactured metallic materials. *Materials (Basel)*, *11*(9), 1566. doi:10.3390/ma11091566 PMID:30200231

Zhang, J., Wang, J., Dong, S., Yu, X., & Han, B. (2019). A review of the current progress and application of 3D printed concrete. *Composites. Part A, Applied Science and Manufacturing*, *125*, 105533. doi:10.1016/j.compositesa.2019.105533

Zheng, S. Y., Liu, Z. W., Kang, H. L., Liu, F., Yan, G. P., & Li, F. (2023). 3D-Printed scaffolds based on poly (Trimethylene carbonate), poly (ε-Caprolactone), and β-Tricalcium phosphate. *International Journal of Bioprinting*, *9*(1), 641. doi:10.18063/ijb.v9i1.641 PMID:36636134

Zhu, K., Fuh, J. Y. H., & Lin, X. (2021). Metal-based additive manufacturing condition monitoring: A review on machine learning based approaches. *IEEE/ASME Transactions on Mechatronics*.

Zolotareva, N. V., Resnyanskaya, A. S., & Ocheredko, Y. A. (2021). Implementation of modeling elements and 3D printing technology for chemical objects in the educational process within the framework of the "University–School" interaction system. In *SHS Web of Conferences* (Vol. 113, p. 00043). EDP Sciences.

カサルト, ミ., クジェ, フ., & プラツ, エ. (2011). *Getting started with the manufacturing process of expandable vinyl aromatic polymers*. Academic Press.

Chapter 6
Unleashing the Future Potential of 4D Printing:
Exploring Applications in Wearable Technology, Robotics, Energy, Transportation, and Fashion

S. Revathi
Department of Computer Science and Engineering, B.S. Abdul Rahman Crescent Institute of Science and Technology, India

M. Babu
https://orcid.org/0000-0001-9034-3952
Department of Mechanical Engineering, SRM Easwari Engineering College, India

N. Rajkumar
Department of Computer Science & Engineering, Alliance College of Engineering and Design, Alliance University, India

Vinod Kumar V. Meti
https://orcid.org/0000-0001-5692-9693
KLE Technological University, India

Sumanth Ratna Kandavalli
https://orcid.org/0000-0003-2195-7568
Department of Mechanical Engineering, Tandon School of Engineering, New York University, USA

Sampath Boopathi
https://orcid.org/0000-0002-2065-6539
Mechanical Engineering, Muthayammal Engineering College, India

ABSTRACT

4D printing technology combines additive manufacturing with materials that can change shape or properties over time, enabling objects to self-assemble, self-repair, and adapt to their environment. It has potential applications in robotics, autonomous systems, energy and environmental systems, and smart materials for energy storage and distribution. The text discusses the potential of 4D printing technology and its role in shaping the future of wearable technology, robotics, energy, transportation, and fashion industries. It looks at future applications of 4D printing in fashion and design, such as dynamic and customizable clothing and accessories, shape-changing jewelry and wearable art, responsive and interactive fashion shows and events, and sustainable and adaptive fashion manufacturing processes. It emphasizes the importance of continued research and development to unlock the full potential of 4D printing and its transformative impact on various industries.

DOI: 10.4018/979-8-3693-2647-3.ch006

1. INTRODUCTION

Additive manufacturing has experienced significant advancements, with 3D printing revolutionizing industries and fostering creativity. However, 4D printing is emerging, offering unprecedented fabrication possibilities by adding the fourth dimension of time, enabling objects to self-transform and adapt to different conditions. 4D printing is a new technology that enhances 3D printing by introducing time into the manufacturing process. It involves creating objects or materials that can change shape, properties, or functionality due to stimuli like heat, moisture, light, or mechanical forces. 4D refers to the spatial dimensions (length, width, and height) plus the temporal dimension. 4D printing relies on smart materials, also known as programmable or shape-memory materials, which can transform when exposed to external triggers like temperature, humidity, pH, or electric current. By integrating these materials into 3D-printed structures, researchers and engineers can create dynamic objects that self-assemble, repair, or adapt to changing conditions (Kantaros et al., 2023; Ntouanoglou et al., 2018).

4D printing involves creating a CAD model, translating it into digital instructions for 3D printers to deposit layers of material, typically polymers or composites, to build structures. The key difference from traditional 3D printing is the careful selection and integration of smart materials. 3D-printed objects undergo post-processing, where they are exposed to a trigger that activates smart materials' shape-changing properties. This activation causes the object to deform, morph, or reconfigure into its final shape, either instantaneously or gradually, depending on the materials and triggering mechanism. 4D printing has numerous applications across various industries, including wearable technology, robotics, energy systems, transportation, and fashion and design. It allows for self-adapting and self-repairing mechanisms in garments, enabling robots to navigate complex environments and perform intricate tasks. Energy systems optimize efficiency and adapt to varying conditions, while transportation is revolutionized by adaptive components. Fashion and design industries can explore new avenues of creativity and personalization by incorporating dynamic elements into clothing and accessories (Pacillo et al., 2021; Zhang et al., 2019).

4D printing technology is still in its early stages, but research and development efforts are advancing its capabilities and potential applications. This innovative approach holds immense potential for various industries, including wearable technology, robotics, energy, transportation, and fashion. By harnessing the dynamic capabilities of 4D printing, we can create smart materials and devices that revolutionize technology interactions, energy efficiency, transportation systems, and fashion and design. 4D printing advancements in wearable technology offer enhanced comfort and functionality by enabling garments to automatically adjust to the wearer's body. The integration of sensors and electronics in wearables can enable real-time monitoring of vital signs, movement tracking, and gesture recognition, opening new avenues in healthcare, sports, and augmented reality. In robotics, 4D printing allows for self-assembling structures and mechanisms that can adapt and reconfigure in response to changing environments, revolutionizing the development of complex robots capable of navigating terrains, performing tasks, and even repairing themselves. This flexibility and versatility have the potential to revolutionize industries like manufacturing, healthcare, and exploration (Kuang et al., 2019; Raina et al., 2021).

4D printing offers potential benefits in the energy sector by creating advanced materials with shape-changing properties. This can be used in smart energy systems like solar panels and energy storage devices that can adjust their shape to maximize efficiency. Additionally, 4D printing technologies can revolutionize transportation by creating adaptive components and structures that enhance vehicle performance, safety, and efficiency (Kumari et al., 2022; Mahmood et al., 2022; Sadasivuni et al., 2019). This includes self-adjusting aerodynamic surfaces for aircraft and 4D-printed tires that automatically adapt to road conditions, reshaping the way we travel and commute. The fashion industry can utilize 4D printing to revolutionize clothing and accessories by incorporating dynamic elements that can change appearance, adapt to different climates, or respond to wearer movements. This convergence of fashion and technology offers self-expression and customization, challenging traditional notions of style and aesthetics. This exploration explores applications in wearable technology, robotics, energy, transportation, and fashion, examining current research and development in these fields. The future of 4D printing is exciting, as materials come alive, objects transform, and innovation boundaries are redefined. Exploring future applications is crucial for advancing research and development in any field, including 4D printing. Here are a few reasons why it is important (Ntouanoglou et al., 2018; Pacillo et al., 2021):

- **Innovation and Progress:** Researchers and developers can push boundaries by envisioning and exploring potential applications of 4D printing. This drives innovation, fostering the development of new techniques, materials, and technologies, leading to advancements that can revolutionize industries, improve quality of life, and address societal challenges.
- **Problem Solving:** Researchers can tackle specific problems and challenges by identifying real-world needs and gaps, tailoring research and development efforts to create practical solutions and maximize the impact of 4D printing technology.
- **Collaboration and Interdisciplinary Approaches:** Interdisciplinary collaboration is crucial for exploring future applications, involving experts from various fields like materials science, engineering, design, and healthcare. This exchange of knowledge and expertise leads to groundbreaking advancements and unlocking new possibilities.
- **Market Expansion and Economic Growth:** Exploring potential applications in 4D printing technologies leads to market expansion, creating new business opportunities, economic growth, investment attraction, and employment. This positioning positions companies and entrepreneurs at the forefront of emerging industries, resulting in economic benefits.

The "Make in India" initiative aims to promote manufacturing in India, transforming the country into a global hub and attracting domestic and foreign investments. 4D printing applications align with this concept in several ways (Kuang et al., 2019; Kumari et al., 2022; Zhang et al., 2019).

- **Technological Advancement:** 4D printing advances manufacturing by enhancing India's capabilities and global competitiveness by embracing cutting-edge technologies and concepts, fostering technological advancement in the sector.
- **Job Creation and Skill Development:** As the manufacturing sector expands and incorporates advanced technologies, it generates employment opportunities. Exploring future applications of 4D printing can lead to the establishment of new businesses, research centers, and manufacturing facilities, creating jobs and boosting skill development among the workforce.
- **Attracting Investments:** By actively exploring and promoting future applications of 4D printing, India can attract investments from both domestic and international companies. This not only strengthens the manufacturing sector but also drives economic growth and contributes to the "Make in India" initiative's objectives.
- **Fostering Innovation and Entrepreneurship:** Exploring future applications of 4D printing encourages innovation and entrepreneurship. It provides opportunities for startups and entrepreneurs to develop unique products, solutions, and services based on 4D printing technology. This

promotes a culture of innovation, supports small and medium enterprises, and nurtures a vibrant ecosystem for manufacturing and technological advancements.

Exploring 4D printing applications is crucial for research, development, innovation, and economic growth. It aligns with the "Make in India" concept, promoting job creation, investment, and entrepreneurship in the manufacturing sector.

2. FUNDAMENTALS OF 4D PRINTING

4D printing builds on 3D printing principles by incorporating time, allowing objects to change shape, properties, or functionality. It involves integrating smart materials into 3D-printed structures, allowing them to undergo pre-defined transformations triggered by environmental conditions. The fundamentals of 4D printing involve design, material science, and additive manufacturing techniques, with key elements including time, programmable materials, and environmental conditions (Mitchell et al., 2018; Subeshan et al., 2021; Tibbits, 2014).

- **Design:** 4D printing begins with the design phase, where computer-aided design (CAD) software is used to create a 3D model of the desired object. Design considerations include incorporating the appropriate smart materials, defining the desired shape transformations, and identifying the triggering mechanisms.
- **Smart Materials:** Smart materials, also known as programmable or shape-memory materials, are a critical component of 4D printing. These materials possess the ability to change their shape or properties when exposed to specific stimuli, such as temperature, humidity, light, or mechanical forces. Shape-memory polymers and shape-memory alloys (such as Nitinol) are commonly used in 4D printing due to their reversible deformations.
- **Additive Manufacturing:** The next step involves the fabrication of the 3D-printed structure using additive manufacturing techniques. Similar to traditional 3D printing, layer-by-layer deposition of materials is carried out based on the CAD model. The choice of printing technology, such as fused deposition modeling (FDM), stereolithography (SLA), or selective laser sintering (SLS), depends on the specific application and the properties of the smart materials used.
- **Triggering Mechanisms:** After the 3D-printed object is fabricated, it undergoes a post-processing step to activate the shape-changing properties of the embedded smart materials. The triggering mechanisms vary depending on the material and the desired response. Examples of triggering mechanisms include temperature changes, exposure to moisture, electrical stimulation, light absorption, or magnetic fields.

4D printing is in its early stages, but significant advancements have been made, including self-folding structures, biomedical implants, and adaptive textiles. However, there are limitations and challenges to be addressed (Javaid & Haleem, 2019; Joshi et al., 2020; Khalid et al., 2022).

- **Material Selection and Compatibility:** Identifying and developing suitable smart materials with the desired properties, responsiveness, and compatibility with 3D printing processes remains a challenge. The availability of a wide range of materials and their integration into multi-material printing systems is essential for expanding the capabilities of 4D printing.

- **Printing Resolution and Complexity:** Achieving high printing resolution and intricate designs while incorporating smart materials is another area of focus. Overcoming the limitations of current 3D printing technologies, such as limited resolution and layer adhesion, is crucial for fabricating complex 4D-printed structures.
- **Triggering Mechanism Control:** Precise control over the triggering mechanisms is essential for achieving predictable and repeatable shape transformations. Developing reliable and scalable methods for activating the smart materials, as well as integrating sensing and feedback mechanisms, is necessary for advancing the field.
- **Scalability and Manufacturing Processes:** As with any new technology, scalability and cost-effectiveness are important factors for practical implementation. Optimizing the manufacturing processes, reducing fabrication time, and improving the reliability and repeatability of shape transformations are areas that require further research and development.

4D printing rapidly evolves due to research, collaborations, and advancements in materials, design techniques, and manufacturing processes. This leads to transformative changes in various industries, despite challenges.

Materials Used in 4D Printing and Their Unique Properties

4D printing uses a variety of smart or programmable materials with unique properties, allowing shape changes and dynamic behaviours in response to external stimuli. Common materials included for 4D printing Technologies are illustrated in Figure 1. And discussed below (Khalid et al., 2022; Mohol & Sharma, 2021; Zhou et al., 2015).

Figure 1. Materials used in 4D printing and their unique properties

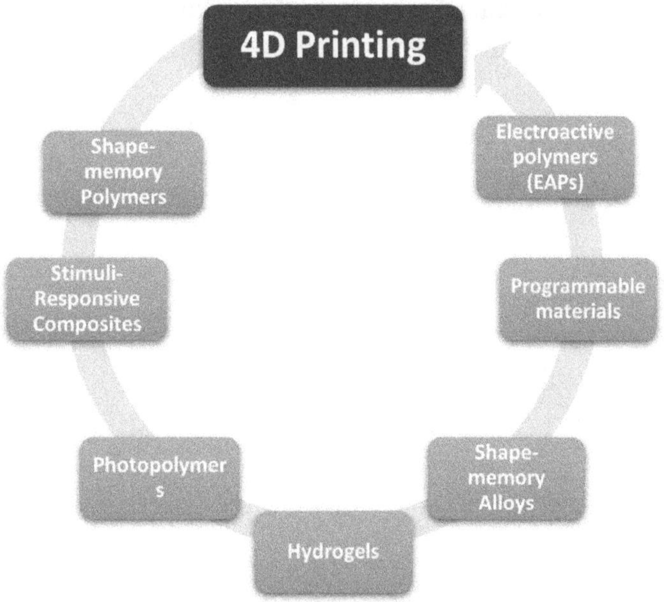

- **Shape-Memory Polymers:** Shape-memory polymers (SMPs) are a class of materials that have the ability to "remember" their original shape and return to it when triggered. They can undergo temporary deformation and recover their initial shape upon exposure to specific stimuli, such as heat, light, or moisture. SMPs offer excellent flexibility, tunable mechanical properties, and can be processed using conventional 3D printing techniques.
- **Shape-Memory Alloys:** Shape-memory alloys (SMAs), such as Nitinol (nickel-titanium alloy), exhibit unique properties, including shape memory effect and superelasticity. SMAs can be deformed and regain their original shape when subjected to a specific temperature change, known as the shape-memory effect. Additionally, they can undergo large elastic deformations without permanent damage, referred to as superelasticity. SMAs are typically used as wires or thin filaments embedded in 3D-printed structures to provide shape-changing capabilities.
- **Hydrogels:** Hydrogels are three-dimensional networks of hydrophilic polymers capable of absorbing and retaining large amounts of water. They can undergo substantial volume changes in response to environmental stimuli, such as temperature, pH, or light. Hydrogels are often employed in biomedical applications due to their biocompatibility and ability to mimic soft tissue properties. They can be 3D-printed using techniques like extrusion or inkjet printing.
- **Photopolymers:** Photopolymers are materials that undergo polymerization or crosslinking when exposed to specific wavelengths of light. They can be solidified or cured layer-by-layer using photopolymerization techniques, such as stereolithography (SLA). Photopolymers offer high resolution and can be tuned to exhibit different mechanical properties, making them suitable for fabricating intricate and detailed 4D-printed structures.
- **Stimuli-Responsive Composites:** Stimuli-responsive composites combine different materials to achieve tailored shape-changing behaviors. These composites often incorporate a matrix material, such as a polymer, reinforced with functional fillers or additives. By incorporating materials with different response mechanisms, such as thermal or electrical conductivity, into the composite, specific shape transformations can be achieved upon exposure to corresponding triggers.

The working principles of 4D printing depend on the specific materials and triggering mechanisms used as shown in Figure 2. The general process involves the following steps (Moroni et al., 2022; Subeshan et al., 2021):

Figure 2. Working principles of 4D printing technology

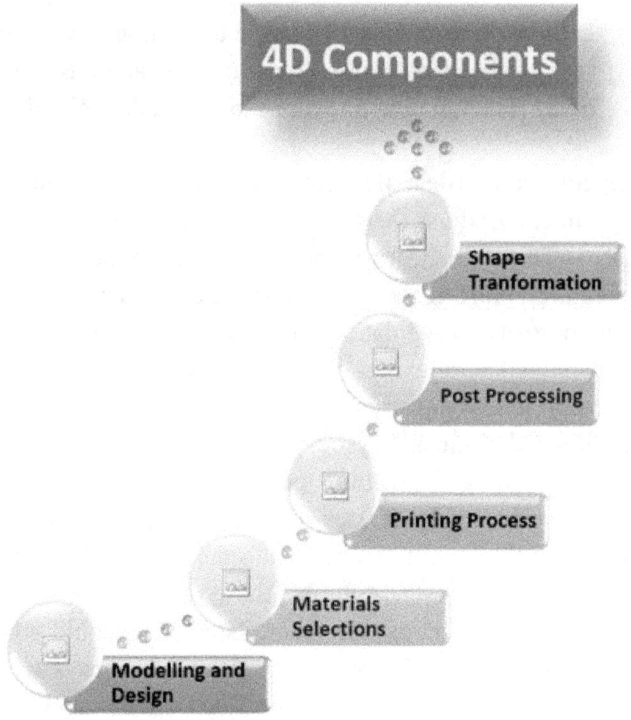

- **Design:** A computer-aided design (CAD) model is created, defining the desired shape, properties, and the transformation behavior of the 4D-printed object.
- **Material Selection:** Suitable smart materials are chosen based on the desired response and compatibility with the 3D printing process.
- **3D Printing:** The CAD model is translated into digital instructions that guide a 3D printer to deposit the chosen materials layer by layer, forming the structure of the object.
- **Post-Processing:** After the 3D printing is complete, the object undergoes a post-processing step to activate the shape-changing properties of the embedded smart materials. This can involve exposing the object to specific stimuli, such as temperature changes, moisture, light, or electrical currents, depending on the material and desired response.
- **Shape Transformation:** Upon activation of the triggering mechanism, the embedded smart materials undergo a physical or chemical change, causing the 4D-printed object to transform its shape or properties according to the pre-designed behavior.

The control and precision of the shape transformation depend on factors such as the design of the object, the choice of smart materials, the triggering mechanism, and the post-processing conditions. Ongoing research and technological advancements aim to refine the working principles of 4D printing, enhancing the predictability, repeatability, and complexity of the shape-changing behaviours.

3. FUTURE 4D APPLICATIONS IN WEARABLE TECHNOLOGY

4D printing has the potential to revolutionize wearable technology by integrating smart materials into textiles and devices, offering enhanced comfort, functionality, and customization (McCann & Bryson, 2009; McLellan et al., 2022). The future applications in wearable technology are elaborated below.

- **Shape-Changing Smart Textiles:** 4D printing enables the creation of shape-changing smart textiles that can dynamically adjust their form, properties, and fit in response to external stimuli or user preferences. These textiles can incorporate embedded smart materials that respond to changes in temperature, moisture, or other environmental factors. For example, a 4D-printed fabric could adapt its porosity to regulate breathability or change its surface texture for improved comfort. Shape-changing smart textiles can enhance user comfort, optimize performance, and enable personalized experiences in various wearable applications, including sports apparel, medical garments, and fashion (McCann & Bryson, 2009).
- **Customizable and Adaptive Wearable Devices:** 4D printing allows for the fabrication of customizable and adaptive wearable devices that can adapt to individual users' unique needs and body shapes. By integrating smart materials into the design of wearable devices, such as smartwatches, fitness trackers, or prosthetic limbs, these devices can dynamically adjust their fit and functionality. For example, a 4D-printed smartwatch band could adapt its shape and tension to provide a personalized and comfortable fit for different users. This level of customization and adaptability enhances user experience, improves functionality, and promotes a more inclusive approach to wearable technology.
- **Interactive Interfaces and Haptic Feedback:** 4D printing can enable the creation of interactive interfaces and haptic feedback systems within wearable devices. By incorporating shape-changing smart materials into the design, wearables can offer tactile feedback and dynamic interfaces that enhance user interactions and augmented reality (AR) experiences. For example, a 4D-printed glove could dynamically adjust its texture or generate localized vibrations to provide haptic feedback in virtual or augmented reality applications. These interactive interfaces and haptic feedback systems can improve immersion, interactivity, and realism in AR experiences, making them more engaging and intuitive.
- **Biometric Monitoring and Healthcare Integration:** 4D-printed wearables can integrate biometric monitoring capabilities and healthcare functionalities, providing personalized health tracking and monitoring. By incorporating sensors and smart materials, these wearables can dynamically adapt to the wearer's body and capture vital signs, such as heart rate, blood pressure, or temperature. For example, a 4D-printed smart band could adjust its tightness based on the wearer's biometric data, ensuring optimal sensor contact and accurate measurements. Additionally, 4D-printed wearables can facilitate the integration of healthcare sensors or drug delivery systems, enabling continuous monitoring and personalized healthcare solutions.

4D printing technology in wearable devices improves functionality, design possibilities, and user interactions. By using shape-changing materials, wearable technology becomes responsive, adaptable, and user-centric, creating a new generation of wearable devices that seamlessly integrate into daily life. This technology offers interactive interfaces, haptic feedback, biometric monitoring, augmented reality experiences, and healthcare functionalities, with potential future applications. By transforming augmented reality interactions and advancing personalized healthcare monitoring and interventions, wearables provide a more immersive and personalized experience for users.

Case Study: Shape-Changing Smart Textiles Using 4D Printing Technology

This case study focuses on the implementation of 4D printing technology in the development of shape-changing smart textiles. Shape-changing smart textiles are innovative materials that can alter their physical characteristics or morphology in response to external stimuli. By integrating 4D printing into the fabrication process, these textiles can achieve dynamic shape transformations, leading to enhanced functionality and versatility in various applications (Figure 3). The specific application chosen for this case study is the development of a shape-changing smart textile for active sportswear. Traditional sportswear fabrics lack the ability to adapt to the body's movements and environmental conditions. The limitations include restricted breathability, limited stretchability, and inadequate moisture management. The goal is to overcome these limitations by integrating 4D printing technology into the textile manufacturing process (Cheng et al., 2021; Ryan et al., 2021).

The decision to integrate 4D printing technology into the development of shape-changing smart textiles is driven by the potential benefits it offers. By utilizing 4D printing, it becomes possible to incorporate responsive materials that can change their shape, texture, or mechanical properties based on external factors such as heat, moisture, or pressure. This integration aims to enhance comfort, flexibility, and performance in sportswear, providing athletes with optimal functionality and support.

Implementation Process

1. Selection of Suitable 4D Printing Materials:

    - Extensive research is conducted to identify suitable 4D printing materials that exhibit the desired shape-changing properties while maintaining comfort and durability.
    - Materials such as shape memory polymers or composites with stimuli-responsive behavior are considered for their ability to transform in response to specific stimuli.

Figure 3. Case study: Shape-changing smart textiles using 4D printing technology

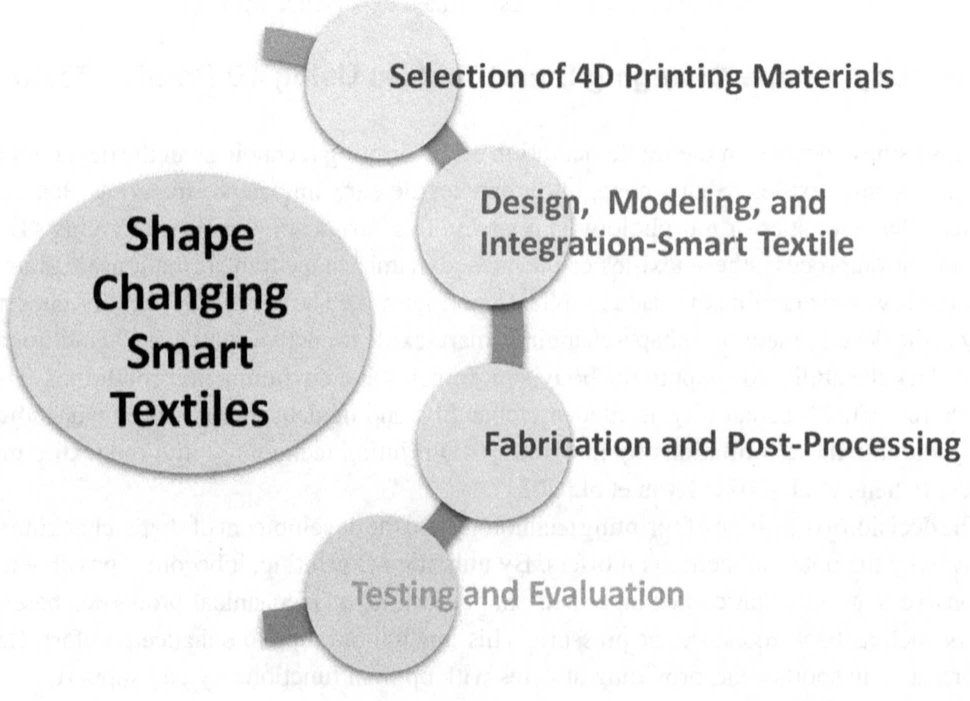

2. Design and Modeling of the Smart Textile:
    - Design considerations are made to incorporate 4D printing elements into the textile structure without compromising the fabric's breathability or flexibility.
    - Computer-aided design (CAD) tools and simulation software are utilized to create digital models and simulate the behavior of the shape-changing smart textile.
3. Integration of 4D Printing Elements:
    - 4D printing techniques, such as multi-material deposition or layer-by-layer printing, are employed to embed the responsive materials into the fabric structure.
    - Advanced printing systems capable of depositing multiple materials with precise control over their spatial distribution are utilized.
4. Fabrication and Post-Processing:
    - The 4D printed smart textile is fabricated using additive manufacturing processes.
    - Post-processing steps, such as curing or annealing, may be applied to activate or enhance the shape-changing properties of the printed elements.
5. Testing and Evaluation:
    - The fabricated shape-changing smart textile undergoes rigorous testing to evaluate its responsiveness, durability, comfort, and performance.
    - Testing may include measuring the textile's shape transformation under various stimuli, assessing breathability and moisture management, and evaluating its mechanical properties.

4D printing technology in shape-changing smart textiles significantly improves performance by transforming shape, texture, and mechanical properties in response to stimuli like body heat or moisture.

This adapts to wearer movements, improves breathability, flexibility, and provides targeted support and compression in various body areas. The smart textile enhances functionality and comfort in sportswear by adjusting its shape, improving range of motion, reducing muscle fatigue, and providing a customized fit. Its 4D printed elements enable precise control, ensuring optimal performance and comfort for athletes during physical activities.

The case study showcases the successful use of 4D printing technology in creating shape-changing smart textiles for active sportswear. This technology enhances functionality, comfort, and performance by integrating elements, resulting in dynamic shape transformations. This case study highlights the potential of 4D printing technology in revolutionizing the textile industry, offering innovative and adaptive materials for various applications.

4. ROBOTICS AND AUTONOMOUS SYSTEMS

4D printing technology holds immense potential in robotics and autonomous systems, enabling self-assembling and self-repairing components, versatile shape-changing robots, adaptive grippers, sensors, soft robotics, and morphological computation advancements. This technology also enables advancements in soft robotics and morphological computation (Li et al., 2017; Zolfagharian et al., 2020). The 4D Printing Technologies on making Robotics and Autonomous Systems are shown in Figure 4.

Figure 4. 4D printing technologies on making robotics and autonomous systems

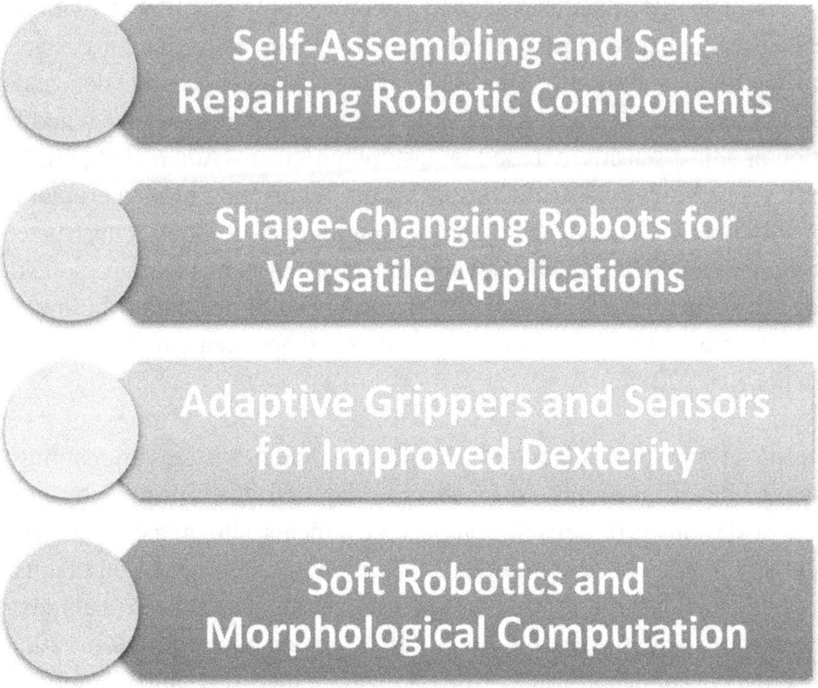

- **Self-Assembling and Self-Repairing Robotic Components:** 4D printing can enable the development of self-assembling and self-repairing robotic components. By utilizing shape-memory polymers or other smart materials, robotic parts can be designed to autonomously transform and assemble into complex structures. This can streamline the manufacturing process and reduce the need for manual assembly. Additionally, self-repairing capabilities can enhance the longevity and reliability of robots by allowing them to detect and repair damages or wear over time. 4D-printed robotic components offer self-assembling and self-repairing capabilities, making them valuable in space exploration, autonomously assembling and repairing critical components without human intervention.
- **Shape-Changing Robots for Versatile Applications:** 4D printing enables the creation of shape-changing robots that can adapt their morphology and functionality to different tasks or environments. By integrating smart materials with the ability to change shape or properties, robots can transform their physical configuration to navigate challenging terrains, manipulate objects of varying sizes and shapes, or adapt to specific tasks. These shape-changing robots offer increased versatility and agility compared to their rigid counterparts. A 4D-printed robot for search and rescue missions can dynamically alter its shape, enabling it to navigate tight spaces, extend its reach, or modify its locomotion pattern based on obstacles or requirements. This allows robots to operate in diverse environments and perform complex tasks more efficiently.
- **Adaptive Grippers and Sensors for Improved Dexterity:** 4D printing can enhance the dexterity and functionality of robotic grippers and sensors. By incorporating smart materials with shape-memory properties or responsive characteristics, robotic grippers can adapt their shape or stiffness to grasp objects of various sizes, shapes, and textures. This adaptability allows robots to handle delicate objects without causing damage or securely grip objects with irregular surfaces. 4D-printed sensors enhance sensing capabilities by dynamically changing shape or properties in response to environmental stimuli. This allows robots to gather accurate data and improve perception of the environment. For instance, a tactile sensor can optimize contact and friction for object manipulation or adjust sensitivity based on task requirements(Adam et al., 2021).
- **Soft Robotics and Morphological Computation:** 4D printing plays a crucial role in advancing the field of soft robotics and morphological computation. Soft robots, constructed with compliant materials, mimic the characteristics and movement patterns of natural organisms, enabling safe interactions with humans and delicate objects. 4D printing techniques allow the integration of smart materials into soft robotic structures, enabling shape-changing capabilities and responsive behavior (Choi et al., 2015).

4D printing technology revolutionizes robotics and autonomous systems by enabling the development of highly adaptive and versatile systems. Soft robots can benefit from 4D printing by incorporating shape-memory polymers or elastomers that enable complex movements, allowing them to navigate challenging terrains and adapt to unpredictable environments. Morphological computation offloads computational complexity to the body, enabling robots to perform computations and decision-making processes through their physical interactions with the environment. This approach allows for more efficient and adaptive robotic behavior, reducing computational load on the central processing unit. Combining 4D printing and robotics offers endless possibilities for designing and developing highly adaptive and versatile systems, including self-assembling and self-repairing components, shape-changing robots, adaptive grippers and sensors, and advancements in soft robotics and morphological computation. These advancements pave the way for robots that can operate in diverse environments, perform complex tasks, and interact intelligently and intuitively.

Case Study: 4D Printing Technology in Commercial Robots Manufacturing

This case study examines the use of 4D printing technology in commercial robotics, focusing on enhancing functionality and performance. It examines challenges, implementation processes, and outcomes achieved through 4D printing integration. The study highlights potential benefits, limitations, and future prospects of 4D printing technology in the robotics industry. This case study examines an industrial pick-and-place robot in a manufacturing facility, primarily used for accurately picking and placing components. The system faces limitations such as adaptability to different shapes, gripping fragile or irregular objects, and manual adjustments for handling different components. The integration of 4D printing technology in robotic systems offers potential benefits in addressing limitations and challenges (Adam et al., 2021; Choi et al., 2015; Zolfagharian et al., 2020). By incorporating 4D printed components, the robot gains enhanced adaptability and gripping capabilities, handling a wider range of component shapes and sizes more efficiently. The shape-changing properties of 4D printed materials enable real-time adjustment of grip and shape, improving overall performance and versatility.

- **Selection of Suitable 4D Printing Materials and Techniques:** Extensive research is conducted to identify suitable 4D printing materials with shape-changing properties, durability, and compatibility with the robotic application. Various 4D printing techniques, such as multi-material deposition, are explored to achieve the desired shape-changing functionality.
- **Design Considerations and Modifications:** The robot's gripper system is redesigned to incorporate 4D printed components that can change their shape and adapt to different objects. Modifications are made to the robot's control system to accommodate the integration of the 4D printed components and enable real-time adjustments.
- **Collaboration With Experts:** Collaboration is established with experts in both 4D printing and robotics to ensure a successful implementation. Expertise from both fields is combined to optimize the design, fabrication, and integration of the 4D printed components into the robotic system.
- **Testing and Validation:** Extensive testing is conducted to evaluate the performance of the 4D printed components in various scenarios and with different objects. The robotic system is tested for its adaptability, gripping capabilities, accuracy, and overall efficiency compared to the previous system. Validation is done through real-world production scenarios to assess the practicality and reliability of the integrated system.

Evaluation of Performance Improvements: The integration of 4D printing technology leads to significant performance improvements in the robotic system. The robot demonstrates enhanced adaptability and gripping capabilities, allowing it to handle a wider range of components, including fragile and irregularly shaped objects. The shape-changing properties of the 4D printed components enable the robot to adjust its grip in real-time, resulting in improved accuracy and efficiency. The integrated system offers enhanced functionality, adaptability, and efficiency. It handles various component shapes and sizes without manual adjustments, increasing productivity and reducing downtime. The shape-changing gripper system ensures a secure grip, minimizing component drop or damage risks. Overall, the robotic system is more versatile and capable of handling diverse manufacturing tasks.

This case study showcases the potential of 4D printing technology in improving industrial robot performance by overcoming limitations. The enhanced functionality, adaptability, and efficiency achieved through 4D printed components demonstrate the transformative impact of this technology in commercial applications.

5. 4D PRINTING IN ENERGY AND ENVIRONMENTAL APPLICATIONS

4D printing technology revolutionizes energy generation, storage, distribution, and sustainability in buildings and infrastructure. It can have transformative impacts in four key areas: energy generation, storage, distribution, and infrastructure sustainability (Ameta et al., 2022; Ruiz-Morales et al., 2017; Vates et al., 2021). The 4D printing technology in various energy and environmental applications are depicted in Figure 4.

Figure 5. 4D printing technology in various energy and environmental applications

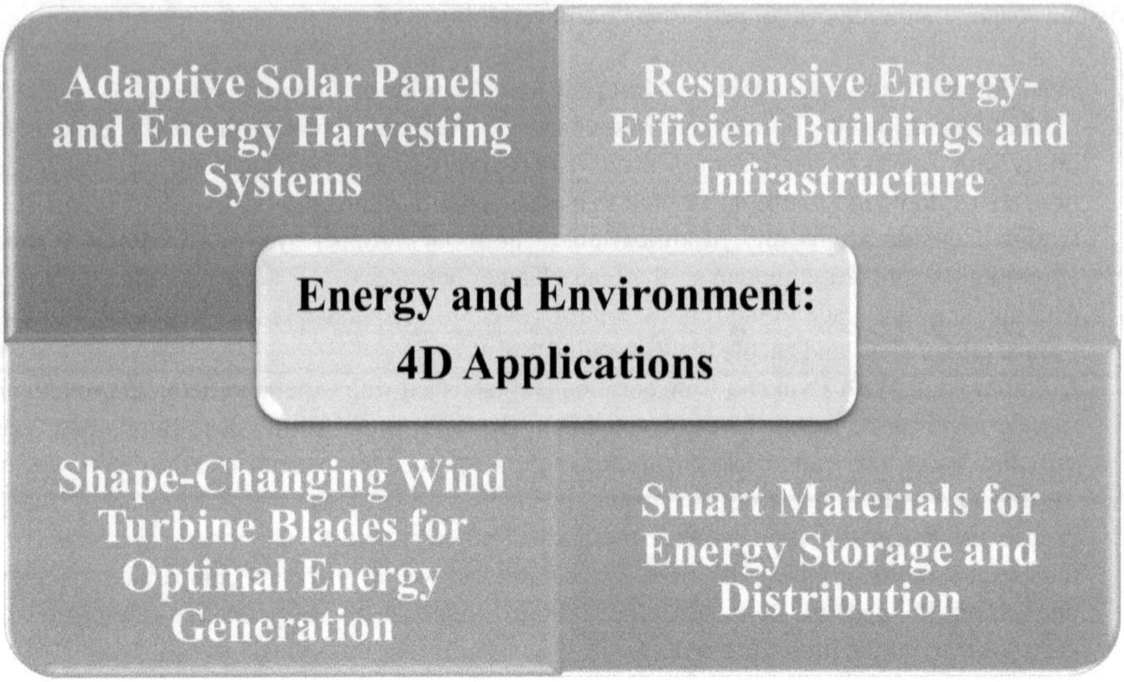

- **Adaptive Solar Panels and Energy Harvesting Systems:** 4D printing can be employed to develop adaptive solar panels and energy harvesting systems that can optimize energy generation based on environmental conditions. By integrating shape-changing materials or mechanisms into solar panels, they can autonomously adjust their orientation or surface area to maximize sunlight absorption. This flexibility enables solar panels to capture more energy throughout the day and adapt to different weather conditions, enhancing overall energy efficiency. 4D-printed energy harvesting systems convert ambient energy, like vibrations or thermal gradients, into usable electrical energy. These systems can adapt their shape and configuration to optimize energy capture and enhance efficiency, enhancing the overall energy harvesting process(Ruiz-Morales et al., 2017).

- **Responsive Energy-Efficient Buildings and Infrastructure:** 4D printing enables the creation of responsive building components and infrastructure systems that can dynamically adapt to changing environmental conditions, promoting energy efficiency. By integrating shape-changing materials into architectural elements, such as windows, shades, or façade systems, buildings can regulate heat, light, and ventilation based on real-time conditions. This adaptability optimizes energy usage by minimizing heating and cooling needs, reducing reliance on artificial lighting, and enhancing overall occupant comfort. Additionally, 4D-printed sensors and actuators can be integrated into building systems to monitor and control energy consumption, optimizing energy efficiency. For example, smart windows can dynamically adjust their transparency or insulation properties in response to sunlight intensity or ambient temperature, reducing the need for heating or cooling systems.
- **Shape-Changing Wind Turbine Blades for Optimal Energy Generation:** Wind turbine efficiency can be significantly improved through 4D printing technology by creating shape-changing turbine blades. These blades can adjust their shape or configuration based on wind conditions to maximize energy generation. By integrating smart materials or mechanisms that respond to wind speed and direction, wind turbine blades can optimize their aerodynamic profile, reducing drag and enhancing power generation. The ability of 4D-printed wind turbine blades to adapt their shape dynamically allows for improved energy capture across a wider range of wind speeds, increasing overall efficiency and output of wind energy systems.
- **Smart Materials for Energy Storage and Distribution:** 4D printing opens up possibilities for developing smart materials that can revolutionize energy storage and distribution. For instance, 4D-printed batteries and energy storage devices can incorporate shape-changing materials to optimize their internal structure or electrode configuration, leading to improved energy storage capacity and faster charging times. These advancements can contribute to the development of more efficient and compact energy storage systems for renewable energy integration and portable electronics. 4D printing smart materials enable responsive energy distribution systems by integrating shape-changing materials into transmission networks, enhancing efficiency and resilience by adapting to demand fluctuations or grid conditions.

4D printing technology offers transformative opportunities in energy and environmental applications, including adaptive solar panels, renewable buildings, wind turbine blades, and smart materials for energy storage and distribution. This promotes sustainable and efficient systems, fostering a greener future.

6. TRANSPORTATION AND AUTOMOTIVE INDUSTRY

4D printing technology can revolutionize automotive design, performance, and user experience in four key areas, transforming vehicle design, performance, and user experience.

- **Self-Adaptive Vehicle Components for Improved Performance:** 4D printing enables the creation of self-adaptive vehicle components that can optimize performance based on real-time conditions. By incorporating shape-changing materials or mechanisms into critical parts, such as suspension systems, aerodynamic elements, or tire treads, vehicles can dynamically adjust their characteristics to adapt to different driving conditions. For example, a 4D-printed suspension system could adapt its stiffness and damping properties to provide optimal handling and ride comfort, both on smooth highways and off-road terrains. This adaptability improves overall performance, safety, and user experience.

- **Shape-Changing Car Bodies for Aerodynamics and Efficiency:** 4D printing offers the potential to design shape-changing car bodies that can dynamically adjust their shape or surface characteristics to optimize aerodynamics and improve fuel efficiency. By integrating smart materials that can change their shape in response to speed or environmental conditions, vehicles can reduce drag, minimize turbulence, and enhance overall aerodynamic performance. For instance, a 4D-printed car body could automatically extend or retract spoilers, adjust air vents, or modify its surface texture to reduce wind resistance and improve efficiency at high speeds. This leads to improved fuel economy and reduced emissions.
- **Customizable and Responsive Interiors for Comfort and User Experience:** 4D printing allows for customizable and responsive interiors that can enhance comfort and user experience. By incorporating shape-changing materials into seating systems, interior panels, or climate control components, vehicles can adapt to the individual preferences and needs of the occupants. For example, a 4D-printed seat could adjust its shape, firmness, or temperature based on the occupant's body characteristics or preferences, providing personalized comfort and support. Moreover, interactive interfaces and displays with shape-changing properties can dynamically adjust their configuration to optimize visibility and accessibility.
- **Self-Repairing and Self-Monitoring Automotive Systems:** 4D printing has the potential to introduce self-repairing and self-monitoring capabilities in automotive systems. By utilizing shape-memory materials or smart sensors, vehicles can detect damages or wear and initiate self-repair processes. For instance, a 4D-printed exterior panel could automatically repair minor scratches or dents by utilizing shape-memory properties to regain its original shape. Additionally, embedded sensors and monitoring systems can continuously assess the performance and condition of various vehicle components, enabling proactive maintenance and minimizing downtime.

4D printing technology in the automotive industry improves performance, aerodynamics, efficiency, and user experience. It offers self-adaptive components, shape-changing car bodies, customizable interiors, and self-repairing systems, contributing to enhanced functionality, comfort, and sustainability. As 4D printing advances, the automotive sector can benefit from smarter, more efficient, and user-centric vehicles.

7. 4D PRINTING TECHNOLOGIES IN FASHION AND DESIGN

4D printing technology in the fashion industry offers innovative, sustainable creations through four key applications: design, fashion, and sustainability (Champeau et al., 2020).

- **Dynamic and Customizable Clothing and Accessories:** 4D printing allows for the creation of dynamic and customizable clothing and accessories that can adapt to the wearer's needs and preferences. By using shape-changing materials, garments can adjust their shape, fit, or functionality based on various factors such as body movement, environmental conditions, or user input. This customization enables personalized and adaptive fashion, providing a unique and comfortable experience for individuals. For example, a 4D-printed dress could change its shape or pattern in response to body temperature or the wearer's mood.

- **Shape-Changing Jewelry and Wearable Art:** 4D printing offers a new dimension to jewelry and wearable art by enabling shape-changing properties. With the use of smart materials, jewelry pieces can transform their shape, texture, or configuration, creating dynamic and interactive designs. For instance, a 4D-printed bracelet may change its shape to fit different wrist sizes, or a necklace may adjust its length or design based on the wearer's preferences. This integration of technology and fashion allows for unique and expressive wearable art pieces (Biswas et al., 2021; McCann & Bryson, 2022).
- **Responsive and Interactive Fashion Shows and Events:** 4D printing technology can enhance fashion shows and events by enabling responsive and interactive elements. By incorporating shape-changing materials or mechanisms into runway designs, stage props, or installations, fashion shows can become immersive experiences for the audience. For example, 4D-printed stage backdrops may change their shape or color to create dynamic visual effects that complement the showcased garments. Additionally, interactive elements, such as touch-sensitive fabrics or sound-reactive accessories, can engage the audience and create memorable fashion experiences.
- **Sustainable and Adaptive Fashion Manufacturing Processes:** 4D printing has the potential to revolutionize fashion manufacturing processes, promoting sustainability and adaptability. By utilizing additive manufacturing techniques, designers can reduce material waste and energy consumption compared to traditional manufacturing methods. Additionally, the ability to create complex geometries and customizable designs through 4D printing allows for efficient production and reduces the need for excessive inventory.

4D printing revolutionizes the fashion industry with its adaptive fashion pieces, promoting sustainable fashion and extending garment lifespan. This technology offers customizable clothing, shape-changing jewelry, responsive fashion shows, and sustainable manufacturing processes. As technology evolves, it offers unique and personalized experiences while minimizing environmental impact, shaping the future of fashion.

Case Study: Shape-Changing Jewelry and Wearable Art Using 4D Printing Technology

This case study focuses on the application of 4D printing technology in the creation of shape-changing jewelry and wearable art. Shape-changing jewelry and wearable art offer a unique and interactive experience by incorporating dynamic elements that can alter their form, texture, or appearance. By leveraging 4D printing technology, these pieces can achieve intricate and complex transformations, pushing the boundaries of traditional jewelry design (Champeau et al., 2020; Leist & Zhou, 2016).

The specific application chosen for this case study is the development of shape-changing jewelry and wearable art for a high-end fashion brand. Traditional jewelry designs lack the ability to adapt to different occasions or reflect the wearer's mood. The objective is to integrate 4D printing technology to create pieces that can dynamically change their shape, color, or pattern, allowing individuals to express their personal style and make a statement. 4D printing technology is being integrated into jewelry and wearable art to create innovative, interactive designs. This technology enables materials to respond to external stimuli, resulting in surprises and versatility. The goal is to redefine jewelry and wearable art, providing captivating and personalized experiences for wearers (Champeau et al., 2020; Choi et al., 2015; McCann & Bryson, 2009; Wiechetek & Gola, 2019).

Implementation Process

- Research identifies shape-changing materials for jewelry and wearable art applications, including shape memory alloys, thermoplastics, and responsive composites. These materials enable controlled shape transformations, making them suitable for various applications.
- Designing jewelry and wearable art incorporates 4D printing elements for aesthetic and functionality. Utilizing CAD tools and simulation software, digital models are created, allowing visualization and optimization of shape-changing features.
- 4D printing techniques like selective laser sintering and fused deposition modeling are used to fabricate shape-changing components, requiring multiple iterations for intricacy and precision.
- 4D printed components are integrated into jewelry or wearable art designs, with post-processing steps like polishing, plating, or gemstone additions to enhance aesthetic appeal and quality.
- Shape-changing jewelry and wearable art undergo thorough testing to assess responsiveness, durability, and aesthetic appeal. This includes assessing shape transformation, evaluating mechanisms, and ensuring comfortable wearability.

4D printing technology improves performance and aesthetic appeal in shape-changing jewelry and wearable art. It allows for dynamic transformations, personalization, and interactivity, allowing individuals to customize accessories to match their style, mood, or occasion. The integration of 4D printing elements creates a sense of wonder and individuality, making the pieces engaging and captivating for both wearers and observers.

The case study showcases 4D printing technology's success in creating shape-changing jewelry and wearable art, revolutionizing traditional design with dynamic transformations and personalized experiences. This enhances surprise, interactivity, and self-expression in these products.

8. CHALLENGES AND FUTURE DIRECTIONS

4D printing faces challenges and requires further research to unlock its full potential. Ethical considerations and societal implications must be addressed for responsible adoption (Javaid & Haleem, 2019; Joshi et al., 2020).

- Technological, material, and regulatory challenges in 4D printing implementation include advancements in materials, techniques, and fabrication processes. Research is ongoing on shape-changing materials and reliable, scalable printing methods, addressing challenges in integrating smart polymers or composites.
- Developing materials with desired properties for shape-changing behavior, durability, and compatibility with 4D printing processes is a significant challenge. Materials should exhibit predictable, repeatable transformations, possess mechanical integrity, and be environmentally sustainable.

- 4D printing demands regulatory challenges to ensure safety, quality control, and compatibility with manufacturing processes. Addressing issues like material safety, intellectual property, and certification is crucial for regulatory bodies.

Research and Development Requirements for Advancing the Field

To unlock the future potential of 4D printing, continued research and development efforts are necessary (Deepak Kumar et al., 2021; Osouli-Bostanabad et al., 2022).

- Material development focuses on shape-changing materials with precise, controllable responses, improved mechanical properties, and environmental sustainability.
- Exploring innovative printing techniques for improved precision, speed, scalability, and material integration.
- Developing advanced design tools and simulation software for optimizing 4D-printed objects.
- Encourage multidisciplinary collaboration among researchers, engineers, material scientists, designers to foster innovation and tackle complex challenges.

Ethical Considerations and Societal Implications of Widespread Adoption are listed here (Biswas et al., 2021; Subeshan et al., 2021).

- 4D printing technology advances raise intellectual property concerns and equity concerns. Balancing innovation and fair access to benefits is crucial, ensuring equitable use and protection of intellectual property rights.
- 4D printing can reduce material waste and promote sustainable manufacturing, but it requires assessing and mitigating its environmental impact throughout its lifecycle, including material sourcing, energy consumption, and end-of-life disposal.
- 4D printing adoption may disrupt industries and job markets, requiring smooth transition and identifying new employment opportunities for economic growth and social impact.

To fully realize the potential of 4D printing, collaboration between researchers, engineers, designers, policymakers, and industry experts is crucial. This approach accelerates innovation, addresses complex problems, and ensures responsible and ethical development of 4D printing technologies and applications. 4D printing has potential but faces challenges in technology, materials, and regulations. Responsible adoption requires research, interdisciplinary collaboration, and ethical considerations to transform industries and achieve positive impacts.

9. CONCLUSION

In conclusion, 4D printing technology holds immense potential to revolutionize various industries and transform the way we design, create, and interact with objects. Throughout this discussion, we have explored some of the future applications of 4D printing in different fields, including wearable technology, robotics, energy, transportation, fashion, and design. Here's a summary of the key applications:

- Wearable Technology: 4D printing enables shape-changing smart textiles, customizable wearable devices, interactive interfaces, and biometric monitoring integration, enhancing comfort, functionality, and user experience.
- Robotics and Autonomous Systems: 4D printing offers self-assembling and self-repairing robotic components, shape-changing robots, adaptive grippers and sensors, and advancements in soft robotics and morphological computation, improving versatility and dexterity.
- Energy and Environmental Applications: 4D printing contributes to adaptive solar panels and energy harvesting systems, responsive and energy-efficient buildings, shape-changing wind turbine blades, and smart materials for energy storage and distribution, promoting sustainability and efficiency.
- Transportation: 4D printing can lead to self-adaptive vehicle components, shape-changing car bodies, customizable and responsive interiors, and self-repairing automotive systems, enhancing performance, aerodynamics, user experience, and sustainability.
- Fashion and Design: 4D printing enables dynamic and customizable clothing and accessories, shape-changing jewelry and wearable art, responsive fashion shows and events, and sustainable manufacturing processes, offering creativity, personalization, and sustainability in the fashion industry.

Continued research and exploration in 4D printing are essential for unlocking its full potential. Technological advancements, material development, and regulatory frameworks require refinement. Interdisciplinary collaboration, involving researchers, engineers, designers, policymakers, and industry experts, is crucial for driving innovation, addressing challenges, and ensuring responsible and ethical adoption.

4D printing has the potential to transform industries by offering customization, adaptability, sustainability, and improved performance. By utilizing its capabilities, we can create dynamic objects and systems that respond to their environment, enhance user experiences, optimize energy usage, and contribute to a more sustainable and efficient future. As research and development continue, we can anticipate the full realization of 4D printing's future potential.

REFERENCES

Adam, G., Benouhiba, A., Rabenorosoa, K., Clévy, C., & Cappelleri, D. J. (2021). 4D Printing: Enabling Technology for Microrobotics Applications. *Advanced Intelligent Systems*, *3*(5), 2000216. doi:10.1002/aisy.202000216

Ameta, K. L., Solanki, V. S., Haque, S., Singh, V., Devi, A. P., & Chundawat, R. S. (2022). Critical appraisal and systematic review of 3D \& 4D printing in sustainable and environment-friendly smart manufacturing technologies. *Sustainable. Materials Technology*, 00481.

Biswas, M. C., Chakraborty, S., Bhattacharjee, A., & Mohammed, Z. (2021). 4D printing of shape memory materials for textiles: Mechanism, mathematical modeling, and challenges. *Advanced Functional Materials*, *31*(19), 2100257. doi:10.1002/adfm.202100257

Champeau, M., Heinze, D. A., Viana, T. N., de Souza, E. R., Chinellato, A. C., & Titotto, S. (2020). 4D printing of hydrogels: A review. *Advanced Functional Materials, 30*(31), 1910606. doi:10.1002/adfm.201910606

Cheng, T., Thielen, M., Poppinga, S., Tahouni, Y., Wood, D., Steinberg, T., Menges, A., & Speck, T. (2021). Bio-Inspired Motion Mechanisms: Computational Design and Material Programming of Self-Adjusting 4D-Printed Wearable Systems. *Advancement of Science, 8*(13), 2100411. doi:10.1002/advs.202100411 PMID:34258167

Choi, J., Kwon, O. C., Jo, W., Lee, H. J., & Moon, M. W. (2015). 4D printing technology: A review. *3D Printing and Additive Manufacturing, 2*(4), 159–167. doi:10.1089/3dp.2015.0039

Deepak Kumar, S., Dewangan, S., Jha, S. K., Parida, S. K., & Behera, A. (2021). 3D and 4D Printing in Industry 4.0: Trends, Challenges, and Opportunities. *Springer Proceedings in Materials, 9*, 579–587. doi:10.1007/978-981-16-0182-8_43

Javaid, M., & Haleem, A. (2019). 4D printing applications in medical field: A brief review. *Clinical Epidemiology and Global Health, 7*(3), 317–321. doi:10.1016/j.cegh.2018.09.007

Joshi, S., Rawat, K., C, K., Rajamohan, V., Mathew, A. T., Koziol, K., Kumar Thakur, V., & A.S.S., B. (2020). 4D printing of materials for the future: Opportunities and challenges. *Applied Materials Today, 18*, 100490. doi:10.1016/j.apmt.2019.100490

Kantaros, A., Ganetsos, T., & Piromalis, D. (2023). 3D and 4D Printing as Integrated Manufacturing Methods of Industry 4.0. *3D and 4D Printing as Integrated Manufacturing Methods of Industry, 4*, 12–22.

Khalid, M. Y., Arif, Z. U., Noroozi, R., Zolfagharian, A., & Bodaghi, M. (2022). 4D printing of shape memory polymer composites: A review on fabrication techniques, applications, and future perspectives. *Journal of Manufacturing Processes, 81*, 759–797. doi:10.1016/j.jmapro.2022.07.035

Kuang, X., Roach, D. J., Wu, J., Hamel, C. M., Ding, Z., Wang, T., Dunn, M. L., & Qi, H. J. (2019). Advances in 4D Printing: Materials and Applications. *Advanced Functional Materials, 29*(2), 1805290. doi:10.1002/adfm.201805290

Kumari, G., Abhishek, K., Singh, S., Hussain, A., Altamimi, M. A., Madhyastha, H., Webster, T. J., & Dev, A. (2022). A voyage from 3D to 4D printing in nanomedicine and healthcare: Part i. *Nanomedicine (London), 17*(4), 237–253. doi:10.2217/nnm-2021-0285 PMID:35109704

Leist, S. K., & Zhou, J. (2016). Current status of 4D printing technology and the potential of light-reactive smart materials as 4D printable materials. *Virtual and Physical Prototyping, 11*(4), 249–262. doi:10.1080/17452759.2016.1198630

Li, X., Shang, J., & Wang, Z. (2017). Intelligent materials: A review of applications in 4D printing. *Assembly Automation, 37*(2), 170–185. doi:10.1108/AA-11-2015-093

Mahmood, A., Akram, T., Chen, H., & Chen, S. (2022). On the Evolution of Additive Manufacturing (3D/4D Printing) Technologies: Materials, Applications, and Challenges. *Polymers, 14*(21), 4698. doi:10.3390/polym14214698 PMID:36365695

McCann, J., & Bryson, D. (2009). Smart Clothes and Wearable Technology. In *Smart Clothes and Wearable Technology*. Woodhead Publishing., doi:10.1533/9781845695668

McCann, J., & Bryson, D. (2022). *Smart clothes and wearable technology*. Woodhead Publishing.

McLellan, K., Sun, Y. C., & Naguib, H. E. (2022). A review of 4D printing: Materials, structures, and designs towards the printing of biomedical wearable devices. *Bioprinting (Amsterdam, Netherlands)*, *27*, e00217. doi:10.1016/j.bprint.2022.e00217

Mitchell, A., Lafont, U., Hołyńska, M., & Semprimoschnig, C. (2018). Additive manufacturing — A review of 4D printing and future applications. *Additive Manufacturing*, *24*, 606–626. doi:10.1016/j.addma.2018.10.038

Mohol, S. S., & Sharma, V. (2021). Functional applications of 4D printing: A review. *Rapid Prototyping Journal*, *27*(8), 1501–1522. doi:10.1108/RPJ-10-2020-0240

Moroni, S., Casettari, L., & Lamprou, D. A. (2022). 3D and 4D Printing in the Fight against Breast Cancer. *Biosensors (Basel)*, *12*(8), 568. doi:10.3390/bios12080568 PMID:35892465

Ntouanoglou, K., Stavropoulos, P., & Mourtzis, D. (2018). 4D printing prospects for the aerospace industry: A critical review. *Procedia Manufacturing*, *18*, 120–129. doi:10.1016/j.promfg.2018.11.016

Osouli-Bostanabad, K., Masalehdan, T., Kapsa, R. M. I., Quigley, A., Lalatsa, A., Bruggeman, K. F., Franks, S. J., Williams, R. J., & Nisbet, D. R. (2022). Traction of 3D and 4D Printing in the Healthcare Industry: From Drug Delivery and Analysis to Regenerative Medicine. *ACS Biomaterials Science & Engineering*, *8*(7), 2764–2797. doi:10.1021/acsbiomaterials.2c00094 PMID:35696306

Pacillo, G. A., Ranocchiai, G., Loccarini, F., & Fagone, M. (2021). Additive manufacturing in construction: A review on technologies, processes, materials, and their applications of 3D and 4D printing. *Material Design & Processing Communications*, *3*(5), e253. doi:10.1002/mdp2.253

Raina, A., Haq, M. I. U., Javaid, M., Rab, S., & Haleem, A. (2021). 4D Printing for Automotive Industry Applications. *Journal of The Institution of Engineers (India): Series D, 102*(2), 521–529. doi:10.1007/s40033-021-00284-z

Ruiz-Morales, J. C., Tarancón, A., Canales-Vázquez, J., Méndez-Ramos, J., Hernández-Afonso, L., Acosta-Mora, P., Rueda, J. R. M., & Fernández-González, R. (2017). Three dimensional printing of components and functional devices for energy and environmental applications. *Energy\&. Environmental Sciences (Ruse)*, *10*(4), 846–859.

Ryan, K. R., Down, M. P., & Banks, C. E. (2021). Future of additive manufacturing: Overview of 4D and 3D printed smart and advanced materials and their applications. *Chemical Engineering Journal*, *403*, 126162. doi:10.1016/j.cej.2020.126162

Sadasivuni, K. K., Deshmukh, K., & Almaadeed, M. A. (2019). *3D and 4D printing of polymer nanocomposite materials: Processes, applications, and challenges.* doi:10.1016/C2018-0-01194-9

Subeshan, B., Baddam, Y., & Asmatulu, E. (2021). Current progress of 4D-printing technology. *Progress in Additive Manufacturing*, *6*(3), 495–516. doi:10.100740964-021-00182-6

Tibbits, S. (2014). 4D Printing: Multi-Material Shape Change. *Architectural Design*, *84*(1), 116–121. doi:10.1002/ad.1710

Vates, U. K., Mishra, S., Kanu, N. J., & ... (2021). Biomimetic 4D printed materials: A state-of-the-art review on concepts, opportunities, and challenges. *Materials Today: Proceedings*, *47*, 3313–3319. doi:10.1016/j.matpr.2021.07.148

Wiechetek, Ł., & Gola, A. (2019). 4D Printing as an Innovative Technology for Creating Agile, Shape Morphing Products Meeting Individual User Needs. *Przedsiębiorczość i Zarządzanie, 20*(12), 23–35. http://yadda.icm.edu.pl/yadda/element/bwmeta1.element.ekon-element-000171570433%0Ahttp://files/280/bwmeta1.element.html

Zhang, Z., Demir, K. G., & Gu, G. X. (2019). Developments in 4D-printing: A review on current smart materials, technologies, and applications. *International Journal of Smart and Nano Materials*, *10*(3), 205–224. doi:10.1080/19475411.2019.1591541

Zhou, Y., Huang, W. M., Kang, S. F., Wu, X. L., Lu, H. B., Fu, J., & Cui, H. (2015). From 3D to 4D printing: Approaches and typical applications. *Journal of Mechanical Science and Technology*, *29*(10), 4281–4288. doi:10.100712206-015-0925-0

Zolfagharian, A., Kaynak, A., Bodaghi, M., Kouzani, A. Z., Gharaie, S., & Nahavandi, S. (2020). Control-based 4D printing: Adaptive 4D-printed systems. *Applied Sciences (Basel, Switzerland)*, *10*(9), 3020. doi:10.3390/app10093020

Chapter 7
Security Incidents and Security Requirements in Internet of Things (IoT) Devices

Pabak Indu
Institute of Engineering and Management, University of Engineering and Management, Kolkata, India & Indian Institute of Information Technology, Allahabad, India

Nabajyoti Mazumdar
Indian Institute of Information Technology, Allahabad, India

Souvik Bhattacharyya
University Institute of Technology, University of Burdwan, India

ABSTRACT

The proliferation of IoT devices has revolutionized daily life, offering unmatched convenience and connectivity but also exposing substantial security vulnerabilities. This chapter delves into security incidents and requirements in IoT devices, emphasizing the need to safeguard devices and their data. It analyzes historical events like the Mirai Botnet attack, Stuxnet worm, and ransomware to highlight the consequences of inadequate security. Exploring security challenges involving CIA triad, this chapter outlines practical measures for enhancing IoT security, including secure device configurations, robust authentication, and continuous monitoring. It also examines existing regulatory frameworks and standards, such as ISO/IEC, and industry-specific guidelines. In conclusion, this chapter underscores the urgency of addressing security incidents and fulfilling security requirements in IoT devices and provides an overview of emerging trends and challenges. It serves as a persuasive call to prioritize IoT device protection to preserve user privacy and interconnected system integrity.

DOI: 10.4018/979-8-3693-2647-3.ch007

1. INTRODUCTION

In this chapter, we embark on a comprehensive exploration of Internet of Things (IoT) devices, which have unequivocally established themselves as indispensable constituents of our quotidian existence. The "Internet of Things" paradigm engenders a complex network interlinking a myriad of tangible entities, spanning from motor vehicles to household appliances and a diverse array of products. These entities are imbued with a suite of sensors, underpinned by sophisticated software, and endowed with the capacity to acquire and disseminate data via the conduit of internet connectivity. These technological entities, often colloquially referred to as "smart devices," encompass a multifarious spectrum of technical contrivances, encompassing smart home appliances, wearable technologies, industrial IoT systems, and healthcare monitoring apparatus.

The ubiquity of IoT devices has ushered in profound metamorphoses across a plethora of sectors, progressively ingratiating themselves as integral facets of our daily regimen (Roman, R., et al., 2013). These technological innovations proffer augmented convenience, automated functionalities, and seamless connectivity, seamlessly assimilating into the fabric of our daily routines. The amalgamation of IoT devices has not only become emblematic of modern living but has also yielded diverse manifestations, such as smart thermostats optimizing domestic energy efficiency and fitness trackers assiduously scrutinizing an individual's physiological well-being.

1.1. The Ascendant Significance of IoT Devices in Contemporary Society

This phase, we endeavor to scrutinize the burgeoning significance of IoT devices within the tapestry of our contemporary lives. Our examination shall be anchored in assessing the ramifications of IoT devices across pivotal domains, including healthcare, transportation, agriculture, and home automation. This analytical endeavor shall pivot around elucidating the salient advantages conferred by these devices, encompassing facets of convenience, efficiency, and connectivity (Atzori, L,et al., 2010).

Within the realm of healthcare, IoT devices have instigated a paradigm shift of notable proportions, particularly manifesting in the domains of remote patient monitoring, telemedicine, and wearable health tracking. These technological enablers are instrumental in effecting continuous surveillance of vital physiological parameters, reinforcing adherence to prescribed therapeutic regimens, and orchestrating bespoke healthcare management paradigms. The aegis of remote patient monitoring, in particular, has empowered healthcare providers with the wherewithal to vigilantly oversee patients from afar, culminating in ameliorated health outcomes and commensurately diminished healthcare expenditures.

IoT devices have not been circumscribed by the confines of the healthcare sphere; they have proffered substantial advantages to the transportation sector. This extends to multifaceted applications ranging from vehicle telematics to fleet management and traffic optimization. Connected vehicles serve as veritable data repositories, aggregating real-time information pertaining to vehicle performance metrics, traffic dynamics, and driver behavioral patterns. These datasets serve as the bedrock for route optimization, preemptive maintenance initiatives, and the amelioration of road safety protocols.

In this scholarly pursuit, we shall unravel the multifaceted tapestry of IoT devices and discern their consequential imprint upon our contemporary human experience.

The integration of IoT devices has led to significant breakthroughs in the field of agriculture, with a special focus on precision farming. The utilisation of Internet of Things (IoT) sensors within agricultural environments facilitates the efficient surveillance and enhancement of irrigation, fertilisation, and livestock well-being, hence leading to heightened agricultural output and the promotion of sustainable farming methodologies.

For home automation, Internet of Things (IoT) devices provide enhanced levels of comfort, security, and energy efficiency etc. Gadgets used for smart home such as motion sensor lights, thermostats, and security cameras, offer the convenience of remote management, enabling homeowners to efficiently and safely manage their properties.

1.2. Navigating Vulnerability of IoT Devices

In this section, we embark on a journey into the intricate realm of security concerns that accompany the world wide adoption of Internet of Things (IoT) devices. Our quest here is to unravel the intricate tapestry of unique security challenges that orbit the utilization of these interconnected wonders. Amongst these challenges lie resource constraints, a multitude of communication protocols, and vulnerabilities that lurk both within the hardware and software domains.

A notable adversary faced in this domain arises from the inherent limitations of resources within IoT devices. These constraints encompass restricted processing capabilities, limited memory capacity, and finite battery life. These inescapable boundaries cast a shadow over the implementation of robust security measures, thereby exposing IoT devices to potential vulnerabilities and the looming specter of exploitative attacks. Moreover, the diverse range of communication protocols employed by IoT devices, spanning the realms of Wi-Fi, Bluetooth, Zigbee, and cellular networks, presents a formidable challenge in the pursuit of ensuring secure and dependable connectivity (Alshaikh, H. et al., 2020).

Another chapter in our exploration unveils the intrinsic vulnerabilities nestled within the hardware and software architecture of IoT devices. A myriad of these devices showcases frailties in their security vulnerabilities, exposing them to potential threat. The existence of inadequate authentication systems, fragile encryption techniques, and inefficient update mechanisms further exacerbates these vulnerabilities.

The presence of these inherent vulnerabilities within the IoT landscape opens the door to a Pandora's box of risks. These include, but are not confined to, the specter of unauthorized access, harrowing data breaches, invasions of privacy, and the looming menace of malevolent exploitation. For instance, the act of gaining unauthorized access to a smart home device can trigger a cascade of events that threaten the user's privacy and even serve as a gateway to launch further attacks on the home network. Similarly, the compromise of an industrial IoT device can have far-reaching consequences, spanning from operational disruptions to financial repercussions, and in the most dire circumstances, potential physical harm.

To chart a safe course through these security challenges, it becomes imperative to instate measures that act as guardians of IoT device integrity, confidentiality, and availability. This necessitates the implementation of stalwart authentication mechanisms, robust encryption protocols, secure firmware update processes, and the judicious use of network segmentation to effectively isolate IoT devices from mission-critical systems. Our journey through the realm of IoT security will unveil the strategies and solutions that illuminate this path to safeguarding our connected future.

2. HISTORICAL INSTANCES ILLUSTRATING VULNERABILITIES IN IOT DEVICES

Recent years have borne witness to a series of noteworthy security incidents that have cast a stark spotlight upon the innate vulnerabilities inherent in Internet of Things (IoT) devices. These real-world events serve as empirical evidence of the multifaceted threats that traverse the landscape of IoT technology.

Among these historical records, the 'Mirai Botnet Attack of 2016' stands as a prominent case study. This incident unfolded as a manifestation of the exploitation of susceptible IoT devices, precipitating the establishment of a substantial botnet. This botnet, in turn, was weaponized to execute a series of distributed denial-of-service (DDoS) assaults of substantial consequence. The event underscores the gravity of vulnerabilities that permeate the IoT ecosystem and their potential for significant disruption (Antonakakis, M. et al. .2017).

The Stuxnet Worm, in the year 2010, specifically targeted industrial control systems by exploiting Internet of Things (IoT) devices, with the primary objective of causing disruption to nuclear facilities (Jiang, X., et al., 2020).

The NotPetya ransomware outbreak of 2017 originated from a software update for Ukrainian accounting systems and quickly propagated to susceptible Internet of Things (IoT) devices, resulting in significant disruptions (Wang, W., et al., 2017).

The 2017 WannaCry ransomware assault was designed to primarily target Internet of Things (IoT) devices that were operating on outdated versions of the Windows operating system. This malicious software encrypted data on these devices and afterwards demanded ransom payments.

The BlueBorne vulnerability, which emerged in 2017, had a significant impact on Internet of Things (IoT) devices equipped with Bluetooth capabilities. This vulnerability allowed for remote code execution and unauthorised control of affected devices (Ujjawal, K. et al., 2018).

The Key Reinstallation Attack (KRACK) of 2017 was aimed at the WPA2 protocol, which is extensively utilised in Wi-Fi communications. This attack had the ability to compromise the security of IoT devices by granting unauthorised access (Vanhoef, M., et al.,2017).

The Triton/Trisis malware, which was detected in 2017, specifically targeted industrial safety systems, hence highlighting the susceptibility of Internet of Things (IoT) equipment to criminal activities (Di Pinto et al. 2018).

In this chapter, we embark on a technical voyage through the turbulent seas of IoT device vulnerabilities. The annals of recent history have unveiled a tapestry of real-world incidents that serve as cautionary tales, illuminating the multifaceted threats woven into the very fabric of IoT technology.

Our journey begins in 2018 with the malevolent VPNFilter malware. Crafted with a sinister intent, it set its sights on infiltrating IoT devices, clandestinely gaining unauthorized access to network traffic, siphoning data, and orchestrating a repertoire of destructive operations (Zhao, H. et al., 2021).

Fast forward to 2020, and we encounter the Ripple20 vulnerabilities—a seismic event in the IoT landscape. These vulnerabilities, akin to seismic fault lines, rendered a plethora of IoT devices susceptible to seismic shocks. Remote code execution, data leakage, and the specter of device hijacking loomed large on the horizon (Rajkumar, V. S, 2021).

2018 introduced us to the Meltdown and Spectre vulnerabilities, akin to fault lines in the IoT bedrock. These fissures provided unauthorized individuals with a gateway to sensitive data, shattering the façade of IoT security (Kocher, P. et al., 2020).

In the following year, 2019, vulnerabilities in D-Link routers came to the fore. These potential chinks in the armor rendered routers susceptible to remote attacks and unauthorized incursions ("Using CVE-2022-4363",2022).

In a parallel narrative of 2019, we encountered the unsettling saga of unauthorized access to Ring security cameras. This incident laid bare the vulnerabilities and privacy concerns that accompany IoT devices employed for residential surveillance (Tuohy, J. P,2023).

The year 2019 also bore witness to the emergence of the URGENT/11 vulnerabilities—an urgent matter indeed. These vulnerabilities acted as conduits for remote code execution, unleashing a potent threat to critical infrastructure ("Using URGENT/11",2023).

As we traverse these technical accounts, we must recognize that they not only underscore the urgency of fortifying IoT device security but also beckon us to explore the robust measures essential for safeguarding IoT ecosystems in an era characterized by relentless interconnectivity.These occurrences highlight the imperative requirement for strong security protocols in order to safeguard Internet of Things (IoT) devices and the interconnected systems they are linked to. Addressing these vulnerabilities is crucial in order to guarantee the secure and dependable functioning of Internet of Things (IoT) technologies across diverse sectors.

The ShadowHammer supply chain attack, which occurred in 2019, involved the compromise of ASUS computer's supply chain. This allowed the attackers to implant a backdoor into IoT devices and selectively target certain systems for surveillance purposes ("Using Operation ShadowHammer",2021).

The CVE-2020-0796, also known as SMBGhost, vulnerability discovered in 2020, pertains to the Microsoft Server Message Block (SMB) protocol. This vulnerability specifically rendered Internet of Things (IoT) devices operating on the Windows platform susceptible to remote code execution attacks (Yaacoub, J. P. A et al.,2020).

2.1 The Effects of Security Incidents on Individuals and Organisations

The ramifications of security incidents on individuals and organisations can be substantial and wide-ranging. The following are several significant consequences that individuals and organisations may encounter due to security incidents in Internet of Things (IoT) devices.

Security incidents have the potential to cause significant financial losses for both individuals and organisations. This encompasses various expenses related to incident response, recovery, legal expenditures, regulatory penalties, and potential financial setbacks resulting from operational disruptions (Kovalchuk, O. et al., 2021).

The occurrence of security incidents can give rise to data breaches, thereby compromising the confidentiality of sensitive information and giving way to infringements upon privacy. This encompasses personal identifiable information (PII), financial data, and other forms of confidential data. Reputational harm and erosion of trust can be consequences of privacy infringements (Sinanaj, G., & Muntermann, J., 2013).

The occurrence of security incidents has the potential to disrupt the regular operations of Internet of Things (IoT) devices and their corresponding systems. The aforementioned consequences encompass downtime, decreased productivity, and disruptions in essential services, thereby affecting both individuals and organisations that heavily depend on these devices for their day-to-day operations (Ingemarsdotter, E et al.,2020).

Certain security incidents have the potential to cause physical harm to infrastructure that is under the control of Internet of Things (IoT) devices. Incidents aimed at industrial Internet of Things (IoT) systems have the potential to result in harm to machinery, equipment, and vital infrastructure, thereby posing safety hazards and substantial financial consequences (Zhang, X. et al., 2020).

The erosion of trust and reputation is a consequence of security incidents, which have a detrimental impact on the confidence placed in IoT devices, service providers, and the broader IoT ecosystem. Reputational damage can have adverse consequences for organisations, resulting in the attrition of customers, partnerships, and potential business prospects (Grover, V., et al. 2018).

Legal and regulatory ramifications may ensue as a result of security incidents, particularly in cases where data breaches transpire or privacy regulations are infringed upon. Organisations may incur penalties, legal actions, and regulatory investigations, which can impose additional financial and reputational burdens (Crossler, R. E. et al., 2013).

Personal safety and security risks can potentially arise, placing individuals in a vulnerable position, contingent upon the specific characteristics of the security incident. The utilisation of compromised Internet of Things (IoT) devices in home security systems or healthcare monitoring devices has the potential to result in physical harm or unauthorised intrusion into private spaces (Konstantinou, C. et al.,2015).

The occurrence of security incidents can elicit psychological and emotional consequences for individuals, manifesting as sensations of violation, insecurity, and mistrust. The aforementioned occurrences have the potential to induce feelings of stress, anxiety, and a heightened perception of vulnerability within the individuals impacted (Ferguson, C. J. et al., 2008).

The prioritisation of IoT device security, the implementation of robust security measures, and the adherence to best practises are imperative for individuals and organisations in order to mitigate potential impacts and safeguard against security incidents within the IoT ecosystem.

2.2 Insights Gained From Previous Incidents

Discover the invaluable insights that lie beneath the surface, waiting to be unearthed. Delve into the depths of past breaches and breaches, and emerge with a newfound understanding of the ever-evolving landscape of security threats. Let the lessons learned.

Discover the invaluable lessons learned from past security incidents, emphasising the utmost significance of embracing tailored security measures for Internet of Things (IoT) devices. Experience these impactful incidents that serve as powerful reminders of the imperative need for proactive safeguards. Safeguard your devices and the networks they are an integral part of, ensuring utmost protection.

1. Discover the power of timely application of patches and updates: a recurring lesson that emphasises the utmost importance of promptly implementing these essential enhancements. Discover the untold tales of countless incidents that unfolded due to neglected vulnerabilities. These vulnerabilities, if only addressed promptly, could have been effortlessly neutralised. Discover the paramount importance of consistently upkeeping IoT devices for individuals and organisations alike. Stay ahead of the curve by swiftly implementing the latest security patches. Discover the power of a proactive approach - the key to effectively mitigating the risk of exploitation. Trust the experts, as cited in the article by Sander-Staudt, M.(2010).
2. Unlock the Power of Robust Authentication Practises: Discover the game-changing secret to safeguarding your IoT devices from unauthorised access. Discover the undeniable importance of

fortifying your online security with robust, one-of-a-kind passwords and the implementation of cutting-edge multi-factor authentication (MFA). Introducing these exceptional security measures adds multiple layers of protection, dramatically diminishing the chances of any unauthorised intrusion (Ferrag, M. A., et al. 2017).

3. Enhance IoT Device Security with the Power of Defense-in-Depth Strategy: Implementing this robust approach is the key to fortifying your devices and staying one step ahead of potential threats. Introducing a cutting-edge approach that encompasses the strategic implementation of a diverse range of security measures. Brace yourself for the unparalleled power of network segmentation, intrusion detection systems, and access control methods. Experience the ultimate protection that leaves no room for compromise. By strategically layering multiple defences, the security posture is elevated to new heights, creating an impenetrable fortress that poses a formidable challenge to any would-be attacker. With each layer meticulously designed to thwart malicious intent, the system becomes an impregnable stronghold, safeguarding valuable assets and sensitive information (José, M. (2023)).
4. Introducing Continuous Monitoring: Unlocking the Power of Swift Security Issue Detection for IoT Devices and Networks. Discover the secret to organisational success: the implementation of robust and dynamic incident response strategies. With these strategies in place, your organisation will be empowered to swiftly and seamlessly combat any security breaches that come its way. Don't let your organisation be caught off guard - take charge and ensure a quick and efficient response to any potential threats. Experience peace of mind with our proactive approach that guarantees the swift detection and resolution of any security events. Trust in our expertise to keep you protected at all times (Mahmoud, R., et al. 2015).

Unlock the boundless potential of IoT security by harnessing the invaluable wisdom gleaned from past incidents. Let these profound insights become the bedrock of your journey, empowering both organisations and individuals to navigate the intricate landscape with unwavering confidence. Supercharge the safeguarding of your IoT devices and the invaluable data they handle by seamlessly incorporating these invaluable lessons into your security practises. Experience unparalleled protection and peace of mind like never before.

It is imperative for organisations to evaluate the security measures implemented by vendors of Internet of Things (IoT) devices and guarantee the adoption of secure supply chains (Kolias, C., et al. 2017). Previous occurrences have illustrated the significance of thoroughly evaluating vendors in terms of their security protocols and verifying the trustworthiness of devices during the procurement phase.

The promotion of user education and awareness plays a vital role in the mitigation of security risks. Disseminating knowledge to individuals and organisations regarding optimal strategies, such as employing robust passwords, adhering to regular software updates, and developing the ability to identify phishing attempts, can effectively mitigate security incidents (Mawel, M. (2022)).

3. THE SECURITY REQUIREMENTS FOR INTERNET OF THINGS (IOT) DEVICES

3.1. Gaining Insight Into the Distinctive Security Challenges Posed by Internet of Things (IoT) Devices

Internet of Things (IoT) devices pose distinct security challenges as a result of their heterogeneous characteristics, limitations in resources, and decentralised architecture. This subsection examines the unique attributes of IoT devices that give rise to security challenges. These attributes include limited computational capabilities, restricted memory capacity, and the vast scale and diverse nature of the IoT ecosystem (Sedrati, A., & Mezrioui, A., 2018). Comprehending these challenges is imperative for discerning and executing suitable security measures.

3.2. The Preservation of Confidentiality in Internet of Things (IoT) Devices

The maintenance of confidentiality in Internet of Things (IoT) devices necessitates safeguarding sensitive information from unauthorised access and disclosure. This subsection provides an analysis of essential security measures aimed at preserving confidentiality in Internet of Things (IoT) devices.

3.2.1. The Topic of Discussion Pertains to the Concepts of Encryption and Data Protection

The utilisation of encryption is of utmost importance in safeguarding the confidentiality of data within Internet of Things (IoT) devices. This subsection delves into the utilisation of cryptographic algorithms and secure communication protocols for the purpose of encrypting data both when it is stored and when it is being transmitted (Sicari, S.,et al., 2015). The paper examines the significance of employing end-to-end encryption, secure key management, and secure storage mechanisms as a means of safeguarding sensitive information from unauthorised access.

3.2.2. Access Control Mechanisms Refer to the Various Methods and Techniques Employed to Regulate and Manage Access to Resources, Systems, or Information Within an Organisation

Access control mechanisms play a crucial role in the enforcement of confidentiality within Internet of Things (IoT) devices. This subsection explores different access control techniques, including role-based access control (RBAC) (Li, F., Zheng, Z., & Jin, C. 2016), attribute-based access control (ABAC), and fine-grained access control policies. The text explores the significance of appropriately configuring access control mechanisms in order to restrict access solely to authorised entities.

3.3. Ensuring the Integrity of Internet of Things (IoT) Devices

Within the intricate framework of Internet of Things (IoT) devices, the concept of integrity assumes paramount importance, for it is the cornerstone upon which we establish the reliability and trustworthiness of these interconnected entities.

3.3.1: The Imperative of Device Authentication

Our scholarly exploration brings us to a critical juncture—device authentication. This facet of IoT security stands as a sentinel, guarding the gates of secure communication and access. In this section, we embark on a meticulous examination of device authentication, a linchpin in our endeavor to fortify the security and integrity of IoT devices.

Device authentication, we soon discern, transcends the realm of mere procedural formality. Rather, it emerges as a pivotal element in the bulwarking of IoT integrity. Our in-depth analysis encompasses a comprehensive survey of authentication mechanisms, ranging from the robustness of digital certificates to the intricate intricacies of public-key infrastructure (PKI) and the nuanced protocols governing mutual authentication.

Our scholarly journey underscores the criticality of robust device authentication measures. In the interconnected milieu of IoT, the stakes are palpably elevated. The specter of unauthorized devices infiltrating or compromising the IoT network looms large. Hence, the ensuing discourse is dedicated to elucidating the path toward ensuring the unassailable trustworthiness and integrity of our IoT ecosystem (HaddadPajouh, H. et al., 2021).

3.3.2. Ensuring Secure Firmware Updates

Preserving the integrity of IoT devices hinges upon the meticulous implementation of secure firmware updates. Within this subsection, we embark on an academic journey, dissecting various mechanisms at our disposal to ensure the secure and trustworthy updating of device firmware (Mtetwa, N. S et al., 2019).

This section encompasses multifaceted strategies, including the deployment of digital signatures, secure bootstrapping procedures, and rigorous firmware validation protocols. These mechanisms serve as our sentinels, fortifying the walls of security around firmware updates.

It is imperative to recognize the paramount significance of guaranteeing both the authenticity and integrity of firmware updates. By doing so, we erect formidable barriers against unauthorized alterations and the insidious installation of malevolent firmware—a defense mechanism indispensable in the IoT landscape.

This academic discourse unearths the intricate intricacies of securing firmware updates, emphasizing the imperative nature of these measures in safeguarding the reliability and trustworthiness of IoT devices in an era fraught with security challenges.

3.4. Ensuring Availability in the Realm of IoT Devices

In our scholarly exploration, we now turn our attention to the indispensable aspect of ensuring the availability of Internet of Things (IoT) devices. This chapter delves into the critical measures required to protect against disruptions and maintain continuous operation, a paramount consideration in the IoT security landscape.

3.4.1. Mitigating DDoS Threats

At the forefront of our discussion lies the formidable challenge of Distributed Denial of Service (DDoS) attacks, a significant threat to the availability of IoT devices. In this subsection, we embark on an academic analysis of the strategies and techniques employed to counter the insidious nature of DDoS attacks.

This section includes a range of defensive maneuvers, such as traffic filtering, rate limiting, and anomaly detection techniques. These measures serve as our sentinels, vigilantly guarding against the disruptive forces of DDoS attacks. This discourse underscores the pivotal role of swift identification and efficient mitigation in preventing service interruptions—a critical defense in our quest to ensure the availability of IoT devices.

3.4.2. The Crucial Role of Redundancy and Failover Mechanisms

We further delve into the realm of system reliability and availability, where the implementation of redundancy and failover mechanisms reigns supreme. This subsection conducts an academic examination of the utilization of redundant components, backup systems, and failover protocols—a triumvirate of strategies that guarantee uninterrupted operation and enhance resilience in the face of failures (Kumar, S., et al. 2020).

This discourse meticulously scrutinizes the significance of fault tolerance and system redundancy, for it is these attributes that stand as bulwarks against disruptions, ensuring the uninterrupted provision of services.

By comprehending these distinct security challenges and addressing the triad of confidentiality, integrity, and availability, both organizations and individuals can bolster the security posture of their IoT deployments and mitigate potential risks.

4. BEST PRACTICES FOR ENSURING SECURITY OF IOT DEVICES

4.1. Forging Secure Device Configurations

4.1.1. The Predicament of Default Passwords and Credentials

Within the sphere of IoT security, a pressing concern takes center stage: the use of default passwords and credentials. This security vulnerability is pervasive, with a multitude of IoT devices being disseminated with passwords that are either generic or easily foreseeable. Such laxity renders these devices vulnerable to unauthorized intrusion, a grave threat to their security.

In this subsection, we undertake an exhaustive academic analysis, delving deep into the risks that default passwords pose. We scrutinize the potential ramifications of neglecting to modify these passwords, shedding light on the profound security implications (Alaba, F. A. et al.,2017).

The paper examines different attack vectors, including brute force attacks and dictionary attacks, which exploit default credentials. In addition, this study examines real-life instances of security breaches that have occurred as a consequence of exploiting default passwords. The subsection additionally offers comprehensive instructions for ensuring secure password management in IoT devices. These guidelines encompass the utilisation of robust and intricate passwords, the enforcement of password rotation policies, and the avoidance of common pitfalls such as employing commonly used or easily predictable passwords.

4.1.2. Delving into Network Segmentation for IoT Security

In this section, we turn our attention to the intricate realm of network segmentation, a fundamental aspect of bolstering the security of Internet of Things (IoT) devices. Consider this as an academic discourse, a deep dive into the intricate facets of network segmentation, akin to a researcher presenting their findings.

4.1.3. Unpacking the Significance of Network Segmentation

Network segmentation, within the realm of IoT security, is more than a mere concept; it is a strategic pillar that demands our scrutiny (Ray, P. P., 2018). In this discussion, we embark on a comprehensive exploration, peeling away the layers to reveal the profound implications of this practice.

Our investigation spans a spectrum of network segmentation strategies, encompassing Virtual Local Area Networks (VLANs) and the meticulous crafting of subnets. Each strategy, akin to a distinct avenue of research, plays a pivotal role in safeguarding our digital domain.

We dissect the intricate mechanisms of network zoning, the art of isolating traffic, and the intricate configurations of firewalls. These components, much like findings in an academic study, collectively contribute to the successful execution of network segmentation.

Furthermore, our discourse extends to the emerging frontiers of Zero Trust Architecture (ZTA), a paradigm shift that promises to reshape our approach to cybersecurity within IoT network segmentation.

However, it is incumbent upon us to acknowledge the complexities and trade-offs inherent in network segmentation. We engage in a rigorous examination of the challenges surrounding the management of segmented networks and their implications for device compatibility.

4.2. Unveiling Secure Communication Protocols

4.2.1. The Crucial Role of Transport Layer Security (TLS)

At the heart of our discourse lies the venerable Transport Layer Security (TLS) protocol, as referenced (Keoh, S. L. et al., 2014). TLS is a cryptographic workhorse, facilitating secure communication across diverse networks. In this section, we embark on a comprehensive exposition of TLS and its pivotal role in ensuring the security of communications among Internet of Things (IoT) devices.

Our analysis begins with a deep dive into the TLS handshake process. It's akin to a secret handshake between trusted partners, involving the exchange of cryptographic keys and the negotiation of cipher suites. The ultimate goal? To establish an impervious channel for secure communication.

We proceed to scrutinize the significance of digital certificates, the guardians of identity verification in this digital realm. These certificates not only vouch for the identity of communicating entities but also safeguard the integrity of the data they transmit.

Yet, our research does not shy away from acknowledging the vulnerabilities and shortcomings that can afflict TLS implementations. We delve into the risks posed by outdated protocols and weak cipher suites, shedding light on the potential pitfalls.

Moreover, our scholarly journey extends to practical recommendations for optimizing TLS configurations. We advocate for the adoption of robust cipher suites, diligent certificate administration, and the implementation of forward secrecy—a multifaceted approach to fortify TLS security.

4.2.2. Fortifying MQTT for Enhanced IoT Security

The Message Queuing Telemetry Transport (MQTT) protocol, as referenced (Marques, G., et al., 2019), stands as a lightweight messaging solution frequently employed in IoT implementations. However, MQTT, by its intrinsic design, does not inherently provide security measures. This section pivots towards the imperative task of fortifying MQTT communications to uphold the tenets of confidentiality, integrity, and authenticity within the IoT domain.

Our exploration delves into the adoption of secure MQTT variants, notably MQTT over TLS (MQTT/TLS) or MQTT over WebSocket Secure (MQTT/WS-Secure). These variants serve as our guardians, activated to enforce encryption, authentication, and access control mechanisms that secure the IoT data.

Furthermore, our study takes a close look at the utilization of client-side certificates, acting as digital passports, to facilitate mutual authentication between MQTT clients and brokers. This two-way trust mechanism ensures that communicating entities are who they claim to be, adding layers of security to MQTT interactions.

Additionally, our research meticulously examines secure configurations for MQTT brokers, with a specific focus on access control lists (ACLs) and message filtering. These configurations are akin to gatekeepers, diligently controlling who can access what, and thus augmenting the security measures within MQTT-based IoT deployments.

4.3. The Significance of Firmware Updates and Patch Management

Regular firmware updates and the meticulous management of patches stand as linchpins in the endeavor to mitigate known vulnerabilities and security flaws within Internet of Things (IoT) devices (Samaila, M. G. et al., 2018). In this section, we embark on an extensive analysis, uncovering the profound importance of maintaining up-to-date firmware and implementing robust patch management procedures.

Our exploration ventures into the unique challenges that arise when updating firmware in the context of IoT. We confront the limitations imposed by resource constraints on IoT devices, acknowledging the complex and heterogeneous nature of the IoT ecosystem.

Furthermore, we scrutinize a spectrum of strategies for the distribution of firmware updates, including the realm of Over-the-Air (OTA) updates, secure boot processes, and the judicious use of version control systems. Each strategy is akin to a tool in our arsenal, designed to navigate the intricacies of IoT firmware management.

Moreover, our research emphasizes the pivotal role of continuous vulnerability monitoring, vendor support, and user awareness in ensuring the timely and efficient handling of patches. We shed light on the significance of vulnerability databases as repositories of knowledge and automated patch management tools as facilitators of patch deployment in extensive IoT deployments.

4.4. Reinforcing IoT Security through Robust Authentication and Authorization

4.4.1. Unpacking the Significance of Two-Factor Authentication (2FA)

Two-Factor Authentication (2FA) emerges as a formidable security paradigm, mandating users to furnish two distinct authentication factors to gain access. Our examination delves into the merits of 2FA in fortifying the security of Internet of Things (IoT) devices, acting as a bulwark against unauthorized access.

Our analysis encompasses an array of authentication factors, encompassing conventional passwords, biometrics, smart cards, and mobile tokens. Each factor represents a unique layer of security, collectively fortifying the 2FA framework.

Furthermore, we underscore the pivotal need for tailored 2FA mechanisms explicitly designed to align with the nuanced functionalities of IoT devices. This includes considerations such as device-based authentication and the seamless integration of biometric authentication through embedded sensors.

Our research extends to the complexities and nuances inherent in deploying 2FA on IoT devices that often operate under resource constraints. This endeavor is akin to optimizing a finely-calibrated system to function efficiently within limited resources.

Additionally, we delve into emerging authentication technologies, notably FIDO (Fast Identity Online), and assess their potential applications within the purview of IoT security.

4.4.2. The Essence of Role-Based Access Control (RBAC)

Role-Based Access Control (RBAC), as elucidated by (Sengupta, J., Ruj, S., & Bit, S. D. 2020), assumes a prominent role as an access control paradigm. It strategically allocates permissions and privileges based on predefined user roles, akin to orchestrating an intricate symphony of access permissions. Join me as we unravel the layers of RBAC and appreciate its profound relevance within the expansive realm of Internet of Things (IoT) devices.

We shall meticulously uncover the inherent advantages of Role-Based Access Control (RBAC) in the systematic management of access privileges for IoT devices. RBAC, as we shall discover, stands as a precise and formidable means of governing access permissions, effectively erecting barricades against unauthorized activities.

Our scholarly odyssey will navigate through the theoretical foundations that underpin roles, permissions, and authorization policies. I shall provide you with clear and methodical guidelines for the seamless implementation of Role-Based Access Control (RBAC) in IoT settings. These guidelines will encompass critical facets such as role allocation, the establishment of role hierarchies, and the unwavering enforcement of policies contingent upon roles.

Furthermore, we shall shed light on the intrinsic benefits of Role-Based Access Control (RBAC) in efficiently overseeing intricate IoT ecosystems, replete with a multitude of users and a diverse array of device categories.

4.5. Examining Continuous Monitoring and Incident Response in IoT

4.5.1. The Crucial Role of Intrusion Detection Systems (IDS)

In the context of IoT, Intrusion Detection Systems (IDS) take on profound importance. They act as vigilant guardians, diligently monitoring IoT devices for any signs of suspicious activities or potential security breaches (Casola, V. et al., 2019). This subsection meticulously dissects the significance of IDS deployment in swiftly identifying and responding to security incidents in the IoT landscape.

We will delve into various manifestations of intrusion detection systems, including network-based IDS (NIDS) and host-based IDS (HIDS), critically evaluating their suitability for integration within IoT environments. The subsequent subsection will underscore the significance of diverse detection methodologies, encompassing anomaly detection, signature-based detection, and behavior-based detection.

Moreover, our research will extend to explore the fusion of IDS with threat intelligence feeds and the utilization of machine learning algorithms to enhance detection capabilities.

Lastly, we will emphasize the pivotal importance of rapid response mechanisms and incident investigation protocols in mitigating the adverse consequences of security incidents. This comprehensive approach ensures that IoT ecosystems remain resilient in the face of evolving threats.

4.5.2. Enhancing IoT Security Through SIEM Integration

SIEM systems stand as formidable pillars in the realm of cybersecurity, offering centralized platforms for the meticulous logging, vigilant monitoring, and meticulous analysis of security events ("Using ISO/IEC 27001:2013",2013). Our research endeavors to dissect the profound implications of deploying SIEM solutions, specifically geared towards aggregating and correlating security events emanating from IoT devices.

Our journey commences by navigating through the multifaceted challenges inherent in managing IoT events. We grapple with the sheer volume of data generated by these devices and the pressing need for real-time analysis. Our research goes in-depth, scrutinizing the diverse functionalities of SIEM systems, with a particular focus on their adeptness in identifying security incidents, promptly generating alerts, and providing invaluable support in forensic investigations.

But our exploration extends beyond the surface. We delve into the intricacies of integrating SIEM with complementary security components, including Intrusion Detection Systems (IDS) and threat intelligence feeds. This integration paves the way for a comprehensive security paradigm meticulously tailored to the intricate demands of IoT environments.

In our quest for thoroughness, we underscore the critical aspects of log management, data retention policies, and compliance obligations, all of which bear substantial significance in the implementation of SIEM solutions within the multifaceted realm of IoT.By adhering to these recommended practises for securing IoT devices, both individuals and organisations can greatly improve the overall security of their IoT deployments. This will result in a decreased likelihood of unauthorised access or data breaches, as well as a reduction in potential security threats within the IoT ecosystem.

5. THE PRESENT DISCOURSE PERTAINS TO THE REGULATORY AND STANDARDS FRAMEWORKS THAT GOVERN THE SECURITY OF THE INTERNET OF THINGS (IOT)

5.1. International Standards Organisations Are Entities That Develop and Publish Standards That Are Recognised and Utilised on a Global Scale

5.1.1. ISO/IEC

The development of standards for IoT security is a collaborative effort between the International Organisation for Standardisation (ISO) and the International Electrotechnical Commission (IEC) ("Using NIST Cybersecurity Framework",2023). These standards offer organisations guidance and recommended practises to improve the security of their Internet of Things (IoT) implementations. The ISO/IEC 27001 standard, entitled "Information Security Management System," outlines the necessary criteria for the establishment, implementation, maintenance, and ongoing enhancement of an information security management system (ISMS). The aforementioned system offers a methodical approach to effectively oversee and safeguard sensitive corporate data, guaranteeing its confidentiality, integrity, and accessibility. The adherence to ISO/IEC 27001 aids organisations in the identification and mitigation of potential security risks that may arise from the utilisation of Internet of Things (IoT) devices and their interconnected networks.

5.1.2. NIST

The National Institute of Standards and Technology (NIST) is widely recognised as a leading institution in the field of cybersecurity, particularly in accordance with the Internet of Things (IoT). NIST offers comprehensive guidelines and recommendations for ensuring the security of IoT systems. The NIST Cybersecurity Framework is a framework that has gained significant adoption and is utilised by various organisations. It offers these organisations a risk-based methodology to effectively manage and enhance their cybersecurity stance. The aforementioned set of core functions, namely identify, protect, detect, respond, and recover, are integral components that aid organisations in formulating efficient security strategies for their Internet of Things (IoT) implementations. Furthermore, NIST Special Publication 800-53 offers an extensive array of security controls designed for federal information systems and organisations. These controls can be utilised to implement strong security measures for Internet of Things (IoT) devices and networks.

5.2. Security Guidelines That Are Specific to the Industry

5.2.1. Deciphering the OWASP IoT Top Ten Project

The OWASP IoT Top Ten Project stands as a beacon in the IoT security landscape, diligently addressing the most critical security risks that pervade Internet of Things (IoT) devices and applications. Our exploration begins with a deep dive into the fundamental mission of this project.

At its core, the OWASP IoT Top Ten Project is a comprehensive compendium. It meticulously identifies and documents the paramount security risks inherent to IoT implementations. Within these documented vulnerabilities, we encounter issues such as feeble authentication protocols, vulnerable web interfaces, and the critical absence of secure update mechanisms.

But this project is more than just a catalog of vulnerabilities; it serves as a guiding light. For organizations navigating the intricate terrain of IoT security, the OWASP Top Ten list is a valuable resource. It not only reveals the unique security challenges posed by IoT but also offers actionable guidance on implementing robust security controls and countermeasures.

5.2.2. The Industrial Internet Consortium (IIC) Has Meticulously Crafted a Comprehensive Security Framework, Which Serves as a Compendium of Guidelines and Best Practices With a Singular Objective: To Bolster the Security Landscape of the Industrial Internet

At its core, this endeavor is championed by the IIC, a highly influential organization wholly dedicated to propelling the advancement of Internet of Things (IoT) technology within industrial domains. The IIC Security Framework is a meticulously designed compendium of directives and best practices. Its purpose is to elevate the security stance of IoT deployments situated within industrial settings, which demand specialized attention. This framework is a multifaceted approach, meticulously curated to fortify IoT systems within these specialized environments. Its cornerstone principles revolve around trustworthiness, scalability, and resilience. The framework provides a protective shield encompassing various dimensions of IoT security. It extends its coverage to device authentication, secure communication protocols, data fortification, and access control mechanisms. Through unwavering adherence to the IIC Security Framework, organizations have the opportunity to construct an impregnable fortress around their industrial IoT deployments, thereby laying a secure foundation for safeguarding these invaluable systems.

5.3. In the Realm of Governmental Laws and Initiatives, There Exists a Topic of Significant Importance That Undeniably Warrants Our Attention

5.3.1. General Data Protection Regulation (GDPR) Is a Legal Framework, Meticulously Established by the European Union (EU) and Judiciously Applicable Within the European Economic Area (EEA), Officially Came Into Effect on the Momentous Date of May 25, 2018

The General Data Protection Regulation (GDPR) stands as an exemplar of a comprehensive data protection policy, one painstakingly crafted by the European Union (EU). Its overarching mission is centered profoundly on the preservation and unwavering safeguarding of individuals' cherished privacy and their invaluable personal data. In the intricate and ever-evolving landscape of the Internet of Things (IoT), the GDPR assumes an unquestionably substantial and consequential role. This significance emanates from its pertinence to the extensive collection and meticulous manipulation of personal data perpetuated by the multifarious IoT devices. Organizations bestowed with the solemn duty of vigilantly safeguarding this treasure trove of personal data bear a stringent and unwavering responsibility. This responsibility finds its anchoring in the unequivocal and scrupulous adherence to the well-articulated provisions meticulously outlined in the General Data Protection Regulation (GDPR).

These provisions encompass, most notably, the imperative of obtaining explicit and unambiguous user consent, the seamless integration of the lofty ideals encapsulated by the privacy-by-design principles into the very fabric of their operational paradigms, and the maintenance of an unwavering and unrelenting commitment to the sacred cause of ensuring the impervious security and impenetrable confidentiality of the invaluable personal data.

In the intricate web of digital governance, compliance with the General Data Protection Regulation (GDPR) transcends the realm of obligation; it emerges as a solemn and pivotal duty. It is a duty that does not merely ensure adherence to the legal framework but also plays an instrumental role in shielding and fortifying the hallowed bastion of individuals' privacy rights. Furthermore, it stands as a beacon, a guiding light that illuminates the path toward responsible and ethical data management within the ever-expanding domain of Internet of Things (IoT) implementations.

5.3.2. The California Consumer Privacy Act (CCPA) Is a Legislative Measure Enacted in the State of California

In the realm of contemporary data protection legislation, the California Consumer Privacy Act (CCPA) assumes a prominent role, particularly within the context of the United States. The core mission of this legislative framework is to confer enhanced control over personal data to consumers, signifying a pivotal shift in the regulatory landscape. This transformative legislation places distinctive obligations upon entities that engage in the processing of personal data, an area of increasing relevance in today's digital age.

Within the purview of the burgeoning Internet of Things (IoT) landscape, where an array of interconnected devices continually harvest copious amounts of personal data, the CCPA takes on even greater significance. It calls upon organizations to exhibit unwavering dedication to compliance, underpinned by a trifecta of key requirements. Firstly, organizations are mandated to provide comprehensive disclosures concerning their data collection practices, enhancing transparency. Secondly, they must secure explicit user consent, thereby aligning data collection and sharing activities with the user's explicit approval. Thirdly, organizations are tasked with implementing mechanisms that empower users with the agency to opt out of data sharing endeavors, fostering individual autonomy and control.

For organizations navigating the IoT ecosystem, meticulous alignment with the stringent stipulations set forth within the CCPA becomes imperative. Beyond the paradigm of regulatory compliance, this engagement serves as a fundamental testament to an organization's unwavering commitment to the preservation of consumer privacy.

In seeking to solidify the security foundations of their IoT deployments and to ensure the confidentiality and integrity of data transmissions across a complex network of interconnected devices, organizations are offered a pivotal opportunity. This opportunity arises through the diligent observance of regulatory frameworks and the resolute adherence to industry-specific security guidelines. The implications of such an approach extend beyond mere compliance; they resonate as a profound demonstration of an organization's dedication to safeguarding the privacy rights of consumers amid the ever-evolving IoT landscape.

6. CONCLUSION

We examined important IoT device security issues in this detailed study. Our analysis examined security occurrences, necessary security measures, effective methodology, legislative frameworks, and the importance of addressing IoT device security concerns. We now comprehend the issues and implications of IoT device security after this extensive research.

Our journey began with a thorough study of IoT security incidents from the past decade. The Mirai botnet attack, Stuxnet worm, and NotPetya ransomware outbreak have highlighted IoT device vulnerabilities and threats. By analysing these incidents, we recognise their significant impact on persons and organisations and get useful insights that can inform our security efforts.

Following that, we addressed IoT device security needs. Our analysis focused on these devices' unique issues, particularly in secrecy, integrity, and availability. We examined secure device settings, strong communication protocols, firmware upgrades and patch management, and robust authentication and authorization techniques to address these issues. These security requirements underpin a resilient IoT security framework.

We also examined IoT security regulations and standards. ISO/IEC 27001 and the NIST Cybersecurity Framework are excellent guides from respected worldwide standards organisations. The OWASP IoT Top Ten Project and the Industrial Internet Consortium (IIC) Security Framework have both provided practical advice for strengthening IoT systems. The General Data Protection Regulation (GDPR) and the California Consumer Privacy Act (CCPA) shape IoT security law and privacy.

In conclusion, IoT device security and incident management are crucial. Security breaches increase as IoT devices become more embedded into our daily lives. Security events can cause unauthorised access, data breaches, privacy violations, and service outages. Protecting IoT devices and the sensitive data they manage requires proactive adoption of sophisticated security mechanisms.

Understanding the diversity, resource constraints, and potential attack vectors of IoT devices helps create comprehensive security measures. These include secure device setups, communication methods, updates, and strong authentication. Continuous monitoring and incident response methods help identify, respond to, and mitigate security problems quickly.

Looking ahead, IoT security will evolve and face new difficulties. IoT ecosystem adoption and complexity introduce new risks and complications. Future improvements may include anomaly identification and threat analysis using machine learning and AI. Data integrity and device identity management can be improved with blockchain technology. Secure hardware and hardware-assisted security measures will also be crucial to IoT device security.

However, these advances will bring new obstacles. Legacy IoT device security, supply chain security, user data privacy, and adaptive security standards and legislation are examples. Vigilance, adaptive security, and proactive threat mitigation are essential in the ever-changing IoT world.

Establishing strong IoT device security requires collaboration between individuals, organisations, and policymakers. Strong password hygiene, regular device updates, and careful data handling are essential for IoT device security. Organisations must prioritise security during IoT device design and development, implement comprehensive security safeguards, and engage in staff security training and awareness programmes. Policymakers help create and enforce IoT security and privacy legislation.

Collaboration among stakeholders is key. Researchers, manufacturers, and security professionals can share information to detect vulnerabilities, establish strong security practises, and respond quickly to emerging threats. Continuous education and awareness initiatives guarantee that all relevant parties understand IoT security and have the competence and resources to mitigate risks.

By tackling IoT device security needs together, we can maximise the potential of networked devices while protecting data confidentiality, integrity, and accessibility. Individuals and organisations can negotiate the changing landscape of IoT security and fully embrace its transformational potential with proactive steps and constant attention.

REFERENCES

Alaba, F. A., Othman, M., Hashem, I. A. T., & Alotaibi, F. (2017). Internet of Things security: A survey. *Journal of Network and Computer Applications, 88*, 10–28. doi:10.1016/j.jnca.2017.04.002

Alshaikh, H., Ramadan, N., & Hefny, H. A. (2020). Ransomware prevention and mitigation techniques. *Int. J. Comput. Appl, 177*(40), 31–39.

Antonakakis, M., April, T., Bailey, M., Bernhard, M., Bursztein, E., Cochran, J., . . . Zhou, Y. (2017). Understanding the mirai botnet. In *26th USENIX security symposium (USENIX Security 17)* (pp. 1093-1110). Academic Press.

Atzori, L., Iera, A., & Morabito, G. (2010). The internet of things: A survey. *Computer Networks, 54*(15), 2787–2805. doi:10.1016/j.comnet.2010.05.010

Casola, V., De Benedictis, A., Riccio, A., Rivera, D., Mallouli, W., & de Oca, E. M. (2019). A security monitoring system for internet of things. *Internet of Things : Engineering Cyber Physical Human Systems, 7*, 100080. doi:10.1016/j.iot.2019.100080

Crossler, R. E., Johnston, A. C., Lowry, P. B., Hu, Q., Warkentin, M., & Baskerville, R. (2013). Future directions for behavioral information security research. *Computers & Security, 32*, 90-101.

CVE-2022-43633: This vulnerability allows network-adjacent attackers to execute arbitrary code on affected installations of D-Link DIR-1. (n.d.). https://www.cvedetails.com/cve/CVE-2022-43633/

Di Pinto, A., Dragoni, Y., & Carcano, A. (2018). TRITON: The first ICS cyber attack on safety instrument systems. *Proc. Black Hat USA, 2018*, 1–26.

Ferguson, C. J., Rueda, S. M., Cruz, A. M., Ferguson, D. E., Fritz, S., & Smith, S. M. (2008). Violent video games and aggression: Causal relationship or byproduct of family violence and intrinsic violence motivation? *Criminal Justice and Behavior, 35*(3), 311–332. doi:10.1177/0093854807311719

Ferrag, M. A., Maglaras, L. A., Janicke, H., Jiang, J., & Shu, L. (2017). Authentication protocols for internet of things: A comprehensive survey. *Security and Communication Networks, 2017*, 2017. doi:10.1155/2017/6562953

Grover, V., Chiang, R. H., Liang, T. P., & Zhang, D. (2018). Creating strategic business value from big data analytics: A research framework. *Journal of Management Information Systems, 35*(2), 388–423. doi:10.1080/07421222.2018.1451951

HaddadPajouh, H., Dehghantanha, A., Parizi, R. M., Aledhari, M., & Karimipour, H. (2021). A survey on internet of things security: Requirements, challenges, and solutions. *Internet of Things : Engineering Cyber Physical Human Systems, 14*, 100129. doi:10.1016/j.iot.2019.100129

Ingemarsdotter, E., Jamsin, E., & Balkenende, R. (2020). Opportunities and challenges in IoT-enabled circular business model implementation–A case study. *Resources, Conservation and Recycling, 162*, 105047. doi:10.1016/j.resconrec.2020.105047

International Organization for Standardization (ISO). (2013). *ISO/IEC 27001:2013 - Information security management systems -- Requirements*. Retrieved from https://www.iso.org/standard/54534.html

Jiang, X., Lora, M., & Chattopadhyay, S. (2020). An experimental analysis of security vulnerabilities in industrial IoT devices. *ACM Transactions on Internet Technology*, *20*(2), 1–24. doi:10.1145/3379542

José, M. (2023). *A Comparative Study on the Performance of Security Mechanisms in Internet of Things Devices*. Academic Press.

Keoh, S. L., Kumar, S. S., & Tschofenig, H. (2014). Securing the internet of things: A standardization perspective. *IEEE Internet of Things Journal*, *1*(3), 265–275. doi:10.1109/JIOT.2014.2323395

Kocher, P., Horn, J., Fogh, A., Genkin, D., Gruss, D., Haas, W., Hamburg, M., Lipp, M., Mangard, S., Prescher, T., Schwarz, M., & Yarom, Y. (2020). Spectre attacks: Exploiting speculative execution. *Communications of the ACM*, *63*(7), 93–101. doi:10.1145/3399742

Kolias, C., Kambourakis, G., Stavrou, A., & Voas, J. (2017). DDoS in the IoT: Mirai and other botnets. *Computer*, *50*(7), 80–84. doi:10.1109/MC.2017.201

Konstantinou, C., Maniatakos, M., Saqib, F., Hu, S., Plusquellic, J., & Jin, Y. (2015, May). Cyber-physical systems: A security perspective. In *2015 20th IEEE European Test Symposium (ETS)* (pp. 1-8). IEEE. 10.1109/ETS.2015.7138763

Kovalchuk, O., Shynkaryk, M., & Masonkova, M. (2021, September). Econometric models for estimating the financial effect of cybercrimes. In *2021 11th International Conference on Advanced Computer Information Technologies (ACIT)* (pp. 381-384). IEEE. 10.1109/ACIT52158.2021.9548490

Kumar, S., Ranjan, P., Singh, P., & Tripathy, M. R. (2020, September). Design and implementation of fault tolerance technique for internet of things (iot). In *2020 12th International Conference on Computational Intelligence and Communication Networks (CICN)* (pp. 154-159). IEEE.

Li, F., Zheng, Z., & Jin, C. (2016). Secure and efficient data transmission in the Internet of Things. *Telecommunication Systems*, *62*(1), 111–122. doi:10.100711235-015-0065-y

Mahmoud, R., Yousuf, T., Aloul, F., & Zualkernan, I. (2015, December). Internet of things (IoT) security: Current status, challenges and prospective measures. In *2015 10th international conference for internet technology and secured transactions (ICITST)* (pp. 336-341). IEEE.

Marques, G., Pitarma, R. M., Garcia, N., & Pombo, N. (2019). Internet of things architectures, technologies, applications, challenges, and future directions for enhanced living environments and healthcare systems: A review. *Electronics (Basel)*, *8*(10), 1081. doi:10.3390/electronics8101081

Mawel, M. (2022). *Exploring the Strategic Cybersecurity Defense Information Technology Managers Can Implement to Reduce Healthcare Data Breaches* [Doctoral dissertation]. Colorado Technical University.

Mtetwa, N. S., Tarwireyi, P., Abu-Mahfouz, A. M., & Adigun, M. O. (2019, November). Secure firmware updates in the internet of things: A survey. In *2019 International Multidisciplinary Information Technology and Engineering Conference (IMITEC)* (pp. 1-7). IEEE. 10.1109/IMITEC45504.2019.9015845

National Institute of Standards and Technology (NIST). (n.d.). *NIST Cybersecurity Framework*. Retrieved from https://www.nist.gov/cyberframework

Operation ShadowHammer: new supply chain attack threatens hundreds of thousands of users worldwide. (2021, May 26). https://www.kaspersky.com/about/press-releases/2019_operation-shadowhammer-new-supply-chain-attack

Rajkumar, V. S., Stefanov, A., Musunuri, S., & de Wit, J. (2021, September). Exploiting ripple20 to compromise power grid cyber security and impact system operations. In *CIRED 2021-The 26th International Conference and Exhibition on Electricity Distribution* (Vol. 2021, pp. 3092-3096). IET. 10.1049/icp.2021.2146

Ray, P. P. (2018). A survey on Internet of Things architectures. *Journal of King Saud University. Computer and Information Sciences*, *30*(3), 291–319. doi:10.1016/j.jksuci.2016.10.003

Roman, R., Zhou, J., & Lopez, J. (2013). On the features and challenges of security and privacy in distributed internet of things. *Computer Networks*, *57*(10), 2266–2279. doi:10.1016/j.comnet.2012.12.018

Samaila, M. G., Neto, M., Fernandes, D. A., Freire, M. M., & Inácio, P. R. (2018). Challenges of securing Internet of Things devices: A survey. *Security and Privacy*, *1*(2), e20. doi:10.1002py2.20

Sander-Staudt, M. (2010). Review of Feminist Bioethics At the Center, On the Margins, edited by Jackie Leach Scully, Laurel E. Baldwin-Ragaven, Petya Fitzpatrick. Philosophy, Ethics, and Humanities in Medicine: PEHM, 5, 18.

Sedrati, A., & Mezrioui, A. (2018). A survey of security challenges in internet of things. Advances in Science. *Technology and Engineering Systems Journal*, *3*(1), 274–280.

Sengupta, J., Ruj, S., & Bit, S. D. (2020). A secure fog-based architecture for industrial Internet of Things and industry 4.0. *IEEE Transactions on Industrial Informatics*, *17*(4), 2316–2324. doi:10.1109/TII.2020.2998105

Sicari, S., Rizzardi, A., Grieco, L. A., & Coen-Porisini, A. (2015). Security, privacy and trust in Internet of Things: The road ahead. *Computer Networks*, *76*, 146–164. doi:10.1016/j.comnet.2014.11.008

Sinanaj, G., & Muntermann, J. (2013). *Assessing corporate reputational damage of data breaches: An empirical analysis*. Academic Press.

Tuohy, J. P. (2023, January 6). Amazon's flying indoor security camera will be at least three years late. *The Verge*. https://www.theverge.com/2023/1/6/23541395/amazon-ring-always-home-cam-release-date-price-ces2023

Ujjawal, K., Garg, S. K., Ali, A., & Singh, D. K. (n.d.). *Security Threats for Short Range Communication Wireless Network on IoT Devices*. Academic Press.

URGENT/11. (2023, August 22). Armis. https://www.armis.com/research/urgent-11/#:~:text=URGENT%2F11%20is%20serious%20as,malware%20into%20and%20within%20networks

Vanhoef, M., & Piessens, F. (2017, October). Key reinstallation attacks: Forcing nonce reuse in WPA2. In *Proceedings of the 2017 ACM SIGSAC Conference on Computer and Communications Security* (pp. 1313-1328). 10.1145/3133956.3134027

Wang, W., Krishna, A., & McFerran, B. (2017). Turning off the lights: Consumers' environmental efforts depend on visible efforts of firms. *JMR, Journal of Marketing Research*, *54*(3), 478–494. doi:10.1509/jmr.14.0441

Yaacoub, J. P. A., Salman, O., Noura, H. N., Kaaniche, N., Chehab, A., & Malli, M. (2020). Cyber-physical systems security: Limitations, issues and future trends. *Microprocessors and Microsystems*, *77*, 103201. doi:10.1016/j.micpro.2020.103201 PMID:32834204

Zhang, X., Upton, O., Beebe, N. L., & Choo, K. K. R. (2020). Iot botnet forensics: A comprehensive digital forensic case study on mirai botnet servers. *Forensic Science International Digital Investigation*, *32*, 300926. doi:10.1016/j.fsidi.2020.300926

Zhao, H., Shu, H., & Xing, Y. (2021, January). A review on IoT botnet. In *The 2nd International Conference on Computing and Data Science* (pp. 1-7). Academic Press.

Chapter 8
Ethics in AI and Virtual Reality: Ensuring Responsible Development

Kriti Saroha
https://orcid.org/0000-0001-9804-771X
Centre for Development of Advanced Computing, Noida, India

Vishal Jain
https://orcid.org/0000-0003-1126-7424
Sharda University, India

ABSTRACT

This chapter explores the ethical considerations that arise at the intersection of artificial intelligence (AI) and virtual reality (VR). It examines the multifaceted ethical challenges posed by the integration of AI and VR technologies, focusing on issues such as privacy, bias, autonomy, social impact, and regulatory frameworks. By analyzing existing literature and real-world cases, this chapter seeks to provide a comprehensive understanding of the ethical dimensions of AI-driven virtual reality experiences.

1. INTRODUCTION

As the fields of artificial intelligence (AI) and virtual reality (VR) continue to advance at an unprecedented pace, their potential to transform various aspects of our lives becomes increasingly apparent. The rapid advancement of these technologies has brought about transformative changes across various sectors. From enhancing entertainment experiences to revolutionizing industries such as healthcare and education, AI and VR hold immense promise. However, with great power comes great responsibility and hence, their responsible development is paramount to avoid unintended consequences. This chapter explores the ethical considerations surrounding the development and deployment of AI and VR technologies, emphasizing the importance of responsible practices to ensure a harmonious integration into society. There is compelling need for exploring the ethical implications of creating and interacting with artificial virtual environments, including questions about the blurring of reality, identity, and morality. Ethics in AI and virtual reality encompasses a wide range of issues/ aspects, all of which are crucial for

DOI: 10.4018/979-8-3693-2647-3.ch008

ensuring the responsible development of these technologies. Some of the key issues included under this umbrella are discussed in subsequent sections.

1.1 Brief Overview of AI and VR Technologies

Artificial Intelligence (AI)

Artificial Intelligence (AI) refers to the simulation of human intelligence processes by computer systems. AI systems can perform tasks that typically require human intelligence, such as problem-solving, decision-making, language understanding, and learning. AI encompasses various techniques, including machine learning, natural language processing, computer vision, and robotics.

AI has found applications in diverse domains, from healthcare and finance to entertainment and autonomous vehicles. Machine learning algorithms, such as neural networks, enable AI systems to analyze large datasets, recognize patterns, and make predictions. AI-driven technologies have the potential to transform industries, enhance efficiency, and introduce new levels of automation (Goodfellow et al., 2016; Russell & Norvig, 2016).

Virtual Reality (VR)

Virtual Reality (VR) is a technology that creates a computer-generated simulated environment, allowing users to interact and immerse themselves in a three-dimensional virtual world. VR typically involves the use of headsets or other devices that provide visual, auditory, and sometimes haptic feedback, creating a sense of presence within the virtual environment.

VR has applications in entertainment, education, training, therapy, and more. It enables users to experience scenarios that may be difficult or impossible to encounter in the physical world. VR experiences can range from immersive gaming environments to realistic architectural walkthroughs and medical simulations (Burdea & Coiffet, 2003; Sherman & Craig, 2018).

The Convergence of AI and VR

AI and VR technologies, though distinct technologies, are increasingly converging to create immersive and intelligent virtual experiences. AI provides the cognitive capabilities necessary to make sense of complex data and interactions within virtual environments. AI enhances VR environments by providing real-time interactions and personalized content, while VR augments AI by creating lifelike simulations for training and testing AI models. VR also enhances the immersive experience by simulating realistic and interactive settings. However, the fusion of these technologies opens up new frontiers but also poses complex ethical challenges that require careful navigation.

As these technologies continue to advance, understanding and addressing the ethical implications of AI-VR integration is crucial for ensuring responsible and beneficial development in both fields. Figure 1. shows the components of a good ethical AI framework as discussed in (Census, n.d.).

Figure 1. Components of a good ethical AI framework (Censius, n.d.)

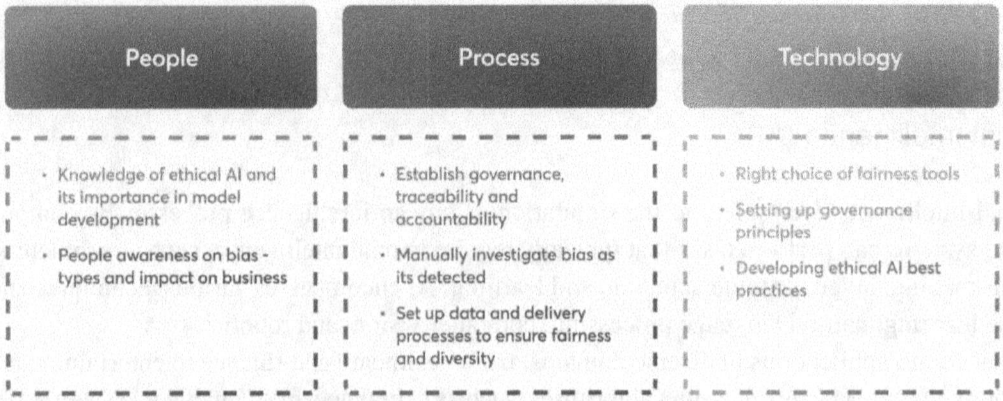

1.2 Importance of Studying Ethics in AI-VR Integration/ Ethical Dimensions in AI-VR Integration

The amalgamation of artificial intelligence (AI) and virtual reality (VR) has ushered in a new era of technological innovation and immersive experiences. However, this synergy also brings forth a host of ethical challenges that span privacy, bias, autonomy, and more that warrant careful examination. Delving into these ethical dimensions is paramount to ensure the responsible and beneficial development of AI-VR technologies. Understanding the importance of studying ethics in AI-VR integration is essential for fostering responsible development, ensuring user well-being, and shaping a future where these technologies can positively impact society. The author in (Bersin, 2019) presents a framework with two dimensions (Fairness and Safety & Trust) to ethics and is shown in Figure 2.

Figure 2. A framework for ethics of data and AI (Bersin, 2019)

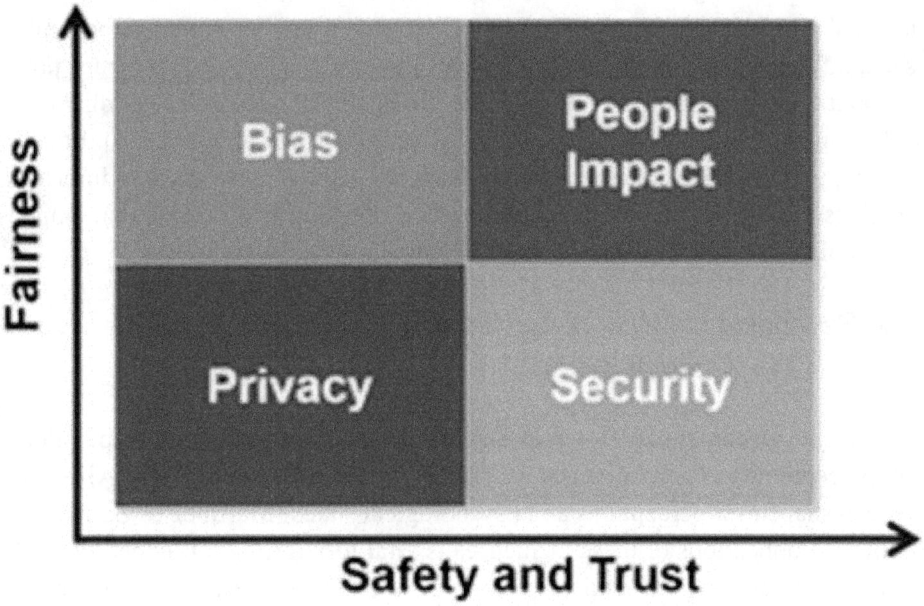

i. User Privacy and Data Protection Concerns in AI-Driven Virtual Reality

The seamless blend of AI and VR often involves the collection, processing, and analysis of vast amounts of user data that raises significant privacy issues. The collection and analysis of user data within immersive environments raise questions about data ownership, consent, and potential misuse. Ethical concerns arise regarding the privacy of personal information, potential data breaches, and the extent to which users are informed and have control over data usage (Smith et al., 2020). Ethical scrutiny is essential to strike a balance between immersive experiences and safeguarding users' personal information. Studying ethics in AI-VR integration helps establish guidelines and safeguards to protect user privacy in immersive *environments*.

ii. Algorithmic Bias and Fairness in AI-Powered VR

AI algorithms used in VR experiences can inadvertently perpetuate biases present in the training data, leading to discriminatory or unfair outcomes (Johnson & Li, 2019). Investigating ethics in AI-VR integration enables the identification and mitigation of biases, ensuring that virtual environments are inclusive and equitable. The ethical dimension of algorithmic bias underscores the need to ensure inclusivity, fairness, and transparency in AI-generated content.

iii. User Autonomy and Informed Consent in AI-Enhanced Virtual Environments

AI's influence in VR experiences blurs the boundary between user agency and algorithmic control. AI technologies can influence the content and experiences presented in VR environments, potentially raising questions about user autonomy and consent. This raises ethical questions regarding user autonomy, consent, and the extent to which users are aware of AI's role (Brown & Lee, 2021). Ethical analysis is crucial to ensuring that users have the necessary control and information to make informed decisions. By exploring ethics in AI-VR integration, researchers can develop frameworks that empower users to make informed choices and retain control over their virtual experiences.

iv. Social and Psychological Well-being/ User Experience and Emotional Manipulation

AI's ability to personalize content in VR environments can lead to emotional manipulation, potentially impacting user perceptions and psychological well-being. The emotional impact of AI-mediated content in VR settings can shape user perceptions and psychological states (Martinez & Garcia, 2018). Understanding the ethical implications of these influences is vital for crafting VR experiences that promote well-being and avoid potential harm. Ethical exploration is also vital to establish guidelines that prevent undue emotional influence while harnessing AI's capabilities for positive experiences.

v. Regulatory and Policy Frameworks

The development of AI-VR technologies is outpacing the formulation of comprehensive regulatory frameworks. The integration of AI and VR poses challenges for existing regulatory frameworks, often failing to account for novel ethical dilemmas. Developing appropriate regulations and policies requires a deep understanding of the ethical implications (White et al., 2022). The study of ethics in AI-VR integration informs the creation of policies that govern these technologies, ensuring alignment with societal values and norms. Ethical analysis guides the creation of frameworks that ensure responsible technology development and deployment.

vi. Long-Term Societal Impact

Ethical considerations in AI-VR integration extend beyond immediate use cases. Researchers must anticipate and address potential long-term effects on culture, social interaction, and the human experience. Studying ethics in AI-VR integration fosters a proactive approach to technology development, encouraging stakeholders to identify and address ethical dilemmas before they become pervasive. As AI-VR technologies continue to shape our digital and physical worlds, a strong ethical foundation ensures that their impact is beneficial and aligned with the values of society.

By engaging in rigorous ethical analysis, researchers, developers, and policymakers can collectively guide the evolution of AI-VR technologies, creating a harmonious balance between technological advancement and ethical responsibility. The study of ethics in AI-VR integration is not just a theoretical exercise; it is a critical step toward shaping a future where these technologies contribute positively to human well-being and progress.

vii. Balancing Efficiency and Ethical Considerations

AI's potential to enhance educational and training experiences in VR raises questions about achieving a balance between efficiency gains and maintaining ethical educational rigor (Jackson & Smith, 2019). Ethical exploration aids in designing AI-VR educational experiences that prioritize meaningful learning outcomes.

2. LITERATURE REVIEW

Developing AI and virtual reality presents several ethical challenges. These challenges include discrimination in AI systems, the lack of semantic and context understanding in AI models, and the use of facial bio-metrics for predictions (Baeza-Yates, 2022). This section presents a comprehensive review of the related work in the area. The authors in (Ribeiro et al., 2016) discuss the importance of explaining the predictions of any classifier, which is relevant to the ethical considerations of AI and VR integration. (Floridi, 2019) provides a theory of philosophy as conceptual design, which can contribute to understanding the ethical dimensions of AI-driven virtual reality experiences. The authors in (Davis & Roblyer, 2005) propose a technology action competence approach for preparing teachers for the "school of tomorrow," which can be relevant to the responsible development of AI and VR in education. In (Gulbahar & Tinmaz, 2006), authors discuss the need for teacher professional development in technology integration, which can inform the ethical considerations of AI and VR in educational settings. (Tintarev & Masthoff, 2012) provide insights into designing and evaluating explanations for recommender systems, which can be relevant to understanding the ethical implications of AI-driven customization options in VR experiences. The authors in (Kim et al., 2019) focus on building user trust in AI-driven virtual environments, which can contribute to the responsible development and deployment of AI and VR technologies. Virtual reality introduces new ethical concerns, including physiological and cognitive impacts, as well as behavioural and social dynamics (Kenwright, 2018). Also, the automation of moral decision-making in AI systems raises methodological and ethical challenges, such as bias mitigation, the lack of ground truth for moral correctness, and the societal implications of algorithmic moral decision-making (Hagendorff & Danks, 2023). Table 1 gives a summarizes the findings of some of the literature reviewed in the area.

Table 1. Summary of literature review

	Papers	Insights	Results & Conclusions (Contributions)	Limitations/Practical Implications
1	Ricardo Baeza-Yates (2022), 'Ethical Challenges in AI', Proceedings of the 15th ACM International Conference on Web Search and Data Mining.	The paper discusses ethical challenges in AI. Ethical challenges in AI addressed through examples - Four specific challenges in AI are discussed: discrimination, lack of semantic understanding, physiognomy, indiscriminate use of computing resources. The paper addresses four generic challenges: (1) too many principles, (2) cultural differences; (3) regulation and (4) their cognitive biases and discusses what the authors can do to address these challenges in the near future.	- Four current specific challenges in AI: discrimination, stupid models, physiognomy, indiscriminate use of computing resources. - Four generic challenges in AI: too many principles, cultural differences, regulation, cognitive biases.	-Addressing discrimination and bias in AI applications - Lack of semantic and context understanding in models. - Identifying and addressing ethical challenges in AI
2	Ben Kenwright (2018), 'Virtual Reality: Ethical Challenges and Dangers [Opinion]', IEEE Technology and Society Magazine	The ethical challenges in developing AI and virtual reality include physiological and cognitive impacts, behavioural and social dynamics, and the need for regulations and guidelines. - Virtual reality (VR) presents ethical challenges and dangers. - - Identifying and managing procedures to address emerging ethical issues will happen not only through regulations and laws, but also through ethics-in-practice (respect, care, morals, and education).	- VR technologies have ethical complexities and potential dangers. - Managing ethical issues requires regulations, ethics-in-practice, and education.	- Lack of information on physiological impacts of VR - Lack of information on user attributes and critical reasoning abilities
3	Thilo Hagendorff, David Danks (2023), 'Ethical and methodological challenges in building morally informed AI systems', AI Ethics 3, 553–566, Springer.	The paper discusses ethical challenges in developing morally informed AI systems, but does not specifically mention virtual reality. - Progress in language models enables simulation of moral agency. - Challenges in bias mitigation, moral correctness, and societal implications. In this paper, the authors provide critical considerations for future research on full artificial moral agency and discuss the challenges of meta-ethics in algorithmic moral decision-making, including bias mitigation, missing ground truth for moral correctness, effects of bounded ethicality in machines, changes in moral norms over time, risks of using morally informed AI systems as actual advice, as well as societal implications.	- Methodological and ethical challenges in building morally informed AI systems. - Critical considerations for future research on artificial moral agency	- Challenges Bias mitigation and missing ground truth for moral "correctness". - Risks of using morally informed AI systems

Continued on following page

Table 1. Continued

	Papers	Insights	Results & Conclusions (Contributions)	Limitations/Practical Implications
4	Jess Whittlestone, S. Clarke (2022), 'AI Challenges for Society and Ethics', arXiv:cs	- AI impacts society, with potential benefits and harm. - AI governance aims to mitigate risks and enable innovation. The role of AI governance is ultimately to take practical steps to mitigate this risk of harm while enabling the benefits of innovation in AI as discussed by the authors, which requires answering challenging empirical questions about current and potential risks and benefits of AI: assessing impacts that are often widely distributed and indirect and making predictions about a highly uncertain future.	- AI governance is crucial for mitigating risks and enabling benefits - Progress has been made in addressing challenges - Progress made on empirical questions about risks and benefits of AI - Challenges remain in implementing high-level principles in practice	- Assessing impacts that are widely distributed and indirect and making predictions about AI. - Mitigating risks and enabling benefits of AI - Putting high-level principles into practice
5	Boddington, P. (2017). 'How AI Challenges Professional Ethics', In: Towards a Code of Ethics for Artificial Intelligence. Artificial Intelligence: Foundations, Theory, and Algorithms. Springer	- AI challenges professional codes of ethics - AI introduces complexity with the behaviour of machines How AI presents particular challenges for developing professional codes of ethics is considered, which means that in AI, there is a particular problem with professional vulnerability in relation to their own products.	- AI presents challenges for developing professional codes of ethics - Professional vulnerability in relation to AI products	- AI work may be carried out by those outside of any formal organisational setting. - Control problem in AI undermines expertise gradient. - Challenges in developing professional codes of ethics - Professional vulnerability in relation to AI products
6	Daniel J. Finnegan, Alexia Zoumpoulaki, Parisa Eslambolchilar (2021), 'Does mixed reality have a Cassandra Complex', Front. Virtual Real., Sec. Virtual Reality and Human Behaviour, Volume 2.	The paper discusses the need for a unified ethical framework in the development and deployment of XR technologies, similar to the challenges faced in AI. - Boom in Virtual, Augmented, and Mixed Reality technologies - Concerns about ethical dilemmas and best practices In this paper, the authors propose that the virtual, augmented, and mixed reality research and development areas need to come together as whole; involving government, industry and science in order to define, develop and decide guidelines and strategies before we replicate the devastating consequences such as decaying trust in technology witnessed in other areas like social media.	- Need for a collective, united nations approach to ethical practice in mixed reality applications. - Importance of proactive approach and collaboration with stakeholders.	- Lack of guidelines and ethical standards - Potential harm to users of XR technologies

Continued on following page

Table 1. Continued

	Papers	Insights	Results & Conclusions (Contributions)	Limitations/Practical Implications
7	Daniel Zeng (2015), 'AI Ethics: Science Fiction Meets Technological Reality', IEEE Intelligent Systems (IEEE), Vol. 30, Iss: 3, pp 2-5,	The ethical challenges in developing AI and virtual reality include accountability, human-AI relations, understanding emotions, and potential impact on consciousness and matter. - Growing ethical issues in AI-enabled technologies - Need for holistic approach in studying these issues, discusses a growing number of ethical issues connected to AI-enabled technologies that need to be studied by using a holistic approach.	- AI ethics is no longer purely philosophical. - AI ethical issues require interdisciplinary research and collaboration.	- AI ethics is no longer just a philosophical topic. - AI ethical issues require interdisciplinary research and collaboration.
8	Cotton, M. (2021). 'The Ethical Dimensions of Virtual Reality', In: Virtual Reality, Empathy and Ethics. Palgrave Macmillan, Cham.	The ethical challenges in developing AI and virtual reality include privacy concerns, potential negative impacts on human behaviour and well-being, and the threat of malicious use. - Ethical concerns of virtual objects in public life In this paper, the authors discuss the ways in which cultural and epistemic fears over virtual objects and environments emerged in the early 1980s as the fear of covert artificial reality was posed in literature and film.	- Virtual objects in public life threaten privacy and trust. - VR impacts human-agent and human-computer interactions. - Examines ethical concerns of virtual reality - Discusses negative impacts and potential benefits of VR	- Lack of computing power for fully immersive VR - Threats to personal privacy, dignity, and political security - Negative impacts on human-agent and human-computer interactions
9	H. A. Shazly, A. Ferraro and K. Bennet (2020), 'Ethical Concerns: An overview of Artificial Intelligence System Development and Life Cycle, IEEE International Symposium on Technology and Society (ISTAS).	The paper discusses the ethical challenges in developing Artificial Intelligent Systems (AIS). Impact on data collection and marketing of data commodities. In this paper, the authors examine how these issues effect ethics throughout the life cycle of the AIS and carries into the life-cycle of the data and examine the impact of these issues on the data collection process and derivative computed Information and Knowledge.	- Ethical concerns arise throughout the life cycle of AI systems. - Data collection processes and derivative information raise ethical challenges. - Examines ethical challenges in Artificial Intelligent Systems.	- Examines ethical challenges in AI system development. - Explores impact on data collection and marketing venues.
10	M. Milossi, E. Alexandropoulou-Egyptiadou and K. E. Psannis (2021), 'AI Ethics: Algorithmic Determinism or Self-Determination? The GPDR Approach', In IEEE Access, vol. 9.	The paper discusses ethical challenges in AI and the need for regulation. - - AI reshapes lives, interactions, and environments. - AI systems act to achieve given goals. In this paper, the authors summarize and critically evaluate the basic principles for the use of AI, with emphasis to the General Data Protection Regulation's (GDPR) approach, concerning data subject consent, data protection principles and data subject's rights in a context of privacy by design architecture. - Focus on consent, privacy, and individual rights	- AI ethics raise concerns about surveillance and manipulation. - The paper highlights the ethical challenges in AI and the need for ethical AI frameworks. - Different countries have different approaches to ethics. - The paper summarizes and evaluates the basic principles for the use of AI, with emphasis on the GDPR principles for data accuracy, storage limitation, and security. - Use of AI and statistical methods for data analytics	- Inaccurate data can harm data subjects. - AI systems can cause wrongful convictions. - Individuals must have control of their own lives - Trustworthiness is a prerequisite for AI uptake - Broad surveillance, manipulation, lack of autonomy, lack of democracy

Continued on following page

Table 1. Continued

	Papers	Insights	Results & Conclusions (Contributions)	Limitations/Practical Implications
11	B. C. Stahl (2021), 'Ethical Issues of AI', Artificial Intelligence for a Better Future, Springer Briefs in Research and Innovation Governance	The ethical challenges in developing AI include concerns about machine learning, societal impacts, and metaphysical issues. This paper discusses the ethical issues that are raised by the development, deployment and use of AI and presents the findings of the SHERPA project, which used case studies and a Delphi study to identify what people perceived to be ethical issues.	- Ethical issues of AI are categorized into three categories: machine learning, artificial general intelligence, and broader socio-technical systems. - The third category, "metaphysical issues," is the most unexplored and relates to fundamental aspects of reality and human nature. - Ethical issues of AI are discussed. - Findings from the SHERPA project is presented.	N/A
12	Michael B. Burns, Gina Lebkuecher, Sophia Rahman, Maya Roytman, Sydney Samoska & Joseph Vukov (2022) 'Extended Frameworks for Extended Reality: Ethical Considerations', AJOB Neuroscience, 13:3, 171-173	The paper discusses ethical considerations in extended reality (XR) applications, but does not specifically address emotional manipulation in AI-driven virtual reality.	- No evidence to support effectiveness of XR interventions - Moral concerns if used for non-rehabilitative purposes	- XR applications in forensic contexts need to be researched for effectiveness. - If effective, XR applications should be analyzed using existing evaluative frameworks.
13	Tusher, H., Nazir, S., Mallam, S. (2022). 'Ethical Considerations for the Application of Virtual Reality in Education and Training', In: International Conference. AHFE Open Access, vol 59., USA.	The paper discusses ethical implications of using VR in education and training.	- Ethical problems and harm of VR in education - Recommendations for ethical use of VR	- Critical evaluation of VR technology for everyday use - Recommendations for ethical use of VR in the future
14	Jon Rueda, Francisco Lara (2020), 'Virtual Reality and Empathy Enhancement: Ethical Aspects', Front. Robot. AI, Sec. Virtual Environments, Vol. 7.	The paper discusses the potential of virtual reality to provoke emotional responses and the ethical considerations surrounding it.	- VR is not the ideal way to enhance empathy. - Fostering empathy through virtual embodiment in avatars.	- VR has various applications in different domains. - Ethical considerations are important in VR use.
15	Cotton, M. (2021). 'Virtual Reality as Ethical Tool', In: Virtual Reality, Empathy and Ethics. Palgrave Macmillan, Cham.	This paper examines the ethical considerations of using virtual reality for emotional manipulation in AI-driven systems.	- Examines application of virtual reality to prosocial behaviour change, news reporting, art, and social justice campaigning. - Critically assesses capacity of VR works to stimulate empathy.	- Application of VR to prosocial behaviour change - Use of VR in news reporting, art, and social justice campaigning

Continued on following page

Table 1. Continued

	Papers	Insights	Results & Conclusions (Contributions)	Limitations/Practical Implications
16	Mitchell, Alanah and Khazanchi, Deepak (2012), 'Ethical Considerations for Virtual Worlds', Proceedings of the 18th Americas Conference on Information Systems, Seattle, Washington	The paper discusses ethical considerations in virtual worlds.	- Starting point for discussing ethics in virtual worlds - Review of virtual worlds and their unique technology capabilities	- Understanding ethical challenges in virtual worlds - Potential research agenda for exploring these considerations
17	Francisco Lopez Luro, Diego Navarro and Veronica Sundstedt (2017), 'Ethical Considerations for the Use of Virtual Reality: An Evaluation of Practices in Academia and Industry', ICAT-EGVE - International Conference on Artificial Reality and Telexistence and Eurographics Symposium on Virtual Environments.	The paper discusses ethical considerations for the use of virtual reality technology.	N/A	- Recommendations for designing and executing VR experiences - Ethical considerations for the use of VR technology
18	Radziwill, Nicole (2019), 'Quality Considerations for Ethical Design of Virtual and Augmented Reality', Software Quality Professional; Milwaukee Vol. 21, Iss. 4, pp 34-47	The paper introduces conscious reality (CoRe) questions as a checklist tool to help developers create ethical virtual reality content.	N/A	- Introduces conscious reality (CoRe) questions checklist tool - Enhances quality and integrity of XR applications

Addressing the ethical dimensions discussed in section 1.2 and section 2, is pivotal to ensure that the fusion of AI and VR technologies leads to responsible and beneficial outcomes. Ethical analysis and discourse play a central role in guiding technological advancements, shaping policies, and fostering an ethical foundation for the evolving landscape of AI-VR integration.

Following sections present discussions on the above-mentioned points/ dimensions.

3. SOCIETAL IMPACT AND PSYCHOLOGICAL CONSEQUENCES OF AI-VR INTEGRATION

The integration of artificial intelligence (AI) and virtual reality (VR) technologies holds transformative potential across various domains. However, this convergence also introduces profound societal and psychological considerations that demand thoughtful examination. Understanding the societal impact and psychological consequences of AI-VR integration is essential for shaping a future where these technologies enhance well-being and promote ethical engagement.

i. Social Interaction and Relationships

AI-VR integration can reshape how people interact, communicate, and form relationships. It has the potential to significantly impact social interaction and relationships in various ways. Here are some potential consequences of AI-VR integration on social interaction and relationships:

- Enhanced Virtual Social Interactions: AI-driven avatars can mimic human expressions and emotions, making virtual interactions more lifelike. Also, AI algorithms can analyze user data to create tailored social experiences, catering to individual preferences and interests.
- Altered Perception of Reality: Extended use of VR may blur the line between virtual and physical reality, challenging traditional concepts of social interaction and relationships. Virtual environments might offer an escape from real-world problems, potentially leading to social withdrawal among some individuals.
- Impact on Communication: VR can capture subtle non-verbal cues, enhancing communication. However, misinterpretation of these cues could occur. VR also enables people worldwide to interact, fostering global connections and multicultural understanding.
- Impact on Social Skills: For some, VR might enhance social skills by providing a controlled environment for practicing interactions. Excessive reliance on virtual interactions could diminish face-to-face social skills in some individuals.

Virtual environments enriched by AI may blur the lines between physical and digital interactions, influencing social norms and behaviours. This shift necessitates ethical exploration to ensure that AI-mediated interactions foster genuine connections and respect cultural nuances (Biocca, 1997). In conclusion, while AI-VR integration offers exciting possibilities for social interaction and relationships, it also raises important ethical, psychological, and societal questions. Striking a balance between the benefits of immersive virtual experiences and the preservation of genuine human connections will be a critical challenge in the coming years. Society must remain mindful of these consequences as these technologies continue to advance.

ii. Digital Identity and Authenticity

The augmentation of VR experiences with AI-generated content raises questions about digital identity and authenticity. As users interact with AI-driven avatars or personalities, the ethical dimension emerges concerning user autonomy, consent, and the potential for identity manipulation (Eslami et al., 2015). Following are some key impacts:

- Creation of Virtual Identities: AI can create highly realistic avatars. Individuals can present themselves differently online, raising questions about authenticity. Users can craft customized virtual personas, leading to the potential for identity manipulation and multiple online identities. Advanced AI techniques could be used to steal someone's virtual identity, leading to financial or reputational damage.

- Challenges to Authenticity: AI-VR integration can facilitate the creation of sophisticated deepfakes, making it difficult to distinguish between real and fake content, impacting trust in digital interactions. Also, AI-powered virtual influencers are becoming popular, challenging the authenticity of online endorsements and interactions.
- Enhanced Authentication Methods: VR can incorporate biometric data (facial recognition, voice patterns) for authentication, offering more secure and convenient identity verification methods. AI can analyze user behaviour in VR environments, adding unique layers of identity verification based on how users interact with virtual spaces.

iii. Emotional Manipulation and Well-Being/ Empathy and Emotional Understanding

AI-driven personalization of VR content can influence user emotions and psychological states. VR can create immersive experiences, helping individuals in long-distance relationships feel closer and more connected. While VR can simulate intimacy, it might create challenges in differentiating between virtual intimacy and genuine emotional connections. AI-powered VR environments thus designed to evoke empathy and emotional understanding present ethical challenges in terms of controlling users' emotional states and ensuring that such experiences align with ethical principles. The ethical concern revolves around preventing undue emotional manipulation while harnessing AI's potential to facilitate positive emotional experiences (Duhigg, 2012; Martinez & Garcia, 2018).

iv. Addiction and Escapism

The immersive nature of AI-enhanced VR experiences can raise concerns about addictive behaviours and excessive escapism due to the immersive and engaging experiences they offer. Excessive use of AI-VR platforms might lead to addiction, impacting real-world relationships and social skills. Ethical analysis is needed to strike a balance between fostering healthy engagement and mitigating potential negative psychological consequences (Lin & Tsai, 2002). Here's how AI-VR integration can impact addiction and escapism:

- Escapism in Virtual Worlds: VR provides highly immersive environments, allowing users to escape from real-life problems and stresses into virtual worlds. For individuals facing challenges in reality, the appeal of VR escapism can lead to addictive behaviours, where they prefer the virtual world over real-life responsibilities.
- Gaming and Entertainment Addiction: VR gaming, especially with AI-driven immersive experiences, can lead to compulsive gaming habits, similar to traditional video game addiction. AI algorithms in VR can adapt games and experiences based on user behaviour, encouraging prolonged engagement and potential addiction.
- Social Interaction and Relationships: Spending excessive time in VR social platforms can lead to reduced physical social interactions, affecting real-life relationships. Developing emotional attachments to AI-driven characters or personas in VR can lead to challenges in differentiating between virtual and real emotions.
- Addressing Addiction and Escapism: AI-VR integration can be used therapeutically to address addiction, offering controlled environments for therapy and rehabilitation. Also, raising awareness

about the potential risks of addiction and providing education about responsible VR use is crucial. Vulnerable individuals, such as those with existing mental health issues, might be more susceptible to VR addiction and escapism. Hence, ensuring users are aware of the addictive potential of AI-VR experiences and providing informed consent before usage is essential.

- Regulation and Policies: Implementing age restrictions and guidelines for the use of AI-VR technologies, especially for immersive and potentially addictive content. Tools and support systems should be developed to monitor VR usage patterns and offer assistance to individuals showing signs of addiction.

While AI-VR integration offers incredible potential for various applications, including education, therapy, and entertainment, it is vital to acknowledge and address the potential risks associated with addiction and escapism. Responsible usage guidelines, education, mental health support, and ethical considerations are necessary to ensure that these technologies are harnessed in ways that benefit users without causing harm.

v. Cultural and Ethical Norms

AI-VR integration might lead to the development of new/ novel social, cultural norms, etiquettes and ethical challenges specific to virtual interactions. Initially, there might be resistance and challenges in accepting AI-driven entities as valid social partners. The globalization of VR experiences infused with AI-generated content necessitates ethical considerations to ensure that diverse perspectives are respected and represented (Consalvo & Ess, 2011).

vi. Therapeutic and Mental Health Applications

Prolonged use of VR can lead to a disconnect from reality, exacerbating mental health issues such as depression and anxiety. Escaping into VR worlds could potentially lead to social isolation if individuals prefer virtual interactions over face-to-face communication or real-world relationships. AI-driven virtual therapists and support systems could aid in addressing mental health issues. The integration of Artificial Intelligence (AI) and Virtual Reality (VR) has transformative potential in the field of therapeutic and mental health applications. Following are the key impacts:

- Virtual Therapy Sessions: VR allows remote access to therapy for individuals in rural or underserved areas, enhancing mental health services' accessibility. AI-driven VR simulations create controlled and safe environments for exposure therapy, aiding in the treatment of phobias, and anxiety disorders.
- Cognitive Behavioral Therapy (CBT): AI-VR applications can provide interactive CBT exercises, allowing patients to practice coping strategies and behavioural interventions in realistic scenarios. AI algorithms can analyze patient data to personalize therapy sessions, adapting scenarios and responses based on the individual's needs.
- Mindfulness and Relaxation: VR environments can simulate peaceful landscapes, aiding mindfulness practices and relaxation techniques. AI can analyze physiological data, providing real-time feedback during relaxation exercises, enhancing their effectiveness.

- Treatment of Phobias: VR facilitates gradual exposure to phobic stimuli or traumatic memories in a controlled manner, helping patients confront and manage their fears. AI algorithms adjust the intensity of stimuli based on the patient's response, optimizing the desensitization process.
- Pain Management: VR distracts patients from pain during medical procedures, reducing the need for anaesthesia and painkillers. AI-VR can incorporate personalized sensory experiences, such as soothing visuals and music, to manage chronic pain and improve patients' overall well-being.
- Social Skills Training: VR scenarios can simulate social situations, helping individuals with social anxiety or autism spectrum disorders practice social interactions. AI algorithms can provide feedback on social cues, helping patients improve their social skills through repeated simulations.
- Early Detection and Monitoring: AI analyzes user behaviour within VR environments, aiding in the early detection of mental health issues based on patterns of interaction and response. VR applications, supported by AI, enable continuous monitoring of patients' mental health, allowing for timely interventions when needed.
- Support for Neurological Disorders: VR combined with AI offers interactive exercises for patients with neurological disorders, supporting cognitive rehabilitation and enhancing brain function. AI analyzes patient performance data to tailor rehabilitation programs, optimizing the effectiveness of interventions for conditions like stroke or traumatic brain injuries.

In summary, the integration of AI and VR in therapeutic and mental health applications revolutionizes the way mental health services are delivered. It enhances accessibility, personalization, and effectiveness of interventions, offering new hope for individuals struggling with various mental health challenges and neurological disorders. Continued research, ethical considerations, and the collaboration between technology experts and mental health professionals are essential to harness the full potential of AI-VR integration in the field of mental health and therapy. While AI-VR integration offers promising applications in therapy and mental health, ethical dimensions arise concerning patient privacy, informed consent, and the potential for AI to influence therapeutic outcomes (Riva et al., 2016).

Considering the societal impact and psychological consequences of AI-VR integration is essential for responsible technology development. Ethical considerations must guide the design, deployment, and use of AI-VR technologies to ensure they contribute positively to individuals, communities, and society at large.

4. LEGAL AND REGULATORY CHALLENGES OF ETHICAL AI-VR INTEGRATION/COMPREHENSIVE REGULATORY FRAMEWORK FOR ETHICAL AI-VR INTEGRATION

The intersection of artificial intelligence (AI) and virtual reality (VR) technologies introduces novel legal and regulatory challenges that require careful consideration. As these technologies advance and become more integrated into various aspects of society, legal frameworks must evolve to address the unique ethical and practical challenges posed by AI-VR integration. Understanding and addressing these challenges are crucial to ensure responsible development, protect user rights, and navigate the evolving landscape of AI-VR technologies. This demands a comprehensive regulatory framework aims to ensure responsible development, deployment, and use of AI-VR systems while safeguarding user rights, data privacy, and societal well-being.

i. Ethical Principles and Guidelines

a. *Transparency and Explainability*: Mandate that AI-VR systems provide clear explanations of AI-driven decisions, content creation, and interactions to users (Laranjeiro et al., 2021).
b. *Algorithmic Fairness*: Enforce measures to mitigate biases in AI algorithms, ensuring equitable representation and fair treatment across diverse user groups (Johnson & Li, 2019).
c. *User Autonomy*: Guarantee user control over AI-VR experiences, enabling customization, personalization, and the ability to set boundaries on AI involvement (Sundar et al., 2021).

ii. Intellectual Property and Copyright

AI-generated content within VR environments raises questions about ownership and protection of intellectual property rights. Determining authorship, ownership, and licensing of AI-driven VR creations presents a complex legal challenge (Samuelson, 2007).

iii. Accountability and Oversight/Liability and Accountability

When AI-driven VR experiences interact with users, the question of liability arises in cases of errors, misinformation, or even accidents. Assigning responsibility between AI systems, VR platform operators, and users requires a nuanced legal framework (Calo, 2010).

a. *Ethical Review Boards*: Establish independent review boards to assess the ethical implications of AI-VR projects before deployment, particularly in sensitive areas like healthcare and education.
b. *Algorithm Auditing*: Enforce regular audits of AI algorithms in VR environments to identify and rectify biases, ensuring that AI-VR interactions align with ethical standards.

iv. Data Protection, Privacy, and Security

The collection and analysis of user data within AI-enhanced VR experiences raise significant concerns about data privacy and security. Advanced AI techniques could be used to steal someone's virtual identity, leading to financial or reputational damage. Establishing robust data protection mechanisms, user consent protocols, and transparency measures are crucial to navigate the legal landscape (Purtova, 2017).

a. *Informed Consent*: Mandate explicit and informed consent for data collection, usage, and sharing within AI-VR systems, ensuring users have a clear understanding of how their data is utilized.
b. *Anonymization*: Require robust anonymization techniques to protect user identities and sensitive information, preventing unauthorized access and data breaches.

v. Consumer Protection and Transparency

As AI-VR integration becomes more prevalent, ensuring that consumers are informed about AI's role and influence in VR environments becomes essential. Legal frameworks must require transparency and disclosure to prevent deceptive practices (Hoffman & Novak, 1996).

vi. Cross-Border Jurisdiction and Data Flow

AI-VR integration can lead to cross-border data flows and jurisdictional challenges. Legal frameworks must address issues related to data localization, data sovereignty, and conflicts of laws (Balkin, 2007).

vii. Ethical and Social Impact Assessments

Incorporating ethical and social impact assessments into legal frameworks can ensure that AI-VR technologies align with societal values and norms. Establishing mechanisms for evaluating and addressing potential societal impacts is crucial (Hildebrandt & Gutwirth, 2016).

viii. Standardization and Certification

Developing industry standards and certifications for AI-VR integration can help ensure compliance with ethical and legal requirements. Such standards can promote responsible development and protect user interests (Dutton et al., 2011).

ix. Cultural Sensitivity and Diversity

a. *Cultural Impact Assessment*: Implement assessments to ensure AI-generated content and interactions within VR environments respect diverse cultural norms and values.
b. *Diverse Representation*: Encourage developers to incorporate diverse perspectives in AI training data to avoid perpetuating cultural stereotypes (Consalvo & Ess, 2011).

x. Education and Awareness

a. *User Education*: Mandate user education initiatives to inform individuals about AI-VR integration, its benefits, risks, and ethical considerations, enabling informed decision-making.
b. *Training for Developers*: Require training and certification for developers working on AI-VR projects, ensuring a comprehensive understanding of ethical guidelines and practices.

xi. Collaboration and Multi-Stakeholder Engagement

a. *Interdisciplinary Collaboration*: Foster collaboration between academia, industry, civil society, policymakers, and users to continuously refine and update the regulatory framework.
b. *Public Consultations*: Conduct regular public consultations to gather input and feedback on AI-VR policies, ensuring that regulations reflect societal values and concerns.

Addressing these legal and regulatory challenges is pivotal for establishing a clear framework that governs AI-VR integration. Collaboration between legal experts, technologists, policymakers, and ethicists is essential to develop comprehensive guidelines that balance technological innovation with ethical and legal considerations. This comprehensive regulatory framework balances technological innovation with ethical considerations, aiming to promote responsible AI-VR integration while safeguarding user rights, societal values, and the well-being of individuals and communities. As AI-VR technologies continue to advance, an adaptive and forward-thinking legal landscape will be crucial to ensure their responsible and beneficial deployment.

5. EDUCATIONAL AND TRAINING IMPLICATIONS OF AI-VR INTEGRATION

The integration of artificial intelligence (AI) and virtual reality (VR) technologies holds transformative potential in the realm of education and training. This convergence offers innovative ways to enhance learning experiences, skill acquisition, and knowledge retention. Understanding the educational and training implications of AI-VR integration is essential for harnessing these technologies to their fullest educational potential while addressing ethical and pedagogical considerations.

i. Personalized Learning and Adaptive Instruction

The integration of Artificial Intelligence (AI) and Virtual Reality (VR) has significant implications for personalized learning and adaptive instruction, transforming the way students learn and educators teach. AI-powered VR environments can adapt content and experiences to individual learners' needs, pace, and learning styles. This personalized approach enhances engagement, self-directed learning, and knowledge mastery (Jackson & Smith, 2019). Here's how AI-VR integration impacts personalized learning and adaptive instruction:

- Personalized Learning Paths: AI analyzes students' learning patterns and performance data to customize learning paths, ensuring each student receives tailored educational content. VR platforms, powered by AI, adapt content difficulty and complexity based on students' proficiency levels, ensuring an appropriate level of challenge for individual learners.
- Real-Time Feedback and Assessment: AI analyzes students' interactions in VR, providing real-time feedback on their performance, allowing immediate corrections and improvements. VR assessments powered by AI offer formative feedback, helping educators understand students' strengths and areas needing improvement, enabling targeted interventions.
- Customized Learning Materials: AI can create customized learning materials, including textbooks, exercises, and multimedia content, tailored to students' learning styles and preferences. VR supports diverse learning styles by offering a range of multimodal experiences, accommodating visual, auditory, and kinesthetic learners.
- Support for Special Education: AI-VR integration provides personalized support for students with special needs, creating adaptive learning experiences catering to their unique requirements. VR can provide sensory stimulation for students with sensory processing disorders, offering controlled and customizable sensory inputs.

ii. Immersive Experiential Learning

AI-driven VR simulations create immersive and interactive learning environments, enhancing student engagement and motivation. VR, augmented by AI, enables learners to experience scenarios that would otherwise be difficult or impossible to recreate in traditional classrooms. VR allows students to perform experiments, explore historical sites, or engage in simulations, providing a hands-on learning experience that is both educational and enjoyable. This immersive experiential learning enhances understanding and retention of complex concepts (Riva et al., 2016). The combination of AI and VR, thus has a profound impact on immersive experiential learning, revolutionizing the way individuals acquire knowledge and skills. Following are some of the ways in which AI-VR integration influences immersive experiential learning:

- Realistic Simulations: AI-driven VR simulations can recreate real-world environments, allowing learners to engage in lifelike scenarios relevant to their field of study or profession. Learners can practice complex tasks, experiments, or procedures in a risk-free virtual environment, enhancing hands-on learning experiences.
- Interactivity and Engagement: AI-VR integration creates interactive and immersive learning environments, promoting active engagement and participation among learners. Learners can assume different roles within VR simulations, promoting empathy and a deeper understanding of diverse perspectives.AI algorithms can also introduce gamification elements, such as challenges, rewards, and leaderboards, increasing motivation and competition among learners.
- Multi-Sensory Learning: VR supports multi-sensory learning experiences, accommodating various learning styles and preferences, including visual, auditory, and kinesthetic learning. AI can provide sensory feedback, replicating sensations like touch or vibrations, enriching the immersive experience and enhancing learning outcomes.
- Skill Mastery and Proficiency: Learners can repeat exercises and tasks within VR simulations until they achieve mastery, ensuring proficiency in specific skills or knowledge areas. AI provides instant feedback on learners' actions, enabling them to correct mistakes immediately and learn from their errors, accelerating the learning process.
- Cultivating Problem-Solving Skills: AI-VR scenarios can present complex, real-world problems that require critical thinking and problem-solving skills, helping learners develop these essential competencies. Learners can face decision-making challenges within VR simulations, allowing them to experience the consequences of their choices in a controlled environment.

iii. Skill Acquisition and Practice

AI-driven simulations in VR settings provide a safe environment for learners to practice skills, make decisions, and receive real-time feedback. AI-VR platforms facilitate continuous or lifelong learning by offering personalized skill development modules for professionals and learners of all ages. AI adjusts the complexity of skill-based VR simulations based on users' performance, ensuring effective skill acquisition and mastery. VR simulations, guided by AI, can be used for certification programs, ensuring professionals are well-prepared for their roles in a realistic virtual environment. AI-VR integration is also used for job-specific training across various industries, allowing professionals to enhance their skills and stay up-to-date with industry standards and practices. This approach is particularly valuable in training professionals for high-stakes and hazardous scenarios (Eggenberger et al., 2016).

iv. Global Collaborative Learning

AI-VR platforms enable collaborative learning experiences, allowing learners from different locations to work together in real time, fostering teamwork and cooperation skills. AI-VR platforms can be designed to accommodate various languages, ensuring inclusivity for diverse linguistic backgrounds. AI-powered VR platforms enable students and educators from around the world to collaborate in shared virtual spaces. This fosters cross-cultural understanding, global awareness with global perspectives, and collaborative problem-solving (Dede, 2009).

v. Data-Driven Insights and Learning Analytics

AI algorithms can analyze learner interactions within VR environments, providing educators with valuable insights into individual progress and group dynamics. These data-driven insights inform instructional strategies and enhance pedagogical outcomes (Sotiriou et al., 2019). Teacher Support and Professional Development: AI analyzes classroom data to provide teachers with insights into student progress, enabling them to make data-informed instructional decisions. VR offers immersive training environments for educators, allowing them to practice teaching techniques and classroom management skills in realistic scenarios.

In summary, AI-VR integration revolutionizes personalized learning and adaptive instruction by providing tailored, interactive, and immersive educational experiences. These advancements have the potential to improve learning outcomes, enhance student engagement, and support educators in their teaching endeavours, making education more accessible, effective, and inclusive for learners of all ages and abilities.

Some of the potential applications of AI in education as depicted in (Kamalov et al., 2023) is shown in Figure 3.

Figure 3. Multifaceted impact of AI in education (Kamalov et al., 2023)

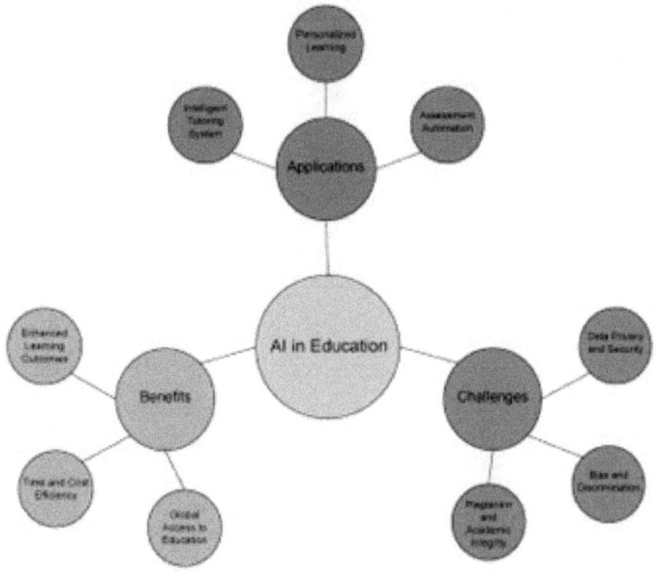

vi. Ethical Considerations in AI-VR Education

Ethical considerations in AI-VR education are crucial to ensuring that the integration of these technologies in learning environments is responsible, fair, and respectful of users' rights and well-being. Here, we discuss some key ethical considerations in AI-VR education. The integration of AI into VR education raises ethical questions regarding data privacy, algorithmic bias, and learner autonomy. VR platforms collect extensive user data. Ethical practices involve ensuring the privacy and security of this data, protecting users from unauthorized access or misuse. Users, especially students, should be fully informed about the data collected, how it will be used, and have the right to consent or opt-out. Ethical AI-VR education should focus on providing equal access to educational resources, avoiding discrimination based on factors like race, gender, socioeconomic status, or disabilities. VR educational content and platforms should be designed to be accessible to all, including individuals with disabilities, ensuring that learning experiences are inclusive. Efforts should be made to ensure that VR technology and related educational content are affordable and accessible to students from diverse socioeconomic backgrounds. Users should have the ability to understand and challenge decisions made by AI systems, especially in educational evaluations and assessments. In VR environments, especially those involving social interactions, it's crucial to establish and maintain appropriate boundaries between educators and students, ensuring a safe and respectful learning environment. Educators and administrators must prevent any form of exploitation or harassment within VR spaces, protecting vulnerable students. VR experiences, while immersive, can lead to excessive screen time. Ethical considerations involve balancing immersive learning with the importance of physical and mental well-being. Ethical design includes features to prevent addiction, especially in educational games, by discouraging overuse and encouraging breaks.

Ethical considerations extend to the long-term societal impact of AI-VR education, including its influence on employment, social skills, and cultural norms. These potential impacts must be carefully considered and addressed. Educational institutions, developers, policymakers, and educators themselves play a significant role in upholding ethical standards in AI-VR education. By being mindful of these ethical considerations, the integration of AI and VR technologies can enhance educational experiences while ensuring the well-being and rights of all learners. Balancing the benefits of AI-enhanced learning with ethical considerations is essential to create a responsible and inclusive educational environment (Brown & Lee, 2021). Figure 4. shows privacy concerns as identified in (Regan & Jesse, 2018).

Figure 4. Privacy concerns identified in (Regan & Jesse, 2018)

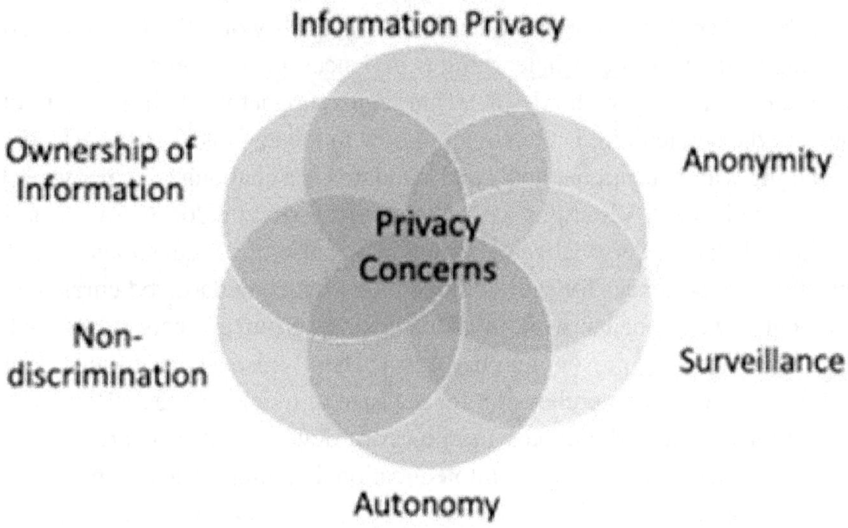

Leveraging the educational and training implications of AI-VR integration requires a thoughtful approach that considers pedagogical effectiveness, learner engagement, and ethical considerations. By harnessing the capabilities of AI and VR, educators can create immersive and personalized learning experiences that empower learners and prepare them for the challenges of an ever-evolving world.

5.1 Balancing Efficiency Gains with Maintaining Educational Integrity in AI-VR Integration

The integration of artificial intelligence (AI) and virtual reality (VR) technologies into education brings the promise of enhanced efficiency and personalized learning experiences. While AI-VR integration offers transformative potential, it also raises critical concerns about maintaining educational integrity. Striking a balance between efficiency gains and upholding the principles of quality education is essential to harness the full benefits of these technologies.

i. Personalized Learning and Efficiency

AI-powered VR environments can tailor educational content to individual learners, enabling efficient adaptive instruction as discussed in section 5. Learners can progress at their own pace, receive targeted interventions, and focus on areas needing improvement, leading to more efficient learning outcomes (Jackson & Smith, 2019).

ii. Challenges to Maintaining Educational Integrity

The integration of Artificial Intelligence (AI) and Virtual Reality (VR) in education brings about various benefits but also poses significant challenges to maintaining educational integrity. The efficiency gains brought by AI-VR integration may raise concerns about the depth and rigor of learning experiences. Ensuring the accuracy and credibility of the content within VR simulations and experiences is crucial. Misinformation or biased content can mislead learners. The quality of VR educational content can vary significantly, leading to inconsistencies in learning experiences and outcomes. Educators might lack the necessary training and familiarity with AI-VR technologies, impacting their ability to effectively integrate these tools into the curriculum. Understanding how to leverage AI-VR for effective teaching and learning while aligning with educational goals and standards is a challenge for many teachers. Ensuring that the immersive experience of VR aligns with educational goals and doesn't overshadow the learning objectives is a delicate balance. Personalized learning in VR also raises questions about how to balance customized educational experiences for individual learners with standardized curricular requirements. Assessing the authenticity of students' work in VR, especially group projects, poses challenges in identifying original contributions and preventing plagiarism. There's also a risk of sacrificing critical thinking, problem-solving, and deep comprehension for the sake of quick progress (Richter & Koch, 2018).

Technical limitations, such as the processing power of devices and software bugs, can disrupt the seamless integration of AI-VR technologies into educational settings. VR equipment requires regular maintenance and technical support, which can be resource-intensive for educational institutions, especially smaller ones with limited budgets. Also, students from disadvantaged backgrounds might lack access to VR technology or high-quality internet connections, creating inequalities in learning opportunities. The cost of VR equipment and software can create disparities between schools and students, affecting the equitable implementation of AI-VR integration.

iii. Ensuring Comprehensive Learning

While AI can identify gaps in knowledge and offer targeted learning paths, maintaining educational integrity requires ensuring a comprehensive and holistic understanding of subjects. Ensuring comprehensive learning in AI-VR integration involves thoughtful planning, pedagogical innovation, and addressing the diverse needs of learners. The discussion emphasizes few points to ensure a well-rounded and effective educational experience in AI-VR integration.

It must be ensured that AI-VR activities align with the curriculum's learning objectives, emphasizing the knowledge, skills, and competencies students are expected to achieve. VR simulations must be developed in a way that they are interactive, engaging, and closely related to real-world scenarios, allowing students to apply theoretical knowledge in practical contexts. The content must cater to different learning styles (visual, auditory, kinesthetic) within VR environments, and accessible and engaging for all types of learners. It must encourage interdisciplinary collaboration by designing projects that require students from different disciplines to work together within VR environments, fostering teamwork, communication skills, problem-solving abilities with diverse perspectives and knowledge exchange. AI algorithms may be utilized to track individual progress and tailor learning pathways, offering personalized content and challenges based on students' strengths, weaknesses, and learning pace. Formative assessments may be integrated within VR experiences, providing feedback to students about their performance, allowing them to understand their progress and areas for improvement. The feedback about students' performance will provide educators with insights to assess learning outcomes and make data-driven instructional decisions as discussed in section 5. The students must be engaged in discussions about the societal impact of AI-VR integration, encouraging them to consider the technology's effects on various communities and professions. There must also be feedback loops/ mechanisms where students and educators can provide input on the effectiveness of AI-VR learning experiences, allowing for continuous improvement and refinement of the content.

By integrating these strategies, educational institutions can create comprehensive AI-VR learning experiences that not only enhance academic knowledge but also develop critical thinking, problem-solving, collaboration, ethical reasoning skills, incorporating diverse perspectives, and opportunities for open-ended exploration, preparing students for the challenges of the future. This (Bolstad et al., 2012).

iv. Ethical Use of AI for Assessment

AI-driven assessment tools in VR environments can enhance efficiency by automatically grading assignments. Educational institutions and developers should be transparent about the algorithms used in AI-VR systems, enabling users to understand how decisions are made. Ethical AI-VR education involves implementing measures to prevent cheating, such as plagiarism detection algorithms, while respecting students' privacy. However, ensuring that these assessments accurately capture students' learning and abilities while preventing cheating is crucial to maintaining the integrity of educational outcomes (Davis & Roblyer, 2005).

v. Fostering Critical Thinking and Creativity

While AI-VR integration can streamline content delivery, educators must prioritize fostering critical thinking, problem-solving, and creativity. VR assignments and projects should encourage creativity and original thinking, ensuring that students are not merely copying or mimicking VR experiences created by others. Designing learning experiences that encourage learners to question, analyze, and synthesize information remains essential (Jonassen, 2010).

vi. Educator Roles and Training

Balancing efficiency and maintaining educational integrity necessitates equipping educators with the skills to effectively integrate AI and VR into their pedagogical practices. Professional development and ongoing training are crucial to ensure educators can guide students through meaningful learning experiences (Gulbahar & Tinmaz, 2006).

Addressing these challenges requires a concerted effort from educators, policymakers, technology developers, and researchers. It involves developing clear guidelines, investing in teacher training, promoting digital inclusion, ensuring content quality, and upholding ethical standards to harness the full potential of AI-VR integration while maintaining educational integrity. Striking the delicate balance between efficiency gains and maintaining educational integrity requires a thoughtful approach that prioritizes learners' holistic development. By leveraging AI-VR technologies to enhance learning experiences while upholding the principles of comprehensive education, educators can create a dynamic and effective learning environment that prepares students for success in a rapidly evolving world.

6. TRANSPARENCY AND EXPLAINABILITY IN AI-VR INTEGRATION

The integration of artificial intelligence (AI) and virtual reality (VR) technologies offers exciting opportunities for immersive and personalized experiences in various domains, including education, healthcare, and entertainment. However, as AI algorithms drive decisions and content creation within VR environments, ensuring transparency and explainability becomes paramount. Understanding the importance of transparency and explainability in AI-VR integration is essential for building trust, enhancing user experiences, and addressing ethical concerns.

i. Transparency in Content Creation

Transparency in content creation plays a pivotal role in AI-VR integration, ensuring ethical practices, user trust, and the responsible deployment of these technologies. Providing users with insights into how AI contributes to the creation of VR content enhances their understanding of the virtual environment. It is essential because transparent content creation processes help identify and eliminate biases in AI algorithms, ensuring that VR experiences do not discriminate against any group based on race, gender, or other factors. Transparency fosters ethical decision-making, ensuring that content creators are aware of the ethical implications of their work and make responsible choices during the development process. Transparency in content creation includes clear communication about how user data is collected, stored, and utilized within AI-VR applications, ensuring user privacy and empowering users to make informed decisions about their participation. Transparent content creation processes maintain the integrity of educational content, ensuring that VR experiences are academically sound, aligned with curricular goals, and provide accurate information to learners.

In summary, transparency in content creation within AI-VR integration is essential for fostering trust, ensuring ethical practices, upholding educational integrity, and promoting a collaborative and informed approach to the development and deployment of AI-driven VR experiences. It serves as a foundation for responsible innovation, encouraging the creation of inclusive, ethical, and effective learning environments. This transparency helps users discern between AI-generated and human-created elements, allowing them to appreciate the technology's role (Tintarev & Masthoff, 2012).

ii. User Trust and Confidence

Transparency and explainability are key factors in building user trust and confidence in AI-VR systems. Transparent practices instil trust in users, including students, educators, and parents, who need assurance that the AI-driven VR content is accurate, unbiased, and designed with their best interests in mind. Providing clear and understandable information about how AI algorithms shape VR experiences enhances user confidence and understanding. When users understand the algorithms behind their VR experiences, how AI influences their VR experiences, they are better equipped to make informed decisions and are more likely to actively engage and interact with the technology (Kim et al., 2019).

iii. Explainable AI Interfaces

Explainable AI (XAI) interfaces are crucial in the context of AI-VR integration, especially in applications, where transparency, understanding, and user trust are paramount. Implementing XAI interfaces in

VR environments can offer users detailed explanations about AI-generated suggestions, predictions, or outcomes. XAI interfaces can visualize complex AI algorithms used in VR experiences, making them understandable to educators, students, and administrators who may not have a technical background. XAI interfaces can analyze user feedback about AI-VR experiences, identifying common issues or errors. This information can be used to enhance AI algorithms and improve user understanding. Users can comprehend errors or inaccuracies in AI-generated content, fostering trust by demonstrating that the system's limitations and mistakes are recognized and addressed. Understanding user interactions through XAI interfaces enables iterative development of AI algorithms, leading to more effective and user-friendly AI-VR content over time. These interfaces help users comprehend the rationale behind AI's decisions, enhancing their control over interactions and trust in the technology (Laranjeiro et al., 2021).

iv. Avoiding Black Box Phenomenon

AI algorithms, especially in deep learning, can be perceived as "black boxes" where their decision-making process is opaque and difficult to comprehend. Ensuring transparency and explainability helps users, developers, and regulators understand how decisions are made within AI-VR systems (Ribeiro et al., 2016).

v. Ethical Accountability

Transparent AI-VR systems enable responsible handling of user data and content creation. When users can trace how their data is used and understand the ethical considerations in content generation, it reinforces the accountability of AI developers and operators (Floridi, 2019).

vi. User-Centric Customization

Transparent AI-VR systems allow users to customize their experiences based on their preferences and values. Users can adjust AI-driven aspects to align with their comfort levels and ethical standards, enhancing user agency and control (Sundar et al., 2018).

vii. Customization and Personalization

Empowering users to customize AI settings in VR experiences gives them control over the extent and nature of AI's influence as discussed in section 5. Customization options could range from adjusting AI-generated content levels to tailoring the style of interactions (Sundar et al., 2021).

viii. User Feedback Loops

Transparency encourages users to provide feedback about their experiences, enabling content creators to refine their creations based on user input, enhancing the overall quality of VR content. Incorporating mechanisms for users to provide feedback on AI-mediated experiences enables iterative improvement and promotes a sense of co-creation. This approach empowers users to shape their virtual interactions and fosters a collaborative relationship with AI (Van Der Linden et al., 2018).

ix. Education and Learning Interfaces

Transparency and explainability in AI-VR integration are crucial for educational contexts. Learners benefit from understanding how AI influences their learning paths and content recommendations, enabling them to make informed decisions about their education. In educational contexts, AI-driven VR platforms can offer learners insights into how AI assists in their learning journeys. Transparent communication helps users understand the lifelong learning opportunities provided by AI-VR integration, promoting ongoing education and skill development. Transparent practices contribute to public understanding of AI technologies, dispelling misconceptions and fostering informed discussions about the potential and limitations of AI-VR integration. Visualizations or explanations of AI's contributions help learners understand how AI supports their educational goals (Heller & Rahal, 2020).

xi. Legal and Regulatory Compliance

Transparent AI-VR systems facilitate compliance with data protection regulations and ethical standards as discussed in section 4. Transparent content creation practices ensure compliance with legal and regulatory frameworks related to data privacy, user rights, and ethical guidelines, protecting both content creators and users from legal complications. Organizations can demonstrate accountability by providing explanations for AI-driven decisions, ensuring alignment with legal requirements (Hoffman & Podgurski, 2017).

By prioritizing transparency and explainability in AI-VR integration, developers and operators can create immersive experiences that empower users, foster trust, and uphold ethical principles. Transparent AI-VR systems ensure that users have insights into how AI influences their interactions and decision-making, enabling them to make informed choices and engage meaningfully in virtual environments.

xii. Enhancing User Understanding and Control Over AI-Mediated Virtual Experiences

The integration of artificial intelligence (AI) and virtual reality (VR) technologies has opened up new possibilities for immersive and personalized experiences. However, ensuring that users have a clear understanding of and control over AI-mediated virtual experiences is essential to foster trust, enable informed decision-making, and promote ethical engagement. By enhancing user understanding and control, AI-VR integration can create more meaningful and empowering interactions.

All the above discussion points at developing clear ethical guidelines and controls for AI-VR integration allows users to set boundaries on AI's involvement. Users can define limits on data usage, AI decision-making, and content generation, enhancing their control and preserving ethical considerations (Floridi et al., 2018).

Empowering users with understanding and control over AI-mediated virtual experiences not only enhances their engagement but also addresses ethical concerns. By incorporating transparency, explainability, customization, and user feedback mechanisms, AI-VR integration can create a symbiotic relationship between users and technology, fostering responsible and meaningful interactions in virtual environments.

7. SOME REAL-WORLD CASE STUDIES WHERE THE INTERSECTION OF AI AND VR TECHNOLOGIES HAS RAISED ETHICAL CONSIDERATIONS

i. Project Debater: AI-Powered Debating in VR

IBM's Project Debater, an AI system designed to engage in meaningful debates with humans, was integrated into a VR environment. Users could engage in debates with Project Debater, blurring the line between human and AI interaction. This raised ethical questions about the potential manipulation of user opinions, AI bias, and the implications of AI-mediated discourse in virtual spaces (Araki & Fujimura, 2021).

ii. Mental Health Therapy in Virtual Reality

VR platforms, enriched with AI-driven analytics, are used in mental health therapy to create immersive environments for exposure therapy and stress reduction. While these technologies offer innovative therapeutic options, ethical considerations include data privacy, informed consent, and ensuring that AI algorithms respect users' emotional states during therapy (Riva et al., 2016).

iii AI-Powered Medical Simulation in VR

AI-driven simulations in VR are employed for medical training and surgical practice. These simulations enable medical professionals to practice procedures in a risk-free environment. Ethical concerns include ensuring that AI accurately represents real-world medical scenarios and that the data used to train AI models is representative and diverse (Chandra et al., 2019).

iv. AI-Driven Content Creation in VR Storytelling

In VR storytelling, AI algorithms are used to dynamically generate narrative elements based on user interactions. While this offers personalized experiences, ethical dilemmas emerge around the authorship of generated content, intellectual property rights, and maintaining the integrity of human creativity (McCormick & Heer, 2017).

v. AI-Enhanced Language Learning in VR

AI-powered language learning platforms integrated into VR environments enable personalized language instruction. Ethical considerations include the potential for AI to reinforce cultural stereotypes, the quality of language instruction provided, and the transparency of AI's pedagogical decisions (Heift & Schulze, 2019).

vi. AI-VR Assisted Architectural Design

Architects use AI-driven VR tools to visualize and iterate designs. Ethical concerns revolve around the potential displacement of human creativity, accountability for design choices made by AI, and ensuring that AI-enhanced designs align with human values (Karakusevic, 2021).

These case studies illustrate the diverse ways in which AI and VR technologies intersect ethically across various sectors. Each example highlights the importance of considering transparency, data privacy, bias mitigation, user agency, and the preservation of human values when integrating AI and VR for meaningful and responsible outcomes.

8. DISCUSSION AND FUTURE DIRECTIONS

Synthesis of Key Findings and Ethical Considerations in AI-VR Integration

The integration of artificial intelligence (AI) and virtual reality (VR) technologies holds immense promise for reshaping various aspects of human experience, from education and healthcare to entertainment and beyond. As AI-VR integration evolves, a synthesis of key findings underscores both the potential benefits and ethical considerations that guide responsible development and deployment.

Key Findings:

i. **Enhanced Experiences**: AI-VR integration offers enhanced, immersive experiences by personalizing content, adapting interactions, and enabling users to engage in lifelike scenarios (Jackson & Smith, 2019; Riva et al., 2016).
ii. **Efficiency and Personalization**: AI-driven VR environments facilitate efficient learning, training, and problem-solving through personalized pathways and adaptive instruction (Kim et al., 2019; Sundar et al., 2021).
iii. **Therapeutic Applications**: AI-powered VR platforms have therapeutic potential in mental health, exposure therapy, and medical training, providing controlled and safe environments for practice (Chandra et al., 2019; Riva et al., 2016).
iv. **Collaboration and Global Reach**: AI-VR integration enables collaborative learning and transcends geographical boundaries, fostering cross-cultural understanding and global interactions (Dede, 2009; Kim et al., 2019).

Ethical Considerations for Responsible AI-VR Integration:

i. **User Empowerment**: Empower users with transparency, customization, and control to shape their AI-VR experiences. Ensuring transparency in AI-VR systems helps build user trust by providing insights into AI's role, decision-making, and content generation (Laranjeiro et al., 2021; Tintarev & Masthoff, 2012).
ii. **Ethical Algorithms**: Develop and implement algorithms that mitigate bias, ensure fairness, and align with ethical standards. AI algorithms can perpetuate biases present in training data, necessitating ongoing monitoring, mitigation strategies, and equitable representation (Johnson & Li, 2019; White et al., 2022).
iii. **User Autonomy and Control**: Balancing efficiency gains with user agency is vital. Users should have control over AI-driven experiences, customization options, and the ability to set boundaries (Brown & Lee, 2021; Sundar et al., 2021).
iv. **Privacy and Data Protection**: Collecting and analyzing user data within AI-VR environments raises privacy concerns, requiring robust data protection mechanisms, ensuring informed consent,

responsible data usage and adhere to stringent data protection measures (Purtova, 2017; Smith et al., 2020).

v. **Cultural Sensitivity**: Create AI-VR content such that AI-VR experiences must respect diverse cultural norms, values, and perspectives, avoiding cultural appropriation and offensive content (Consalvo & Ess, 2011; Kim et al., 2019).

vi. **Educational Integrity**: AI-VR integration should uphold educational rigor, prioritizing critical thinking, and comprehensive learning, ensuring that AI-enhanced experiences do not compromise educational quality (Bolstad et al., 2012; Richter & Koch, 2018).

vii. **Ongoing Monitoring**: Continuously monitor AI-VR systems for biases, algorithmic performance, and ethical implications.

The synthesis of key findings and ethical considerations underscores the need for a multidisciplinary approach, involving technologists, educators, ethicists, policymakers, and users. Responsible AI-VR integration is a dynamic endeavour that requires constant vigilance, adaptation, and ethical reflection to ensure that these technologies enrich human experiences while upholding ethical values and societal well-being.

8.1 Implications for Future Research, Technology Development, and Policy-Making in AI-VR Integration

The convergence of artificial intelligence (AI) and virtual reality (VR) technologies presents a rapidly evolving landscape that holds significant potential across various domains. As AI-VR integration continues to advance, several implications emerge for future research, technology development, and policy-making to ensure responsible and beneficial outcomes.

i. Research Directions

a. *Ethical AI-VR Frameworks*: Future research should focus on developing comprehensive ethical frameworks that guide AI-VR integration, addressing transparency, bias mitigation, data privacy, and user autonomy (Floridi et al., 2018).

b. *Algorithmic Fairness*: Research should delve into methods for ensuring fairness in AI-VR algorithms, preventing biases in content generation, and ensuring equitable access to immersive experiences (Johnson & Li, 2019).

c. *User-Centric Design*: Exploring user preferences, perceptions, and experiences in AI-VR integration can guide the design of personalized and user-centric virtual environments (Sundar et al., 2021).

ii. Technology Development

a. *Explainable AI-VR Interfaces*: Developers should prioritize creating intuitive and transparent interfaces that explain AI's role and decision-making within VR environments, ensuring users can comprehend and control their experiences (Laranjeiro et al., 2021).

b. *AI-VR Personalization*: Further development of AI-driven personalization techniques can enhance user engagement and learning outcomes while maintaining educational integrity (Jackson & Smith, 2019).
c. *Data Privacy Solutions*: Innovations in privacy-preserving AI algorithms and data anonymization techniques are essential to protect user data and ensure compliance with data protection regulations (Purtova, 2017).

iii. Policy-Making

a. *Ethical Guidelines and Standards:* Policymakers should collaborate with experts to develop clear and comprehensive ethical guidelines for AI-VR integration, addressing issues such as data privacy, algorithmic bias, and user consent (Hildebrandt & Gutwirth, 2016).
b. *Regulation and Compliance*: Robust regulatory frameworks should be established to ensure AI-VR technologies adhere to ethical and legal standards, promoting responsible development and deployment (Dutton et al., 2011).
c. *Collaboration and Multi-Stakeholder Involvement*: Policymakers should foster collaboration between academia, industry, civil society, and users to develop and implement AI-VR policies that reflect diverse perspectives and expertise.

The implications for future research, technology development, and policy-making emphasize the need for interdisciplinary collaboration and a proactive approach to addressing ethical, technical, and societal challenges. By aligning research, development, and policies, AI-VR integration can be harnessed to create meaningful, inclusive, and responsible virtual experiences that benefit individuals and society as a whole.

REFERENCES

Araki, Y., & Fujimura, T. (2021). VR Debates with Project Debater. *IBM Journal of Research and Development, 65*(5/6), 5:1-5:12.

Baeza-Yates, R. (2022). Ethical Challenges in AI. *Proceedings of the 15th ACM International Conference on Web Search and Data Mining.*

Balkin, J. M. (2007). The First Amendment and the second commandment. *New York University Law Review, 81*(5), 1639–1683.

Bersin, J. (2019). *The Ethics of People Analytics and AI in the Workplace: Four Dimensions of Trust.* The Medium.

Biocca, F. (1997). The Cyborg's Dilemma: Progressive Embodiment in Virtual Environments. *Journal of Computer-Mediated Communication, 3*(2), JCMC321. doi:10.1111/j.1083-6101.1997.tb00070.x

Bolstad, R., Gilbert, J., McDowall, S., Bull, A., Boyd, S., & Hipkins, R. (2012). *Supporting Future-oriented Learning and Teaching—A New Zealand Perspective.* Ministry of Education.

Brown, L., & Lee, E. (2021). Autonomy and Consent in AI-Enhanced Virtual Environments. *Journal of Virtual Ethics*, *6*(1), 45–62.

Burdea, G., & Coiffet, P. (2003). *Virtual Reality Technology*. John Wiley & Sons. doi:10.1162/105474603322955950

Calo, R. (2010). Robots and Privacy. *Harvard Law Review*, *154*(2), 1671–1762.

Censius. (n.d.). *What is Ethical AI - Responsible AI*. Censius.

Chandra, M., Glassman, D., & Frantz, S. (2019). Exploring the Impact of Mixed Reality on Robotic Surgical Training. *Journal of Robotic Surgery*, *13*(4), 579–583. PMID:31555957

Consalvo, M., & Ess, C. (2011). *The Handbook of Internet Studies*. Wiley-Blackwell. doi:10.1002/9781444314861

Davis, N. E., & Roblyer, M. D. (2005). Preparing Teachers for the "School of Tomorrow": A Technology Action Competence Approach. *British Journal of Educational Technology*, *36*(2), 237–254.

Dede, C. (2009). Immersive Interfaces for Engagement and Learning. *Science*, *323*(5910), 66–69. doi:10.1126cience.1167311 PMID:19119219

Duhigg, C. (2012). *The Power of Habit: Why We Do What We Do in Life and Business*. Random House.

Dutton, W. H., Dopatka, A., Hills, M., Law, G., & Nash, V. (2011). *Freedom of Connection - Freedom of Expression: The Changing Legal and Regulatory Ecology Shaping the Internet*. Oxford Internet Institute.

Eggenberger, T., Schmid Mast, M., & Muff, B. (2016). Influence of Simulated Patients' Affective Tone of Voice on Student Learning and Emotional Responses—A Randomized Controlled Trial. *Patient Education and Counseling*, *99*(2), 273–282.

Eslami, M., Rickman, A., Vaccaro, K., Aleyasen, A., Vuong, A., Karahalios, K., & Hamilton, K. (2015). I Always assumed that I wasn't really that close to [her]: Reasoning about Invisible Algorithms in News Feeds. *Proceedings of the Eighth International Conference on Weblogs and Social Media*, 1-10. 10.1145/2702123.2702556

Floridi, L. (2019). *The Logic of Information: A Theory of Philosophy as Conceptual Design*. Oxford University Press. doi:10.1093/oso/9780198833635.001.0001

Floridi, L., Cowls, J., Beltrametti, M., Chatila, R., Chazerand, P., Dignum, V., ... Luetge, C. (2018). AI4People—an Ethical Framework for a Good AI Society: Opportunities, Risks, Principles, and Recommendations. *Minds and Machines*, *28*(4), 689–707. doi:10.100711023-018-9482-5 PMID:30930541

Goodfellow, I., Bengio, Y., & Courville, A. (2016). *Deep Learning*. MIT Press.

Gulbahar, Y., & Tinmaz, H. (2006). A Case for Teacher Professional Development in Technology Integration. *Journal of Technology and Teacher Education*, *14*(4), 729–740.

Hagendorff, T., & Danks, D. (2023). Ethical and methodological challenges in building morally informed AI systems. *AI and Ethics*, *3*(2), 553–566. doi:10.100743681-022-00188-y

Heift, T., & Schulze, M. (2019). Natural Language Processing in CALL. The Cambridge Handbook of CALL, 216-236.

Heller, R. S., & Rahal, M. (2020). The Impacts of AI on Education: Insights from the AI and Education Community. *Information and Learning Science*, *121*(1/2), 1–16.

Hildebrandt, M., & Gutwirth, S. (2016). *Profiling the European Citizen: Cross-disciplinary Perspectives*. Springer.

Hoffman, D. L., & Novak, T. P. (1996). Marketing in Hypermedia Computer-Mediated Environments: Conceptual Foundations. *Journal of Marketing*, *60*(3), 50–68. doi:10.1177/002224299606000304

Hoffman, L. J., & Podgurski, A. (2017). Big Data's Disparate Impact. *Minnesota Law Review*, *101*(1), 86–150.

Jackson, K., & Smith, T. (2019). Ethical Considerations in AI-VR Education: Balancing Efficiency and Rigor. *Educational Ethics Quarterly*, *24*(4), 315–332.

Johnson, I. M., & Li, F. (2019). Fairness and Abstraction in Sociotechnical Systems. *Proceedings of the 2019 AAAI/ACM Conference on AI, Ethics, and Society*, 217-223.

Johnson, M., & Li, Q. (2019). Algorithmic Bias in Virtual Reality: Implications for Ethics. *Ethics in Technology and Society*, *14*(3), 210–225.

Jonassen, D. H. (2010). *Learning to Solve Problems: A Handbook for Designing Problem-Solving Learning Environments*. Routledge. doi:10.4324/9780203847527

Kamalov, F., Calonge, D. S., & Gurrib, I. (2023). New Era of Artificial Intelligence in Education: Towards a Sustainable Multifaceted Revolution. *Sustainability (Basel)*, *15*(16), 12451. doi:10.3390u151612451

Karakusevic, P. (2021). Architects and AI: An Ethical Discussion. *The Architectural Review*, *249*(1487), 12–19.

Kenwright, B. (2018). Virtual Reality: Ethical Challenges and Dangers. *IEEE Technology and Society Magazine*, *37*(4), 20–25. doi:10.1109/MTS.2018.2876104

Kim, B. Y., Song, M., & Ahn, J. (2019). Building User Trust in AI-Driven Virtual Reality. *Journal of Human-Computer Interaction*, *35*(4), 375–396.

Laranjeiro, N., Rodrigues, R., Marques, T., & Jorge, J. A. (2021). Investigating Explainable AI Interfaces for Collaborative Creative VR Applications. *International Journal of Human-Computer Studies*, *147*, 102544.

Lin, S. J., & Tsai, C. C. (2002). Sensation Seeking and Internet dependence of Taiwanese high school adolescents. *Computers in Human Behavior*, *18*(4), 411–426. doi:10.1016/S0747-5632(01)00056-5

Martinez, A., & Garcia, S. (2018). Emotional Manipulation in AI-Driven Virtual Reality: Ethical Considerations. *Virtual Ethics Journal*, *3*(2), 120–138.

McCormick, T. H., & Heer, J. (2017). Narrative Visualization: Telling Stories with Data. *IEEE Transactions on Visualization and Computer Graphics*, *24*(1), 451–460. PMID:27875161

Purtova, N. (2017). *The Right to Be Forgotten: A Transatlantic Perspective*. Cambridge University Press.

Regan, P. M., & Jesse, J. (2018). Ethical challenges of edtech, big data and personalized learning: Twenty-first century student sorting and tracking. *Ethics and Information Technology*, *21*(3), 167–179. doi:10.100710676-018-9492-2

Ribeiro, M. T., Singh, S., & Guestrin, C. (2016). "Why Should I Trust You?" Explaining the Predictions of Any Classifier. *Proceedings of the 22nd ACM SIGKDD International Conference on Knowledge Discovery and Data Mining*, 1135-1144. 10.1145/2939672.2939778

Richter, T., & Koch, S. C. (2018). *Digital Learning Environments: New Possibilities and Opportunities*. Springer.

Riva, G., Baños, R. M., Botella, C., Mantovani, F., & Gaggioli, A. (2016). Transforming Experience: The Potential of Augmented Reality and Virtual Reality for Enhancing Personal and Clinical Change. *Frontiers in Psychiatry*, *7*, 164. doi:10.3389/fpsyt.2016.00164 PMID:27746747

Russell, S. J., & Norvig, P. (2016). *Artificial Intelligence: A Modern Approach*. Pearson Education.

Samuelson, P. (2007). Challenges in Mapping the Public Domain. *Journal of the Copyright Society of the U.S.A.*, *55*(4), 1–17.

Sherman, W. R., & Craig, A. B. (2018). *Understanding Virtual Reality: Interface, Application, and Design*. Morgan Kaufmann.

Smith, J., Johnson, A., & Williams, R. (2020). Privacy Challenges in AI-Driven Virtual Reality. *Journal of Ethics and Technology*, *10*(2), 87–104.

Sotiriou, S., Retalis, S., & Bulus, M. (2019). Data Mining in the Context of Immersive Virtual Reality Environments for Learning. *IEEE Transactions on Learning Technologies*, *13*(3), 517–526.

Sundar, S. S., Kang, H., Oprean, D., & Waddell, T. F. (2018). Anonymity, Privacy, and Perceived Surveillance in the Virtual School: A Naturalistic Case Study. *Internet Research*, *28*(5), 1169–1188.

Sundar, S. S., Kim, J., & Han, S. H. (2021). Interplay of Machine Agency, Media Richness, and Personalization in Persuasive Technologies. *International Journal of Human-Computer Interaction*, *37*(6), 548–562.

Tintarev, N., & Masthoff, J. (2012). Designing and Evaluating Explanations for Recommender Systems. In Recommender Systems Handbook (pp. 479-510). Springer.

Van Der Linden, J. L., Maibach, E., & Leiserowitz, A. (2018). Improving Public Engagement with Climate Change: Five "Best Practice" Insights from Psychological Science. *Perspectives on Psychological Science*, *13*(4), 492–498. PMID:29961412

White, P., Thompson, L., & Turner, R. (2022). Legal and Ethical Challenges of AI-VR Integration. *Journal of AI and Virtual Reality Law*, *8*(1), 35–58.

Chapter 9
From Code to Care and Navigating Ethical Challenges in AI Healthcare

Sourav Madhur Dey
University of Burdwan, India

Pushan Dutta
https://orcid.org/0000-0002-4765-3864
Amity University, India

ABSTRACT

Artificial intelligence (AI) has become a transformative force in the healthcare industry, offering unprecedented opportunities for improved diagnostics, patient treatment, and outcomes. However, its integration into healthcare systems has also brought to light a host of ethical concerns that require careful scrutiny. This chapter delves into the intricate nexus of ethics and AI in healthcare, shedding light on the multifaceted implications and challenges that arise. AI technologies such as machine learning (ML) and data analytics (DS) have immense potential to revolutionize healthcare. They can enhance diagnostic accuracy, enable the treatment of a larger number of patients, and improve patient outcomes. However, their implementation is not without ethical quandaries. These primarily revolve around data privacy, bias mitigation, transparency, responsibility, and patient independence. Transparency and interpretability are other essential aspects of the ethical discourse surrounding AI in healthcare.

INTRODUCTION

The expeditious progression of artificial intelligence (AI) has inaugurated a novel epoch in the realm of healthcare. AI technologies are being incorporated into diverse domains of healthcare, encompassing diagnostic and therapeutic procedures, administrative functions, and patient-centered services. Although these advancements exhibit significant potential for enhancing patient outcomes and optimizing healthcare efficiency, they also present substantial ethical dilemmas. This article aims to examine the

DOI: 10.4018/979-8-3693-2647-3.ch009

ethical considerations associated with artificial intelligence (AI) in the healthcare sector. It will utilize a comprehensive analysis of existing literature to offer valuable perspectives on the intricate realm of AI ethics within this specific field. The healthcare industry is undergoing a significant transformation due to the advent of Artificial Intelligence (AI), which is altering the methods employed by medical practitioners in the diagnosis, treatment, and management of diseases. Artificial intelligence (AI) exhibits significant potential for improving healthcare outcomes; nevertheless, it also introduces a multitude of ethical dilemmas that necessitate comprehensive scrutiny and deliberate resolutions. This article presents an extensive examination of the ethical intricacies associated with artificial intelligence (AI) in the healthcare sector, offering insights into the diverse aspects of this significant matter.

The Ethical Imperative in Healthcare

The incorporation of ethical considerations has consistently had a pivotal position within the realm of healthcare. The core concepts of beneficence, non-maleficence, autonomy, and justice serve as the foundational pillars that underpin healthcare decisions and procedures. With the growing use of artificial intelligence (AI) in the healthcare sector, the ethical considerations associated with its use are confronted with novel dimensions and complexities. Ethical issues have long been a fundamental aspect of the healthcare field, with guiding concepts including beneficence, non-maleficence, autonomy, and justice. The aforementioned principles serve as the foundation for the ethical responsibilities of healthcare practitioners in promoting patient welfare, preventing harm, upholding autonomy, and equitably allocating healthcare resources. The integration of AI technologies into healthcare systems presents new ethical considerations, highlighting the need for a comprehensive framework to guide ethical decision-making.

The ethical obligation within the healthcare field is a concept that is both transcendent and essential, requiring deep reflection and examination. It prompts a persistent pursuit to understand its inherent importance and lasting pertinence. Located at the focal point of healthcare practice and policy, this ethical obligation emanates with a radiant and multidimensional brightness, exerting its moral guidance on the intricate tapestry of human welfare. In order to comprehensively understand the significance of the ethical obligation within the healthcare field, it is important to conduct an in-depth analysis of the fundamental nature of this complex concept. The ethical obligation in the field of healthcare fundamentally represents a deep reverence for the inherent worth of human beings, a notion that is universally applicable and not subject to the constraints of time, culture, or situation. The healthcare sector, being a domain where matters of life, suffering, and vulnerability intersect, bears the weighty duty of protecting and upholding the intrinsic value and dignity of each person.

The concept of human dignity is deeply ingrained in the ethical framework, serving as a fundamental basis for the concepts of beneficence, non-maleficence, autonomy, and justice that form the foundation of healthcare ethics. The aforementioned statement highlights the ethical duty to advance the welfare of persons (beneficence), refrain from causing harm (non-maleficence), uphold their autonomy, and provide fair and equal access to healthcare resources (justice).

Within the complex realm of medical decision-making, the ethical imperative assumes a crucial role as a guiding principle, directing healthcare professionals and politicians towards actions that uphold the inherent value and sanctity of each individual's life. The aforementioned statement highlights the imperative for individuals in the healthcare profession to approach their work with a steadfast commitment to the well-being of patients and communities, surpassing personal motivations or convenience. Healthcare, which is deeply interconnected with the human condition, consistently encounters the presence of many forms of pain, including physical, emotional, and existential, without faltering. The ethical imperative, which is rooted in compassion, emphasizes the moral obligation to mitigate suffering and provide comfort to others experiencing discomfort. Healthcare practitioners are bound by the ethical principle of beneficence, which not only imposes an ethical obligation but also represents a moral summons. The ethical obligation to act in a morally upright manner is not solely a theoretical concept, but rather a pragmatic instruction that drives healthcare professionals to approach the distress of their patients with both compassion and expertise. It cultivates a dedication to alleviating suffering, promoting healing, and improving overall well-being.

The principle of non-maleficence, which entails the ethical need to prevent injury, serves as a stinging reminder that in the endeavor to achieve healthcare objectives, the potential for harm must be diligently safeguarded against. Healthcare practitioners are ethically obligated to utilize their skills with scrupulous caution, prioritizing the minimization of potential harm, even when dealing with intricate medical operations. The idea of autonomy, which entails the ability to make informed decisions and determine one's own course of action, is highly regarded within the ethical framework of healthcare, as it serves to empower individuals. The aforementioned statement confers upon individuals the authoritative entitlement to exercise autonomy in matters pertaining to their well-being, physical beings, and forthcoming prospects. This entitlement is regarded as sacred and absolute, hence prohibiting any infringement upon it. Autonomy in the healthcare field is often regarded as a fundamental aspect of patient-centered care. This concept emphasizes the shift of healthcare providers from being solely responsible for medical knowledge to actively supporting patients in making informed decisions. The ethical obligation necessitates the dissemination of information, the fostering of trust, and the safeguarding of individual autonomy. The emergence of sophisticated technology, such as artificial intelligence, enhances the importance of autonomy. Healthcare professionals and technologists are morally obligated to address the ethical complexities associated with AI-driven suggestions, in order to safeguard patients' ability to make independent decisions, especially when confronted with intricate algorithms. Transparency and informed consent are ethical imperatives that arise under the autonomy framework, granting individuals the required knowledge to navigate the digital healthcare ecosystem.

Justice, an esteemed guardian of fair distribution of resources, plays a crucial role in the ethical framework of healthcare. The concept encapsulates the notion that healthcare resources, including medical care, treatments, and research opportunities, should be allocated in a manner that is equitable and impartial, without any kind of prejudice, discrimination, or unwarranted advantage. The cultivation of equitable healthcare policies and practices is vital in order to address and mitigate healthcare inequities, hence fostering societal well-being and cohesion. In the period characterized by the proliferation of sophisticated technology and the emergence of artificial intelligence, the ethical obligation emphasizes the moral responsibility to traverse the digital realm with an unyielding dedication to principles of fairness and equity. There is a need for thorough examination of AI algorithms in order to address prejudice, ensure fairness, and prevent algorithmic discrimination. The concept of justice serves as a moral guiding principle, necessitating the endeavor to achieve fairness in the allocation of healthcare resources led by artificial intelligence.

The ethical imperative within the healthcare field is not a mere conceptual idea, but rather a lasting and fundamental guiding principle that directs both healthcare practice and policy. The underlying significance of this phenomenon is in its deep respect for the inherent worth of individuals, its empathetic attention to mitigating distress, its enabling support for self-governance, and its steadfast commitment to fairness. The ethical imperative holds significant importance within the complicated realm of healthcare ethics, serving as a fundamental and essential framework that guides decision-making processes in healthcare. The responsibility to protect the sanctity of life, ameliorate suffering, empower individuals, and promote societal fairness is a transcendent mandate that applies universally across different temporal and spatial contexts. This mandate compels healthcare practitioners, policymakers, and society at large to prioritize these principles. The acknowledgment of the inherent importance of the ethical obligation in the field of healthcare necessitates our acceptance of an ethical covenant. This covenant resonates with the enduring dedication to promote positive actions, prevent harm, uphold individual autonomy, and strive for fairness. Within the dynamic and always changing realm of healthcare, this covenant serves as a guiding principle, shedding light on the trajectory towards ethical healthcare practice and policy, wherein the utmost importance is placed on the dignity, well-being, and rights of persons.

The ethical principles of beneficence, which entails the requirement to act in the best interests of patients, and non-maleficence, which involves the duty to refrain from causing damage, hold significant importance in the field of healthcare. The utilization of artificial intelligence (AI) in the healthcare sector holds the potential to augment the principle of beneficence by enhancing the accuracy of diagnoses, effectiveness of treatments, and the overall quality of patient care. Machine learning algorithms possess the capability to evaluate vast datasets, enabling the identification of patterns, forecast generation, and provision of assistance to physicians in making well-informed judgments. For example, artificial intelligence (AI) has the potential to enhance the prompt identification of diseases, hence potentially enhancing the efficacy of treatment interventions. However, a significant ethical dilemma emerges in the imperative to guarantee the reliability and safety of AI systems. Artificial intelligence (AI), like to any technological system, is susceptible to errors, biases, and misinterpretations of data. Therefore, it is imperative to develop systems that can check the precision and security of AI algorithms in order to sustain the ideals of beneficence and non-maleficence.

Artificial intelligence (AI) possesses the capacity to significantly augment the positive impact of healthcare by enhancing the precision of diagnoses, the efficacy of treatments, and the overall well-being of patients. Machine learning algorithms possess the capability to evaluate extensive quantities of medical data in order to detect patterns and generate predictions that may be elusive to human clinicians. For instance, artificial intelligence (AI) has the potential to aid in the timely identification of diseases such as cancer, thereby enhancing the likelihood of effective therapeutic interventions. Nevertheless, an important aspect to consider in the context of beneficence is non-maleficence, which entails the need to prevent harm. Artificial intelligence (AI) systems, like to other technological advancements, are susceptible to errors and biases. The potential for significant harm arises when patients and healthcare providers place unwavering reliance in AI suggestions, as inaccurate predictions or misdiagnoses might have detrimental consequences. Consequently, it is vital from an ethical standpoint to ensure the safety and dependability of AI algorithms.

Autonomy refers to the capacity of an individual or entity to make independent decisions and act accordingly. The preservation of patient autonomy continues to be of paramount importance within the context of artificial intelligence. The autonomy of patients to make well-informed choices regarding their healthcare should be respected, and it is imperative that artificial intelligence (AI) does not compromise this fundamental concept. An ethical consideration arises from the possibility of AI-powered nudges or recommendations exerting influence over patient decision-making. As an illustration, an artificial intelligence (AI) system could propose a specific course of treatment, perhaps leading patients to have a sense of obligation to adhere to the algorithm's recommendation without a comprehensive grasp of the potential consequences. Furthermore, concerns regarding transparency and explainability come to the forefront. It is imperative that patients are provided with comprehensive information regarding the decision-making process employed by artificial intelligence (AI) algorithms in generating recommendations. The opaqueness inherent in many AI models can provide challenges for patients and healthcare practitioners in comprehending and placing confidence in the decision-making mechanism.

The concept of justice is a fundamental principle in various fields of study, including philosophy, law. The concept of justice is concerned with ensuring equitable allocation of healthcare resources and equal opportunities to access healthcare services. The implementation of AI in healthcare, if not executed with equity, has the potential to worsen existing gaps in healthcare. There exist apprehensions over the potential of artificial intelligence (AI) to unintentionally reinforce biases that are inherent in the data employed for its training. For instance, in cases where historical healthcare data exhibits biases towards specific demographic groups, the utilization of AI algorithms may accidentally result in discriminatory outcomes pertaining to diagnosis and treatment recommendations for those groups. In addition, the substantial expenses linked to the adoption of artificial intelligence can give rise to a discrepancy in the availability of sophisticated healthcare services. The use of AI technology in healthcare may be hindered in smaller healthcare facilities and impoverished populations due to limited financial resources, which could result in a disparity in the quality of healthcare services, also referred to as a "digital divide."

Navigating Ethical Challenges

In order to acquire a more profound comprehension of the ethical dilemmas encountered in the realm of AI healthcare, we direct our attention towards the elucidations offered by extant scholarly works. These subjects have been thoroughly investigated by scholars and experts, who have provided useful viewpoints and recommendations.

Bias and Fairness

Bias is a prevalent ethical dilemma that permeates the field of AI healthcare. The analysis of relevant literature highlights that artificial intelligence (AI) algorithms, when trained on biased data, have the potential to perpetuate and exacerbate pre-existing imbalances within the healthcare sector. An investigation conducted by Williams et al. (2020) revealed that a commonly employed algorithm for the distribution of healthcare resources exhibited a systematic bias in favor of white patients at the expense of Black patients.

In order to mitigate bias and foster equity, scholars and healthcare professionals are actively investigating approaches such as the implementation of debiasing algorithms, the augmentation of training data with diverse samples, and the execution of comprehensive audits on artificial intelligence (AI) systems. The primary objective of these endeavors is to guarantee that artificial intelligence (AI) in the field of healthcare is not solely characterized by its precision, but also by its fairness and impartiality.

The incorporation of Artificial Intelligence (AI) into the healthcare sector has emerged as a significant catalyst, holding the potential to augment the processes of diagnosis, treatment, and patient care. Nevertheless, the progression of technology in the field of healthcare has not been without ethical considerations, with bias emerging as a prominent worry that permeates the landscape of artificial intelligence in healthcare. This extensive literature review explores the various aspects of bias in artificial intelligence (AI) healthcare. It synthesizes findings from a wide range of academic sources, providing insights into the difficulties and potential solutions associated with tackling this significant issue.

The presence of bias in AI healthcare extends beyond the inherent limits of algorithms, encompassing historical healthcare data, societal inequities, and the human elements associated with the development and implementation of AI. As we traverse this intricate landscape, the scholarly literature offers a multitude of aspects to consider, encompassing biases related to race, gender, socioeconomic status, and data analysis. These multifaceted dimensions call for a thorough and nuanced investigation.

Racial Bias in AI Healthcare

Racial bias is a significant and worrisome manifestation of bias within AI healthcare, as AI algorithms demonstrate discrepancies in their recommendations and diagnoses that are contingent upon the race or ethnicity of patients. In a seminal study conducted by Williams et al. (2020), it was revealed that a healthcare resource allocation algorithm exhibited systematic bias against Black patients, while favoring white ones. This discovery shed light on the concerning fact that artificial intelligence algorithms, when trained on biased data, not only inherit but also perpetuate these biases, hence worsening disparities in healthcare.

Additionally, scholarly literature emphasizes the issue of racial and ethnic minorities being inadequately represented in datasets used for training artificial intelligence systems. This shortcoming further amplifies the presence of prejudice inside these systems. Efforts aimed at mitigating racial bias involve the reevaluation of data collection methods, the establishment of varied and representative training data, and the implementation of machine learning approaches that prioritize fairness. According to Shao et al. (2022), Academic scholars argue for the use of proactive techniques aimed at addressing racial bias in artificial intelligence (AI) healthcare systems, with the goal of promoting fair delivery of treatment.

The issue of racial bias in AI healthcare is a matter of concern that occurs when machine learning algorithms demonstrate inequalities in their predictions, diagnoses, or recommendations based on the race or ethnicity of individuals. Presented below are several illustrative instances that exemplify the presence of racial bias within artificial intelligence (AI) healthcare systems.

The estimation of Glomerular Filtration Rate (GFR): The presence of bias in a given situation or context. The AI-driven glomerular filtration rate (GFR) estimation tool repeatedly demonstrates a tendency to underestimate renal function in Black individuals when compared to their White counterparts. If the training dataset used for the AI model mostly consists of data from individuals of White ethnicity and exhibits limited racial diversity, the algorithm may fail to adequately consider the biological differences in kidney function that exist among various racial populations.

The utilization of AI algorithms for the interpretation of pulmonary function tests may result in diagnostic inaccuracies for lung disorders such as asthma or chronic obstructive pulmonary disease (COPD) among Black patients. This bias might be attributed to lower anticipated values for lung function in this demographic group. If the reference datasets utilized for the interpretation of pulmonary function tests predominantly consist of populations that are not of Black ethnicity, the AI model may not yield precise evaluations for individuals of African origin.

The utilization of an AI tool for cardiovascular risk assessment exhibits disparities in assigning greater risk ratings to Black patients, thereby resulting in the implementation of more aggressive and potentially unwarranted therapies. The presence of biased historical data or disproportionate representation of cardiovascular disease cases among Black populations has the potential to cause an overestimation of risk in artificial intelligence (AI) models. This, in turn, may contribute to disparities in healthcare provision.

The utilization of artificial intelligence (AI) algorithms in pain assessment has been found to potentially result in disparities in the evaluation of pain levels between Black and White patients. This discrepancy may lead to insufficient pain management for Black patients. The presence of historical biases in pain assessment and documentation, along with the dearth of diverse pain-related data, can exert an impact on artificial intelligence (AI) algorithms, hence compromising their capacity to effectively evaluate and address pain experienced by persons from various racial origins.

The accuracy of AI dermatological tools in identifying skin disorders may be compromised when applied to persons with darker skin tones, potentially resulting from a bias towards photos of patients with lighter skin tones. The training datasets utilized in dermatological artificial intelligence (AI) systems may exhibit limitations in effectively capturing the whole spectrum of skin tones, hence resulting in challenges when it comes to accurately identifying and diagnosing skin problems in individuals with darker complexions.

The presence of bias in maternal mortality risk prediction models based on artificial intelligence (AI) is a concern, as it may lead to an underestimation of the risk faced by pregnant individuals of Black ethnicity. This, in turn, can contribute to the existing disparities observed in maternal healthcare outcomes. The presence of historical maternal mortality data that is influenced by bias, along with structural inequalities in healthcare access and quality, has the potential to result in erroneous risk evaluations inside artificial intelligence (AI) models.

The phenomenon of biased prioritization in healthcare resource allocation pertains to the potential for an AI system employed in this context to exhibit a preference for allocating medical interventions to White patients over Black patients. This preference, if present, can contribute to the perpetuation of gaps in access to vital care between these two racial groups. If there are racial prejudices or injustices evident in past healthcare resource allocation data, it is possible that AI algorithms could perpetuate these biases when making judgments on resource allocation. The mitigation of racial bias in AI healthcare necessitates a collaborative endeavor involving the diversification of training data, consistent auditing and evaluation of AI models to ensure fairness, and the formulation of ways to effectively counteract bias. Ensuring that AI technologies do not perpetuate healthcare gaps and instead offer equitable care for patients of diverse racial and ethnic backgrounds is of utmost importance.

Gender Bias in AI Healthcare

Gender bias is an additional area of concern, since AI systems have shown discrepancies in diagnosing and treating individuals depending on their gender. Quer et al. (2021) conducted a study which shown that artificial intelligence (AI) algorithms employed in the field of cardiac care displayed notable gender discrepancies in risk prediction. Specifically, the algorithms repeatedly underestimated the danger faced by women. The presence of gender bias in the assessment and management of cardiovascular diseases carries significant ramifications, emphasizing the crucial need to overcome this bias within the realm of artificial intelligence (AI) healthcare. The scholarly literature places significant emphasis on the importance of transparency in artificial intelligence (AI) algorithms. Researchers strongly advocate for the creation of interpretable models that can provide insights into the various elements that contribute to gender-based inequalities (Adadi & Berrada, 2018). Furthermore, there is a need to emphasize the need of diversifying training data and conducting thorough examinations of algorithms in order to guarantee gender justice in the field of AI healthcare.

Gender bias in AI healthcare can appear in diverse manners, arising from both the use of data for training AI models and the conception and execution of these models. The occurrence of gender bias in AI healthcare can be elucidated as follows:

The issue of imbalanced training data is being addressed. Gender bias may manifest itself when the training data employed in the development of AI healthcare models lacks gender balance. In the event that the dataset is largely composed of data from a single gender, the AI model may encounter challenges in effectively generalizing its predictions and recommendations to the other gender. This might potentially result in disparities or discrepancies in the outcomes produced by the model. Women have been traditionally underrepresented in clinical trials and medical research, especially in certain areas of study. If artificial intelligence (AI) models are trained with biased data, there is a risk that they may not sufficiently consider gender-specific aspects within the healthcare domain. The topic of discussion pertains to clinical documentation and diagnosis. Gender bias may be present among healthcare providers when they record patient symptoms, complaints, or medical histories. The aforementioned bias has the potential to manifest itself in medical records, which could subsequently be utilized by AI models for the sake of diagnostic or treatment recommendations. The interpretation of medical tests and diagnostic imaging might also give rise to gender bias. For instance, AI systems utilized in mammography may mostly rely on data derived from women, which could result in less than ideal performance when interpreting mammograms obtained from transgender or non-binary individuals.

The selection of characteristics or variables included in AI models has the potential to induce gender bias in algorithmic design. The inclusion of select gender-specific characteristics in the model while excluding others may lead to predictions that are biased. The algorithms themselves may possess inherent biases. As an instance, when an algorithm is trained using textual data sourced from the internet, it has the potential to acquire and reproduce prevailing gender prejudices that are inherent in online material.

The Implicit Bias of Developers: The individuals involved in the development and implementation of AI healthcare models may possess underlying gender biases that can potentially impact the design and decision-making processes of these models. Unintentionally, the model's behavior may exhibit certain biases. Bias may arise during the procedures of data collection and categorization, as the subjective choices made during these stages can potentially manifest gender prejudices or presumptions.

The concept of feedback loops refers to a mechanism in which the output of a system is sent back into the system as input, resulting in the presence of biases and stereotypes that can be perpetuated by AI models through the dissemination of forecasts that are influenced by subjective viewpoints. For instance, in the event that a diagnostic instrument frequently demonstrates an inability to accurately identify specific health issues in one gender, healthcare practitioners may exhibit a decreased inclination to include those conditions in their list of potential diagnoses for that particular gender. Consequently, this perpetuates the existing bias. The potential consequences of biased or inaccurate suggestions from AI systems on patients include the development of mistrust towards the technology, which in turn may result in inequities in healthcare seeking behavior.

The issue of insufficient diversity among development teams: The presence of homogeneous development teams with insufficient diversity has the potential to unintentionally incorporate gender bias into AI healthcare models. The inclusion of a wide range of opinions is crucial in order to effectively uncover and mitigate bias during the development process.

The mitigation of gender bias in AI healthcare necessitates the implementation of a comprehensive and multifaceted strategy. This encompasses strategies such as enhancing the representation of gender diversity in training data, performing comprehensive audits of AI models to identify and address bias, raising awareness among developers and healthcare practitioners regarding the presence of bias, and adhering to ethical guidelines that prioritize fairness and equity in the context of AI healthcare applications. Ensuring that AI technologies in the healthcare sector do not perpetuate gender inequities or inequalities in medical treatment and diagnosis is of utmost importance.

Socioeconomic Bias in AI Healthcare

Socioeconomic bias, often intertwined with disparities in healthcare access and outcomes, is another dimension of bias in AI healthcare. The literature elucidates how AI algorithms may inadvertently perpetuate socioeconomic disparities by relying on data that reflects existing inequalities in healthcare access and resource allocation (Rice & Smith, 2001). Consequently, individuals from lower socioeconomic strata may face compounded disadvantages when interacting with AI-driven healthcare systems.

To address socioeconomic bias, the literature underscores the importance of enhancing the representativeness of training datasets and adopting approaches that mitigate the impact of socioeconomic factors on AI predictions. Additionally, ethical guidelines are advocated for to ensure that AI technologies are deployed in a manner that promotes healthcare equity, regardless of socioeconomic status.

Data-Driven Bias in AI Healthcare

Data-driven bias, stemming from the inherent biases in historical healthcare data, poses a substantial challenge in AI healthcare. The literature contends that AI models trained on biased data may perpetuate discriminatory practices and generate erroneous predictions. For example, Amann, J., et al. (2020) identified data-driven bias in predictive models for healthcare costs, revealing that AI algorithms may inadvertently reinforce existing healthcare disparities.

Data-driven bias in AI healthcare is a phenomenon where machine learning algorithms, particularly those used for diagnosis, treatment recommendations, or predictive modeling, exhibit biased behavior due to the inherent biases present in the training data. Here are some examples that illustrate data-driven bias in AI healthcare:

An AI algorithm trained on historical patient data for cardiovascular risk prediction consistently underestimates the risk for women compared to men. If the training dataset is predominantly composed of male patients or lacks diversity in gender representation, the algorithm may not learn the nuanced risk factors that are relevant to female patients, leading to biased predictions.

An AI-based skin cancer diagnosis tool consistently misclassifies skin lesions in individuals with darker skin tones as benign when they are malignant. If the training data primarily consists of images of skin lesions from individuals with lighter skin tones, the AI algorithm may not have learned to accurately detect and diagnose skin cancer in individuals with diverse skin colors.

An AI system for treatment recommendations suggests costly treatments for patients with private insurance but recommends less expensive options for patients with public insurance. If the training data reflects healthcare patterns that are influenced by socioeconomic factors, such as insurance type or income level, the AI algorithm may inadvertently perpetuate disparities in treatment recommendations.

An AI model for disease outbreak prediction consistently overestimates the risk of an infectious disease in a particular geographic region, leading to unnecessary interventions and resource allocation. If historical disease data used to train the AI model is biased towards a specific region or lacks adequate representation from other areas, the model may not generalize well to different geographical contexts.

An AI-powered medication prescription system frequently recommends lower doses of certain medications for elderly patients, potentially resulting in inadequate treatment. If the training data includes a limited number of elderly patients or if medication dosages in the data are primarily based on younger populations, the AI algorithm may not account for age-related variations in medication responses.

Natural Language Processing NLP-based AI systems for medical record analysis may struggle to accurately interpret and extract information from non-English medical records, leading to errors in patient histories and diagnoses. If the training data predominantly consists of English-language medical records, the NLP model may perform less effectively when confronted with records in other languages, potentially compromising patient care for non-English-speaking populations.

AI-driven genetic screening tools may provide less accurate risk assessments for certain genetic conditions in populations with genetic diversity not well-represented in the training data. Genetic databases used for training AI models may be skewed towards specific ethnic or racial groups, leading to inaccuracies in risk assessments for individuals from underrepresented backgrounds.

Addressing data-driven bias in AI healthcare requires careful consideration of the diversity and representativeness of training data, ongoing monitoring for bias, and the development of mitigation strategies to ensure that AI systems provide fair and equitable healthcare outcomes for all patients. To combat data-driven bias, scholars advocate for rigorous data preprocessing techniques that identify and rectify bias in training data. Additionally, the literature highlights the importance of ongoing monitoring and auditing of AI systems to detect and rectify bias as it emerges in real-world healthcare applications.

Human Factors and Bias in AI Healthcare

Beyond algorithmic and data-driven bias, the literature also underscores the role of human factors in propagating bias in AI healthcare. Biases held by developers, clinicians, and healthcare practitioners can shape the design and deployment of AI systems, leading to unintended consequences. This human bias may manifest in the choice of data sources, the development of algorithms, and the interpretation of AI-generated recommendations.

To address human factors and bias in AI healthcare, the literature emphasizes the importance of diversity and inclusivity in AI development teams, as well as ongoing training and education to raise awareness about bias and its potential consequences. Additionally, clear guidelines and ethical frameworks are recommended to ensure that human biases do not unduly influence AI-driven healthcare decisions.

Bias in AI healthcare is a multifaceted and pervasive challenge that demands rigorous attention and proactive mitigation strategies. The literature review has illuminated key dimensions of bias, including racial, gender, socioeconomic, data-driven, and human factors bias, all of which intersect and interact within the AI healthcare ecosystem. While AI holds immense promise in healthcare, it is imperative to address bias comprehensively to ensure equitable, fair, and accurate healthcare delivery. Efforts to mitigate bias in AI healthcare must encompass diverse and representative training data, transparency in algorithmic decision-making, ongoing monitoring and auditing, and the cultivation of ethical guidelines and frameworks. The literature provides a rich tapestry of insights and recommendations, serving as a valuable resource for researchers, healthcare practitioners, policymakers, and technologists as they navigate the complex landscape of bias in AI healthcare. By addressing bias effectively, the healthcare community can harness the full potential of AI while upholding the principles of fairness, equity, and patient-centered care.

Transparency and Explainability

The reoccurring subject in the literature pertains to the absence of transparency and explainability in AI models. Scholars have emphasized the necessity of "interpretable" artificial intelligence (AI) systems that possess the capability to offer elucidation regarding their decision-making mechanisms. The absence of transparency in AI suggestions may lead to difficulties in establishing confidence between patients and healthcare practitioners.

The significance of model interpretability in the healthcare domain is underscored in the research conducted by Amann, J., et al. (2020). The authors contend that the integration of simpler, interpretable models with complicated AI models is imperative. This augmentation would enable the provision of valuable insights into the rationale behind certain decisions. The utilization of the "glass-box" methodology has the potential to bolster trust and foster improved decision-making processes.

Informed Consent and Autonomy

The scholarly literature places significant emphasis on the necessity of obtaining informed permission within the domain of artificial intelligence (AI) in healthcare. It is imperative to ensure that patients are sufficiently educated regarding the use of artificial intelligence (AI) in their healthcare, and that they possess the agency to either accept or decline AI-generated recommendations. The issues associated with getting informed consent in situations where artificial intelligence (AI) systems undergo constant updates and algorithm enhancements are discussed in a study conducted by Loftus, T. J., et al. (2020).

In order to tackle this difficulty, scholars suggest the establishment of explicit protocols for obtaining informed permission, which encompass the dissemination of comprehensible details regarding the involvement, potential advantages, and constraints of artificial intelligence (AI). This facilitates the ability of patients to make well-informed decisions while simultaneously upholding their autonomy.

Data Privacy and Security

The ethical considerations around data privacy and security in the field of AI healthcare are of considerable importance. The existing body of literature indicates that healthcare data, which frequently encompasses confidential patient information, is susceptible to breaches and unauthorized utilization. The preservation of patient privacy is of utmost importance in the context of AI systems, which heavily depend on extensive datasets. Academic researchers have conducted investigations into several strategies aimed at safeguarding privacy in the context of artificial intelligence, including but not limited to federated learning and differential privacy. These methodologies enable artificial intelligence models to acquire knowledge from data without directly accessing individual health records, hence reducing privacy concerns.

Professional Responsibility

The literature also emphasizes the ethical obligation of healthcare providers. It is imperative for clinicians to exercise caution and refrain from unquestioningly relying on AI advice. Instead, they should engage in a critical evaluation of these recommendations, taking into account the specific circumstances of their patients. The significance of upholding human supervision in AI healthcare systems to ensure the alignment of decisions with patient interests is underscored in a study conducted by Boretti, A. (2023). In addition, it is imperative for healthcare practitioners to be knowledgeable with artificial intelligence (AI) technology and the ethical considerations associated with their implementation. The acquisition of ongoing education and training is important in order to safely navigate the ever-changing terrain of artificial intelligence in the healthcare sector.

Accountability and Liability

The literature underscores the significance of accountability and liability in the context of AI healthcare. The increasing integration of AI systems into medical decision-making raises inquiries regarding the allocation of responsibility in cases involving errors, malfunctions, or bad effects. There may be a necessity for the adaptation of conventional medical liability frameworks in order to effectively address the distinct difficulties presented by artificial intelligence (AI).

Willems et al. (2023) contend that a reassessment of prevailing legal and ethical norms is necessary to delineate unambiguous mechanisms of responsibility for artificial intelligence (AI) healthcare systems. This encompasses the identification and delineation of the respective duties and obligations of AI developers, healthcare providers, and regulatory entities in guaranteeing the secure and morally sound implementation of AI technology within the healthcare sector. The establishment of a comprehensive framework of accountability is crucial in safeguarding the rights and interests of patients.

Regulatory and Ethical Frameworks

The scholarly literature underscores the importance of establishing comprehensive regulatory and ethical frameworks to provide guidance for the advancement, implementation, and supervision of artificial intelligence (AI) in the healthcare sector. The current regulations frequently fail to keep up with the swift advancements in artificial intelligence (AI), resulting in a legal void that necessitates attention in order to guarantee the ethical application of AI.

Umbrello et al. (2021) contend that there is a need to establish regulatory norms specifically tailored to artificial intelligence (AI), which should address concerns related to justice, transparency, accountability, and data privacy. It is imperative that these frameworks possess the ability to adapt and respond to the dynamic nature of AI technology, while also offering explicit directives for developers, healthcare providers, and governments.

The ethical requirement of providing patients with knowledge regarding artificial intelligence (AI) in the healthcare sector has been emphasized in scholarly literature. It is imperative that patients receive comprehensive information regarding the existence and use of artificial intelligence (AI) in their healthcare, alongside a thorough understanding of its constraints and potential hazards. Patients who possess knowledge and actively participate in their healthcare are more capable of making independent decisions regarding their medical treatment. Levin-Zamir et al. (2018) underscore the significance of patient education initiatives that foster digital health literacy and offer patients the necessary tools to comprehend suggestions given by artificial intelligence. These projects serve to augment patient autonomy and cultivate a collaborative approach between patients and healthcare providers.

Indian Experience

The utilization of Artificial Intelligence (AI) in the healthcare sector is experiencing significant traction in India, mirroring the trend observed in numerous other nations. Artificial intelligence (AI) possesses the capacity to substantially enhance healthcare results, optimize operational efficiency, and elevate the quality of patient care. The following are few salient aspects pertaining to the implementation of artificial intelligence (AI) in the healthcare sector within the context of India:

1. The application of artificial intelligence (AI) is being leveraged to facilitate the analysis and interpretation of medical imaging modalities, including X-rays, magnetic resonance imaging (MRI), and computed tomography (CT) scans. The utilization of this technology has the potential to facilitate the timely identification of many medical conditions, such as cancer, hence enhancing the precision of diagnostic procedures.
2. The use of Electronic Health Records (EHRs) in healthcare institutions in India is increasing, and the utilization of artificial intelligence (AI) can aid in the effective management and extraction of valuable insights from these records. This, in turn, has the potential to enhance the quality of patient care.
3. The adoption of telemedicine in India was expedited by the COVID-19 pandemic. AI-driven chatbots and virtual assistants are employed for the purpose of first patient engagements and the evaluation of symptoms.
4. Predictive Analytics: Artificial intelligence has the capability to evaluate patient data in order to forecast occurrences of disease outbreaks, anticipate patient outcomes, and determine the necessary healthcare resources. This application is particularly advantageous in the realm of public health management.
5. Drug discovery and development involve the utilization of artificial intelligence (AI) and machine learning techniques to facilitate the identification of prospective drugs and forecast their efficacy.
6. Personalized Medicine: Artificial intelligence (AI) assists in customizing treatment strategies for specific patients by utilizing their genetic and clinical data, hence enhancing therapy efficacy.
7. Health chatbots: Health chatbots have emerged as a valuable tool in the healthcare industry, serving to address inquiries pertaining to health, provide medical guidance, and furnish knowledge regarding symptoms, diseases, and treatment alternatives.
8. The integration of artificial intelligence (AI) algorithms in the field of radiology has facilitated the interpretation of medical pictures and the identification of anomalies, hence resulting in a reduction in the diagnostic time required by radiologists.
9. Public health initiatives encompass the utilization of artificial intelligence (AI) in disease surveillance, the monitoring of disease spread, and the oversight of public health programs.
10. Remote patient monitoring involves the utilization of artificial intelligence (AI) in wearable devices and applications to remotely monitor the health of patients, with a particular focus on those suffering from chronic ailments.

The implementation of Artificial Intelligence (AI) in the healthcare sector has the capacity to bring about a transformative shift in the medical domain of India, hence enhancing the quality of patient care, diagnosis, and treatment. Nevertheless, there are a number of notable obstacles that must be tackled in order to achieve successful integration. This extensive discourse aims to explore the various issues associated with the use of artificial intelligence (AI) in the healthcare sector in India, offering a thorough examination and valuable perspectives.

The healthcare industry produces substantial quantities of confidential patient data, hence rendering data privacy and security a paramount consideration. The Personal Data Protection Bill (PDPB) in India aims to establish regulations pertaining to the acquisition and utilization of personal data, encompassing healthcare data as well. Nevertheless, numerous healthcare organizations, particularly those of smaller scale, may have challenges in executing the requisite data protection protocols. Healthcare providers have significant challenges in ensuring compliance with data protection legislation, such as the Personal Data Protection Bill (PDPB). Compliance necessitates significant financial investments and a high level of technological knowledge. The issue of data breaches continues to be a prominent worry, as it poses a substantial risk wherein unauthorized individuals may obtain patients' health records. These records often encompass sensitive personal, financial, and medical data.

The implementation of data localization rules, as specified in the Personal Data Protection Bill (PDPB), might result in increased expenses and intricacies for healthcare organizations, especially those that rely on cloud-based platforms. The acquisition of informed consent for the utilization of data in artificial intelligence (AI) applications presents difficulties, since patients may possess an incomplete comprehension of the ramifications associated with the disclosure of their data. It is imperative that the process of obtaining consent is characterized by transparency and simplicity. The current legal landscape for artificial intelligence (AI) in the healthcare sector in India is undergoing continuous change. To ensure the appropriate advancement and implementation of AI systems, it is imperative to establish a comprehensive and strong framework that addresses both regulatory and ethical considerations. The importance of ethical considerations is commensurate with the potential impact of AI on patient outcomes and well-being. The absence of comprehensive and tailored rules pertaining to artificial intelligence (AI) in the healthcare sector poses significant difficulties for healthcare organizations in effectively navigating and ensuring adherence to regulatory requirements. The lack of clear regulations can also serve as a deterrent to both investment and innovation.

One of the primary considerations in this study revolves around ethical concerns. The tough challenge lies in guaranteeing that AI systems are used to enhance patient well-being and avoid the perpetuation of biases or discrimination towards specific groups. The prioritization of developing ethical and explainable AI models is of utmost importance. The process of data standardization refers to the establishment and implementation of consistent and uniform formats, structures, and definitions for data across an The lack of defined data formats and sharing protocols among healthcare providers can impede the progress of AI systems that depend on interoperable data.

India's healthcare infrastructure exhibits heterogeneity, resulting in variations in both access to and quality of healthcare services across different regions. The presence of this discrepancy has the potential to impact the acceptance and advantages of artificial intelligence (AI) within the healthcare sector. The digital divide refers to the inequitable availability of high-speed internet and digital technology in rural and underserved regions. This disparity can impose limitations on the efficacy of telemedicine, remote monitoring, and other healthcare solutions driven by artificial intelligence. The limitations imposed by available resources. Smaller healthcare institutions especially those situated in economically challenged locations may encounter challenges due to limited financial and technical resources, which may impede the successful application of artificial intelligence (AI) technologies.

The disparity in healthcare services between urban and rural areas is a substantial concern. Although artificial intelligence (AI) has the potential to mitigate this gap, its effectiveness is contingent upon concurrent investments in infrastructure development and training initiatives.

The imperative for effective deployment lies in adequately equipping healthcare workers to collaborate with AI systems and adopting new technologies. A pressing requirement exists for the development of comprehensive training programs aimed at equipping healthcare professionals with the necessary knowledge and abilities to proficiently utilize artificial intelligence (AI) solutions. This encompasses the comprehension of AI outputs, the integration of AI into clinical workflows, and the assurance that AI serves as a supplement to, rather than a replacement for, their knowledge. The reluctance to embrace change, particularly in relation to emerging technologies, might impede the integration and utilization of artificial intelligence (AI) within the healthcare industry. This resistance is frequently grounded in apprehension regarding potential job displacement, which poses a significant barrier to the acceptance and adoption of AI among healthcare workers. The acquisition of fundamental knowledge and comprehension of artificial intelligence (AI) ideas and terminology is crucial for healthcare workers to facilitate efficient communication and foster productive collaboration.

The financial implications associated with the development, implementation, and upkeep of AI systems may provide a significant obstacle to entry, particularly for healthcare facilities of smaller scale and underprivileged regions. The initial expenditures associated with the integration of artificial intelligence (AI) systems, encompassing hardware, software, and training, can be considerable. Smaller healthcare providers may encounter challenges in obtaining financial resources for such expenditures. The allocation of supplementary financial resources is necessary for the continuous maintenance and updating of artificial intelligence (AI) systems. The challenge lies in ensuring the sustainability of these charges.

The measurement of return on investment (ROI) for artificial intelligence (AI) in the healthcare sector presents a considerable challenge due to the inherent uncertainty associated with factors such as long-term benefits, including enhanced patient outcomes and decreased operational expenses. Patients may possess incomplete comprehension regarding the capacities and constraints of artificial intelligence (AI) within the healthcare domain, hence giving rise to skepticism and opposition.

CONCLUSION

The application of AI in medicine presents a significant opportunity to realize significant improvements in patient care as well as operational efficiencies. Nonetheless, it does so while also posing intricate ethical concerns that call for careful thought. In the context of artificial intelligence, ethical principles like as beneficence, non-maleficence, autonomy, and justice continue to play an important role in healthcare, but they take on new meanings. A examination of the relevant literature suggests that important areas of concern include, among other things, issues of bias and fairness, transparency and explainability, informed consent and autonomy, data privacy and security, and professional accountability. Researchers and practitioners in the healthcare industry are actively working to address these difficulties by developing techniques to reduce prejudice, improve transparency, safeguard patient privacy, and encourage informed consent.

To successfully navigate the ethical problems presented by AI in healthcare, a multidisciplinary approach is required. This approach must involve collaboration amongst ethicists, technologists, policymakers, and healthcare practitioners. It is crucial to find a balance between maximizing the potential benefits of AI and respecting the ethical standards that form the basis of medical practice. If we do this, we may ensure that artificial intelligence acts as a useful tool in the healthcare industry, thereby enhancing patient outcomes while also respecting the rights and values of individuals.

REFERENCES

Adadi, A., & Berrada, M. (2018). Peeking inside the black-box: A survey on explainable artificial intelligence (XAI). *IEEE Access : Practical Innovations, Open Solutions*, *6*, 52138–52160. doi:10.1109/ACCESS.2018.2870052

Amann, J., Blasimme, A., Vayena, E., Frey, D., & Madai, V. I. (2020). Explainability for artificial intelligence in healthcare: A multidisciplinary perspective. *BMC Medical Informatics and Decision Making*, *20*(1), 1–9. doi:10.118612911-020-01332-6 PMID:33256715

Boretti, A. (2023). Ethical reflections on AI taking decisions for incapacitated patients. *Ethique & Santé*, *20*(3), 174–179. doi:10.1016/j.etiqe.2023.06.001

Levin-Zamir, D., & Bertschi, I. (2018). Media health literacy, eHealth literacy, and the role of the social environment in context. *International Journal of Environmental Research and Public Health*, *15*(8), 1643. doi:10.3390/ijerph15081643 PMID:30081465

Loftus, T. J., Tighe, P. J., Filiberto, A. C., Efron, P. A., Brakenridge, S. C., Mohr, A. M., Rashidi, P., Upchurch, G. R. Jr, & Bihorac, A. (2020). Artificial intelligence and surgical decision-making. *JAMA Surgery*, *155*(2), 148–158. doi:10.1001/jamasurg.2019.4917 PMID:31825465

Quer, G., Arnaout, R., Henne, M., & Arnaout, R. (2021). Machine learning and the future of cardiovascular care: JACC state-of-the-art review. *Journal of the American College of Cardiology*, *77*(3), 300–313. doi:10.1016/j.jacc.2020.11.030 PMID:33478654

Rice, N., & Smith, P. C. (2001). Ethics and geographical equity in health care. *Journal of Medical Ethics*, *27*(4), 256–261. doi:10.1136/jme.27.4.256 PMID:11479357

Shao, P., Wu, L., Chen, L., Zhang, K., & Wang, M. (2022). FairCF: Fairness-aware collaborative filtering. *Science China. Information Sciences*, *65*(12), 222102. doi:10.100711432-020-3404-y

Umbrello, S., & Van de Poel, I. (2021). Mapping value sensitive design onto AI for social good principles. *AI and Ethics*, *1*(3), 283–296. doi:10.100743681-021-00038-3 PMID:34790942

Willems, W., Heltzel, A., Nabuurs, J., Broerse, J., & Kupper, F. (2023). Welcome to the fertility clinic of the future! Using speculative design to explore the moral landscape of reproductive technologies. *Humanities & Social Sciences Communications*, *10*(1), 1–12. doi:10.105741599-023-01674-2

Williams, J. C., Anderson, N., Mathis, M., Sanford, E. III, Eugene, J., & Isom, J. (2020). Colorblind algorithms: Racism in the era of COVID-19. *Journal of the National Medical Association*, *112*(5), 550–552. doi:10.1016/j.jnma.2020.05.010 PMID:32563687

Chapter 10

Machine Learning and Sentiment Analysis: Analyzing Customer Feedback

Namita Sharma
Sharda University, India

Vishal Jain
https://orcid.org/0000-0003-1126-7424
Sharda University, India

ABSTRACT

In today's digitally interconnected world, customer feedback has become a goldmine of valuable information for businesses seeking to improve their products, services, and overall customer experience. Analysing this data is instrumental in boosting business. Machine learning and sentiment analysis have emerged as powerful tools in processing and extracting valuable insights from customer feedback. MonkeyLearn, Lexalytics are some of the sentiment analysis tools which are well suited for processing customer feedback. Sentiment analysis powered by machine learning algorithms automates the process of extracting insights from unstructured textual data. This chapter will explore the underlying principles of machine learning algorithms and their roles in automating sentiment analysis from diverse sources such as online reviews, social media, surveys, and customer support interactions. Through real-world case studies and practical examples, readers will discover how to harness the power of sentiment analysis to gain actionable insights and effectively measure customer satisfaction.

1. INTRODUCTION

In today's dynamic business landscape, understanding and acting upon customer feedback is paramount for the success of any organization. Customer feedback provides invaluable insights into the strengths and weaknesses of products or services, enabling companies to refine their offerings and enhance customer

DOI: 10.4018/979-8-3693-2647-3.ch010

satisfaction. However, with the sheer volume of feedback generated across various platforms, manually analysing and extracting meaningful information can be a daunting task.

This is where machine learning and sentiment analysis step in as powerful tools. Machine learning, a subset of artificial intelligence, empowers systems to learn and make predictions or decisions without explicit programming. When applied to customer feedback, it can automate the process of extracting sentiments, trends, and patterns, saving time and resources.

Sentiment analysis, also known as opinion mining, is a specific application of machine learning. It involves using algorithms to automatically classify and quantify the sentiment expressed in text data, such as customer reviews, social media posts, or survey responses. By discerning whether feedback is positive, negative, or neutral, sentiment analysis provides actionable insights for businesses to tailor their strategies, refine their products, and ultimately, enhance the customer experience.

In this chapter, we will delve deeper into the fascinating world of machine learning and sentiment analysis applied to customer feedback. We'll explore the underlying principles, methodologies, and benefits of these technologies, and discuss how they can revolutionize the way businesses perceive and respond to customer sentiment.

Machine learning and sentiment analysis play a crucial role in understanding and extracting insights from customer feedback. This process involves using computational techniques to automatically identify and categorize opinions expressed in text data, such as reviews, comments, or survey responses. Figure 1 illustrates a step-by-step guide on how to approach sentiment analysis using machine learning:

1.Data Collection and Preprocessing:

Gather a diverse set of customer feedback data. This can come from sources like product reviews, social media comments, customer support interactions, and surveys. Clean and preprocess the data. This includes tasks like removing irrelevant characters, converting text to lowercase, removing stop words, and performing tokenization.

2.Labeling:

Manually label a subset of your data with sentiment labels (e.g., positive, negative, neutral). This labelled dataset will be used to train your machine learning model.

3.Feature Extraction:

Convert the pre-processed text data into a numerical format that can be used by a machine learning algorithm. Common techniques include TF-IDF (Term Frequency-Inverse Document Frequency) or word embeddings like Word2Vec or GloVe.

4.Model Selection:

Choose a suitable machine learning model for sentiment analysis. Common choices include:
Naive Bayes: Simple and fast, often used as a baseline.
Support Vector Machines (SVM): Effective for text classification tasks.

Deep Learning Models (e.g., LSTM, CNN): Can capture complex relationships in text data but may require larger datasets.

5.Model Training:

Train the selected model on the labelled dataset. Use techniques like cross-validation to ensure robustness.

6.Model Evaluation:

Assess the performance of the model using metrics like accuracy, precision, recall, and F1-score. Consider using techniques like k-fold cross-validation to get a more reliable estimate of performance.

7.Hyperparameter Tuning:

Fine-tune the model's hyperparameters to improve its performance. This might involve adjusting learning rates, regularization parameters, etc.

8.Model Deployment:

Once satisfied with the performance, deploy the model in your production environment. This can be in the form of an API that takes text input and returns sentiment predictions.

9.Monitoring and Updating:

Continuously monitor the model's performance in real-world scenarios. If the distribution of feedback changes over time, retraining the model with new data may be necessary.

10.Interpretation and Visualization:

Understand which features or words are influential in determining sentiment. This can help in gaining insights into what aspects of your product or service are driving customer sentiment.

Remember, the success of a sentiment analysis system depends heavily on the quality and diversity of the training data, so make sure to continually update and refine your dataset as trends and customer sentiments evolve.

Figure 1. Flowchart of machine learning and sentiment analysis for analysing customer feedback

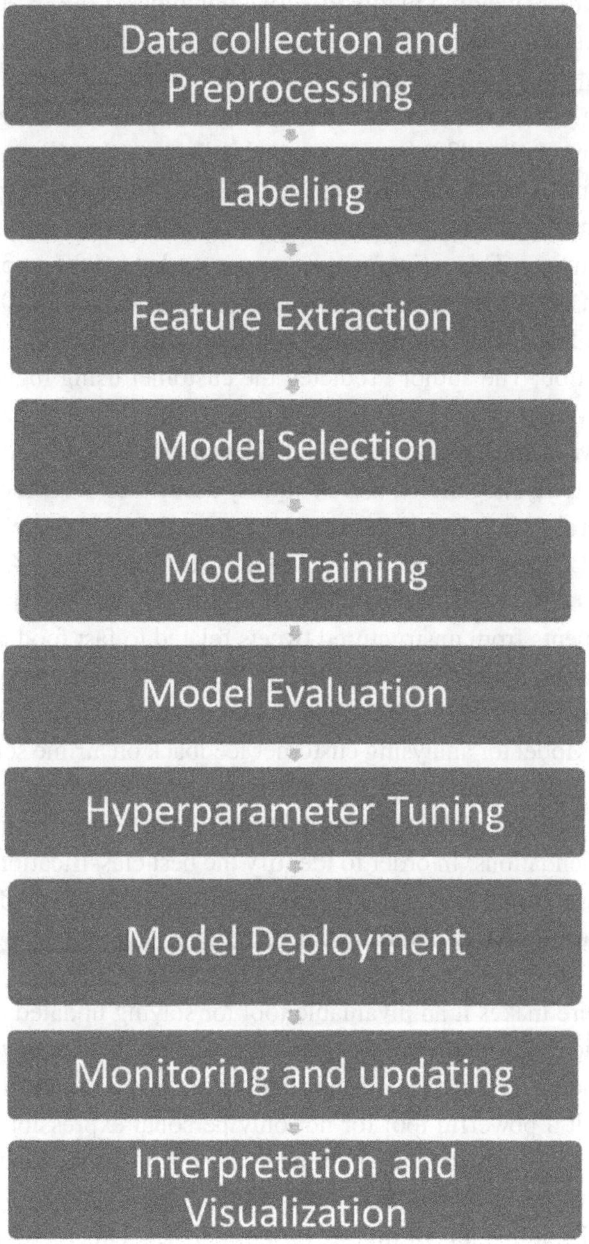

2. LITERATURE SURVEY

Sentiment analysis, also known as opinion mining, has garnered significant attention in recent years due to its potential to extract valuable insights from unstructured text data. In the context of customer feedback, sentiment analysis plays a pivotal role in understanding and categorizing customer sentiments, thereby aiding businesses in making data-driven decisions to enhance customer satisfaction and loyalty.

Numerous researchers have employed machine learning and deep learning techniques to analyse diverse feedback from various sources, yielding highly effective outcomes. Loukili et al. (2023) evaluate various supervised machine learning models based on performance metrics to ascertain the most effective model for consumer sentiment analysis in the context of a women's clothing e-commerce store. Their focus centres on analysing customer comments pertaining to the diverse range of products offered by the store. Khin Sandar Kyaw et al. (2023) focusses on using business intelligent framework in sentiment analysis for digital marketing. Qorich, Mohammed et al. (2023) conducted experiments on an Amazon reviews dataset, employing stop words in conjunction with a CNN model to categorize text reviews into negative and positive sentiments. This refinement led to a remarkable 90% improvement in the accuracy of sentiment classification on the Amazon review dataset. Atre, Ruchita (2022) perform behavioural analysis on data retrieved from Amazon reviews. These comments are divided into four categories: happy, up, down and rejection. The author Predicted the customer using logistic regression and Naive bayes algorithm. Satuluri Vanaja et al() leverages Amazon customer review data to extract aspect terms from each review. It involves identifying the Parts-of-Speech and applying classification algorithms to ascertain the levels of positivity, negativity, and neutrality associated with each review.

Mujahid, Muhammad et al. (2023) employed a range of deep ensemble models, including combinations of BiLSTM and GRU (BiLSTM+GRU), LSTM and GRU (LSTM+GRU), GRU and recurrent neural network (GRU+RNN), as well as BiLSTM and RNN (BiLSTM+RNN). These models were utilized to discern customer sentiments from unstructured tweets related to fast food restaurants. The study revealed that the deep ensemble models outperformed the lexicon-based approach, with BiLSTM+GRU achieving the highest accuracy of 95.31% for three-class sentiment classification. Patel et al. (2022) used Language Representation Model for analysing customer feedback on airline services. Bezek, Ufuk et al. (2020) and Kumar, Sachin (2019) analyses airline tweets using various machine learning algorithm. Jain, Praphula Kumar at el. (2022) used qualitative and quantitative contents of online reviews for predicting airline customers' recommendations. In order to identify the best classification algorithm for sentiment analysis of a specific dataset, Iqbal et al. (2020) compares the predictive performance of a number of well-known supervised learning-based classification techniques, including Gaussian Nave Bayes, Decision Tree, Support Vector Machines, and Random Forest, among others.

Twitter's real-time nature makes it an invaluable tool for staying updated on current events, trends, and conversations worldwide. The platform has given a voice to millions, allowing them to express opinions, share experiences, and engage in discussions on a wide array of topics. Its unique blend of brevity and immediacy has made it a powerful tool for not only personal expression, but also for businesses, celebrities, and public figures to connect with their audiences. Aljedaani, Wajdi et al. (2022) discovered that models exhibit superior performance when trained using the sentiments assigned by TextBlob in comparison to the original sentiments within the Twitter dataset. This trend was consistent across the dataset, demonstrating the effectiveness of TextBlob-assigned sentiments in training sentiment analysis models. Kalaivani (2022) performed comparative analysis of sentiment classification using machine learning techniques on Twitter data and used Naive Bayes and SVM for sentiment classification.

Customer reviews play a pivotal role in shaping the success of products and sellers on Amazon. Sinnasamy, Thilageswari et al. (2022) showed that TF-IDF method with N-gram shows unigram with Support Vector Machine learning with highest accuracy results for Amazon product customers' reviews. Dadhich, Anjali et al. (2021) examines and assesses the methods for automatically identifying sentiments conveyed in English text for products on Amazon and Flipkart. The techniques employed include Naive Bayes, Logistic Regression, SentiWordNet, Random Forest, and K-Nearest Neighbour. Mobile banking has revolutionized the way individuals and businesses manage their finances, providing a convenient and accessible means to carry out banking operations from virtually anywhere with an internet or cellular connection. Rahman, Nurazzah Abd et al. (2022) identified keywords associated with customer feedback on mobile banking, categorized the sentiments, and assessed the accuracy using supervised machine learning algorithms, specifically Support Vector Machine (SVM) and Naïve Bayes (NB). Adak, Anirban et al. (2022) objective was to assess machine learning (ML) and deep learning (DL) models alongside explainable artificial intelligence (XAI) techniques for predicting customer sentiments in the Food Delivery Services (FDS) sector. Their analysis led to the conclusion that future research endeavours should prioritize the utilization of DL models for sentiment analysis within the FDS domain. Additionally, incorporating XAI methods will be crucial to enhance the interpretability and transparency of these models. Kaur, Parneet (2022) in 2022 performed Sentiment analysis using web scraping for live news data with machine learning algorithms. Web scraping is a technique used to extract information from websites. It involves automated software programs (often referred to as "bots" or "crawlers") that navigate through web pages, access the underlying HTML code, and extract specific data for further use or analysis. This data can include text, images, links, and various types of structured content. Kaur, Parneet (2022) utilized supervised machine learning algorithms, including Naïve Bayes and Logistic Regression, on real-time news data to obtain refined outcomes for news articles, specifically focusing on metrics like accuracy, precision, and recall. Ajitha, P, Sivasangari (2021) developed a sentiment analysis tool centered around feature extraction by integrating various machine learning algorithms. The primary aim of this endeavour was to address the challenge of data overload . Rezapour, Mahdi (2021) employed the Synthetic Minority Over-sampling Technique (SMOTE) to tackle the issue of class imbalance within shopping review data, which predominantly consisted of positive reviews with a limited proportion of negative ones. The study incorporated algorithms including Naïve Bayes (NB), Support Vector Machine (SVM), and Decision Tree (DT). Interestingly, the findings indicated that the Decision Tree algorithm demonstrated superior performance compared to the other machine learning methods. Yechuri, Praveen Kumar et al. (2021) employed a deep learning Recurrent Neural Network (RNN) for predicting sentiment in movie reviews. The study also implemented sentence vectorization techniques to address the variability in sentence structure and form.

Ramos C et al. (2023) introduces a decision-support system designed to assess consumer satisfaction by leveraging feedback obtained from customers' experiences with a transfer company operating in the Algarve region of Portugal. Modern eateries now favor receiving online orders, as it serves a dual purpose of gathering valuable customer feedback and streamlining order management effortlessly. Kumar D. et al. (2020) study delves into restaurant reviews, uncovering valuable insights often overlooked or not accounted for in ratings. The research employs a combined approach, utilizing two distinct datasets of restaurant reviews. Machine learning algorithms such as Naïve Bayes and Logistic Regression are employed initially for classifying reviews into relevant aspects, followed by sentiment analysis.

Aimal, Mohammad et al. (2021) identified negativity factors from social media text corpus using sentiment analysis method. Twitter and Facebook tweets are used for classifying them in negative classes. Khalid, Madiha (2020) employed a voting classifier known as Gradient Boosted Support Vector Machine (GBSVM), which combines the strengths of gradient boosting and support vector machines. This ensemble classifier was utilized for sentiment classification of unstructured reviews. Renga, Shreyas et al. (2020) used Naive Bayes, Support vector machine (svm) and Logistic regression to analyse the feedbacks and the reviews given by the customers in hotel management. Singh, S. et al. (2020) aim to measure customer opinion on services provided by public transports through sentiment and accuracy is calculated with Naïve Bayes and Logistic Regression. Sharma, Dipti et al. (2019) explores sentiment analysis for social media utilizing a Support Vector Machine (SVM) classifier in machine learning. The research paper suggests a novel hybrid feature selection approach that combines Particle Swarm Optimization (PSO) with Cuckoo Search. Given the subjective nature of social media reviews, this hybrid technique surpasses the performance of conventional methods.

3. METHODOLOGY

3.1. Data Collection and Preprocessing

Data collection and preprocessing are foundational steps in building a sentiment analysis model. Here's a step-by-step guide for both:

1.Data Collection:

Determine where you will gather customer feedback from. Common sources include: Customer reviews (e.g., Amazon, Yelp, TripAdvisor, Social media platforms (e.g., Twitter, Facebook), Surveys and feedback form, Customer support chat logs, Email correspondence with customers. If using social media, identify specific keywords or hashtags related to your product or service. This helps in filtering out relevant data.Use web scraping tools or APIs to extract data from websites, or access APIs provided by social media platforms for public data.Respect privacy laws and terms of service for the platforms you're collecting data from. Anonymize or aggregate data if necessary. Set up a data storage system that maintains the integrity and confidentiality of the data. For ongoing analysis, set up automated processes to collect new customer feedback as it comes in.

2. Data Preprocessing:

If you're collecting data from various sources, extract the relevant text from the dataset. This might involve removing HTML tags, extracting email bodies, etc.

Lowercasing: Convert all text to lowercase to ensure uniformity.

Tokenization: Split sentences or paragraphs into individual words or tokens. This stage is crucial for subsequent processing. Punctuation, symbols, and numerical characters may not have substantial relevance in sentiment analysis and can be eliminated. Likewise, common words like "and," "the," and "is," which hold limited sentiment-related information, should also be removed. Consider using techniques like "not" handling (e.g., converting "not good" to "not_good") to ensure the model captures negations correctly. Emojis and emoticons can carry sentiment information. Decide whether to keep them as is or convert them to text equivalents. Depending on the quality of the data, you may want to perform spell-checking or correction.

If there's a significant class imbalance, consider techniques like oversampling, under sampling, or using weighted loss functions.

Utilize vectorization techniques such as TF-IDF (Term Frequency-Inverse Document Frequency) or word embeddings (e.g., Word2Vec, GloVe) to transform textual data into numerical representations. Ensure to partition your pre-processed data into training, validation, and test sets. Keep in mind that the performance of your sentiment analysis model significantly relies on the quality of your data and the thoroughness of your preprocessing efforts. Take time to clean and prepare the data properly for the best results.

3.2. Labeling

Labelling data is a crucial step in training a sentiment analysis model. It involves assigning a sentiment label (e.g., positive, negative, neutral) to a given piece of text. The first step is to decide on the specific sentiment categories you want to classify the feedback into. Common categories include Positive, Negative, and Neutral. You can further refine this by adding more granular categories like Very Positive, Very Negative, Slightly Positive, SlightlyNegative, etc., depending on your specific use case. Collect a diverse set of customer feedback data. This data can be obtained from sources like customer reviews, surveys, social media comments, or any other relevant channels. Ensure that the data is representative of the kind of feedback you expect to encounter in real-world scenarios. Manual Annotation involves reading each feedback and assigning an appropriate sentiment label. You can use a tool to streamline this process, or you can create a spreadsheet where you record the text and its corresponding sentiment label. If you have a large dataset, you may consider using a crowdsourcing platform to get human annotators to label the data. Tools like Amazon Mechanical Turk can be used for crowdsourcing. Provide clear guidelines to the annotators to ensure they have a common understanding of the sentiment categories. Use examples to illustrate what each category means. Consider conducting training sessions or providing a guideline document.

If you have multiple annotators, calculate the inter-annotator agreement to ensure consistency in labelling. This helps identify cases where annotators might be interpreting sentiment differently.

Spot Check Annotators' Work: Review a subset of annotated data to ensure the quality and consistency of the labels. Provide feedback to annotators if necessary. Some feedback may be ambiguous or hard to classify. In such cases, consider creating an "Uncertain" or "Ambiguous" category to handle these cases.

Ensure that your dataset is balanced across different sentiment categories. If one category is significantly overrepresented, it can bias the model's training.

Segment your annotated dataset into training, validation, and test subsets. This facilitates training your model on one portion, fine-tuning hyperparameters on another, and assessing its performance on a third. In cases where one sentiment class is notably underrepresented, contemplate employing methods such as oversampling, under sampling, or employing specialized loss functions to rectify the imbalance .Before using the labelled data to train a model, conduct a final review to ensure there are no errors or inconsistencies in the labels. Remember, labelling data is a crucial step that significantly impacts the performance of your sentiment analysis model. Take your time and ensure high-quality annotations for the best results.

3.3. Feature Extraction

Feature extraction plays a pivotal role in sentiment analysis as it entails converting text data into a format suitable for training a machine learning model. Here are some prevalent techniques employed for feature extraction in sentiment analysis:

Figure 2. Feature extraction techniques

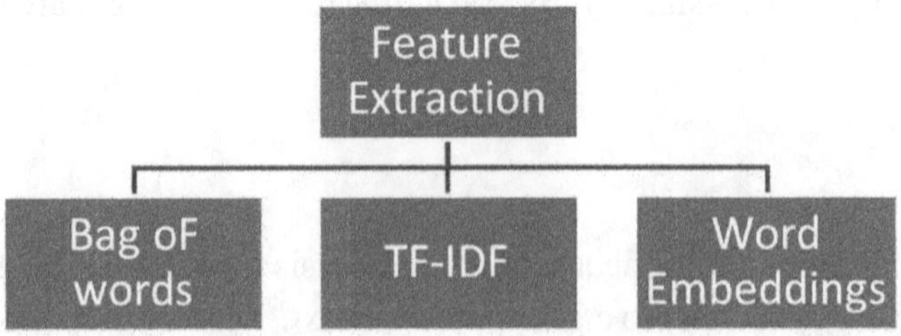

Bag of Words (BoW):

Bag of Words (BoW) encodes text as an unstructured assembly of words or tokens. It establishes a lexicon containing all distinct words in the dataset and tallies the occurrences of each word in a particular text. This process results in a sparse matrix where each row corresponds to a text, and each column corresponds to a word present in the lexicon.

Term Frequency-Inverse Document Frequency (TF-IDF):

TF-IDF is a statistical metric employed to assess the significance of a word in a document in comparison to a set of documents (corpus). It takes into account both the frequency of the term in the document (TF) and its scarcity in the corpus (IDF). This leads to a weighted representation of words presented in the form of a matrix.

Word Embeddings:

Word embeddings represent words as dense vectors in a continuous vector space. Techniques like Word2Vec, GloVe, and FastText learn these vector representations by considering the context in which words appear. These embeddings capture semantic relationships between words.

N-grams refer to sequential groupings of N items, typically words, from a specific sample of text or speech. They can capture contextual information, especially when used alongside techniques like BoW or TF-IDF. For instance, bigrams consider pairs of adjacent words. POS tagging assigns a part of speech (e.g., noun, verb, adjective) to each word in a sentence. This information can be used as features in sentiment analysis, as different parts of speech may carry different sentiment information. Dependency parsing analyses the grammatical structure of a sentence and represents it as a directed graph. Features derived from dependency relationships can be used to capture syntactic information relevant to sentiment. Lexicons are dictionaries or lists of words associated with sentiment scores. They assign a sentiment score to each word based on its semantic meaning. For example, the AFINN-111 lexicon assigns each word a sentiment score ranging from -5 to +5.Extract features related to emotional content. This can involve identifying emoticons, emojis, and specific words or phrases associated with emotions.

Determine the subjectivity of the text (e.g., objective, subjective). Subjective text may carry more sentiment information. Features like the length of the text, number of sentences, and average sentence length can provide additional context. SRL involves identifying the semantic roles of words in a sentence (e.g., agent, patient). This can be used to extract features related to the roles of entities in a statement.

Keep in mind that the selection of a feature extraction technique should be tailored to the unique attributes of your dataset and the requirements of the sentiment analysis task. It's often beneficial to try multiple techniques and evaluate their performance to determine which one works best for your particular application.

3.4. Model Selection

Selecting an appropriate model for sentiment analysis hinges on several considerations, such as the dataset's size, the intricacy of the task, and the available resources. Below are some prevalent models frequently employed in sentiment analysis:

1.Naive Bayes:

Naive Bayes is a swift and straightforward algorithm that demonstrates effectiveness in text classification endeavours, including sentiment analysis. It assumes independence between features, which might not always hold in natural language, but it can still be effective.

2.Support Vector Machines (SVM):

SVMs are powerful classifiers that can be applied to both linear and non-linear problems. They work well for sentiment analysis, especially when combined with appropriate feature extraction techniques like TF-IDF or word embeddings.

3.Logistic Regression:

Logistic regression can be used for binary sentiment analysis tasks. It's relatively simple and interpretable, making it a good choice for some applications.

4.Random Forest and Gradient Boosting:

Ensemble methods like Random Forest and Gradient Boosting can be used for sentiment analysis tasks. They often provide high accuracy and can handle more complex relationships between features.

5.Neural Networks:

Deep learning models, particularly recurrent neural networks (RNNs) and convolutional neural networks (CNNs), possess the capability to discern intricate patterns within textual data. Long Short-Term Memory networks (LSTMs) and Gated Recurrent Units (GRUs) are widely favoured for tasks involving sequences, such as sentiment analysis.

6.Transformer-based Models:

Cutting-edge models such as BERT, GPT, and their derivatives have set the standard in natural language processing tasks, including sentiment analysis. They have achieved excellent results on various benchmarks.

7.Bidirectional Encoder Representations from Transformers (BERT):

BERT is a model based on the transformer architecture, and it undergoes pre-training on an extensive corpus of text data. Fine-tuning BERT for sentiment analysis tasks often leads to impressive results.8. BERT-based Transfer Learning Models:

Models like RoBERTa, ALBERT, and DistilBERT are variations of BERT that have been fine-tuned for specific tasks. They can be useful for sentiment analysis as well.

9.ULMFiT (Universal Language Model Fine-tuning):

ULMFiT stands for Universal Language Model Fine-tuning. It is a transfer learning approach that involves refining a pre-trained language model for a particular task. This technique has demonstrated remarkable effectiveness across a range of Natural Language Processing tasks, including sentiment analysis.

10.CNN-LSTM Hybrid Models:

Combining convolutional layers with recurrent layers can be effective for extracting features from text data, especially when there are local and global patterns to consider.

11.Ensemble Models:

Combining multiple models (e.g., bagging, boosting) can often lead to improved performance in sentiment analysis tasks.

When choosing a model, consider the following parameters mentioned in Fig 1.3.

Data Size: Larger datasets often allow for more complex models. If you have a small dataset, simpler models like Naive Bayes or Logistic Regression might be more appropriate.

Computational Resources: Deep learning models, especially large transformer models like BERT, can be resource-intensive to train and deploy. Consider your available computational resources.

Interpretability: Depending on your use case, you may need a model that provides interpretable results. In such cases, simpler models like Logistic Regression may be preferred.

Time Sensitivity: Some models are faster to train and make predictions than others. Consider the time constraints of your application.

Pre-trained Models: Utilizing pre-trained models and fine-tuning them on your specific task can often lead to better performance, especially in situations where you have limited training data.

Figure 3. Parameters to consider for choosing a model

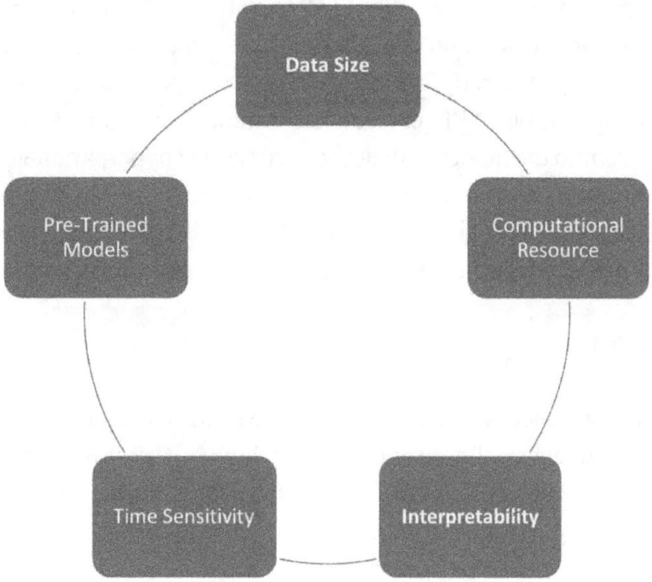

It's recommended to experiment with different models and evaluate their performance using validation data to determine which one works best for your specific sentiment analysis task.

3.5. Model Training

Training a sentiment analysis model involves using a labelled dataset to teach the model how to predict sentiment based on text input. The first step is to clean and preprocess the customer feedback data as discussed earlier. This includes tasks like tokenization, stop word removal, stemming/lemmatization, and feature extraction. After preprocessing convert the sentiment labels (e.g., positive, negative, neutral) into numerical values. For example, you might use 0 for negative, 1 for neutral, and 2 for positive. Partition the pre-processed data into three subsets: training, validation, and test. The training set is employed to train the model, the validation set assists in fine-tuning hyperparameters and mitigating overfitting, while the test set is reserved for assessing the model's performance. Choose a suitable machine learning or deep learning model for sentiment analysis. Options include Naive Bayes, Logistic Regression, SVM, Random Forest, LSTM, BERT, and others, depending on your data size, complexity, and resources. Set up the chosen model with appropriate parameters. For deep learning models, initialize the architecture, embedding layers, etc. For machine learning models, set up the feature space and choose the algorithm. Define a loss function that the model will try to minimize during training. For sentiment analysis, common loss functions include categorical cross-entropy or binary cross-entropy. Choose an optimization algorithm (e.g., Adam, RMSProp) to update the model's parameters. Feed the training data into the model and use backpropagation (for neural networks) or gradient descent (for other models) to update the weights. This is done over multiple epochs (iterations) until the loss converges or a stopping criterion is met.

Utilize the validation set to keep track of the model's performance throughout the training process. Make necessary adjustments to hyperparameters, such as learning rate and batch size, based on the validation performance to safeguard against overfitting. After training is complete, evaluate the model's performance on the test set. Typical evaluation metrics encompass accuracy, precision, recall, F1-score, and ROC-AUC. The specific metrics chosen should align with the nature of your sentiment analysis task. Depending on the performance, you might need to fine-tune hyperparameters or even retrain the model with different settings. Once you're satisfied with the model's performance, deploy it in your desired environment (e.g., web application, API service). Continuously monitor the model's performance in production. If necessary, retrain the model with new data or adjust hyperparameters to maintain accuracy.

Remember, it's important to keep track of different experiments, record hyperparameters, and save the best-performing models and associated weights. Additionally, always test your model on real-world data before deploying it in a production environment to ensure it performs as expected.

3.6. Model Evaluation

Assessing the model's performance is a pivotal stage in the sentiment analysis process. This process aids in comprehending the effectiveness of your model and whether it attains the targeted level of accuracy and dependability. Here are some common techniques for evaluating sentiment analysis models:

1. Confusion Matrix:

A confusion matrix furnishes a comprehensive breakdown of the model's performance, delineating true positives, true negatives, false positives, and false negatives. From this, you can calculate metrics like accuracy, precision, recall, and F1-score.

2. Accuracy:

Accuracy measures the overall correctness of the model's predictions. It is calculated as (TP + TN) / (TP + TN + FP + FN). However, accuracy may not be the best metric if there is class imbalance.

3. Precision:

Precision is computed as the proportion of true positives divided by the sum of true positives and false positives. It indicates how many of the predicted positive instances are actually correct. Precision = TP / (TP + FP).

4. Recall (Sensitivity):

Recall is the ratio of true positives to the sum of true positives and false negatives. It indicates how many of the actual positive instances were correctly predicted. Recall = TP / (TP + FN).

a) F1-Score:

The F1-score is the harmonic mean of precision and recall. It provides a balance between precision and recall, giving you an overall measure of model performance. F1-Score = 2 * (Precision * Recall) / (Precision + Recall).

ROC-AUC:

b) Receiver Operating Characteristic - Area Under the Curve measures the model's ability to distinguish between the positive and negative classes. It is particularly useful when dealing with imbalanced datasets.

c) Precision-Recall Curve:

This curve shows the trade-off between precision and recall at different classification thresholds. It can be helpful when you have imbalanced classes or are more concerned with false positives than false negatives (or vice versa).

d) Mean Absolute Error (MAE) and Mean Squared Error (MSE)** (for regression tasks)**:

If sentiment labels are continuous or ordinal, you may use regression metrics like MAE and MSE to evaluate how well the model's predictions align with the actual values.

5. Cross-Validation:

Employ methods like k-fold cross-validation to evaluate the model's performance across various subsets of the data. This ensures that the model's effectiveness remains consistent and isn't contingent on a specific training-validation partition.

6. Domain-specific Metrics:

Depending on your specific use case, you may define custom evaluation metrics that are more relevant to your domain. For example, if certain sentiments are more critical than others, you might weigh them differently in your evaluation.

7. Error Analysis:

Analyse the misclassified samples to gain insights into why the model made certain mistakes. This can help identify areas for improvement in the model or in the data preprocessing steps.

8. Human Evaluation:

In some cases, you might conduct human evaluations to validate the model's predictions. This could involve having human annotators independently label a subset of the data and comparing their labels to the model's predictions.

Remember that the choice of evaluation metric depends on the specific requirements of your sentiment analysis task. It's also important to consider the potential biases in the data and the implications of false positives and false negatives in your application.

3.7. Hyperparameter Tuning

Hyperparameter tuning involves determining the optimal configuration of hyperparameters for a machine learning model. It's crucial for optimizing the performance of a sentiment analysis model. Identify which hyperparameters need to be tuned. These could include learning rate, batch size, dropout rate (for neural networks), regularization strength, and others specific to the chosen model. Determine the range or discrete values for each hyperparameter that you want to explore. For example, learning rates might range from 0.001 to 0.1, or you might choose between different dropout rates (e.g., 0.2, 0.3, 0.4).

There are various methods for hyperparameter tuning:

Grid Search: Exhaustively searches through a specified hyperparameter grid.

Random Search: Randomly samples hyperparameters from the search space.

Bayesian Optimization: Uses probabilistic models to make informed decisions about which hyperparameters to try next.

Genetic Algorithms: Mimics the process of natural selection to optimize hyperparameters.

Use k-fold cross-validation to assess the model's performance for each combination of hyperparameters. This helps prevent overfitting during hyperparameter tuning. Choose an appropriate evaluation metric (e.g., accuracy, F1-score, ROC-AUC) that aligns with the goal of your sentiment analysis task. Depending on the chosen method (e.g., grid search, random search), iteratively train and evaluate the model using different combinations of hyperparameters.

Compare the performance of different models with different hyperparameter configurations. Look for trends and identify which hyperparameters have the most impact on performance. Based on the initial results, you may decide to refine the search space for certain hyperparameters. For example, if a certain range of learning rates is performing well, you might want to narrow down the search to that range. If necessary, repeat the hyperparameter tuning process with a more focused search space or different tuning method. After hyperparameter tuning, evaluate the final model on the test set to ensure that the chosen hyperparameters generalize well to new data. If you have a set of well-tuned models, consider using ensemble techniques to combine their predictions. This can often lead to further improvements in performance. Record the best hyperparameters and the corresponding performance metrics. This documentation is crucial for reproducibility and for understanding the model's behaviour in the future.

Remember that hyperparameter tuning is an iterative process, and it's important to carefully balance between underfitting and overfitting. Additionally, be mindful of computational resources, as hyperparameter tuning can be resource-intensive, especially for deep learning models.

3.8. Model Deployment

Model deployment involves making your sentiment analysis model accessible and usable in a real-world setting. Decide where you want to deploy your model. Common options include:

Cloud platforms (e.g., AWS, Google Cloud, Azure), On-premises servers, Edge devices (if your model is lightweight and suitable for deployment on devices). If you're using a deep learning model or a complex ensemble, consider containerizing it using tools like Docker. This makes it easier to manage dependencies and ensure consistent behaviour across different environments. If you're deploying your model on a cloud platform, consider creating an API (Application Programming Interface) to facilitate interactions with your model. This allows other applications to send data for sentiment analysis and receive the results. Serialize your trained model so that it can be saved to a file and loaded back into memory during deployment. This is important for maintaining the model's state. If you plan to create a web-based application for customer feedback analysis, you'll need to design the front-end (user interface) and back-end (server-side logic). Depending on your chosen environment, deploy the model using the appropriate tools provided by the platform. For example: If using AWS, you might use SageMaker for hosting models. If using Google Cloud, you might use AI Platform for model hosting.

If you've created an API, set up an endpoint where data can be sent for sentiment analysis. This endpoint should handle requests, pass them to the model, and return the results. Ensure that any data sent to the model for analysis undergoes the same preprocessing steps that were applied during training. This ensures consistency in results. Add error handling mechanisms to gracefully handle situations where the model encounters unexpected or erroneous data. If your application handles sensitive information, consider implementing security measures, such as encryption, authentication, and access controls. Implement logging to keep track of model predictions, errors, and other relevant information. Set up monitoring to ensure that the model is performing as expected in a production environment.

Before deploying the model in a production environment, thoroughly test it with a variety of inputs to ensure it behaves as expected.

If you anticipate a high volume of requests, implement mechanisms for scaling your application and load balancing to distribute the requests across multiple servers. Document the deployment process, including any configurations, dependencies, and API documentation. Consider implementing versioning to keep track of changes to the deployed model.

If applicable, set up a CI/CD pipeline to automate the deployment process, making it easier to roll out updates and improvements. Remember to thoroughly test your deployed model and continuously monitor its performance in the production environment to ensure it meets your performance requirements.

3.9. Monitoring and Updating

Monitoring and updating your sentiment analysis model is crucial for maintaining its effectiveness and relevance over time. Implement real-time monitoring to track the performance of the sentiment analysis system as it processes customer feedback. This can include metrics like accuracy, precision, recall, and user feedback. Regularly review misclassified samples to understand why the model made certain mistakes. This can help identify areas for improvement in the model or data preprocessing steps. Monitor data drift to ensure that the distribution of incoming customer feedback data remains consistent with the training data. Sudden shifts in data distribution may indicate the need for retraining. Collect and incorporate user feedback on the model's predictions. This feedback can be used to identify areas where the model may be struggling and to update the training data or retrain the model accordingly. Continuously monitor key performance metrics such as accuracy, precision, recall, F1-score, and any other relevant metrics. Set up alerts for significant drops in performance. Regularly evaluate the model for bias and fairness, especially if it is used in a context where fairness is critical (e.g., for making decisions about individuals).Monitor the response times of the model and ensure that it can handle the expected load of incoming customer feedback data. Ensure that the model is compliant with privacy and security regulations. Monitor for any potential vulnerabilities or breaches.

Updating

Continue to collect new customer feedback data to ensure that the model remains up-to-date with the latest trends and sentiments. Periodically reannotate a portion of the dataset to account for any changes in language usage, context, or sentiment expressions. Schedule regular retraining of the model using the updated dataset. This is particularly important if there have been significant changes in customer feedback patterns. Revisit hyperparameter tuning periodically, especially if there are changes in the dataset or if you notice a drop in model performance. Consider whether a different model architecture or type may be more suitable based on the evolving nature of your customer feedback data. Implement incremental learning techniques, where the model is updated with new data without having to retrain on the entire dataset. Maintain version control for both the model and the data used for training. This allows for easy comparison of performance between different iterations. Implement A/B testing to compare the performance of the updated model against the previous version. This helps ensure that the updates lead to actual improvements. Keep detailed records of all updates, including changes to the model, hyperparameters, and the training data. This documentation is crucial for tracking the model's progress. Communicate updates and improvements to relevant stakeholders, including team members, clients, or end-users.

Remember to carefully track the impact of any updates to ensure they lead to improved performance. Additionally, always test the updated model on real-world data before deploying it in a production environment.

3.10. Interpretation and Visualization

Interpreting and visualizing the results of sentiment analysis is crucial for extracting actionable insights from customer feedback.

Interpretation

1.Sentiment Distribution:

Analyse the distribution of sentiments (positive, negative, neutral) in the customer feedback. This provides an overview of the overall sentiment makeup. Plot sentiment scores or percentages over time to identify trends and patterns in customer sentiment. This can be helpful for tracking changes in sentiment related to specific events or marketing campaigns. Compare sentiment scores between different products, services, or departments to identify areas of strength and areas that may require improvement. Identify and extract key phrases or keywords associated with positive or negative sentiments. This helps pinpoint specific areas of concern or praise mentioned by customers. Apply topic modelling techniques to group customer feedback into topics or themes. This allows for a deeper understanding of the common issues or subjects mentioned by customers. Use emotion analysis to understand the emotional tone conveyed in the feedback. This can provide additional context and insights beyond just sentiment.

Visualization

Use bar charts to visualize the distribution of sentiment categories (positive, negative, neutral) in customer feedback. This provides a clear overview of sentiment proportions. Plot sentiment scores or percentages over time to track changes and trends in customer sentiment. This can help identify patterns or correlations with specific events. Create heatmaps to visualize sentiment scores by different categories (e.g., product features, customer demographics). This can highlight areas of strength or concern. Display sentiment distribution for different products or services in a stacked format for easy comparison. This allows for a visual comparison of sentiment across different categories. Use scatter plots to visualize the relationship between sentiment scores and other variables (e.g., product ratings, customer satisfaction scores). This can reveal potential correlations. Generate word clouds to visually represent the most frequently occurring words in customer feedback. Customize the word cloud's appearance based on sentiment to highlight positive or negative sentiments. If applicable, use maps to visualize sentiment scores by location, helping identify geographic trends in customer feedback. This is especially useful for businesses with multiple physical locations. Create an interactive dashboard that combines various visualizations for a comprehensive view of customer sentiment. Tools like Tableau or Power BI can be useful for this. Use clustering algorithms to group similar topics together and visualize them in a hierarchical manner. This helps organize and interpret the topics extracted from customer feedback. Compare sentiment scores across different products, services, or customer segments using charts or graphs. This can reveal performance disparities between different areas of your business.

Remember to annotate visualizations with relevant information and insights to make them easily interpretable for stakeholders. Additionally, ensure that the visualizations align with the goals and objectives of your sentiment analysis.

4. USE CASES OF MACHINE LEARNING IN SENTIMENT ANALYSIS

Machine learning plays a pivotal role in sentiment analysis across various industries and applications. Companies use sentiment analysis to track mentions, comments, and conversations about their brand on platforms like Twitter, Facebook, and Instagram. This helps in understanding customer sentiment, identifying potential issues, and shaping marketing strategies. On 9th of April, 2017, United Airlines forcibly removed a passenger from an overbooked flight. This incident got captured by other passengers on their smartphones and got posted on Facebook which got viewed by 6.8 million times in just 24 hours. The United Airlines CEO apologised just next afternoon for this incident (n.d.).

Real-time sentiment analysis of customer feedback involves the use of machine learning models to quickly process and classify sentiments as they are generated. This can be particularly useful in scenarios where immediate response or action is required. Expedia Canada ran a marketing campaign 'escape winter' where they used a screeching violin as their background sound. People noticed it and took it to social media platforms, forums and Expedia quickly removed the add (n.d.).

The "Voice of Customer" (VoC) is a term used in marketing and business to refer to the feedback and opinions expressed by customers regarding their experiences with a product, service, or brand. It encompasses the collective perceptions, preferences, expectations, and suggestions shared by customers through various channels. Analysing the Voice of Customer is a crucial aspect of understanding and meeting customer needs and expectations. Brazilian government used a tool developed my McKinsey called City Voices and conducted citizen surveys across 150 metrics . Applying sentiment analysis over these surveys helped the Brazilian government to mine the most urgent needs of the people and understand the need of the citizen so that they can reform their public policy (Monkeylearn, n.d.).

Sentiment analysis can be used to analyse customer reviews and feedback to improve product recommendation algorithms. By understanding the sentiments associated with products, e-commerce platforms can make more personalized and accurate product suggestions. A large number of reviews from Amazon, Shop Cloes and Flicker were collected and regression model was used to analyse the sentiments of people using these reviews and designed a hybrid recommendation system (HRS) (AI Multiple, n.d.). HRS reliably anticipates customer sentiment when making purchases from a specific supplier.

Smartphones are designed to perform a variety of tasks beyond voice calls and text messaging, including browsing the internet, sending emails, running apps, playing multimedia, and much more. They have become an integral part of modern life, providing users with access to a wide array of information and services on the go. Sentiments in customer reviews for Samsung, Apple, Huawei, Oppo, and Xiaomi, were investigated using various machine learning models to gauge the precision of sentiment score predictions. In the realm of expensive smartphones, customers exhibit a more favourable sentiment towards both Apple and Samsung products. Conversely, within the lower price range, Samsung smartphones stand out as the most satisfying choice for customers (AI Multiple, n.d.).

5. CONCLUSION

The integration of machine learning in sentiment analysis has ushered in a new era of understanding and leveraging customer feedback. Its ability to process vast amounts of unstructured text data and discern nuanced sentiments has revolutionized how businesses interpret and respond to customer sentiments. The depth and accuracy of insights derived from machine learning models have empowered organizations to make data-driven decisions, refine products and services, and optimize customer experiences.

Moreover, the adaptability of machine learning models across various industries and applications underscores their versatility and broad-reaching impact. From e-commerce platforms to healthcare providers, sentiment analysis driven by machine learning has become an indispensable tool for gaining competitive advantage and enhancing customer satisfaction.

However, it is important to acknowledge that the effectiveness of machine learning in sentiment analysis hinges on the quality and diversity of the training data, as well as the selection and fine-tuning of appropriate algorithms. Furthermore, ongoing refinement and adaptation of models to changing linguistic patterns and contexts is essential for maintaining high levels of accuracy and relevance.

As technology continues to advance, the potential for machine learning in sentiment analysis is boundless. With the advent of more sophisticated algorithms and the integration of multi-modal data, we can anticipate even more refined and precise sentiment analysis in the future. In this rapidly evolving landscape, businesses that harness the power of machine learning for sentiment analysis are poised to gain a competitive edge, foster customer loyalty, and drive innovation in their respective domains.

6. FUTURE SCOPE

The future scope of using machine learning in sentiment analysis is poised to be incredibly promising, with several exciting developments on different horizon. Future models are likely to become increasingly adept at discerning fine-grained sentiments. This means they will be able to detect more nuanced emotions and attitudes, providing businesses with deeper insights into customer feedback. Machine learning models will become more proficient at understanding context. This will enable them to accurately interpret sarcasm, irony, and other forms of contextual language, which can often be challenging for current models. Future sentiment analysis models will integrate multiple forms of data, including text, images, audio, and video. This will allow for a more comprehensive and holistic analysis of sentiments, especially in platforms like social media, where content is highly diverse. Advanced machine learning models will be capable of analysing sentiment in multiple languages. This will be crucial for businesses operating in global markets where customer feedback is provided in different languages.

As computing power continues to advance, real-time sentiment analysis will become more prevalent. This will be particularly important in industries like customer service, where immediate response to feedback is crucial . Future models will excel at analysing sentiment in conversational settings, such as chatbots, social media interactions, and customer service dialogues. This will enable businesses to address customer concerns and feedback more effectively. Machine learning models will become better at creating user profiles based on sentiment data. This will allow for highly personalized marketing and customer engagement strategies tailored to individual preferences and emotions. With the rise of augmented reality (AR), virtual reality (VR), and mixed reality (MR), sentiment analysis will extend beyond traditional text-based interactions to encompass sentiment expressed in immersive environments.

Future advancements in sentiment analysis will place a strong emphasis on addressing bias in data and algorithms. This will ensure that sentiment analysis models are fair and provide accurate insights across diverse demographics. Future developments will focus on implementing robust security measures to protect customer data during sentiment analysis, ensuring compliance with evolving privacy regulations.

In all the future of machine learning in sentiment analysis holds immense potential for transforming how businesses understand and respond to customer feedback. The integration of advanced technologies and methodologies will lead to more accurate, contextually-aware, and versatile sentiment analysis models, ultimately driving improved customer experiences and business outcomes.

REFERENCES

Adak, A., Pradhan, B., & Shukla, N. (2022). Sentiment Analysis of Customer Reviews of Food Delivery Services Using Deep Learning and Explainable Artificial Intelligence: Systematic Review. *Foods*, *11*(10), 1500. Advance online publication. doi:10.3390/foods11101500 PMID:35627070

AI Multiple. (n.d.). https://research.aimultiple.com/sentiment-analysismachinelearning/#:~:text=Researchers%20combined%20various%20machine%20 learning,accuracy%20of%20predicting%20sentiment%20scores

Aimal, M., Bakhtyar, M., Baber, J., Lakho, S., Mohammad, U., Ahmed, W., & Karim, J. (2021). *Identifying negativity factors from social media text corpus using sentiment analysis method*. Academic Press.

Ajitha, P., Sivasangari, A., Immanuel Rajkumar, R., & Poonguzhali, S. (2021). Design of text sentiment analysis tool using feature extraction based on fusing machine learning algorithms. *Journal of Intelligent & Fuzzy Systems*, *40*(4), 6375–6383. Advance online publication. doi:10.3233/JIFS-189478

Aljedaani, W., Rustam, F., Mkaouer, M. W., Ghallab, A., Rupapara, V., Washington, P. B., Lee, E., & Ashraf, I. (2022). Sentiment analysis on Twitter data integrating TextBlob and deep learning models: The case of US airline industry. *Knowledge-Based Systems*, *255*, 109780. Advance online publication. doi:10.1016/j.knosys.2022.109780

Atre, R., & Tapaswi, N. (2022). A Prediction of Customer Behavior using Logistic Regression, Naives-bayes Algorithm. *International Journal of Computer Applications*, *183*(50), 31–35. Advance online publication. doi:10.5120/ijca2022921904

Bezek, U., & Shams, P. (2020). Analysis of Airline Tweets by Using Machine Learning Methods. *International Journal of Engineering Research and Applications*, *10*. Www.Ijera.Com

Dadhich, A., & Thankachan, B. (2021). Social & Juristic challenges of AI for Opinion Mining Approaches on Amazon & Flipkart Product Reviews Using Machine Learning Algorithms. *SN Computer Science*, *2*(3), 180. Advance online publication. doi:10.100742979-021-00554-3

Iqbal, Z., Yadav, M., & Masood, S. (2020). Implementation Of Supervised Learning Techniques For Sentiment Analysis Of Customer Tweets On Airline Services. *International Journal of Engineering Applied Sciences and Technology*, *5*(3), 352–357. Advance online publication. doi:10.33564/IJEAST.2020.v05i03.056

Jain, P. K., Patel, A., Kumari, S., & Pamula, R. (2022). Predicting airline customers' recommendations using qualitative and quantitative contents of online reviews. *Multimedia Tools and Applications*, *81*(5), 6979–6994. Advance online publication. doi:10.100711042-022-11972-7 PMID:35035267

Kalaivani, M. S., Jayalakshmi, S., & Priya, R. (2022). Comparative analysis of sentiment classification using machine learning techniques on Twitter data. *International Journal of Health Sciences*, 8273–8280. Advance online publication. doi:10.53730/ijhs.v6nS2.7098

Kaur, P. (2022). Sentiment analysis using web scraping for live news data with machine learning algorithms. *Materials Today: Proceedings*, *65*, 3333–3341. Advance online publication. doi:10.1016/j.matpr.2022.05.409

Khalid, M., Ashraf, I., Mehmood, A., Ullah, S., Ahmad, M., & Choi, G. S. (2020). GBSVM: Sentiment classification from unstructured reviews using ensemble classifier. *Applied Sciences (Basel, Switzerland)*, *10*(8), 2788. Advance online publication. doi:10.3390/app10082788

Kumar, D., Choubey, A., & Singh, M. P. (2020). Restaurant Review Classification and Analysis. *Journal of Engineering Sciences*, *11*(8).

Kumar, S., & Zymbler, M. (2019). A machine learning approach to analyze customer satisfaction from airline tweets. *Journal of Big Data*, *6*(1), 62. Advance online publication. doi:10.118640537-019-0224-1

Loukili, M., Messaoudi, F., & el Ghazi, M. (2023). Sentiment Analysis of Product Reviews for E-Commerce Recommendation based on Machine Learning. *International Journal of Advances in Soft Computing and Its Applications*, *15*(1). Advance online publication. doi:10.15849/IJASCA.230320.01

Monkeylearn. (n.d.). https://monkeylearn.com/sentiment-analysis/

Mujahid, M., Rustam, F., Alasim, F., Siddique, M., & Ashraf, I. (2023). What people think about fast food: Opinions analysis and LDA modeling on fast food restaurants using unstructured tweets. *PeerJ. Computer Science*, *9*, e1193. Advance online publication. doi:10.7717/peerj-cs.1193 PMID:37346556

Patel, A., Oza, P., & Agrawal, S. (2022). Sentiment Analysis of Customer Feedback and Reviews for Airline Services using Language Representation Model. *Procedia Computer Science*, *218*, 2459–2467. Advance online publication. doi:10.1016/j.procs.2023.01.221

Qorich, M., & el Ouazzani, R. (2023). Text sentiment classification of Amazon reviews using word embeddings and convolutional neural networks. *The Journal of Supercomputing*, *79*(10), 11029–11054. Advance online publication. doi:10.100711227-023-05094-6

Rahman, N. A., Idrus, S. D., & Adam, N. L. (2022). Classification of customer feedbacks using sentiment analysis towards mobile banking applications. *IAES International Journal of Artificial Intelligence*, *11*(4), 1579. Advance online publication. doi:10.11591/ijai.v11.i4.pp1579-1587

Ramos, C. M. Q., Cardoso, P. J. S., Fernandes, H. C. L., & Rodrigues, J. M. F. (2023). A Decision-Support System to Analyse Customer Satisfaction Applied to a Tourism Transport Service. *Multimodal Technologies and Interaction*, *7*(1), 5. Advance online publication. doi:10.3390/mti7010005

Renga, S., Ganapathy, A., & Ram Varma, T. H. (2020). Customer review analysis - Multi-label classification and sentiment analysis. *International Research Journal of Computer Science*, *07*(04), 28–32. Advance online publication. doi:10.26562/irjcs.2020.v0704.001

Rezapour, M. (2021). Sentiment classification of skewed shoppers' reviews using machine learning techniques, examining the textual features. *Engineering Reports*, *3*(1), e12280. Advance online publication. doi:10.1002/eng2.12280

Sharma, D., & Sabharwal, M. (2019). Sentiment analysis for social media using SVM classifier of machine learning. *International Journal of Innovative Technology and Exploring Engineering, 8*(9). doi:10.35940/ijitee.I1107.0789S419

Singh, S., & Pareek, A. (2020). Improving Public Transport Services using Sentiment Analysis of Twitter data. *Journal of Information and Computational Science*, *10*(1).

Sinnasamy, T., & Sjaif, N. N. A. (2022). Sentiment Analysis using Term based Method for Customers' Reviews in Amazon Product. *International Journal of Advanced Computer Science and Applications*, *13*(7). Advance online publication. doi:10.14569/IJACSA.2022.0130780

Tepsongkroh, P., Thongkamkaew, C., & Sasha, F. (2023). Business Intelligent Framework Using Sentiment Analysis for Smart Digital Marketing in the E-Commerce Era. *Asia Social Issues*, *16*(3), e252965. Advance online publication. doi:10.48048/asi.2023.252965

Yechuri, P. K., & Ramadass, S. (2021). Classification of Image and Text Data Using Deep Learning-Based LSTM Model. *TS. Traitement du Signal*, *38*(6), 1809–1817. Advance online publication. doi:10.18280/ts.380625

Chapter 11
Machine Learning and Sentiments Analysis:
Analyzing Customer Reviews

Pradeep Kumar Singh
Sharda University, India

Showmik Setta
https://orcid.org/0000-0003-1852-2440
Techno India Hooghly, Dharampur, India

Akhilesh Kumar Singh
Sharda University, India

Amit Pratap Singh
Sharda University, India

ABSTRACT

A significant amount of user-generated material, notably in the form of customer evaluations, has been produced in recent years as a result of the exponential rise of digital platforms. Utilizing this vast amount of data through cutting-edge methods like machine learning and sentiment analysis has become essential for organizations looking to learn insightful things about their customers' attitudes. This chapter explores how machine learning and sentiment analysis dynamically intersect when used to analyze customer evaluations. The chapter analyses how machine learning algorithms can be efficiently used to uncover complex patterns and feelings hidden in various consumer feedback through a thorough study. By using cutting-edge methodology, it reveals the intrinsic polarity and emotional undertones of these evaluations, offering insightful information about how customers feel. The chapter further illustrates how machine learning-driven sentiment analysis is used in practice across a variety of industries, shedding light on how it influences strategic business choices.

DOI: 10.4018/979-8-3693-2647-3.ch011

1. INTRODUCTION

Nowadays product-based businesses are significantly growth too faster in the online mode rather than traditional business approach. Logistics plays a crucial and indispensable role in ensuring products reach their intended destinations successfully. In the online business process, customer reviews and product ratings play a pivotal role in determining the future success of a product. These reviews offer valuable insights that assist business owners in making informed decisions about each individual product. To further enhance this decision-making process, businesses can leverage various machine learning approaches (Behera et al., 2020; Patel et al., 2023; Tepsongkroh et al., 2023).

This paper aims to explore valuable tools and techniques for combining Machine Learning with Sentiment Analysis. It delves into how these methodologies can efficiently analyze sentiments in various data types, particularly in customer reviews, leading to better business decisions and improved customer experience intelligent (Somani et al., 2022; Patel et al., 2023; Tepsongkroh et al., 2023).

Machine Learning algorithms can efficiently process and analyze large volumes of customer reviews, extracting meaningful patterns and trends from the data. This enables businesses to identify common themes, sentiments, and topics mentioned by customers, helping them understand what aspects of their products or services are well-received or need improvement (Somani et al., 2022).

Sentiment Analysis, in particular, allows businesses to determine the overall sentiment expressed in customer reviews, whether positive, negative, or neutral. This helps in quantifying customer satisfaction levels and gauging the sentiment towards specific features or aspects of the products (Somani et al., 2022; Wankhade et al., 2022).

By combining Machine Learning with Sentiment Analysis, businesses can gain a comprehensive understanding of customer sentiments, preferences, and pain points. This data-driven approach empowers them to make informed decisions, optimize their products or services, and enhance the overall (Somani et al., 2022). The remainder of this chapter's substance is divided into the following sections: Literature Review, Motivation, Experimental Tools and Technique Analysis, Comparative Analysis, and Conclusion and Future Directions.

2. LITERATURE REVIEW

In this section, we conduct a thorough literature review on the diverse applications of machine learning and sentiment analysis, exploring their usage across various domains and industries. Kyaw et al. (2023) introduced with the applications of sentiment analysis in E-commerce systems, highlighting its crucial role in uncovering business intelligence for intelligent digital marketing within E-commerce platforms, from a technical standpoint. Dey et al. (2020) conducted a comparison between two machine learning approaches to analyze customer sentiment in Amazon product reviews. It explores how reviews play a crucial role in understanding product quality. By considering various factors like product quality, content, timing of the review concerning product durability, and historical positive customer reviews, the study aims to influence product rankings effectively. Puh et al. (2023) introduced with customer reviews from TripAdvisor were analyzed to predict tourist satisfaction regarding specific places or services. The study employed various methods, including machine learning algorithms like Naïve Bayes and support vector machines, as well as deep learning approaches like bidirectional long short-term memory (BiLSTM). The experimental results revealed that BiLSTM outperformed other methods, enabling tourist service providers to efficiently process large amounts of data and obtain accurate customer feedback. Sentiment analysis offers additional advantages, such as shaping marketing strategies, classifying textual data, and enhancing overall service quality within the tourism industry. Kaur et al. (2023) propose a novel sentiment analysis technique that utilizes a robust hybrid approach to efficiently mine consumer reviews for summarization. The process begins with an effective pre-processing step to eliminate stop words, digits, and irrelevant elements. Subsequently, the preprocessed reviews are fed into a hybrid feature engineering technique, combining review-related and aspect-related features to form a hybrid feature vector (HFV). This approach enables the handling of ambiguous and inconsistent sentences while conducting sentiment analysis effectively. Another proposed research paper by Khan et al. (2020), the focus is on the movie review domain. They aim to summarize thousands of movie reviews to aid viewers (customers) in quickly assessing a movie and deciding whether to watch it. Additionally, these review summaries will be valuable for movie service providers like Netflix, helping them swiftly comprehend customer watching patterns and interests. Yi et al. (2020) research focuses on the application of Machine Learning algorithms for learning, analyzing, and classifying product and shop information based on customer experiences. The data used for analysis consists of product information and customer reviews collected from the benchmark Unified Computing System (UCS), a server used for evaluating hardware and software management. The research findings demonstrate that the proposed HRS system outperforms other approaches, with higher values of MAPE (Mean Absolute Percentage Error) at 96% and accuracy of approximately 98%. The mean absolute error of the HRS system is nearly 0.6, indicating a highly effective performance. Pavitha et al. (2022) proposes a movie recommendation system that utilizes Cosine Similarity to suggest similar movies based on the user's choice. In contrast to existing systems, this approach incorporates sentiment analysis using two supervised machine learning algorithms, Naïve Bayes (NB) Classifier and Support Vector Machine (SVM) Classifier, to determine whether a movie is worth the user's time. The comparison between NB and SVM reveals that SVM achieves an accuracy score of 98.63%, surpassing NB's accuracy score of 97.33%, making SVM the preferred choice for sentiment analysis. This system aims to enhance user experience by providing more personalized and valuable movie recommendations. Zad et al. (2021) conducted an extensive and thorough review. of recent text-based sentiment analysis pipelines, covering various stages such as preprocessing, aspect extraction, feature selection, and classification techniques. Additionally, it explores the diverse applications of sentiment analysis in social media, marketing, and product reviews.

3. MOTIVATION

Over the last decade, the emergence of online e-commerce has significantly transformed our society, revolutionizing businesses across all scales, from small to medium and large-scale enterprises. One crucial aspect that has played a pivotal role in shaping the future prospects of companies and products is customer purchasing reviews, both in textual and rating formats. Customer reviews have become a powerful tool for businesses, as they offer valuable insights into customer opinions and sentiments. Positive reviews can enhance a company's reputation, attract new customers, and build trust, while negative reviews can help identify areas for improvement and drive product enhancements. The abundance of customer review data has paved the way for the development of new fields like business intelligence. By utilizing various machine learning approaches, segmentation analysis, data visualization, and data labeling techniques, businesses can derive deeper insights from customer feedback. This data-driven approach allows companies to identify patterns, trends, and preferences, enabling them to make informed decisions and create tailored marketing strategies.E-commerce websites leverage this wealth of customer review data to showcase best-selling products, top-rated items, and most frequently purchased items. These intelligent features help customers in their decision-making process and boost sales for businesses. As the field of business intelligence continues to evolve, there are exciting prospects for harnessing customer review data to gain a competitive edge in the market. By leveraging the power of machine learning and data analytics, companies can tailor their offerings to meet customer demands, improve customer satisfaction, and drive overall business growth. As this field advances, businesses will have new opportunities to stay ahead in the competitive market and ensure a successful future.

4. EXPERIMENTAL TOOLS AND TECHNIQUE ANALYSIS

Researchers have employed a diverse array of tools and techniques for conducting sentiment analysis on customer reviews in their studies. However, certain methods (Figure 1) frequently employed hold significant importance, as they facilitate comparisons across various research approaches.

Figure 1. Basic architecture for segmentation analysis on customer review data

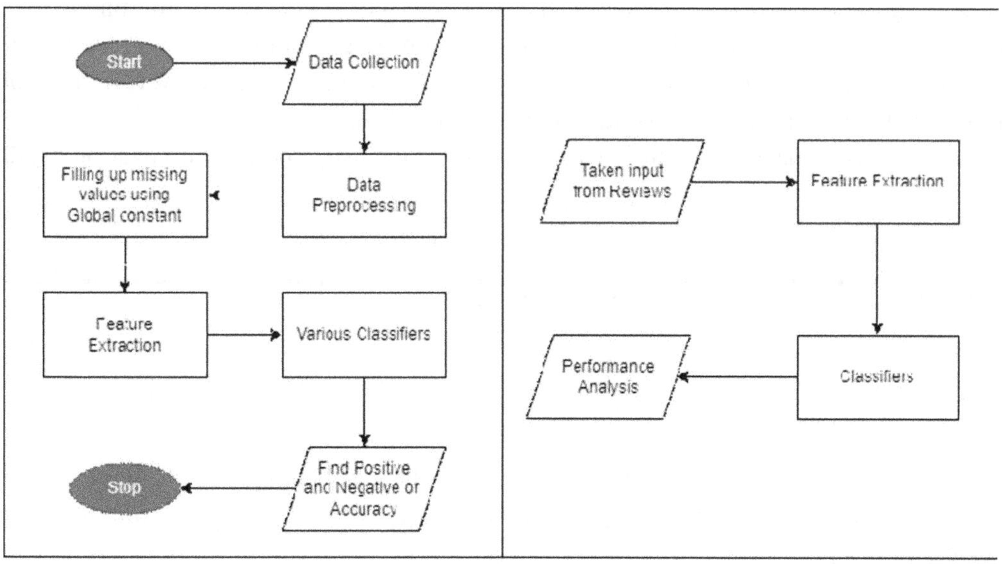

4.1 Lexicon-Based Approach

The lexicon-based approach is a prominent methodology in sentiment analysis, which hinges on the utilization of pre-established sentiment lexicons or dictionaries. These lexicons encompass words or phrases that have been attributed polarity labels like positive, negative, or neutral, grounded in their established emotional associations. This technique offers a valuable mechanism for quantifying sentiment conveyed within a given text.

One prevalent technique for sentiment calculation within the lexicon-based approach is the scoring method. In this method, each word within the text is endowed with a sentiment score from the lexicon, and these individual scores are cumulatively combined to ascertain the holistic sentiment of the text. For instance, if the lexicon designates "excellent" with a positive score of +1 and "poor" with a negative score of -1, a sentence such as "The service was excellent, though the packaging was poor" would yield a net score of 0, indicating a neutral sentiment. Mathematically, the sentiment score for a given text can be expressed as:

$$Sentimentscore = \sum_{i=1}^{n} Score\left(w_i\right) \text{(i)}$$

Where:

- n represents the count of words within the text.
- w_i Symbolizes the ith word in the text.
- *Score*(w_i) Corresponds to the sentiment score attributed to thei^{th}word from the lexicon.

A more sophisticated approach involves integrating sentiment intensities and managing negations. Some lexicons provide gradations of intensity for sentiment-bearing words, facilitating more nuanced sentiment analysis. Furthermore, adeptly handling negations (e.g., "not good") is crucial for precisely capturing the intricacies of sentiment. One strategy for negation handling is inverting the polarity of words positioned within a certain proximity to the negation term.

To elucidate, a sentiment calculation that incorporates intensity scores and negation handling can be portrayed as:

$$Sentimentscore = \sum_{i=1}^{n} \left(Intensity\left(w_i\right) \times Negation\_weight\left(w_i\right) \right) \text{(ii)}$$

Where:

- *Intensity*(w_i) Alludes to the intensity score linked to the ith word as per the lexicon.
- *Negation_weight*(w_i) Signifies a weight assigned to the ith word based on its proximity to a negation term.

The lexicon-based approach in sentiment analysis is predicated upon leveraging pre-established sentiment lexicons to allocate sentiment scores to words in a text. The accumulation of these scores facilitates the computation of the overall sentiment conveyed within the text, and more advanced variations of this approach incorporate intensity scores and negate handling to enhance the precision of sentiment interpretation.Bonta et al. have effectively demonstrated the application of Lexicon-Based Approaches (Figure 2), employing a range of techniques, within their proposed research paper (Bonta et al., 2019).

The corpus-based approach involves analyzing language patterns within extensive collections of text to extract meaningful insights and information. This technique focuses on deriving knowledge from large datasets, enabling a deeper understanding of linguistic trends and context. Rice et al. have showcased the effectiveness of the corpus-based approach in gauging sentiment from extensive benchmarking data in the realm of computational linguistics. They highlight enhanced accuracy compared to standard sentiment dictionaries. Moreover, their method proves valuable in analyzing the language of US federal appellate court decisions (Rice & Zorn, 2021).

Figure 2. Lexicon-based architecture

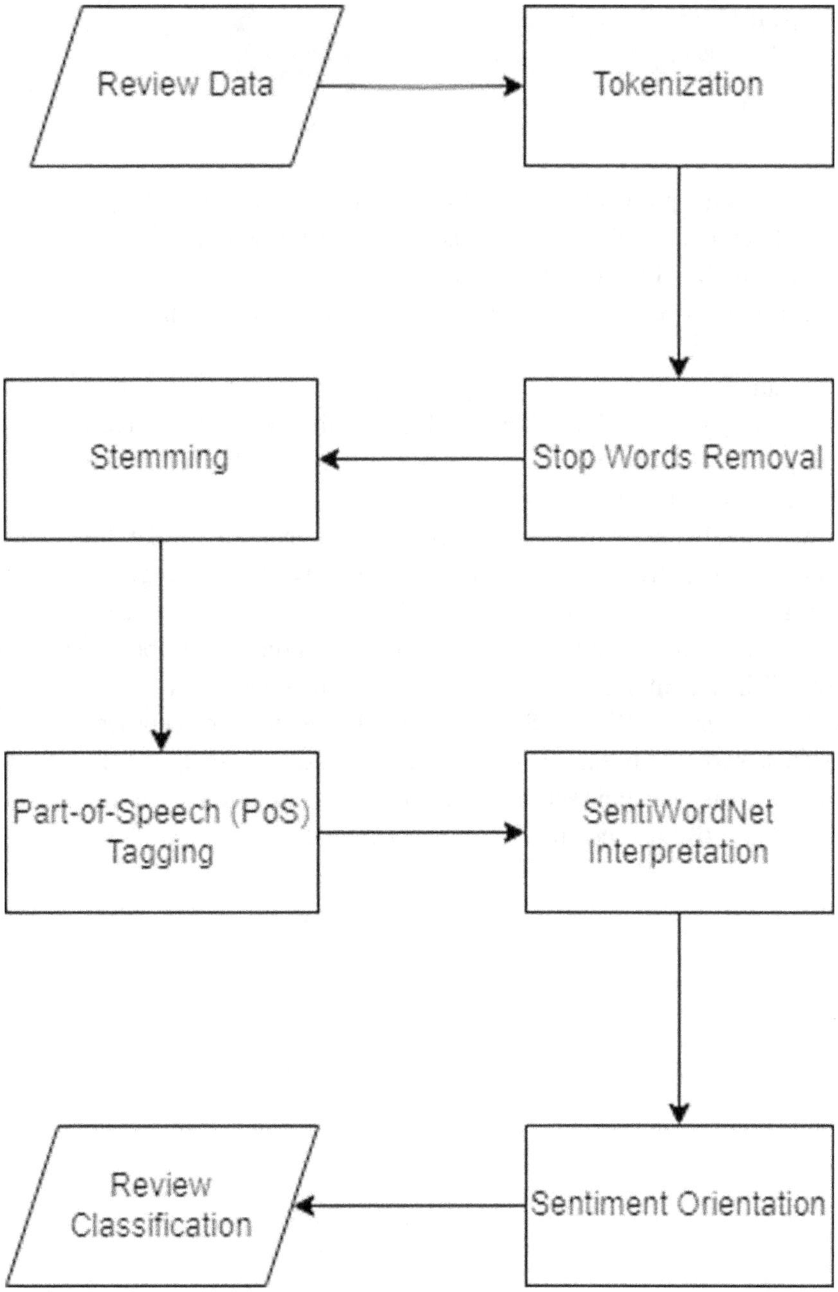

4.2 Naïve Bayes Classifier

The Naive Bayes Classifier, when applied to sentiment analysis, employs a mathematical approach to predict the sentiment expressed in text. This method utilizes the principles of Bayes' theorem to calculate the likelihood of a particular sentiment category given the words present in the text. Mathematically, the Naive Bayes Classifier estimates the probability of a sentiment label S given a set of words W as:

$$P(S|W) = \frac{P(W|S) - P(S)}{P(W)} \text{ (iii)}$$

Where:

- $P(S|W)$ Represents the probability of sentiment S given words W.
- $P(W|S)$ is the likelihood of observing words W given sentiment S.
- $P(S)$ is the prior probability of sentiment S.
- $P(W)$ serves as the normalizing factor ensuring probabilities sum up to 1.

The "Naive" assumption in this classifier implies that the occurrence of each word is independent of the others, simplifying calculations. Despite this simplification, the Naive Bayes Classifier often performs well in practice for sentiment analysis tasks, as it can effectively capture word frequencies associated with different sentiments.

In the context of sentiment analysis, the classifier calculates the probabilities for each sentiment category (e.g., positive, negative, neutral) and assigns the text to the category with the highest probability. This approach makes the Naive Bayes Classifier a valuable tool for sentiment analysis tasks, as it leverages probabilities and conditional likelihoods to make predictions about the sentiment conveyed within textual data. Thwe et al. introduce an open-source methodology that involves the collection of tweets through the Twitter API (Fig 3). Subsequently, they engage in preprocessing, exploration, and visualization of these gathered tweets. This approach to sentiment analysis relies on the extraction of textual data from online discourse and subsequently categorizes individuals' viewpoints into three distinct categories: positive, negative and neutral (Thwe et al., 2021).

Figure 3. Naive Bayes classifier for sentiment analysis

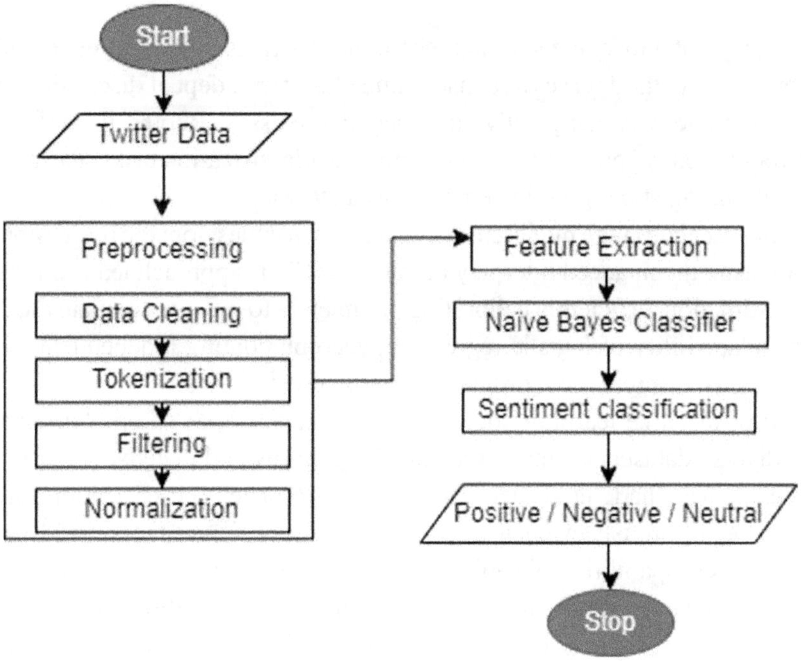

4.3 Support Vector Machine

The Support Vector Machine (SVM) is a segmentation analysis tool that utilizes mathematical techniques to classify data points into separate segments. It achieves this by identifying a hyperplane that optimally separates these segments while maximizing the margin between them. Mathematically, given a dataset with features x_i and corresponding labels y_i, the SVM seeks to find the hyperplane defined by

$f(x) = w*x+b$ (iv)

Here, *w*represents the weight vector perpendicular to the hyperplane, *b* is the bias term, and *x* is the input feature vector. The SVM aims to minimize *w*while ensuring the constraint

$y_i(w*x_i+b\geq 1)$ (v)

holds for all data points.This mathematical formulation allows the SVM to identify the hyperplane that best segregates data points into different segments, making it a valuable tool for accurate segmentation analysis.Gunawan et al. conducted a study to categorize restaurant customer satisfaction in Jakarta. They employed the Support Vector Machine (SVM) and compared it with the Naive Bayes classifier (NB). The findings revealed an increase in SVM accuracy from 77% to 79% (Gunawan et al., 2023).

4.4 Logistic Regression

Logistic regression, a pivotal machine learning technique, operates by effectively blending input values with weight factors. This method serves as a discerning classifier, adept at discerning the essential input attributes that differentiate between positive and negative classes. Rooted in probabilistic regression analysis, logistic regression is optimally suited for intricate classification tasks. Particularly in the realm of binary classification, logistic regression emerges as a stalwart.

As the complexity escalates with numerous explanatory variables, logistic regression deftly computes the odds ratio, capturing the nuanced interplay of variables. This approach leans on the tenets of Maximum Likelihood Estimation, efficiently calibrating parameters to best encapsulate the data's intricacies. Noteworthy is the adaptability of logistic regression, accommodating independent variables spanning the gamut of continuous, discrete (be it ordinal or nominal) categories.

In the vanguard of machine learning, logistic regression stands as an emblem of versatility, effectively navigating diverse datasets to unveil meaningful patterns and decisively classify entities across multifarious contexts. Wankhade et al. delve into the realm of text classification through the lens of machine learning. They rigorously evaluate a trio of models like Naïve Bayes, and Logistic Regression, illuminating their distinct capabilities. Notably, among this diverse array of classification algorithms, the logistic regression method emerges as a harbinger of accuracy augmentation. With precision and finesse, it refines the accuracy levels, significantly elevating the classification process. This strategic utilization of logistic regression showcases its paramountcy in enhancing accuracy, reaffirming its pivotal role in advancing the efficacy of text classification methodologies (Wankhade et al., 2017).

4.5 Decision Tree

The Decision Tree approach, a cornerstone of machine learning, illuminates the intricate terrain of decision-making. This method artfully carves a trail of sequential choices, rooted in input features, to unveil informed conclusions. Its hallmark lies in its lucid interpretability, unveiling the rationale behind intricate decisions. Beyond its transparency, the Decision Tree method finds solace in its adaptability, spanning classifications, regressions, and strategic systems. Its capacity to seamlessly intertwine simplicity with analytical acumen cements its position as an enduring and indispensable entity within the panorama of machine learning strategies. Aouad et al. introduce a versatile methodology named Market Segmentation Trees (MSTs). This innovative approach constructs lucid decision trees that seamlessly integrate both market segmentation and response modeling. MSTs hold the potential to revolutionize personalized decision-making across a multitude of applications, exemplifying their adaptability and significance in diverse contexts (Aouad et al., 2023).

4.6 Sparse Self-Attentive Network

The SpSAN architecture (Figure 4) presents a paradigm shift in sentiment analysis for consumer reviews. This innovative model comprises three integral components, each enhancing its efficacy. First, the Embedding layer employs BERT as an initialization platform, deftly generating word representations. Second, the Sparse Self-attention Fine-tune layer uniquely leverages sparse transformation in lieu of the conventional softmax function, fostering efficient computations. Lastly, the output layer brings the model's insights to fruition. This synthesis of advanced techniques encapsulates the SpSAN architecture's potential to revolutionize sentiment analysis, exemplifying its ingenuity in processing and interpreting complex textual data with unparalleled acumen (Jain et al., 2023).

Figure 4. SpSAN basic architecture

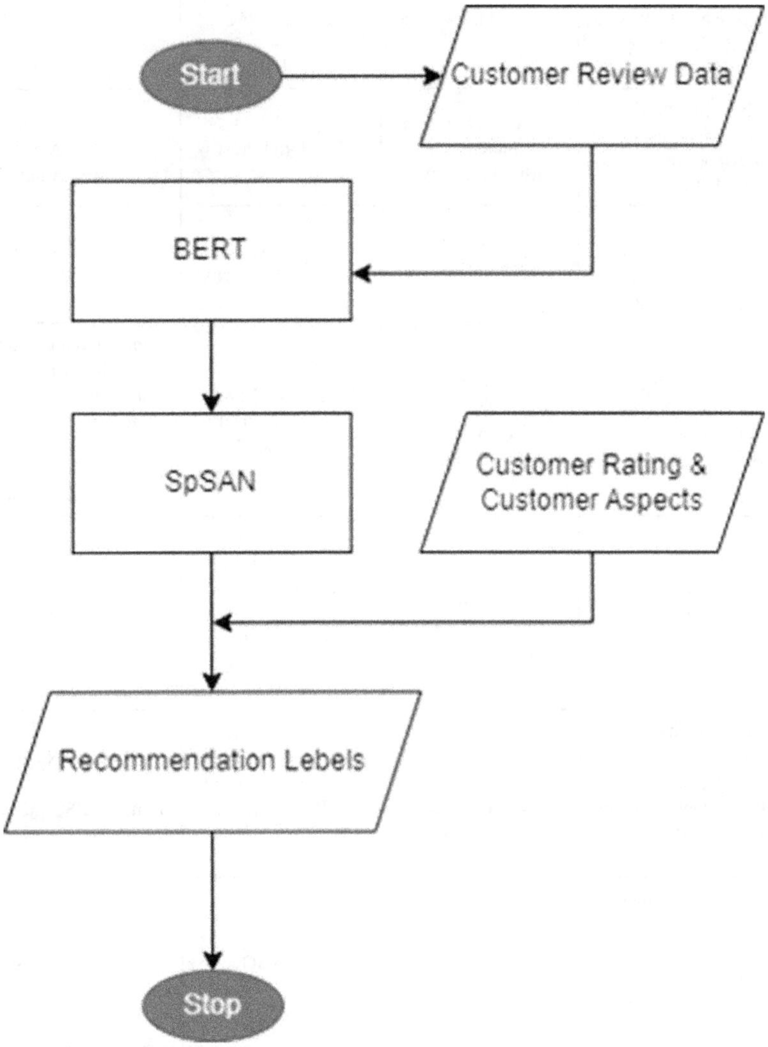

5. COMPARATIVE ANALYSIS

In this section, we have compiled a tabular format presenting insights extracted from the most recently utilized or proposed classifiers found in various contemporary research papers related to our focal topic.

Table 1. Machine learning models

<table>
<tr><th rowspan="2">Sl. NO</th><th colspan="4">Machine Learning Models</th></tr>
<tr><th>Research Paper Title</th><th>Dataset</th><th>Classifiers</th><th>Accuracy / Results / Analysis</th></tr>
<tr><td>1</td><td>A Comparative Study of Support Vector Machine and Naive Bayes Classifier for Sentiment Analysis on Amazon Product Reviews (Dey et al., 2020)</td><td>Amazon Book data</td><td>Linear SVM</td><td>84%</td></tr>
<tr><td>2</td><td>Sentiment Analysis of a Product based on User Reviews using Random Forests Algorithm (Singh & Sarraf, 2020)</td><td>live data of certain e-commerce sites: customer reviews</td><td>Random Forest</td><td>A neutrality score
A positivity score
A negativity score</td></tr>
<tr><td>3</td><td>Deep learning model based on expectation-confirmation theory to predict customer satisfaction in hospitality service (Oh et al., 2022)</td><td>Kaggle customer reviews written in English.</td><td>Deep learning, Fused model, LSTM</td><td>83.54% (Images)
87.94% (Review comments)</td></tr>
<tr><td>4</td><td>Mining the text of online consumer reviews to analyze brand image and brand positioning (Alzate et al., 2022)</td><td>Consumer reviews from the website of a top 50 US cosmetics retailer</td><td>Clustering, LIWC "Psychological processes"</td><td>Upon delving into visualization methods for clustering, it becomes evident that the implementation of LIWC (Linguistic Inquiry and Word Count) is producing valuable outcomes, shedding light on emotional and psychological brand connections.</td></tr>
<tr><td>5</td><td>Restaurant recommender system based on sentiment analysis (Asani et al., 2021)</td><td>TripAdvisor website has been used and comments from 100 different users</td><td>Wu–Palmer method, A novel recommendation system is proposed, rooted in the context-aware approach.</td><td>92.80%</td></tr>
<tr><td>6</td><td>A Hybrid Method for Customer Segmentation in Saudi Arabia Restaurants Using Clustering, Neural Networks and Optimization Learning Techniques (Alghamdi, 2023)</td><td>Saudi Arabia restaurants registered in TripAdvisor</td><td>PSO-ANN, k-means-PSO-ANN</td><td>PSO-ANN (MSE = 0.09847; R2 = 0.98764),
k-means-PSO-ANN (MSE = 0.09847; R2 = 0.98764)</td></tr>
<tr><td>7</td><td>Sentiment Analysis for E-Commerce Product
Reviews in Chinese Based on Sentiment Lexicon
and Deep Learning (Yang et al., 2020)</td><td>Book reviews collected from Dangdang.com</td><td>SLCABG</td><td>93.50%</td></tr>
<tr><td>8</td><td>Sentiment Analysis of Consumer Reviews Using Deep Learning (Iqbal et al., 2022)</td><td>Amazon-Fine-Food-Reviews, Cell Phones and Accessories, Amazon-Products,IMDB, Yelp</td><td>Recurrent neural network-based LSTM, word embedding vector model</td><td><table><tr><th rowspan="2">Datasets</th><th colspan="3">Accuracy</th></tr><tr><th>Model 1</th><th>Model 2</th><th>Model 3</th></tr><tr><td>Amazon-Fine-Food-Reviews</td><td>87</td><td>87</td><td>87</td></tr><tr><td>Cell Phones and Accessories</td><td>87</td><td>88</td><td>88</td></tr><tr><td>Amazon-Products</td><td>97</td><td>96</td><td>95</td></tr><tr><td>IMDB</td><td>75</td><td>74</td><td>69</td></tr><tr><td>Yelp</td><td>83</td><td>82</td><td>83</td></tr></table></td></tr>
<tr><td>9</td><td>Sentiment Analysis on Consumer Reviews of Amazon Products (Rashid & Huang, 2021)</td><td>Amazon Products Review</td><td>Monkey Learn API, chi-square test</td><td>Exploring visualization methods and statistical data analysis to gain insights into Amazon product reviews</td></tr>
</table>

Continued on following page

Table 1. Continued

Sl. NO	Machine Learning Models			
	Research Paper Title	**Dataset**	**Classifiers**	**Accuracy / Results / Analysis**
10	Classification of Customer Reviews Using Machine Learning Algorithms (Noori, 2021)	TripAdvisor	SVM, ANN, NB, DT, C4.5 and kNN	DT and C4.5 attained the highest accuracy (both 98.9%) in classifying reviews
11	Are customer star ratings and sentiments aligned? A deep learning study of the customer service experience in tourism destinations (Bigne et al., 2023)	TripAdvisor (destination - Venice)	LSTM, NLP and ANN	Utilizing visualization techniques and statistical data analysis for deeper insights into the TripAdvisor destination of Venice
12	Sentiment Analysis of Customers' Reviews Using a Hybrid Evolutionary SVM-Based Approach in an Imbalanced Data Distribution (Obiedat et al., 2022)	Jeeran website restaurant reviews in jordan	PSO-SVM+ BSMOTE	80%
13	A deep learning-based model using hybrid feature extraction approach for consumer sentiment analysis (Kaur & Sharma, 2023)	SemEval-2014 restaurant reviews data set, Sentiment140. and STS-Gold	Hybrid Feature Vector (HFV) + LSTM	Datasets: Accuracy SemEval-2014: 90 Sentiment140: 92 STS-Gold: 90
14	SpSAN: Sparse self-attentive network-based aspect-aware model for sentiment analysis (Jain et al., 2023)	Skytrax reviews Data (LCC and FSNC airline)	Sparse Self-Attention Network (SpSAN)	91%
15	A Deep Learning-based Sentiment Analysis Approach for Online Product Ranking with Probabilistic Linguistic Term Sets. (Liu et al., 2023)	Raw user reviews	Probabilities Linguistic Term Set (PLTS), DL-based approach	-
16	An NLP-Deep Learning approach for Product Rating Prediction Based on Online Reviews and Product Features (Amirifar et al., 2023)	Amazon (Laptops)	Radial Basis Function Neural Network	84.01%
17	Game theory and MCDM-based unsupervised sentiment analysis of restaurant reviews (Punetha & Jain, 2023)	TripAdvisor, Yelp	MCDM + game theory and Proposed model	89%
18	Learning consumer preferences from online textual reviews and ratings based on the aggregation-disaggregation paradigm with attitudinal Choquet integral (Yang et al., 2023)	Tripadvisor	Attitudinal Choquet Integral (ACI) and the aggregation-disaggregation paradigm in the NAROR	This suggested approach demonstrates favorable outcomes concerning individual customer preferences, utilizing an additive value function.
19	A Sentiment Analysis of Star-rating: a Cross-Cultural Perspective (Wan & Nakayama, 2022)	Yelp.com, Dianping. com	IBM Watson Explorer Content Analytics, Text Analysis and Knowledge Mining	when evaluating rating data for international destinations, consumers should be cautious about relying solely on rating distribution and average rating information, given that these data are predominantly provided by local customers

Continued on following page

Table 1. Continued

Sl. NO	Machine Learning Models			
	Research Paper Title	Dataset	Classifiers	Accuracy / Results / Analysis
20	Sentiment Analysis of Text Reviews Using Lexicon-Enhanced Bert Embedding (LeBERT) Model with Convolutional Neural Network (Mutinda et al., 2023)	Yelp, IMDB, Amazon Dataset	LeBERT + CNN	Datasets: Accuracy Yelp dataset: 88.2 IMDB dataset: 86.1 Amazon Dataset: 82.4

6. CONCLUSION AND FUTURE DIRECTIONS

In conclusion, this research has successfully conducted a comprehensive comparative study of various segmentation classifiers, employing machine learning techniques to assess their performance. Through this investigation, it has become evident that the format of customer review data significantly impacts the outcomes of sentiment analysis and accuracy measurement.

One of the key findings of this study is that the format of customer review data is of paramount importance. When customer reviews are presented in text format, such as tweets, sentiment analysis emerges as a valuable tool for determining whether the sentiment is positive, negative, or neutral. On the other hand, when customer review data is structured around numerical ratings, accuracy measurement becomes an effective choice for evaluating the results. Therefore, the choice of analysis technique should align with the data format to ensure accurate and meaningful insights.

Additionally, the dataset used in the analysis has emerged as a critical factor influencing the performance and results of the classifiers. While our comparative study revealed that most classifiers achieved accuracy rates exceeding 90%, it's essential to recognize that performance varies significantly when applied to different datasets. This underscores the importance of dataset selection and highlights the need for classifiers that can adapt to diverse data sources.

In practical terms, the insights gained from this research have significant implications for industries and businesses reliant on customer reviews for decision-making. By understanding the nuances of different data formats and their impact on classifier performance, organizations can make more informed choices regarding the analytical tools and techniques they employ. Moreover, the recognition of dataset variability emphasizes the importance of ongoing monitoring and adaptation in the field of machine learning and sentiment analysis.

In a nutshell, this study offers significant value to researchers and practitioners specializing in natural language processing and machine learning. It emphasizes the crucial importance of meticulously evaluating data formats and selecting appropriate datasets when developing proficient segmentation analysis systems. As the field advances, this research plays a vital role in advancing the pursuit of precise and meaningful insights derived from customer review data. Machine learning and sentiment analysis are two tools used to analyze customer reviews, and this discipline is still developing as technology and research advance. Following are some potential developments and trends in these areas:

A Fine-Grained Analysis of Sentiment: Text is often categorized as positive, negative, or neutral by modern sentiment analysis methods. More in-depth sentiment analysis that determines particular sentiments and characteristics of text will be the focus of further developments. This might include detecting emotions like joy, frustration, trust, or fear and connecting them to specific features of a good or service that was stated in the review.

Multifunctional Analysis: It will be more crucial to incorporate both textual and visual reviews from customers (such as photos and videos). A more thorough understands of consumer mood and feedback may be obtained by combining natural language processing with computer vision.

The Context-Specific Analysis: The context of review writing will be taken into account by upcoming sentiment analysis models. More accurate sentiment analysis can be achieved by knowing the historical background of an item or service as well as the reviewer's previous opinions.

Architectures for Deep Learning: The development of sentiment analysis models will continue to be driven by developments in deep learning architectures like transformers. Longer text sequences can be handled by these models, which can also pick up more nuanced language patterns.

Analysis of Sentiment From Various Domains: There will be an increase in the use of specialized sentiment analysis models designed for certain businesses or domains (such as healthcare or finance). These models can handle complexity and language distinctive to a particular topic better.

Analysis of Sentiment Based on Aspects: Aspect-based sentiment analysis will advance beyond general sentiment. It entails determining customer sentiment towards particular product features or qualities identified in a review, giving businesses useful information for enhancing their products and services.

Multilingual Sentiment Analysis: The demand for sentiment analysis across several languages will rise as businesses grow internationally. There will be a demand for multilingual models that can identify sentiment in many languages.

Real-Time Analysis: To rapidly fix problems and make adjustments, businesses will need to be able to analyze client sentiment in real-time. The creation of effective and quick sentiment analysis algorithms will be required.

Reasonable AI: Businesses will need sentiment analysis algorithms with increased readability and openness. It will be crucial to develop approaches to justify the sentiments attached to texts, especially in regulated businesses.

Ethical Importance: The ethical issues within privacy, bias, and fairness will be more crucial as sentiment analysis becomes more popular. To ensure responsible and objective analysis, researchers and developers will need to solve these concerns.

Analysis of User-Generated Content: Sentiment analysis will be extended beyond customer reviews to include user-generated content on social media sites, forums, and other online communities. This wider perspective can offer insightful information on trends and public opinion.

AI and Human Collaboration: Combining the advantages of human analysts and artificial intelligence will remain popular. While human analysts can provide context and make strategic decisions, AI can help automate sentiment analysis tasks.

In conclusion, technological developments, enhanced context awareness, domain-specific customization, and ethical considerations will all play a role in the development of sentiment analysis in customer evaluations. These trends will influence the development of sentiment analysis tools as businesses work to comprehend and react to user input more efficiently. This chapter illustrates the transformative influence of sentiment research on improving customer experiences, brand management, and product creation through instructive case studies. Furthermore, this chapter acts as a road map for scholar, researchers, and technocrats in guiding and leading them through the complex environment of sentiment analysis powered by machine learning in the context of customer evaluations. It also emphasizes in understanding customer sentiment, motivating wise choices, and cultivating long-lasting customer connections in different domains of real time applications.

REFERENCES

Alghamdi, A. (2023). A Hybrid Method for Customer Segmentation in Saudi Arabia Restaurants Using Clustering, Neural Networks and Optimization Learning Techniques. *Arabian Journal for Science and Engineering*, *48*(2), 2021–2039. doi:10.100713369-022-07091-y PMID:35910042

Alzate, M., Arce-Urriza, M., & Cebollada, J. (2022). Mining the text of online consumer reviews to analyze brand image and brand positioning. *Journal of Retailing and Consumer Services, 67*. doi:10.1016/j.jretconser.2022.102989

Amirifar, T., Lahmiri, S., & Zanjani, M. K. (2023). An NLP-Deep Learning Approach for Product Rating Prediction Based on Online Reviews and Product Features. *IEEE Transactions on Computational Social Systems*, 1–13. Advance online publication. doi:10.1109/TCSS.2023.3290558

Aouad, A., Elmachtoub, A. N., Ferreira, K. J., & McNellis, R. (2023). Market segmentation trees. *Manufacturing & Service Operations Management*, *25*(2), 648–667. doi:10.1287/msom.2023.1195

Asani, E., Vahdat-Nejad, H., & Sadri, J. (2021). Restaurant recommender system based on sentiment analysis. *Machine Learning with Applications, 6*. doi:10.1016/j.mlwa.2021.100114

Behera, R. K., Gunasekaran, A., Gupta, S., Kamboj, S., & Bala, P. K. (2020). Personalized digital marketing recommender engine. *Journal of Retailing and Consumer Services*, *53*, 101799. doi:10.1016/j.jretconser.2019.03.026

Bigne, E., Ruiz, C., Perez-Cabañero, C., & Cuenca, A. (2023). Are customer star ratings and sentiments aligned? A deep learning study of the customer service experience in tourism destinations. *Service Business*, *17*(1), 281–314. doi:10.100711628-023-00524-0

Bonta, V., Kumaresh, N., & Janardhan, N. (2019). A comprehensive study on lexicon based approaches for sentiment analysis. *Asian Journal of Computer Science and Technology*, *8*(S2), 1–6. doi:10.51983/ajcst-2019.8.S2.2037

Dadhich, A., & Thankachan, B. (2022). Sentiment Analysis of Amazon Product Reviews Using Hybrid Rule-Based Approach. In A. K. Somani, A. Mundra, R. Doss, & S. Bhattacharya (Eds.), *Smart Systems: Innovations in Computing. Smart Innovation, Systems and Technologies* (Vol. 235). Springer. doi:10.1007/978-981-16-2877-1_17

Dey, S., Wasif, S., Tonmoy, D. S., Sultana, S., Sarkar, J., & Dey, M. (2020). A Comparative Study of Support Vector Machine and Naive Bayes Classifier for Sentiment Analysis on Amazon Product Reviews. *2020 International Conference on Contemporary Computing and Applications (IC3A),* 217-220. 10.1109/IC3A48958.2020.233300

Gunawan, L., Anggreainy, M. S., Wihan, L., Lesmana, G. Y., & Yusuf, S. (2023). Support vector machine based emotional analysis of restaurant reviews. *Procedia Computer Science*, *216*, 479–484. doi:10.1016/j.procs.2022.12.160

Iqbal, A., Amin, R., Iqbal, J., Alroobaea, R., Binmahfoudh, A., & Hussain, M. (2022). Sentiment Analysis of Consumer Reviews Using Deep Learning. *Sustainability (Basel)*, *14*(17), 10844. doi:10.3390u141710844

Jain, P. K., Quamer, W., Pamula, R., & Saravanan, V. (2023). SpSAN: Sparse self-attentive network-based aspect-aware model for sentiment analysis. *Journal of Ambient Intelligence and Humanized Computing*, *14*(4), 3091–3108. doi:10.100712652-021-03436-x

Kaur, G., & Sharma, A. (2023). A deep learning-based model using hybrid feature extraction approach for consumer sentiment analysis. *Journal of Big Data*, *10*(1), 5. doi:10.118640537-022-00680-6 PMID:36686621

Khan, A., Gul, M. A., Zareei, M., Biswal, R. R., Zeb, A., Naeem, M., Saeed, Y., & Salim, N. (2020). Movie review summarization using supervised learning and graph-based ranking algorithm. *Computational Intelligence and Neuroscience*, *2020*, 1–14. doi:10.1155/2020/7526580 PMID:32565772

Liu, Z., Liao, H., Li, M., Yang, Q., & Meng, F. (2023). A Deep Learning-Based Sentiment Analysis Approach for Online Product Ranking With Probabilistic Linguistic Term Sets. *IEEE Transactions on Engineering Management*, 1–18. Advance online publication. doi:10.1109/TEM.2023.3271597

Mutinda, J., Mwangi, W., & Okeyo, G. (2023). Sentiment Analysis of Text Reviews Using Lexicon-Enhanced Bert Embedding (LeBERT) Model with Convolutional Neural Network. *Applied Sciences (Basel, Switzerland)*, *13*(3), 1445. doi:10.3390/app13031445

Noori, B. (2021). Classification of Customer Reviews Using Machine Learning Algorithms. *Applied Artificial Intelligence*, *35*(8), 567–588. doi:10.1080/08839514.2021.1922843

Obiedat, R., Qaddoura, R., Al-Zoubi, A. M., Al-Qaisi, L., Harfoushi, O., Alrefai, M., & Faris, H. (2022). Sentiment Analysis of Customers' Reviews Using a Hybrid Evolutionary SVM-Based Approach in an Imbalanced Data Distribution. *IEEE Access : Practical Innovations, Open Solutions*, *10*, 22260–22273. doi:10.1109/ACCESS.2022.3149482

Oh, S., Ji, H., Kim, J., Park, E., & del Pobil, A. P. (2022). Deep learning model based on expectation-confirmation theory to predict customer satisfaction in hospitality service. *Information Technology & Tourism*, *24*(1), 109–126. doi:10.100740558-022-00222-z

Patel, Oza, & Agrawal. (2023). Sentiment Analysis of Customer Feedback and Reviews for Airline Services using Language Representation Model. *Procedia Comput. Sci*, *218*, 2459 – 2467.

Pavitha, N., Pungliya, V., Raut, A., Bhonsle, R., Purohit, A., Patel, A., & Shashidhar, R. (2022). Movie recommendation and sentiment analysis using machine learning. *Global Transitions Proceedings*, *3*(1), 279–284. doi:10.1016/j.gltp.2022.03.012

Puh, K., & Bagić Babac, M. (2023). Predicting sentiment and rating of tourist reviews using machine learning. *Journal of Hospitality and Tourism Insights*, *6*(3), 1188–1204. doi:10.1108/JHTI-02-2022-0078

Punetha, N., & Jain, G. (2023). Game theory and MCDM-based unsupervised sentiment analysis of restaurant reviews. *Applied Intelligence*, *53*(17), 20152–20173. Advance online publication. doi:10.100710489-023-04471-1 PMID:37363390

Rashid, A., & Huang, C. Y. (2021). Sentiment Analysis on Consumer Reviews of Amazon Products. *International Journal of Computer Theory and Engineering*, *13*(2), 7. doi:10.7763/IJCTE.2021.V13.1287

Rice, D. R., & Zorn, C. (2021). Corpus-based dictionaries for sentiment analysis of specialized vocabularies. *Political Science Research and Methods*, *9*(1), 20–35. doi:10.1017/psrm.2019.10

Singh, S. N., & Sarraf, T. (2020). Sentiment Analysis of a Product based on User Reviews using Random Forests Algorithm. *2020 10th International Conference on Cloud Computing, Data Science & Engineering (Confluence),* 112-116. 10.1109/Confluence47617.2020.9058128

Tepsongkroh, P., Thongkamkaew, C., & Sasha, F. (2023). Business Intelligent Framework Using Sentiment Analysis for Smart Digital Marketing in the E-Commerce Era. *Asia Social Issues*, *16*(3), e252965. doi:10.48048/asi.2023.252965

Thwe, P., Aung, Y. Y., & Lwin, C. C. (2021). Naïve Bayes Classifier for sentiment analysis. *International Journal Of All Research Writings*, *3*(7), 32–35.

.Wan, Y., & Nakayama, M. (2022). *A sentiment analysis of star-rating: a cross-cultural perspective*. Academic Press.

Wankhade, M., Rao, A. C. S., Dara, S., & Kaushik, B. (2017, September). A sentiment analysis of food review using logistic regression. In *International Conference on Machine Learning and Computational Intelligence-2017* (pp. 2456-3307). Academic Press.

Wankhade, M., Rao, A. C. S., & Kulkarni, C. (2022). A survey on sentiment analysis methods, applications, and challenges. *Artificial Intelligence Review*, *55*(7), 5731–5780. doi:10.100710462-022-10144-1

Yang, L., Li, Y., Wang, J., & Sherratt, R. S. (2020). Sentiment Analysis for E-Commerce Product Reviews in Chinese Based on Sentiment Lexicon and Deep Learning. *IEEE Access : Practical Innovations, Open Solutions*, *8*, 23522–23530. doi:10.1109/ACCESS.2020.2969854

Yang, Zhu, Liao, & Wu. (2023). Learning consumer preferences from online textual reviews and ratings based on the aggregation-disaggregation paradigm with attitudinal Choquet integral. *Economic Research-EkonomskaIstraživanja, 36*(2). doi:10.1080/1331677X.2022.2106282

Yi, S., & Liu, X. (2020). Machine learning based customer sentiment analysis for recommending shoppers, shops based on customers' review. *Complex & Intelligent Systems*, *6*(3), 621–634. doi:10.100740747-020-00155-2

Zad, S., Heidari, M., Jones, J. H., & Uzuner, O. (2021). A survey on concept-level sentiment analysis techniques of textual data. In *2021 IEEE World AI IoT Congress (AIIoT).* IEEE. 10.1109/AIIoT52608.2021.9454169

Chapter 12

Unleashing Customer Insights:
Harnessing Machine Learning Approaches for Sentiment Analyzing and Leveraging Customer Feedback

Debosree Ghosh
https://orcid.org/0009-0005-5585-5588
Shree Ramkrishna Institute of Science and Technology, India

ABSTRACT

This chapter explores the integration of machine learning with customer sentiment analysis to unveil insights from customer feedback. It emphasizes the importance of understanding customer sentiment for enhancing satisfaction and making informed decisions. The chapter covers various machine learning approaches including supervised and unsupervised learning, as well as deep learning models. Preprocessing techniques and feature engineering methods for textual data are discussed. The challenges of sentiment analysis, such as sarcasm and context, are addressed, along with practical applications in product development, brand management, and personalized marketing. Ethical considerations are highlighted. Overall, this chapter provides valuable insights on leveraging machine learning for customer sentiment analysis.

INTRODUCTION

In today's digital age, customers are more vocal than ever before. They are constantly sharing their opinions, experiences, and feedback on social media, review sites, and other online platforms. This wealth of data provides businesses with a unique opportunity to understand customer sentiment and gain insights into how they can improve their products and services. This chapter explores the intersection of machine learning and customer sentiment analysis, focusing on how machine learning approaches can be harnessed to analyze and leverage customer feedback effectively.

DOI: 10.4018/979-8-3693-2647-3.ch012

Literature on Sentiment Analysis

The research on sentiment analysis is extensive and growing rapidly.

Turney (2002): Turney proposed a simple approach to sentiment analysis using point wise mutual information (PMI). PMI is a measure of the association between two words, and Turney used it to identify the sentiment of words by their association with known positive and negative words.

Pang and Lee (2002): Pang and Lee proposed a supervised approach to sentiment analysis using machine learning. They trained a classifier to predict the sentiment of sentences by using a set of labelled examples.

Liu et al. (2005): Liu et al. proposed a feature-based approach to sentiment analysis. They identified a set of features that are useful for predicting sentiment, such as the presence of certain words or phrases, and used these features to train a classifier.

Since these early works, there have been many advances in the field of sentiment analysis. New ML algorithms have been developed, and researchers have explored new ways to leverage customer feedback data for sentiment analysis.

Literature on Sentiment Analysis for Customer Feedback

There is a growing body of research on using sentiment analysis to analyse customer feedback.

Hu and Liu (2004): Hu and Liu proposed a method for using sentiment analysis to identify customer opinion leaders. They used a graph-based approach to identify customers who are highly influential in social networks.

Wang et al. (2011): Wang et al. proposed a method for using sentiment analysis to identify product defects. They used sentiment analysis to identify customer reviews that express negative sentiment about specific product features.

Asur and Huberman (2010): Asur and Huberman proposed a method for using sentiment analysis to predict stock market movements. They used sentiment analysis to identify positive and negative sentiment about companies in social media data, and found that this sentiment could be used to predict stock prices.

These studies demonstrate the potential of sentiment analysis for analysing customer feedback. Sentiment analysis can be used to identify customer opinion leaders, identify product defects, predict customer churn, and more.

Understanding Customer Sentiment

An overview of consumer sentiment analysis and its importance in the corporate world is given in this section. It looks at how important it is to comprehend the feelings, desires, and views of customers as well as how sentiment analysis can provide insightful information.

Sentiment analysis is the technique of identifying opinions, feelings, and other subjective information in text. It can be applied to comprehend consumer perceptions of a brand, service, or product. Sentiment analysis may be done automatically with the use of advanced tools like machine learning. Businesses may recognize positive, negative, and neutral sentiment automatically by using machine learning algorithms on consumer input. Afterwards, by using this data, corporate decisions may be made more effectively and customer happiness can be raised.

Customer sentiment quantifies the opinions that consumers have about a brand, service, or product. It may be neutral, negative, or positive. Customers who express positive emotion are happy with the goods or service, whereas those who express negative sentiment are not. Customers that express neutral sentiment are neither happy nor unhappy.

Customer sentiment can be measured in a variety of ways. Using surveys is one approach. Customers can be directly questioned via surveys about how satisfied they are with a good or service. Using social media is an additional technique to gauge consumer mood. A product or service's positive, negative, and neutral sentiment can be determined by analyzing social media posts.

Introduction to Machine Learning

This part explains the fundamentals of machine learning to lay the groundwork. It highlights the significance of fundamental ideas in sentiment analysis by explaining terms like reinforcement learning, supervised learning, and unsupervised learning.

A potent tool for analyzing consumer feedback and spotting underlying patterns and trends is machine learning (ML). Businesses may automatically discern between positive, negative, and neutral sentiment by using machine learning algorithms to customer feedback. Afterwards, by using this data, corporate decisions may be made more effectively and customer happiness can be raised.

The particular business goals will determine which machine learning approach is best. If the only objective is to distinguish between positive, negative, and neutral sentiment, supervised learning might be a suitable choice. However, if the goal is to identify more nuanced sentiment or uncover hidden patterns, then unsupervised learning may be a better choice.

In addition to the ML approach, there are a number of other factors that need to be considered when analyzing customer feedback. These factors include the type of data, the size of the dataset, and the desired level of accuracy. For example, if the data is very noisy or the dataset is small, then it may be difficult to achieve high accuracy.

There are a variety of ML approaches that can be used for sentiment analysis. Some of the most common approaches include:

Lexicon-based approaches: These approaches use a dictionary of words and phrases with known sentiment scores to classify text as positive, negative, or neutral.

Machine learning classifiers: These approaches train a classifier on a set of labelled training data to predict the sentiment of new text.

Deep learning models: These models are trained on large amounts of unlabelled text data to learn to identify sentiment.

Preprocessing and Feature Engineering for Sentiment Analysis

This section delves into the preprocessing steps necessary for customer feedback analysis, including text cleaning, tokenization, and normalization. It also explores feature engineering techniques like bag-of-words, TF-IDF, and word embedding's to represent textual data effectively.

Data Cleaning and Normalization

Before performing sentiment analysis, it is essential to preprocess the customer feedback data to remove noise and inconsistencies. Data cleaning involves removing irrelevant characters, punctuation, and special symbols. Additionally, normalization techniques like converting text to lowercase, handling contractions, and removing stop words can help standardize the text and reduce dimensionality.

Tokenization and Part-of-Speech Tagging

Tokenization is the process of breaking down the text into individual words or tokens. This step helps in organizing the data and separating meaningful units for analysis. Part-of-speech (POS) tagging assigns grammatical tags to each token, such as noun, verb, adjective, or adverb. POS tagging aids in capturing the contextual information and can be useful in sentiment analysis.

Feature Extraction Techniques

Feature extraction plays a critical role in sentiment analysis as it involves transforming the text data into a numerical representation that machine learning algorithms can understand.

Bag-of-Words and N-Grams

The bag-of-words (BoW) model represents the text as a collection of words, disregarding grammar and word order. It creates a vocabulary of unique words and counts the occurrence of each word in the document. N-grams are extensions of the BoW model, where consecutive sequences of words are considered as features. By capturing word frequencies and patterns, BoW and N-grams provide valuable information for sentiment analysis.

TF-IDF (Term Frequency-Inverse Document Frequency)

TF-IDF is a statistical measure used to evaluate the importance of a term in a document within a collection of documents. It combines term frequency (TF), which measures the frequency of a term in a document, and inverse document frequency (IDF), which penalizes terms that appear in many documents. TF-IDF helps in capturing the relevance of words in the context of a specific document and the entire corpus.

Word Embedding

Word embeddings represent words as dense numerical vectors in a continuous space, capturing semantic relationships between words. Popular word embedding techniques like Word2Vec and GloVe use neural networks to learn word representations based on the context in which they appear. Word embeddings can capture subtle linguistic nuances and contribute to improved sentiment analysis accuracy.

Feature engineering is the process of choosing and modifying the retrieved features in order to improve the sentiment analysis model's predicting ability. Model performance can be enhanced by methods such as dimensionality reduction (e.g., Principal Component Analysis) and feature selection techniques (e.g., chi-square, information gain).

The selection of preprocessing and feature engineering methods needs to be carefully thought out in light of the language, sentiment analysis task, and data properties. Finding the best methods for a certain dataset may need some trial and error and fine-tuning. By effectively preprocessing and engineering features, sentiment analysis models can capture the nuanced aspects of customer feedback, leading to more accurate sentiment predictions and better insights for businesses.

Supervised Learning for Sentiment Analysis

It addresses well-known models, including decision trees, Naive Bayes, and Support Vector Machines (SVM), outlining their advantages, disadvantages, and factors to take into account when choosing a model. A set of labeled data, such as customer reviews that have been manually categorized as good, negative, or neutral, is used to train a model in supervised learning. Next, the model gains the ability to recognize the characteristics linked to every sentiment category. New customer reviews can be classified by the model once it has been trained.

Support Vector Machines (SVM)

Support Vector Machines are powerful and widely used classifiers in sentiment analysis. SVM aims to find an optimal hyperplane that separates data points of different sentiment classes with the largest margin. It works by mapping the input data into a higher-dimensional feature space and finding a decision boundary that maximally separates the sentiment classes.

Naive Bayes Classifier

Naive Bayes is a probabilistic classifier based on Bayes' theorem with the assumption of independence among features. Despite its simplifying assumptions, Naive Bayes has shown good performance in sentiment analysis tasks. It calculates the probability of a document belonging to each sentiment class based on the occurrence of words and uses these probabilities to classify the document.

Decision Trees and Random Forests

Decision trees partition the feature space into smaller regions based on a set of if-else conditions. Each leaf node represents a sentiment class label. Decision trees are interpretable and can capture nonlinear relationships. Random Forests, an ensemble method, combine multiple decision trees to improve generalization and reduce over fitting.

Neural Networks for Sentiment Analysis

Deep neural networks, such as Multilayer Perceptron's (MLPs) and Recurrent Neural Networks (RNNs), have gained popularity in sentiment analysis due to their ability to capture complex patterns in data. MLPs consist of multiple layers of interconnected neurons and can learn intricate relationships between input features and sentiment labels. RNNs, particularly Long Short-Term Memory (LSTM) and Gated Recurrent Unit (GRU) networks, are capable of capturing sequential dependencies in text data, making them suitable for sentiment analysis.

Model Evaluation and Selection

The performance of supervised learning models in sentiment analysis is assessed using evaluation metrics such as accuracy, precision, recall, and F1-score. Cross-validation techniques, like k-fold cross-validation, can be employed to estimate the model's generalization ability. Hyper parameter tuning, through techniques like grid search or Bayesian optimization, can optimize model performance by selecting the best combination of hyper parameters.

It is important to note that the choice of the supervised learning approach depends on various factors, including the nature of the dataset, the available computational resources, and the specific requirements of the sentiment analysis task. Experimentation and model comparison are essential to identify the most suitable algorithm for a given application.

Unsupervised Learning Approach for Sentiment Analysis

This section examines unsupervised learning methods for sentiment analysis, such as topic modeling strategies like Latent Dirichlet Allocation (LDA) and clustering algorithms like k-means and hierarchical clustering. It talks about how to use them to find themes and patterns in customer reviews.

Unsupervised learning can also be used to analyze client feedback. Unsupervised learning involves not using labeled data to train the model. Rather, without any prior information, the model learns to recognize patterns and trends in the data. Outliers can be found, hidden correlations can be found, and client segments can be identified using this method.

Clustering Methods

Clustering algorithms group similar data points together based on their inherent patterns or similarities. In the context of sentiment analysis, clustering techniques can identify groups of customer feedback that share similar sentiment characteristics. K-means clustering, hierarchical clustering, and density-based clustering algorithms (e.g., DBSCAN) are commonly used for unsupervised sentiment analysis. Clusters can then be analyzed to infer sentiment patterns and identify sentiment orientations.

Latent Dirichlet Allocation (LDA)

LDA is a probabilistic topic modeling technique that identifies latent topics within a collection of documents. In sentiment analysis, LDA can uncover underlying themes or topics in customer feedback data. By assigning words to different topics and estimating the topic distribution within each document, LDA can help reveal sentiment-related topics and their prevalence in the dataset. This can provide valuable insights into customer sentiment patterns and sentiments associated with specific topics.

Topic Modeling for Sentiment Analysis

Beyond LDA, other topic modeling techniques, such as Non-Negative Matrix Factorization (NMF), can also be applied to sentiment analysis. NMF decomposes the customer feedback matrix into non-negative basis vectors, each representing a topic. By extracting latent topics from the data, NMF can uncover sentiment-related topics and facilitate sentiment analysis at a topic level. This allows for a more granular understanding of sentiment in different aspects of customer feedback.

Unsupervised learning techniques offer benefits in identifying underlying sentiment patterns and structures in consumer feedback data. They do, however, also provide difficulties. Evaluation is more difficult in the absence of ground truth sentiment labeling, and unsupervised result interpretation may be arbitrary. To validate the patterns found, careful thought should be devoted to choosing the best clustering or topic modeling techniques, adjusting parameters, and doing qualitative analysis.

Sentiment analysis findings can be further improved by combining unsupervised learning with additional strategies like rule-based or lexicon-based approaches. Hybrid models can improve the accuracy and interpretability of sentiment analysis in customer feedback analysis by combining supervised and unsupervised learning approaches, thereby utilizing the advantages of both paradigms.

Deep Learning Approaches for Sentiment Analysis

Recurrent neural networks (RNNs), convolutional neural networks (CNNs), and transformer models are a few examples of the deep learning architectures that are introduced in this section. It examines the ways in which these models are particularly good at capturing sentiment analysis's semantic knowledge, long-term dependencies, and contextual information.

Using neural network topologies to identify intricate patterns and semantic representations in consumer feedback data, deep learning has become a potent method in sentiment analysis. Sentiment analysis is one of the natural language processing problems where deep learning models have shown state-of-the-art performance.

Recurrent Neural Networks (RNNs)

Recurrent Neural Networks are designed to process sequential data, making them well-suited for sentiment analysis tasks where the order of words in a sentence matters. RNNs utilize recurrent connections to capture dependencies between words across time steps. Long Short-Term Memory (LSTM) and Gated Recurrent Unit (GRU) are popular variations of RNNs that can mitigate the vanishing gradient problem and model long-term dependencies. By analyzing the sequential nature of customer feedback, RNNs can capture contextual information and temporal dynamics, improving sentiment analysis accuracy.

Convolutional Neural Networks (CNNs)

Convolutional Neural Networks have traditionally been used in image recognition tasks, but they have also shown effectiveness in sentiment analysis. CNNs leverage convolutional filters to capture local patterns in text data. By applying multiple filters of varying sizes, CNNs can learn features at different levels of granularity. This allows them to capture both local word-level features and higher-level syntactic and semantic structures. CNNs are particularly effective at identifying important n-grams or phrases that contribute to sentiment polarity.

Transfer Learning and Pertained Models

In sentiment analysis, transfer learning—a method where a model trained on a huge dataset is optimized for a particular task—has shown promise. Sentiment analysis is just one of the many natural language processing tasks in which pertained models, like BERT (Bidirectional Encoder Representations from Transformers) and GPT (Generative Pertained Transformer), have demonstrated outstanding performance. These algorithms successfully capture contextual and semantic information since they have been trained on large corpora. Transfer learning allows exploiting the knowledge obtained from large-scale datasets even with insufficient labeled data by tailoring existing models to sentiment analysis applications.

For sentiment analysis, deep learning models need a lot of labeled data and a lot of processing power to train. They do, however, have advantages when it comes to catching minute linguistic details, contextual awareness, and distant relationships. They have the potential to handle challenging sentiment analysis scenarios, such as sarcasm, irony, and sentiment in context.

Deep learning model fine-tuning entails choosing suitable architectures, tackling issues like over fitting and interpretability of the model, and optimizing hyper parameters. Strategies like regularization, attention mechanisms, and dropout can be used to improve model performance and address frequent problems.

The investigation of transformer-based architectures and self-attention processes, among other ongoing developments in deep learning, present encouraging directions for enhancing the precision and resilience of sentiment analysis.

Sentiment analysis methods based on deep learning have demonstrated remarkable efficacy in discerning the subtle nuances of client sentiment. Businesses may improve their products, services, and overall customer experiences by using these models to get a more thorough knowledge of customer feedback and make data-driven decisions.

Leveraging Sentiment Analysis to Unleash Customer Insights

Businesses can leverage sentiment analysis to unleash customer insights in a variety of ways.

Identify product or service defects: Businesses can use sentiment analysis to identify customer feedback that mentions product or service defects. This feedback can then be used to fix the defects and improve the customer experience.

Predict customer churn: Businesses can use sentiment analysis to predict which customers are likely to churn. This information can then be used to develop targeted retention programs.

Improve customer support: Businesses can use sentiment analysis to identify customer support tickets that indicate customer dissatisfaction. These tickets can then be prioritized and resolved quickly.

Personalize customer experiences: Businesses can use sentiment analysis to understand individual customer preferences. This information can then be used to personalize customer experiences, such as by recommending products or services that the customer is likely to be interested in.

Handling Challenges in Sentiment Analysis

This section addresses common challenges in sentiment analysis, such as handling sarcasm, irony, and sentiment in context. It discusses techniques like sentiment lexicons, context-aware models, and attention mechanisms to address these challenges and improve the accuracy of sentiment analysis results.

Sarcasm and Irony Detection

Sarcasm and irony often involve the use of language that expresses sentiments opposite to the literal meaning. To handle sarcasm and irony in sentiment analysis, advanced techniques can be employed. One approach is to incorporate sentiment lexicons that capture the polarity of words in different contexts. Additionally, contextual analysis and semantic understanding techniques, such as deep learning models with attention mechanisms, can help identify sarcastic or ironic expressions.

Sentiment in Context

Understanding sentiment in context is crucial for accurate sentiment analysis. The sentiment expressed by a word or phrase can vary depending on its surrounding context. Techniques like syntactic and semantic parsing, dependency parsing, and semantic role labeling can help capture the relationships between words and disambiguate their sentiments within a sentence or document. Context-aware models, such as contextual word embeddings like ELMo, BERT, or GPT, can effectively incorporate contextual information for sentiment analysis.

Noisy or Unstructured Data

Customer feedback data can be noisy, containing grammatical errors, misspellings, abbreviations, or informal language. Data preprocessing techniques, including spell-checking, correcting errors, and normalizing abbreviations, can help clean the data and improve sentiment analysis results. Additionally, techniques like data augmentation, where synthetic data is generated to expand the training set, can help mitigate the impact of noisy data. Handling unstructured data, such as free-form text or social media posts, may require specific techniques like topic modeling or natural language understanding to extract sentiment-related information.

Domain Adaptation

Sentiment analysis models trained on one domain may not perform optimally when applied to another domain due to differences in language use and sentiment expressions. Domain adaptation techniques can be employed to adapt sentiment analysis models to specific domains by leveraging domain-specific labeled data or using transfer learning approaches. Fine-tuning pertained models on domain-specific data or incorporating domain-specific sentiment lexicons can improve sentiment analysis accuracy within a particular domain.

Evaluation and Validation

Evaluating the performance of sentiment analysis models is crucial. It is essential to use appropriate evaluation metrics such as accuracy, precision, recall, and F1-score. Additionally, validation techniques like cross-validation or hold-out validation can provide insights into model generalization and performance. It is also recommended to conduct qualitative analysis, including manual annotation of a subset of data, to validate the sentiment predictions and identify potential misclassifications or limitations of the model.

Leveraging Customer Sentiment

This section explores practical applications of sentiment analysis in leveraging customer feedback. It discusses how sentiment analysis can support various business areas, including product development, marketing campaigns, customer service enhancement, and brand reputation management.

Product Development

Customer sentiment analysis provides valuable feedback on existing products or services. By analyzing customer sentiments, businesses can identify areas for improvement, understand customer needs, and prioritize feature enhancements. This feedback-driven approach enables organizations to develop products that align with customer expectations, leading to increased customer satisfaction and loyalty.

Marketing Campaigns

Understanding customer sentiment helps businesses develop effective marketing campaigns. By analyzing sentiment, organizations can identify key themes, preferences, and pain points that resonate with customers. This insight enables businesses to tailor their messaging, design targeted campaigns, and deliver personalized content that aligns with customer sentiment. By incorporating customer sentiment analysis into marketing strategies, organizations can enhance engagement, drive conversions, and build stronger brand connections.

Customer Service Enhancement

Customer sentiment analysis plays a vital role in enhancing customer service experiences. By analyzing sentiment in customer feedback, businesses can identify patterns and trends related to customer satisfaction, service quality, and support issues. This insight enables organizations to proactively address customer concerns, improve response times, and personalize interactions. By leveraging sentiment analysis in customer service, businesses can optimize customer experiences, foster loyalty, and drive positive word-of-mouth.

Brand Reputation Management

Sentiment analysis helps businesses monitor and manage their brand reputation. By analyzing sentiment in online conversations, reviews, and social media mentions, organizations can gauge the sentiment surrounding their brand. This information allows businesses to identify potential reputation risks, respond to negative sentiment, and capitalize on positive sentiment. Proactively managing brand reputation based on sentiment analysis helps maintain a positive brand image, attract new customers, and retain existing ones.

Market Research and Competitive Analysis

Sentiment analysis provides valuable insights into customer opinions, preferences, and market trends. By analyzing sentiment in customer feedback and reviews, businesses can identify emerging trends, assess market demand, and gather competitive intelligence. This information helps organizations make data-driven decisions, refine their market positioning, and gain a competitive edge. Sentiment analysis in market research enables businesses to stay ahead of market dynamics and adapt their strategies accordingly.

Practical Applications of Sentiment Analysis

Sentiment analysis has a wide range of practical applications across various industries. By analyzing and understanding customer sentiment, businesses can gain valuable insights that inform decision-making, improve products and services, and enhance customer experiences.

Product and Service Improvement

Sentiment analysis can help businesses identify areas for product and service enhancement. By analyzing customer feedback, organizations can uncover recurring themes, identify specific pain points, and understand customer satisfaction levels. This information can guide product development efforts, enable targeted improvements, and drive innovation based on customer needs and preferences.

Brand Monitoring and Reputation Management

Monitoring and managing brand reputation is critical in today's digital landscape. Sentiment analysis enables organizations to track online mentions, reviews, and social media conversations about their brand. By analyzing sentiment in real-time, businesses can identify positive and negative sentiment trends, detect potential reputation risks, and take proactive measures to address customer concerns or mitigate negative sentiment.

Customer Service Enhancement

Sentiment analysis can play a crucial role in improving customer service experiences. By analyzing customer feedback across various channels, such as call center recordings, chat logs, and customer surveys, organizations can identify common issues and sentiment patterns. This information helps businesses optimize customer service processes, address recurring problems, and personalize interactions to meet individual customer needs, ultimately enhancing overall customer satisfaction.

Market Research and Competitive Analysis

Sentiment analysis provides valuable insights into consumer preferences, opinions, and trends. By analyzing customer feedback and sentiment related to specific products or industry trends, businesses can gain a competitive edge. This information helps identify market gaps, assess product positioning, and monitor consumer sentiment towards competitors. Sentiment analysis also enables organizations to conduct sentiment-based market research and assess the potential success of new product launches or marketing campaigns.

Personalized Marketing and Recommendation Systems

Sentiment analysis can contribute to personalized marketing efforts by understanding individual customer preferences and sentiments. By analyzing past interactions, reviews, and feedback, businesses can tailor marketing messages, offers, and recommendations to specific customer segments. Sentiment analysis can also help identify influencers or brand advocates among customers, enabling targeted marketing initiatives and maximizing the impact of promotional activities.

It is important for businesses to integrate sentiment analysis into their existing data analytics and business intelligence workflows to maximize the value derived from customer feedback.

Ethical Considerations

Given the sensitive nature of customer data, this section emphasizes the ethical considerations in sentiment analysis. It discusses privacy protection, data anonymization, and the responsible use of customer feedback, highlighting the importance of complying with ethical guidelines and regulations.

Privacy and Data Protection

Respecting user privacy and safeguarding customer data should be a top priority. Organizations must obtain appropriate consent when collecting customer feedback data for sentiment analysis. It is important to adhere to data protection regulations and implement robust security measures to protect sensitive customer information. Anonymizing or pseudonymizing data can further ensure privacy.

Bias and Fairness

Bias in sentiment analysis can lead to unfair or discriminatory outcomes. It is essential to address biases related to gender, race, ethnicity, or other protected attributes. Care should be taken to ensure that sentiment analysis models and algorithms are trained on diverse and representative datasets. Regular evaluation and monitoring of model performance for bias and fairness can help mitigate any unintended biases.

Transparency and Explainability

Customers should be informed about the use of sentiment analysis on their feedback and understand how their data is being analyzed. Providing clear explanations about the purpose and process of sentiment analysis fosters transparency and builds trust. Organizations should strive to make sentiment analysis models and decisions explainable to stakeholders, enabling them to understand the factors influencing sentiment predictions.

Accountability and Responsible Use

Organizations must take responsibility for the decisions made based on sentiment analysis. It is important to avoid making high-stakes decisions solely based on automated sentiment analysis, especially in sensitive areas such as hiring or financial decision-making. Human oversight and intervention should be incorporated to ensure that sentiment analysis results are interpreted and used responsibly.

Continuous Monitoring and Improvement

Ethical considerations in sentiment analysis require continuous monitoring and improvement. Regular audits of sentiment analysis models should be conducted to identify potential biases or ethical concerns. Feedback loops should be established to incorporate user feedback and address any unintended consequences. Organizations should be open to feedback and adapt their practices accordingly to ensure ethical and responsible use of sentiment analysis.

It is essential to establish clear policies and guidelines for the ethical use of sentiment analysis, encompassing privacy, bias mitigation, transparency, and accountability. Collaboration with legal and ethics experts can provide valuable insights and guidance in navigating ethical challenges. By adopting ethical practices in sentiment analysis, organizations can build trust with customers, protect their reputation, and ensure the responsible use of customer feedback data.

Benefits of Using ML to Analyze Customer Feedback

There are a number of benefits to using ML to analyze customer feedback. These benefits include:

Enhanced accuracy: A great degree of accuracy can be achieved in the identification of sentiment by training ML algorithms. This can assist companies in making more informed judgments about how to enhance their goods and services.

Lower expenses: Machine learning can automate the consumer feedback analysis procedure. Businesses can save money and time by doing this.

Better insights: ML can assist companies in comprehending the requirements and preferences of their clients on a deeper level. Utilizing this data will boost customer happiness and enhance the customer experience.

Early warning system: Machine learning (ML) can be used to spot possible issues with goods or services before they get out of hand. This can assist companies in making necessary corrections and preventing client complaints.

Challenges of Using ML to Analyze Customer Feedback

There are also a number of challenges to using ML to analyze customer feedback. These challenges include:

Data availability: ML algorithms require large amounts of data to train. This data may not always be available, especially for small businesses.

Data quality: The quality of the data can impact the accuracy of the ML algorithms. If the data is noisy or incomplete, then the algorithms may not be able to identify sentiment accurately.

Model complexity: ML algorithms can be complex and difficult to interpret. This can make it difficult for businesses to understand how the algorithms are making decisions.

Case Studies

Case Study 1: Amazon

Sentiment analysis is a tool that Amazon uses to examine user evaluations and find flaws in products. Afterwards, Amazon uses these comments to raise the caliber of its goods. For instance, Amazon employed sentiment analysis to determine that a specific smartphone model's battery life was a source of complaints from customers. After looking into the matter, Amazon discovered that the battery was faulty. All impacted devices had their batteries changed by Amazon, and consumers who had already bought the product were given a refund.

Case Study 2: Netflix

Netflix use sentiment analysis as a tool to learn about its users' tastes and suggest TV series and films that they will probably like. Netflix gathers information about the watching preferences, reviews, and search terms of its users. Sentiment analysis is then used to examine this data in order to determine the categories of films and television series that viewers are most drawn to. Netflix then makes customer-specific content recommendations based on this data.

Case Study 3: Airbnb

Airbnb use sentiment analysis to find customer reviews that highlight unfavourable encounters. The Airbnb platform is then enhanced based on these comments, giving users a better overall experience. For instance, sentiment analysis was utilized by Airbnb to determine that certain of its listings' cleanliness was a source of complaints from customers. Subsequently, Airbnb launched a new initiative to assist hosts in making their listings cleaner.

Case Study 4: Delta Air Lines

Sentiment analysis is a tool that Delta Air Lines uses to monitor customer happiness and pinpoint areas for improvement. Customer feedback is gathered by Delta through surveys, social media, and customer support tickets. Sentiment analysis is then applied to this data in order to determine both positive and negative customer sentiment. Delta makes use of this data to pinpoint areas in which its goods, services, and customer support could be enhanced.

Case Study 5: Starbucks

Starbucks develops new goods and services by using sentiment analysis to learn about consumer preferences. Starbucks gathers customer input via surveys, social media, and customer support tickets. Sentiment analysis is then used to examine this data in order to determine the categories of goods and services that consumers are most interested in. Starbucks makes use of this data to create fresh goods and services that are probably going to be well-liked by consumers.

CONCLUSION

With the use of machine learning (ML), one can examine client feedback and find hidden recurring trends and patterns. When utilizing ML, there are quite a number of issues to take into account. Businesses may improve the way they employ machine learning (ML) to enhance the services and goods they offer by having a better knowledge of these problems. In conclusion, this chapter offers a thorough examination of machine learning techniques for assessing and utilizing consumer sentiment. It gives readers the skills and resources they need to glean useful information from customer feedback, empowering companies to improve customer happiness and make well-informed decisions. The chapter ends with case examples and a discussion of new developments and directions in machine learning and sentiment analysis. It explores areas such as sentiment analysis in social media, multimodal sentiment analysis, and the integration of explainable AI techniques. It emphasizes the need for continued research and innovation to advance the field and maximize the value of customer sentiment analysis.

REFERENCES

Asur, S., & Huberman, B. A. (2010). Predicting the future with social media: The case of stock market predictions. In *Proceedings of the 2010 IEEE International Conference on Intelligence and Security Informatics (ISI)* (pp. 391-399). IEEE.

Eyheramendy, S., Lewis, D., & Madigan, D. (2003) On the naive bayes model for text categorization. Proceedings Artificial Intelligence & Statistics 2003.

Friedman, N., Geiger, D., & Goldszmidt, M. (1997). Bayesian network classifiers. *Machine Learning, 29*(2/3), 31–163. doi:10.1023/A:1007465528199

Hu, M., & Liu, B. (2004). Mining and summarizing customer reviews. In *Proceedings of the 2004 ACM SIGKDD International Conference on Knowledge Discovery and Data Mining (KDDM)* (pp. 168-177). ACM.

Liu, B. (2015). *Sentiment Analysis: Mining Opinions, Sentiments, and Emotions*. Morgan Kaufmann. doi:10.1017/CBO9781139084789

Liu, B., Hu, M., & Cheng, J. (2005). A Survey on Sentiment Analysis. *Proceedings of the 40th Annual Meeting of the Association for Computational Linguistics (ACL '05).*

Liu, B., Hu, M., & Cheng, J. (2005). Opinion observer: An automated approach to mining and summarizing customer reviews. In *Proceedings of the 2005 ACM SIGKDD International Conference on Knowledge Discovery and Data Mining (KDDM)* (pp. 419-428). ACM.

Pang, B., & Lee, L. (2002). A sentimental education: Sentiment analysis using subjectivity and polarity of text. In *Proceedings of the 2002 Conference on Empirical Methods in Natural Language Processing (EMNLP)* (pp. 280-289). Academic Press.

Shashank, S., & Goyal, V. (2023). *Unleashing Customer Insights: Harnessing Machine Learning Approaches for Sentiment Analyzing and Leveraging Customer Feedback.* Springer Nature Singapore Pte Ltd.

Tiwari, A., Singh, G., & Kumar, S. (2021). *Unveiling Customer Sentiment: Harnessing Machine Learning Approaches for Analyzing and Leveraging Customer Feedback.* Springer Nature Switzerland AG.

Turney, P. D. (2002). Thumbs up or thumbs down? Semantic orientation applied to unsupervised classification of reviews. In *Proceedings of the 40th Annual Meeting of the Association for Computational Linguistics (ACL)* (pp. 417-424). ACL.

Wang, H., He, Y., & Ji, D. (2011). A novel method for product defect identification using machine learning and sentiment analysis. In *Proceedings of the 2011 IEEE International Conference on Intelligent Systems and Applications (ISA)* (pp. 1-6). IEEE.

Chapter 13
Safety for Digital Immersive Environments and Social Economic Dynamics Based on Designing the Metaverse

S. Vinoth Kumar
Vel Tech Rangarajan Dr. Sagunthala R&D Institute of Science and Technology, India

Vishnu Kumar Kaliappan
KPR Institute of Engineering and Technology, India

A. Suresh
Vellore Institute of Technology, Chennai, India

B. Suresh Kumar
The Kavery Engineering College, India

S. V. Manikanthan
Melange Academic Research Associates, Puducherry, India

ABSTRACT

The Metaverse is a network of 3D virtual worlds that combines real-world and virtual experiences and offers ways for multimodal communication and experiences in a range of settings. The third wave of the World Wide Web revolution, known as the metaverse, is based on cutting-edge technologies like artificial intelligence and greater reality. Here, through an analysis of the literature and a synthesis of best practices for creating metaverse educational settings, the authors revise learning throughout the metaverse and suggest a fresh and cutting-edge theoretical framework. By doing this, they intend to show that the SED model-based computer simulation experiment method is a scientific empirical approach that has more benefits than other methods for empirical study in economics now in use. A virtual world with physics, finances, society, and governance that is close to and exists alongside reality can be created using the digital twin approach. The SED model may be fully utilized to create a market and a virtual financial system.

DOI: 10.4018/979-8-3693-2647-3.ch013

1. INTRODUCTION

How swiftly it is expanding is shown by the fact that Geppetto has 200 million members and Animal Crossing is holding the election in the metaverse. An interesting fact about Roblox is that it has 150 million monthly active users (MAU), 2/3 of who are US children between the ages of 9 and 12, and 1/3 of them are under the threshold of 18. Early metaverse studies conducted in 2007 concentrated on Second Life. However, the current Metaverse is based on Generation Z social standards, which hold that a person's online and offline identities are same. Because the current Metaverse is different from the previous one due to the increasing prevalence of social events and supplies, a new definition is consequently necessary.

Three stages of evolution can be seen in this metaverse vision. When our real environments are digitalized and have the potential to occasionally reflect modifications to their virtual parallels, we start with the concept of "digital twins." According to the natural world, digital twins produce 'many' virtual worlds that are digital replicas of the real world, and human users who use their characters to create new things in these virtual worlds are said to be digital natives (Lee et al., 2021). It's vital to remember that these virtual worlds will first have information silos due to their limited access to one another and the real world. Then they will gradually join together to form a vast landscape. In the end, the digital real world and virtual world merge, the last phase of the cohabitation of physical and virtual reality resembling the surreal). A physical and virtual world that is so integrated provides meet the enormous needs of a permanent, 3D virtual environment is the metaverse.

Technologies other than the web, networking sites, playing games, and simulated settings should be taken into account to achieve the metaverse. The metaverse is being built on the foundation of the emergence of AR and VR, high-speed networks, edge computing, machine learning, and hyper-ledgers. We define the principles of the metaverse and its technological singularity from a technical perspective. To provide a critical perspective for creating the metaverse, which consists of everlasting, shared, simultaneous, and 3D virtual places combined into a perceived virtual cosmos, this essay evaluates the existing technologies and technical infrastructures. The article makes three contributions.

Figure 1. Significant the metaverse

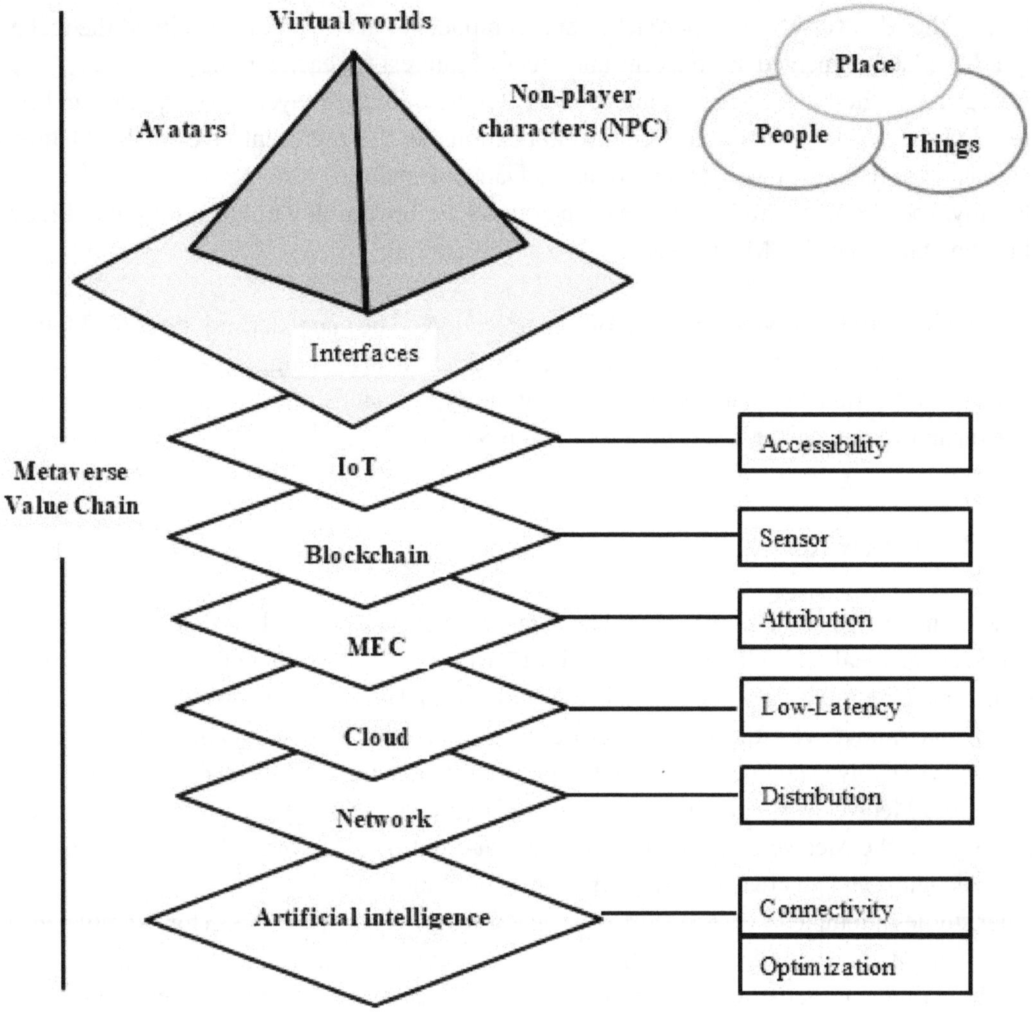

In 2021 and 2022, the Metaverse received a lot of public attention in Figure 1. It gained notoriety, which caused businesses, investors, and users to change their priorities. Investments in technologies connected to the Metaverse increased dramatically, and Metaverse tokens saw tremendous growth (Dolata & Schwabe, 2023). Additional symptoms include Facebook changing its name to Meta and Microsoft completing the largest takeover deal in history by buying a virtual reality (VR) startup for USD 68.7 billion.

The Metaverse's broad breadth makes it difficult for us to fully comprehend how it functions, why it is necessary, and what it is even capable of (Park & Kim, 2022). We need multidisciplinary cooperation and studies with the behavioural and social science research of the Metaverse to effectively address these issues.

These are the study's three primary contributions:

- We suggest a technological foundation for the metaverse that paves the route for its realization.

- Summarized technologies' proposed metaverse taxonomy is utilized to categorize laboratory studies. Hardware, software, contents, user interaction, executions, and apps make up our categorization of the Metaverse's key approaches and component parts. We have outlined the technologies that have lately emerged as concerns and areas of interest for each strategy.
- Using the methodology outlined above, we categorise Ready Player One, Roblox, and Facebook research in movies, video games, and publications as the representative of the Metaverse and characterize the most recent technological advancements.
- Finally, social effects, limitations, and open tasks are broken down into issues and directions for building an immersive Metaverse.

The rest of this study is divided into the following sections. The many definitions of the Metaverse and avatar are organised chronologically in Section 2. Section 3 lists and suggests the methods and materials are required, Section 4 concludes by discussing the experiment's results, our opinion, and proposed areas for further research. The answer is provided in Section 5.

2. RELATED WORKS

The present knowledge of the Metaverse is based on Generation Z societal views that the online persona is the same as the ideal self (Tlili et al., 2022). Furthermore, it is likely that electronic identities utilized online mirror and represents real identities discovered in actual physical settings found in online contexts. It is said that an innovative view is necessary because Generation Z's ascent and influence have caused the Metaverse to evolve and become distinct from what it once was. Additionally, as compared to prior versions of the Metaverse, the rapid advancement of mobile technology and deep learning has made it simpler to get to the Metaverse from anywhere and at any time, improved the precision of visual and linguistic recognition, and created settings that are more immersive.

Earlier studies attempted to use 3D virtual space to create creative artworks (for example, visualizing enigmatic concepts, communicating abstract biological genomics ideas, and testing new concepts (for instance, including abstract artworks in buildings) (Lee et al., 2021). 'Azimuth' seeks to present the new subject in simple-to-understand yet creative ways. The magic nature known as 'the Aleph' appears as a cyberspace entity in this work. Additionally, computational artists collaborate with scientists to present publicly accessible, aesthetically pleasing visualizations of genome sequencing data.

"A 3D-based augmented reality in which daily activities and economic life are conducted through avatars representing the real themselves," according to Go and his colleagues, is what they referred to as the Metaverse (Tlili et al., 2022). According to Lee and his coworkers, a "metaverse" is a setting where "social, economic, and cultural events are carried out in it to create value" and "virtual and reality interact and coevolve." These two definitions suggest that the Metaverse is more than just a merging of the physical and virtual worlds; rather, it is a continuation of the physical world within the virtual world to produce an ecosystem that combines both (physical and virtual) worlds.

A range of immersive technologies known as "Extended Reality" or "Cross Reality" (XR) generate electronic, digital settings where data are symbolised and displayed (Kaddoura & Al Husseiny, 2023). The three components of XR are VR, augmented reality (AR), and mixed reality (MR). People observe and interact with a fully or partially artificial digital space produced by technology in all XR aspects.

Virtual reality is an entirely artificial environment created digitally. Users behave similarly to how they would in the real world, feel because they are in another realm, and experience immersion.

In his book Snow Crash, Neal Stephenson introduced the concept of the "Metaverse," a setting where software agents and human avatars could interact in a three-dimensional virtual environment much as it would in the real world (Weinberger, 2022). There have been numerous manifestations of the idea of the metaverse, or online computer-mediated interaction that mimics offline interaction. Long before Instagram announced in 2021 that it would change its name to Meta; metaverses were known by names like MUDs (Multi-User Dungeons), Collaboration Virtual Environments (CVEs), Massively Multiplayer mode Online Role-Playing Games (MMORPGs), and open-ended 3D virtual worlds.

Data-driven intelligent urbanism and structure urbanism have given the globally operating platform companies the chance to advance individuals of thinking and create complex platforms as a result of the permeability of urban society by online platforms in terms of data infrastructures, financial procedures, and governance models (Bibri et al., 2022). One of these platforms is the enormous ecosystem application known as the Metaverse, which is powered by cutting-edge computers and immersive technology. Research in this area often focuses primarily on two strands, which are typical of the introduction of new highly disruptive technologies, given the current development phase of the Metaverse as a worldwide platform being introduced in 2021 by Meta.

The Metaverse is built on technologies that allow for multimodal conversations with digital individuals, things, and settings (Mystakidis, 2022). Stereoscopic displays that can transmit the sense of depth enable the computational quality of the XR system. With distinct and somewhat different representations for each eye that mimic sight in actual situations, this is feasible. High-resolution XR displays enable a large user field of vision that can range from 90 to 180 degrees. Compared to 2D systems, XR systems also provide greater aural experiences. The creation of soundscapes that notably improve immersion in AR and VR is made possible by 3D, spatial, or binaural sound.

Historically, Neal Stephenson's science fiction book Snow Crash, which was published in 1992, is credited with popularising the term "Metaverse." In Snow Crash, Stephenson imagined readers retreating into a virtual world to escape the harsh realities of a global economic collapse. Stephenson's works contain a variety of concepts and ideas, including as the use of "headsets" and "goggles" that allowed readers to immerse themselves in a hypothetical pre-VR world before spectacles and methods, driving the worldwide market for these goods in profitable directions (Allam et al., 2022).

In Narin (2021) an immersive user experience for the home automation system in virtual reality was made. They described the protocols required for the connections between the home server, metaverse client, and metaverse server. The best way to successfully define the brand's interface and incorporate their brand into the Metaverse, according to experts, is to choose target audiences, focus on their current behaviors and trends, conduct an updated competitive analysis of the metaverse adoption, look for natural variations to their current providing, and identify the best possibilities. But while the majority of businesses concentrate on the rewards and possible opportunities offered by the Metaverse, risk ought to be a key consideration.

Essentially, a person's avatar's mental or behavioral characteristics in the metaverse, such as confidence, communication, and comprehension, are determined by the metaverse's technological abilities, which also impact the quality of interactions between a person and his or her virtual (Chang et al., 2023). As a result, interaction and communication will be made easier and the virtual world of the metaverse will continue to improve, leading to a variety of outcomes. This is accomplished through the mental state and behavior of avatars. According to the concept, metaverse technologies need to be able to communicate, provide, communicate, and offer teamwork tools that can affect how people and their manifestations are represented in the multiverse, such as presence and engagement.

In Zhang et al. (2022) the digital twin offers a resource model for combining virtual and traditional schooling as well. Based on digital twin and VR visual recognition technology, along with the actual requirements of teaching rhythmic athletics, the author created an appropriate auxiliary teaching system to increase the efficiency of rhythmic gymnastics instruction. The authors created a machine learning and digital twin-based matching teacher ability rating model to research ways to enhance instructors' instructional skills.

3. METHODS AND MATERIALS

Based on contrasts of comparable concepts, this section explains the notions of the Metaverse, avatar, and extended reality (XR). The avatar is the user's alter ego and acts as the focal point in the virtual world known as the "Metaverse" (Dwivedi et al., 2022). The avatar is the user. XR serves as the conduit between users in the real world and characters in the Metaverse.

Figure 2. The metaverse's safety and privacy threats

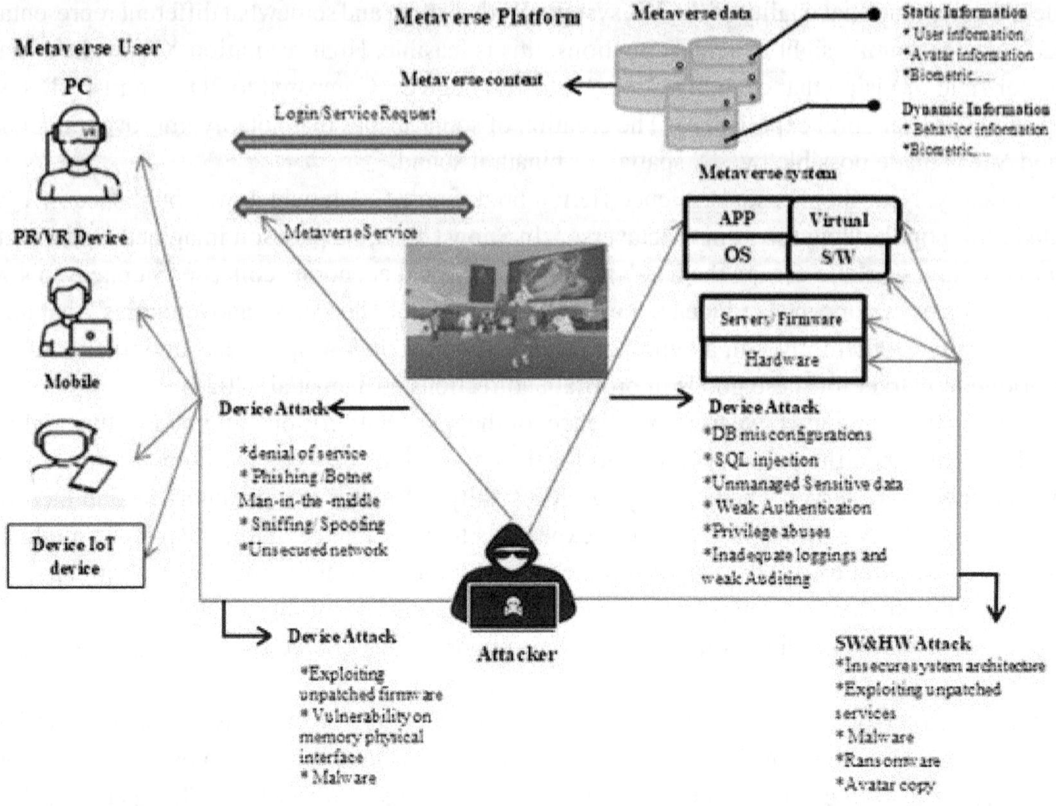

The Function of the Metaverse as a Tool

By accomplishing jobs that are difficult to conduct in the real world, such as investigating isolated locations, granting psychological assistance, and educating recruits for warfare, the metaverse strengthens the real world in numerous instances. It serves in the place of normal circumstances (including offices, SNS, in-person classes, and medical care) and permits actions that would be challenging or unattainable to accomplish in reality because of issues like an expense. As a kind of instrument, the virtual world minimizes complications (such as in aircraft technology) and enhances consistency compared with a multimodal perspective. Without bias or social discrimination, it is allowed to replicate social difficulties, moral disputes, and policy-related concerns. The multiverse is better suited for business for the reason client experience analysis is far more reliable than an assessment of surveys that depends on user feedback. Users commonly believe that they consume more water than usual when comparing it to soda intake; however, records of users preserved in the metaverse can assist with the genuine study. This section examines more specific possible safety risks and challenges, as shown in Figure 2.

Figure 3. Metaverse applications as a tool and a target

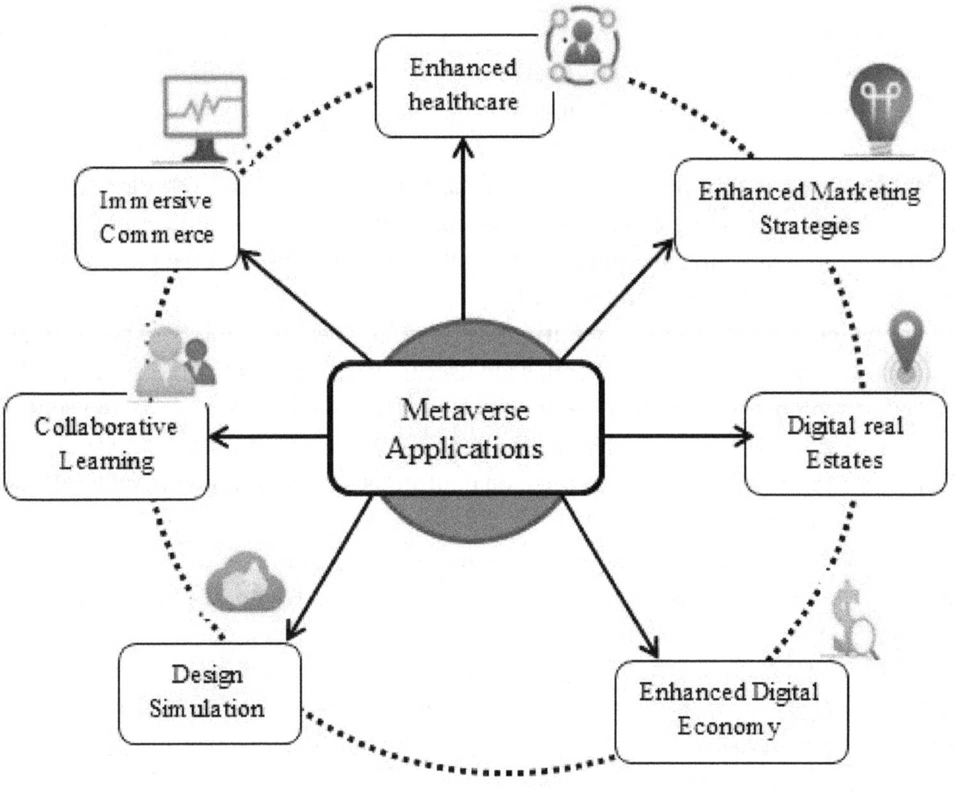

Uses

This current metaverse receives greater focus than previous versions because is more economically beneficial. The applications are classified as "metaverse as a technique" and "metaverse as a theory." as depicted in Figure 3. The phrase "metaverse as a tool" implies the consumption of the metaverse to deal with problems and challenges in the physical realm. The phrase "metaverse as a target" illustrates the way the virtual world itself can accomplish goals like spreading the metaverse as well as earning money. In comparison with "metaverse as a tool" apps, "metaverse as target" technologies are autonomous and highly dependent on the virtual world.

Metaverse as a Goal

The concept of the metaverse originally served as an algorithm for reflecting on physical reality, although, individuals recognized value and social relationships in the parallel universe.

Significant Problems and Possibilities Associated with Sustainability, Safety, and Cross-Disciplinary Suggestions

The realm of the metaverse provides advantages as well as challenges. The prior study has concentrated primarily on hardware (like HMDs) and software (like VR) applications. In the following paragraphs, we cover three viewpoints: environmental sustainability, assurance, and under-researched cross-disciplinary concerns.

Ecological Responsibility: The metaverse's managing framework requires a lot of patrons to function effectively to remain feasible, and flawless functions are reachable regardless of fairly fundamental handheld devices. Environmental planning involves taking the flexibility of the present moment limited ecosystem consideration for long-term reliability.

Robust Interface: The long-term viability of the virtual world is contingent on an interface that's easy to use. Holograms and eye-attached optics are useful modifications to both augmented reality and virtual reality. An additional comprehensive approach needs to be employed to give the consumer a real-time, accurate image (e.g., enhancing the display concentration for the intended portion). In addition, the HMDs investigate and take advantage of personal information concerning eye motion, concentration flashing, grinning, and orientation.

Durable Communication: The metaphysical universe needs communication to thrive. Debates between users and conversations with non-player characters (NPCs) are two distinct kinds of interaction. Through social networking, individuals generally interact with other individuals in their native language and English. Yet an application that roughly translates and offers natural expressions via interpretation is required for individuals who speak multiple languages to interact with a metaverse.

Privacy and Assurance: Although substantial studies on metaverse technology, privacy and security in the multiverse have drawn inadequate focus. In the realm of metaphysics, safety, and confidentiality are essential concerns, just like on social networking websites. To locate a user, attackers can track and accumulate real-time authentication methods (such as expressions on the face and vocal inflections) and metaverse user habits (such as their interactions with fellow users and purchasing movements).

Safeguarding Data: An individual's avatar, or substitute self-importance, develops numerous kinds of information in the virtual world, including secret details (such as messages, voicemails, and videos), proprietary knowledge utilized for a place of employment, and personally identifiable data that are needed for products and services to function. Security hazards to such information will consequently persist. It is conceivable to intentionally distort and breach private data and assets preserved in a virtual environment, metaverse platform, or application system.

Security: The metaphysical realm systems feature a far greater capacity for vulnerable data gathering than conventional mechanisms, which brings about a serious threat to user confidentiality. In the Metaverse, a renowned writer raised issues regarding privacy and suggested remedies, especially those associated with avatars and other components of the metaverse that don't end.

Software Protection: The safekeeping of the metaverse platform itself needs to be strengthened most of all. There are numerous diverse kinds of security concerns in the metaverse, just like there are within current software systems (such as vulnerable system design, unprotected software, malware, and ransomware). Additionally, there is the possibility that young people could be faced with violent or pornographic material. For instance, some hackers invaded Roblox, a sample metaverse. Hackers used ransomware to temporarily shut down the Roblox system and demanded payment in Robux, the game's virtual coin.

Hardware Security: Certain gadgets (such as HMDs, VR headsets, and IoT technologies) can be utilized for material authorization and identity. Without employing a login and password, they could enable clients to circumvent the requisite authorization and encryption procedures. Sensors might additionally be equipped with biometric data, which could also involve movement monitoring. As a consequence, fraudulent attackers can remotely supervise connected gadgets, seize a piece of specific device information (such as gaze knowledge, functions in the virtual world, etc.), or work together with the central management server in metaverse systems if they successfully hijack the user or administrator rights of the equipment using the security flaws of metaverse mobile phones.

Network Protection: Metaverse applications generally don't implement encryption for communication over networks, especially those between Avatars or from a user's gadget to the platform. Hackers may therefore employ sniffer or spoofing attempts on a virtual framework to intercept emails or obtain valuable data. Network connections, therefore, have to be encrypted by employing a reliable and efficient cryptographic algorithm, according to the data and circumstances at hand in the metaverse.

Difficulties and Possibilities: In the multiverse, secure and confidential information is essential. In the metaphysical context, they are considered vital elements that require to be continually controlled throughout every phase of the delivery process. That is, throughout initial implementation by performing decommissioning, security and privacy should be kept in account and regulated across management. We can stick to the "security by design" paradigm to adequately ensure security and privacy. "Safety by architecture" is a cyber-security plan that enables an enterprise to codify the framework of its construction projects implement its data security procedures, and become integrated security into its IT management procedures.

Constructing Trust Metric

Quantifying the reliability of an organization is denoted with the trust metric R. This measurement is an amalgamated measure that incorporates into consideration the four essential behavioral characteristics of honesty (O), reputation (E), cooperation (P), and competence (M). The trust score R_{nu}, which determines how trustworthy organization u is in the eyes of entity n, can be mathematically written as

$$R_{nu} = x_o O_{nu} + x_e E_{nu} + x_p P_{nu} + x_m M_{nu} \tag{1}$$

The terms x_o, x_e, x_p, and x_m in this formula believe for the proportional weights allocated to honesty, reputation, cooperation, and competence, respectively. This guarantees that x_o+x_e+x_p+x_m=1. The parameters that follow have been employed for evaluating those component's scores that form together the trust metric:

Honesty O_{nu}: The reliability of organization n as examined through u regarding p interactions can be measured by this attribute. It can be expressed mathematically as

$$O_{nu} = \frac{1}{q}\sum_{i=1}^{q} N_{nu}^{i} \tag{2}$$

Here, N_{nu}^{i} expresses the truthfulness of the i-th interaction of n with u. This is coded for various behaviours like honesty and dishonesty which means the codes are indicated as 0 and 1 respectively.

Reputation E_{nu}: This element captures what entity n is recognized by entity u, which is defined by n's interactions with all other entities u, with $m \neq u$

$$E_{nu} = \frac{1}{j}\sum_{m=1, m \neq u}^{j} R_{mn} \tag{3}$$

Here, the aggregate entities n has had interactions with which is symbolized as j.

Cooperativeness P_{nu}: The statistic indicates the possibility of entity n collaborating with entity u throughout s interactions:

$$P_{nu} = \frac{1}{s}\sum_{i=1}^{s} K_{nu}^{i} \tag{4}$$

With an overall rating of 1 for cooperative behavior and 0 for non-cooperation, K_{nu}^{i} in the formula reflects how cooperatively n performed throughout its i-th interaction with u, Competence M_{nu}: This element assesses an entity's capacity to supply u with high-quality service throughout s interactions:

$$M_{nu} = \frac{1}{s}\sum_{i=1}^{s} L_{nu}^{i} \tag{5}$$

In the present scenario, the expression "L_{nu}^{i}" indicates the standard of n's last interaction with u when measured by a reasonable quality metric. The allocation of weights for x_o, x_e, x_p, and x_m takes place to comply with the necessities and guidelines inherent to the multiverse circumstances.

The normalized honesty value throughout every instance is going to remain constant despite the component from which the network has been observed, imagining honesty is symmetric (i.e., N_{nu}=N_{un} for each interaction between n and u).

We must define O as the unchanging truth in every aspect, for that reason

$$O = \sum_{n=1}^{s} \sum_{u=1,u\neq n}^{s} O_{nu}$$

Assuming through the symmetry,

$$O = \sum_{n=1}^{s} \sum_{u=1,u\neq n}^{s} O_{un}$$

Which is further reduces to

$$O / s^2 = O' / s^2$$

As a consequence, honesty tends to remain uniform throughout every entity.

The boundary of [0, 1] is present in each of the components O_{nu}, E_{nu}, P_{nu}, and M_{nu}. Due to that

$$x_o + x_e + x_p + x_m = 1$$

If each one of these variables is at its highest point, R_{nu} will attain the highest possible value, leading to

$$R_{nu,max} = x_o + x_e + x_p + x_m = 1$$

The trust ratings of entities that have greater launching trust levels will be more adversely affected by adjustments to the assigned weights of the reliability score aspects stipulated that every single one of the trust ratings is calibrated to 1.

When you do a slight variation α in weight x*o* then it will end up resulting in an alteration in the trust score since $Rn_{u=}On_{u.}$ Providing

$$R_{nu} = x_o O_{nu} + x_e E_{nu} + x_p P_{nu} + x_m M_{nu}$$

and because

$$x_o + x_e + x_p + x_m = 1$$

It is present as

$$O_{nu} = \left(R_{nu} - x_e E_{nu} - x_p P_{nu} - x_m M_{nu} \right) / x_o$$

triggering a modification in the trust score that is proportional

$$\alpha R_{nu} / R_{nu} = \alpha / \left(1 - x_e E_{nu} / R_{nu} - x_p P_{nu} / R_{nu} - x_m M_{nu} / R_{nu}\right)$$

Taking into account these parameters eliminate a smaller amount out of the denominator, it can be observed that the change in relative value is bigger for entities that have greater beginning trust scores.

Method for Distributing Resources

Trust scores are extremely important to the computational resource management methodology. In order to confirm that the allocation of resources R is in line with the associated trust scores, we add a fairness coefficient v_n that assumes a mechanism for regulation. The mathematical expression of the computing energy provided to entity n is

$$E_n = E_{total} \times V_n \times \frac{R_n}{\sum_{u=1}^{s} R_u} \tag{6}$$

In the above formula, the value of the denominator reflects the whole trust scores of every single entity, R_n corresponds to the entity n's trust score, and E_{total} symbolizes the total computational assets that are now accessible.

The fairness component V_n is estimated through the logistical equation that creates an effortless change that is flexible, encouraging better resource allocation for entities with trust scores that are significantly greater than the average (Guo & Gao, 2022). The expression of this function is

$$V_n = \frac{1}{1 + e^{-\gamma\left(R_n - R_{avg}\right)}} \tag{7}$$

In this expression, R_{avg} indicates for the mean trust score, γ is an adaptable element that adjusts the curve's steepness, and f is the organic logarithm's base. The implementation of the fairness coefficient culminates in an equitable and proportionate allocation technique, fostering equity to motivate constructive behavior inside the metaverse.

V_n is the fairness coefficient which is indicated as

$$V_n = \frac{1}{1 + e^{-\gamma\left(R_n - R_{avg}\right)}} \tag{8}$$

The exponent's value starts to decrease as R_n advances, leading to $e^{-\gamma\left(R_n - R_{avg}\right)}$ to minimize. As an outcome, the denominator's total worth reduces, which improves the value of V_n.

Exponent turns into 0 and V_n examines to 0.5 in which $R_n = R_{avg}$.

$$V_n = \frac{1}{1 + e^0} = \frac{1}{1 + 1} = \frac{1}{2} \tag{9}$$

R_n Generally approaches the integer infinity, $e^{-\gamma(R_n - R_{avg})}$ goes to zero, and V_n moves to one in the following manner:

$$\lim_{R_n \to +\infty} V_n = \frac{1}{1+0} = 1 \tag{10}$$

R_n Generally approaches the negative infinity, $e^{-\gamma(R_n - R_{avg})}$ goes to infinity, and V_n moves to 0.5 which is indicated in the below expression:

$$\lim_{R_n \to -\infty} V_n = \frac{1}{1+\infty} = \frac{1}{\infty} = 0 \tag{11}$$

Improvement of Performance and the Prevention of Latency

TBRA attempts to minimize latency and boost metaverse functionality by allowing resources from reliable entities. It assures that sustainable corporations receive the instruments they require to manage efficient operations, eliminating possible bottlenecks that lead to noteworthy latency. An organization n's latency A has an inverse correlation with the resources E_n it has been supplied, and it can be characterized as

$$A_n = \frac{\beta}{E_n} \tag{12}$$

where β is a fixed value that varies depending on specific parameters of the metaverse environment. By E_n the derivative of A_n is thought as

$$\frac{dA_n}{dE_n} = -\frac{\beta}{E_n^2} \tag{13}$$

E_n is positive, hence any positive number's square, E_n^2, also happens to be positive. As a consequence, the derived value $\frac{dA_n}{dE_n}$ is negative, suggesting that A_n shrinks as E_n improves. Thus, the theorem is established.

Justification. Since E_n approaches infinity the limit of A_n is assumed as:

$$\lim_{E_n \to +\infty} A_n = \lim_{E_n \to +\infty} \frac{\beta}{E_n} = 0 \tag{14}$$

This points out that the latency encountered by an entity decreases gradually to zero as the assets assigned to it increase arbitrarily big. Let's get started now to investigate the overall latency minimization rate. The derived value of A_n in conjunction with E_n is

$$\frac{dA_n}{dE_n} = -\frac{\beta}{E_n^2} \tag{15}$$

The magnitude of this rate diminishes as E_n expands which suggests that the postponement A_n simplifies at a declining rate as supplies expand. This rate of transformation resembles a hyperbolic decay framework.

Reliable Resource Collaborating on for Computers

By correlating the distribution of resources with entity credibility, the TBRA methodology promises a secure operating platform. Resources are removed from entities getting involved with malicious activity or falling short to perform their agreements, boosting a safe virtual world. This connection can be expressed in the unique model as

$$\Delta E_n = -\delta \Delta \mathrm{R}n \tag{16}$$

where ΔR_n is the change in entity n's trust score, ΔE_n is the change in resources assigned to it, and δ is a proportionality constant. The safeguarding of the metaverse as an entire entity n is assured by this equation, which indicates how entities participating in threatening behavior will have their resources dropped.

Considering the connection

$$\Delta E_n = -\delta \Delta \mathrm{R}n \tag{17}$$

For a particular entity n, any changes to its trust score ΔR_n will lead to a modification to the allocation of its resources ΔE_n which is directly correlated to R_n with the proportionality constant $-\delta$.

Let us say ΔR_n<0 (i.e., entity n's trust rating sinks). If we apply this to our bond, we figure out that

$$\Delta E_n = -\delta\left(-\left|\Delta R_n\right|\right) = \delta\left|\Delta R_n\right| > 0 \tag{18}$$

On the other hand, assuming that ΔR_n>0 (i.e., entity n's trust score grows). When we implement this to the bond we share, we observe that

$$\Delta E_n = -\delta \mathrm{I} \Delta \mathrm{R}n_{\mathrm{I}} < 0 \tag{19}$$

The aforementioned results show that a drop in trust score leads to an equivalent increase in resources allocated, and inversely. By modifying resource allocation as a consequence of modifications in trust scores, the trustworthiness-based resource allocation (TBRA) methodology encourages trustworthy computing circumstances.

Decreased Latency Based on Credibility

The third component of our plan of action is a reputation-based procedure constructed to tackle metaverse latency issues. The basic premise behind this mechanism is to continuously track how different entities function and give esteem feedback correspondingly. These scores for credibility are then used for resource allocation and latency supervision, and Algorithm 2 showcases every step of the method.

Analysis of Reputation Score

By examining its historical latency information an n entity's reliability score, authorized as E_n, is established. The score given here reflects how well the entity executes with regard to of latency as time passes. We compute this achievement using the formula given below:

$$E_n(r) = \frac{1}{S}\sum_{m=1}^{S} A_{n,u} \tag{20}$$

Where $A_{n,u}$ the latency of the m-th interaction and S is the aggregate amount of interactions the entity n has experienced up to time r.

The Digital Society and the Metaverse

Access to the metaverse, a completely immersive digital environment, is made possible by an avatar with a virtual time-space continuum. The metaverse architecture, which integrates the digital, human, and physical worlds, is shown in Figure 4 in a very thorough manner.

Figure 4. Integration of the human and physical worlds with digital realms in a metaverse architecture

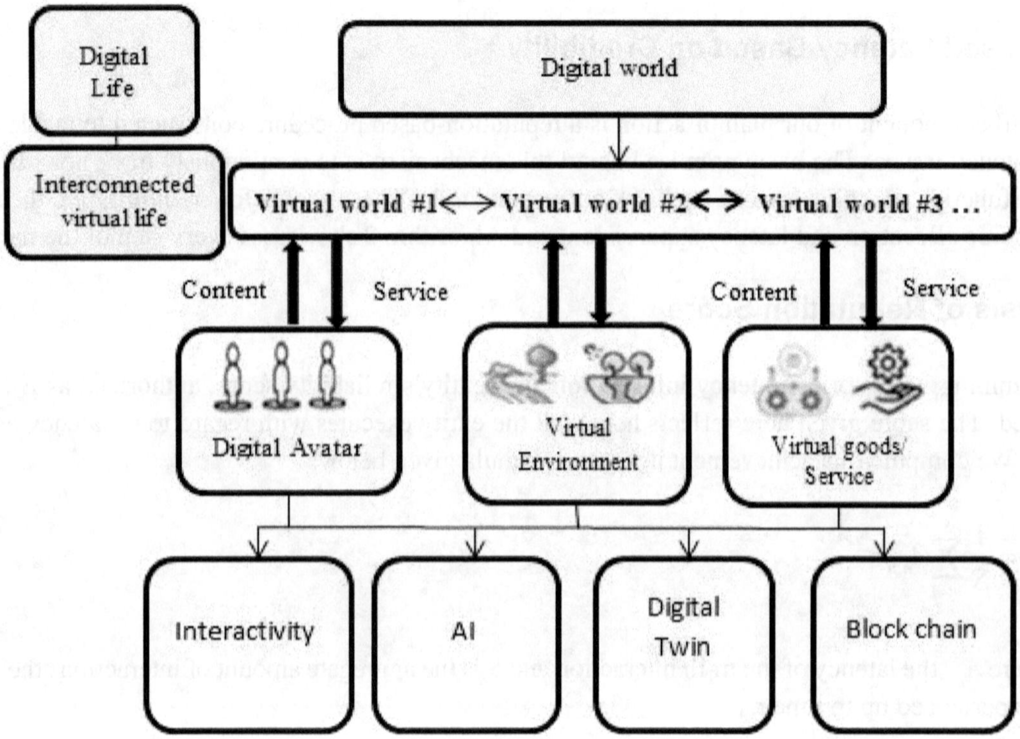

The metaverse, which offers more logical means of interacting between people and technology (Sá & Serpa, 2023), will alter the future and even human beings. The metaverse will link people's physical and digital representations in the virtual and physical worlds, as well as their many modes of contact and interaction.

In the metaverse, communication flits back and forth between the physical world and the digital one. The procedure can get more complicated when people interact virtually while conversing physically in the same location. This occurs when people switch between online and offline contexts and vice versa. The metaverse, which provides more logical ways for humans and technology to interact, will change the future and even individuals. The physical and digital representations of individuals in the virtual and real worlds, as well as their many means of communication and interaction, will be connected via the metaverse. The physical world and the digital one is frequently in touch with one another in the metaverse. When people converse literally in the same place while interacting electronically, the process can become more challenging. This happens when users go back and forth between offline and online settings.

Technologies for the Metaverse Framework

The multidisciplinary ecosystem known as the Metaverse was developed by integrating several other technologies into various layers of its overall architecture. A 3D rendition of the current internet is available. Several elements interact between the real and virtual worlds in a metaverse scenario. Customers are one of the most important elements among them. A user can engage with the virtual worlds using a variety of gadgets, such as head-mounted displays or AR/VR glasses.

Users are able to interact and carry out various tasks virtually thanks to these devices. The relationship between the physical and virtual worlds also relies on IoT networks that virtual service providers (VSPs), and physical service providers (PSPs) (Ali et al., 2023). Digital twins are created using data that is gathered from the physical world using IoT and sensor networks. The physical service providers (PSPs) and virtual service providers (VSPs) support the upkeep of the metaverse's virtual and physical settings. Figure 5 and the discussion that follows discuss a few of those vital technologies.

Figure 5. Building block of Metaverse

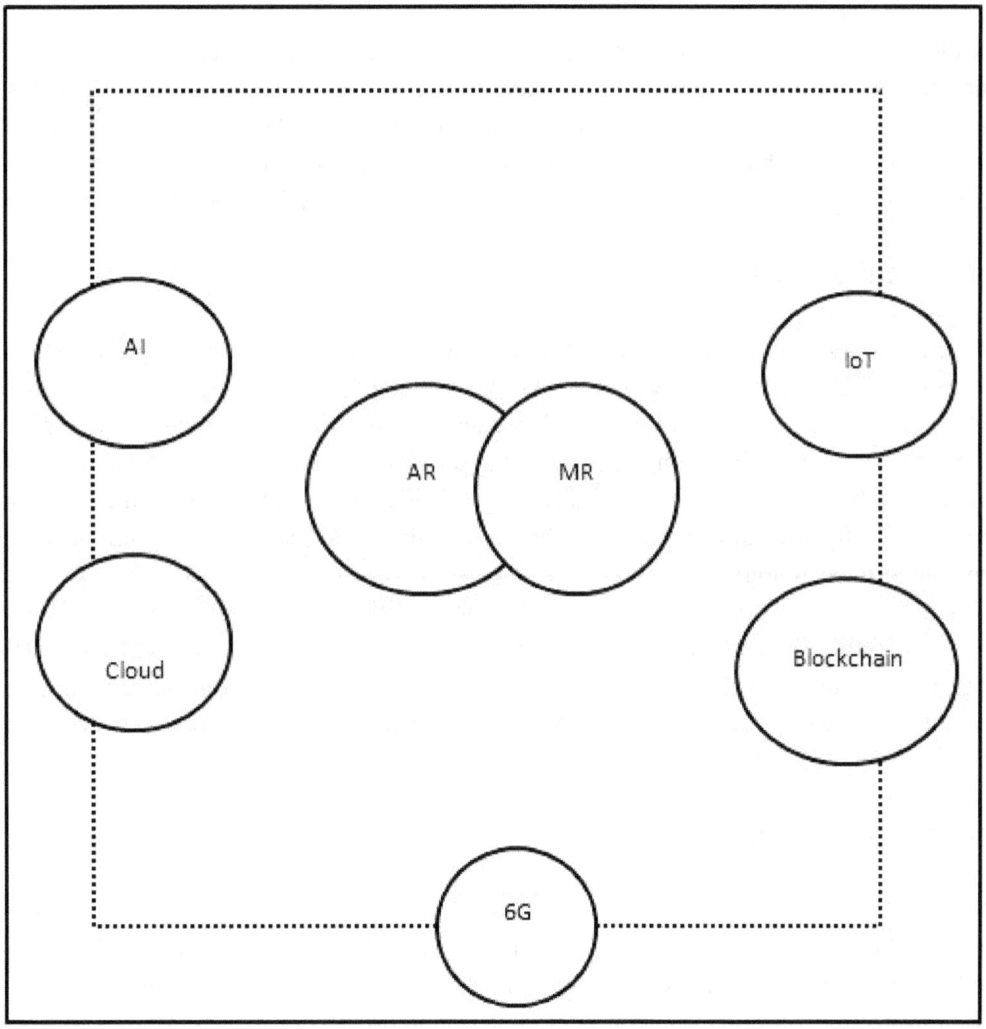

Virtual Reality (VR)

With the assistance of VR glasses or a display mounted on the head (HMD), consumers of virtual reality (VR) can recreate a moment. Using software and hardware elements, allows consumers to completely immerse themselves within a 3D digital environment. Furthermore, it delivers cutting-edge technological capabilities and a smooth and rich experience enabling people in the virtual universe to be in control of the moment. Despite virtual reality (VR) infrastructure is not an innovative concept, it became quite common when the parallel universe was created. In 2016, there was a total of 2.3 billion USD invested in VR businesses; by 2025, that amount is predicted to climb to 20.9 billion USD. Technological titans like Google, Meta (formerly Facebook), Apple, HTC, Sony, and many more are researching VR hardware which involves haptic gloves, optical trackers, 3D mice, movement controllers' omnidirectional treadmills (ODts), etc.

These electronic devices have outstanding characteristics such as the embedded CPUs as well as the all-in-one performance of the Oculus Quest 2. Many countries, including China, the United States, South Korea, and Japan, have chosen to focus on the VR industry as a crucial technological advancement area with the possibility for enhancing their total savings. VR technology is currently administered in the medical field for surgeries, physiotherapy, anxiety and discomfort relief, cognitive rehabilitation, etc.

Extended Reality (XR)

VR, AR, and mixed reality (MR) all have been incorporated underneath the umbrella term "extended reality." All blended virtual and tangible settings are included. In 1960, the extended reality initially appeared in the context of historical events. Subsequently, literally every industry, including mining, healthcare, manufacturing, education, etc., employs significant use of this modern technology. It delivers an enormous number of apps and a ton of difficulty levels in a simulated environment. Subsequently, literally every industry, including mining, healthcare, manufacturing, education, etc., employs significant use of this modern technology.

It delivers an enormous number of apps and a ton of difficulty levels in the virtual world. Three primary virtual reality method categories have been utilized in the healthcare industry: haptic device simulators, head-mounted displays (HMDs), and computer-based simulations. Haptic simulators were the most widely utilized and appreciated of these three technologies, which is why they are commonly used during surgeries and other therapies for patients.

AR: Augmented Reality

One of the innovations that have altered how the universe displays is what's known as augmented reality. Augmented reality (AR), basically merges with manmade items with virtual overlays, and boosts the user's understanding of the genuine surroundings. In other senses, the concept of augmented reality is the process of introducing digital information to the physical world by overlaying digital images on top of it.

Pokemon Go, which enables us to explore the world around us via our smartphones and may overlay digital characters, is one of the most successful manifestations of augmented reality. Similar to this, users utilize numerous Snapchat filters to improve our physical appearances in their social media pictures such as bunny ears, multiple kinds of cosmetics, etc.

When they want to do surgery, surgeons and medical professionals make use of augmented reality, which supplements the body section that requires surgical attention and aids them throughout the process. By integrating 3D patient images over real pictures of the surgical area, the visualization is strengthened. With outstanding precision, it assists in patient survival. Several well-known AR technologies are the Magic Leap, Google Glass, and Microsoft's HoloLens.

Networking and the Internet of Things

To enable users to link and interact with an enormous variety of devices, including smart watches, smartphones, healthcare equipment, etc., the IoT supplies a broad spectrum of innovations, including sensors, wireless networks, and nanotechnology. IoT along with additional technologies are altering human existence in addition to enhancing everyday activities. This improves our standards of life as a consequence. It frequently gets used in healthcare, allowing patients and physicians access to facilities.

Because of the use of various IoT devices, individuals can be electronically tracked, enhancing the standard of healthcare while decreasing expenditures. The ecological system of the metaverse is contingent upon this advanced technology. By embracing IoT methods, the meta verse's possibilities get enhanced. Virtual service vendors will be able to bring together the digital twins mainly to the IoT devices' impulses to collect and perceive the physical condition of the assets.

Edge Computing

The latest concept in processing is edge/cloud computing, where processing duties have been carried out at the boundary of the network. Through the implementation of this approach, computing resources will be delivered closer to the source of the data. The increase of data volume continues to grow day by day as an outcome of the IoT and peripheral devices.

As a direct consequence, there are additionally several kinds of difficulties, including data privacy, energy consumption, security issues, and bottlenecks in real-time operations. Edge computing is a new computation mode that is nearer to the boundary of the network equipment, was presented as a solution to these obstacles. It promotes data optimization, security and privacy, and real-time business.

Artificial Intelligence

The extensively used technique of AI has implications for a broad spectrum of business sectors, including manufacturing, human resources, agriculture, healthcare, and business. Robots can mimic the human brain through the use of artificial intelligence, which additionally enables them to acquire knowledge from their experiences just like people do. It performs different duties according to experience. Machine learning, deep learning, computer vision, and many more subfields are all part of artificial intelligence. Supervised learning, unsupervised learning, and reinforcement training are the three categories of computational learning, which is one of the many branches of AI.

While unsupervised learning and reinforcement learning are used for unlabeled data, supervised learning needs labeled data in order to train the model. A particular type of machine learning termed deep learning incorporates neural networks patterned after biological neurons. Beginning with the data, deep learning generates characteristics. In addition, it requires greater quantities of information than traditional machine learning methods do.

The main piece of technology that will develop, support, and aid in the actualization of the metaverse concept is AI. Machine learning, reinforcement learning, computer vision, deep learning etc. are a few instances of artificial intelligence algorithms that serve as the "key" to integrating the gap that exists between the virtual and physical worlds. Artificial intelligence technologies permit the parallel universe to get involved in economic and social activities that transcend the real world in a secure and free manner.

Electronic Twin

A digital twin is a replica of an actual object in digital form. In the virtual world, a synthetic replica of real objects is made. It is currently used to a variety of industries, which comprises production, medical care, and smart city development. The actual product, its digital procreation or virtual equivalent, and the transfer of data between the real and virtual objects constitute the three primary components of this sort of technology. The digital twin was crucial in the field of health care during the COVID-19 pandemic. Wearable technology, such as cellphones, permitted healthcare professionals to visually observe patients while capturing their essential measures, such as blood pressure, temperature, and heart rate.

Machine Learning

A machine is able to notice and recognize images because of computer vision. It permits XR devices to identify and understand visual data from real-world surroundings, aiding in the development of virtual environments. The recreation of 3D objects in the internet is made achievable by the incorporation of this kind of technology in large-scale AR/VR and XR apps. A more effectively and efficiently precise user experience in a 3D immersive world is now being built in the multiverse leveraging computer vision-based algorithms. Implementing one of the most sophisticated methodologies, such as Mask RCNN, YOLO, etc., computer vision algorithms can carry out object recognition, object classification, object categorization, and object localization with great reliability. Since avatars must have the ability to detect and comprehend the habits of other fictional characters, computer vision may also be employed for identifying movements and gestures, which somewhat additionally constitute crucial parts of the multiverse.

Blockchain

A distributed ledger, or blockchain technology, is composed of consecutive blocks attached to each other and carrying the value of the hash of the previous block's header. It makes use of electronic signatures for storing data in a decentralized network. All data which has been recorded is not capable of modification. Although blockchain technology is primarily utilized in the banking industry, it can additionally be relevant to other industries, such as asset tracking, risk management, education, cyber security, healthcare, and social services.

Blockchain in the realm of metaphysics can be made use for medical purposes to safeguard patient data confidentially. Enhancing the confidentiality of a patient's medical record as an outcome Data on the individual which has been preserved in the blockchain cannot be altered or deleted. It also simplifies the administration of computerized healthcare data and promotes quicker and cheaper therapies for patients. Furthermore, the program provides instruments for seamless integration, integrity, data security, and data collaborate.

With enhanced network safety, blockchain technology regulates every communication throughout the physical and virtual worlds. For the purpose of keeping track of everything that you do, all the trading platforms are additionally captured. This characteristic in blockchain technology empowers healthcare professionals to immediately examine and fully understand patients' medical histories.

Avatar

The Hindi word "Avatar" refers to the Hindu god's physical manifestation as a person or animal in the real world. Humans appear as virtual avatars in the metaverse that are exact replicas of real people. Users have the option to change their avatars' appearance in any way they see fit. A scenario in a sophisticated game, like Fortnite, serves as a good illustration. Avatars have been employed in the healthcare industry to offer patient monitoring, therapy, testing, and instructional training for nurses, doctors, and other medical professionals. It improves visualization in a virtual setting, enabling surgeons to carry out intricate surgeries with ease.

Virtual Stitching and Fitting Technology: Its Basis and Uses

To accomplish the virtual simulation of apparel modeling layout, three-dimensional apparel casting involves virtual simulation studies for designer costumes. The virtual simulation, virtual sewing, clothing distortion limitation management, and crash recognition of two-dimensional chopping elements can be implemented using costume clothes sewing, design, and fitting. The technological device may promote the exchange of created and well-established styles, color matching, layout dispersion, etc. At the same time, virtual reality programs use two-dimensional cutting technology In order to accomplish human body collision identification and accomplish the procedure for the transformation of two-dimensional cutting components to three-dimensional elements, 2-dimensional chopping components are utilized for digital sewing.

The aforementioned virtual stitching technology is right now extremely widespread in China: Shanghai Jiana Textile Technology Co., Ltd., French Ooster Company, and Korea Crow Company created the Clothing Layout Optimization 3D virtual tailoring software, that somewhat is a virtual stitching solution for clothing. It develops smart merchandise design software that involves virtual stitching, human body scans, and modeling presentation. The German Assyst technology has been separated into multiple components which enable precise 2-D cutting and drawing.

The seamless interaction between the three-dimensional scanning table and the three-dimensional modeling is made achievable by the computerized weaving of items, the digital trying-on of three-dimensional apparel, and the MTM tailor-made technology coupled with anthropometric measurement data. For an amalgamated and better observing position, augmented reality (AR) technology superimposes virtual items on real objects using three-dimensional technology. In accordance with virtual reality (VR) technology, augmented reality (AR) technology effortlessly combines real-world objects with digital virtual data and makes use of the design features of computer-related software to bring online technologies to the reality of life.

To improve the impact of augmented reality via communication with the external environment, augmented reality (AR) technology overlays electronic simulated data and real-world objects into the identical viewpoint area, permitting learners to find virtual pictures and data in a real-world setting. The greater the extent to which the real world and electronic data cross over, the more vital it is for learners to actively engage in conversations and the more successful the educational environment's augmented reality is. Holographic glasses and other electronic devices are often utilized in AR technology to boost the realistic feel and proportionality of education and to comprehend data as well as surrounding environments.

In this section, it is crucial to differentiate clearly among MR, AR, and VR methodologies. Since AR technology is built on VR technology, the physical and virtual worlds are more closely connected. Embedding the physical environment in the technology of computers means overlapping real objects upon an image generated by software so that a third party can view both virtual objects and the real world. The amalgamation of the imaginary and tangible can more successfully showcase the numerous advantages of AR technology and improve the reality effect.

Through the process of a combination of real-world environments, MR technology is going to perform visualization simulations employing the corresponding virtual reality and augmented reality innovations. In simple terms, virtual reality (VR) technology has its foundation in an imaginary setting, augmented reality (AR) methodology combines digital and physical worlds, and mixed reality (MR) technology is an improvement in conjunction with modifications that further boosts interactive behavior.

Figure 6. Variations and interconnections among the three VR, AR, and MR methodologies

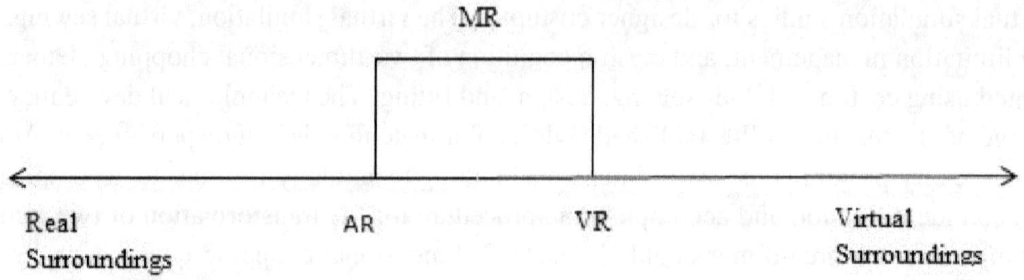

Figure 6 highlights the variations and interconnections amongst all three VR, AR, and MR techniques. It is evident that, in terms of efficiency, *AR+VR<MR*. This MR technology is an advancement and incorporation of virtual reality and augmented reality technologies and their hardware.

4. IMPLEMENTATION AND EXPERIMENTAL PARTS

The establishment of the interactive portal for art design education will convert art design works into digital cultural expressions.

Table 1. Detailed score for system interaction

Sample Set	Proposed Method	BPNN
200	81.47	79.3
300	77.95	69.64
400	90.73	79.77
500	76.88	67.5
600	77.57	71.48
700	94.13	81.34
800	97.69	87.79
900	97.99	87.02

Table 1 displays the interactive score results derived from the created VR modeling system.

Figure 7. Score for system interaction

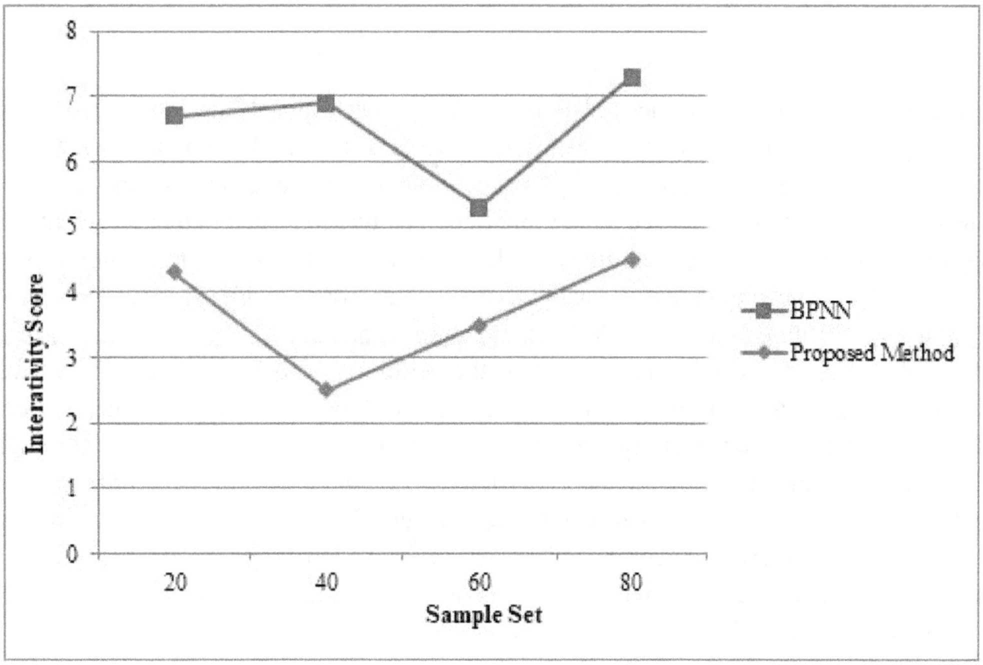

Figure 7 indicates that this platform has improved communication and a better user experience in comparison to other methods. Smaller feature maps recommend that a greater number of details about the image are lost due to multiple levels of output characteristic maps having different sizes. If just the outcome of a single layer is utilized as the coding result, it is not advantageous for the entire network to get maximal use of feature data since the output feature map of a single layer is comparatively single in scale and the abstract grade of characteristics is steady.

Figure 8. Developing the algorithm

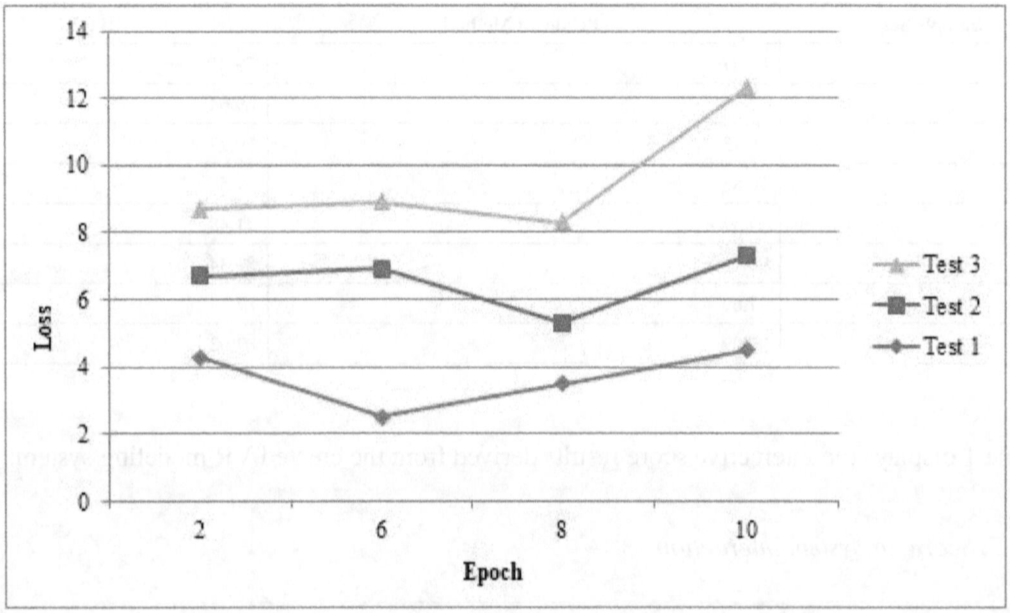

Semantic data is progressively encoded as network component levels are introduced, suggesting a decline in the geographic accuracy of the feature map while a boost in the channel size. A high degree of semantic information has been projected by the decoding unit to the target domain space, revealing a spike in feature map resolution and an overall reduction in feature map stream measurement. The actual depth map matching the input image should be made visible during DNN training as monitoring data. In the trial phase, DNN determines the relevant depth map in accordance with the input test image. Figure 8 demonstrates the learning phase of the VR visualization algorithm.

Under the visual 3D reconstruction procedures, the depth map and camera's internal as well as external citation matrices can be used to recreate three-dimensional point clouds, efficiently converting the depth maps spatial coordinates to the 3D point cloud's. The level of accuracy of the calibration of the cameras internal and external component matrices, in conjunction with the depth map's effectiveness, is what determines how well clouds can be reproduced. Both the internal and external parameter matrices for a specific camera photography technology are locked in, rendering the overall performance of the depth map the key variable limiting the precision of 3D point cloud reconstruction. The error of the algorithm is demonstrated in Table 2.

Table 2. Comparison of errors using an algorithm

Repetitions	Advanced Technique	BPNN
41	0.730	0.699
81	0.744	0.67
121	0.729	0.54
161	0.655	0.51
201	0.626	0.467
241	0.645	0.415
281	0.603	0.366

The weaknesses across multiple techniques demonstrate a fewer patterns during training as rapidly as achievable, although the VR visualization exploration presented in this paper has clear advantages.

Table 3. Comparison of accuracy using algorithms

Repetitions	Advanced Technique	BPNN
41	82.97	93.68
81	82.3	94.05
121	83.73	93.42
161	83.52	93.74
201	83.31	97.32
241	73.77	95.43
281	85.78	92.26

The output feature maps across numerous layers of the generator are utilized as input in this approach, and the geographical grouping of the attribute maps from various layers and the multi-level feature clustering are the outcomes that make the technology combination achievable. The modeling precision of the approach is highlighted in Table 3 and Figure 9.

Figure 9. Algorithm accuracy comparisons

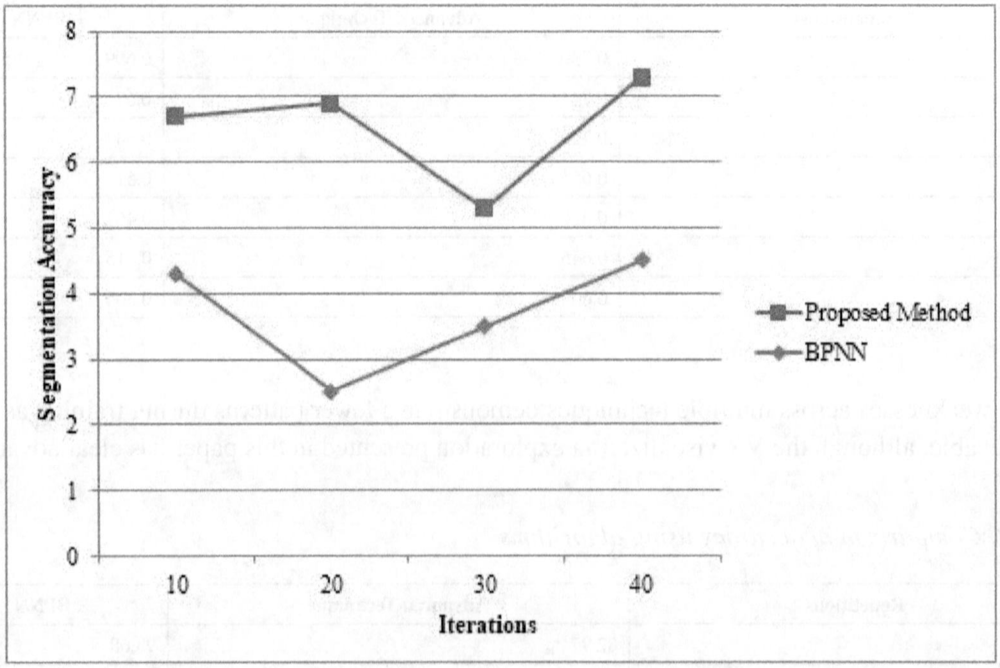

The graphic knowledge evidence that the precision of this approach is greater than 95% is known here. Every single neuron is utilized during network forecasting, which may be considered an amalgamation of the multiple networks formed while learning.

Figure 10. Comparing the percentage of incorrect pixels in every picture

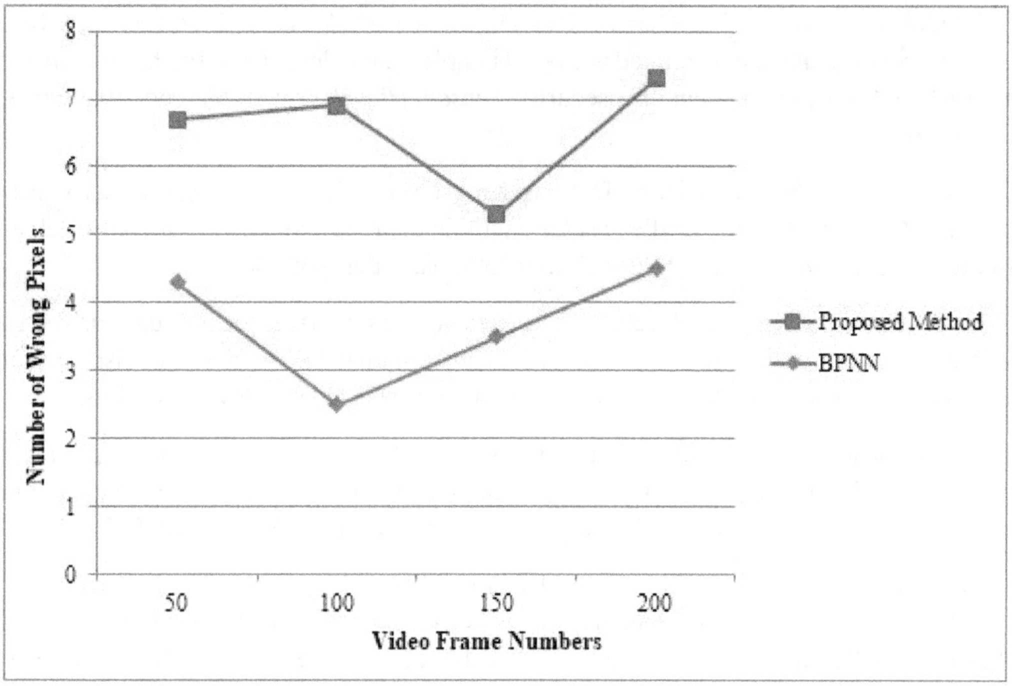

Figure 10 renders it clear that, for a significant number of video frames, the categorization outcomes of the VR visualization model used in this paper are greater compared to those derived from different approaches.

5. CONCLUSION

The metaverse, which was created as an imitation of the natural world, offers an appropriate working environment for researchers in all subjects, from health to activities, from education to the arts, and it covers all topics linked to people and society. This study investigates academic studies and deals with the scientific side of metaverse studies. The concept of the metaverse has been explained in most papers in the literature. Some have imagined the interactions between sociocultural conversations, faith, artwork, and learning throughout the metaverse, while some have implemented metaverse applications in certain fields. This study looked at academic studies carried out in the last 20 years concurrent with technological advancements like 3D, AR, and VR.

In this article, an artificial intelligence and CAD-based VR visualization model is built in Metaverse to enhance Italian design education both theoretically and practically. The experimental findings demonstrate that this method's modelling accuracy is greater than 95%, surpassing that of the contrasting algorithm.

REFERENCES

Ali, S., Abdullah, Armand, T. P. T., Athar, A., Hussain, A., Ali, M., Yaseen, M., Joo, M.-I., & Kim, H.-C. (2023). Metaverse in healthcare integrated with explainable ai and blockchain: Enabling immersiveness, ensuring trust, and providing patient data security. *Sensors (Basel)*, *23*(2), 565. doi:10.339023020565 PMID:36679361

Allam, Z., Sharifi, A., Bibri, S. E., Jones, D. S., & Krogstie, J. (2022). The metaverse as a virtual form of smart cities: Opportunities and challenges for environmental, economic, and social sustainability in urban futures. *Smart Cities*, *5*(3), 771–801. doi:10.3390martcities5030040

Bibri, S. E., Allam, Z., & Krogstie, J. (2022). The Metaverse as a virtual form of data-driven smart urbanism: Platformization and its underlying processes, institutional dimensions, and disruptive impacts. *Computational Urban Science*, *2*(1), 24. doi:10.100743762-022-00051-0 PMID:35974838

Chang, V., Strittmatter, S., Jesus, V., Golightly, L., Ni, P., & Hall, K. (2023, April). Exploring Risks in the Metaverse in an Immersive Digital Economy. In *5th International Conference on Finance, Economics, Management and IT Business* (pp. 107-113). SciTePress. 10.5220/0011990900003494

Dwivedi, Y. K., Hughes, L., Baabdullah, A. M., Ribeiro-Navarrete, S., Giannakis, M., Al-Debei, M. M., Dennehy, D., Metri, B., Buhalis, D., Cheung, C. M. K., Conboy, K., Doyle, R., Dubey, R., Dutot, V., Felix, R., Goyal, D. P., Gustafsson, A., Hinsch, C., Jebabli, I., ... Wamba, S. F. (2022). Metaverse beyond the hype: Multidisciplinary perspectives on emerging challenges, opportunities, and agenda for research, practice and policy. *International Journal of Information Management*, *66*, 102542. doi:10.1016/j.ijinfomgt.2022.102542

Guo, H., & Gao, W. (2022). Metaverse-powered experiential situational English-teaching design: An emotion-based analysis method. *Frontiers in Psychology*, *13*, 859159. doi:10.3389/fpsyg.2022.859159 PMID:35401297

Kaddoura, S., & Al Husseiny, F. (2023). The rising trend of Metaverse in education: Challenges, opportunities, and ethical considerations. *PeerJ. Computer Science*, *9*, e1252. doi:10.7717/peerj-cs.1252 PMID:37346578

Lee, L. H., Braud, T., Zhou, P., Wang, L., Xu, D., Lin, Z., . . . Hui, P. (2021). *All one needs to know about metaverse: A complete survey on technological singularity, virtual ecosystem, and research agenda.* arXiv preprint arXiv:2110.05352.

Lee, L. H., Lin, Z., Hu, R., Gong, Z., Kumar, A., Li, T., . . . Hui, P. (2021). *When creators meet the metaverse: A survey on computational arts.* arXiv preprint arXiv:2111.13486.

Mystakidis, S. (2022). Metaverse. *Encyclopedia*, *2*(1), 486–497. doi:10.3390/encyclopedia2010031

Narin, N. G. (2021). A content analysis of the metaverse articles. *Journal of Metaverse*, *1*(1), 17–24.

Park, S. M., & Kim, Y. G. (2022). A metaverse: Taxonomy, components, applications, and open challenges. *IEEE Access : Practical Innovations, Open Solutions*, *10*, 4209–4251. doi:10.1109/ACCESS.2021.3140175

Sá, M. J., & Serpa, S. (2023). Metaverse as a learning environment: Some considerations. *Sustainability (Basel)*, *15*(3), 2186. doi:10.3390u15032186

Tlili, A., Huang, R., Shehata, B., Liu, D., Zhao, J., Metwally, A. H. S., Wang, H., Denden, M., Bozkurt, A., Lee, L.-H., Beyoglu, D., Altinay, F., Sharma, R. C., Altinay, Z., Li, Z., Liu, J., Ahmad, F., Hu, Y., Salha, S., ... Burgos, D. (2022). Is Metaverse in education a blessing or a curse: A combined content and bibliometric analysis. *Smart Learning Environments*, *9*(1), 1–31. doi:10.118640561-022-00205-x

Tlili, A., Huang, R., Shehata, B., Liu, D., Zhao, J., Metwally, A. H. S., Wang, H., Denden, M., Bozkurt, A., Lee, L.-H., Beyoglu, D., Altinay, F., Sharma, R. C., Altinay, Z., Li, Z., Liu, J., Ahmad, F., Hu, Y., Salha, S., ... Burgos, D. (2022). Is Metaverse in education a blessing or a curse: A combined content and bibliometric analysis. *Smart Learning Environments*, *9*(1), 1–31. doi:10.118640561-022-00205-x

Weinberger, M. (2022). What Is Metaverse? A Definition Based on Qualitative Meta-Synthesis. *Future Internet*, *14*(11), 310. doi:10.3390/fi14110310

Zhang, G., Cao, J., Liu, D., & Qi, J. (2022). Popularity of the metaverse: Embodied social presence theory perspective. *Frontiers in Psychology*, *13*, 997751. doi:10.3389/fpsyg.2022.997751 PMID:36248483

Chapter 14
Critical Success Factors (CSFs) of Industry Centre of Excellence (ICoE) Performance at Majlis Amanah Rakyat (MARA) Technical and Vocational Education

Rozita Razali
Majlis Amanah Rakyat (MARA), Kuala Lumpur, Malaysia & Universiti Teknologi Malaysia, Malaysia

Syuhaida Ismail
Universiti Teknologi Malaysia, Malaysia

Mohamad Syazli Fathi
https://orcid.org/0000-0002-0474-6278
Universiti Teknologi Malaysia, Malaysia

ABSTRACT

Industry collaboration between technical and vocational education and training (TVET) institutions and industries is essential for Malaysia to reach 35% of its labour force being high-skilled workers. Hence, this chapter will identify the challenges that obstruct ICoE from performing at MARA institutions and propose the critical success factors (CSFs) of ICoE's good performance as per industry standards at TVET institutions. The systematic literature review (SLR) reveals that the management of the ICoE is confronted with significant obstacles, primarily stemming from diverse organisational approaches that can potentially complicate the functions of the ICoE. In addition, the talent in the focus area of ICoE is among the CSFs to ensure ICoE performance's success. Therefore, to ensure the successful performance of ICoE, TVET institutions have to prepare the expertise and choose the focus area wisely before establishing ICoE to attract industries collaboration.

DOI: 10.4018/979-8-3693-2647-3.ch014

1. INTRODUCTION

Technical and Vocational Education and Training (TVET) refers to a specific component of the educational process that encompasses the study of technologies, related sciences, and the acquisition of practical skills, attitudes, understanding, and knowledge pertaining to occupations in diverse sectors of economic and social life that is in addition to the general education. (United Nations Educational, Scientific and Cultural Organization, 2015). TVET has gained attention from stakeholders amongst the public because of its ability to contribute towards economic growth and provide a skilful workforce. TVET is an alternative path for developing high-skilled workers and responding to the economy's labour market needs and strengthening society (Malaysia Ministry of Education, 2015; Petnuchová et al., 2012).

In accordance with Strategic Thrust 3 outlined in the Shared Prosperity Vision 2030, Malaysia has set a goal to achieve a 35% representation of highly skilled workers within the employment market (Ministry of Economic Affairs, 2019). According to the Pocket Stats Quarter 4 2020 report, the proportion of high-skilled workers is at 30.7%, whereas semi-skilled workers account for 59.5% and low-skilled workers make up 11.7% of the workforce (Malaysia Department of Statistics, 2020). In order to attain a workforce composed of 35% highly skilled individuals by the year 2025, and to provide support for the Economic Transformation Programme (ETP) implemented by the Malaysian government, it is imperative for Malaysia to augment the enrolment of Technical and Vocational Education and Training (TVET) students (Malaysia Ministry of Education, 2015). TVET providers in private sectors and public sectors across ministries and agencies thus require strategic decisions and address the emerging labour market by achieving the national targets by 2025.

1.1 Industries Collaboration in Technical and Vocational Education and Training (TVET) Institutions

Technical and Vocational Education and Training (TVET) institutions may take collaboration efforts because of differing agendas. The most notable highlight to assure collaborative achievement is enhancing research development and commercialisation potentials, upgrading technical skills, minimising demand and supply mismatch, and increase graduate employability (Kamaliah et al., 2018; Raihan, 2014). One of the strategies is to provide TVET education attractive career development and academic progression for TVET graduates.

Strategic collaboration has the ability to bridge the skills gap and technology gap by leading the graduates to possess the relevant skills for industrialisation that are necessary to enhance graduate employability (Ali, Triyono & Koehler, 2020; Kenayathulla, Ahmad & Idris, 2019). Simultaneously, this would reduce the workforce mismatch between supply and demand in various sectors of the economy.

This initiative also offers human capital with competence, competitiveness, and adaptability to the ever-changing work environment. The cooperation aims to address the skills and competency gap among graduates of TVET programmes by aligning their skills with the specific requirements of the industry. The collaboration also allows industries to facilitate an industry-led curriculum to ensure the contents are relevant to various industries' current technologies. The model in Figure 1 shows that the coordination synergy between institutions and industries is required to produce a productive workforce (Cheong & Lee, 2016; Jee-Peng., 2013). Being a demand and industry-driven institution contributes to economic and social growth by lifting the employees from poverty (Arthur-Mensah & Alagaraja, 2013; Cheong & Lee, 2016).

Figure 1. The conceptual framework for a system approach to workforce development. Reprinted from "What Matters for Workforce Development: A Framework and Tool for Analysis" by Jee-Peng et al., 2013, SABER Working Paper Series, 6, p. 8. Copyright 2013 by Education Department, Human Development Network, World Bank.

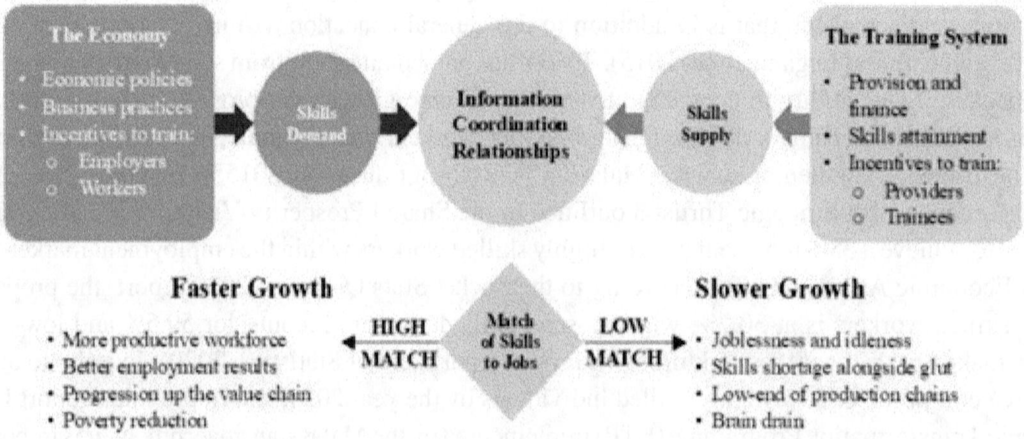

1.2 Industry Centre of Excellence (ICOE)

The Industry Centre of Excellence (ICoE) represents the pinnacle of strategic partnership between Technical and Vocational Education and Training (TVET) institutions and industries. The term employed in this study is the Industry Centre of Excellence (ICoE), as it pertains to the creation of ICoEs through collaborations between academic institutions and industries, with a primary emphasis on technological advancements and industry specialisation. The ICoE is an organisational entity or collaborative facility that fosters the advancement of research and development, innovation, consultation, commercialisation and training in alignment with the specific focal areas of diverse sectors. Its primary objective is to uphold elevated standards of conduct and achievement in these focus areas.

The primary focus of a Centre of Excellence (CoE) is on areas of science and technologies that exhibit high potential for growth. Consequently, CoEs possess the capacity to harness and produce novel knowledge by means of strategic partnerships between academic institutions and industries (Adenfelt & Lagerström, 2006; Ghazinoory, Ameri & Farnoodi, 2013; Hellström, 2018; Palaiologk, Koller & Wierse, 2016). The CoE model as illustrated in Table 1 demonstrates that a CoE is structured to unite several teams with the shared objective of promoting customer centricity, quality and innovation (Hogan & Volini, 2011; Marciniak, 2012). Despite significant challenges, CoE serves as a hub for disseminating and exchanging training guidelines, best practices, and shared strategic objectives (Dahm., 2020; Larsen, 2020).

Table 1. Centre of excellence (CoE) model

Philosophy Behind the Model	Advisory Organisation, Consultative Service Relationship
Nature of services	Judgement-based
Value proposition	Improved business outcomes
Process of a value proposition	Access to otherwise unavailable capabilities, higher-level skills and experience
Criteria for choosing a location	Cost is secondary
Criteria for labour selection	Capability is primary, while cost is secondary
Organisational structure and governance	Service levels and customer service procedures are negotiated between functional heads and internal customers, usually reports to functions
Measurement systems	Evaluative, outcome-based
Ensuring customer service	The actual professional who does the work
Demand for services	Episodic, event-driven

Note. Reprinted from "Next-generation service delivery model" by Hogan & Volini, 2011, Globalization Today, p. 26-30. Copyright 2011 by International Association of Outsourcing Professionals (IAOP).

The establishment of ICoE ensures that instructors and students of institutions conduct research and development or innovation of new products or services that help the industries to commercialise. However, the establishment and management of ICoE are complicated. Hence, it requires clear strategic orientation to ensure the successful performance of ICoE. Therefore, this paper sets its objectives to identify the current challenges that obstruct ICoE to perform at TVET institutions and propose the critical success factors (CSFs) of ICoE's good performance as per industry standard at TVET institutions.

2. METHODOLOGY

The literature search resulted in a total of 54 publications, which were obtained through database searching as well as other sources. These publications are related to various topics including Technical and Vocational Education and Training (TVET), Centre of Excellence (CoE), Critical Success Factors (CSFs) and Preferred Reporting Items for Systematic reviews and Meta-Analyses (PRISMA). After eliminating duplicate papers, a total of 47 articles were found to be significant to the study. The technique employed in this study involved conducting a systematic literature review (SLR). A total of 47 publications were first reviewed, and after excluding seven (7) articles that were specifically connected to CoE in Security, Healthcare, and Disaster Management, 40 articles were deemed eligible and appraised for inclusion in the study. The practises employed by the CoE are deemed unsuitable for conducting frequency and content analysis. Twenty publications were included in the research to investigate the critical success factors associated with establishing, operating, and managing the centres. This information was obtained using a desk study, as seen in Figure 2.

Furthermore, the methods of frequency and content analysis were used to identify, categorise and arrange the challenges and CSFs in various CoE projects of different sectors, including education, Information System (IS), Information Technologies (IT), Artificial Intelligence (AI), Business Process Management (BPM), Pharmaceutical, sustainable development, nanotechnology, humanities and electronics. The primary rationale for using SLR is the fairness and reliability in synthesising the current work (Ayat et al., 2020).

The Industry Centre of Excellence (ICoE) outcomes are influenced by a set of primary success criteria, as identified in a systematic literature review (SLR). The researchers employed frequency and content analysis methodologies to establish record and classify the success factors discussed in the chosen scholarly articles. This research presents a comprehensive analysis of 20 publications related to Centres of Excellence (CoE), identifying 17 distinct sets of Critical Success Factors (CSFs). The relative relevance of these characteristics is determined by the frequency of their occurrence in the literature (Ayat et al., 2020; Nasir & Sahibuddin, 2011). The measure of the occurrence frequency of CSFs refers to the quantity of scholarly articles in which the relevant elements have been examined and discussed. All critical success factors (CSFs), both those that have been extensively debated and others that have received less attention, have been compiled and organised in a table for the chosen literature. The literature highlights the occurrence's importance from the researcher's standpoint. Nevertheless, a few of the variables have a low frequency. However, this study maintains the perspective that these factors are critical success factors (CSFs) due to the prevalence of such findings in prior research, namely Baraldi & Ratajczak-Mrozek (2019), Mohan et al. (2010) and V.Tadwalker (2008) also included these low frequency variables in their respective studies.

Figure 2. PRISMA flow of systematic literature review. Adoption from "Preferred Reporting Items for Systematic Reviews and Meta-Analyses: The PRISMA Statement" by Moher et al., 2009, PLoS Medicine, 6. Copyright 2009 by PLoS Medicine.

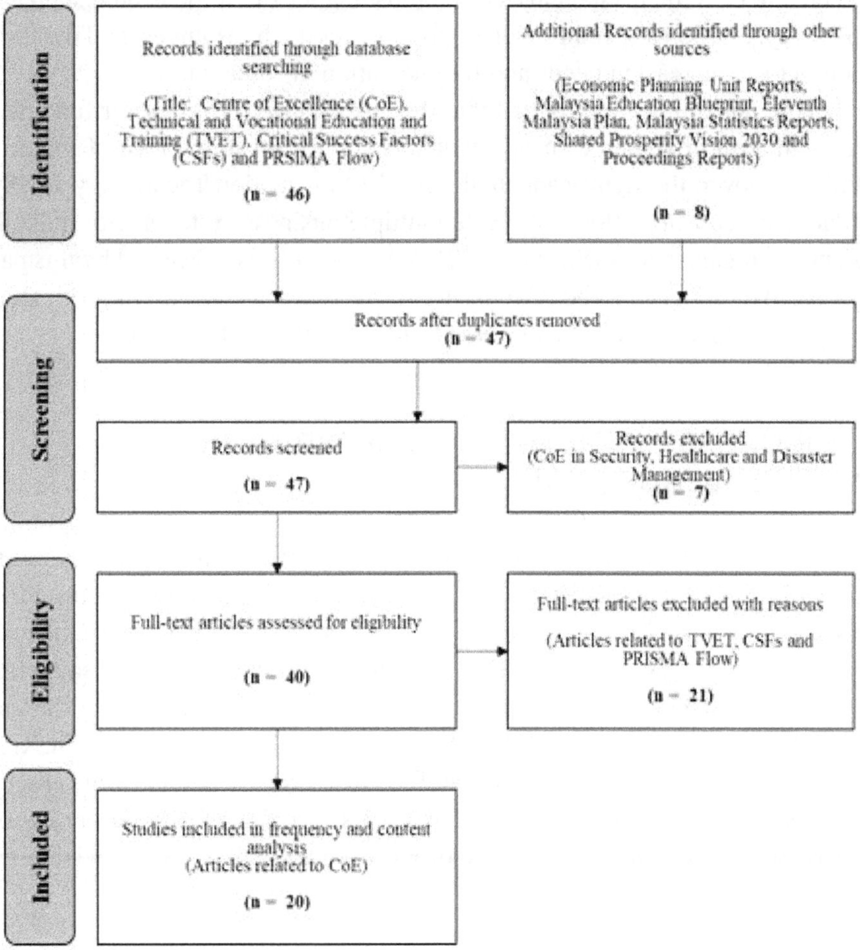

3. CHALLENGES OF INDUSTRY CENTRE OF EXCELLENCE (ICOE) PERFORMANCE

Reports related to the study on the demand and supply of human capital on Technical Vocational Education and Training (TVET) alarmed that the collaboration between industries and TVET institutions rarely reaches the breadth and depth necessary to develop high-quality programmes (Economic Planning Unit, 2016). This is further supported by literature which found that about 40% of the successful projects resulted in major impact and about 60% of the projects failed to reach their expected outcomes (Pertuzé et al., 2010). Hence, it is undoubtful that establishing an ICoE requires commitment from both parties, namely institution and industry.

Establishing a Centre of Excellence (CoE) could result in several advantages. However, many challenges could occur in the CoE's operation (Li, Chen & Su, 2018; Marciniak, 2012). Through the systematic literature review (SLR), many challenges hinder CoE activities' success, such as different operational approaches using CoE designations and managing a CoE network and the differences in strategies or priorities that can further complicate the ICoE functions. In addition, according to Hellström (2018), there are three main challenges of establishing a CoE: a focus on resource concentration and interdisciplinarity, dilution and redirection of possible research resources, and the fast expansion of higher education to meet increasing needs and fragmentation of research.

While one CoE in humanities highlighted that the size of the CoE grant for funding impacted the research activities in term of resource spending, it was significant in the area of impacts (Borlaug & Langfeldt, 2020). Moreover, the significant challenges for Information Technology and System-related CoE involved data and reporting silos that create multiple business systems with redundant functions as current practices in organisations (Sherman, 2014). However, it is suggested by this paper that all of these challenges faced by underachieved ICoE have a strong relationship with the critical success factors (CSFs) of ICoE performance that will be discussed further in the next section.

4. CRITICAL SUCCESS FACTORS (CSFS) OF INDUSTRY CENTRE OF EXCELLENCE (ICOE)

Project success criteria are defined as a collection of guidelines or rules used to measure or evaluate project success, while critical success factors (CSFs) can be defined as facts or circumstances influencing project outcomes or project success (Ayat., 2020). CSFs studies are useful for making sense of issues that include several possible factors that affect the result and propose realistic suggestions based on those factors (Remus & Wiener, 2010). Multiple critical success factors (CSFs) of the Industry Centre of Excellence (ICoE) have been discovered through Systematic Literature Review (SLR). Furthermore, practical recommendations for implementation at Technical and Vocational Education and Training (TVET) institutions have been proposed. Table 2 presents a comprehensive overview of the Critical Success Factors (CSFs) of the Integrated Centre of Excellence (ICoE) as documented in a total of 20 scholarly publications.

Table 2. Critical success factors (CSFs) of industry centre of excellence (ICoE) identified across 20 publications

Critical Success Factors (CSFs)		Literature Citation	Citation Count in the Literature (n = 20)	
			Frequency	(%)
1	People (specialist, expertise in critical areas, high-quality personnel, research team)	(Aleksey et al., 2015; Aruba Centre of Excellence for Sustainable Development of SIDS, 2019; Baraldi & Ratajczak-Mrozek, 2019; Borlaug & Langfeldt, 2020; Chang, 2014; Dahm et al., 2020; Daragmeh, Drane & Light, 2012; Grady, 2004; Hellström, 2018; Hogan & Volini, 2011; Li, Chen & Su, 2018; Marciniak, 2012; Sherman, 2014; Mickle, 2007; Mohan et al., 2010; Palaiologk, Koller & Wierse, 2016; V.Tadwalker, 2008; Yamanaka, 2009)	18	90%
2	Strategic orientation, strategic vision, proactive and provident strategy, build agile and adaptable plans, commitment	(Aruba Centre of Excellence for Sustainable Development of SIDS, 2019; Baraldi & Ratajczak-Mrozek, 2019; Chang, 2014; Dahm et al., 2020; Daragmeh, Drane & Light, 2012; Ghazinoory, Ameri & Farnoodi, 2013; Hellström, 2018; Hogan & Volini, 2011; Li, Chen & Su, 2018; Sherman, 2014; Mickle, 2007; Mohan et al., 2010; Palaiologk, Koller & Wierse, 2016; V.Tadwalker, 2008)	14	70%
3	Infrastructure and facilities including open and sharing system platforms, data security	(Aleksey et al., 2015; Aruba Centre of Excellence for Sustainable Development of SIDS, 2019; Baraldi & Ratajczak-Mrozek, 2019; Chang, 2014; Dahm et al., 2020; Grady, 2004; Hogan & Volini, 2011; Li, Chen & Su, 2018; Sherman, 2014; Mickle, 2007; Mohan et al., 2010; Palaiologk, Koller & Wierse, 2016; V.Tadwalker, 2008; Yamanaka, 2009)	14	70%
4	Establish a relationship or interaction with other institutions	(Aleksey et al., 2015; Aruba Centre of Excellence for Sustainable Development of SIDS, 2019; Borlaug & Langfeldt, 2020; Chang, 2014; Dahm et al., 2020; Daragmeh, Drane & Light, 2012; Li, Chen & Su, 2018; Mickle, 2007; Mohan et al., 2010; Palaiologk, Koller & Wierse, 2016; Yamanaka, 2009)	11	55%
5	Organisation support and inter-department collaboration; tolerant to failure and courage to take the risk in innovation	(Baraldi & Ratajczak-Mrozek, 2019; Daragmeh, Drane & Light, 2012; Grady, 2004; Hellström, 2018; Hogan & Volini, 2011; Li, Chen & Su, 2018; Sherman, 2014; Mickle, 2007; Palaiologk, Koller & Wierse, 2016; V.Tadwalker, 2008)	10	50%
6	Funding, sponsorship or grant	(Aleksey et al., 2015; Borlaug & Langfeldt, 2020; Grady, 2004; Hogan & Volini, 2011; Li, Chen & Su, 2018; Sherman, 2014; Mickle, 2007; Mohan et al., 2010)	8	40%
7	Coordinated training or build new skill sets	(Aleksey et al., 2015; Li, Chen & Su, 2018; Sherman, 2014; Mohan et al., 2010; V.Tadwalker, 2008)	5	25%
8	Fast adaptation: Proper interaction with a changing environment or flexible approach of the process	(Aruba Centre of Excellence for Sustainable Development of SIDS, 2019; Baraldi & Ratajczak-Mrozek, 2019; Ghazinoory, Ameri & Farnoodi, 2013; Marciniak, 2012; V.Tadwalker, 2008)	5	25%
9	Sharing the best practices, knowledge sharing and transfer	(Baraldi & Ratajczak-Mrozek, 2019; Li, Chen & Su, 2018; Marciniak, 2012; Sherman, 2014)	4	20%
10	Government support	(Aruba Centre of Excellence for Sustainable Development of SIDS, 2019; Ghazinoory, Ameri & Farnoodi, 2013; Hogan & Volini, 2011; Li, Chen & Su, 2018)	4	20%
11	Focus on new development; numbers of new products	(Baraldi & Ratajczak-Mrozek, 2019; Chang, 2014; Li, Chen & Su, 2018)	3	15%
12	Location	(Aruba Centre of Excellence for Sustainable Development of SIDS, 2019; Chang, 2014; Yamanaka, 2009)	3	15%
13	Policies or legal framework	(Li, Chen & Su, 2018; Sherman, 2014; Palaiologk, Koller & Wierse, 2016)	3	15%
14	Module or contents	(Daragmeh, Drane & Light, 2012; Grady, 2004)	2	10%
15	Encourage entrepreneurship start-up	(Mohan et al., 2010)	1	5%
16	Current products and services	(V.Tadwalker, 2008)	1	5%
17	Trust and commitment	(Baraldi & Ratajczak-Mrozek, 2019)	1	5%

5. DISCUSSION

The top five critical success factors (CSFs) are determined by their frequency of occurrence, with a threshold of 50%, following the suggestion by Nasir & Sahibuddin (2011). This paper found that the Industry Centre of Excellence (ICoE) performance depends on experts on the focus area, clear strategic orientation, organisation support, facilities and multi-relationship with other institutions or triple-helix model of innovations.

The primary objective of establishing an International Centre of Excellence (ICoE) is to ensure the inclusion of subject matter specialists who possess specialised knowledge and expertise in the designated focal area. The experts or specialists from the ICoE possess extensive technical expertise and relevant professional experiences that enable them to effectively address highly intricate issues within the designated area. The expert possesses exceptional skills and expertise, enabling them to effectively carry out and manage all operations associated with the ICoE. Moreover, they possess the ability to identify issues within the designated area of emphasis and propose practical and feasible solutions. The professionals additionally offer advisory assistance for the improvement of project technology and advisory services to various institutions and businesses.

The impactful outcomes and operational excellence of ICoE are from the provident strategic orientation and goals. It gives the centre autonomy to research and strategic decisions about the research focus areas and collaboration. The goals of the ICoE are expressed as the desire to enhance the industrial capacity to align with national objectives, foster the development of a highly skilled labour force, enhance education and training, and tackle additional complicated national requirements. Collaborations between institutions and industries with congruent objectives and comprehensive strategies generated greater impacts (Palaiologk, Koller & Wierse, 2016).

The organisation with clear strategic ICoE goals will support all the centre activities. The organisation believes ICoE is the collaboration tools mechanism that can integrate innovation, increase organisation effectiveness, develop expertise with specialisation, and increase economic growth by leveraging or creating new technologies.

The infrastructures and facilities are the criteria for establishing ICoE, thus guaranteed the excellence performance of ICoE. Industries mainly have generously invested in developing facilities better than Technical and Vocational Education and Training (TVET) institutions laboratories or workshops (Li, Chen & Su, 2018). The collaboration through the establishment of ICoE can encourage research networks to enter institutions, also allowing industry talents to enter institutions and vice versa, such as by sharing infrastructure, the participation of end-users in research and mixed sectoral governing boards, where the significant outcome is the knowledge and technology transfer through ICoE. Creating new research-based businesses, retaining domestic companies, commercialising new products or services and attracting investment is seen as the most influential with direct capacity building in socio-economic growth. Sharing facilities also expose the students in TVET institutions to the current and emerging industrialisation by minimising infrastructure maintenance costs and becoming very cost-effective for both parties (Palaiologk, Koller & Wierse, 2016).

The triple helix model or innovation also contributes to the ICoE performance. The model refers to a series of interactions between government (TVET institutions in a government agency), other institutions (universities) and industries to promote economic and social growth through the establishment of ICoE. This can gather core knowledge, technologies and expertise (Hellström, 2018). The virtues of the transfer and interaction of expertise with industrial partners are fundamental to ICoE success. This interaction can revitalise the academic system by creating interdisciplinary knowledge transfer, adapting academic programmes to the needs of industrialisation, stimulating research development and attracting talent.

6. CONCLUSION

In recent years, there has been a notable increase in the focus on the transition pathway from Technical and Vocational Education and Training (TVET). This heightened attention aims to enhance the earning potential and career advancement prospects for individuals who have completed the TVET programmes. In order to facilitate a seamless progression from TVET to higher education, numerous educational institutions across the globe have demonstrated effective collaboration through the establishment of Industry Centres of Excellence (ICoEs). The Malaysian government has demonstrated a notable dedication to rejuvenating the sector in recent years. However, the primary focus has been on augmenting the enrolment rate in TVET and establishing strategic coordination across TVET institutions. The collaborative programme additionally guarantees adaptable transition opportunities for the transfer of knowledge and technology, while also providing TVET graduates with exposure to both existing and new technologies.

It is suggested that ICoE partners demonstrate to each other the presence of strong drivers for problem-solving and collaboration to ensure the formulation of strategic decisions in overcoming the challenges of running complex workflows at scale (Dahm et al., 2020; Larsen, 2020). Based on the awareness of the ICoE complexity and the ability to attract challenges, this paper has successfully identified the critical success factors (CSFs) as the critical contingencies for forming collaboration and propose CSFs for measuring the performance of ICoE, which is the ultimate goals of strategic collaboration between TVET institutions and industries. The strategic collaboration between TVET institutions and industries would help the Malaysian's economic growth by increasing productivity, competitiveness and innovations and bringing benefits to the Malaysia society by improving efficiency and creating job opportunities with the development of new emerging technologies (Palaiologk, Koller & Wierse, 2016).

REFERENCES

Adenfelt, M., & Lagerström, K. (2006). Knowledge Development and Sharing in Multinational Corporations: The Case of a Centre of Excellence and a Transnational Team. *International Business Review, 15*(4), 381–400. doi:10.1016/j.ibusrev.2006.05.002

Aleksey, N. Y., Kirill, S. K., Irina, N. K., & Nikita, V. M. (2015). Creation of Technical University Center of Excellence. *Procedia: Social and Behavioral Sciences, 166*, 235–239. doi:10.1016/j.sbspro.2014.12.517

Ali, M., Triyono, B., & Koehler, T. (2020). Evaluation of Indonesian Technical and Vocational Education in Addressing the Gap in Job Skills Required by Industry. *Proceeding - 2020 3rd International Conference on Vocational Education and Electrical Engineering: Strengthening the framework of Society 5.0 through Innovations in Education, Electrical, Engineering and Informatics Engineering, ICVEE 2020.* 10.1109/ICVEE50212.2020.9243222

Arthur-Mensah, N., & Alagaraja, M. (2013). Exploring Technical Vocational Education and Training Systems in Emerging Markets: A Case Study on Ghana. *European Journal of Training and Development, 37*(9), 835–850. doi:10.1108/EJTD-04-2013-0037

Aruba Centre of Excellence for Sustainable Development of SIDS (2019). *One Happy Island Working towards One Happy Planet - Lessons Learned by the SDG Commission of Aruba: Initial Phase of Institutional Arrangements for Localizing the SDGs.* Author.

Ayat, M., Imran, M., Ullah, A., & Kang, C. W. (2020). Current Trends Analysis and Prioritization of Success Factors: A Systematic Literature Review of ICT Projects. *International Journal of Managing Projects in Business.*

Baraldi, E., & Ratajczak-Mrozek, M. (2019). From Supplier to Center of Excellence and beyond: The Network Position Development of a Business Unit within "IKEA Industry." *Journal of Business Research, 100*, 1–15. doi:10.1016/j.jbusres.2019.03.008

Borlaug, S. B., & Langfeldt, L. (2020). One Model Fits All? How Centres of Excellence Affect Research Organisation and Practices in the Humanities. *Studies in Higher Education, 45*(8), 1746–1757. doi:10.1080/03075079.2019.1615044

Chang, Y. (2014). *Cisco Chooses to Be Smart in Songdo - Cisco's Global Center of Excellence in Korea develops smart city solutions for the Internet of Everything era.* Invest Korea.

Cheong, K., & Lee, K.-H. (2016). Malaysia's Education Crisis - Can TVET Help? *Malaysian Journal of Economic Studies : Journal of the Malaysian Economic Association and the Faculty of Economics and Administration, University of Malaya, 53*, 115–134.

Dahm, J. P., Richards, D. F., Black, A., Bertsch, A. D., Grinberg, L., Karlin, I., Kokkila-Schumacher, S., Leon, E. A., Neely, J. R., Pankajakshan, R., & Pearce, O. (2020). Sierra Center of Excellence: Lessons Learned. *IBM Journal of Research and Development, 64*(3/4), 1–14. doi:10.1147/JRD.2019.2961069

Daragmeh, A. K., Drane, D., & Light, G. (2012). Needs Assessment and Beyond in the Setup of Centers for Teaching and Learning Excellence: An-Najah University Center as a Case Study. *Procedia: Social and Behavioral Sciences, 47*, 841–847. doi:10.1016/j.sbspro.2012.06.745

Economic Planning Unit (EPU). (2016). *Study on the Demand and Supply of Human Capital on Technical Vocational Education and Training (TVET).* Final Report Volume I – Main Report. 2. Malaysia: Economic Planning Unit.

Ghazinoory, S., Ameri, F., & Farnoodi, S. (2013). An Application of the Text Mining Approach to Select Technology Centers of Excellence. *Technological Forecasting and Social Change, 80*(5), 918–931. doi:10.1016/j.techfore.2012.09.001

Grady, H. M. (2004). Centers for Excellence in Engineering Education: A Case Study. *Proceedings - Frontiers in Education Conference, 3*, 1–5. 10.1109/FIE.2004.1408680

Hellström, T. (2018). Centres of Excellence and Capacity Building: From Strategy to Impact. *Science & Public Policy, 45*(4), 543–552. doi:10.1093cipolcx082

Hogan, S., & Volini, E. (2011). Next-generation service delivery model – Expanding the value-creation menu for consumer packaged goods organizations. In Globalization Today (pp. 26-30). New York: International Association of Outsourcing Professionals (IAOP).

Jee-Peng, T., Kiong Hock, L., Alexandria, V., & Joy Yoo-Jeung, N. (2013) What Matters for Workforce Development: A Framework and Tool for Analysis. *SABER Working Paper Series*, 6.

Kamaliah, S., Roslan, S., Bakar, A. R., & Ghiami, Z. (2018). The Effect of Supervised Work Experience on the Acquisition of Employability Skills among Malaysian Students. *Higher Education, Skills and Work-based Learning*, *8*(4), 354–364. doi:10.1108/HESWBL-05-2016-0028

Kenayathulla, H. B., Ahmad, N. A., & Idris, A. R. (2019). Gaps between Competence and Importance of Employability Skills: Evidence from Malaysia. *Higher Education Evaluation and Development*, *13*(2), 97–112. doi:10.1108/HEED-08-2019-0039

Larsen, K. (2020). Managing the Complexity of Centres of Excellence: Accommodating Diversity in Institutional Logics. *Tertiary Education and Management*, *26*(3), 295–310. doi:10.100711233-019-09053-w

Li, F., Chen, J., & Su, Y. S. (2018). Managing the University-Industry Collaborative Innovation in China: The Case of Zhejiang NHU Company. *Journal of Organizational Change Management*, *31*(1), 62–82. doi:10.1108/JOCM-04-2017-0148

Malaysia Department of Statistics. (2020). *Pocket Stats Q3 2020, 4, 82*. Department of Statistics.

Malaysia Ministry of Education. (2015). *Malaysia Education Blueprint 2015-2025 (Higher Education)*. Ministry of Education.

Marciniak, R. (2012). *Center of Excellence as a Next Step for Shared Service Center*. Academic Press.

Mengist, W., Soromessa, T., & Legese, G. (2020). Method for Conducting Systematic Literature Review and Meta-Analysis for Environmental Science Research. *MethodsX*, *7*, 100777. doi:10.1016/j.mex.2019.100777 PMID:31993339

Mickle, M. H. (2007). Establishment of the University of Pittsburgh RFID Center of Excellence. *IEEE Communications Magazine*, *45*(4), 14–16. doi:10.1109/MCOM.2007.348672

Ministry of Economic Affairs. (2019). *Summary Shared Prosperity Vision 2030 Restructuring the Priorities of Malaysia's Development*. Ministry of Economic Affairs.

Mohan, S., Bhat, N., Pratap, R., Jamadagni, H. S., Shivashankar, S. A., Ananthasuresh, G. K., Venkataraman, V., Vinoy, K. J., Vasi, J. M., Ramgopal Rao, V., Kottantharayil, A., & Contractor, A. Q. (2010). Centers of Excellence in Nanoelectronics in India. *Biennial University/Government/Industry Microelectronics Symposium - Proceedings*, 1–4.

Moher, D., Liberati, A., Tetzlaff, J., Altman, D. G., & Group, T. P. (2009). Preferred Reporting Items for Systematic Reviews and Meta-Analyses: The PRISMA Statement. *PLoS Medicine*, 6. PMID:19621072

Nasir, M. H. N., & Sahibuddin, S. (2011). Critical Success Factors for Software Projects: A Comparative Study. *Scientific Research and Essays*, *6*(10), 2174–2186. doi:10.5897/SRE10.1171

Palaiologk, A., Koller, B., & Wierse, A. (2016). Centre of Excellence for HPC and Engineering: Concept Development. *eChallenges e-2015 Conference Proceedings*, 1–10.

Pertuzé, J. A., Calder, E. S., Edward, M., & Lucas, W. A. (2010). Best Practices for Collaboration Best Practices for Industry. *MIT Sloan Management Review*, *51*, 83–90.

Petnuchová, Horňáková, Podařil, Štúr, Ridzoňová, & Novota. (2012). Vocational Education and Training in OECD Countries. *2012 15th International Conference on Interactive Collaborative Learning, ICL 2012*, 10–15.

Raihan, A. (2014). Collaboration between TVET Institutions and Industries in Bangladesh to Enhance Employability Skills. *International Journal of Engineering and Technical Research*, *2*, 50.

Remus, U., & Wiener, M. (2010). A Multi-Method, Holistic Strategy for Researching Critical Success Factors in IT Projects. *Information Systems Journal*, *20*(1), 25–52. doi:10.1111/j.1365-2575.2008.00324.x

Sherman, R. (2014). *Centers of Excellence. Business Intelligence Guidebook From Data Integration to Analytics*. Elsevier Inc.

Tadwalker, V. S. (2008). Create Centre of Excellence (CoE) for Better Business. Satyam Computer Services Ltd.

United Nations Educational, Scientific and Cultural Organization (UNESCO). (2015). Proposal for the Revision of the 2001 Revised Recommendation concerning Technical and Vocational Education. *38th General Conference*, 1-16.

Yamanaka, Y. (2009). Introduction to Global COE Program; Establishment of Center for Integrated Field Environmental Science (IFES). *International Symposium on "Impact of Climate Change on Region Specific Systems."*

Compilation of References

.Wan, Y., & Nakayama, M. (2022). *A sentiment analysis of star-rating: a cross-cultural perspective*. Academic Press.

AbadiM.AgarwalA.BarhamP.BrevdoE.ChenZ.CitroC.CorradoG. S.DavisA.DeanJ.DevinM.GhemawatS.GoodfellowI. HarpA.IrvingG.IsardM.JiaY.JozefowiczR.KaiserL.KudlurM.ResearchG. (2016). *TensorFlow: Large-Scale Machine Learning on Heterogeneous Distributed Systems*. https://arxiv.org/abs/1603.04467v2

Abdella, S., Youssef, S. H., Afinjuomo, F., Song, Y., Fouladian, P., Upton, R., & Garg, S. (2021). 3D Printing of thermosensitive drugs. *Pharmaceutics*, *13*(9), 1524. doi:10.3390/pharmaceutics13091524 PMID:34575600

Abdulhameed, O., Al-Ahmari, A., Ameen, W., & Mian, S. H. (2019). Additive manufacturing: Challenges, trends, and applications. *Advances in Mechanical Engineering*, *11*(2), 1687814018822880. doi:10.1177/1687814018822880

Abramushkina, O.I., Uzorina, M.I., Surikov, P.V., & Ushakova, O.B. (2021). Investigation of the rheological behavior of ABS plastic grades for the production of filaments for 3D printing by layer-by-layer deposition. *Plasticheskie Massy*.

Adadi, A., & Berrada, M. (2018). Peeking inside the black-box: A survey on explainable artificial intelligence (XAI). *IEEE Access : Practical Innovations, Open Solutions*, *6*, 52138–52160. doi:10.1109/ACCESS.2018.2870052

Adak, A., Pradhan, B., & Shukla, N. (2022). Sentiment Analysis of Customer Reviews of Food Delivery Services Using Deep Learning and Explainable Artificial Intelligence: Systematic Review. *Foods*, *11*(10), 1500. Advance online publication. doi:10.3390/foods11101500 PMID:35627070

Adam, G., Benouhiba, A., Rabenorosoa, K., Clévy, C., & Cappelleri, D. J. (2021). 4D Printing: Enabling Technology for Microrobotics Applications. *Advanced Intelligent Systems*, *3*(5), 2000216. doi:10.1002/aisy.202000216

Additive Manufacturing. (n.d.). https://www.additivemanufacturing.media/articles/finally-a-polypropylene-you-can-3d-print

Adel, A. (2022). Future of industry 5.0 in society: human-centric solutions, challenges and prospective research areas. *Journal of Cloud Computing, 11*(1), 1–15. doi:10.1186/s13677-022-00314-5

Adenfelt, M., & Lagerström, K. (2006). Knowledge Development and Sharing in Multinational Corporations: The Case of a Centre of Excellence and a Transnational Team. *International Business Review*, *15*(4), 381–400. doi:10.1016/j.ibusrev.2006.05.002

Afzal, M. A., Gu, Z., Afzal, B., & Bukhari, S. U. (2023). Cognitive Workload Classification in Industry 5.0 Applications: Electroencephalography-Based Bi-Directional Gated Network Approach. *Electronics, 12*(19), 4008. doi:10.3390/electronics12194008

Agha, A., Waheed, W., Alamoodi, N., Mathew, B., Alnaimat, F., Abu-Nada, E., & Alazzam, A. (2022). A review of cyclic olefin copolymer applications in microfluidics and microdevices. *Macromolecular Materials and Engineering*, *307*(8), 2200053. doi:10.1002/mame.202200053

Agrawal, D., & Madaan, J. (2023). A structural equation model for big data adoption in the healthcare supply chain. *International Journal of Productivity and Performance Management*, *72*(4), 917–942. doi:10.1108/IJPPM-12-2020-0667

Ahmad, S., Yew, K., Lang, M., & Peng, W. (2018). Resources, Conservation & Recycling Sustainable product design and development : A review of tools, applications and research prospects. *Resources, Conservation and Recycling*, *132*(January), 49–61. doi:10.1016/j.resconrec.2018.01.020

AI Multiple. (n.d.). https://research.aimultiple.com/sentiment-analysismachinelearning/#:~:text=Researchers%20combined%20various%20machine%20learning,accuracy%20of%20predicting%20sentiment%20scores

Aimal, M., Bakhtyar, M., Baber, J., Lakho, S., Mohammad, U., Ahmed, W., & Karim, J. (2021). *Identifying negativity factors from social media text corpus using sentiment analysis method.* Academic Press.

Ajitha, P., Sivasangari, A., Immanuel Rajkumar, R., & Poonguzhali, S. (2021). Design of text sentiment analysis tool using feature extraction based on fusing machine learning algorithms. *Journal of Intelligent & Fuzzy Systems*, *40*(4), 6375–6383. Advance online publication. doi:10.3233/JIFS-189478

Alaba, F. A., Othman, M., Hashem, I. A. T., & Alotaibi, F. (2017). Internet of Things security: A survey. *Journal of Network and Computer Applications*, *88*, 10–28. doi:10.1016/j.jnca.2017.04.002

Alabdulatif, A., Thilakarathne, N. N., & Kalinaki, K. (2023). A Novel Cloud Enabled Access Control Model for Preserving the Security and Privacy of Medical Big Data. *Electronics (Basel)*, *12*(12), 2646. doi:10.3390/electronics12122646

Aleksey, N. Y., Kirill, S. K., Irina, N. K., & Nikita, V. M. (2015). Creation of Technical University Center of Excellence. *Procedia: Social and Behavioral Sciences*, *166*, 235–239. doi:10.1016/j.sbspro.2014.12.517

Alghamdi, A. (2023). A Hybrid Method for Customer Segmentation in Saudi Arabia Restaurants Using Clustering, Neural Networks and Optimization Learning Techniques. *Arabian Journal for Science and Engineering*, *48*(2), 2021–2039. doi:10.100713369-022-07091-y PMID:35910042

Ali, M., Triyono, B., & Koehler, T. (2020). Evaluation of Indonesian Technical and Vocational Education in Addressing the Gap in Job Skills Required by Industry. *Proceeding - 2020 3rd International Conference on Vocational Education and Electrical Engineering: Strengthening the framework of Society 5.0 through Innovations in Education, Electrical, Engineering and Informatics Engineering, ICVEE 2020.* 10.1109/ICVEE50212.2020.9243222

Alifui-Segbaya, F. (2018). Toxicological assessment of photopolymers in additive manufacturing using the innovative zebrafish embryo model. School of Dentistry and Oral Health, Griffith Health, Griffith University.

Ali, S., Abdullah, Armand, T. P. T., Athar, A., Hussain, A., Ali, M., Yaseen, M., Joo, M.-I., & Kim, H.-C. (2023). Metaverse in healthcare integrated with explainable ai and blockchain: Enabling immersiveness, ensuring trust, and providing patient data security. *Sensors (Basel)*, *23*(2), 565. doi:10.339023020565 PMID:36679361

Aljedaani, W., Rustam, F., Mkaouer, M. W., Ghallab, A., Rupapara, V., Washington, P. B., Lee, E., & Ashraf, I. (2022). Sentiment analysis on Twitter data integrating TextBlob and deep learning models: The case of US airline industry. *Knowledge-Based Systems*, *255*, 109780. Advance online publication. doi:10.1016/j.knosys.2022.109780

Allam, Z., Sharifi, A., Bibri, S. E., Jones, D. S., & Krogstie, J. (2022). The metaverse as a virtual form of smart cities: Opportunities and challenges for environmental, economic, and social sustainability in urban futures. *Smart Cities*, *5*(3), 771–801. doi:10.3390martcities5030040

Alli, A. A., Kassim, K., Mutwalibi, N., Hamid, H., & Ibrahim, L. (2021). Secure Fog-Cloud of Things: Architectures, Opportunities and Challenges. In M. Ahmed & P. Haskell-Dowland (Eds.), *Secure Edge Computing* (1st ed., pp. 3–20). CRC Press. doi:10.1201/9781003028635-2

Alojaiman, B. (2023). Technological Modernizations in the Industry 5.0 Era: A Descriptive Analysis and Future Research Directions. *Processes, 11*(5), 1318. doi:10.3390/pr11051318

Alqoud, A., Schaefer, D., & Milisavljevic-Syed, J. (2022). Industry 4.0: A systematic review of legacy manufacturing system digital retrofitting. *Manufacturing Review, 9*, 32. doi:10.1051/mfreview/2022031

Alshaikh, H., Ramadan, N., & Hefny, H. A. (2020). Ransomware prevention and mitigation techniques. *Int. J. Comput. Appl, 177*(40), 31–39.

Altıparmak, S. C., Yardley, V. A., Shi, Z., & Lin, J. (2021). Challenges in additive manufacturing of high-strength aluminium alloys and current developments in hybrid additive manufacturing. *International Journal of Lightweight Materials and Manufacture, 4*(2), 246–261. doi:10.1016/j.ijlmm.2020.12.004

Alvarez Quiñones, L. I., Lozano-Moncada, C. A., & Bravo Montenegro, D. A. (2023). Machine learning for predictive maintenance scheduling of distribution transformers. *Journal of Quality in Maintenance Engineering, 29*(1), 188–202. doi:10.1108/JQME-06-2021-0052

Alzate, M., Arce-Urriza, M., & Cebollada, J. (2022). Mining the text of online consumer reviews to analyze brand image and brand positioning. *Journal of Retailing and Consumer Services, 67.* doi:10.1016/j.jretconser.2022.102989

Amann, J., Blasimme, A., Vayena, E., Frey, D., & Madai, V. I. (2020). Explainability for artificial intelligence in healthcare: A multidisciplinary perspective. *BMC Medical Informatics and Decision Making, 20*(1), 1–9. doi:10.118612911-020-01332-6 PMID:33256715

Ameta, K. L., Solanki, V. S., Haque, S., Singh, V., Devi, A. P., & Chundawat, R. S. (2022). Critical appraisal and systematic review of 3D \& 4D printing in sustainable and environment-friendly smart manufacturing technologies. *Sustainable. Materials Technology*, 00481.

Amirifar, T., Lahmiri, S., & Zanjani, M. K. (2023). An NLP-Deep Learning Approach for Product Rating Prediction Based on Online Reviews and Product Features. *IEEE Transactions on Computational Social Systems*, 1–13. Advance online publication. doi:10.1109/TCSS.2023.3290558

Amponsah, A. A., Adekoya, A. F., & Weyori, B. A. (2022). A novel fraud detection and prevention method for healthcare claim processing using machine learning and blockchain technology. *Decision Analytics Journal, 4*, 100122. doi:10.1016/j.dajour.2022.100122

Andreacola, F. R., Capasso, I., Pilotti, L., & Brando, G. (2021). Influence of 3d-printing parameters on the mechanical properties of 17-4PH stainless steel produced through Selective Laser Melting. *Frattura ed Integrità Strutturale, 15*(58), 282-295.

Anshasi, R. J., Alsyouf, A., Alhazmi, F. N., & AbuZaitoun, A. T. (2022). A Change Management Approach to Promoting and Endorsing Ergonomics within a Dental Setting. *International Journal of Environmental Research and Public Health, 19*(20), 13193. doi:10.3390/ijerph192013193 PMID:36293773

Antonakakis, M., April, T., Bailey, M., Bernhard, M., Bursztein, E., Cochran, J., . . . Zhou, Y. (2017). Understanding the mirai botnet. In *26th USENIX security symposium (USENIX Security 17)* (pp. 1093-1110). Academic Press.

Aouad, A., Elmachtoub, A. N., Ferreira, K. J., & McNellis, R. (2023). Market segmentation trees. *Manufacturing & Service Operations Management, 25*(2), 648–667. doi:10.1287/msom.2023.1195

Araki, Y., & Fujimura, T. (2021). VR Debates with Project Debater. *IBM Journal of Research and Development, 65*(5/6), 5:1-5:12.

Arciniega-Rocha, R. P., Erazo-Chamorro, V. C., & Szabo, G. (2023). The prevention of industrial manual tool accidents considering occupational health and safety. *Safety (Basel, Switzerland), 9*(3), 51. doi:10.3390afety9030051

Arkouli, Z., Michalos, G., & Makris, S. (2022). On the selection of ergonomics evaluation methods for human centric manufacturing tasks. *Procedia CIRP, 107*, 89–94. doi:10.1016/j.procir.2022.04.015

Arshad, M., Brohi, M. N., Soomro, T. R., Ghazal, T. M., Alzoubi, H. M., & Alshurideh, M. (2023). NoSQL: Future of BigData Analytics Characteristics and Comparison with RDBMS. *Studies in Computational Intelligence, 1056*, 1927–1951. doi:10.1007/978-3-031-12382-5_106

Arthur-Mensah, N., & Alagaraja, M. (2013). Exploring Technical Vocational Education and Training Systems in Emerging Markets: A Case Study on Ghana. *European Journal of Training and Development, 37*(9), 835–850. doi:10.1108/EJTD-04-2013-0037

Aruba Centre of Excellence for Sustainable Development of SIDS (2019). *One Happy Island Working towards One Happy Planet - Lessons Learned by the SDG Commission of Aruba: Initial Phase of Institutional Arrangements for Localizing the SDGs*. Author.

Asani, E., Vahdat-Nejad, H., & Sadri, J. (2021). Restaurant recommender system based on sentiment analysis. *Machine Learning with Applications, 6*. doi:10.1016/j.mlwa.2021.100114

Asicioglu, F., Yilmaz, A. S., de Kinder, J., Pekacar, I., & Gelir, A. (2022). A novel 3D scan-based optical method for analyzing lines drawn at different pen pressure. *Forensic Science International, 338*, 111388. doi:10.1016/j.forsciint.2022.111388 PMID:35907278

Aslam, F., Aimin, W., Li, M., & Ur Rehman, K. (2020). Innovation in the era of IoT and industry 5.0: Absolute innovation management (AIM) framework. *Information (Basel), 11*(2), 124. doi:10.3390/info11020124

Asur, S., & Huberman, B. A. (2010). Predicting the future with social media: The case of stock market predictions. In *Proceedings of the 2010 IEEE International Conference on Intelligence and Security Informatics (ISI)* (pp. 391-399). IEEE.

Atmadi, A., Stephenson, D. A., & Liang, S. Y. (2001). *Cutting Fluid Aerosol from Splash in Turning: Analysis for Environmentally Conscious Machining*. Academic Press.

Atre, R., & Tapaswi, N. (2022). A Prediction of Customer Behavior using Logistic Regression, Naivesbayes Algorithm. *International Journal of Computer Applications, 183*(50), 31–35. Advance online publication. doi:10.5120/ijca2022921904

Atzori, L., Iera, A., & Morabito, G. (2010). The internet of things: A survey. *Computer Networks, 54*(15), 2787–2805. doi:10.1016/j.comnet.2010.05.010

Aurich, J. C., Linke, B., Hauschild, M., Carrella, M., & Kirsch, B. (2013). CIRP Annals - Manufacturing Technology Sustainability of abrasive processes. *CIRP Annals - Manufacturing Technology, 62*(2), 653–672. doi:10.1016/j.cirp.2013.05.010

Awan, U., Bhatti, S. H., Shamim, S., Khan, Z., Akhtar, P., & Balta, M. E. (2022). The Role of Big Data Analytics in Manufacturing Agility and Performance: Moderation–Mediation Analysis of Organizational Creativity and of the Involvement of Customers as Data Analysts. *British Journal of Management, 33*(3), 1200–1220. doi:10.1111/1467-8551.12549

Ayat, M., Imran, M., Ullah, A., & Kang, C. W. (2020). Current Trends Analysis and Prioritization of Success Factors: A Systematic Literature Review of ICT Projects. *International Journal of Managing Projects in Business*.

Babu, S. S., Raghavan, N., Raplee, J., Foster, S. J., Frederick, C., Haines, M., & Dehoff, R. R. (2018). Additive manufacturing of nickel superalloys: Opportunities for innovation and challenges related to qualification. *Metallurgical and Materials Transactions. A, Physical Metallurgy and Materials Science*, *49*(9), 3764–3780. doi:10.100711661-018-4702-4

Baeza-Yates, R. (2022). Ethical Challenges in AI. *Proceedings of the 15th ACM International Conference on Web Search and Data Mining.*

Bag, S., Dhamija, P., Singh, R. K., Rahman, M. S., & Sreedharan, V. R. (2023). Big data analytics and artificial intelligence technologies based collaborative platform empowering absorptive capacity in health care supply chain: An empirical study. *Journal of Business Research*, *154*, 113315. doi:10.1016/j.jbusres.2022.113315

Bala, M., & Verma, D. (2018). A critical review of digital marketing. M. Bala, D. Verma (2018). A Critical Review of Digital Marketing. International Journal of Management. *IT & Engineering*, *8*(10), 321–339.

Balkin, J. M. (2007). The First Amendment and the second commandment. *New York University Law Review*, *81*(5), 1639–1683.

Baraldi, E., & Ratajczak-Mrozek, M. (2019). From Supplier to Center of Excellence and beyond: The Network Position Development of a Business Unit within "IKEA Industry." *Journal of Business Research*, *100*, 1–15. doi:10.1016/j.jbusres.2019.03.008

Barazanchi, A., Li, K. C., Al-Amleh, B., Lyons, K., & Waddell, J. N. (2020). Mechanical properties of laser-sintered 3D-printed cobalt chromium and soft-milled cobalt chromium. *Prosthesis*, *2*(4), 28. doi:10.3390/prosthesis2040028

Barbosa, L., Lopes, T. G., Aguiar, P. R., de Oliveira, R. G. Junior, & França, T. V. (2021). Evaluating Temperature Influence on Low-Cost Microphone Response for 3D Printing Process Monitoring. *Engineering Proceedings*, *10*(1), 67.

Baruti, R. (2023). *Analysis and Implementation of a Business Intelligence QlikView application for logistic and procurement management. Sews Cabind case for the shortage problem.* Academic Press.

Baser, P., & Saini, J. R. (2023). AI-Based Intelligent Solution in Legal Profession. *Lecture Notes in Networks and Systems*, *516*, 75–84. doi:10.1007/978-981-19-5221-0_8

Batwara, A., & Verma, P. (2016). *Influence of process parameters on surface roughness and material removal rate during turning in cnc lathe – an artificial neural network and surface*. Academic Press.

Batwara, A., Sharma, V., Makkar, M., & Giallanza, A. (2022). An Empirical Investigation of Green Product Design and Development Strategies for Eco Industries Using Kano Model and Fuzzy AHP. *Sustainability (Basel)*, *14*(14), 8735. Advance online publication. doi:10.3390u14148735

Batwara, A., Sharma, V., Makkar, M., & Giallanza, A. (2023). Towards smart sustainable development through value stream mapping – a systematic literature review. *Heliyon*, *9*(5), e15852. doi:10.1016/j.heliyon.2023.e15852 PMID:37215771

Beard, L., & Aghassibakes, N. (2021). Tableau (version 2020.3). *Journal of the Medical Library Association: JMLA*, *109*(1), 159. doi:10.5195/jmla.2021.1135

Bedmar, J., Riquelme, A., Rodrigo, P., Torres, B., & Rams, J. (2021). Comparison of different additive manufacturing methods for 316l stainless steel. *Materials (Basel)*, *14*(21), 6504. doi:10.3390/ma14216504 PMID:34772039

Behera, R. K., Gunasekaran, A., Gupta, S., Kamboj, S., & Bala, P. K. (2020). Personalized digital marketing recommender engine. *Journal of Retailing and Consumer Services*, *53*, 101799. doi:10.1016/j.jretconser.2019.03.026

Belhadi, A., Zkik, K., Cherrafi, A., Yusof, S. M., & El fezazi, S. (2019). Understanding Big Data Analytics for Manufacturing Processes: Insights from Literature Review and Multiple Case Studies. *Computers & Industrial Engineering*, *137*, 106099. doi:10.1016/j.cie.2019.106099

Bell, C. (2014). *Maintaining and troubleshooting your 3D printer*. Apress. doi:10.1007/978-1-4302-6808-6

Berselli, G., Vertechy, R., Pellicciari, M., & Vassura, G. (2011). Hyperelastic modeling of rubber-like photopolymers for additive manufacturing processes. In M. Hoque (Ed.), *Rapid Prototyping Technology-Principles and Functional Requirements* (pp. 135–152). IntechOpen Ltd. doi:10.5772/20174

Bersin, J. (2019). *The Ethics of People Analytics and AI in the Workplace: Four Dimensions of Trust*. The Medium.

Bezek, U., & Shams, P. (2020). Analysis of Airline Tweets by Using Machine Learning Methods. *International Journal of Engineering Research and Applications*, *10*. Www.Ijera.Com

Bharadiya, J. P. (2023). Artificial Intelligence in Transportation Systems A Critical Review. *American Journal of Computing and Engineering*, *6*(1), 34–45. doi:10.47672/ajce.1487

Bhatt, H., Bahuguna, R., Singh, R., Gehlot, A., Akram, S. V., Priyadarshi, N., & Twala, B. (2022). Artificial Intelligence and Robotics Led Technological Tremors: A Seismic Shift towards Digitizing the Legal Ecosystem. *Applied Sciences*, *12*(22), 11687. doi:10.3390/app122211687

Bibri, S. E., Allam, Z., & Krogstie, J. (2022). The Metaverse as a virtual form of data-driven smart urbanism: Platformization and its underlying processes, institutional dimensions, and disruptive impacts. *Computational Urban Science*, *2*(1), 24. doi:10.100743762-022-00051-0 PMID:35974838

Bigne, E., Ruiz, C., Perez-Cabañero, C., & Cuenca, A. (2023). Are customer star ratings and sentiments aligned? A deep learning study of the customer service experience in tourism destinations. *Service Business*, *17*(1), 281–314. doi:10.100711628-023-00524-0

Bikas, H., Stavropoulos, P., & Chryssolouris, G. (2016). Additive manufacturing methods and modelling approaches: A critical review. *International Journal of Advanced Manufacturing Technology*, *83*(1-4), 389–405. doi:10.100700170-015-7576-2

Biocca, F. (1997). The Cyborg's Dilemma: Progressive Embodiment in Virtual Environments. *Journal of Computer-Mediated Communication*, *3*(2), JCMC321. doi:10.1111/j.1083-6101.1997.tb00070.x

Biswas, M. C., Chakraborty, S., Bhattacharjee, A., & Mohammed, Z. (2021). 4D printing of shape memory materials for textiles: Mechanism, mathematical modeling, and challenges. *Advanced Functional Materials*, *31*(19), 2100257. doi:10.1002/adfm.202100257

Blakey-Milner, B., Gradl, P., Snedden, G., Brooks, M., Pitot, J., Lopez, E., Leary, M., Berto, F., & Du Plessis, A. (2021). Metal additive manufacturing in aerospace: A review. *Materials & Design*, *209*, 110008. doi:10.1016/j.matdes.2021.110008

Bogue, R. (2013). 3D printing: The dawn of a new era in manufacturing? *Assembly Automation*, *33*(4), 307–311. doi:10.1108/AA-06-2013-055

Bolstad, R., Gilbert, J., McDowall, S., Bull, A., Boyd, S., & Hipkins, R. (2012). *Supporting Future-oriented Learning and Teaching—A New Zealand Perspective*. Ministry of Education.

Bonada, J., Xuriguera, E., Calvo, L., Poudelet, L., Cardona, R., Padilla, J. A., Niubó, M., & Fenollosa, F. (2019). Analysis of printing parameters for metal additive manufactured parts through Direct Ink Writing process. *Procedia Manufacturing*, *41*, 666–673. doi:10.1016/j.promfg.2019.09.056

Bonta, V., Kumaresh, N., & Janardhan, N. (2019). A comprehensive study on lexicon based approaches for sentiment analysis. *Asian Journal of Computer Science and Technology*, *8*(S2), 1–6. doi:10.51983/ajcst-2019.8.S2.2037

Boretti, A. (2023). Ethical reflections on AI taking decisions for incapacitated patients. *Ethique & Santé*, *20*(3), 174–179. doi:10.1016/j.etiqe.2023.06.001

Borgia, S., Pellegrinelli, S., Bianchi, G., & Leonesio, M. (2014). A reduced model for energy consumption analysis in milling. *Procedia CIRP*, *17*, 529–534. doi:10.1016/j.procir.2014.01.105

Borlaug, S. B., & Langfeldt, L. (2020). One Model Fits All? How Centres of Excellence Affect Research Organisation and Practices in the Humanities. *Studies in Higher Education*, *45*(8), 1746–1757. doi:10.1080/03075079.2019.1615044

Boubekri, N., Shaikh, V., & Foster, P. R. (2010). A technology enabler for green machining: Minimum quantity lubrication (MQL). *Journal of Manufacturing Technology Management*, *21*(5), 556–566. doi:10.1108/17410381011046968

Brown, L., & Lee, E. (2021). Autonomy and Consent in AI-Enhanced Virtual Environments. *Journal of Virtual Ethics*, *6*(1), 45–62.

Burdea, G., & Coiffet, P. (2003). *Virtual Reality Technology*. John Wiley & Sons. doi:10.1162/105474603322955950

Burton, G., Goo, C., Zhang, Y., & Jun, M. B. G. (2014). Use of vegetable oil in water emulsion achieved through ultrasonic atomization as cutting fluids in micro-milling. *Journal of Manufacturing Processes*, *16*(3), 405–413. Advance online publication. doi:10.1016/j.jmapro.2014.04.005

Calo, R. (2010). Robots and Privacy. *Harvard Law Review*, *154*(2), 1671–1762.

Carausu, C. (n.d.). *Selection of Subtractive Manufacturing Technology Versus Additive Manufacturing Technology for Rapid Prototyping of a Polymeric Product*. Academic Press.

Casola, V., De Benedictis, A., Riccio, A., Rivera, D., Mallouli, W., & de Oca, E. M. (2019). A security monitoring system for internet of things. *Internet of Things : Engineering Cyber Physical Human Systems*, *7*, 100080. doi:10.1016/j.iot.2019.100080

Censius. (n.d.). *What is Ethical AI - Responsible AI*. Censius.

Champeau, M., Heinze, D. A., Viana, T. N., de Souza, E. R., Chinellato, A. C., & Titotto, S. (2020). 4D printing of hydrogels: A review. *Advanced Functional Materials*, *30*(31), 1910606. doi:10.1002/adfm.201910606

Chander, B., Pal, S., De, D., & Buyya, R. (2022). Artificial Intelligence-based Internet of Things for Industry 5.0. *Internet of Things : Engineering Cyber Physical Human Systems*, 3–45. doi:10.1007/978-3-030-87059-1_1

Chandra, M., Glassman, D., & Frantz, S. (2019). Exploring the Impact of Mixed Reality on Robotic Surgical Training. *Journal of Robotic Surgery*, *13*(4), 579–583. PMID:31555957

Chang, T., Liu, C., Young, L., Wang, V., Jian, S., & Bao, B. (2012). Science of the Total Environment. *The Science of the Total Environment*, *416*, 89–96. doi:10.1016/j.scitotenv.2011.11.071 PMID:22221876

Chang, V., Strittmatter, S., Jesus, V., Golightly, L., Ni, P., & Hall, K. (2023, April). Exploring Risks in the Metaverse in an Immersive Digital Economy. In *5th International Conference on Finance, Economics, Management and IT Business* (pp. 107-113). SciTePress. 10.5220/0011990900003494

Chang, Y. (2014). *Cisco Chooses to Be Smart in Songdo - Cisco's Global Center of Excellence in Korea develops smart city solutions for the Internet of Everything era*. Invest Korea.

Cheng, T., Thielen, M., Poppinga, S., Tahouni, Y., Wood, D., Steinberg, T., Menges, A., & Speck, T. (2021). Bio-Inspired Motion Mechanisms: Computational Design and Material Programming of Self-Adjusting 4D-Printed Wearable Systems. *Advancement of Science*, *8*(13), 2100411. doi:10.1002/advs.202100411 PMID:34258167

Cheong, K., & Lee, K.-H. (2016). Malaysia's Education Crisis - Can TVET Help? *Malaysian Journal of Economic Studies : Journal of the Malaysian Economic Association and the Faculty of Economics and Administration, University of Malaya*, *53*, 115–134.

Chi, H. R., & Radwan, A. (2023). Full-Decentralized Federated Learning-Based Edge Computing Peer Offloading Towards Industry 5.0. *IEEE International Conference on Industrial Informatics (INDIN)*. 10.1109/INDIN51400.2023.10218137

Choi, J., Kwon, O. C., Jo, W., Lee, H. J., & Moon, M. W. (2015). 4D printing technology: A review. *3D Printing and Additive Manufacturing, 2*(4), 159–167. doi:10.1089/3dp.2015.0039

Choi, J.-S., Choi, S.-W., & Lee, E.-B. (2023). Modeling of Predictive Maintenance Systems for Laser-Welders in Continuous Galvanizing Lines Based on Machine Learning with Welder Control Data. *Sustainability (Basel), 15*(9), 7676. doi:10.3390u15097676

Chua, C. K., & Sing, S. L. (2022). Editors' foreword to the inaugural issue of Materials Science in Additive Manufacturing. *Materials Science in Additive Manufacturing, 1*(1), 2. doi:10.18063/msam.v1i1.2

Çinar, Z. M., Nuhu, A. A., Zeeshan, Q., Korhan, O., Asmael, M., & Safaei, B. (2020). Machine Learning in Predictive Maintenance towards Sustainable Smart Manufacturing in Industry 4.0. *Sustainability, 12*(19), 8211. doi:10.3390/su12198211

Cohen, Y., Faccio, M., Pilati, F., & Yao, X. (2019). Design and management of digital manufacturing and assembly systems in the Industry 4.0 era. *International Journal of Advanced Manufacturing Technology*, *105*(9), 3565–3577. doi:10.100700170-019-04595-0

Consalvo, M., & Ess, C. (2011). *The Handbook of Internet Studies*. Wiley-Blackwell. doi:10.1002/9781444314861

Crossler, R. E., Johnston, A. C., Lowry, P. B., Hu, Q., Warkentin, M., & Baskerville, R. (2013). Future directions for behavioral information security research. *Computers & Security, 32*, 90-101.

CVE-2022-43633: This vulnerability allows network-adjacent attackers to execute arbitrary code on affected installations of D-Link DIR-1. (n.d.). https://www.cvedetails.com/cve/CVE-2022-43633/

da Silva, E. H. D. R., Shinohara, A. C., de Lima, E. P., Angelis, J., & Machado, C. G. (2019). Reviewing Digital Manufacturing concept in the Industry 4.0 paradigm. *Procedia CIRP*, *81*, 240–245. doi:10.1016/j.procir.2019.03.042

Da Silva, E. R., Shinohara, A. C., Nielsen, C. P., de Lima, E. P., & Angelis, J. (2020). Operating Digital Manufacturing in Industry 4.0: The role of advanced manufacturing technologies. *Procedia CIRP*, *93*, 174–179. doi:10.1016/j.procir.2020.04.063

Dadhich, A., & Thankachan, B. (2021). Social & Juristic challenges of AI for Opinion Mining Approaches on Amazon & Flipkart Product Reviews Using Machine Learning Algorithms. *SN Computer Science*, *2*(3), 180. Advance online publication. doi:10.100742979-021-00554-3

Dadhich, A., & Thankachan, B. (2022). Sentiment Analysis of Amazon Product Reviews Using Hybrid Rule-Based Approach. In A. K. Somani, A. Mundra, R. Doss, & S. Bhattacharya (Eds.), *Smart Systems: Innovations in Computing. Smart Innovation, Systems and Technologies* (Vol. 235). Springer. doi:10.1007/978-981-16-2877-1_17

Dahm, J. P., Richards, D. F., Black, A., Bertsch, A. D., Grinberg, L., Karlin, I., Kokkila-Schumacher, S., Leon, E. A., Neely, J. R., Pankajakshan, R., & Pearce, O. (2020). Sierra Center of Excellence: Lessons Learned. *IBM Journal of Research and Development*, *64*(3/4), 1–14. doi:10.1147/JRD.2019.2961069

Dai, H. N., Wang, H., Xu, G., Wan, J., & Imran, M. (2019). Big data analytics for manufacturing internet of things: Opportunities, challenges and enabling technologies. *Enterprise Information Systems*, *14*(9–10), 1279–1303. doi:10.1080/17517575.2019.1633689

Daniel, T. O., Nmadu, D., Ali, S. O., Amadi, S. O., & Onuegbu, S. C. (2022). Liquid deposition modelling 3D printing of semiconductor tin sulphide (SnS) thin film for application in optoelectronic and electronic devices. *Revista Mexicana de Física*, *68*(5). Advance online publication. doi:10.31349/RevMexFis.68.051001

Daoudi, N., Smail, Z., & Aboussaleh, M. (2023). *Machine Learning Based Predictive Maintenance: Review, Challenges and Workflow*. doi:10.1007/978-3-031-43524-9_6

Daragmeh, A. K., Drane, D., & Light, G. (2012). Needs Assessment and Beyond in the Setup of Centers for Teaching and Learning Excellence: An-Najah University Center as a Case Study. *Procedia: Social and Behavioral Sciences*, *47*, 841–847. doi:10.1016/j.sbspro.2012.06.745

Das, L., Bibhu, V., Logeswaran, R., Dadhich, K., & Sharma, B. (2023). *AI Model for Blockchain Based Industrial IoT and Big Data*. doi:10.1007/978-3-031-31952-5_3

Davenport, T., & Kalakota, R. (2019). The potential for artificial intelligence in healthcare. *Future Healthcare Journal*, *6*(2), 94–98. doi:10.7861/futurehosp.6-2-94 PMID:31363513

Davis, N. E., & Roblyer, M. D. (2005). Preparing Teachers for the “School of Tomorrow”: A Technology Action Competence Approach. *British Journal of Educational Technology*, *36*(2), 237–254.

Dede, C. (2009). Immersive Interfaces for Engagement and Learning. *Science*, *323*(5910), 66–69. doi:10.1126cience.1167311 PMID:19119219

Deepak Kumar, S., Dewangan, S., Jha, S. K., Parida, S. K., & Behera, A. (2021). 3D and 4D Printing in Industry 4.0: Trends, Challenges, and Opportunities. *Springer Proceedings in Materials*, *9*, 579–587. doi:10.1007/978-981-16-0182-8_43

Dey, S., Wasif, S., Tonmoy, D. S., Sultana, S., Sarkar, J., & Dey, M. (2020). A Comparative Study of Support Vector Machine and Naive Bayes Classifier for Sentiment Analysis on Amazon Product Reviews. *2020 International Conference on Contemporary Computing and Applications (IC3A)*, 217-220. 10.1109/IC3A48958.2020.233300

Di Francesco, M., Marchesi, L., & Porcu, R. (2023). Kryptosafe: managing and trading data sets using blockchain and IPFS. *Proceedings - 2023 IEEE/ACM 6th International Workshop on Emerging Trends in Software Engineering for Blockchain, WETSEB 2023*, 5–8. 10.1109/WETSEB59161.2023.00006

Di Nardo, M., & Yu, H. (2021). Special issue “Industry 5.0: The prelude to the sixth industrial revolution”. *Applied System Innovation*, *4*(3), 45. doi:10.3390/asi4030045

Di Pinto, A., Dragoni, Y., & Carcano, A. (2018). TRITON: The first ICS cyber attack on safety instrument systems. *Proc. Black Hat USA*, *2018*, 1–26.

Dilberoglu, U. M., Gharehpapagh, B., Yaman, U., & Dolen, M. (2017). The role of additive manufacturing in the era of industry 4.0. *Procedia Manufacturing*, *11*, 545–554. doi:10.1016/j.promfg.2017.07.148

Dixit, S., & Liu, S. (2022). Laser Additive Manufacturing of High-Strength Aluminum Alloys: Challenges and Strategies. *Journal of Manufacturing and Materials Processing*, *6*(6), 156. doi:10.3390/jmmp6060156

Djebara, A., Songmene, V., & Bahloul, A. (2013). *Effects of machining conditions on specific surface of PM 2 . 5 emitted during metal cutting*. Academic Press.

Dodziuk, H. (2016). Applications of 3D printing in healthcare. *Kardiochirurgia i Torakochirurgia Polska/Polish. The Journal of Thoracic and Cardiovascular Surgery*, *13*(3), 283–293.

Dominguez, J., & Gonzalez, P. (2022, June). Micro-Architected Lattice-Based Mesh for Fiber Filters: A Novel Additive Manufacturing Architecture for Molded Fiber Tooling. In *International Manufacturing Science and Engineering Conference* (*Vol. 85802*, p. V001T04A002). American Society of Mechanical Engineers. 10.1115/MSEC2022-85305

Dong, F., Hua, Y., & Yu, B. (2018). Peak carbon emissions in China: Status, key factors and countermeasures-A literature review. *Sustainability (Basel)*, *10*(8), 2895. Advance online publication. doi:10.3390u10082895

Du Nguyen, H., & Tran, K. P. (2023). Artificial Intelligence for Smart Manufacturing in Industry 5.0: Methods, Applications, and Challenges. *Springer Series in Reliability Engineering*, (Part F4), 5–33. doi:10.1007/978-3-031-30510-8_2

Du Nguyen, H., Tran, P. H., Do, T. H., & Tran, K. P. (2023). Quality Control for Smart Manufacturing in Industry 5.0. *Springer Series in Reliability Engineering*, (Part F4), 35–64. doi:10.1007/978-3-031-30510-8_3

Du, W., Ren, X., Chen, Y., Ma, C., Radovic, M., & Pei, Z. (2018, June). Model guided mixing of ceramic powders with graded particle sizes in binder jetting additive manufacturing. In *International Manufacturing Science and Engineering Conference* (*Vol. 51357*, p. V001T01A014). American Society of Mechanical Engineers. 10.1115/MSEC2018-6651

Duflou, J. R., Sutherland, J. W., Dornfeld, D., Herrmann, C., Jeswiet, J., Kara, S., Hauschild, M., & Kellens, K. (2012). CIRP Annals - Manufacturing Technology Towards energy and resource efficient manufacturing : A processes and systems approach. *CIRP Annals - Manufacturing Technology*, *61*(2), 587–609. doi:10.1016/j.cirp.2012.05.002

Duhigg, C. (2012). *The Power of Habit: Why We Do What We Do in Life and Business*. Random House.

Dündar, C. (2018, September). A Human-Centered Approach to Hazard Evaluation Checklists for the Risk of Back Pain in Manual Handling Tasks. *Proceedings of the Human Factors and Ergonomics Society Annual Meeting*, *62*(1), 870–874. doi:10.1177/1541931218621198

Dutton, W. H., Dopatka, A., Hills, M., Law, G., & Nash, V. (2011). *Freedom of Connection - Freedom of Expression: The Changing Legal and Regulatory Ecology Shaping the Internet*. Oxford Internet Institute.

Du, W., Ren, X., Pei, Z., & Ma, C. (2020). Ceramic binder jetting additive manufacturing: A literature review on density. *Journal of Manufacturing Science and Engineering*, *142*(4), 040801. doi:10.1115/1.4046248

Dwivedi, Y. K., Hughes, L., Baabdullah, A. M., Ribeiro-Navarrete, S., Giannakis, M., Al-Debei, M. M., Dennehy, D., Metri, B., Buhalis, D., Cheung, C. M. K., Conboy, K., Doyle, R., Dubey, R., Dutot, V., Felix, R., Goyal, D. P., Gustafsson, A., Hinsch, C., Jebabli, I., ... Wamba, S. F. (2022). Metaverse beyond the hype: Multidisciplinary perspectives on emerging challenges, opportunities, and agenda for research, practice and policy. *International Journal of Information Management*, *66*, 102542. doi:10.1016/j.ijinfomgt.2022.102542

Dzogbewu, T. C., & du Preez, W. B. (2021). Additive manufacturing of titanium-based implants with metal-based antimicrobial agents. *Metals*, *11*(3), 453. doi:10.3390/met11030453

Economic Planning Unit (EPU). (2016). *Study on the Demand and Supply of Human Capital on Technical Vocational Education and Training (TVET)*. Final Report Volume I – Main Report. 2. Malaysia: Economic Planning Unit.

Eggenberger, T., Schmid Mast, M., & Muff, B. (2016). Influence of Simulated Patients' Affective Tone of Voice on Student Learning and Emotional Responses—A Randomized Controlled Trial. *Patient Education and Counseling*, *99*(2), 273–282.

Elbardisy, H. M., Richter, E. M., Crapnell, R. D., Down, M. P., Gough, P. G., Belal, T. S., & Banks, C. E. (2020). Versatile additively manufactured (3D printed) wall-jet flow cell for high performance liquid chromatography-amperometric analysis: Application to the detection and quantification of new psychoactive substances (NBOMes). *Analytical Methods*, *12*(16), 2152–2165. doi:10.1039/D0AY00500B

Elkaseer, A., Chen, K. J., Janhsen, J. C., Refle, O., Hagenmeyer, V., & Scholz, S. G. (2022). Material jetting for advanced applications: A state-of-the-art review, gaps and future directions. *Additive Manufacturing*, *60*, 103270. doi:10.1016/j.addma.2022.103270

Elsayed, H., Zocca, A., Schmidt, J., Günster, J., Colombo, P., & Bernardo, E. (2018). Bioactive glass-ceramic scaffolds by additive manufacturing and sinter-crystallization of fine glass powders. *Journal of Materials Research*, *33*(14), 1960–1971. doi:10.1557/jmr.2018.120

Eos. (n.d.). https://www.eos.info/en/3d-printing-materials/metals/cobalt-chrome

Ervural, B. C., & Ervural, B. (2018). *Overview of Cyber Security in the Industry 4.0 Era*. doi:10.1007/978-3-319-57870-5_16

Eslami, M., Rickman, A., Vaccaro, K., Aleyasen, A., Vuong, A., Karahalios, K., & Hamilton, K. (2015). I Always assumed that I wasn't really that close to [her]: Reasoning about Invisible Algorithms in News Feeds. *Proceedings of the Eighth International Conference on Weblogs and Social Media*, 1-10. 10.1145/2702123.2702556

Espinoza, J., Xu, N. Y., Nguyen, K. T., & Klonoff, D. C. (2021). The Need for Data Standards and Implementation Policies to Integrate CGM Data into the Electronic Health Record. *Journal of Diabetes Science and Technology*, *17*(2), 495–502. doi:10.1177/19322968211058148 PMID:34802286

Eyheramendy, S., Lewis, D., & Madigan, D. (2003) On the naive bayes model for text categorization. Proceedings Artificial Intelligence & Statistics 2003.

Fahim, K. E., Kalinaki, K., & Shafik, W. (2023). Electronic Devices in the Artificial Intelligence of the Internet of Medical Things (AIoMT). In Handbook of Security and Privacy of AI-Enabled Healthcare Systems and Internet of Medical Things (pp. 41–62). CRC Press. https://doi.org/ doi:10.1201/9781003370321-3

Faidallah, R. F., Szakál, Z., & Oldal, I. (2021). Introduction to 3d printing: Techniques, materials and agricultural applications. *Hungarian Agricultural Engineering*, (40), 47–58. doi:10.17676/HAE.2021.40.47

Fantechi, A., Gnesi, S., Livi, S., & Semini, L. (2021). A spaCy-based tool for extracting variability from NL requirements. *ACM International Conference Proceeding Series, Part F171625-B*, 32–35. 10.1145/3461002.3473074

Farashi, S., & Vafaee, F. (2022). Effect of printing parameters on the tensile strength of FDM 3D samples: a meta-analysis focusing on layer thickness and sample orientation. *Progress in Additive Manufacturing*, 1-18.

Farina, I., Singh, N., Colangelo, F., Luciano, R., Bonazzi, G., & Fraternali, F. (2019). High-performance nylon-6 sustainable filaments for additive manufacturing. *Materials (Basel)*, *12*(23), 3955. doi:10.3390/ma12233955 PMID:31795290

Fast-Berglund, Å., Gong, L., & Li, D. (2018). Testing and validating Extended Reality (xR) technologies in manufacturing. *Procedia Manufacturing*, *25*, 31–38. doi:10.1016/j.promfg.2018.06.054

Fatih, M., & Öztürk, S. (2019). Experimental study of newly structural design grinding wheel considering response surface optimization and Monte Carlo simulation. *Measurement*, *147*, 106825. doi:10.1016/j.measurement.2019.07.053

Fazal, N., Haleem, A., Bahl, S., Javaid, M., & Nandan, D. (2022). Digital Management Systems in Manufacturing Using Industry 5.0 Technologies. *Lecture Notes in Mechanical Engineering*, 221–234. doi:10.1007/978-981-16-8341-1_18

Fenza, G., Orciuoli, F., Peduto, A., & Postiglione, A. (2023). Healthcare Conversational Agents: Chatbot for Improving Patient-Reported Outcomes. *Lecture Notes in Networks and Systems, 661*, 137–148. https://doi.org/ doi:10.1007/978-3-031-29056-5_14/COVER

Ferguson, C. J., Rueda, S. M., Cruz, A. M., Ferguson, D. E., Fritz, S., & Smith, S. M. (2008). Violent video games and aggression: Causal relationship or byproduct of family violence and intrinsic violence motivation? *Criminal Justice and Behavior, 35*(3), 311–332. doi:10.1177/0093854807311719

Ferrag, M. A., Maglaras, L. A., Janicke, H., Jiang, J., & Shu, L. (2017). Authentication protocols for internet of things: A comprehensive survey. *Security and Communication Networks, 2017*, 2017. doi:10.1155/2017/6562953

Ferreira, I., Vale, D., Machado, M., & Lino, J. (2019). Additive manufacturing of polyethylene terephthalate glycol/carbon fiber composites: An experimental study from filament to printed parts. *Proceedings of the Institution of Mechanical Engineers, Part L: Journal of Materials: Design and Applications, 233*(9), 1866-1878.

Ferretti, P., Leon-Cardenas, C., Santi, G. M., Sali, M., Ciotti, E., Frizziero, L., & Liverani, A. (2021). Relationship between FDM 3D printing parameters study: Parameter optimization for lower defects. *Polymers, 13*(13), 2190. doi:10.3390/polym13132190 PMID:34209372

Flores Ituarte, I., Wiikinkoski, O., & Jansson, A. (2018). Additive manufacturing of polypropylene: A screening design of experiment using laser-based powder bed fusion. *Polymers, 10*(12), 1293. doi:10.3390/polym10121293 PMID:30961218

Floridi, L. (2019). *The Logic of Information: A Theory of Philosophy as Conceptual Design*. Oxford University Press. doi:10.1093/oso/9780198833635.001.0001

Floridi, L., Cowls, J., Beltrametti, M., Chatila, R., Chazerand, P., Dignum, V., ... Luetge, C. (2018). AI4People—an Ethical Framework for a Good AI Society: Opportunities, Risks, Principles, and Recommendations. *Minds and Machines, 28*(4), 689–707. doi:10.100711023-018-9482-5 PMID:30930541

Fongsamootr, T., Thawon, I., Tippayawong, N., Tippayawong, K. Y., & Suttakul, P. (2022). Effect of print parameters on additive manufacturing of metallic parts: Performance and sustainability aspects. *Scientific Reports, 12*(1), 19292. doi:10.103841598-022-22613-2 PMID:36369254

Foteinopoulos, P., Esnault, V., Komineas, G., Papacharalampopoulos, A., & Stavropoulos, P. (2020). Cement-based additive manufacturing: Experimental investigation of process quality. *International Journal of Advanced Manufacturing Technology, 106*(11-12), 4815–4826. doi:10.100700170-020-04978-8

Frank, A. G., Dalenogare, L. S., & Ayala, N. F. (2019). Industry 4.0 technologies: Implementation patterns in manufacturing companies. *International Journal of Production Economics, 210*, 15–26. doi:10.1016/j.ijpe.2019.01.004

Franki, V., Majnarić, D., & Višković, A. (2023). A Comprehensive Review of Artificial Intelligence (AI) Companies in the Power Sector. *Energies, 16*(3), 1077. doi:10.3390/en16031077

Fratila, D., & Radu, A. (2010). *Modeling and comparing of steady thermal state at gear milling by conventional and environment-friendly cooling method*. doi:10.1007/s00170-009-2238-x

Fratila, D. (2009). Evaluation of near-dry machining effects on gear milling process efficiency. *Journal of Cleaner Production, 17*(9), 839–845. doi:10.1016/j.jclepro.2008.12.010

Friedman, N., Geiger, D., & Goldszmidt, M. (1997). Bayesian network classifiers. *Machine Learning, 29*(2/3), 31–163. doi:10.1023/A:1007465528199

Furka, S., Furka, D., Dadi, N. C. T. C. T., Palacka, P., Hromníková, D., Santana, J. A. D., & Bujdak, J. (2021). Novel antimicrobial materials designed for the 3D printing of medical devices used during the COVID-19 crisis. *Rapid Prototyping Journal, 27*(5), 890–904. doi:10.1108/RPJ-09-2020-0219

Furness, R., Stoll, A., Nordstrom, G., Martini, G., Johnson, J., Loch, T., & Klosinski, R. (2006). Minimum Quantity Lubrication (MQL) machining for complex powertrain components. *Proceedings of the International Conference on Manufacturing Science and Engineering,* 1–9. 10.1115/MSEC2006-21112

Gao, W., Zhang, Y., Ramanujan, D., Ramani, K., Chen, Y., Williams, C. B., Wang, C. C. L., Shin, Y. C., Zhang, S., & Zavattieri, P. D. (2015). The status, challenges, and future of additive manufacturing in engineering. *Computer Aided Design, 69*, 65–89. doi:10.1016/j.cad.2015.04.001

Garetti, M., & Taisch, M. (2012). Production Planning & Control : The Management of Operations Sustainable manufacturing : trends and research challenges. Taylor & Francis.

Gatões, D., Alves, R., Alves, B., & Vieira, M. T. (2022). Selective Laser Melting and Mechanical Properties of Stainless Steels. *Materials (Basel), 15*(21), 7575. doi:10.3390/ma15217575 PMID:36363178

Gbededo, M. A., Liyanage, K., & Garza-Reyes, J. A. (2018). Towards a Life Cycle Sustainability Analysis: A systematic review of approaches to sustainable manufacturing. *Journal of Cleaner Production, 184*, 1002–1015. doi:10.1016/j.jclepro.2018.02.310

Gerrikagoitia, J. K., Unamuno, G., Urkia, E., & Serna, A. (2019). Digital manufacturing platforms in the industry 4.0 from private and public perspectives. *Applied Sciences (Basel, Switzerland), 9*(14), 2934. doi:10.3390/app9142934

Ghadimi, P., Li, W., Kara, S., & Herrmann, C. (2014). Integrated Material and Energy Flow Analysis towards Energy Efficient Manufacturing. *Procedia CIRP, 15*, 117–122. doi:10.1016/j.procir.2014.06.010

Ghazinoory, S., Ameri, F., & Farnoodi, S. (2013). An Application of the Text Mining Approach to Select Technology Centers of Excellence. *Technological Forecasting and Social Change, 80*(5), 918–931. doi:10.1016/j.techfore.2012.09.001

Ghobakhloo, M., & Iranmanesh, M. (2021). Digital transformation success under Industry 4.0: A strategic guideline for manufacturing SMEs. *Journal of Manufacturing Technology Management, 32*(8), 1533–1556. doi:10.1108/JMTM-11-2020-0455

Ghobakhloo, M., Iranmanesh, M., Mubarak, M. F., Mubarik, M., Rejeb, A., & Nilashi, M. (2022). Identifying industry 5.0 contributions to sustainable development: A strategy roadmap for delivering sustainability values. *Sustainable Production and Consumption, 33*, 716–737. doi:10.1016/j.spc.2022.08.003

Gogoi & Jeyapoovan. (2016). Design and analysis of 3d printing pen. *International Journal of Engineering Sciences & Research Technology.*

Gokhare, V. G., Raut, D. N., & Shinde, D. K. (2017). A review paper on 3D-printing aspects and various processes used in the 3D-printing. *International Journal of Engineering Research & Technology (Ahmedabad), 6*(06), 953–958.

Golovianko, M., Terziyan, V., Branytskyi, V., & Malyk, D. (2023). Industry 4.0 vs. Industry 5.0: Co-existence, Transition, or a Hybrid. *Procedia Computer Science, 217*, 102-113.

Gong, K., Liu, H., Huang, C., Cao, Z., Fuenmayor, E., & Major, I. (2022). Hybrid Manufacturing of Acrylonitrile Butadiene Styrene (ABS) via the Combination of Material Extrusion Additive Manufacturing and Injection Molding. *Polymers, 14*(23), 5093. doi:10.3390/polym14235093 PMID:36501488

Goodfellow, I., Bengio, Y., & Courville, A. (2016). *Deep Learning*. MIT Press.

Grady, H. M. (2004). Centers for Excellence in Engineering Education: A Case Study. *Proceedings - Frontiers in Education Conference, 3*, 1–5. 10.1109/FIE.2004.1408680

Graybill, B., Li, M., Malawey, D., Ma, C., Alvarado-Orozco, J. M., & Martinez-Franco, E. (2018, June). Additive manufacturing of nickel-based superalloys. In *International Manufacturing Science and Engineering Conference* (*Vol. 51357*, p. V001T01A015). American Society of Mechanical Engineers.

Grover, V., Chiang, R. H., Liang, T. P., & Zhang, D. (2018). Creating strategic business value from big data analytics: A research framework. *Journal of Management Information Systems*, *35*(2), 388–423. doi:10.1080/07421222.2018.1451951

Gualtieri, L. (2021). *Methodologies and guidelines for the design of safe and ergonomic collaborative robotic assembly systems in industrial settings* [Doctoral dissertation]. Free University of Bozen-Bolzano.

Gualtieri, L., Palomba, I., Merati, F. A., Rauch, E., & Vidoni, R. (2020). Design of human-centered collaborative assembly workstations for the improvement of operators' physical ergonomics and production efficiency: A case study. *Sustainability (Basel)*, *12*(9), 3606. doi:10.3390u12093606

Guerra, A. J., Lammel-Lindemann, J., Katko, A., Kleinfehn, A., Rodriguez, C. A., Catalani, L. H., & Dean, D. (2019). Optimization of photocrosslinkable resin components and 3D printing process parameters. *Acta Biomaterialia*, *97*, 154–161. doi:10.1016/j.actbio.2019.07.045 PMID:31352105

Gulbahar, Y., & Tinmaz, H. (2006). A Case for Teacher Professional Development in Technology Integration. *Journal of Technology and Teacher Education*, *14*(4), 729–740.

Gunawan, L., Anggreainy, M. S., Wihan, L., Lesmana, G. Y., & Yusuf, S. (2023). Support vector machine based emotional analysis of restaurant reviews. *Procedia Computer Science*, *216*, 479–484. doi:10.1016/j.procs.2022.12.160

Guo, H., & Gao, W. (2022). Metaverse-powered experiential situational English-teaching design: An emotion-based analysis method. *Frontiers in Psychology*, *13*, 859159. doi:10.3389/fpsyg.2022.859159 PMID:35401297

Guo, N., & Leu, M. C. (2013). Additive manufacturing: Technology, applications, and research needs. *Frontiers of Mechanical Engineering*, *8*(3), 215–243. doi:10.100711465-013-0248-8

Guo, Z., Grijpma, D., & Poot, A. (2020). Leachable poly (trimethylene carbonate)/CaCO3 composites for additive manufacturing of microporous vascular structures. *Materials (Basel)*, *13*(15), 3435. doi:10.3390/ma13153435 PMID:32759759

Gupta, K. (2020). A review on green machining techniques. *Procedia Manufacturing*, *51*(2019), 1730–1736. doi:10.1016/j.promfg.2020.10.241

Gupta, K., Laubscher, R. F., Davim, J. P., & Jain, N. K. (2016). Recent developments in sustainable manufacturing of gears: A review. *Journal of Cleaner Production*, *112*, 3320–3330. doi:10.1016/j.jclepro.2015.09.133

Gupta, N., Weber, C., & Newsome, S. (2012). *Additive manufacturing: status and opportunities*. Science and Technology Policy Institute.

HaddadPajouh, H., Dehghantanha, A., Parizi, R. M., Aledhari, M., & Karimipour, H. (2021). A survey on internet of things security: Requirements, challenges, and solutions. *Internet of Things : Engineering Cyber Physical Human Systems*, *14*, 100129. doi:10.1016/j.iot.2019.100129

Hagendorff, T., & Danks, D. (2023). Ethical and methodological challenges in building morally informed AI systems. *AI and Ethics*, *3*(2), 553–566. doi:10.100743681-022-00188-y

Haghdadi, N., Laleh, M., Moyle, M., & Primig, S. (2021). Additive manufacturing of steels: A review of achievements and challenges. *Journal of Materials Science*, *56*(1), 64–107. doi:10.100710853-020-05109-0

Han, S. B., Lee, Y. S., Park, S. H., & Song, H. (2023). Ti-containing 316L stainless steels with excellent tensile properties fabricated by directed energy deposition additive manufacturing. *Materials Science and Engineering A*, *862*, 144414. doi:10.1016/j.msea.2022.144414

Heift, T., & Schulze, M. (2019). Natural Language Processing in CALL. The Cambridge Handbook of CALL, 216-236.

Heisel, U., & Schaal, M. (2009). Burr formation in short hole drilling with minimum quantity lubrication. *Production Engineering*, *3*(2), 157–163. doi:10.100711740-009-0153-5

Heller, R. S., & Rahal, M. (2020). The Impacts of AI on Education: Insights from the AI and Education Community. *Information and Learning Science*, *121*(1/2), 1–16.

Hellström, T. (2018). Centres of Excellence and Capacity Building: From Strategy to Impact. *Science & Public Policy*, *45*(4), 543–552. doi:10.1093cipolcx082

Hemmerle, A. (2020). *BMW Group applies AI solutions to increase paint shop quality*. BMW. https://www.press.bmwgroup.com/global/article/detail/T0307724EN/bmw-group-applies-ai-solutions-to-increase-paint-shop-quality?language=en

Hildebrandt, M., & Gutwirth, S. (2016). *Profiling the European Citizen: Cross-disciplinary Perspectives*. Springer.

Hmeidat, N. S., Kemp, J. W., & Compton, B. G. (2018, March). High-strength epoxy nanocomposites for 3D printing. *Composites Science and Technology*, *160*, 9–20. Advance online publication. doi:10.1016/j.compscitech.2018.03.008

Hoffman, D. L., & Novak, T. P. (1996). Marketing in Hypermedia Computer-Mediated Environments: Conceptual Foundations. *Journal of Marketing*, *60*(3), 50–68. doi:10.1177/002224299606000304

Hoffman, L. J., & Podgurski, A. (2017). Big Data's Disparate Impact. *Minnesota Law Review*, *101*(1), 86–150.

Hogan, S., & Volini, E. (2011). Next-generation service delivery model – Expanding the value-creation menu for consumer packaged goods organizations. In Globalization Today (pp. 26-30). New York: International Association of Outsourcing Professionals (IAOP).

Hoyos-Ruiz, J., Martínez-Cadavid, J. F., Osorio-Gómez, G., & Mejía-Gutiérrez, R. (2017). Implementation of ergonomic aspects throughout the engineering design process: Human-Artefact-Context analysis. *International Journal on Interactive Design and Manufacturing*, *11*(2), 263–277. doi:10.100712008-015-0282-3

Huang, S., Wang, B., Li, X., Zheng, P., Mourtzis, D., & Wang, L. (2022). Industry 5.0 and Society 5.0—Comparison, complementation, and co-evolution. *Journal of Manufacturing Systems*, *64*, 424–428. doi:10.1016/j.jmsy.2022.07.010

Hudak, R., Schnitzer, M., & Zivcak, J. (2021, January). Additive Manufacturing in Medicine and Tissue Engineering: Plenary Talk. In *2021 IEEE 19th World Symposium on Applied Machine Intelligence and Informatics (SAMI)* (pp. 11-12). IEEE.

Hu, M., & Liu, B. (2004). Mining and summarizing customer reviews. In *Proceedings of the 2004 ACM SIGKDD International Conference on Knowledge Discovery and Data Mining (KDDM)* (pp. 168-177). ACM.

Ilham, A., Arafat, A., Rifelino, R., & Nurdin, H. (2022). Pengaruh nozzle temperature dan layer height hasil 3d printing terhadap uji bending materiai abs. *Jurnal Vokasi Mekanika*, *4*(1), 144–150. doi:10.24036/vomek.v4i1.332

Imambi, S., Prakash, K. B., & Kanagachidambaresan, G. R. (2021). PyTorch. *EAI/Springer Innovations in Communication and Computing*, 87–104. https://doi.org/ doi:10.1007/978-3-030-57077-4_10/COVER

Ingemarsdotter, E., Jamsin, E., & Balkenende, R. (2020). Opportunities and challenges in IoT-enabled circular business model implementation–A case study. *Resources, Conservation and Recycling*, *162*, 105047. doi:10.1016/j.resconrec.2020.105047

Ingrassia, T., Nigrelli, V., Ricotta, V., & Tartamella, C. (2017). Process parameters influence in additive manufacturing. In *Advances on Mechanics, Design Engineering and Manufacturing: Proceedings of the International Joint Conference on Mechanics, Design Engineering & Advanced Manufacturing (JCM 2016), 14-16 September, 2016, Catania, Italy* (pp. 261-270). Springer International Publishing. 10.1007/978-3-319-45781-9_27

International Organization for Standardization (ISO). (2013). *ISO/IEC 27001:2013 - Information security management systems -- Requirements.* Retrieved from https://www.iso.org/standard/54534.html

Iqbal, A., Amin, R., Iqbal, J., Alroobaea, R., Binmahfoudh, A., & Hussain, M. (2022). Sentiment Analysis of Consumer Reviews Using Deep Learning. *Sustainability (Basel), 14*(17), 10844. doi:10.3390u141710844

Iqbal, Z., Yadav, M., & Masood, S. (2020). Implementation Of Supervised Learning Techniques For Sentiment Analysis Of Customer Tweets On Airline Services. *International Journal of Engineering Applied Sciences and Technology, 5*(3), 352–357. Advance online publication. doi:10.33564/IJEAST.2020.v05i03.056

Ivanov, D. (2023). The Industry 5.0 framework: Viability-based integration of the resilience, sustainability, and human-centricity perspectives. *International Journal of Production Research, 61*(5), 1683–1695. doi:10.1080/00207543.2022.2118892

Jackson, K., & Smith, T. (2019). Ethical Considerations in AI-VR Education: Balancing Efficiency and Rigor. *Educational Ethics Quarterly, 24*(4), 315–332.

Jain, H., Dhupper, R., Shrivastava, A., Kumar, D., & Kumari, M. (2023). AI-enabled strategies for climate change adaptation: Protecting communities, infrastructure, and businesses from the impacts of climate change. *Computational Urban Science, 3*(1), 1–17. doi:10.100743762-023-00100-2 PMID:36685089

Jain, P. K., Patel, A., Kumari, S., & Pamula, R. (2022). Predicting airline customers' recommendations using qualitative and quantitative contents of online reviews. *Multimedia Tools and Applications, 81*(5), 6979–6994. Advance online publication. doi:10.100711042-022-11972-7 PMID:35035267

Jain, P. K., Quamer, W., Pamula, R., & Saravanan, V. (2023). SpSAN: Sparse self-attentive network-based aspect-aware model for sentiment analysis. *Journal of Ambient Intelligence and Humanized Computing, 14*(4), 3091–3108. doi:10.100712652-021-03436-x

Jaksic, N. I. (2015, June). BYOE: Using 3D Pens for Enhancement and Rework of 3D-Printed Parts. In *2015 ASEE Annual Conference & Exposition* (pp. 26-317). 10.18260/p.23656

Jamwal, A., Agrawal, R., Sharma, M., & Giallanza, A. (2021). Industry 4.0 technologies for manufacturing sustainability: A systematic review and future research directions. *Applied Sciences (Basel, Switzerland), 11*(12), 5725. doi:10.3390/app11125725

Javaid, M., & Haleem, A. (2019). 4D printing applications in medical field: A brief review. *Clinical Epidemiology and Global Health, 7*(3), 317–321. doi:10.1016/j.cegh.2018.09.007

Javaid, M., Haleem, A., Singh, R. P., Suman, R., & Gonzalez, E. S. (2022). Understanding the adoption of Industry 4.0 technologies in improving environmental sustainability. *Sustainable Operations and Computers, 3*, 203–217. doi:10.1016/j.susoc.2022.01.008

Javaid, M., Haleem, A., Singh, R. P., Suman, R., & Rab, S. (2021). Role of additive manufacturing applications towards environmental sustainability. *Advanced Industrial and Engineering Polymer Research, 4*(4), 312–322. doi:10.1016/j.aiepr.2021.07.005

Jayal, A. D., Badurdeen, F., Dillon, O. W. Jr, & Jawahir, I. S. (2010). Sustainable manufacturing: Modeling and optimization challenges at the product, process and system levels. *CIRP Journal of Manufacturing Science and Technology*, *2*(3), 144–152. doi:10.1016/j.cirpj.2010.03.006

Jee-Peng, T., Kiong Hock, L., Alexandria, V., & Joy Yoo-Jeung, N. (2013) What Matters for Workforce Development: A Framework and Tool for Analysis. *SABER Working Paper Series*, 6.

Jeong, H. Y., & Yi, G. (2014). A service based adaptive u-learning system using UX. *TheScientificWorldJournal*, *2014*, 2014. doi:10.1155/2014/109435 PMID:25147832

Jeon, H., Park, J., Kim, S., Park, K., & Yoon, C. (2020). Effect of nozzle temperature on the emission rate of ultrafine particles during 3D printing. *Indoor Air*, *30*(2), 306–314. doi:10.1111/ina.12624 PMID:31743481

Jiang, C. P., Cheng, Y. C., Lin, H. W., Chang, Y. L., Pasang, T., & Lee, S. Y. (2022). Optimization of FDM 3D printing parameters for high strength PEEK using the Taguchi method and experimental validation. *Rapid Prototyping Journal*, *28*(7), 1260–1271. doi:10.1108/RPJ-07-2021-0166

Jiang, Q., Zhang, P., Yu, Z., Shi, H., Wu, D., Yan, H., & Tian, Y. (2021). A review on additive manufacturing of pure copper. *Coatings*, *11*(6), 740. doi:10.3390/coatings11060740

Jiang, X., Lora, M., & Chattopadhyay, S. (2020). An experimental analysis of security vulnerabilities in industrial IoT devices. *ACM Transactions on Internet Technology*, *20*(2), 1–24. doi:10.1145/3379542

Jin, M., Neuber, C., & Schmidt, H. W. (2020). Tailoring polypropylene for extrusion-based additive manufacturing. *Additive Manufacturing*, *33*, 101101. doi:10.1016/j.addma.2020.101101

Johnson, I. M., & Li, F. (2019). Fairness and Abstraction in Sociotechnical Systems. *Proceedings of the 2019 AAAI/ACM Conference on AI, Ethics, and Society*, 217-223.

Johnson, M., Jain, R., Brennan-Tonetta, P., Swartz, E., Silver, D., Paolini, J., Mamonov, S., & Hill, C. (2021). Impact of Big Data and Artificial Intelligence on Industry: Developing a Workforce Roadmap for a Data Driven Economy. *Global Journal of Flexible Systems Managment*, *22*(3), 197–217. doi:10.100740171-021-00272-y

Johnson, M., & Li, Q. (2019). Algorithmic Bias in Virtual Reality: Implications for Ethics. *Ethics in Technology and Society*, *14*(3), 210–225.

Johnston, T. G., Fellin, C. R., Carignano, A., & Nelson, A. (2019, May). Additive manufacturing of catalytically active living material hydrogels. In *Micro-and Nanotechnology Sensors, Systems, and Applications XI* (Vol. 10982, pp. 19–26). SPIE. doi:10.1117/12.2518653

Jonassen, D. H. (2010). *Learning to Solve Problems: A Handbook for Designing Problem-Solving Learning Environments*. Routledge. doi:10.4324/9780203847527

José, M. (2023). *A Comparative Study on the Performance of Security Mechanisms in Internet of Things Devices*. Academic Press.

Joshi, S., Rawat, K., C, K., Rajamohan, V., Mathew, A. T., Koziol, K., Kumar Thakur, V., & A.S.S., B. (2020). 4D printing of materials for the future: Opportunities and challenges. *Applied Materials Today*, *18*, 100490. doi:10.1016/j.apmt.2019.100490

Jovane, F., Yoshikawa, H., Alting, L., Boër, C. R., Westkamper, E., Williams, D., Tseng, M., Seliger, G., & Paci, A. M. (2008). The incoming global technological and industrial revolution towards competitive sustainable manufacturing. *CIRP Annals - Manufacturing Technology*, *57*(2), 641–659. doi:10.1016/j.cirp.2008.09.010

Junankar, A. A., Parate, S. R., Dethe, P. K., Dhote, N. R., Gadkar, D. G., Gadkar, D. D., & Gajbhiye, S. A. (2020). A review: Enhancement of turning process performance by effective utilization of hybrid nanofluid and MQL. *Materials Today: Proceedings, 38*, 44–47. doi:10.1016/j.matpr.2020.05.603

Jung, H. D., Jang, T. S., Lee, J. E., Park, S. J., Son, Y., & Park, S. H. (2019). Enhanced bioactivity of titanium-coated polyetheretherketone implants created by a high-temperature 3D printing process. *Biofabrication, 11*(4), 045014. doi:10.1088/1758-5090/ab376b PMID:31365916

Kaddoura, S., & Al Husseiny, F. (2023). The rising trend of Metaverse in education: Challenges, opportunities, and ethical considerations. *PeerJ. Computer Science, 9*, e1252. doi:10.7717/peerj-cs.1252 PMID:37346578

Kalaivani, M. S., Jayalakshmi, S., & Priya, R. (2022). Comparative analysis of sentiment classification using machine learning techniques on Twitter data. *International Journal of Health Sciences*, 8273–8280. Advance online publication. doi:10.53730/ijhs.v6nS2.7098

Kalia, K., Francoeur, B., Amirkhizi, A., & Ameli, A. (2022). In situ foam 3D printing of microcellular structures using material extrusion additive manufacturing. *ACS Applied Materials & Interfaces, 14*(19), 22454–22465. doi:10.1021/acsami.2c03014 PMID:35522894

Kalinaki, K., Fahadi, M., Alli, A. A., Shafik, W., Yasin, M., & Mutwalibi, N. (2023). Artificial Intelligence of Internet of Medical Things (AIoMT) in Smart Cities: A Review of Cybersecurity for Smart Healthcare. In Handbook of Security and Privacy of AI-Enabled Healthcare Systems and Internet of Medical Things (pp. 271–292). CRC Press. https://doi.org/ doi:10.1201/9781003370321-11

Kalinaki, K., Namuwaya, S., Mwamini, A., & Namuwaya, S. (2023). Scaling Up Customer Support Using Artificial Intelligence and Machine Learning Techniques. In *Contemporary Approaches of Digital Marketing and the Role of Machine Intelligence* (pp. 23–45). IGI Global. doi:10.4018/978-1-6684-7735-9.ch002

Kalinaki, K., Shafik, W., Gutu, T. J. L., & Malik, O. A. (2023). Computer Vision and Machine Learning for Smart Farming and Agriculture Practices. In *Artificial Intelligence Tools and Technologies for Smart Farming and Agriculture Practices* (pp. 79–100). IGI Global. doi:10.4018/978-1-6684-8516-3.ch005

Kalinaki, K., Thilakarathne, N. N., Mubarak, H. R., Malik, O. A., & Abdullatif, M. (2023). Cybersafe Capabilities and Utilities for Smart Cities. In *Cybersecurity for Smart Cities* (pp. 71–86). Springer. doi:10.1007/978-3-031-24946-4_6

Kamaliah, S., Roslan, S., Bakar, A. R., & Ghiami, Z. (2018). The Effect of Supervised Work Experience on the Acquisition of Employability Skills among Malaysian Students. *Higher Education, Skills and Work-based Learning, 8*(4), 354–364. doi:10.1108/HESWBL-05-2016-0028

Kamalov, F., Calonge, D. S., & Gurrib, I. (2023). New Era of Artificial Intelligence in Education: Towards a Sustainable Multifaceted Revolution. *Sustainability (Basel), 15*(16), 12451. doi:10.3390u151612451

Kantaros, A., Ganetsos, T., & Piromalis, D. (2023). 3D and 4D Printing as Integrated Manufacturing Methods of Industry 4.0. *3D and 4D Printing as Integrated Manufacturing Methods of Industry, 4*, 12–22.

Karakusevic, P. (2021). Architects and AI: An Ethical Discussion. *The Architectural Review, 249*(1487), 12–19.

Karanth, S., Benefo, E. O., Patra, D., & Pradhan, A. K. (2023). Importance of artificial intelligence in evaluating climate change and food safety risk. *Journal of Agriculture and Food Research, 11*, 100485. doi:10.1016/j.jafr.2022.100485

Kaur, G., & Sharma, A. (2023). A deep learning-based model using hybrid feature extraction approach for consumer sentiment analysis. *Journal of Big Data, 10*(1), 5. doi:10.118640537-022-00680-6 PMID:36686621

Kaur, P. (2022). Sentiment analysis using web scraping for live news data with machine learning algorithms. *Materials Today: Proceedings*, *65*, 3333–3341. Advance online publication. doi:10.1016/j.matpr.2022.05.409

Kechagias, J. D., Vidakis, N., Petousis, M., & Mountakis, N. (2022). A multi-parametric process evaluation of the mechanical response of PLA in FFF 3D printing. *Materials and Manufacturing Processes*, *38*(8), 941–953. doi:10.1080/10426914.2022.2089895

Kejriwal, M. (2023). *AI in Practice and Implementation: Issues and Costs*. doi:10.1007/978-3-031-19039-1_2

Kenayathulla, H. B., Ahmad, N. A., & Idris, A. R. (2019). Gaps between Competence and Importance of Employability Skills: Evidence from Malaysia. *Higher Education Evaluation and Development*, *13*(2), 97–112. doi:10.1108/HEED-08-2019-0039

Kenwright, B. (2018). Virtual Reality: Ethical Challenges and Dangers. *IEEE Technology and Society Magazine*, *37*(4), 20–25. doi:10.1109/MTS.2018.2876104

Keoh, S. L., Kumar, S. S., & Tschofenig, H. (2014). Securing the internet of things: A standardization perspective. *IEEE Internet of Things Journal*, *1*(3), 265–275. doi:10.1109/JIOT.2014.2323395

Khalid, M. Y., Arif, Z. U., Noroozi, R., Zolfagharian, A., & Bodaghi, M. (2022). 4D printing of shape memory polymer composites: A review on fabrication techniques, applications, and future perspectives. *Journal of Manufacturing Processes*, *81*, 759–797. doi:10.1016/j.jmapro.2022.07.035

Khalid, M., Ashraf, I., Mehmood, A., Ullah, S., Ahmad, M., & Choi, G. S. (2020). GBSVM: Sentiment classification from unstructured reviews using ensemble classifier. *Applied Sciences (Basel, Switzerland)*, *10*(8), 2788. Advance online publication. doi:10.3390/app10082788

Khalid, M., & Peng, Q. (2021). Investigation of printing parameters of additive manufacturing process for sustainability using design of experiments. *Journal of Mechanical Design*, *143*(3), 032001. doi:10.1115/1.4049521

Khan, A., Gul, M. A., Zareei, M., Biswal, R. R., Zeb, A., Naeem, M., Saeed, Y., & Salim, N. (2020). Movie review summarization using supervised learning and graph-based ranking algorithm. *Computational Intelligence and Neuroscience*, *2020*, 1–14. doi:10.1155/2020/7526580 PMID:32565772

Khan, S. U., Khan, N., Ullah, F. U. M., Kim, M. J., Lee, M. Y., & Baik, S. W. (2023). Towards intelligent building energy management: AI-based framework for power consumption and generation forecasting. *Energy and Building*, *279*, 112705. doi:10.1016/j.enbuild.2022.112705

Kilkki, D. S. K. (2011). *User-centered design of an instruction manual for a research vehicle*. Academic Press.

Kim, B. Y., Song, M., & Ahn, J. (2019). Building User Trust in AI-Driven Virtual Reality. *Journal of Human-Computer Interaction*, *35*(4), 375–396.

Kocher, P., Horn, J., Fogh, A., Genkin, D., Gruss, D., Haas, W., Hamburg, M., Lipp, M., Mangard, S., Prescher, T., Schwarz, M., & Yarom, Y. (2020). Spectre attacks: Exploiting speculative execution. *Communications of the ACM*, *63*(7), 93–101. doi:10.1145/3399742

Kolias, C., Kambourakis, G., Stavrou, A., & Voas, J. (2017). DDoS in the IoT: Mirai and other botnets. *Computer*, *50*(7), 80–84. doi:10.1109/MC.2017.201

Konieczny, B., Szczesio-Wlodarczyk, A., Sokolowski, J., & Bociong, K. (2020). Challenges of Co–Cr alloy additive manufacturing methods in dentistry—The current state of knowledge (systematic review). *Materials (Basel)*, *13*(16), 3524. doi:10.3390/ma13163524 PMID:32785055

Königstorfer, F., & Thalmann, S. (2022). AI Documentation: A path to accountability. *Journal of Responsible Technology, 11*, 100043. doi:10.1016/j.jrt.2022.100043

Konstantinou, C., Maniatakos, M., Saqib, F., Hu, S., Plusquellic, J., & Jin, Y. (2015, May). Cyber-physical systems: A security perspective. In *2015 20th IEEE European Test Symposium (ETS)* (pp. 1-8). IEEE. 10.1109/ETS.2015.7138763

Korniejenko, K., Łach, M., Chou, S. Y., Lin, W. T., Cheng, A., Hebdowska-Krupa, M., & Mikuła, J. (2020). Mechanical properties of short fiber-reinforced geopolymers made by casted and 3D printing methods: A comparative study. *Materials (Basel), 13*(3), 579. doi:10.3390/ma13030579 PMID:31991886

Koshiyama, A., Kazim, E., & Treleaven, P. (2022). Algorithm Auditing: Managing the Legal, Ethical, and Technological Risks of Artificial Intelligence, Machine Learning, and Associated Algorithms. *Computer, 55*(4), 40–50. doi:10.1109/MC.2021.3067225

Kovalchuk, O., Shynkaryk, M., & Masonkova, M. (2021, September). Econometric models for estimating the financial effect of cybercrimes. In *2021 11th International Conference on Advanced Computer Information Technologies (ACIT)* (pp. 381-384). IEEE. 10.1109/ACIT52158.2021.9548490

Kozak, J., Zakrzewski, T., Witt, M., & Dębowska-Wąsak, M. (2021). Selected problems of additive manufacturing using SLS/SLM processes. *Transactions on Aerospace Research, 2021*(1), 24–44. doi:10.2478/tar-2021-0003

Kreft, K., Lavrič, Z., Stanić, T., Perhavec, P., & Dreu, R. (2022). Influence of the Binder Jetting Process Parameters and Binder Liquid Composition on the Relevant Attributes of 3D-Printed Tablets. *Pharmaceutics, 14*(8), 1568. doi:10.3390/pharmaceutics14081568 PMID:36015194

Kristiawan, R. B., Imaduddin, F., Ariawan, D., & Arifin, Z. (2021). A review on the fused deposition modeling (FDM) 3D printing: Filament processing, materials, and printing parameters. *Open Engineering, 11*(1), 639–649. doi:10.1515/eng-2021-0063

Kuang, X., Roach, D. J., Wu, J., Hamel, C. M., Ding, Z., Wang, T., Dunn, M. L., & Qi, H. J. (2019). Advances in 4D Printing: Materials and Applications. *Advanced Functional Materials, 29*(2), 1805290. doi:10.1002/adfm.201805290

Kumar, S. (2020). Additive manufacturing processes. Springer.

Kumar, S., Ranjan, P., Singh, P., & Tripathy, M. R. (2020, September). Design and implementation of fault tolerance technique for internet of things (iot). In *2020 12th International Conference on Computational Intelligence and Communication Networks (CICN)* (pp. 154-159). IEEE.

Kumar, D., Choubey, A., & Singh, M. P. (2020). Restaurant Review Classification and Analysis. *Journal of Engineering Sciences, 11*(8).

Kumari, G., Abhishek, K., Singh, S., Hussain, A., Altamimi, M. A., Madhyastha, H., Webster, T. J., & Dev, A. (2022). A voyage from 3D to 4D printing in nanomedicine and healthcare: Part i. *Nanomedicine (London), 17*(4), 237–253. doi:10.2217/nnm-2021-0285 PMID:35109704

Kumar, S., & Zymbler, M. (2019). A machine learning approach to analyze customer satisfaction from airline tweets. *Journal of Big Data, 6*(1), 62. Advance online publication. doi:10.118640537-019-0224-1

Kunle, S., & Corresponding, K. (2013). *Performance Evaluation of Vegetable Oil-Based Cutting Fluids in Mild Steel Machining*. Academic Press.

Kurfess, T. R., Saldana, C., Saleeby, K., & Dezfouli, M. P. (2020). A review of modern communication technologies for digital manufacturing processes in industry 4.0. *Journal of Manufacturing Science and Engineering, 142*(11), 110815. doi:10.1115/1.4048206

Laranjeiro, N., Rodrigues, R., Marques, T., & Jorge, J. A. (2021). Investigating Explainable AI Interfaces for Collaborative Creative VR Applications. *International Journal of Human-Computer Studies, 147*, 102544.

Larsen, K. (2020). Managing the Complexity of Centres of Excellence: Accommodating Diversity in Institutional Logics. *Tertiary Education and Management, 26*(3), 295–310. doi:10.100711233-019-09053-w

Leal, R., Barreiros, F. M., Alves, L., Romeiro, F., Vasco, J. C., Santos, M., & Marto, C. (2017). Additive manufacturing tooling for the automotive industry. *International Journal of Advanced Manufacturing Technology, 92*(5-8), 1671–1676. doi:10.100700170-017-0239-8

Lecis, N., Beltrami, R., & Mariani, M. (2021). Binder jetting 3D printing of 316 stainless steel: Influence of process parameters on microstructural and mechanical properties. *La Metallurgia Italiana, 113*, 31–41.

Lee, I., & Mangalaraj, G. (2022). Big Data Analytics in Supply Chain Management: A Systematic Literature Review and Research Directions. *Big Data and Cognitive Computing, 6*(1), 17. doi:10.3390/bdcc6010017

Lee, L. H., Braud, T., Zhou, P., Wang, L., Xu, D., Lin, Z., . . . Hui, P. (2021). *All one needs to know about metaverse: A complete survey on technological singularity, virtual ecosystem, and research agenda.* arXiv preprint arXiv:2110.05352.

Lee, L. H., Lin, Z., Hu, R., Gong, Z., Kumar, A., Li, T., . . . Hui, P. (2021). *When creators meet the metaverse: A survey on computational arts.* arXiv preprint arXiv:2111.13486.

Leist, S. K., & Zhou, J. (2016). Current status of 4D printing technology and the potential of light-reactive smart materials as 4D printable materials. *Virtual and Physical Prototyping, 11*(4), 249–262. doi:10.1080/17452759.2016.1198630

Leng, J., Sha, W., Wang, B., Zheng, P., Zhuang, C., Liu, Q., Wuest, T., Mourtzis, D., & Wang, L. (2022). Industry 5.0: Prospect and retrospect. *Journal of Manufacturing Systems, 65*, 279–295. doi:10.1016/j.jmsy.2022.09.017

Leng, J., Wang, D., Shen, W., Li, X., Liu, Q., & Chen, X. (2021). Digital twins-based smart manufacturing system design in Industry 4.0: A review. *Journal of Manufacturing Systems, 60*, 119–137. doi:10.1016/j.jmsy.2021.05.011

Leng, J., Zhong, Y., Lin, Z., Xu, K., Mourtzis, D., Zhou, X., Zheng, P., Liu, Q., Zhao, J. L., & Shen, W. (2023). Towards resilience in Industry 5.0: A decentralized autonomous manufacturing paradigm. *Journal of Manufacturing Systems, 71*, 95–114. doi:10.1016/j.jmsy.2023.08.023

Levin-Zamir, D., & Bertschi, I. (2018). Media health literacy, eHealth literacy, and the role of the social environment in context. *International Journal of Environmental Research and Public Health, 15*(8), 1643. doi:10.3390/ijerph15081643 PMID:30081465

Li, F., Chen, J., & Su, Y. S. (2018). Managing the University-Industry Collaborative Innovation in China: The Case of Zhejiang NHU Company. *Journal of Organizational Change Management, 31*(1), 62–82. doi:10.1108/JOCM-04-2017-0148

Li, F., Zheng, Z., & Jin, C. (2016). Secure and efficient data transmission in the Internet of Things. *Telecommunication Systems, 62*(1), 111–122. doi:10.100711235-015-0065-y

Lin, S. J., & Tsai, C. C. (2002). Sensation Seeking and Internet dependence of Taiwanese high school adolescents. *Computers in Human Behavior, 18*(4), 411–426. doi:10.1016/S0747-5632(01)00056-5

Liu, J., Nguyen-Van, V., Panda, B., Fox, K., du Plessis, A., & Tran, P. (2022). Additive manufacturing of sustainable construction materials and form-finding structures: a review on recent progresses. *3D Printing and Additive Manufacturing, 9*(1), 12-34.

Liu, B. (2015). *Sentiment Analysis: Mining Opinions, Sentiments, and Emotions.* Morgan Kaufmann. doi:10.1017/CBO9781139084789

Liu, B., Hu, M., & Cheng, J. (2005). A Survey on Sentiment Analysis. *Proceedings of the 40th Annual Meeting of the Association for Computational Linguistics (ACL '05).*

Liu, B., Hu, M., & Cheng, J. (2005). Opinion observer: An automated approach to mining and summarizing customer reviews. In *Proceedings of the 2005 ACM SIGKDD International Conference on Knowledge Discovery and Data Mining (KDDM)* (pp. 419-428). ACM.

Liu, C., Le, L., Zhang, M., & Ding, J. (2022). Tunable Large-Scale Compressive Strain Sensor Based on Carbon Nanotube/Polydimethylsiloxane Foam Composites by Additive Manufacturing. *Advanced Engineering Materials, 24*(6), 2101337. doi:10.1002/adem.202101337

Liu, H., & Ling, D. (2020). Sustainable Computing : Informatics and Systems Value chain reconstruction and sustainable development of green manufacturing industry. *Sustainable Computing : Informatics and Systems, 28*, 100418. doi:10.1016/j.suscom.2020.100418

Liu, X., Liu, Z., Chen, P. Q., Xie, Z. Y., Lai, B. J., Zhan, B., & Lao, J. R. (2021). Human reliability evaluation based on objective and subjective comprehensive method used for ergonomic interface design. *Mathematical Problems in Engineering, 2021*, 1–16. doi:10.1155/2021/5560519

Liu, Z., Liao, H., Li, M., Yang, Q., & Meng, F. (2023). A Deep Learning-Based Sentiment Analysis Approach for Online Product Ranking With Probabilistic Linguistic Term Sets. *IEEE Transactions on Engineering Management*, 1–18. Advance online publication. doi:10.1109/TEM.2023.3271597

Li, X., Shang, J., & Wang, Z. (2017). Intelligent materials: A review of applications in 4D printing. *Assembly Automation, 37*(2), 170–185. doi:10.1108/AA-11-2015-093

Li, Y., Liu, W., Zhang, Y., Zhang, W., Gao, C., Chen, Q., & Ji, Y. (2023). Interactive Real-Time Monitoring and Information Traceability for Complex Aircraft Assembly Field Based on Digital Twin. *IEEE Transactions on Industrial Informatics, 19*(9), 9745–9756. doi:10.1109/TII.2023.3234618

Loftus, T. J., Tighe, P. J., Filiberto, A. C., Efron, P. A., Brakenridge, S. C., Mohr, A. M., Rashidi, P., Upchurch, G. R. Jr, & Bihorac, A. (2020). Artificial intelligence and surgical decision-making. *JAMA Surgery, 155*(2), 148–158. doi:10.1001/jamasurg.2019.4917 PMID:31825465

Lopatina, Y., & Filippova, A. (2020). Research of composition porosity based on 3d-printed frames and impregnated with epoxy resin. *Modern Power Engineering (MPMB 2020) IOP Conf. Series: Materials Science and Engineering, 963*.10.1088/1757-899X/963/1/012031

Loukili, M., Messaoudi, F., & el Ghazi, M. (2023). Sentiment Analysis of Product Reviews for E-Commerce Recommendation based on Machine Learning. *International Journal of Advances in Soft Computing and Its Applications, 15*(1). Advance online publication. doi:10.15849/IJASCA.230320.01

Lu, Y., Zheng, H., Chand, S., Xia, W., Liu, Z., Xu, X., Wang, L., Qin, Z., & Bao, J. (2022). Outlook on human-centric manufacturing towards Industry 5.0. *Journal of Manufacturing Systems, 62*, 612–627. doi:10.1016/j.jmsy.2022.02.001

Łyszczarz, E., Brniak, W., Szafraniec-Szczęsny, J., Majka, T. M., Majda, D., Zych, M., & Jachowicz, R. (2021). The impact of the preparation method on the properties of orodispersible films with aripiprazole: Electrospinning vs. casting and 3D printing methods. *Pharmaceutics, 13*(8), 1122. doi:10.3390/pharmaceutics13081122 PMID:34452083

Maghazei, O., & Netland, T. (2020). Drones in manufacturing: Exploring opportunities for research and practice. *Journal of Manufacturing Technology Management, 31*(6), 1237–1259. doi:10.1108/JMTM-03-2019-0099

Mahmood, A., Akram, T., Chen, H., & Chen, S. (2022). On the Evolution of Additive Manufacturing (3D/4D Printing) Technologies: Materials, Applications, and Challenges. *Polymers*, *14*(21), 4698. doi:10.3390/polym14214698 PMID:36365695

Mahmood, M. A., Ur Rehman, A., Ristoscu, C., Demir, M., Popescu-Pelin, G., Pitir, F., & Mihailescu, I. N. (2022). Advances in Laser Additive Manufacturing of Cobalt–Chromium Alloy Multi-Layer Mesoscopic Analytical Modelling with Experimental Correlations: From Micro-Dendrite Grains to Bulk Objects. *Nanomaterials (Basel, Switzerland)*, *12*(5), 802. doi:10.3390/nano12050802 PMID:35269291

Mahmoud, R., Yousuf, T., Aloul, F., & Zualkernan, I. (2015, December). Internet of things (IoT) security: Current status, challenges and prospective measures. In *2015 10th international conference for internet technology and secured transactions (ICITST)* (pp. 336-341). IEEE.

Malaysia Department of Statistics. (2020). *Pocket Stats Q3 2020, 4, 82.* Department of Statistics.

Malaysia Ministry of Education. (2015). *Malaysia Education Blueprint 2015-2025 (Higher Education).* Ministry of Education.

Mallegni, N., Milazzo, M., Cristallini, C., Barbani, N., Fredi, G., Dorigato, A., & Danti, S. (2023). Characterization of Cyclic Olefin Copolymers for Insulin Reservoir in an Artificial Pancreas. *Journal of Functional Biomaterials*, *14*(3), 145. doi:10.3390/jfb14030145 PMID:36976069

Manning, K. L., Feder, J., Kanellias, M., Murphy, J. III, & Morgan, J. R. (2020). Toward automated additive manufacturing of living bio-tubes using ring-shaped building units. *SLAS Technology*, *25*(6), 608–620. doi:10.1177/2472630320920896 PMID:32452278

Marciniak, R. (2012). *Center of Excellence as a Next Step for Shared Service Center.* Academic Press.

Marques, G., Pitarma, R. M., Garcia, N., & Pombo, N. (2019). Internet of things architectures, technologies, applications, challenges, and future directions for enhanced living environments and healthcare systems: A review. *Electronics (Basel)*, *8*(10), 1081. doi:10.3390/electronics8101081

Marseguerra, M., & Zio, E. (2000). Optimizing maintenance and repair policies via a combination of genetic algorithms and Monte Carlo simulation. *Reliability Engineering & System Safety*, *68*(1), 69–83. doi:10.1016/S0951-8320(00)00007-7

Martinez, A., & Garcia, S. (2018). Emotional Manipulation in AI-Driven Virtual Reality: Ethical Considerations. *Virtual Ethics Journal*, *3*(2), 120–138.

Mathiyazhagan, K., Sengupta, S., & Mathivathanan, D. (2019). Challenges for implementing green concept in sustainable manufacturing: a systematic review. In Opsearch (Vol. 56, Issue 1). Springer India. doi:10.100712597-019-00359-2

Matsuoka, H., Ryu, T., Nakae, T., Shutou, S., & Kodera, T. (2013). *Fundamental Research on Hobbing with Minimal Quantity Lubrication of Cutting Oil.* Academic Press.

Mawel, M. (2022). *Exploring the Strategic Cybersecurity Defense Information Technology Managers Can Implement to Reduce Healthcare Data Breaches* [Doctoral dissertation]. Colorado Technical University.

McCann, J., & Bryson, D. (2009). Smart Clothes and Wearable Technology. In *Smart Clothes and Wearable Technology.* Woodhead Publishing., doi:10.1533/9781845695668

McCann, J., & Bryson, D. (2022). *Smart clothes and wearable technology.* Woodhead Publishing.

McCormick, T. H., & Heer, J. (2017). Narrative Visualization: Telling Stories with Data. *IEEE Transactions on Visualization and Computer Graphics*, *24*(1), 451–460. PMID:27875161

McLellan, K., Sun, Y. C., & Naguib, H. E. (2022). A review of 4D printing: Materials, structures, and designs towards the printing of biomedical wearable devices. *Bioprinting (Amsterdam, Netherlands)*, *27*, e00217. doi:10.1016/j.bprint.2022.e00217

Meinert, E., Khan, A., Iyawa, G., & Vărzaru, A. A. (2022). Assessing Artificial Intelligence Technology Acceptance in Managerial Accounting. *Electronics*, *11*(14), 2256. doi:10.3390/electronics11142256

Mengist, W., Soromessa, T., & Legese, G. (2020). Method for Conducting Systematic Literature Review and Meta-Analysis for Environmental Science Research. *MethodsX*, *7*, 100777. doi:10.1016/j.mex.2019.100777 PMID:31993339

Mhlanga, D. (2023). Artificial Intelligence and Machine Learning for Energy Consumption and Production in Emerging Markets: A Review. *Energies*, *16*(2), 745. doi:10.3390/en16020745

Mickle, M. H. (2007). Establishment of the University of Pittsburgh RFID Center of Excellence. *IEEE Communications Magazine*, *45*(4), 14–16. doi:10.1109/MCOM.2007.348672

Ministry of Economic Affairs. (2019). *Summary Shared Prosperity Vision 2030 Restructuring the Priorities of Malaysia's Development*. Ministry of Economic Affairs.

Mishra, R. R., Sahoo, A. K., Panda, A., Kumar, R., Das, D., & Routara, B. C. (2020). MQL machining of high strength steel: A case study on surface quality characteristic. *Materials Today: Proceedings*, *26*, 2616–2618. doi:10.1016/j.matpr.2020.02.552

Mitchell, A., Lafont, U., Hołyńska, M., & Semprimoschnig, C. (2018). Additive manufacturing — A review of 4D printing and future applications. *Additive Manufacturing*, *24*, 606–626. doi:10.1016/j.addma.2018.10.038

Mitrovic, R., Miskovic, Z., Ristivojevic, M., Dimic, A., Danko, J., Bucha, J., & Rackov, M. (2018, July). Determination of optimal parameters for rapid prototyping of the involute gears. *IOP Conference Series. Materials Science and Engineering*, *393*(1), 012105. doi:10.1088/1757-899X/393/1/012105

Mohammed, A., & Al-Saadi, N. T. K. (2020). Ultra-high early strength cementitious grout suitable for additive manufacturing applications fabricated by using graphene oxide and viscosity modifying agents. *Polymers*, *12*(12), 2900. doi:10.3390/polym12122900 PMID:33287399

Mohan, S., Bhat, N., Pratap, R., Jamadagni, H. S., Shivashankar, S. A., Ananthasuresh, G. K., Venkataraman, V., Vinoy, K. J., Vasi, J. M., Ramgopal Rao, V., Kottantharayil, A., & Contractor, A. Q. (2010). Centers of Excellence in Nanoelectronics in India. *Biennial University/Government/Industry Microelectronics Symposium - Proceedings*, 1–4.

Moher, D., Liberati, A., Tetzlaff, J., Altman, D. G., & Group, T. P. (2009). Preferred Reporting Items for Systematic Reviews and Meta-Analyses: The PRISMA Statement. *PLoS Medicine*, 6. PMID:19621072

Mohiuddin Babu, M., Akter, S., Rahman, M., Billah, M. M., & Hack-Polay, D. (2022). The role of artificial intelligence in shaping the future of Agile fashion industry. *Production Planning and Control*, 1–15. Advance online publication. doi:10.1080/09537287.2022.2060858

Mohol, S. S., & Sharma, V. (2021). Functional applications of 4D printing: A review. *Rapid Prototyping Journal*, *27*(8), 1501–1522. doi:10.1108/RPJ-10-2020-0240

Moldavska, A., & Welo, T. (2017). The concept of sustainable manufacturing and its definitions: A content-analysis based literature review. *Journal of Cleaner Production*, *166*, 744–755. doi:10.1016/j.jclepro.2017.08.006

Monkeylearn. (n.d.). https://monkeylearn.com/sentiment-analysis/

Montoya-Reyes, M., Gil-Samaniego-Ramos, M., González-Angeles, A., Mendoza-Muñoz, I., & Navarro-González, C. R. (2020). Novel ergonomic triad model to calculate a sustainable work index for the manufacturing industry. *Sustainability (Basel), 12*(20), 8316. doi:10.3390u12208316

Moon, D., Lee, M. G., Sun, J. Y., Song, K. H., & Doh, J. (2022). Jammed Microgel-Based Inks for 3D Printing of Complex Structures Transformable via pH/Temperature Variations. *Macromolecular Rapid Communications, 43*(19), 2200271. doi:10.1002/marc.202200271 PMID:35686322

Moroni, S., Casettari, L., & Lamprou, D. A. (2022). 3D and 4D Printing in the Fight against Breast Cancer. *Biosensors (Basel), 12*(8), 568. doi:10.3390/bios12080568 PMID:35892465

Msallem, B., Sharma, N., Cao, S., Halbeisen, F. S., Zeilhofer, H. F., & Thieringer, F. M. (2020). Evaluation of the dimensional accuracy of 3D-printed anatomical mandibular models using FFF, SLA, SLS, MJ, and BJ printing technology. *Journal of Clinical Medicine, 9*(3), 817. doi:10.3390/jcm9030817 PMID:32192099

Mtetwa, N. S., Tarwireyi, P., Abu-Mahfouz, A. M., & Adigun, M. O. (2019, November). Secure firmware updates in the internet of things: A survey. In *2019 International Multidisciplinary Information Technology and Engineering Conference (IMITEC)* (pp. 1-7). IEEE. 10.1109/IMITEC45504.2019.9015845

Muhammad, A. R., Sakura, R. R., Dwilaksana, D., & Trifiananto, M. (2022). Layer Height, Temperature Nozzle, Infill Geometry and Printing Speed Effect on Accuracy 3D Printing PETG. *REM (Rekayasa Energi Manufaktur) Jurnal, 7*(2), 81–88.

Muhindo, D., Elkanayati, R., Srinivasan, P., Repka, M. A., & Ashour, E. A. (2023). Recent advances in the applications of additive manufacturing (3D printing) in drug delivery: A comprehensive review. *AAPS PharmSciTech, 24*(2), 57. doi:10.120812249-023-02524-9 PMID:36759435

Mujahid, M., Rustam, F., Alasim, F., Siddique, M., & Ashraf, I. (2023). What people think about fast food: Opinions analysis and LDA modeling on fast food restaurants using unstructured tweets. *PeerJ. Computer Science, 9*, e1193. Advance online publication. doi:10.7717/peerj-cs.1193 PMID:37346556

Mujber, T. S., Szecsi, T., & Hashmi, M. S. (2004). Virtual reality applications in manufacturing process simulation. *Journal of Materials Processing Technology, 155*, 1834–1838. doi:10.1016/j.jmatprotec.2004.04.401

Müller, J. (2020). Enabling technologies for Industry 5.0. European Commission.

Munechika, D., Wang, Z. J., Reidy, J., Rubin, J., Gade, K., Kenthapadi, K., & Chau, D. H. (2022). Visual Auditor: Interactive Visualization for Detection and Summarization of Model Biases. *Proceedings - 2022 IEEE Visualization Conference - Short Papers, VIS 2022*, 45–49. 10.1109/VIS54862.2022.00018

Murkute, Gaikwad, Kathar, Sanap, & Raut. (2022). 3D printing technology and short introduction in 3D bio-printed matrices for in vitro tumor model. *International Journal of Science & Engineering Development Research, 7*(2), 217 – 228.

Mutinda, J., Mwangi, W., & Okeyo, G. (2023). Sentiment Analysis of Text Reviews Using Lexicon-Enhanced Bert Embedding (LeBERT) Model with Convolutional Neural Network. *Applied Sciences (Basel, Switzerland), 13*(3), 1445. doi:10.3390/app13031445

Mystakidis, S. (2022). Metaverse. *Encyclopedia, 2*(1), 486–497. doi:10.3390/encyclopedia2010031

Nambiar, A., & Mundra, D. (2022). An Overview of Data Warehouse and Data Lake in Modern Enterprise Data Management. *Big Data and Cognitive Computing, 6*(4), 132. doi:10.3390/bdcc6040132

Namtao, M., Larcher, S., Gavazzeni, C., & Angelo Porcelli, G. (2023). *Enel automates large-scale power grid asset management and anomaly detection using Amazon SageMaker | AWS Machine Learning Blog*. Amazon. https://aws.amazon.com/blogs/machine-learning/enel-automates-large-scale-power-grid-asset-management-and-anomaly-detection-using-amazon-sagemaker/

Narin, N. G. (2021). A content analysis of the metaverse articles. *Journal of Metaverse*, *1*(1), 17–24.

Nasir, M. H. N., & Sahibuddin, S. (2011). Critical Success Factors for Software Projects: A Comparative Study. *Scientific Research and Essays*, *6*(10), 2174–2186. doi:10.5897/SRE10.1171

National Institute of Standards and Technology (NIST). (n.d.). *NIST Cybersecurity Framework*. Retrieved from https://www.nist.gov/cyberframework

Ngo, T. D., Kashani, A., Imbalzano, G., Nguyen, K. T., & Hui, D. (2018). Additive manufacturing (3D printing): A review of materials, methods, applications and challenges. *Composites. Part B, Engineering*, *143*, 172–196. doi:10.1016/j.compositesb.2018.02.012

Nigenda, D., Karnin, Z., Zafar, M. B., Ramesha, R., Tan, A., Donini, M., & Kenthapadi, K. (2022). Amazon SageMaker Model Monitor: A System for Real-Time Insights into Deployed Machine Learning Models. *Proceedings of the ACM SIGKDD International Conference on Knowledge Discovery and Data Mining*, 3671–3681. 10.1145/3534678.3539145

Nikolic, B., Ignjatic, J., Suzic, N., Stevanov, B., & Rikalovic, A. (2017). Predictive manufacturing systems in industry 4.0: Trends, benefits and challenges. *Annals of DAAAM & Proceedings, 28.*

Nofar, M., Utz, J., Geis, N., Altstädt, V., & Ruckdäschel, H. (2022). Foam 3D printing of thermoplastics: A symbiosis of additive manufacturing and foaming technology. *Advancement of Science*, *9*(11), 2105701. doi:10.1002/advs.202105701 PMID:35187843

Noori, B. (2021). Classification of Customer Reviews Using Machine Learning Algorithms. *Applied Artificial Intelligence*, *35*(8), 567–588. doi:10.1080/08839514.2021.1922843

Nti, I. K., Quarcoo, J. A., Aning, J., & Fosu, G. K. (2022). A mini-review of machine learning in big data analytics: Applications, challenges, and prospects. *Big Data Mining and Analytics*, *5*(2), 81–97. doi:10.26599/BDMA.2021.9020028

Ntouanoglou, K., Stavropoulos, P., & Mourtzis, D. (2018). 4D printing prospects for the aerospace industry: A critical review. *Procedia Manufacturing*, *18*, 120–129. doi:10.1016/j.promfg.2018.11.016

Obiedat, R., Qaddoura, R., Al-Zoubi, A. M., Al-Qaisi, L., Harfoushi, O., Alrefai, M., & Faris, H. (2022). Sentiment Analysis of Customers' Reviews Using a Hybrid Evolutionary SVM-Based Approach in an Imbalanced Data Distribution. *IEEE Access : Practical Innovations, Open Solutions*, *10*, 22260–22273. doi:10.1109/ACCESS.2022.3149482

Obikawa, T., Kamata, Y., & Shinozuka, J. (2006). *High-speed grooving with applying MQL.* doi:10.1016/j.ijmachtools.2005.11.007

Oh, S., Ji, H., Kim, J., Park, E., & del Pobil, A. P. (2022). Deep learning model based on expectation-confirmation theory to predict customer satisfaction in hospitality service. *Information Technology & Tourism*, *24*(1), 109–126. doi:10.100740558-022-00222-z

Okkalidis, N. (2022). 3D printing methods for radiological anthropomorphic phantoms. *Physics in Medicine and Biology*, *67*(15), 15TR04. doi:10.1088/1361-6560/ac80e7 PMID:35830787

Operation ShadowHammer: new supply chain attack threatens hundreds of thousands of users worldwide. (2021, May 26). https://www.kaspersky.com/about/press-releases/2019_operation-shadowhammer-new-supply-chain-attack

Osouli-Bostanabad, K., Masalehdan, T., Kapsa, R. M. I., Quigley, A., Lalatsa, A., Bruggeman, K. F., Franks, S. J., Williams, R. J., & Nisbet, D. R. (2022). Traction of 3D and 4D Printing in the Healthcare Industry: From Drug Delivery and Analysis to Regenerative Medicine. *ACS Biomaterials Science & Engineering*, *8*(7), 2764–2797. doi:10.1021/acsbiomaterials.2c00094 PMID:35696306

Öztürk, S., & Fatih, M. (2019). *Modeling and optimization of machining parameters during grinding of flat glass using response surface methodology and probabilistic uncertainty analysis based on Monte Carlo simulation.* doi:10.1016/j.measurement.2019.05.098

Pacillo, G. A., Ranocchiai, G., Loccarini, F., & Fagone, M. (2021). Additive manufacturing in construction: A review on technologies, processes, materials, and their applications of 3D and 4D printing. *Material Design & Processing Communications*, *3*(5), e253. doi:10.1002/mdp2.253

Pack, R. C., Romberg, S. K., Badran, A. A., Hmeidat, N. S., Yount, T., & Compton, B. G. (2020). Carbon fiber and syntactic foam hybrid materials via core–shell material extrusion additive manufacturing. *Advanced Materials Technologies*, *5*(12), 2000731. doi:10.1002/admt.202000731

Palaiologk, A., Koller, B., & Wierse, A. (2016). Centre of Excellence for HPC and Engineering: Concept Development. *eChallenges e-2015 Conference Proceedings*, 1–10.

Panagou, S., Neumann, W. P., & Fruggiero, F. (2023). A scoping review of human robot interaction research towards Industry 5.0 human-centric workplaces. *International Journal of Production Research*, 1–17. Advance online publication. doi:10.1080/00207543.2023.2172473

Panariello, D., Grazioso, S., Caporaso, T., Di Gironimo, G., & Lanzotti, A. (2021). User-centered approach for design and development of industrial workplace. *International Journal on Interactive Design and Manufacturing*, *15*(1), 121–123. doi:10.100712008-020-00737-x

Pang, B., & Lee, L. (2002). A sentimental education: Sentiment analysis using subjectivity and polarity of text. In *Proceedings of the 2002 Conference on Empirical Methods in Natural Language Processing (EMNLP)* (pp. 280-289). Academic Press.

Papetti, A., Gregori, F., Pandolfi, M., Peruzzini, M., & Germani, M. (2020). A method to improve workers' well-being toward human-centered connected factories. *Journal of Computational Design and Engineering*, *7*(5), 630–643. doi:10.1093/jcde/qwaa047

Park, S. M., & Kim, Y. G. (2022). A metaverse: Taxonomy, components, applications, and open challenges. *IEEE Access : Practical Innovations, Open Solutions*, *10*, 4209–4251. doi:10.1109/ACCESS.2021.3140175

Parupelli, S., & Desai, S. (2019). A comprehensive review of additive manufacturing (3d printing): Processes, applications and future potential. *American Journal of Applied Sciences*, *16*(8), 244–272. doi:10.3844/ajassp.2019.244.272

Paschek, D., Luminosu, C.-T., & Ocakci, E. (2022). *Industry 5.0 Challenges and Perspectives for Manufacturing Systems in the Society 5.0.* doi:10.1007/978-981-16-7365-8_2

Patel, Oza, & Agrawal. (2023). Sentiment Analysis of Customer Feedback and Reviews for Airline Services using Language Representation Model. *Procedia Comput. Sci, 218*, 2459 – 2467.

Patel, A., Oza, P., & Agrawal, S. (2022). Sentiment Analysis of Customer Feedback and Reviews for Airline Services using Language Representation Model. *Procedia Computer Science*, *218*, 2459–2467. Advance online publication. doi:10.1016/j.procs.2023.01.221

Patel, R., Dhimmar, V., Kagzi, S., & Patel, M. (2022). Investigation of Fused Deposition Modelling Process Parameters in 3D Printing for Composite Material (Poly Lactic Acid and Banana Fibre). *International Journal of Automotive and Mechanical Engineering*, *19*(3), 10028–10038. doi:10.15282/ijame.19.3.2022.14.0774

Paudel, P., Kwon, Y. J., Kim, D. H., & Choi, K. H. (2022). Industrial Ergonomics Risk Analysis Based on 3D-Human Pose Estimation. *Electronics (Basel)*, *11*(20), 3403. doi:10.3390/electronics11203403

Paul, M., Roenspieß, A., Mentler, T., & Herczeg, M. (2014). The usability engineering repository (UsER). *Software Engineering*.

Pavitha, N., Pungliya, V., Raut, A., Bhonsle, R., Purohit, A., Patel, A., & Shashidhar, R. (2022). Movie recommendation and sentiment analysis using machine learning. *Global Transitions Proceedings*, *3*(1), 279–284. doi:10.1016/j.gltp.2022.03.012

Paz, E., Jiménez, M., Romero, L., Espinosa, M. D. M., & Domínguez, M. (2021). Characterization of the resistance to abrasive chemical agents of test specimens of thermoplastic elastomeric polyurethane composite materials produced by additive manufacturing. *Journal of Applied Polymer Science*, *138*(32), 50791. doi:10.1002/app.50791

Peerzada, A. B., Rangaraju, P., Roberts, J., & Biehl, A. (2022). Influence of External Vibration on the Gravitational Flow Characteristics of Cementitious Materials: A Perspective from Application in Additive Manufacturing. *Transportation Research Record: Journal of the Transportation Research Board*, *2676*(7), 379–394. doi:10.1177/03611981221078572

Peng, Q. (2007). Virtual reality technology in product design and manufacturing. *Proceedings of the Canadian Engineering Education Association (CEEA)*.

Pérez, L., Rodríguez-Jiménez, S., Rodríguez, N., Usamentiaga, R., & García, D. F. (2020). Digital twin and virtual reality-based methodology for multi-robot manufacturing cell commissioning. *Applied Sciences (Basel, Switzerland)*, *10*(10), 3633. doi:10.3390/app10103633

Pertuzé, J. A., Calder, E. S., Edward, M., & Lucas, W. A. (2010). Best Practices for Collaboration Best Practices for Industry. *MIT Sloan Management Review*, *51*, 83–90.

Petnuchová, Horňáková, Podařil, Štúr, Ridzoňová, & Novota. (2012). Vocational Education and Training in OECD Countries. *2012 15th International Conference on Interactive Collaborative Learning, ICL 2012*, 10–15.

Pires, L. S. O., Afonso, D. G., Fernandes, M. H. F. V., & de Oliveira, J. M. M. (2023). Improvement of processability characteristics of porcelain-based formulations toward the utilization of 3D printing technology. *3D Printing and Additive Manufacturing, 10*(2), 298-309.

Prescott, B. (2016). *Artificial intelligence approach improves accuracy in breast cancer diagnosis*. Harvard Medical School. https://hms.harvard.edu/news/better-together

Priana, A. J., Tolle, H., Aknuranda, I., & Arisetijono, E. (2018). User Experience Design of Stroke Patient Communications Using Mobile Finger (MOFI) Communication Board With User Center Design Approach. *International Journal of Interactive Mobile Technologies*, *12*(2), 162. doi:10.3991/ijim.v12i2.7937

Puh, K., & Bagić Babac, M. (2023). Predicting sentiment and rating of tourist reviews using machine learning. *Journal of Hospitality and Tourism Insights*, *6*(3), 1188–1204. doi:10.1108/JHTI-02-2022-0078

Punetha, N., & Jain, G. (2023). Game theory and MCDM-based unsupervised sentiment analysis of restaurant reviews. *Applied Intelligence*, *53*(17), 20152–20173. Advance online publication. doi:10.100710489-023-04471-1 PMID:37363390

Purtova, N. (2017). *The Right to Be Forgotten: A Transatlantic Perspective*. Cambridge University Press.

Putrama, I. M., & Martinek, P. (2023). A hybrid architecture for secure Big-Data integration and sharing in Smart Manufacturing. *Proceedings of the International Spring Seminar on Electronics Technology*. 10.1109/ISSE57496.2023.10168508

Qiu, X., Cai, Z., & Peng, H. (2023). Predefined Time Consensus Control of Nonlinear Multi-agent Systems for Industry 5.0. *IEEE Transactions on Consumer Electronics*, 1. doi:10.1109/TCE.2023.3319477

Qorich, M., & el Ouazzani, R. (2023). Text sentiment classification of Amazon reviews using word embeddings and convolutional neural networks. *The Journal of Supercomputing*, *79*(10), 11029–11054. Advance online publication. doi:10.100711227-023-05094-6

Quer, G., Arnaout, R., Henne, M., & Arnaout, R. (2021). Machine learning and the future of cardiovascular care: JACC state-of-the-art review. *Journal of the American College of Cardiology*, *77*(3), 300–313. doi:10.1016/j.jacc.2020.11.030 PMID:33478654

Rabiei, F., Rahimi, A. R., Hadad, M. J., & Ashrafijou, M. (2015). Performance improvement of minimum quantity lubrication (MQL) technique in surface grinding by modeling and optimization. *Journal of Cleaner Production*, *86*, 447–460. doi:10.1016/j.jclepro.2014.08.045

Rad, A. S. (2008). *Persual on synthesis, pattern and applications of polyurethane as functional macromolecule*. Academic Press.

Rahman, N. A., Idrus, S. D., & Adam, N. L. (2022). Classification of customer feedbacks using sentiment analysis towards mobile banking applications. *IAES International Journal of Artificial Intelligence*, *11*(4), 1579. Advance online publication. doi:10.11591/ijai.v11.i4.pp1579-1587

Raihan, A. (2014). Collaboration between TVET Institutions and Industries in Bangladesh to Enhance Employability Skills. *International Journal of Engineering and Technical Research*, *2*, 50.

Raina, A., Haq, M. I. U., Javaid, M., Rab, S., & Haleem, A. (2021). 4D Printing for Automotive Industry Applications. *Journal of The Institution of Engineers (India): Series D*, *102*(2), 521–529. doi:10.1007/s40033-021-00284-z

Rajkumar, V. S., Stefanov, A., Musunuri, S., & de Wit, J. (2021, September). Exploiting ripple20 to compromise power grid cyber security and impact system operations. In *CIRED 2021-The 26th International Conference and Exhibition on Electricity Distribution* (Vol. 2021, pp. 3092-3096). IET. 10.1049/icp.2021.2146

Ramos, C. M. Q., Cardoso, P. J. S., Fernandes, H. C. L., & Rodrigues, J. M. F. (2023). A Decision-Support System to Analyse Customer Satisfaction Applied to a Tourism Transport Service. *Multimodal Technologies and Interaction*, *7*(1), 5. Advance online publication. doi:10.3390/mti7010005

Rashid, A., & Huang, C. Y. (2021). Sentiment Analysis on Consumer Reviews of Amazon Products. *International Journal of Computer Theory and Engineering*, *13*(2), 7. doi:10.7763/IJCTE.2021.V13.1287

Ray, P. P. (2018). A survey on Internet of Things architectures. *Journal of King Saud University. Computer and Information Sciences*, *30*(3), 291–319. doi:10.1016/j.jksuci.2016.10.003

Recalde, I., Gualdrón-Reyes, A. F., Echeverría-Arrondo, C., Villanueva-Antolí, A., Simancas, J., Rodriguez-Pereira, J., & Sans, V. (2023). Vitamins as Active Agents for Highly Emissive and Stable Nanostructured Halide Perovskite Inks and 3D Composites Fabricated by Additive Manufacturing. *Advanced Functional Materials*, *33*(8), 2210802. doi:10.1002/adfm.202210802

Regan, P. M., & Jesse, J. (2018). Ethical challenges of edtech, big data and personalized learning: Twenty-first century student sorting and tracking. *Ethics and Information Technology*, *21*(3), 167–179. doi:10.100710676-018-9492-2

Remus, U., & Wiener, M. (2010). A Multi-Method, Holistic Strategy for Researching Critical Success Factors in IT Projects. *Information Systems Journal*, *20*(1), 25–52. doi:10.1111/j.1365-2575.2008.00324.x

Renga, S., Ganapathy, A., & Ram Varma, T. H. (2020). Customer review analysis - Multi-label classification and sentiment analysis. *International Research Journal of Computer Science*, *07*(04), 28–32. Advance online publication. doi:10.26562/irjcs.2020.v0704.001

Research, G. E. (2023). *Predictive Maintenance*. General Electric. https://www.ge.com/research/project/predictive-maintenance

Revilla-León, M., Sadeghpour, M., & Özcan, M. (2020). A review of the applications of additive manufacturing technologies used to fabricate metals in implant dentistry. *Journal of Prosthodontics*, *29*(7), 579–593. doi:10.1111/jopr.13212 PMID:32548890

Rezapour, M. (2021). Sentiment classification of skewed shoppers' reviews using machine learning techniques, examining the textual features. *Engineering Reports*, *3*(1), e12280. Advance online publication. doi:10.1002/eng2.12280

Ribeiro, M. T., Singh, S., & Guestrin, C. (2016). "Why Should I Trust You?" Explaining the Predictions of Any Classifier. *Proceedings of the 22nd ACM SIGKDD International Conference on Knowledge Discovery and Data Mining*, 1135-1144. 10.1145/2939672.2939778

Rice, D. R., & Zorn, C. (2021). Corpus-based dictionaries for sentiment analysis of specialized vocabularies. *Political Science Research and Methods*, *9*(1), 20–35. doi:10.1017/psrm.2019.10

Rice, N., & Smith, P. C. (2001). Ethics and geographical equity in health care. *Journal of Medical Ethics*, *27*(4), 256–261. doi:10.1136/jme.27.4.256 PMID:11479357

Richter, T., & Koch, S. C. (2018). *Digital Learning Environments: New Possibilities and Opportunities*. Springer.

Righetti, G., Zilio, C., Savio, G., Meneghello, R., Calati, M., & Mancin, S. (2021, November). Experimental pressure drops during the water flow into porous materials realized via additive manufacturing. *Journal of Physics: Conference Series*, *2116*(1), 012059. doi:10.1088/1742-6596/2116/1/012059

Riva, G., Baños, R. M., Botella, C., Mantovani, F., & Gaggioli, A. (2016). Transforming Experience: The Potential of Augmented Reality and Virtual Reality for Enhancing Personal and Clinical Change. *Frontiers in Psychiatry*, *7*, 164. doi:10.3389/fpsyt.2016.00164 PMID:27746747

Roman, R., Zhou, J., & Lopez, J. (2013). On the features and challenges of security and privacy in distributed internet of things. *Computer Networks*, *57*(10), 2266–2279. doi:10.1016/j.comnet.2012.12.018

Romeijn, T., Behrens, M., Paul, G., & Wei, D. (2022). Instantaneous and long-term mechanical properties of Polyethylene Terephthalate Glycol (PETG) additively manufactured by pellet-based material extrusion. *Additive Manufacturing*, *59*, 103145. doi:10.1016/j.addma.2022.103145

Rožanec, J. M., Novalija, I., Zajec, P., Kenda, K., Tavakoli Ghinani, H., Suh, S., Veliou, E., Papamartzivanos, D., Giannetsos, T., Menesidou, S. A., Alonso, R., Cauli, N., Meloni, A., Recupero, D. R., Kyriazis, D., Sofianidis, G., Theodoropoulos, S., Fortuna, B., Mladenić, D., & Soldatos, J. (2023). Human-centric artificial intelligence architecture for industry 5.0 applications. *International Journal of Production Research*, *2023*(20), 6847–6872. doi:10.1080/00207543.2022.2138611

Ruiz-Morales, J. C., Tarancón, A., Canales-Vázquez, J., Méndez-Ramos, J., Hernández-Afonso, L., Acosta-Mora, P., Rueda, J. R. M., & Fernández-González, R. (2017). Three dimensional printing of components and functional devices for energy and environmental applications. *Energy \&. Environmental Sciences (Ruse)*, *10*(4), 846–859.

Russell, S. J., & Norvig, P. (2016). *Artificial Intelligence: A Modern Approach*. Pearson Education.

Ryan, K. R., Down, M. P., & Banks, C. E. (2021). Future of additive manufacturing: Overview of 4D and 3D printed smart and advanced materials and their applications. *Chemical Engineering Journal*, *403*, 126162. doi:10.1016/j.cej.2020.126162

Sadasivuni, K. K., Deshmukh, K., & Almaadeed, M. A. (2019). *3D and 4D printing of polymer nanocomposite materials: Processes, applications, and challenges.* doi:10.1016/C2018-0-01194-9

Šafka, J., Ackermann, M., Véle, F., Macháček, J., & Henyš, P. (2021). Mechanical properties of polypropylene: Additive manufacturing by multi jet fusion technology. *Materials (Basel)*, *14*(9), 2165. doi:10.3390/ma14092165 PMID:33922827

Saha, A., Johnston, T. G., Shafranek, R. T., Goodman, C. J., Zalatan, J. G., Storti, D. W., & Nelson, A. (2018). Additive manufacturing of catalytically active living materials. *ACS Applied Materials & Interfaces*, *10*(16), 13373–13380. doi:10.1021/acsami.8b02719 PMID:29608267

Sakib-Uz-Zaman, C., & Khondoker, M. A. H. (2023). A Review on Extrusion Additive Manufacturing of Pure Copper. *Metals*, *13*(5), 859. doi:10.3390/met13050859

Salari, F., Bosetti, P., & Sglavo, V. M. (2022). Binder Jetting 3D Printing of Magnesium Oxychloride Cement-Based Materials: Parametric Analysis of Manufacturing Factors. *Journal of Manufacturing and Materials Processing*, *6*(4), 86. doi:10.3390/jmmp6040086

Salmi, M., Ituarte, I. F., Chekurov, S., & Huotilainen, E. (2016). Effect of build orientation in 3D printing production for material extrusion, material jetting, binder jetting, sheet object lamination, vat photopolymerisation, and powder bed fusion. *International Journal of Collaborative Enterprise*, *5*(3-4), 218–231. doi:10.1504/IJCENT.2016.082334

Sá, M. J., & Serpa, S. (2023). Metaverse as a learning environment: Some considerations. *Sustainability (Basel)*, *15*(3), 2186. doi:10.3390u15032186

Samaila, M. G., Neto, M., Fernandes, D. A., Freire, M. M., & Inácio, P. R. (2018). Challenges of securing Internet of Things devices: A survey. *Security and Privacy*, *1*(2), e20. doi:10.1002py2.20

Samuelson, P. (2007). Challenges in Mapping the Public Domain. *Journal of the Copyright Society of the U.S.A.*, *55*(4), 1–17.

Sander-Staudt, M. (2010). Review of Feminist Bioethics At the Center, On the Margins, edited by Jackie Leach Scully, Laurel E. Baldwin-Ragaven, Petya Fitzpatrick. Philosophy, Ethics, and Humanities in Medicine: PEHM, 5, 18.

Santosh, K., & Gaur, L. (2021). *Artificial Intelligence and Machine Learning in Public Healthcare*. Springer Singapore. doi:10.1007/978-981-16-6768-8

Schönherr, J. A., Baumgartner, S., Hartmann, M., & Stampfl, J. (2020). Stereolithographic additive manufacturing of high precision glass ceramic parts. *Materials (Basel)*, *13*(7), 1492. doi:10.3390/ma13071492 PMID:32218270

Sedrati, A., & Mezrioui, A. (2018). A survey of security challenges in internet of things. Advances in Science. *Technology and Engineering Systems Journal*, *3*(1), 274–280.

Self, J. L., Xiao, H., Hausladen, M. M., Bramanto, R. A., Usgaonkar, S. S., & Ellison, C. J. (2022). Camphene as a Mild, Bio-Derived Porogen for Near-Ambient Processing and 3D Printing of Porous Thermoplastics. *ACS Applied Materials & Interfaces*, *14*(43), 49244–49253. doi:10.1021/acsami.2c16192 PMID:36279408

Sengupta, J., Ruj, S., & Bit, S. D. (2020). A secure fog-based architecture for industrial Internet of Things and industry 4.0. *IEEE Transactions on Industrial Informatics*, *17*(4), 2316–2324. doi:10.1109/TII.2020.2998105

Sezen, B., & Çankaya, S. Y. (2013). Effects of green manufacturing and eco-innovation on sustainability performance. *Procedia: Social and Behavioral Sciences*, *99*, 154–163. doi:10.1016/j.sbspro.2013.10.481

Sgarbossa, F., Grosse, E. H., Neumann, W. P., Battini, D., & Glock, C. H. (2020). Human factors in production and logistics systems of the future. *Annual Reviews in Control*, *49*, 295–305. doi:10.1016/j.arcontrol.2020.04.007

Shahrubudin, N., Lee, T. C., & Ramlan, R. (2019). An Overview on 3D Printing Technology: Technological, Materials, and Applications. *2nd International Conference on Sustainable Materials Processing and Manufacturing (SMPM 2019).*

Shakor, P., Nejadi, S., Paul, G., & Malek, S. (2019). Review of emerging additive manufacturing technologies in 3D printing of cementitious materials in the construction industry. *Frontiers in Built Environment*, *4*, 85. doi:10.3389/fbuil.2018.00085

Shao, P., Wu, L., Chen, L., Zhang, K., & Wang, M. (2022). FairCF: Fairness-aware collaborative filtering. *Science China. Information Sciences*, *65*(12), 222102. doi:10.100711432-020-3404-y

Sharma, D., & Sabharwal, M. (2019). Sentiment analysis for social media using SVM classifier of machine learning. *International Journal of Innovative Technology and Exploring Engineering, 8*(9). doi:10.35940/ijitee.I1107.0789S419

Shashank, S., & Goyal, V. (2023). *Unleashing Customer Insights: Harnessing Machine Learning Approaches for Sentiment Analyzing and Leveraging Customer Feedback.* Springer Nature Singapore Pte Ltd.

Sherman, R. (2014). *Centers of Excellence. Business Intelligence Guidebook From Data Integration to Analytics.* Elsevier Inc.

Sherman, W. R., & Craig, A. B. (2018). *Understanding Virtual Reality: Interface, Application, and Design.* Morgan Kaufmann.

Sherrod, L. (2023). *Supply Chain Optimization: How AI is Improving Efficiency and Reducing Costs.* LinkedIn. https://www.linkedin.com/pulse/supply-chain-optimization-how-ai-improving-efficiency-larry-sherrod

Shukla, A., & Dhir, S. (2016). Tools for data visualization in business intelligence: Case study using the tool Qlikview. *Advances in Intelligent Systems and Computing*, *434*, 319–326. doi:10.1007/978-81-322-2752-6_31

Sicari, S., Rizzardi, A., Grieco, L. A., & Coen-Porisini, A. (2015). Security, privacy and trust in Internet of Things: The road ahead. *Computer Networks*, *76*, 146–164. doi:10.1016/j.comnet.2014.11.008

Sieradzka, M., Fabia, J., Biniaś, D., Graczyk, T., & Fryczkowski, R. (2021). High-impact polystyrene reinforced with reduced graphene oxide as a filament for fused filament fabrication 3D printing. *Materials (Basel)*, *14*(22), 7008. doi:10.3390/ma14227008 PMID:34832407

Silva, H., António, N., & Bacao, F. (2022). A Rapid Semi-automated Literature Review on Legal Precedents Retrieval. Lecture Notes in Computer Science (Including Subseries Lecture Notes in Artificial Intelligence and Lecture Notes in Bioinformatics), 13566, 53–65. doi:10.1007/978-3-031-16474-3_5

Silva, S., Nuzum, A. K., & Schaltegger, S. (2019). Stakeholder expectations on sustainability performance measurement and assessment. A systematic literature review. *Journal of Cleaner Production*, *217*, 204–215. doi:10.1016/j.jclepro.2019.01.203

Sinanaj, G., & Muntermann, J. (2013). *Assessing corporate reputational damage of data breaches: An empirical analysis.* Academic Press.

Singh, B., & Verma, H. K. (2021). Dawn of Big Data with Hadoop and Machine Learning. *Machine Learning and Data Science: Fundamentals and Applications*, 47–65. doi:10.1002/9781119776499.ch3

Singh, S. N., & Sarraf, T. (2020). Sentiment Analysis of a Product based on User Reviews using Random Forests Algorithm. *2020 10th International Conference on Cloud Computing, Data Science & Engineering (Confluence)*, 112-116. 10.1109/Confluence47617.2020.9058128

Singh, A., Philip, D., & Ramkumar, J. (2015). Quantifying green manufacturability of a unit production process using simulation. *Procedia CIRP*, *29*, 257–262. doi:10.1016/j.procir.2015.01.034

Singh, A., Philip, D., & Ramkumar, J. (2016a). Green Index quantification of a unit manufacturing process through simulation experiments. *Procedia CIRP*, *41*, 1131–1136. doi:10.1016/j.procir.2016.05.073

Singh, S. K., Yang, L. T., & Park, J. H. (2023). FusionFedBlock: Fusion of blockchain and federated learning to preserve privacy in industry 5.0. *Information Fusion*, *90*, 233–240. doi:10.1016/j.inffus.2022.09.027

Singh, S., & Pareek, A. (2020). Improving Public Transport Services using Sentiment Analysis of Twitter data. *Journal of Information and Computational Science*, *10*(1).

Sinnasamy, T., & Sjaif, N. N. A. (2022). Sentiment Analysis using Term based Method for Customers' Reviews in Amazon Product. *International Journal of Advanced Computer Science and Applications*, *13*(7). Advance online publication. doi:10.14569/IJACSA.2022.0130780

Skobelev, P. O., & Borovik, S. Y. (2017). On the way from Industry 4.0 to Industry 5.0: From digital manufacturing to digital society. *Industry 4.0*, *2*(6), 307-311.

Smith, J., Johnson, A., & Williams, R. (2020). Privacy Challenges in AI-Driven Virtual Reality. *Journal of Ethics and Technology*, *10*(2), 87–104.

Song, H. C., Ray, N., Sokolov, D., & Lefebvre, S. (2017). Anti-aliasing for fused filament deposition. *Computer Aided Design*, *89*, 25–34. doi:10.1016/j.cad.2017.04.001

Soori, M., Arezoo, B., & Dastres, R. (2023). Artificial intelligence, machine learning and deep learning in advanced robotics, a review. *Cognitive Robotics*, *3*, 54–70. doi:10.1016/j.cogr.2023.04.001

Sotiriou, S., Retalis, S., & Bulus, M. (2019). Data Mining in the Context of Immersive Virtual Reality Environments for Learning. *IEEE Transactions on Learning Technologies*, *13*(3), 517–526.

Srinivasan, D., Meignanamoorthy, M., Ravichandran, M., Mohanavel, V., Alagarsamy, S. V., Chanakyan, C., Sakthivelu, S., Karthick, A., Prabhu, T. R., & Rajkumar, S. (2021). 3D printing manufacturing techniques, materials, and applications: An overview. *Advances in Materials Science and Engineering*, *2021*, 1–10. doi:10.1155/2021/5756563

Starke, A. D., & Lee, M. (2022). Unifying Recommender Systems and Conversational User Interfaces. *ACM International Conference Proceeding Series*. 10.1145/3543829.3544524

Stefano, J. S., Kalinke, C., da Rocha, R. G., Rocha, D. P., da Silva, V. A. O. P., Bonacin, J. A., & Muñoz, R. A. A. (2022). *Electrochemical (bio) sensors enabled by fused deposition modeling-based 3D printing: A guide to selecting designs, printing parameters, and post-treatment protocols*. Academic Press.

Stiles, A., Tison, T. A., Pruitt, L., & Vaidya, U. (2022). Photoinitiator selection and concentration in photopolymer formulations towards large-format additive manufacturing. *Polymers*, *14*(13), 2708. doi:10.3390/polym14132708 PMID:35808752

Straub, J. (2015). Initial work on the characterization of additive manufacturing (3D printing) using software image analysis. *Machines*, *3*(2), 55–71. doi:10.3390/machines3020055

Subeshan, B., Baddam, Y., & Asmatulu, E. (2021). Current progress of 4D-printing technology. *Progress in Additive Manufacturing*, *6*(3), 495–516. doi:10.100740964-021-00182-6

Sumalatha, M., Malleswara Rao, J. N., & Supraja Reddy, B. (2021). Optimization Of Process Parameters In 3d Printing-Fused Deposition Modeling Using Taguchi Method. *IOP Conference Series. Materials Science and Engineering*, *1112*(1), 1112. doi:10.1088/1757-899X/1112/1/012009

Sun, C., Wang, Y., McMurtrey, M. D., Jerred, N. D., Liou, F., & Li, J. (2021). Additive manufacturing for energy: A review. *Applied Energy*, *282*, 116041. doi:10.1016/j.apenergy.2020.116041

Sundar, S. S., Kang, H., Oprean, D., & Waddell, T. F. (2018). Anonymity, Privacy, and Perceived Surveillance in the Virtual School: A Naturalistic Case Study. *Internet Research*, *28*(5), 1169–1188.

Sundar, S. S., Kim, J., & Han, S. H. (2021). Interplay of Machine Agency, Media Richness, and Personalization in Persuasive Technologies. *International Journal of Human-Computer Interaction*, *37*(6), 548–562.

Suta, M. J., Béresová, M., Csámer, L., Csík, A., & Hegedűs, C. (2022). Evaluation of Polyjet and SLA 3D printers. *Fogorvosi Szemle*, *115*(2), 64-68.

Sutton, J. (2019). *Evaluation of Lignin-containing Photopolymers for use in Additive Manufacturing*. Academic Press.

Tadwalker, V. S. (2008). Create Centre of Excellence (CoE) for Better Business. Satyam Computer Services Ltd.

Tai, B. L., Stephenson, D. A., Furness, R. J., & Shih, A. J. (2014). Minimum Quantity Lubrication (MQL) in Automotive Powertrain Machining. *Procedia CIRP*, *14*, 523–528. doi:10.1016/j.procir.2014.03.044

Takahashi & Kim. (2019). 3D Pen + 3D Printer: Exploring the Role of Humans and Fabrication Machines in Creative Making. *Conference: the 2019 CHI Conference*.10.1145/3290605.3300525

Tang, S., Ummethala, R., Suryanarayana, C., Eckert, J., Prashanth, K. G., & Wang, Z. (2021). Additive Manufacturing of Aluminum-Based Metal Matrix Composites—A Review. *Advanced Engineering Materials*, *23*(7), 2100053. doi:10.1002/adem.202100053

Taylor, P., Dasch, J., Arcy, J. D., Gundrum, A., Sutherland, J., Johnson, J., Dasch, J., Arcy, J. D., Gundrum, A., Sutherland, J., Johnson, J., & Carlson, D. (n.d.). *in Automotive Plants. December 2014*, 37–41. doi:10.1080/15459620500377659

Taylor, P., Filipovic, A., & Stephenson, D. A. (2007). *Machining Science and Technology : A Minimum Quantity Lubrication (MQL) Applications in Automotive Power-Train Machining*. doi:10.1080/10910340500534258

Tay, Y. W. D., Lim, J. H., Li, M., & Tan, M. J. (2022). Creating functionally graded concrete materials with varying 3D printing parameters. *Virtual and Physical Prototyping*, *17*(3), 662–681. doi:10.1080/17452759.2022.2048521

Teodorico, C., Carmina, S., Anastasia, S., Roberto, G., Francesco, T., & Maria, R. (2014). Noise and cardiovascular effects in workers of the sanitary fixtures industry. *International Journal of Hygiene and Environmental Health*. Advance online publication. doi:10.1016/j.ijheh.2014.09.007 PMID:25455423

Tepsongkroh, P., Thongkamkaew, C., & Sasha, F. (2023). Business Intelligent Framework Using Sentiment Analysis for Smart Digital Marketing in the E-Commerce Era. *Asia Social Issues*, *16*(3), e252965. Advance online publication. doi:10.48048/asi.2023.252965

Tewani, H., Hinaus, M., Talukdar, M., Sone, H., & Prabhakar, P. (2022). *Architected syntactic foams: a tale of additive manufacturing and reinforcement parameters*. arXiv preprint arXiv:2211.00955.

Thiede, S., Posselt, G., & Herrmann, C. (2013). CIRP Journal of Manufacturing Science and Technology SME appropriate concept for continuously improving the energy and resource efficiency in manufacturing companies. *CIRP Journal of Manufacturing Science and Technology*, *6*(3), 204–211. doi:10.1016/j.cirpj.2013.02.006

Thwe, P., Aung, Y. Y., & Lwin, C. C. (2021). Naïve Bayes Classifier for sentiment analysis. *International Journal Of All Research Writings*, *3*(7), 32–35.

Tibbits, S. (2014). 4D Printing: Multi-Material Shape Change. *Architectural Design*, *84*(1), 116–121. doi:10.1002/ad.1710

Tichý, T., Šefl, O., Veselý, P., Dušek, K., & Bušek, D. (2021). Mathematical Modelling of Temperature Distribution in Selected Parts of FFF Printer during 3D Printing Process. *Polymers*, *13*(23), 4213. doi:10.3390/polym13234213 PMID:34883715

Tintarev, N., & Masthoff, J. (2012). Designing and Evaluating Explanations for Recommender Systems. In Recommender Systems Handbook (pp. 479-510). Springer.

Tiwari, A., Singh, G., & Kumar, S. (2021). *Unveiling Customer Sentiment: Harnessing Machine Learning Approaches for Analyzing and Leveraging Customer Feedback*. Springer Nature Switzerland AG.

Tlili, A., Huang, R., Shehata, B., Liu, D., Zhao, J., Metwally, A. H. S., Wang, H., Denden, M., Bozkurt, A., Lee, L.-H., Beyoglu, D., Altinay, F., Sharma, R. C., Altinay, Z., Li, Z., Liu, J., Ahmad, F., Hu, Y., Salha, S., ... Burgos, D. (2022). Is Metaverse in education a blessing or a curse: A combined content and bibliometric analysis. *Smart Learning Environments*, *9*(1), 1–31. doi:10.118640561-022-00205-x

Tosto, C., Pergolizzi, E., Blanco, I., Patti, A., Holt, P., Karmel, S., & Cicala, G. (2020). 18 July 2020, Epoxy Based Blends for Additive Manufacturing by Liquid Crystal Display (LCD) Printing: The Effect of Blending and Dual Curing on Daylight Curable Resins. *Polymers*, *12*(7), 1594. doi:10.3390/polym12071594 PMID:32708360

Tshephe, T. S., Akinwamide, S. O., Olevsky, E., & Olubambi, P. A. (2022). Additive manufacturing of titanium-based alloys-A review of methods, properties, challenges, and prospects. *Heliyon*, *8*(3), e09041. doi:10.1016/j.heliyon.2022.e09041 PMID:35299605

Tuohy, J. P. (2023, January 6). Amazon's flying indoor security camera will be at least three years late. *The Verge*. https://www.theverge.com/2023/1/6/23541395/amazon-ring-always-home-cam-release-date-price-ces2023

Turney, P. D. (2002). Thumbs up or thumbs down? Semantic orientation applied to unsupervised classification of reviews. In *Proceedings of the 40th Annual Meeting of the Association for Computational Linguistics (ACL)* (pp. 417-424). ACL.

Ujjawal, K., Garg, S. K., Ali, A., & Singh, D. K. (n.d.). *Security Threats for Short Range Communication Wireless Network on IoT Devices*. Academic Press.

Umbrello, S., & Van de Poel, I. (2021). Mapping value sensitive design onto AI for social good principles. *AI and Ethics*, *1*(3), 283–296. doi:10.100743681-021-00038-3 PMID:34790942

United Nations Educational, Scientific and Cultural Organization (UNESCO). (2015). Proposal for the Revision of the 2001 Revised Recommendation concerning Technical and Vocational Education. *38th General Conference*, 1-16.

URGENT/11. (2023, August 22). Armis. https://www.armis.com/research/urgent-11/#:~:text=URGENT%2F11%20is%20serious%20as,malware%20into%20and%20within%20networks

Uriondo, A., Esperon-Miguez, M., & Perinpanayagam, S. (2015). The present and future of additive manufacturing in the aerospace sector: A review of important aspects. *Proceedings of the Institution of Mechanical Engineers. Part G, Journal of Aerospace Engineering*, *229*(11), 2132–2147. doi:10.1177/0954410014568797

Vafadar, A., Guzzomi, F., Rassau, A., & Hayward, K. (2021). Advances in metal additive manufacturing: A review of common processes, industrial applications, and current challenges. *Applied Sciences (Basel, Switzerland)*, *11*(3), 1213. doi:10.3390/app11031213

Vambol, O., Kondratiev, A., Purhina, S., & Shevtsova, M. (2021). Determining the parameters for a 3D-printing process using the fused deposition modeling in order to manufacture an article with the required structural parameters. *Eastern-European Journal of Enterprise Technologies*, *2*(1 (110)), 70–80. doi:10.15587/1729-4061.2021.227075

Van Der Linden, J. L., Maibach, E., & Leiserowitz, A. (2018). Improving Public Engagement with Climate Change: Five "Best Practice" Insights from Psychological Science. *Perspectives on Psychological Science*, *13*(4), 492–498. PMID:29961412

van Oudenhoven, B., Van de Calseyde, P., Basten, R., & Demerouti, E. (2022). Predictive maintenance for industry 5.0: Behavioural inquiries from a work system perspective. *International Journal of Production Research*. Advance online publication. doi:10.1080/00207543.2022.2154403

Vanhoef, M., & Piessens, F. (2017, October). Key reinstallation attacks: Forcing nonce reuse in WPA2. In *Proceedings of the 2017 ACM SIGSAC Conference on Computer and Communications Security* (pp. 1313-1328). 10.1145/3133956.3134027

Vasconcelos, J., Sardinha, M., Vicente, C., & Reis, L. (2022). Additive Manufacturing of Glass-Ceramic Parts from Recycled Glass Using a Novel Selective Powder Deposition Process. *Applied Sciences (Basel, Switzerland)*, *12*(24), 13022. doi:10.3390/app122413022

Vates, U. K., Mishra, S., Kanu, N. J., & ... (2021). Biomimetic 4D printed materials: A state-of-the-art review on concepts, opportunities, and challenges. *Materials Today: Proceedings*, *47*, 3313–3319. doi:10.1016/j.matpr.2021.07.148

Velankar, M., & Kulkarni, P. (2023). Music Recommendation Systems: Overview and Challenges. *Signals and Communication Technology*, 51–69. doi:10.1007/978-3-031-18444-4_3

Veleva, S. S., & Tsvetanova, A. I. (2020, September). Characteristics of the digital marketing advantages and disadvantages. *IOP Conference Series. Materials Science and Engineering*, *940*(1), 012065. doi:10.1088/1757-899X/940/1/012065

Ventola, C. L. (2014). Medical applications for 3D printing: Current and projected uses. *P&T*, *39*(10), 704. PMID:25336867

Vidakis, N., Kechagias, J. D., Petousis, M., Vakouftsi, F., & Mountakis, N. (2023). The effects of FFF 3D printing parameters on energy consumption. *Materials and Manufacturing Processes*, *38*(8), 915–932. doi:10.1080/10426914.2022.2105882

Vila, C., Abellán-nebot, J. V., Albiñana, J. C., & Hernández, G. (2015). An approach to Sustainable Product Lifecycle Management (Green PLM). *Procedia Engineering*, *132*, 585–592. doi:10.1016/j.proeng.2015.12.608

Vora, L. K., Gholap, A. D., Jetha, K., Thakur, R. R. S., Solanki, H. K., & Chavda, V. P. (2023). Artificial Intelligence in Pharmaceutical Technology and Drug Delivery Design. *Pharmaceutics*, *15*(7), 1916. doi:10.3390/pharmaceutics15071916

Wagner, M. A., Engel, J., Hadian, A., Clemens, F., Rodriguez-Arbaizar, M., Carreño-Morelli, E., & Spolenak, R. (2022). Filament extrusion-based additive manufacturing of 316L stainless steel: Effects of sintering conditions on the microstructure and mechanical properties. *Additive Manufacturing*, *59*, 103147. doi:10.1016/j.addma.2022.103147

Wang, C., & Yin, L. (2023). Defining Urban Big Data in Urban Planning: Literature Review. *Journal of Urban Planning and Development*, *149*(1), 04022044. doi:10.1061/(ASCE)UP.1943-5444.0000896

Wang, H., He, Y., & Ji, D. (2011). A novel method for product defect identification using machine learning and sentiment analysis. In *Proceedings of the 2011 IEEE International Conference on Intelligent Systems and Applications (ISA)* (pp. 1-6). IEEE.

Wang, W., Krishna, A., & McFerran, B. (2017). Turning off the lights: Consumers' environmental efforts depend on visible efforts of firms. *JMR, Journal of Marketing Research*, *54*(3), 478–494. doi:10.1509/jmr.14.0441

Wang, W., Shao, H., Liu, X., & Yin, B. (2020). Printing direction optimization through slice number and support minimization. *IEEE Access : Practical Innovations, Open Solutions*, *8*, 75646–75655. doi:10.1109/ACCESS.2020.2980282

Wang, Y., Müllertz, A., & Rantanen, J. (2022). Additive manufacturing of solid products for oral drug delivery using binder jetting three-dimensional printing. *AAPS PharmSciTech*, *23*(6), 196. doi:10.120812249-022-02321-w PMID:35835970

Wani, Z. K., & Abdullah, A. B. (2020, September). A Review on metal 3D printing; 3D welding. *IOP Conference Series. Materials Science and Engineering*, *920*(1), 012015. doi:10.1088/1757-899X/920/1/012015

Wankhade, M., Rao, A. C. S., Dara, S., & Kaushik, B. (2017, September). A sentiment analysis of food review using logistic regression. In *International Conference on Machine Learning and Computational Intelligence-2017* (pp. 2456-3307). Academic Press.

Wankhade, M., Rao, A. C. S., & Kulkarni, C. (2022). A survey on sentiment analysis methods, applications, and challenges. *Artificial Intelligence Review*, *55*(7), 5731–5780. doi:10.100710462-022-10144-1

Wanniarachchi, C. T., Arjunan, A., Baroutaji, A., & Singh, M. (2022). Mechanical performance of additively manufactured cobalt-chromium-molybdenum auxetic meta-biomaterial bone scaffolds. *Journal of the Mechanical Behavior of Biomedical Materials, 134*, 105409.

Warsi, M. H., Yusuf, M., Al Robaian, M., Khan, M., Muheem, A., & Khan, S. (2018). 3D printing methods for pharmaceutical manufacturing: Opportunity and challenges. *Current Pharmaceutical Design*, *24*(42), 4949–4956. doi:10.2174/1381612825666181206121701 PMID:30520367

Wawrla, L., Maghazei, O., & Netland, P. D. T. (2019). Applications of drones in warehouse operations. *ETH Zurich*, (August), 13.

Weinberger, M. (2022). What Is Metaverse? A Definition Based on Qualitative Meta-Synthesis. *Future Internet*, *14*(11), 310. doi:10.3390/fi14110310

Weisgrab, G., Guillaume, O., Guo, Z., Heimel, P., Slezak, P., Poot, A., Grijpma, D., & Ovsianikov, A. (2020). 3D Printing of large-scale and highly porous biodegradable tissue engineering scaffolds from poly (trimethylene-carbonate) using two-photon-polymerization. *Biofabrication*, *12*(4), 045036. doi:10.1088/1758-5090/abb539 PMID:33000766

White, P., Thompson, L., & Turner, R. (2022). Legal and Ethical Challenges of AI-VR Integration. *Journal of AI and Virtual Reality Law*, *8*(1), 35–58.

Wickramasinghe, K. C., Sasahara, H., Rahim, E. A., & Perera, G. I. P. (2020). Green Metalworking Fluids for sustainable machining applications: A review. *Journal of Cleaner Production*, *257*, 120552. Advance online publication. doi:10.1016/j.jclepro.2020.120552

Wiechetek, Ł., & Gola, A. (2019). 4D Printing as an Innovative Technology for Creating Agile, Shape Morphing Products Meeting Individual User Needs. *Przedsiębiorczość i Zarządzanie, 20*(12), 23–35. http://yadda.icm.edu.pl/yadda/element/bwmeta1.element.ekon-element-000171570433%0Ahttp://files/280/bwmeta1.element.html

Willems, W., Heltzel, A., Nabuurs, J., Broerse, J., & Kupper, F. (2023). Welcome to the fertility clinic of the future! Using speculative design to explore the moral landscape of reproductive technologies. *Humanities & Social Sciences Communications*, *10*(1), 1–12. doi:10.105741599-023-01674-2

Williams, J. C., Anderson, N., Mathis, M., Sanford, E. III, Eugene, J., & Isom, J. (2020). Colorblind algorithms: Racism in the era of COVID-19. *Journal of the National Medical Association*, *112*(5), 550–552. doi:10.1016/j.jnma.2020.05.010 PMID:32563687

Willson, J. M., Grinshpun, V. S., & Santos, R. (1998). *U.S. Patent No. 5,789,456*. Washington, DC: U.S. Patent and Trademark Office.

Wohlers, T., Gornet, T., Mostow, N., Campbell, I., Diegel, O., Kowen, J., ... Peels, J. (2016). *History of additive manufacturing*. Academic Press.

Wohlgenannt, I., Simons, A., & Stieglitz, S. (2020). Virtual Realist. *Business & Information Systems Engineering*, *62*(5), 455–461. doi:10.100712599-020-00658-9

Wong, K. V., & Hernandez, A. (2012). A review of additive manufacturing. *International Scholarly Research Notices*.

Wu, Y., Lu, Y., Zhao, M., Bosiakov, S., & Li, L. (2022). A Critical Review of Additive Manufacturing Techniques and Associated Biomaterials Used in Bone Tissue Engineering. *Polymers*, *14*(10), 2117. doi:10.3390/polym14102117 PMID:35631999

Xian, W., Yu, K., Han, F., Fang, L., He, D., & Han, Q. L. (2023). Advanced Manufacturing in Industry 5.0: A Survey of Key Enabling Technologies and Future Trends. *IEEE Transactions on Industrial Informatics*, 1–15. Advance online publication. doi:10.1109/TII.2023.3274224

Xu, X., Lu, Y., Vogel-Heuser, B., & Wang, L. (2021). Industry 4.0 and Industry 5.0—Inception, conception, and perception. *Journal of Manufacturing Systems*, *61*, 530–535. doi:10.1016/j.jmsy.2021.10.006

Yaacoub, J. P. A., Salman, O., Noura, H. N., Kaaniche, N., Chehab, A., & Malli, M. (2020). Cyber-physical systems security: Limitations, issues and future trends. *Microprocessors and Microsystems*, *77*, 103201. doi:10.1016/j.micpro.2020.103201 PMID:32834204

Yamanaka, Y. (2009). Introduction to Global COE Program; Establishment of Center for Integrated Field Environmental Science (IFES). *International Symposium on "Impact of Climate Change on Region Specific Systems."*

Yang, Zhu, Liao, & Wu. (2023). Learning consumer preferences from online textual reviews and ratings based on the aggregation-disaggregation paradigm with attitudinal Choquet integral. *Economic Research-EkonomskaIstraživanja*, *36*(2). doi:10.1080/1331677X.2022.2106282

Yang, L., Li, Y., Wang, J., & Sherratt, R. S. (2020). Sentiment Analysis for E-Commerce Product Reviews in Chinese Based on Sentiment Lexicon and Deep Learning. *IEEE Access : Practical Innovations, Open Solutions*, *8*, 23522–23530. doi:10.1109/ACCESS.2020.2969854

Yang, S. (2022, September). Introduction and future outlook of the 3D printing technology. In *International Conference on Mechanical Design and Simulation (MDS 2022)* (Vol. 12261, pp. 240-246). SPIE. 10.1117/12.2639668

Yao, Z., Desmouceaux, Y., Cordero-Fuertes, J. A., Townsley, M., & Clausen, T. (2022). Aquarius - Enable Fast, Scalable, Data-Driven Service Management in the Cloud. *IEEE Transactions on Network and Service Management*, *19*(4), 4028–4044. doi:10.1109/TNSM.2022.3197130

Yasmin, A., Tasneem, S., & Fatema, K. (2015). Effectiveness of digital marketing in the challenging age: An empirical study. *International Journal of Management Science and Business Administration, 1*(5), 69-80.

Yechuri, P. K., & Ramadass, S. (2021). Classification of Image and Text Data Using Deep Learning-Based LSTM Model. *TS. Traitement du Signal*, *38*(6), 1809–1817. Advance online publication. doi:10.18280/ts.380625

Yin, Y., Stecke, K. E., & Li, D. (2017). The evolution of production systems from Industry 2.0 through Industry 4.0. *International Journal of Production Research*, *56*(1–2), 848–861. doi:10.1080/00207543.2017.1403664

Yi, S., & Liu, X. (2020). Machine learning based customer sentiment analysis for recommending shoppers, shops based on customers' review. *Complex & Intelligent Systems*, *6*(3), 621–634. doi:10.100740747-020-00155-2

Yousefnezhad, N., Malhi, A., & Främling, K. (2020). Security in product lifecycle of IoT devices: A survey. *Journal of Network and Computer Applications*, *171*(June), 102779. doi:10.1016/j.jnca.2020.102779

Yuri, K., Hyun-Jung, Y., Bum-Keun, K., & Hee-Don, C. (2022). Choi Yun-Sang, 3D Printing Technology: Food Tech Analysis. *Resour Sci Res*, *4*(1), 1–11. doi:10.52346/rsr.2022.4.1.1

Zad, S., Heidari, M., Jones, J. H., & Uzuner, O. (2021). A survey on concept-level sentiment analysis techniques of textual data. In *2021 IEEE World AI IoT Congress (AIIoT)*. IEEE. 10.1109/AIIoT52608.2021.9454169

Zadpoor, A. A. (2018). Frontiers of additively manufactured metallic materials. *Materials (Basel)*, *11*(9), 1566. doi:10.3390/ma11091566 PMID:30200231

Zhang, G., & Wei, H. (n.d.). *Selection of optimal process parameters for gear hobbing under cold air minimum quantity lubrication cutting environment*. Academic Press.

Zhang, C., Wang, Z., Zhou, G., Chang, F., Ma, D., Jing, Y., Cheng, W., Ding, K., & Zhao, D. (2023). Towards new-generation human-centric smart manufacturing in Industry 5.0: A systematic review. *Advanced Engineering Informatics*, *57*, 102121. doi:10.1016/j.aei.2023.102121

Zhang, G., Cao, J., Liu, D., & Qi, J. (2022). Popularity of the metaverse: Embodied social presence theory perspective. *Frontiers in Psychology*, *13*, 997751. doi:10.3389/fpsyg.2022.997751 PMID:36248483

Zhang, J., Wang, J., Dong, S., Yu, X., & Han, B. (2019). A review of the current progress and application of 3D printed concrete. *Composites. Part A, Applied Science and Manufacturing*, *125*, 105533. doi:10.1016/j.compositesa.2019.105533

Zhang, L., Zhou, L., Ren, L., & Laili, Y. (2019). Modeling and simulation in intelligent manufacturing. *Computers in Industry*, *112*, 103123. doi:10.1016/j.compind.2019.08.004

Zhang, X., Upton, O., Beebe, N. L., & Choo, K. K. R. (2020). Iot botnet forensics: A comprehensive digital forensic case study on mirai botnet servers. *Forensic Science International Digital Investigation*, *32*, 300926. doi:10.1016/j.fsidi.2020.300926

Zhang, Z., Demir, K. G., & Gu, G. X. (2019). Developments in 4D-printing: A review on current smart materials, technologies, and applications. *International Journal of Smart and Nano Materials*, *10*(3), 205–224. doi:10.1080/19475411.2019.1591541

Zhao, H., Shu, H., & Xing, Y. (2021, January). A review on IoT botnet. In *The 2nd International Conference on Computing and Data Science* (pp. 1-7). Academic Press.

Zheng, S. Y., Liu, Z. W., Kang, H. L., Liu, F., Yan, G. P., & Li, F. (2023). 3D-Printed scaffolds based on poly (Trimethylene carbonate), poly (ε-Caprolactone), and β-Tricalcium phosphate. *International Journal of Bioprinting*, *9*(1), 641. doi:10.18063/ijb.v9i1.641 PMID:36636134

Zhou, Y., Huang, W. M., Kang, S. F., Wu, X. L., Lu, H. B., Fu, J., & Cui, H. (2015). From 3D to 4D printing: Approaches and typical applications. *Journal of Mechanical Science and Technology*, *29*(10), 4281–4288. doi:10.100712206-015-0925-0

Zhu, K., Fuh, J. Y. H., & Lin, X. (2021). Metal-based additive manufacturing condition monitoring: A review on machine learning based approaches. *IEEE/ASME Transactions on Mechatronics*.

Zhu, X., Xiao, Y., Xiao, G., & Deng, X. (2022). Research on Driving Factors of Collaborative Integration Implementation of Lean-Green Manufacturing System with Industry 4.0 Based on Fuzzy AHP-DEMATEL-ISM: From the Perspective of Enterprise Stakeholders. *Processes (Basel, Switzerland), 10*(12), 1–24. doi:10.3390/pr10122714

Zolfagharian, A., Kaynak, A., Bodaghi, M., Kouzani, A. Z., Gharaie, S., & Nahavandi, S. (2020). Control-based 4D printing: Adaptive 4D-printed systems. *Applied Sciences (Basel, Switzerland), 10*(9), 3020. doi:10.3390/app10093020

Zolotareva, N. V., Resnyanskaya, A. S., & Ocheredko, Y. A. (2021). Implementation of modeling elements and 3D printing technology for chemical objects in the educational process within the framework of the "University–School" interaction system. In *SHS Web of Conferences* (Vol. 113, p. 00043). EDP Sciences.

カサルト, ミ., クジェ, フ., & プラツ, エ. (2011). *Getting started with the manufacturing process of expandable vinyl aromatic polymers*. Academic Press.

About the Contributors

Ahdi Hassan has been Associate or Consulting Editor of numerous journals and also served the editorial review board from 2013- to till now. He has a number of publications and research papers published in various domains. He has given contribution with the major roles such as using modern and scientific techniques to work with sounds and meanings of words, studying the relationship between the written and spoken formats of various Asian/European languages, developing the artificial languages in coherence with modern English language, and scientifically approaching the various ancient written material to trace its origin. He teaches topics connected but not limited to communication such as English for Young Learners, English for Academic Purposes, English for Science, Technology and Engineering, English for Business and Entrepreneurship, Business Intensive Course, Applied Linguistics, interpersonal communication, verbal and nonverbal communication, cross cultural competence, language and humor, intercultural communication, culture and humor, language acquisition and language in use.

Pushan Kumar Dutta is an Assistant Professor at Amity University Kolkata, where he teaches and conducts research in the field of Electronics and Communication Engineering. He has a PhD from Jadavpur University, India and a post-doctorate from the Erasmus Mundus Leaders programme, as well as multiple certifications from LinkedIn and Udemy. With over 12 years of experience, Dr. Dutta has a diverse and interdisciplinary research portfolio, spanning topics such as data mining, AI, edge computing, federated learning, predictive analytics, earthquake precursor study, sustainability, industry 5.0, machine ethics, and intelligent systems for biomedical. He has edited over 20 books for prestigious publishers such as Springer, Elsevier, and CRC, and published over 130 articles in scopus indexed journals and conferences. He has also received several honors and awards, such as the Young Faculty in Engineering award in 2018. He is a member of the technical programming committee for various prominent conferences and a keynote speaker at international events. He also coordinates sports and innovation competitions at his university and mentors students and young innovators. He is a passionate educator, a dedicated researcher, and an influential voice in studies related to digital transformation and studies related to data science.

* * *

Suresh A. is with School of Computer Science and Engineering, Vellore Institute of Technology, Chennai, 600127, Tamilnadu, India.

Suresh Kumar B. is with Department of Electronics and Communication Engineering, The Kavery Engineering College, Mechery, Salem, Tamil Nadu, India.

Sampath Boopathi is an accomplished individual with a strong academic background and extensive research experience. He completed his undergraduate studies in Mechanical Engineering and pursued his postgraduate studies in the field of Computer-Aided Design. Dr. Boopathi obtained his Ph.D. from Anna University, focusing his research on Manufacturing and optimization. Throughout his career, Dr. Boopathi has made significant contributions to the field of engineering. He has authored and published over 160 research articles in internationally peer-reviewed journals, highlighting his expertise and dedication to advancing knowledge in his area of specialization. His research output demonstrates his commitment to conducting rigorous and impactful research. In addition to his research publications, Dr. Boopathi has also been granted one patent and has three published patents to his name. This indicates his innovative thinking and ability to develop practical solutions to real-world engineering challenges. With 17 years of academic and research experience, Dr. Boopathi has enriched the engineering community through his teaching and mentorship roles. He has served in various engineering colleges in Tamilnadu, India, where he has imparted knowledge, guided students, and contributed to the overall academic development of the institutions. Dr. Sampath Boopathi's diverse background, ranging from mechanical engineering to computer-aided design, along with his specialization in manufacturing and optimization, positions him as a valuable asset in the field of engineering. His research contributions, patents, and extensive teaching experience exemplify his expertise and dedication to advancing engineering knowledge and fostering innovation.

Subash C. is a passionate undergraduate student specializing in mechatronics at Kumaraguru College of Technology, Coimbatore, Tamil Nadu, India. Subash C has already shown remarkable dedication to IoT in healthcare, machine learning in agriculture, additive manufacturing, material optimization, robotics, and industrial automation, with notable academic achievements and involvement. He published research and review articles in Scopus-indexed international journals and conferences. He is currently working on Emerging Technologies to Enhance Human-Machine Interaction and the Evolution of Industry 4.0 to 5.0, offering a unique take on his work.

Mohamad Syazli Fathi is a highly accomplished academic and researcher with a wealth of experience in construction management, project management, system engineering, and sustainable development. He currently serves as an Associate Professor at Razak Faculty of Technology & Informatics, Universiti Teknologi Malaysia Kuala Lumpur. In addition to his academic role, Mohamad Syazli has held several key leadership positions at UTM, including Deputy Dean for Research, Development & Innovation (FTIR), Deputy Director for Occupational Safety, Health & Environment (OSHE), Deputy Director for the Centre for General Courses & Co-curriculum (CGCC), and Head of Construction Quality and Maintenance research group. These positions have allowed him to contribute significantly to the development and administration of various academic and research initiatives at UTM. With a strong interest in student development through co-curricular activities, Mohamad Syazli has led initiatives involving community engagement, entrepreneurship, sports, culture, innovation, leadership, volunteerism, and university social responsibility. He has also served as an academic coordinator, academic advisor, and civil engineering student society advisor, demonstrating his commitment to fostering the growth and development of students. Prior to his academic career, Mohamad Syazli worked in private sectors managing various private and national projects, including the construction of Electrical and Telecommunications Substation projects and the Malaysian flagship Telehealth project under the Multimedia Super Corridor (MSC). This experience has given him valuable insights into project management, engineering informatics, safety and system engineering, and sustainable development, which he has brought to his academic work. Overall, Mohamad Syazli is a distinguished academic and leader who has made significant contributions to the field of construction management, project management, and sustainable development. His expertise and experience have positioned him as a valuable academician.

Syuhaida Ismail is working as Associate Professor at Universiti Teknologi Malaysia, Malaysia.

Vishal Jain is presently working as an Associate Professor at Department of Computer Science and Engineering, Sharda School of Engineering and Technology, Sharda University, Greater Noida, U. P. India. Before that, he has worked for several years as an Associate Professor at Bharati Vidyapeeth's Institute of Computer Applications and Management (BVICAM), New Delhi. He has more than 14 years of experience in the academics. He obtained Ph.D (CSE), M.Tech (CSE), MBA (HR), MCA, MCP and CCNA. He has authored more than 90 research papers in reputed conferences and journals, including Web of Science and Scopus. He has authored and edited more than 30 books with various reputed publishers, including Elsevier, Springer, Apple Academic Press, CRC, Taylor and Francis Group, Scrivener, Wiley, Emerald, NOVA Science and IGI-Global. His research areas include information retrieval, semantic web, ontology engineering, data mining, ad hoc networks, and sensor networks. He received a Young Active Member Award for the year 2012–13 from the Computer Society of India, Best Faculty Award for the year 2017 and Best Researcher Award for the year 2019 from BVICAM, New Delhi.

Vishnu Kumar Kaliappan is with Department of Computer Science and Engineering, KPR Institute of Engineering and Technology, Coimbatore, Tamil Nadu - 641407, India.

Kassim Kalinaki (MIEEE) is a passionate technologist, researcher, and educator with more than ten years of experience in industry and academia. He received his Diploma in Computer engineering from Kyambogo University, a BSc in computer science and engineering, and an MSc. Computer Science and Engineering from Bangladesh's Islamic University of Technology (IUT). Since 2014, He has been lecturing at the Islamic University in Uganda (IUIU), where he most recently served as the Head of Department Computer Science department (2019-2022). Currently, he's pursuing his Ph.D. in Computer Science at the School of Digital Science at Universiti Brunei Darussalam (UBD) since January 2022 and is slated to complete in August 2025. He's the founder and principal investigator of Borderline Research Laboratory (BRLab) and his areas of research include Ecological Informatics, Data Analytics, Computer Vision, ML/DL, Digital Image Processing, Cybersecurity, IoT/AIoMT, Remote Sensing, and Educational Technologies. He has authored and co-authored several published peer-reviewed articles in renowned journals and publishers, including in Springer, Elsevier, Taylor and Francis, Emerald and IEEE.

Daphne Teck Ching Lai is a Senior Assistant Professor at the School of Digital Science, Universiti Brunei Darussalam. She received her B. Sc. in Computer Science from Strathclyde University in 2004, MSc from University of Kent, Canterbury in 2006 and Ph. D. from University of Nottingham, UK in 2014. She worked at Hosei University, Japan in 2018 under the Hosei International Fund Foreign Scholars Fellowship. Her research interests lie in Clustering, Evolutionary Computation and Data Science.

S. V. Manikanthan is a Director of Melange Academic Research Associates, Puducherry, India.

Dhanasekaran P. is working at the Department of Electronics and Communication Engineering, The Kavery Engineering College, Mechery, Salem, Tamil Nadu, India.

Pavithra R. is currently working at the Department of Computer Science and Engineering, Dr. N.G.P. Institute of Technology, Coimbatore, Tamil Nadu - 641048, India.

Roshan R. P. is currently pursuing an undergraduate degree in the Department of Mechatronics Engineering at Kumaraguru College of Technology, Coimbatore, Tamilnadu, India. Published Research and Review articles in Scopus indexed International Journals and Conferences and patents. Research interests include Additive Manufacturing, Material Optimization, Robotics and Industrial Automation. Currently, conducting research on the Evolution of Industry 4.0 to 5.0 with a focus on enhancing human-machine interaction in Industry 5.0.

Sivaramakrishnan Rajendar is working at the Department of Computer Science and Engineering, KPR Institute of Engineering and Technology, Coimbatore, Tamil Nadu, India.

Rozita Razali is Senior Executive di Majlis Amanah Rakyat (MARA), Selangor, Malaysia.

Illavarasi S. is currently working at the Department of Computer Science and Engineering, Sengunthar Engineering College, Erode, Tamil Nadu-637205, India.

Vinoth Kumar S. is with Department of Computer Science and Engineering, School of Computing, Vel Tech Rangarajan Dr. Sagunthala R&D Institute of Science and Technology, Chennai, Tamil Nadu, India.

Umar Yahya is a Senior Lecturer of Computer Science at the Islamic University in Uganda, Kampala Uganda. He is also the Head of Motion Analysis Research Laboratory at the same University. His research interests include, Computational Biomechanics, IoT, Intelligent Systems, Applied AI, Emerging Technologies, and Innovation Management. He holds a PhD in Computer Science from Universiti Brunei Darussalam, Brunei.

Index

V

W

www.ingramcontent.com/pod-product-compliance
Lightning Source LLC
LaVergne TN
LVHW080632011026
849160LV00014B/1193
9798369346624